Jan. 2006

Ex Corde Ecclesiae

Ex Corde Ecclesiae

DOCUMENTS CONCERNING RECEPTION AND IMPLEMENTATION

edited by

ALICE GALLIN, O. S. U.

University of Notre Dame Press
Notre Dame, Indiana

Library of Congress Cataloging in-Publication Data

Ex corde ecclesiae : documents concerning reception and implementation /
edited by Alice Gallin.
   p.   cm.
  ISBN 0-268-02966-0 (cloth : alk. paper)
  1. Catholic Church. Pope (1978–2005 : John Paul II). Ex corde ecclesiae.
2. Universities and colleges (Canon law)—Sources.   3. Christian education
(Canon law)—Sources.   4. Catholic universities and colleges—United States—
Sources.   I. Gallin, Alice.
  KBU3054E9   2005
  378'.071273—dc22

2005034400

In announcing the reception of the *recognitio* for the document "*Ex Corde Ecclesiae*: An Application to the United States" submitted to the Holy See by the National Conference of Catholic Bishops, the president of the Conference, Most Reverend Joseph A. Fiorenza, expressed his appreciation for the work done by the Implementation Committee. He noted in particular the outstanding leadership of its chairman, Bishop John J. Leibrecht: "He has been extraordinarily perceptive and prudent in dealing with a complex matter whose ramifications extend from theology and canon law to issues of academic administration and civil law."

In gratitude for such leadership, I dedicate this book to Bishop Leibrecht and his co-workers on the Implementation Committee.

Contents

Acknowledgments

There are many persons to whom I owe a debt of gratitude for their help in the preparation of this book. Without the encouragement of Bishop John Leibrecht I would never have ventured to attempt it, and without the friendly support of my Ursuline sisters and the leadership of the College of New Rochelle I might have never completed it. Financial support from a foundation that prefers to remain anonymous, and a very flexible schedule as a Scholar-in-Residence, gave me the time and leisure to focus my attention on the project.

For inspiration, I looked to two colleagues who worked tirelessly behind the scenes. Rev. Terrence Toland, S.J., dedicated himself to the task of conducting the wide consultations for the *Ex Corde Ecclesiae* Implementation Committee at each step of the way, and traveled the country from September 1994 to February 1997 to assist those engaged in dialogue. His tact, language skills, and astute analysis were invaluable. The late Rev. James Sauvé, S.J., made a major contribution in Rome by translating and interpreting the Implementation Committee's point of view to the Congregation for Catholic Education, and vice versa. I want to pay tribute to these priest-scholars who served us so well.

I would like to express my gratitude to all of the archivists who served me so generously at the Association of Catholic Colleges and Universities, the Association of Jesuit Colleges and Universities, and the National Conference of Catholic Bishops (United States Conference of Catholic Bishops). I also thank Sister Dorothy Ann Kelly, O.S.U., and Dr. Stephen Sweeny for giving me access, for purposes of comparison, to their files in the president's office of the College of New Rochelle. The technical preparation of the documents for publication required knowledge and skill which I lacked, but which Ms. Jillian De Four of the Academic Computing Office at the College of New Rochelle ably and graciously supplied. Once again, my editor at the University of Notre Dame Press has been of invaluable help and I am deeply grateful to her. Without her there would be no finished product. However, I take full responsibility for the content and interpretation in the book.

The text of *Ex Corde Ecclesiae* is reprinted from my *American Catholic Higher Education: Essential Documents, 1967–1990*, as it appeared in *Origins*.

Documents reproduced from *Origins* and from the ACCU's *Current Issues in Catholic Education* do not require specific permission.

Lisa Sowle Cahill, Joseph A. Komonchak, Avery Dulles, S.J., James H. Provost, and Sharon Euart, R. S. M., have kindly granted permission for publication of the essays they submitted to the Implementation Committee.

Permission to reprint Douglas Laycock's "The Rights of Religious Academic Communities" from the *Journal of College and University Law* was granted by the National Association of College and University Attorneys.

All documents not otherwise identified are from my personal files.

Introduction

The Reception and Implementation of *Ex Corde Ecclesiae*

Why did it take ten years for the American bishops, working with their higher education consultants, to complete a document applying Pope John Paul II's apostolic constitution *Ex Corde Ecclesiae* to the Catholic colleges and universities in the United States? One way to answer that question is to examine the work of the Implementation Committee of the National Conference of Catholic Bishops (NCCB). For the historian, the drafts of a document are as important as the final version in ascertaining the purpose and biases of those who produced it and in judging the outcome of their labor. To appreciate the difficulty of the bishops' task and the length of time it took, one must have listened to the dialogue among members of the committee, read hundreds of responses to questions and drafts sent to a wide group of interested parties (the "consultations"), and analyzed the changes from one draft to another. In the long run, the process followed by this committee is a model for the development of authentic interaction between bishops and their people in the decision-making tasks of the Catholic community. Within the church, as Cardinal Bernardin so strongly urged, we must search for "common ground" to heal the divisions among us and to permit us to enjoy true collegiality in the work of the church. This requires patient dialogue.

Therefore, it seems important to me to bring together in once place crucial documents of the NCCB Implementation Committee, which in December 1990 was given the task of "applying" *Ex Corde Ecclesiae* to the Catholic colleges and universities in the United States. The episcopal members of the committee and their consultants never expected their assignment to take over a decade to complete. Yet they continued to give their time and effort to the task as the years went by. They engaged in a give-and-take of forceful argument in their attempt to listen and respond to the numerous consultations they conducted among bishops, college and university presidents, theologians and canon lawyers, sponsoring religious communities, and Catholic learned societies. Unwilling to allow disagreement to cut off debate, they met at two-day sessions two or three times a year for ten years, read hundreds of pages of consultation responses, and struggled to find consensus in their understanding of the place of the Catholic university in the church and in society.

1

In this volume, I present documents that were produced by the committee or material given to the committee members that presumably influenced their thinking. My introductory narrative is based, in addition, on relevant portions of the annual NCCB meetings of the bishops as well as some background materials in the files of the NCCB and the Association of Catholic Colleges and Universities (ACCU). Although the work of this committee, especially the drafts that seemed to introduce episcopal control over university policies, received considerable attention in the media, that attention is not my topic here. My primary focus is the text of the many drafts of documents. An analysis of these drafts indicates the impact of the process of wide consultation on the work of the committee. I also include communications from the chairman to the committee and to the various constituencies that the committee served: Catholic colleges and universities, religious communities that founded and/or sponsored these institutions, learned societies, and the entire body of bishops. In addition, I include the instructions from the Congregation for Catholic Education in Rome directed to conferences of bishops on how to "apply" *Ex Corde Ecclesiae,* and the responses from the committee to the Congregation, which were of great significance. An end product of the committee's work was presented to the American bishops for their vote on two occasions, once in 1996 and again in 1999. The 1999 version was formally "recognized" by the Holy See in May 2000.

As one who was named to the committee as a "resource person," I attended all but one of its meetings, participated fully in its discussions, and received and studied all of the consultation materials. The documents in this volume are in my personal files and have been checked against those in the files of the Association of Catholic Colleges and Universities, the Association of Jesuit Colleges and Universities (AJCU), and the United States Conference of Catholic Bishops (USCCB, the name by which the National Conference of Catholic Bishops has been known since 2001). I have relied on the minutes of committee meetings in my introduction but have not identified individuals who expressed opinions either at the meetings or in communications to Bishop Leibrecht and/or the committee, since these discussions were not intended for publication. My references to the chairman, Bishop John Leibrecht, whose leadership was crucial in guiding the work of the committee, are the exception. His collaborative attitude, which mandated the widest possible consultation at every step in the journey from December 1990 to 2000, gave witness to the meaning of the term "partnership" and accounts in large measure for the committee's persistent effort to achieve consensus among participants with fundamental differences of opinion.

The introductory narrative represents my understanding of the various stages in the development of the final text and my evaluation of the process followed by the committee in its search for consensus. Since my version may not agree with that of other participants in the discussions, I look forward to the kind of continuing dialogue that the American bishops and Catholic universities have endorsed as the necessary means of implementing *Ex Corde Ecclesiae*. It is my hope that this collection of relevant source documents will assist others in evaluating the work of the committee and the Application of *Ex Corde Ecclesiae*—an evaluation called for in the text itself.

In my epilogue, I call attention to projects undertaken on American Catholic college and university campuses to implement *Ex Corde Ecclesiae* in the light of their specific missions and capabilities as academic institutions. In the 1990s, the faculties and administrators of such institutions, grateful for John Paul II's emphasis on the role of the Catholic university in mediating faith to cultures, intensified efforts already evident in the 1989 National Congress of Church-Related Higher Education, which had sought ways of expressing the uniqueness of "church-related" institutions within the academic community. With the promulgation of *Ex Corde Ecclesiae* the discussion on campuses turned specifically to questions of *Catholic* identity and the call to a renewal of the Catholic intellectual tradition. New programs explored Catholic dimensions of university life and mission in curricular and co-curricular areas, bringing together representatives from various institutions to share their experiences as they tried to acknowledge and enrich the tradition of Catholic learning within the context of American higher education. Initiatives undertaken on individual campuses are also part of the "reception and implementation" (in the broad sense) of the apostolic letter, and although it is too early to carry out a study of such initiatives on more than two hundred campuses, we can cite some models and suggest a list of relevant publications. It is important to recognize the positive "reception" of *Ex Corde Ecclesiae* and the efforts to "implement" it by colleges and universities, despite the many objections voiced to some of its "norms." The attention given to these norms in public discourse, especially the one requiring a *mandatum* for theologians, may have obscured such efforts, but in the long run, they may have the greatest effect on Catholic higher education in the United States.

EX CORDE ECCLESIAE

By the time John Paul II issued his apostolic constitution *Ex Corde Ecclesiae* in 1990, its message had been discussed and debated by the leadership of Catholic universities for twenty-five years. In 1965 the Assembly of the International

Federation of Catholic Universities (IFCU), meeting in Tokyo, had agreed to develop a statement on Catholic universities based on the spirit of the Vatican II document *Gaudium et Spes* ("The Church in the Modern World"). This led to regional meetings, including one at Land-O-Lakes in Wisconsin, where IFCU delegates from North America produced the famous 1967 "Land O'Lakes" statement. This was later merged with other regional statements and led to a statement adopted by delegates to the Second International Congress of Catholic Universities, which became the 1972 document "The Catholic University in the Modern World." This was then submitted to the Sacred Congregation for Catholic Education, whose Prefect, Cardinal Gabriel Marie Garrone, returned it with the request that it be disseminated to all Catholic universities. It was to be accompanied by a letter from the Prefect, which made it clear that while the document had merit, it left points to be addressed—points that would clarify the canonical relation of universities to the church.[1] The document and letter were distributed in April 1973.

In the following year, authorities in Rome, aware of the increasing laicization of boards of trustees of Catholic colleges and universities in the United States, raised this question with the American bishops: "Are these institutions still Catholic?" In many cases, this laicization involved a transfer of property from the founding religious community of the college or university to the legal board of trustees, now composed of a majority of lay persons. In most cases, the religious communities did not request authorization from Rome for alienation of property (a term of church law) because they regarded their action as simply transferring university property—which they held "in trust"—to new boards of trustees now composed of both lay and religious members. To them, university property belonged to a civil corporation and thus no permission other than that required by civil law was needed for their actions.[2] Hence, the question from Roman authorities, "Are they still Catholic?" did not make much sense to them. However, the officials at the Roman Curia viewed all property of religious institutes as "church" property and did not accept the opinion of the American colleges.

I have discussed elsewhere the development of *Ex Corde Ecclesiae*. In this introduction I focus on the ten years after it was promulgated, by describing and documenting its reception and implementation, in the official sense of these terms, by the American bishops and the authorities of the Catholic college and university communities.[3] To evaluate the reception of *Ex Corde Ecclesiae*, however, we must recall the process by which the apostolic letter had been developed, a process that included intensive consultation over a period of thirty years. It had required an enormous amount of time and energy on the part of both bishops and presidents throughout the world, and in 1990 the American bishops were confident that the matter was closed.

This extensive process had included the following phases:

1. Discussions that took place during the revision of the Code of Canon Law. A first draft of the proposed revision of the 1917 code was reviewed by selected canonists in 1977; subsequent drafts were presented for review in 1978 and 1980. American Catholic universities responded both individually, and collectively through their association (ACCU). Since the 1917 code had no canons specifically directed at higher education, proposed new statutes on higher education in the drafts were vigorously opposed by the universities as unnecessary and inappropriate for American institutions. Five representatives of ACCU and NCCB met with John Paul II in March 1982 and made a strong effort to point out the difficulties in reconciling the new canons with the practices of American higher education. The delegation requested that either these canons be deleted from the proposed code or that Rome grant the United States a dispensation from them. When the final code was issued in 1983, however, it still contained the troublesome canons.[4]

2. In 1985 the Sacred Congregation for Catholic Education sent the first draft of what would become *Ex Corde Ecclesiae* to bishops and university presidents around the world with a request for their responses. The draft had already been critiqued by selected "periti" (experts in particular fields). It was described as a way to "flesh out" the Code of Canon Law and as a "schema" for a document on Catholic universities and all institutions of higher learning. The Congregation received some 650 responses, which it collated and distributed in 1985 to all bishops and universities for further critique.[5] On the basis of these consultations, the Congregation prepared a second draft, which was circulated in 1988 with the announcement that a meeting of delegates would be held in Rome in April 1989 to discuss the draft. In the United States, sixteen presidential delegates were elected by their colleagues and four bishops were elected by the National Conference of Catholic Bishops.[6] At the eight-day meeting in Rome, large and small groups debated the draft, refined wording, and finally achieved consensus on an acceptable document. They handed in recommendations to the Congregation and elected fifteen members to return in September to assist in the final process. By then, another draft had been prepared and distributed based on the recommendations from the delegates, with an invitation to readers to submit any final comments. The committee of fifteen suggested further refinement of language on some points. Nearly a year later, on August 15, 1990, the apostolic constitution *Ex Corde Ecclesiae* was promulgated (**Doc. 1**). It was a tribute to the value of extended consultation and dialogue.

3. One of the notable features of *Ex Corde Ecclesiae* resulting from the 1989 Rome meeting was a change in the concept of "norms" as universal. Relying on the principle of subsidiarity[7] and recognizing the vast differences in the cultural contexts of Catholic universities around the world, the authors of the final document confided the implementation of the "norms" to the national hierarchies. The "norms" had already gone through several iterations; in one draft there were forty-nine; in another, seventy-two. The final text had only eleven norms, and the last four were "transitional" or dealt with the time of implementation and possible changes in the future.

When the apostolic constitution was released on August 15, 1990, several features made it more acceptable to the Catholic higher education community in the United States than the earlier drafts. Indeed, the full text was praised by many academics across a wide spectrum of opinion. They regarded the theme of inculturation, stressed by John Paul II, as a useful concept in developing mission statements for contemporary Catholic colleges and universities. Mindful that demographic changes in faculty and students as well as societal and cultural changes had had an impact on the "Catholic identity" of colleges, many of their presidents welcomed the clear call to renew their distinctive institutional mission.[8] An editorial in *America* stated: "The reaction has been largely positive because of three gratifying elements: the process of drawing up the document, the product itself, and the procedure recommended for implementing the norms."[9] It emphasized the fact that comments and suggestions sent to the Congregation had been heard. The ACCU expressed approval that so many of the criticisms of earlier drafts had been taken seriously, that the number of norms had been severely reduced, and that the implementation had been placed in the hands of the national hierarchy instead of the Sacred Congregation.[10] One of the best known scholars of American Catholic history, Dr. Philip Gleason, summed up the reasons for this positive reception of the text: "The final document *Ex Corde Ecclesiae* itself could be called a happy synthesis in that it avoids what academics found most objectionable in earlier Roman initiatives, while embodying papal encouragement, challenge, and admonition."[11]

The next step would be the application of the document to the American scene. The National Conference of Catholic Bishops was asked to develop an application of *Ex Corde Ecclesiae* to the institutions in the United States, to come into effect on the first day of the academic year 1991. Instead, this second part of the process took ten years (1991–2000). The ten years of work of the NCCB Implementation Committee is the subject of this book.

EFFORTS AT IMPLEMENTATION: PHASE I, 1990–1996

In December 1990, Archbishop Daniel Pilarczyk, the chair of the NCCB, appointed an episcopal committee of seven members of the hierarchy, chaired by Bishop John Leibrecht of Springfield–Cape Giradeau. Pilarczyk also invited eight university and college presidents to assist the bishops in the task of creating "ordinances" that would apply the apostolic constitution to the United States. In addition, he asked six individuals to serve as "resource persons" (**Doc. 2**).[12] In referring to the Implementation Committee, unless noted otherwise, I refer to all participants in the life of the committee: bishops, presidents, and resource persons (in the committee documents, presidents and resource persons are sometimes referred to as consultants).

The committee held its first meeting on February 19–20, 1991, where Bishop Leibrecht made it clear that the task of the committee was to study carefully the whole of *Ex Corde Ecclesiae* and not merely its norms. Despite this clear intent on the part of the committee, however, it was the section of general norms, especially article 4, paragraph 3, that received the most attention for the next ten years. Paragraph 3 reads: "In particular, Catholic theologians, aware that they fulfill a mandate [*mandatum*] received from the church, are to be faithful to the magisterium of the church as the authentic interpreter of sacred Scripture and sacred tradition." The note to this paragraph (note 50) cites canon 812 in support: "It is necessary that those who teach theological disciplines in any institute of higher studies have a mandate from the competent ecclesiastical authority."[13]

Several members of the Implementation Committee had served together on the Bishops and Presidents' Committee (a joint committee of NCCB and ACCU in existence since 1974) and had represented the United States at the meeting in Rome in April 1989 regarding *Ex Corde Ecclesiae*. Because they had attended the Rome meeting, they were somewhat surprised when Bishop Leibrecht shared with them new "directives" for implementation that had come from the Sacred Congregation for Catholic Education, dated January 21, 1991 (**Doc. 3**). They had understood their task to be that of applying the apostolic constitution to the United States in the light of the local cultural context and legal system. They had not expected formal directives from Rome about how to do their job. The committee agreed to address its task as the members understood it and not attempt to follow all the specific directives they had now received. In this, they relied on the text of *Ex Corde Ecclesiae* itself: *"The general norms are to be applied concretely at the local and regional levels by episcopal conferences and other*

*assemblies of Catholic hierarchy in conformity with the Code of Canon Law and
complementary church legislation, taking into account the statutes of each university or institute and, as far as possible and appropriate, civil law"* (general norms,
article 1, paragraph 2, emphasis mine). In the years that followed, the debate
generated by the committee's work would often reveal the tension between the
two phrases "in conformity with the Code of Canon Law and complementary
church legislation" and "taking into account the statutes of each university or
institute and, as far as possible and appropriate, civil law."

During its first meeting in February 1991 the committee also divided itself
into five subgroups, each of which would deal with certain topics: (1) the implementation of the four characteristics of "Catholic identity" of a university as
given in *Ex Corde Ecclesiae*; (2) roles and relationships (of university to bishop,
of theologian to university and to bishop, and perhaps of sponsoring religious
community to university); (3) the teaching of theology and Catholic doctrine;
(4) the role of campus ministry—accountable to both the university and the
wider church community and bishop—in a university's mission of evangelization; and (5) the task of writing a general introduction that would serve to place
a final "Application" in the context of American life. The subgroups were asked
to present their reports at the next meeting, in September 1991. Both bishops
and presidents were members of each subgroup, a fact that favored a significant
exchange of opinions and a spirit of collaboration in the task ahead.

Once they began work, however, committee members soon recognized that
no matter what topic had been assigned to them, one of the difficult points to
implement would be the paragraph based on canon 812, dealing with theologians. The committee concluded that they had to undertake a serious study of
the meaning of a *mandatum* from theological, ecclesiological, and canonical perspectives, since any attempt to implement this norm in the context of American
higher education required agreement within the committee on the definition of
the term *mandatum*. Canon 812 in the revised Code of Canon Law (1983) was
a new canon that had not been in the 1917 code or in any of the documents of
Vatican II. Based on the discussion at the September 1991 meeting, therefore,
the committee suggested inviting some experts to present their analyses to the
committee.

Three eminent scholars, Dr. Lisa Cahill, Rev. Joseph A. Komonchak, and
Rev. Avery Dulles, S.J., were invited to prepare papers exploring the meaning of
such a *mandatum*. The authors presented their papers to the committee at its
meeting of September 9–10, 1992, and discussed them at length with the committee. Hence, a reading of these papers is essential to appreciating the ecclesial
issues (**Docs. 4, 5, and 6**).

In his paper Father Dulles pointed out that the term *canonical mission* had been used in early drafts of canon 812 to describe the requirements for a theologian teaching in a Catholic university, but at the 1981 meeting of the Committee for the Revision of the Code this term had been changed to *mandatum*.[14] The term *mandatum* now appearing in canon 812 and cited in *Ex Corde Ecclesiae* (in note 50) was sufficiently ambiguous to warrant a detailed study by the Implementation Committee. It is worth noting that two distinguished canonists, Sister Sharon Euart, R.S.M., and Rev. Frederick McManus, served as resource persons at the committee meetings and were of significant help in explicating the canonical history for members of the committee; in addition, several bishop members were canon lawyers. As the committee discussions proceeded, canon 812 requiring a *mandatum* proved to be the key issue in the difficult struggle to reach consensus on implementing the norms in the apostolic letter for the United States.

At the close of the September 1992 meeting, Bishop Leibrecht asked committee members to reflect on the presentations of Cahill, Dulles, and Komonchak and to develop a list of questions regarding the *mandatum* for discussion at the November 1992 meeting. He also informed the committee that a request by Archbishop Pilarczyk for postponement of the presentation of ordinances to the Sacred Congregation by December 31, 1992, had been accepted, and that Rome would consider a further postponement of six months. By now, the fundamental differences between the bishops and presidents on the committee regarding the *mandatum* were becoming clear. One bishop expressed his concern about rushing the process, to the detriment of extensive consultation. He noted that based on his and other bishops' conversations with bishops in other countries, their submission of ordinances was proceeding even more slowly than in the United States. However, it was also noted that most European, Latin American, and Asian countries did not have the same kind of Catholic universities as in the United States, and their concerns were different.

When the committee met in November 1992, its discussion was wide-ranging and respectful, but it was unable to find a way of presenting canon 812 that would not infringe on academic freedom and institutional autonomy. At several points committee members suggested asking Rome for an indult (a special exemption from church law), but the majority of the bishops on the committee thought that the NCCB would not agree to ask for one.[15] At the end of the meeting the committee agreed to a tentative text regarding the mandate:

> In view of their mutual desire to maintain the Catholic identity of the university/college . . . university authorities and the local Bishop, according

to their own proper roles, will seek to promote the teaching of Catholic theology in communion with the church. To achieve this purpose, university authorities shall make known that the church expects Catholic teachers of theological disciplines to request a mandate from the diocesan bishop. In turn, the bishop will invite the Catholic teacher to request the mandate and, after appropriate review, respond to the request. (Minutes of the November 1992 meeting)

Nevertheless, committee members were dissatisfied with their work, and they agreed with the chair's proposal to select a single writer to create a draft of the ordinances (the specific norms intended to "apply" the general norms in *Ex Corde Ecclesiae*), based on the committee's discussion thus far. This draft should be submitted to the full committee for their review and approval at the January 1993 meeting. According to plan, a few members of the committee would serve as consultants to the selected writer. In the meantime, the chair would inform all the American bishops and presidents of Catholic colleges and universities that following the committee's review, they would receive a draft text for discussion and their responses, which should be sent back to the committee. Bishop Leibrecht explained the entire process of wide consultation that the committee intended to follow in his letter to all bishops and presidents of December 30, 1992. He also noted that Cardinal Laghi of the Sacred Congregation had encouraged this wide process of consultation (**Doc. 7**).

When the committee met in January 1993, it had on the table a seven-page draft submitted by the designated writer. The committee proceeded to analyze it, one ordinance (norm) at a time. Members agreed that the introduction to the document should present a forceful description of the unique American context for any norms that were presented. Beyond that, however, the discussion of the draft resembled any project where a committee tries to write a document: statements and terms were examined for various interpretations, possible misunderstandings by the media, their impact on academic faculties, whether they would meet expectations from Rome, and so forth. The committee spent two long days massaging the text in the hope of reaching consensus. Certain points were crucial: (1) the importance of not involving a bishop in the hiring process of a college or university; (2) recognition of the responsibility of a bishop for the teaching of Catholic doctrine within his diocese and the need to reconcile that with academic freedom of the professors of theological disciplines; (3) disagreement about the description of the role of the president of a Catholic university with regard to "promoting" or "*seeking* to promote" the teaching of Catholic theology in communion with the church; and (4) whether a Catholic university could be assumed to be a "community of faith." A lengthy theological discussion ensued here about the possibility of an institution making an act of faith. Only a high level of patient explanation and good will, as well as a sense of humor at some points, held the committee together.

A question arose during the meeting as to the procedure for voting on the ordinances. The committee asked for guidance from Sister Euart in her role as Associate General Secretary of NCCB. She gave a formal reply in a memo to Bishop Leibrecht, which, in turn, he shared with the committee.[16] Since the Implementation Committee was an ad hoc committee of NCCB, only the bishops on the committee could vote on the final document to be submitted for vote to the body of all bishops. However, the committee itself could decide on a way to register the opinions of all who were participating in the work of the committee. The bishops on the committee agreed that each ordinance should be voted on separately by the two main groups on the committee: first the bishops and then the presidents. Bishop Leibrecht described this agreement and the voting procedure in a memo to the presidents on the committee of March 18, 1993 (**Doc. 8**).

At the next meeting, on March 26, 1993, each proposed ordinance, with any amendments that had been suggested at the January meeting, was examined and debated anew. The chair and the members labored patiently to reach consensus but could not reach agreement on any action (approval, disapproval, or no action). In the end, they voted to send the current draft, without committee action, to the various constituencies.

This was done in Bishop Leibrecht's memo to all American bishops and presidents of May 4, 1993 (**Doc. 9**), which clearly stated that the enclosed draft ordinances were from the bishop members of the committee. Bishop Leibrecht stated that only the bishops on the committee had voted on the final draft, although the presidents and resource persons "participated fully in all discussions prior to the bishops' decisions about the text. On some matters during discussion, bishops and presidents agreed . . ."; in other cases they "found themselves unanimously with opposing views on a particular proposal. In some discussions neither the bishops nor the presidents were, among themselves, unanimous. . . . Votes among the bishops were unanimous on the ordinances finally presented in the accompanying draft." No breakdown of the separate votes of bishops and presidents on the committee was provided, although in his internal March 18 memo to president members, Bishop Leibrecht had stated that the bishops on the committee favored having such a notation on each ordinance because they thought that "most notations of votes by bishops and presidents on ordinances would show a common ground." Perhaps the intervening discussions had highlighted differences rather than agreements.

In the May 4 memo accompanying the draft ordinances, Bishop Leibrecht urged the widest possible consultation on the ordinances. Discussions should include academic faculty, administrators, trustees, religious superiors of religious communities that sponsored some of the colleges, and Catholic learned societies. If possible, there should also be conversations among representatives of the colleges in a particular diocese with the bishop of that diocese. In other words, the memo displayed a strong effort to "consult" all who might be involved in carrying out the norms. Responses were due by December 31, 1993.

During 1993 the committee received and studied two critiques of the draft ordinances from canon lawyers. The critique by Rev. James Provost, a canon lawyer at The Catholic University of America, was prepared at the request of ACCU and distributed by Mr. Ben Lopez, executive director of ACCU, in a memo of September 8, 1993, to all presidents of Catholic colleges and universities and to the Implementation Committee (**Doc. 10**). Although his critique was regarded by Father Provost as merely "initial reflections" on the proposed ordinances, it furnished the committee with a close analysis of each ordinance, including useful explanations of canonical terms in *Ex Corde Ecclesiae* and in these proposed norms. Sister Sharon Euart's critique was one she also presented on November 8, 1993, at a meeting sponsored by the Cleveland Diocesan Tribunal (**Doc. 11**). The committee also received and reflected on articles published in *America, Commonweal,* and *First Things* as well as relevant essays and book reviews in canon law and theology journals.

Even before the May 1993 draft, several academic conferences had been devoted to *Ex Corde Ecclesiae* and its potential impact on American Catholic colleges and universities. A conference at Fordham University in the fall of 1992 had addressed the future of institutions which identified themselves as "Catholic"— hospitals, social agencies, and educational endeavors, including Catholic universities. (The proceedings were published in 1992 as *The Future of Institutional Ministries: A Continuing Conversation*).[17] A symposium on the apostolic letter held at Georgetown University in April 1993 highlighted the issue of Catholic identity and its meaning in contemporary American society. Major presenters on relevant topics included Philip Gleason, on historical background; Joseph Komonchak, on ecclesiological perspective; Michael Buckley, S.J., on a theological view of the "identity" question; James Provost, on canonical issues; Philip Burling and Gregory Moffatt, on legal complexities; and Jaroslav Pelikan, reflecting on Cardinal Newman's view of the Catholic university. A prepared response to the Burling and Moffat presentation was delivered by Charles Wilson, whose viewpoint can be found in more detail in his published essay (**Doc. 13**).

The publication in late 1993 of these symposium papers as *Catholic Universities in Church and Society*[18] provided first-rate resources for debate in the academic arena. The May 1993 draft of the ordinances was included as an appendix.

During the 1993–94 academic year, numerous articles appeared in print both for and against the draft ordinances. In addition, the ACCU board, fourteen presidents of Catholic research universities, and groups such as the Fellowship of Catholic Scholars submitted opinions to Bishop Leibrecht for the committee.[19] The arguments in the various responses received by the committee were clear and forceful from both bishops and university presidents. All respondents hoped for a way of strengthening the bonds between them in the service of the mission of Catholic higher education, but they were divided as to how to achieve this goal. For some respondents, the goal required canonical and juridical clarification of the relationship of the local bishop to the universities within his diocese. Others argued that the goal could be achieved without such canonical norms. Many of the latter began to link their arguments to the concept of *communio,* a term used to describe relationships within the early church and one which implied "shared responsibilities" among all the people of God. If this reality could be acknowledged, they maintained, issues of difference could be resolved by respectful dialogue. Various respondents emphasized the negative practical repercussions of the proposed *mandatum* for theologians. They argued that it was unenforceable and would lead to confrontation rather than *communio.*

By the annual meeting of ACCU in February 1994, opinions on the draft ordinances of May 1993 had been fully developed and articulated. Bishop Leibrecht agreed to speak to the college presidents at the ACCU meeting on February 2, 1994, and expressed his desire to hear from them. Following his presentation (**Doc. 15**), Bishop James Malone and Archbishop Oscar Lipscomb, also bishop members of the Implementation Committee, presented the rationale behind the draft. Reaction from the floor was quick and negative. The majority of the presidents who spoke stated that the draft ordinances were unacceptable and dangerous to the status of American Catholic colleges and universities. Their position was not surprising; it had been strongly expressed in five regional meetings sponsored by ACCU during 1993 and had been submitted earlier to the Implementation Committee with a cover letter of November 10, 1993, from Author Hughes, the president of the University of San Diego and current chair of ACCU. A synthesis of the regional meetings had also been submitted to the committee dated November 12, 1993 (see **Doc. 14** for Hughes' letter and the synthesis).

To deal with this obvious "nonreception" of the ordinances by the presidents of Catholic colleges and universities, the committee went back to the drawing board. In a meeting on March 21, 1994, the committee focused on the discussion at the ACCU meeting of February 2 and on two major suggestions made at the time: (1) to widen participation in the dialogue and (2) to extend the period for discussions. The president members of the committee insisted that opposition to the norms should not be construed as opposition to *Ex Corde Ecclesiae*. Their problem was that the ordinances were simply unworkable in the environment of American higher education. Bishop Leibrecht informed the committee that the NCCB was considering hiring a project director to manage the extended dialogue and assessment of the May 1993 draft ordinances and had requested from Rome an extension of the deadline for implementation. The committee passed a resolution in favor of the search for a project director, who could facilitate the dialogue and coordinate research into legal, theological and canonical issues. FADICA (Foundations and Donors Interested in Catholic Activities) had agreed to consider a proposal for funding. Bishop Leibrecht communicated this plan to all bishops and university and college presidents, as well as the learned societies and religious communities, in a memo of April 11, 1994 (**Doc. 16**).

Many of the objections to the draft ordinances had referred to serious legal problems and court cases that might result from trying to enforce them. At its March 21 meeting the committee also heard from Mark Chopko, the general counsel for NCCB and USCC (the United States Catholic Conference, the administrative arm of NCCB). He maintained that some of the legal concerns were overblown and presented expert opinions that did not foresee dire consequences. However, citing contrary legal opinions, various committee members (including bishops, presidents, and resource persons) urged further investigation of the liabilities connected with even the appearance of giving bishops authority over the hiring and firing of theologians on the faculties of Catholic colleges and universities. Bishop Leibrecht urged all participants in discussions in the coming months to give careful attention to the legal issues. (For published discussions of such issues, see **Docs. 12 and 13**).[20]

Finally, at the meeting on March 21 the committee members expressed once again their own views on the proposed ordinances, emphasizing the lack of attention to the peculiar American situation in which Catholic universities were private and independent institutions, not state-controlled or pontifical universities granting Vatican degrees. They urged that this unique situation be highlighted in the introduction to any future document. Once again, they subjected each ordinance to a detailed analysis, uncovering points of ambiguity as well as frank disagreements among committee members about the ways in which the Catholic identity of a college or university could be manifested. The chair repeated his commitment to broad consultation and stated that he would explain to all the bishops and presidents the new process of dialogue that the committee was proposing, as done on July 8 (**Doc. 18**). The new plan was, first of all, to discuss basic themes relating to Catholic higher education in order to clarify the underlying purposes of the ordinances. This would take place in fall 1994, paving the way for further dialogue in spring 1995 on the *mandatum* and related matters. Once the first step had been accomplished, the committee could more readily address the question of applying *Ex Corde Ecclesiae* to the American schools.

In a conference call on August 26, 1994, the committee agreed to a schedule of meetings for the coming year. Responses to the new round of consultation on basic themes of Catholic identity were to be submitted to the committee by December 10, 1994, for discussion. Following the further dialogue in spring 1995, the bishop members of the committee would then draft new ordinances and send them to all bishops, in preparation for a discussion at the NCCB meeting in November 1995. Bishop Leibrecht expressed his hope that the bishops would engage in conversation with college and university personnel to ascertain their receptivity to the revised set of ordinances.

It was clear by this time that all decisions regarding the process would be made by the chair only after consultation with both the bishop members and the invited presidents and resource persons. This created an environment of respect and mutual appreciation. Consultations were not window-dressing but rather a genuine effort to hear from all those who would be affected by the final outcome.

The work of the committee was greatly enhanced by the appointment of Rev. Terrence Toland, S.J., as project director. In announcing this appointment in a memo of August 25, 1994, to bishops, presidents, learned societies, and other experts, Bishop Leibrecht described Father Toland's responsibilities as, in particular, facilitating regional discussions and assuming responsibility for the efficient conducting of the consultations. Once Father Toland was on board, he attended regional meetings of bishops, presidents, and others, listened to their concerns, and reported back to the committee. To help focus discussions, his office developed and disseminated a bibliography.

At its meeting on January 27, 1995, the committee discussed the responses received from the fall 1994 dialogues, which had been grouped around the themes suggested for discussion as a result of the concerns expressed by college and university presidents in their ACCU meeting in 1994. Bishop Leibrecht informed the presidents at the ACCU meeting on February 1, 1995, that in response to their nonreception of the proposed ordinances of May 1993, the committee had taken those ordinances "off the table" (**Doc. 20**).[21] New proposals would be based both on the recent and ongoing dialogues that focused on Catholic identity, the relation between faith and culture, and pastoral ministry on campus, and on those to be held in the spring of 1995 on the *mandatum* and other related topics. Bishop James Malone added to this the importance of conducting conversations about the notion of *communio,* especially the concept of "shared responsibility" in light of "shared duties" (also **Doc. 20**). Referring to the relationship of the bishop of a diocese to Catholic colleges and universities within *communio,* he expressed his belief that as a result of the present dialogues, "we are moving forward together, talking to each other, respecting each other." He summed up the new atmosphere: "The time we are spending together—bishops and Catholic higher education people—is paying dividends." He added, however, that it was necessary to move on "to some conclusion, however provisional." It was not enough to agree on the theory of *communio;* we must move on to the practice of *communio.* The goal was now identified as understanding the "value" underlying each ordinance and then trying to construct *nonjuridical* ways of attaining the goal within the context of contemporary American higher education (emphasis mine). Bishop Leibrecht reminded the ACCU audience that, according to *Ex Corde Ecclesiae,* the university itself is the agent responsible for the Catholic identity of the institution. Others within the institution share that responsibility, and "the bishop's role is to promote and assist in the preservation and strengthening of their Catholic identity" (*Ex Corde Ecclesiae,* part 1, para. 28).

In a follow-up memo of February 10, 1995 (**Doc. 21**), Leibrecht explored possible means of attaining the goals agreed on by the committee: (1) promoting Catholic theology taught in a manner faithful to scripture, tradition, and the magisterium; (2) recognizing the legitimate place of theology as a discipline in the university; and (3) stimulating bishops' support for creative work of theologians. He proposed a number of questions relating particularly to the values underlying the *mandatum,* for discussion by those at universities in the spring 1995 dialogues:

1. How does your current program in theology/religious studies achieve the values/goals mentioned in ECE (*Ex Corde Ecclesiae*)?
2. What is needed in your program for a better achievement of the goals and values of ECE?
3. How do you envision hiring faculty committed to such goals? and, How can you facilitate the present faculty members' consideration of them?
4. Are there opportunities for interdisciplinary discussions where theological traditions can be explored by faculty from many disciplines?
5. What is the meaning of evangelization in ECE as it might relate to universities?

These questions were suggested as conversation starters. No written responses were required. During 1995, as in 1994, there was constant public discussion about the significance of *Ex Corde Ecclesiae*. In August 1995, for example, a conference at the University of St. Thomas, St. Paul, Minnesota, cosponsored by ACCU, was devoted to the theme of "Catholic Higher Education: Practice and Promise." For three days, approximately 450 faculty, administrators, bishops, trustees, leaders of student services and campus ministries, and admissions and financial aid officers listened to major presentations on the current crisis of Catholic identity on campuses and debated long and hard about solutions to the ongoing tension between the institutional autonomy of universities and the place of the university within the church. Speakers included Cardinal Pio Laghi, Secretary of the Sacred Congregation for Catholic Education, Margaret O'Brien Steinfels, Peter Steinfels, Rev. J. Bryan Hehir, and Edgar F. Beckham.[22] Many participants commented on the positive climate at this meeting, which seemed to mark a change from previous meetings. Discussion focused not on the question of the *mandatum* but rather on the compelling challenge from *Ex Corde Ecclesiae* to enliven the commitment of believers to the role of the Catholic university as the mediator of faith to cultures. It was also an opportunity for participants to describe new initiatives on college campuses that had been inspired by a post–Vatican II understanding of Catholic identity—that is, witnessing to the values of the Gospel in meeting the needs of our times.[23]

In August 1995 Bishop Leibrecht sent a memo to all bishops and presidents enclosing the latest effort on the part of the committee, entitled "*Ex Corde Ecclesiae*: An Application to the United States" (**Doc. 22**). This draft, which replaced the rejected 1993 draft ordinances, had resulted from the consultations of 1994 and 1995 as analyzed by the committee. Leibrecht proposed that this new version be discussed by groups of bishops, presidents, trustees, and academic faculty between the end of August and the next meeting of NCCB on November 13–16, 1995. Reactions and comments should be brought to the NCCB meeting, where the draft document would be discussed by the full body of bishops. It would not be voted on, however, until the following year. The decision to delay a final NCCB vote arose from concern that short-circuiting local and regional discussions would, in the end, militate against good long-term relations between bishops and universities.

Three significant documents accompanied the August 25 draft. The first was a brief summary of background history. In the second, Bishop Leibrecht provided some interpretive comments. He noted that the implementation of canon 812 must be consistent with the context of American higher education and that it should further the values explicated in *Ex Corde Ecclesiae,* namely, mutual trust between college/university and church authorities; close and consistent cooperation between university/college and church authorities; and continuing dialogue among these authorities. Each of these desirable outcomes had specific implications.

The third accompanying document was a brief canonical rationale for the committee's assumption that through the development of these relationships, the purpose of canon 812 would be achieved, namely, the "safeguarding of the orthodoxy of church teaching within Catholic colleges and universities." It pointed out that this safeguarding must be done within the wider goal of *Ex Corde Ecclesiae,* which is to fulfill a Catholic mission and identity as "a bridge between the Gospel and culture." Hence, the crucial emphasis on the American cultural context. It advocated seeking a balance between "guaranteeing institutional autonomy and academic freedom, on the one hand, and respect for church authority and loyal assent, on the other." The conclusion of this canonical rationale was that the goal of canon 812 could be achieved by a nonjuridical application of the *mandatum.* (Critics, of course, labeled this a refusal to implement canon 812.)

It is interesting to note that the framework for this new draft of the Application was taken from another pontifical document issued on May 22, 1994, entitled "The Church's Presence in the University and in University Culture." It states that "by its very existence, the Catholic university achieves its aim of guaranteeing, in institutional form, a Christian presence in the university world" (**Doc. 17**). The presidents of American Catholic colleges wanted to stress this understanding of their mission and of the inculturation that it required (see **Doc. 19**).

The proposed text of the Application, dated August 25, 1995, resulted in numerous responses. These were distributed to all the members and resource persons on the Implementation Committee for their study and analysis. At the NCCB meeting on November 13–16, 1995, Bishop Leibrecht reported on the progress of the Implementation Committee thus far. Other members of the committee, including Cardinal Hickey and Bishop Malone, expressed their support for the draft and their belief that real progress had occurred in the dialogues still going on. Some bishops raised questions concerning canon 812. The suggestion in the draft that a 1989 NCCB document, "Doctrinal Responsibilities: Approaches to Promoting Cooperation and Resolving Misunderstandings between Bishops and Theologians," should provide the due process needed to resolve disputes between bishops and theologians appeared to some as "a way around canon 812." The danger of "secularization" of Catholic colleges and universities surfaced in the discussion several times. Some bishops stressed the need for strong church authority (exercised either by the local bishop or a religious community) over institutions of higher education. Others insisted on the need to support the leaders of Catholic higher education, especially lay leaders, as they sought ways of articulating a Catholic identity in today's intellectual climate, instead of focusing on the need for outside authority to mandate such commitment.

At its next meeting, on January 26, 1996, the Implementation Committee considered each of the points made at the November meeting of NCCB, as well as certain written responses. On February 23, 1996, a revised text of the Application was sent to all bishops and presidents, religious communities who sponsored colleges and universities, and learned societies (see **Doc. 24**). Once more they were asked to discuss it and to submit their responses to the next NCCB meeting, in June 1996. Bishop Leibrecht informed recipients that after the NCCB meeting and a meeting of the Implementation Committee later in June, a newly revised text would be sent for final comments before the NCCB meeting in November 1996. At that time, according to plan, a vote would be taken. Bishop Leibrecht expressed his conviction that *Ex Corde Ecclesiae* was the basic text and that nothing new should be added to it. In his cover letter to the draft sent on February 23, 1996, he wrote, "In decisions about proposed revisions, the Committee members kept in mind that the Apostolic Constitution itself is the primary text offering guidance for the future" (also **Doc. 24**). It was important to reiterate this message, since some respondents to the August 25 draft had suggested changes that would run counter to the papal directives in *Ex Corde Ecclesiae* itself. (For examples, see **Doc. 23** and the later **Doc. 27**).[24] These suggested changes came in consultations from individuals as well as certain faculty at Catholic colleges who belonged to the Fellowship of Catholic Scholars and the Cardinal Newman Society. *First Things* also carried articles with the same point of view.

Once again, the issue of the *mandatum* marked the divide among the respondents to the draft of August 25, 1995. Some favored a clear and unambiguous insistence on a juridical *mandatum* for all Catholic teachers of theological disciplines in all Catholic colleges.[25] Others held out for a further study of canon 812 and of ways to achieve the goal of the canon without provoking a confrontation between the Sacred Congregation in Rome and the American bishops and institutions of higher education. In its recent drafts, the Implementation Committee had proposed placing the emphasis on an institution's responsibility for its Catholic identity and remanding the questions related to canon 812 for further study.

The key to understanding both the draft of August 25, 1995, and the draft of February 23, 1996, is found in their treatment of part 1, paragraph 28 of *Ex Corde*

Ecclesiae, which describes the pastoral relationship that should exist between bishops and universities. Such a relationship is characterized by "mutual trust, close and consistent cooperation and continuing dialogue." The drafts analyze each of these phrases and spell out their implications. The February 23 draft alludes to canon 812 only in very general terms: "[I]t follows . . . that the institution, following its own procedures in the hiring and retention of professionally qualified faculty and staff, seeks individuals who are committed to the Catholic tradition or, if not Catholic, who are aware and respectful of that tradition." (The wording of the August 25 draft is substantially the same.) The bishop's role is basically a pastoral one: "[A]ware of the contributions made by theologians to Church and academy, the local bishop in accord with his ecclesial responsibility, in circumstances where he questions whether or not an individual theologian is presenting authentic Catholic teaching, shall follow *established procedures* [as noted in "Doctrinal Responsibilities"] and take appropriate action" (emphasis in original).

At the June 1996 meeting of the NCCB, Bishop Leibrecht explained the committee's approach, which was based on the Holy Father's encouragement to develop "personal and pastoral relationships" between Catholic institutions of higher education and church authority (**Doc. 25**). After five years of work by the committee, Leibrecht understood the necessary tension between the pastoral responsibility of a bishop to participate in the life of a university in his diocese and his obligation not to be involved in the internal governance of the institution. The committee was also anxious to avoid creating new problems by involving the university administration in the question of religious orthodoxy of theologians. Its new approach was to identify the values inherent in canon 812 and then find ways of promoting them without invoking a juridical norm, which might have unintended consequences for universities. Thus, the recent drafts focused on the responsibilities of the institution for its Catholic identity and defined the bishop's responsibility as that of correcting by public statement what he regards as teaching contrary to Catholic tradition. Nevertheless, the committee still recognized that the *mandatum* needed additional attention and recommended that the NCCB undertake further study.

The bishops and the universities continued to send in comments on the draft of February 23, 1996. The great majority of them approved of its pastoral tone. Many noted that the dialogues thus far between bishops, university presidents, and theologians had been fruitful. In response to the consultations, the committee distributed another draft on August 2, 1996 (**Doc. 26**). It retained the pastoral emphasis and the reference to "Doctrinal Responsibilities."

The major point of disagreement with the recent drafts was still canon 812; not all of the respondents were convinced that the committee's reliance on further conversations between bishops and presidents and on their mutual trust would be a sufficient means of dealing with a theologian who, in the opinion of the local bishop, was not teaching "in communion with the church." The reliance in these drafts on "Doctrinal Responsibilities" was unacceptable to some in light of that document's ambiguous status—it was approved by NCCB but had no *recognitio* from Rome, and thus lacked the status of law. It was also not clear how it would cover canon 812. For example, one bishop pointed out that the process suggested in "Doctrinal Responsibilities" only took effect after some indication that the professor was not teaching in accord with Catholic doctrine, whereas canon 812 placed the action of the granting of the *mandatum* at the time of hiring. One bishop wrote, "The present draft appears to bridge the gap 'regarding the mandatum' and incorporates the values without raising unnecessary concerns or problems for those involved in the ministry of Catholic higher education." Another bishop, however, wrote, "Advocating a non-juridical application of the mandatum really amounts to an oxymoron! . . . Either canon 812 should be observed or an indult should be requested formally." Many respondents praised the process followed by the Implementation Committee. Others, however, denounced it as a capitulation by the bishops to the leaders of Catholic higher education (see, for example, **Doc. 27**).

The months leading up to November 1996 were busy ones for those gathering the submissions to the Implementation Committee and for the committee itself, as it tried to come up with yet another draft of the Application. Changes were still being suggested right up to the NCCB meeting and in the discussion at the meeting itself. The final draft, presented for a vote on November 13, 1996, followed the basic thrust of relying on the relationships to be developed between bishops and universities to carry forward the message of *Ex Corde Ecclesiae*. The pastoral tone of the February 1996 draft was maintained, and the question of the *mandatum* was dealt with in a note promising further study by NCCB. On November 13, 1996, the full body of American bishops voted 224 to 6 in favor of the document, a record-breaking endorsement of its contents (**Doc. 28**). Following the vote of the bishops, the document was submitted to the Congregation for Catholic Education in Rome for its approval (the *recognitio*).

Briefly, what can be said of the reception of this presumably final version of the Application? At the annual meeting of the ACCU in February 1997, its executive director, Dr. Monika Hellwig, expressed the generally positive reaction of the Catholic college and university presidents.[26] She pointed out that the canonical aspects of *Ex Corde Ecclesiae* were "provisionally settled" and that colleges and universities should now attend to the basic non-canonical content of the document, including ways to pass on their Catholic heritage to lay leadership. The positive responses to "*Ex Corde Ecclesiae*: An Application to the United States" passed by the bishops in November 1996 were based on the assumption that the question of the *mandatum* had been temporarily postponed. In the media, individual college presidents were quoted as being pleased with the work of the Implementation Committee. Peter Steinfels, in his column in the *New York Times* on November 14, 1996, voiced general satisfaction at the results of the six-year consultation but also pointed out the objections to the final document on the part of the Cardinal Newman Society and the Fellowship of Catholic Scholars, who had expressed their dismay at the weakness of the ordinances[27] and had offered alternatives that would have clearly required Catholic colleges and universities to comply with a more restrictive interpretation of *Ex Corde Ecclesiae*.

EFFORTS AT IMPLEMENTATION: PHASE II, 1997–2000

This was not the end of the story. In a brief letter of May 6, 1997, to Bishop Leibrecht (**Doc. 30**), Bishop Anthony M. Pilla, president of NCCB, informed him that he had received personally from Cardinal Laghi, under date of April 23, 1997, a formal response (**Doc. 29**) to the request for a *recognitio* of the Application submitted to the Sacred Congregation the previous November.[28] Bishop Pilla urgently requested that Bishop Leibrecht reconvene the Implementation Committee to consider the "observations" of the Congregation criticizing the submitted Application. For the most part, these concerned the lack of juridical provisions in what was termed the "first draft" of the ordinances designed to implement the general norms contained in *Ex Corde Ecclesiae*. The Congregation requested a "second draft." It faulted the ordinances of the Application for not following the directives of January 21, 1991. This response was puzzling in view of the fact that Archbishop Laghi had been informed early in the process that the 1991 directives did not seem useful to the committee in carrying out its task of adapting the general norms to American legal and educational institutions. In a letter of April 17, 1991, for example, the executive director of ACCU had written to Archbishop Laghi that the directives seemed to her and to certain others involved in the implementation process as contradictory to the general understanding at the meeting in Rome in April 1989 — namely, that the specific application of the norms would be made by national conferences of bishops to ensure harmony with their distinctive academic cultures and legal systems. In his response of May 31, 1991, Archbishop Laghi agreed with the intent to respect

the cultural diversity among Catholic universities worldwide but also emphasized the "reality of Catholic identity common and essential to all of them." He
regarded the invitation to the national conferences of bishops to identify the
different types of institutions of higher education in their countries as a recognition of cultural diversity, but he also wanted the bishops to "assume a new interest and responsibility with regard to Catholic universities, as a way of promoting, in the local Church, the university's Catholic identity."[29]

This exchange of letters in 1991 foreshadowed the very real conflict in 1997,
when the Sacred Congregation criticized the ordinances in the Application of
November 1996 for not having a sufficiently juridical character. The Congregation pointed out that the lack of a "juridical instrument" for the resolution of
"tensions, crises, or problems" could hinder the effective functioning of the
Catholic university as both Catholic and university. The meaning of this observation, however, was not self-evident. In addition, the Congregation gave specific directions as to the placement of such juridical elements in the text. The
Congregation desired an implementation of the general norms of *Ex Corde Ecclesiae* that would clearly specify the juridical elements required by the norms.
In short, it was clearly not satisfied with the pastoral approach taken by the
American bishops. The Implementation Committee was therefore reconvened
(**Doc. 31**). More important, a new subcommittee was established by Bishop Pilla,
as head of NCCB, with the task of responding to the need for canonical lan-
guage and, in particular, dealing with canon 812. Bishop Pilla appointed Car-
dinal Anthony Bevilacqua as chair of the subcommittee. Other members were
Bishop Raymond Burke, Bishop Thomas Doran, Cardinal Adam Maida, and
Rev. Msgr. John Alesandro, all canon lawyers.

For further clarification as to the Sacred Congregation's instructions, Bishop
Leibrecht and three other bishops from the Implementation Committee (Cardinal James Hickey, Cardinal Adam Maida, and Archbishop Francis Schulte),
along with Reverend Terrence Toland, S.J., and Msgr. Thomas McDade from the
NCCB/USCC staff, met with Cardinal Laghi and his staff in Rome on June 26,
1997. In his report of July 3 to all bishops, presidents, and others who had been
involved in the earlier consultations (**Doc. 32**), Bishop Leibrecht stated that the
meeting was helpful and that the bishops present had told Cardinal Laghi that
some of the observations from the Congregation could be incorporated without much difficulty, but others needed further study and reflection. Not surprisingly, the greatest amount of time at the meeting had been devoted to a discussion of canon 812. A news release of July 1, 1997, reported on this meeting and
added: "Attention was given to how Catholic colleges and universities carry
out their programs for students, to the expectations of parents, and to how

the institutions offer high levels of scholarship and ensure authentically Catholic teaching."

The subcommittee began its work in June 1997 and by July 15–16 had submitted a preliminary report (**Doc. 33**), which suggested retaining the pastoral approach of the 1996 document and adding a second part devoted to "particular norms," which would incorporate the "necessary juridical elements" required by the Sacred Congregation. The subcommittee stated its belief that the *mandatum* could be based on the theological concept of *communio*.

While the document itself does not indicate to whom it was sent, one may infer that it was distributed only to the bishops on the Implementation Committee, since it includes the statement that "when the subcommittee's draft reaches a certain stage, consultation should include a discussion with the presidents of Catholic colleges and universities currently serving as consultants to the *Ex Corde Ecclesiae* committee." For the first time, a distinction had been made in the distribution of materials between the bishops on the Implementation Committee (technically, the real, voting members) and the presidents and resource persons. This distinction in distribution had not existed previously in the internal processes of the committee. The additional statement that consultation would extend to "other representatives of Catholic colleges and universities who have made observations and comments on the Application" also struck some readers as implying that the nonepiscopal "members" (all of whom had been appointed by the chair of NCCB) did not genuinely represent Catholic higher education. Unfortunately, this seemed to suggest that there was now a lack of trust on the part of the subcomittee in the presidents and resource persons on the full committee, and this cast a shadow over the necessary collaboration.

In a letter to Cardinal Bevilacqua on August 21, 1997, Bishop Leibrecht informed him that the Implementation Committee had met by conference call and agreed to the plan for a two-part document that had been proposed (**Doc. 34**). He indicated that the committee hoped for a meeting with the subcommittee in the fall to discuss the next draft of the Application and to consider the steps to be taken regarding consultations. When Bishop Leibrecht spoke of the Implementation Committee, he always meant the bishops, presidents, and resource persons who served on it.

The subcommittee and the Implementation Committee met jointly on January 28, 1998, and August 28, 1998. At each meeting a draft proposed by the subcommittee was thoroughly discussed, with no final consensus on the canonical norms as they were now being presented.[30] At the August 28 meeting, the members of the Implementation Committee were unable to decide on any formal action regarding the most recent draft (i.e., to accept, edit, or reject it) and therefore agreed that the chair should send the draft to the same groups involved in the pre-1997 consultations—all bishops, presidents of Catholic colleges and universities, officers of learned societies, and sponsoring religious communities—for their discussion and response. This was done under date of October 15, 1998 (**Doc. 35**). The draft sent out with this communication from Bishop Leibrecht was actually a revision prepared by the subcommittee after the joint meeting in August, dated September 27, 1998. It was intended as the basis for dialogue with local bishops before the NCCB meeting on November 16–19, 1998, where it would be discussed and where changes might still be suggested. A vote on a new Application was not planned until 1999, so that all the different groups being consulted would have time to send responses to their local bishops or to the Implementation Committee.

A study of the different drafts of the Application in 1997 and 1998 reveals several points where consensus could not be reached, but the heart of the problem was the description of the relationship between the universities and the Catholic hierarchy. Was the university "within the church," as some early drafts had it? Or was it more accurate, as in the September 27, 1998, draft, to speak of the university as "a vital institution in the communion of the church"? Behind this verbal struggle lay certain fundamentally differing ecclesiologies.

With regard to the norms, an important change is evident in article 1 of the September 1998 draft, where the text states that in the application of *Ex Corde Ecclesiae* to Catholic universities, account must be taken of "relevant provisions of applicable federal and state law, regulations and procedures," namely, the role of state constitutions and laws in granting charters and accreditation of programs to colleges and universities. This was directed at the bishops implementing *Ex Corde Ecclesiae,* not the universities. Another significant addition was to article 2.5b: a Catholic university should affirm its essential Catholic identity "with due regard for academic freedom and the conscience of every individual." While these may seem small changes, the committee had learned that when dealing with canon law, one needs to include points of interpretation that qualify the law. One interesting concept to track when comparing the various drafts is "portability" with regard to the *mandatum.* The Implementation Committee took the position that once a theologian received a *mandatum,* it should be valid wherever he or she taught. The Sacred Congregation, however, supported the prerogative of the local bishop to reject a *mandatum* granted by a bishop in another diocese. In the draft and in the final document a phrase is inserted to that effect: "without prejudice to the rights of the local bishop" (in article 4.4e.4b of the final document).

By now, the drafts of "*Ex Corde Ecclesiae*: An Application to the United States" had two parts: Part I, which resembled the 1996 draft passed by the NCCB; and Part II (containing the articles noted above), which applied the general norms of *Ex Corde Ecclesiae* within the context of the Code of Canon Law and complementary church legislation to the Catholic colleges and universities in the United States. The latest draft (September 1998) was submitted to all bishops for discussion at the November 1998 NCCB meeting (**Doc. 36**). It was also distributed to the presidents of colleges and universities, sponsoring religious communities, and the learned societies. A few changes were proposed at the November 1998 NCCB meeting, and some objections were raised regarding the "juridical elements" now in place. Bishop Leibrecht stressed the fact that the theological concept underlying the current document was still that of *communio*, but some of the bishops insisted that the ongoing dialogues were more in keeping with that concept than were the juridical elements that had been added in Part II of the document. On the other hand, certain bishops seemed intent on meeting Rome's demands. They were no longer willing to hold out for modifications relevant to the American context, which had been repeatedly sought by the Implementation Committee. At the close of the NCCB discussion, Bishop Leibrecht urged continued discussions by all bishops with the other constituencies. He requested a report on such discussions by May 1, 1999. The plan still was to hold a vote on a final draft at the November 1999 NCCB meeting.

Responses during the following year (November 1998 to November 1999) were numerous and, predictably, in disagreement. Many who responded could live with Part I, but Part II (the norms) was unacceptable. Furthermore, some of its norms appeared to go beyond the general norms of *Ex Corde Ecclesiae*. The canonists on the subcommittee clearly had done what they had been asked to do, but the full Implementation Committee was not prepared to endorse their work without further amendment.

To discuss the September 1998 draft, the bishops convened meetings with college and university administrators and theologians. Some dialogues also included trustees. In many cases, reports on the dialogues were cosigned by the local bishop and the representatives of the universities. Many requested a return to the document passed in 1996. Although a few reports favored a juridical framework for defining the church-university relationship, most did not. Some requested more time and perhaps a five-year moratorium on implementing the juridical norms. Some called for yet more attention to the potential legal challenges. Some proposed a form of accreditation for theologians through some kind of review process that would focus on the conformity of their teaching to the magisterium, but most did not. Many of the criticisms could be summed up in the following statement from one university report: "The clash between the language of *communio* in Part I with the thrust and language of the Ordinances in Part II is deafening."

Several bishops argued for more discussion on the basic points of disagreement, especially academic freedom and institutional autonomy. One expressed the frustration felt by himself and the university faculties in his diocese at the continued discussion of the implementation of *Ex Corde Ecclesiae,* given that Rome had apparently not heard the message from the bishops in their approval of the 1996 document. From the perspective of the American bishops, they had made every effort in drafting that document to avoid harming universities while at the same time protecting their responsibilities. Now, the canonists on the subcommittee seemed solely intent on compliance with the legal imperatives of the Roman Congregation—which was, of course, the task given to them.

At the ACCU annual meeting in February 1999, the Board of Directors put forward a resolution declaring that the Application, as now proposed, had "unintended negative consequences legally, academically, and financially, and that it is further impracticable, counter-productive, and unclear in certain canonical implications." Due to insufficient time for discussion at the business meeting, however, the ACCU chose not to vote on the resolution. Instead, ACCU staff prepared alternative proposals that were distributed to members for critique and then submitted to the Implementation Committee on April 28, 1999 (**Doc. 37**). Many of the subsequent responses from sessions of bishops and university administrators, from individuals, and from groups such as the presidents and board chairs of the twenty-eight Jesuit universities referenced these "Alternatives" and offered support for them. Continuing problem areas as reported in the responses to the draft were (1) the meaning of the term "faithful Catholic"; (2) references in the draft Application to percentages of trustees and faculty who should be "faithful Catholics"; (3) the distinction of six categories of Catholic universities with respect to their canonical standing, although *Ex Corde Ecclesiae* had distinguished only two categories; and, of course (4) the *mandatum.*

In April 1999, representatives of ACCU and AJCU met in Rome with Cardinal Laghi, Prefect of the Sacred Congregation for Catholic Education, Archbishop Joseph Pittau, Secretary of the Congregation, and their staff to discuss the basic problems in trying to create a juridical structure that would not impinge on the academic freedom and governmental autonomy of universities. Interestingly, while Cardinal Laghi insisted that the norms must implement *Ex Corde Ecclesiae* and the Code of Canon Law (1983 revision), he did not bring up the directives of January 1991 at this meeting, nor had he referred to them at the 1995 conference at St. Thomas University (mentioned above); this was in marked contrast to the Bevilacqua subcommittee, which kept referring to the directives as instructions that must be followed.

In response to the request of Bishop Leibrecht for input on the proposed draft, the Catholic learned societies, which had been part of the ongoing discussions from the time of the revision of the Code, now drew up formal responses to the Implementation Committee. Each organization focused on the aspect of the draft that most concerned them: the College Theology Society (CTS) and the Catholic Theological Society of America (CTSA) analyzed the effect it would have on theologians, while the Canon Law Society of America (CLSA) concentrated on the lanaguage used regarding the *mandatum*. The Board of Governors of CLSA presented opinions from several canonists on what the *mandatum* was and what it was not; such language found its way into the final Application. Two of the canonists cited supported the *mandatum* with the qualification that it be implemented by a national board of bishops, theologians, and other individuals, in order to give some uniformity to the way the *mandatum* was granted or withdrawn. (See, for example, **Docs. 38, 39**).

Several bishops, individually and in concert with the colleges in their dioceses, also urged acceptance of the "Alternatives" proposed by ACCU. Since the Implementation Committee did not receive any record of the Bevilacqua subcommittee's final deliberations, however, we can only surmise that the ACCU alternatives did not receive serious consideration.

When the bishops met in November 1999 they engaged in a lengthy debate on the proposed Application brought to the floor by the Implementation Committee for a vote.[31] A few amendments were offered by the committee itself, and in the debate a few more were offered, but most of the latter were rejected by the full body of bishops. In terms of the overall content of the document, especially the *mandatum*, it was clear that the majority of the bishops thought that continued discussion was by now pointless. Archbishop Pilarczyk, however, insisted that the procedure to be adopted regarding the *mandatum* "should guarantee that there will not be room for the unlikely but not impossible capricious action of a bishop in the distant future." He and others wanted to ensure that when specific procedures for the *mandatum* were drawn up at a later date, these procedures would come back to the body of bishops for approval. Some voices still urged against a vote at this time, given uncertainties about legal consequences. Nevertheless, the majority of bishops seemed intent on bringing an end to the long debate on implementing *Ex Corde Ecclesiae,* at the cost of submitting to Rome's demands for juridical elements in the document and giving up the struggle for the modifications relevant to the American context that had been repeatedly sought by the Implementation Committee.

In the ongoing discussions before the final NCCB vote, it was clear that past dialogues between bishops and presidents had been a source of increased mutual understanding, despite disagreements. Some of the disputed issues were dealt with in the final draft by the use of flexible expressions: for example, by stating that "as far as possible" the trustees should be Catholics and that hiring should "[take] into consideration legal restrictions." One canonist pointed out that since the Application was to be a canonical document, it was important to clarify its terms in the text and not leave this matter to the notes; by the time readers consulted the notes, an unofficial interpretation of the text would already be cause for vocal public dissent. On the other hand, to some bishops it seemed preferable to leave a certain amount of ambiguity in the text.

What was the interaction of the Implementation Committee and the Bevilacqua subcommittee in the development of the final draft? Before the November 1999 meeting of NCCB, members of the Implementation Committee had received and studied the consultation responses and held another long conference call meeting on June 2, 1999, in which they prepared for a meeting with the subcommittee on June 28–29, 1999. On June 28 the full Implementation Committee and the Bevilacqua subcommittee went over the draft together, with members of the Implementation Committee emphasizing the objectionable points. The executive director of ACCU requested a consideration of the Alternatives submitted to the committee in April, but the subcommittee made no response. On June 29, only the bishops on the Implementation Committee (i.e., the actual NCCB committee proper) met with the subcommittee and worked on a new draft. The next step was to send the draft to the NCCB Administrative Committee. It accepted the draft for the agenda and sent it to the full Conference of Bishops for a vote at the November 1999 meeting. Once the document was on the bishops' agenda for a vote, the Implementation Committee ceased to exist. At the meeting of the full National Conference of Bishops on November 17, 1999, the Application passed by a vote of 223 to 31 (**Doc. 40**).

It did not take long for commentators to wonder at the remarkable turnaround on the part of the bishops—from the 224 to 6 vote in favor of the 1996 draft, to the 223 to 31 vote on the final draft with its added juridical requirements. Nevertheless, on May 3, 2000, the Congregation for Bishops in Rome (the formal grantor, after approval by the Congregation for Catholic Education) granted the *recognitio*, affirming that these norms were in conformity with the universal law of the church (**Doc. 41**). The Application would become effective on May 3, 2001. But, in terms of demonstrating respect for dialogue and collaboration among bishops, as well as between them and the universities, a final action on the part of the Sacred Congregation for Catholic Education undermined much of what had been accomplished. The Congregation at this late date insisted, as a condition for granting the *recognitio,* on a note underscoring the right of a local bishop not to accept the principle that the *mandatum* was portable—a principle that had been debated and accepted by the American bishops. In the history of the National Conference of Catholic Bishops, this was one more case of its authority being subordinated to the will of individual local bishops, a more fundamental issue in church governance than that of the *mandatum.*

With the exception of the Fellowship of Catholic Scholars and the Cardinal Newman Society, the Catholic higher education community remained unconvinced of the value of the new juridical approach in the Application. They continued to point out that they were anxious to attend to the questions of Catholic identity posed by *Ex Corde Ecclesiae* but that the dialogues between bishops and universities over the past ten years had amply demonstrated the efficacy of the pastoral rather than the juridical approach. Nevertheless, the text of the Application was now in place. After all the hope generated by the dialogues and by the collaborative spirit of the Implementation Committee, this was a tremendous disappointment to many. Moreover, the way the Bevilacqua subcommittee functioned between 1997 and 1999 stood in complete contrast to the functioning of the full committee. This approach was reminiscent of a top-down mode of decision making, including behind-the-scenes discussions not shared with the full Implementation Committee. It encouraged the widespread suspicion that many bishops acted out of fear that they would be criticized by Rome as giving in to the higher education community if they allowed extra time for consultation. To the consultants on the committee, in particular, it seemed that the former open collaboration and shared responsibility engendered by the work of the committee from 1990 to 1996 had been jettisoned for fear of offending Rome.

IMPLEMENTATION BEGINS: THE GUIDELINES

The Application stipulated that the U.S. bishops should develop a procedure for requesting and granting or withdrawing the *mandatum.* This further task was entrusted to a new committee under the chairmanship of Archbishop Daniel Pilarczyk. Other members were Cardinal Anthony Bevilacqua, Bishop Edward Braxton, Bishop Thomas G. Doran, and Bishop Donald Wuerl, with consultants Professor Terrence Tilly of Dayton University; James J. Conn, S.J., canonist at Fordham University; Maureen Fay, O.P., president of the University of Detroit Mercy; and Professor Daniel Finn of St. John's University, Collegeville, Minnesota. At the November 1999 bishops' meeting it had been quite clear that the anxiety of theologians regarding the possibility of arbitrary action by a local bishop was a major factor in the resistance to the *mandatum*. It seemed wise to move as quickly as possible to set up guidelines. Archbishop Pilarczyk therefore engaged in conference calls as well as written correspondence with the other members of the committee and developed a draft proposal, which the committee addressed at the first meeting on November 1, 2000. They also discussed relevant issues that had been raised in past consultations. Probably the most important was the issue of due process and how that could be guaranteed. The theologians on the committee pressed for a more adequate description of the procedure for granting or refusing to grant the *mandatum*. One of the resources for their discussion was a sixty-one-page report prepared and disseminated by CTSA in September 2000 entitled "Theologians, Catholic Higher Education, and the *Mandatum*" (**Doc. 43**), which explored every angle of the canonical requirement. At the end of the first meeting the committee agreed that Professor Finn should speak on behalf of theologians at the next bishops' meeting, in only two weeks.[32]

At the meeting on November 15, 2000, Archbishop Pilarczyk reported for the committee and introduced Professor Finn. Finn's presentation stressed the role of Catholic universities in maintaining a balance within higher education between the wisdom of our faith and the wisdom of secular knowledge. To accomplish this task, the Catholic theologian and the church needed academic credibility. Some theologians feared "that the *mandatum* threatens the church's mission to the world in which Catholic higher education plays a central role." Finn reviewed the concerns expressed since the 1999 vote and urged the bishops to read the CTSA report and discuss it with theologians. Archbishop Pilarczyk added that the committee was planning a one-day workshop for bishops, in which they could discuss the issues and work toward a common understanding regarding the granting of the *mandatum*. This would also help bishops prepare for the June 2001 NCCB meeting, when a vote on guidelines was planned. In the ensuing discussion, some very real divisions among the bishops surfaced concerning the relationship of the university to the theologians on its faculty, as well as to the bishop. Questions by bishops about the appropriate reasons for not granting or for withdrawing a *mandatum* led to a clear statement by Archbishop Pilarczyk that in such a case, there must be "specific and detailed evidence" to support such a decision and it must be put in writing. Bishop Leibrecht pointed out the importance of not harming reputations or livelihoods.

Subsequently, the committee set a date of May 30, 2001, for a meeting between bishops with Catholic colleges and universities in their dioceses and a number of theologians, university presidents, canonists, and legal experts. Materials prepared by CTSA and CTS were sent in advance to all bishops.[33] An outline for the meeting, giving a canonist's perspective, was prepared by Sister Sharon Euart, R.S.M. This document was perhaps the clearest and most intelligible analysis of the process that had been followed by the committee in seeking useful guidelines for the *mandatum*. When the matter came to the June 2001 meeting of NCCB, this kind of preparation paid off.[34] Following questions for clarification and a brief discussion, the bishops passed the "Guidelines Concerning the Academic Mandatum in Catholic Universities" by voice vote (**Doc. 44**).

It is important to note that this document as published by NCCB states that only those guidelines which repeat a norm of the Application have the force of canon law. It also states that the accompanying "Resource Companion" (which provides examples for bishops in offering the *mandatum*) was not submitted to the Conference of Bishops for a vote but was developed by the USCCB staff in consultation with the committee to assist those who requested a specific protocol for the granting of the *mandatum*. Finally, it states that these guidelines should be reviewed after five years by a committee appointed by the president of the National Conference of Bishops. In the meantime, the Bishops and Presidents' Committee will serve as resource for information and guidance on matters connected with the *mandatum*.

The ten years between the promulgation of *Ex Corde Ecclesiae* in August 1990 and the final action of the bishops in June 2001 regarding the *mandatum* have demonstrated the importance of dialogue between the bishops and the academic community. If the complicated relationship between them, based on different understandings of the nature and mission of a Catholic college or university, is to be honest and productive, both sides must be willing to continue their debate. The mission of the Catholic university, as reiterated in *Ex Corde Ecclesiae*, is to mediate faith to cultures, but this concept requires a common understanding of the terms *mediation* and *inculturation,* as well as a clear commitment to a Catholic intellectual journey that is open to more than one theological tradition. Only with this common understanding in place will the church and the university, in their interaction, be able to make a significant contribution to the social, economic, religious, and intellectual life of our global society.

In his statement at the time of his promulgation of the Application (**Doc. 42**), Bishop Joseph Fiorenza, president of USCCB, called attention to the importance of the dialogue that had preceded *Ex Corde Ecclesiae*: "The continuation of this dialogue should be a permanent result of applying *Ex Corde Ecclesiae* to Catholic higher education in the United States." Will there be sufficient trust on both sides to make that a reality? Will the lessons learned in this ten-year dialogue be remembered?

NOTES

1. Discussions leading up to the issuing of *Ex Corde Ecclesiae* are covered in detail in Alice Gallin, *Negotiating Identity: Catholic Higher Education since 1960* (Notre Dame, Ind.: University of Notre Dame Press, 2000). Documents relevant to the discussions are in Alice Gallin, ed., *American Catholic Higher Education: Essential Documents, 1967–1990* (Notre Dame, Ind.: University of Notre Dame Press, 1992). The reservations expressed by Cardinal Garrone on behalf of the Congregation are extremely important in that they were the source of continual disagreement between the Holy See and the American bishops and college presidents. The "improvement" that the Congregation sought in the document was closely related to its objections in 1997 to the 1996 document "*Ex Corde Ecclesiae*: An Application to the United States." In 1973 Rome was insistent on formal statutory acknowledgment of the university's "character and commitment" as Catholic and on the establishment of "efficacious instruments" of self-regulation in areas of faith, morality, and discipline. See Gallin, *Essential Documents*, 60. These were the same points that were raised with regard to the 1996 Application.

2. These questions are dealt with in Alice Gallin, *Independence and a New Partnership in Catholic Higher Education* (Notre Dame, Ind.: University of Notre Dame Press, 1996), which presents seven case studies demonstrating the variety of processes followed by Catholic colleges and universities in transferring governance to lay-religious boards in the 1960s and 1970s.

3. Part of the process by which an ecclesial document is interpreted is the "reception" of it by the church at large. For a theological explanation of this principle, see Giuseppe Alberigo, Jean-Pierre Jossua, and Joseph A. Komonchak, *The Reception of Vatican II*, trans. Matthew J. O'Connell (Washington, D.C.: The Catholic University of America Press, 1987). See especially the article by Alberigo, 1–24. The canonist James Coriden has defined the canonical doctrine of reception as "a principle asserting that for a law or rule to be an effective guide for the believing community it must be accepted by that community." See his "The Canonical Doctrine of Reception," *The Jurist* 50 (1990): 58–82.

4. All drafts and responses are in Gallin, *Essential Documents*, 153–172. The delegation that visited John Paul II in 1982 is covered in Gallin, *Negotiating Identity*, 149–150.

5. See Gallin, *Essential Documents*, 293–322. The summary document helped American bishops and universities understand the issues in countries other than the United States. The numerical breakdown of the responses was very useful in interpreting them. The summary was dated April 15, 1988, so nearly three years of reflection had intervened since the first draft was issued.

6. The bishop delegates from NCCB were Daniel Kucera, James Malone, Francis Schulte, and Paul Waldschmidt. The presidents' representatives were Dorothy Brown, Patrick Ellis, Paul Reiss, William Byron, S.J., Edward Malloy, C.S.C., Thomas Scanlon, F.S.C., Joseph O'Hare, S.J., Frank Kerins, Sally Furay, R.S.C.J., J. Donald Monan, S.J.,

Joseph Hagen, Dorothy Ann Kelly, O.S.U., Ray Fitz, S.M., Bridgid Driscoll, R.S.H.M., Alice Gallin, O.S.U., and Magdalen Coughlin, S.S.J. The three chosen from the latter group to represent the delegation at the follow-up meeting in September were Sally Furay, R.S.C.J., Joseph O'Hare, S.J., and Edward Malloy, C.S.C.

7. The principle of subsidiarity was explained by Pope Pius XII in 1946 in his address to newly created cardinals. Referring to the use made of this term by Pius XI with reference to the social order (i.e., the principle that what individual human beings can do by themselves and by their own forces should not be taken from them and assigned to the community), Pius XII said that it was a valid concept for the life of the church as well, "without prejudice to its hierarchical structure." This text was quoted in "Doctrinal Responsibilities" (an NCCB document, June 17, 1989), 26.

8. This positive view was expressed by several university presidents, including some who had been outstanding critics of earlier drafts: William Byron, S.J., of The Catholic University of America, J. Donald Monan, S.J., of Boston College, Edward Malloy, C.S.C., of the University of Notre Dame, and William Rewak, S.J., of Santa Clara. Their organization, the ACCU, also expressed its satisfaction with the final document and looked forward to exploring the major area of a Catholic university's mission as identified in *Ex Corde Ecclesiae,* namely, the mediation of faith to cultures.

9. *America,* October 20, 1990, 259.

10. Approval of the document seemed to come from all sectors of Catholic colleges and universities. See, for example, issues from this period of the *Update* of ACCU and the *FCS Newsletter* of the Fellowship of Catholic Scholars, two organizations whose opinions are usually contradictory.

11. Philip Gleason, "The American Background of *Ex Corde Ecclesiae,*" in John Langan, S.J., ed., *Catholic Universities in Church and Society: A Dialogue on Ex Corde Ecclesiae* (Washington, D.C.: Georgetown University Press, 1993), 2.

12. Members of the committee were Cardinal James Hickey, Archbishop Oscar Lipscomb, Archbishop Adam Maida, Archbishop Francis Schulte, Bishop James Griffin, Bishop John Leibrecht, Bishop James Malone, Dr. Dorothy McKenna Brown, Rev. William Byron, S.J., Brother Raymond Fitz, S.M., Dr. Norman Francis, Sister Karen Kennelly, C.S.J., Rev. Edward Malloy, C.S.C., Rev. J. Donald Monan, S.J., and Dr. Matthew Quinn. Resource people to assist the committee were Sister Sharon Euart, R.S.M., Sister Alice Gallin, O.S.U., Rev. Charles Hagan, John Liekweg, Msgr. Frederick McManus, and Sister Lourdes Sheehan, R.S.M. (**Doc. 2**).

13. A lengthy commentary on the meaning of canon 812 is found in *The Code of Canon Law, Text and Commentary,* ed. James Coriden et al. (Mahwah, N.J.: Paulist Press 1985). It is reprinted in Gallin, *Essential Documents,* 184–186.

14. This change was made at the request of Archbishop Bernardin, a representative of NCCB, at the last meeting of the Commission for the Revision of the Code. According to Bernardin, "several of us did express reservations about the implications for our country." It was proposed that this canon (767, later 812) be deleted. Instead, the commission agreed to change the term from *canonical mission* to *mandatum.* The reason given was that the *mandatum* was not fully equal to a canonical mission. This action was reported in *Communicationes Acta Commissionis* and described in a letter from Cardinal Bernardin to the author of September 15, 1995. *Canonical mission* is the term used in the encyclical *Sapientia Christiana* (April 15, 1979) with reference to teachers in ecclesiastical universities and

faculties, that is, those erected or canonically approved by the Apostolic See and with the right to confer academic degrees by the authority of the Holy See. All who teach disciplines in such universities concerning faith or morals must receive a *canonical mission*. In the draft of the new Code of Canon Law, the requirement was extended to theology professors in all institutions of Catholic higher education. The change from *canonical mission* to *mandatum* for the latter group indicated that there was a distinction but led only to more ambiguity. The question now was, what did the statement that a *mandatum* was "not fully equal" to the canonical mission mean?

Many canonical questions had already been dealt with at length in the Commentary of the Code of Canon Law issued in 1983. The same analysis was now necessary for the specific reference to the *mandatum* in *Ex Corde Ecclesiae*. During the entire decade of the 1990s, canonists addressed the question in scholarly articles and journals of opinion. For the best summary, see note 13 above and various articles in *The Jurist*.

15. An indult had already been informally requested in 1982, when the Code was under revision, by the delegation from ACCU that visited John Paul II. See Gallin, *Negotiating Identity*, 145 and 148–151. Cardinal Bernardin and others also requested an indult at the meeting of the Code Commission in 1981, but instead *canonical mission* was changed to *mandatum*.

16. Memo to Bishop Leibrecht from Sr. Sharon Euart, R.S.M., February 8, 1993.

17. Charles J. Fahey and Mary Ann Lewis, eds., *The Future of Institutional Ministries: A Continuing Conversation* (New York: Third Age Center, Fordham, 1992).

18. John P. Langan, S.J., ed., *Catholic Universities in Church and Society* (full citation in note 11 above).

19. For examples of divergent points of view, see Robert F. Sasseen, "Authority and the Academy," in *FCS Newsletter*, June 1993, 21–24, and Ladislas Orsy, "Bishops and Universities: Dominion or Communion," in *America*, November 20, 1993, 11–16. See also J.A. Dinoia, O.P., "Communion and Magisterium: Teaching Authority and the Culture of Grace," in *Modern Theology* 9, no. 4 (October 1993): 403–418, and a special collection of opinions in *Commonweal*, November 19, 1993, 14–25.

20. Since several of the legal opinions shared with the committee had been given to individual clients among the presidents, they are not available for publication. They generally supported the opinion of Charles Wilson, which he presented orally at a meeting of ACCU as well as the April 1993 Georgetown University symposium mentioned previously, and later published in *Current Issues in Catholic Higher Education* (**Doc. 13**). See also the paper by Philip Burling and Gregory T. Moffatt and the responses to it by Wilson and David Thomas Link, also from the Georgetown symposium, published in Langan, *Catholic Universities in Church and Society*, 153–195. An opinion closer to Chopko's was that of Douglas Laycock, published as "The Rights of Religious Academic Communities," in *The Journal of College and University Law* 20, no. 1 (Summer 1993) (**Doc. 12**) and sent to the committee on April 7, 1994. Mr. Chopko later submitted a memorandum to the committee dated August 20, 1998, in which his opinions were more nuanced. He still maintained that the *mandatum* could be reconciled with the Supreme Court decisions regarding direct government financial aid, but he anticipated difficulties if the universities were expected to make hiring decisions based on religious affiliation of applicants.

21. Reported in *Origins* 24, no. 35 (February 16, 1995): 577–582. A sidebar contains quotes from a review of the meeting by Jerry Filteau of Catholic News Service: "[The

reports presented] and the mood of the meeting itself stood in sharp contrast to last year's assembly, when the same education heads found themselves at an apparent impasse with the bishops over proposed norms."

22. Their papers are published in ACCU, *Occasional Papers on Catholic Higher Education* 1, no. 1 (November 1995). (The numbering of this issue, which may be confusing to librarians, is due to a changed format.) The papers highlight issues discussed widely throughout the 1990s. A sense of urgency pervaded the comments of the speakers and the responses of the participants. Both Margaret Steinfels and Peter Steinfels suggested that the Catholic colleges and universities were at a crucial turning point. Cardinal Laghi's presentation and his participation in the discussions at the meeting indicated his knowledge of American Catholic colleges and universities, acquired during the ten years he had served as papal nuncio in Washington, D.C.

23. Some of these initiatives are described in the epilogue.

24. The hundreds of responses received by Father Toland's office were carefully categorized by source (bishops, presidents, joint meetings of colleges and bishops, learned societies, and individuals) and were distributed to all the members and consultants on the committee on a regular basis. Hence, the entire committee could prepare for each meeting in a systematic way and evaluate all the information efficiently. (This process seems to explain some of the strong committee support for the final text of November 1996.)

25. A few canonists, for instance, James Conn, S.J., held that the Catholic theologians in *all* universities, secular as well as Catholic, needed a *mandatum*.

26. See *Update* 24, no. 4 (March–April 1997).

27. A similar negative reaction was expressed by Helen Hull Hitchcock, a member of the board of directors of the Fellowship of Catholic Scholars and a leader in the movement "Women for Faith and Family." She called the document "a studied avoidance of the papal statement." *Crisis,* November 1996, as quoted in *Catholic International,* May 2000, 154.

28. A *recognitio* is the formal approval by Congregations of the Roman Curia of a document from a conference of bishops. Cardinal Laghi also explained in his letter that the *recognitio* had to come from the Congregation of Bishops, after it had received the approval of the Congregation for Catholic Education and the opinion of the Pontifical Council for the Interpretation of Texts. This explanation of the Roman process in reviewing a document came as a surprise to those who had worked on *Ex Corde Ecclesiae* and its implementation, since they assumed that the *recognitio* would come from the Congregation for Catholic Education, the partner in their many meetings and conversations during the past decade.

29. Laghi-Gallin correspondence, ACCU files and the author's personal files.

30. These two drafts of the subcommittee, in the author's personal files, were classified as "confidential" so that they would not lead to public discussion before the Implementation Committee had time to work on them. Unfortunately, the USCCB has declined to declassify them at the time of preparing this volume because of their policies regarding confidential materials. Thus I have been unable to include these texts.

31. Minutes of the NCCB meeting, November 15–18, 1999, USCCB files.

32. Report on the meeting of the Ad Hoc Committee on the *mandatum,* November 1, 2000, USCCB files.

33. Memo from Archbishop Daniel Pilarczyk to all bishops, January 16, 2001.

34. Minutes of the NCCB meeting, June 14–16, 2001, USCCB files.

Documents

1 | *Ex Corde Ecclesiae*

John Paul II

August 15, 1990

INTRODUCTION

1. Born from the heart of the church, a Catholic university is located in that course of tradition which may be traced back to the very origin of the University as an institution. It has always been recognized as an incomparable center of creativity and dissemination of knowledge for the good of humanity. By vocation, the *universitas magistrorum et scholarium* is dedicated to research, to teaching, and to the education of students who freely associate with their teachers in a common love of knowledge.[1] With every other university it shares that *gaudium de veritate,* so precious to Saint Augustine, which is that joy of searching for, discovering, and communicating truth in every field of knowledge.[2] A Catholic university's privileged task is "to unite existentially by intellectual effort two orders of reality that too frequently tend to be placed in opposition as though they were antithetical: the search for truth and the certainty of already knowing the fount of truth."[3]

2. For many years I myself was deeply enriched by the beneficial experience of university life: the ardent search for truth and its unselfish transmission to youth and to all those learning to think rigorously, so as to act rightly and to serve humanity better.

The official document, *Constitutio Apostolica de Universitatibus Catholicis,* was published by Libreria Editrice Vaticana in 1990. It has commonly been referred to as *Ex Corde Ecclesiae* and is so designated in this book. This version is based on an English version published by Libreria Editrice Vaticana and distributed by the Sacred Congregation for Catholic Education. Printed in *Origins* 20, no. 17 (October 4, 1990): 265–276. Reprinted from Alice Gallin, O.S.U., ed., *American Catholic Higher Education: Essential Documents, 1967–1990* (Notre Dame, Ind.: University of Notre Dame Press, 1992), 413–437.

Therefore, I desire to share with everyone my profound respect for Catholic universities and to express my great appreciation for the work that is being done in them in the various spheres of knowledge. In a particular way, I wish to manifest my joy at the numerous meetings which the Lord has permitted me to have in the course of my apostolic journeys with the Catholic university communities of various continents. They are for me a lively and promising sign of the fecundity of the Christian mind in the heart of every culture. They give me a well-founded hope for a new flowering of Christian culture in the rich and varied context of our changing times, which certainly face serious challenges but which also bear so much promise under the action of the Spirit of truth and of love.

It is also my desire to express my pleasure and gratitude to the very many Catholic scholars engaged in teaching and research in non-Catholic universities. Their task as academics and scientists, lived out in the light of the Christian faith, is to be considered precious for the good of the universities in which they teach. Their presence, in fact, is a continuous stimulus to the selfless search for truth and for the wisdom that comes from above.

3. Since the beginning of this pontificate, I have shared these ideas and sentiments with my closest collaborators, the cardinals, with the Congregation for Catholic Education, and with men and women of culture throughout the world. In fact, the dialogue of the church with the cultures of our times is that vital area where "the future of the church and of the world is being played out as we conclude the twentieth century."[4] There is only one culture: that of man, by man, and from man.[5] And thanks to her Catholic universities and their humanistic and scientific inheritance, the church, expert in humanity, as my predecessor Paul VI expressed it at the United Nations,[6] explores the mysteries of humanity and of the world, clarifying them in the light of revelation.

4. It is the honor and responsibility of a Catholic university to consecrate itself without reserve to the cause of truth. This is its way of serving at one and the same time both the dignity of man and the good of the church, which has "an intimate conviction that truth is (its) real ally . . . and that knowledge and reason are sure ministers to faith."[7] Without in any way neglecting the acquisition of useful knowledge, a Catholic university is distinguished by its free search for the whole truth about nature, man, and God. The present age is in urgent need of this kind of disinterested service, namely of proclaiming the meaning of truth, that fundamental value without which freedom, justice, and human dignity are extinguished. By means of a kind of universal humanism, a Catholic university is completely dedicated to the research of all aspects of truth in their essential connection with the supreme Truth, who is God. It does this without fear, but rather with enthusiasm, dedicating itself to every path of knowl-

edge, aware of being preceded by him who is "the Way, the Truth, and the Life,"[8] the Logos, whose Spirit of intelligence and love enables the human person with his or her own intelligence to find the ultimate reality of which he is the source and end and who alone is capable of giving fully that wisdom without which the future of the world would be in danger.

5. It is in the context of the impartial search for truth that the relationship between faith and reason is brought to light and meaning. The invitation of Saint Augustine, *"Intellege ut credas; crede ut intellegas,"*[9] is relevant to Catholic universities that are called to explore courageously the riches of revelation and of nature so that the united endeavor of intelligence and faith will enable people to come to the full measure of their humanity, created in the image and likeness of God, renewed even more marvelously, after sin, in Christ, and called to shine forth in the light of the Spirit.

6. Through the encounter which it establishes between the unfathomable richness of the salvific message of the Gospel and the variety and immensity of the fields of knowledge in which that richness is incarnated by it, a Catholic university enables the church to institute an incomparably fertile dialogue with people of every culture. Man's life is given dignity by culture, and, while he finds his fullness in Christ, there can be no doubt that the Gospel which reaches and renews him in every dimension is also fruitful for the culture in which he lives.

7. In the world today, characterized by such rapid developments in science and technology, the tasks of a Catholic university assume an ever greater importance and urgency. Scientific and technological discoveries create an enormous economic and industrial growth, but they also inescapably require the correspondingly necessary search for meaning in order to guarantee that the new discoveries be used for the authentic good of individuals and of human society as a whole. If it is the responsibility of every university to search for such meaning, a Catholic university is called in a particular way to respond to this need: Its Christian inspiration enables it to include the moral, spiritual, and religious dimension in its research and to evaluate the attainments of science and technology in the perspective of the totality of the human person.[10]

In this context, Catholic universities are called to a continuous renewal, both as "universities" and as "Catholic." For, "What is at stake is the very meaning of scientific and technological research, of social life and of culture, but, on an even more profound level, what is at stake is the very meaning of the human person." Such renewal requires a clear awareness that, by its Catholic character, a university is made more capable of conducting an impartial search for truth, a search that is neither subordinated to nor conditioned by particular interests of any kind.

8. Having already dedicated the apostolic constitution *Sapientia Christiana* to ecclesiastical faculties and universities,[11] I then felt obliged to propose an analogous document for Catholic universities as a sort of *magna carta,* enriched by the long and fruitful experience of the church in the realm of universities and open to the promise of the future achievements that will require courageous creativity and rigorous fidelity.

9. The present document is addressed especially to those who conduct Catholic universities, to the respective academic communities, to all those who have an interest in them, particularly the bishops, religious congregations, and ecclesial institutions, and to the numerous laity who are committed to the great mission of higher education. Its purpose is that "the Christian mind may achieve, as it were, a public, persistent, and universal presence in the whole enterprise of advancing higher culture and that the students of these institutions become people outstanding in learning, ready to shoulder society's heavier burdens and to witness the faith to the world."[12]

10. In addition to Catholic universities, I also turn to the many Catholic institutions of higher education. According to their nature and proper objectives, they share some or all of the characteristics of a university, and they offer their own contribution to the church and to society, whether through research, education, or professional training. While this document specifically concerns Catholic universities, it is also meant to include all Catholic institutions of higher education engaged in instilling the Gospel message of Christ in souls and cultures.

Therefore, it is with great trust and hope that I invite all Catholic universities to pursue their irreplaceable task. Their mission appears increasingly necessary for the encounter of the church with the development of the sciences and with the cultures of our age.

Together with all my brother bishops who share pastoral responsibility with me, I would like to manifest my deep conviction that a Catholic university is without any doubt one of the best instruments that the church offers to our age which is searching for certainty and wisdom. Having the mission of bringing the good news to everyone, the church should never fail to interest herself in this institution. By research and teaching, Catholic universities assist the church in the manner most appropriate to modern times to find cultural treasures both old and new, *"nova et vetera,"* according to the words of Jesus.[13]

11. Finally, I turn to the whole church, convinced that Catholic universities are essential to her growth and to the development of Christian culture and human progress. For this reason, the entire ecclesial community is invited to give its support to Catholic institutions of higher education and to assist them

in their process of development and renewal. It is invited in a special way to guard the rights and freedom of these institutions in civil society, and to offer them economic aid, especially in those countries where they have more urgent need of it, and to furnish assistance in founding new Catholic universities wherever this might be necessary.

My hope is that these prescriptions, based on the teaching of Vatican Council II and the directives of the Code of Canon Law, will enable Catholic universities and other institutions of higher studies to fulfil their indispensable mission in the new advent of grace that is opening up to the new millennium.

I. IDENTITY AND MISSION

THE IDENTITY OF A CATHOLIC UNIVERSITY

1. Nature and Objectives

12. Every Catholic university, as a university, is an academic community which, in a rigorous and critical fashion, assists in the protection and advancement of human dignity and of a cultural heritage through research, teaching, and various services offered to the local, national, and international communities.[14] It possesses that institutional autonomy necessary to perform its functions effectively and guarantees its members academic freedom, so long as the rights of the individual person and of the community are preserved within the confines of the truth and the common good.[15]

13. Since the objective of a Catholic university is to assure in an institutional manner a Christian presence in the university world confronting the great problems of society and culture,[16] every Catholic university, as Catholic, must have the following essential characteristics:

"1. A Christian inspiration not only of individuals but of the university community as such.
2. A continuing reflection in the light of the Catholic faith upon the growing treasury of human knowledge, to which it seeks to contribute by its own research.
3. Fidelity to the Christian message as it comes to us through the Church.
4. An institutional commitment to the service of the people of God and of the human family in their pilgrimage to the transcendent goal which gives meaning to life."[17]

14. "In the light of these four characteristics, it is evident that besides the teaching, research, and services common to all universities, a Catholic university, by institutional commitment, brings to its task the inspiration and light of the Christian message. In a Catholic university, therefore, Catholic ideals, attitudes, and principles penetrate and inform university activities in accordance with the proper nature and autonomy of these activities. In a word, being both a university and Catholic, it must be both a community of scholars representing various branches of human knowledge, and an academic institution in which Catholicism is vitally present and operative."[18]

15. A Catholic university, therefore, is a place of research, where scholars scrutinize reality with the methods proper to each academic discipline, and so contribute to the treasury of human knowledge. Each individual discipline is studied in a systematic manner; moreover, the various disciplines are brought into dialogue for their mutual enhancement.

In addition to assisting men and women in their continuing quest for the truth, this research provides an effective witness, especially necessary today, to the church's belief in the intrinsic value of knowledge and research.

In a Catholic university, research necessarily includes (a) the search for an integration of knowledge, (b) a dialogue between faith and reason, (c) an ethical concern, and (d) a theological perspective.

16. Integration of knowledge is a process, one which will always remain incomplete; moreover, the explosion of knowledge in recent decades, together with the rigid compartmentalization of knowledge within individual academic disciplines, makes the task increasingly difficult. But a university, and especially a Catholic university, "has to be a 'living union' of individual organisms dedicated to the search for truth. . . . It is necessary to work towards a higher synthesis of knowledge, in which alone lies the possibility of satisfying that thirst for truth which is profoundly inscribed on the heart of the human person."[19] Aided by the specific contributions of philosophy and theology, university scholars will be engaged in a constant effort to determine the relative place and meaning of each of the various disciplines within the context of a vision of the human person and the world that is enlightened by the Gospel, and therefore by a faith in Christ, the Logos, as the center of creation and of human history.

17. In promoting this integration of knowledge, a specific part of a Catholic university's task is to promote dialogue between faith and reason, so that it can be seen more profoundly how faith and reason bear harmonious witness to the unity of all truth. While each academic discipline retains its own integrity and has its own methods, this dialogue demonstrates that "methodical research

within every branch of learning, when carried out in a truly scientific manner and in accord with moral norms, can never truly conflict with faith. For the things of the earth and the concerns of faith derive from the same God."[20] A vital interaction of two distinct levels of coming to know the one truth leads to a greater love for truth itself, and contributes to a more comprehensive understanding of the meaning of human life and of the purpose of God's creation.

18. Because knowledge is meant to serve the human person, research in a Catholic university is always carried out with a concern for the ethical and moral implications both of its methods and of its discoveries. This concern, while it must be present in all research, is particularly important in the areas of science and technology. "It is essential that we be convinced of the priority of the ethical over the technical, of the primacy of the person over things, of the superiority of the spirit over matter. The cause of the human person will only be served if knowledge is joined to conscience. Men and women of science will truly aid humanity only if they preserve the 'sense of the transcendence of the human person over the world and of God over the human person.'"[21]

19. Theology plays a particularly important role in the search for a synthesis of knowledge as well as in the dialogue between faith and reason. It serves all other disciplines in their search for meaning, not only by helping them to investigate how their discoveries will affect individuals and society, but also by bringing a perspective and an orientation not contained within their own methodologies. In turn, interaction with these other disciplines and their discoveries enriches theology, offering it a better understanding of the world today, and making theological research more relevant to current needs. Because of its specific importance among the academic disciplines, every Catholic university should have a faculty, or at least a chair, of theology.[22]

20. Given the close connection between research and teaching, the research qualities indicated above will have their influence on all teaching. While each discipline is taught systematically and according to its own methods, interdisciplinary studies, assisted by a careful and thorough study of philosophy and theology, enable students to acquire an organic vision of reality and to develop a continuing desire for intellectual progress. In the communication of knowledge, emphasis is then placed on how human reason in its reflection opens to increasingly broader questions, and how the complete answer to them can only come from above through faith. Furthermore, the moral implications that are present in each discipline are examined as an integral part of the teaching of that discipline so that the entire educative process be directed toward the whole development of the person. Finally, Catholic theology, taught in a manner faithful

to Scripture, tradition, and the church's magisterium, provides an awareness of the Gospel principles which will enrich the meaning of human life and give it a new dignity.

Through research and teaching the students are educated in the various disciplines so as to become truly competent in the specific sectors in which they will devote themselves to the service of society and of the church, but at the same time prepared to give the witness of their faith to the world.

2. The University Community

21. A Catholic university pursues its objectives through its formation of an authentic human community animated by the spirit of Christ. The source of its unity springs from a common dedication to the truth, a common vision of the dignity of the human person, and, ultimately, the person and message of Christ which gives the institution its distinctive character. As a result of this inspiration, the community is animated by a spirit of freedom and charity; it is characterized by mutual respect, sincere dialogue, and protection of the rights of individuals. It assists each of its members to achieve wholeness as human persons; in turn, everyone in the community helps in promoting unity, and each one, according to his or her role and capacity, contributes toward decisions which affect the community, and also toward maintaining and strengthening the distinctive Catholic character of the institution.

22. University teachers should seek to improve their competence and endeavor to set the content, objectives, methods, and results of research in an individual discipline within the framework of a coherent world vision. Christians among the teachers are called to be witnesses and educators of authentic Christian life, which evidences an attained integration between faith and life, and between professional competence and Christian wisdom. All teachers are to be inspired by academic ideals and by the principles of an authentically human life.

23. Students are challenged to pursue an education that combines excellence in humanistic and cultural development with specialized professional training. Most especially, they are challenged to continue the search for truth and for meaning throughout their lives, since "the human spirit must be cultivated in such a way that there results a growth in its ability to wonder, to understand, to contemplate, to make personal judgments, and to develop a religious, moral, and social sense."[23] This enables them to acquire or, if they have already done so, to deepen a Christian way of life that is authentic. They should realize the responsibility of their professional life, the enthusiasm of being the trained 'leaders' of

tomorrow, of being witness to Christ in whatever place they may exercise their profession.

24. Directors and administrators in a Catholic university promote the constant growth of the university and its community through a leadership of service; the dedication and witness of the non-academic staff are vital for the identity and life of the university.

25. Many Catholic universities were founded by religious congregations and continue to depend on their support; those religious congregations dedicated to the apostolate of higher education are urged to assist these institutions in the renewal of their commitment, and to continue to prepare religious men and women who can positively contribute to the mission of a Catholic university.

Laypeople have found in university activities a means by which they too could exercise an important apostolic role in the church and, in most Catholic universities today, the academic community is largely composed of laity; in increasing numbers, lay men and women are assuming important functions and responsibilities for the direction of these institutions. These lay Catholics are responding to the church's call "to be present, as signs of courage and intellectual creativity, in the privileged places of culture, that is, the world of education—school and university."[24] The future of Catholic universities depends to a great extent on the competent and dedicated service of lay Catholics. The church sees their developing presence in these institutions both as a sign of hope and as a confirmation of the irreplaceable lay vocation in the church and in the world, confident that laypeople will, in the exercise of their own distinctive role, "illumine and organize these (temporal) affairs in such a way that they always start out, develop, and continue according to Christ's mind, to the praise of the Creator and the Redeemer."[25]

26. The university community of many Catholic institutions includes members of other Churches, ecclesial communities and religions, and also those who profess no religious belief. These men and women offer their training and experience in furthering the various academic disciplines or other university tasks.

3. The Catholic University in the Church

27. Every Catholic university, without ceasing to be a university, has a relationship to the church that is essential to its institutional identity. As such, it participates most directly in the life of the local church in which it is situated; at the same time, because it is an academic institution and therefore a part of the international community of scholarship and inquiry, each institution participates in and contributes to the life and the mission of the universal church, assuming

consequently a special bond with the Holy See by reason of the service to unity which it is called to render to the whole church. One consequence of its essential relationship to the church is that the institutional fidelity of the university to the Christian message includes a recognition of and adherence to the teaching authority of the church in matters of faith and morals. Catholic members of the university community are also called to a personal fidelity to the church with all that this implies. Non-Catholic members are required to respect the Catholic character of the university, while the university in turn respects their religious liberty.[26]

28. Bishops have a particular responsibility to promote Catholic universities, and especially to promote and assist in the preservation and strengthening of their Catholic identity, including the protection of their Catholic identity in relation to civil authorities. This will be achieved more effectively if close personal and pastoral relationships exist between university and church authorities characterized by mutual trust, close and consistent cooperation, and continuing dialogue. Even when they do not enter directly into the internal governance of the university, bishops "should be seen not as external agents but as participants in the life of the Catholic university."[27]

29. The church, accepting "the legitimate autonomy of human culture and especially of the sciences," recognizes the academic freedom of scholars in each discipline in accordance with its own principles and proper methods,[28] and within the confines of the truth and the common good.

Theology has its legitimate place in the university alongside other disciplines. It has proper principles and methods which define it as a branch of knowledge. Theologians enjoy this same freedom so long as they are faithful to these principles and methods.

Bishops should encourage the creative work of theologians. They serve the church through research done in a way that respects theological method. They seek to understand better, further develop, and more effectively communicate the meaning of Christian revelation as transmitted in Scripture and tradition and in the church's magisterium. They also investigate the ways in which theology can shed light on specific questions raised by contemporary culture. At the same time, since theology seeks an understanding of revealed truth whose authentic interpretation is entrusted to the bishops of the church,[29] it is intrinsic to the principles and methods of their research and teaching in their academic discipline that theologians respect the authority of the bishops and assent to Catholic doctrine according to the degree of authority with which it is taught.[30] Because of their interrelated roles, dialogue between bishops and theologians is essential; this is especially true today, when the results of research are so quickly and so widely communicated through the media.[31]

B. The Mission of Service of a Catholic University

30. The basic mission of a university is a continuous quest for truth through its research, and the preservation and communication of knowledge for the good of society. A Catholic university participates in this mission with its own specific characteristics and purposes.

1. Service to Church and Society

31. Through teaching and research, a Catholic university offers an indispensable contribution to the church. In fact, it prepares men and women who, inspired by Christian principles and helped to live their Christian vocation in a mature and responsible manner, will be able to assume positions of responsibility in the church. Moreover, by offering the results of its scientific research, a Catholic university will be able to help the church respond to the problems and needs of this age.

32. A Catholic university, as any university, is immersed in human society; as an extension of its service to the church, and always within its proper competence, it is called on to become an ever more effective instrument of cultural progress for individuals as well as for society. Included among its research activities, therefore, will be a study of serious contemporary problems in areas such as the dignity of human life, the promotion of justice for all, the quality of personal and family life, the protection of nature, the search for peace and political stability, a more just sharing in the world's resources, and a new economic and political order that will better serve the human community at a national and international level. University research will seek to discover the roots and causes of the serious problems of our time, paying special attention to their ethical and religious dimensions.

If need be, a Catholic university must have the courage to speak uncomfortable truths which do not please public opinion, but which are necessary to safeguard the authentic good of society.

33. A specific priority is the need to examine and evaluate the predominant values and norms of modern society and culture in a Christian perspective, and the responsibility to try to communicate to society those ethical and religious principles which give full meaning to human life. In this way a university can

contribute further to the development of a true Christian anthropology, founded on the person of Christ, which will bring the dynamism of the creation and redemption to bear on reality and on the correct solution to the problems of life.

34. The Christian spirit of service to others for the promotion of social justice is of particular importance for each Catholic university, to be shared by its teachers and developed in its students. The church is firmly committed to the integral growth of all men and women.[32] The Gospel, interpreted in the social teachings of the church, is an urgent call to promote "the development of those peoples who are striving to escape from hunger, misery, endemic diseases, and ignorance; of those who are looking for a wider share in the benefits of civilization and a more active improvement of their human qualities; of those who are aiming purposefully at their complete fulfillment."[33] Every Catholic university feels responsible to contribute concretely to the progress of the society within which it works: For example it will be capable of searching for ways to make university education accessible to all those who are able to benefit from it, especially the poor or members of minority groups who customarily have been deprived of it. A Catholic university also has the responsibility, to the degree that it is able, to help to promote the development of the emerging nations.

35. In its attempts to resolve these complex issues that touch on so many different dimensions of human life and of society, a Catholic university will insist on cooperation among the different academic disciplines, each offering its distinct contribution in the search for solutions; moreover, since the economic and personal resources of a single institution are limited, cooperation in common research projects among Catholic universities, as well as with other private and governmental institutions, is imperative. In this regard, and also in what pertains to the other fields of the specific activity of a Catholic university, the role played by various national and international associations of Catholic universities is to be emphasized. Among these associations the mission of the International Federation of Catholic Universities, founded by the Holy See,[34] is particularly to be remembered. The Holy See anticipates further fruitful collaboration with this federation.

36. Through programs of continuing education offered to the wider community, by making its scholars available for consulting services, by taking advantage of modern means of communication, and in a variety of other ways, a Catholic university can assist in making the growing body of human knowledge and a developing understanding of the faith available to a wider public, thus expanding university services beyond its own academic community.

37. In its service to society, a Catholic university will relate especially to the academic, cultural, and scientific world of the region in which it is located.

Original forms of dialogue and collaboration are to be encouraged between the Catholic universities and the other universities of a nation on behalf of development, of understanding between cultures, and of the defense of nature in accordance with an awareness of the international ecological situation.

Catholic universities join other private and public institutions in serving the public interest through higher education and research; they are one among the variety of different types of institutions that are necessary for the free expression of cultural diversity, and they are committed to the promotion of solidarity and its meaning in society and in the world. Therefore they have the full right to expect that civil society and public authorities will recognize and defend their institutional autonomy and academic freedom; moreover, they have the right to the financial support that is necessary for their continued existence and development.

2. *Pastoral Ministry*

38. Pastoral ministry is that activity of the university which offers the members of the university community an opportunity to integrate religious and moral principles with their academic study and nonacademic activities, thus integrating faith with life. It is part of the mission of the church within the university, and is also a constitutive element of a Catholic university itself, both in its structure and in its life. A university community concerned with promoting the institution's Catholic character will be conscious of this pastoral dimension and sensitive to the ways in which it can have an influence on all university activities.

39. As a natural expression of the Catholic identity of the university, the university community should give a practical demonstration of its faith in its daily activity, with important moments of reflection and of prayer. Catholic members of this community will be offered opportunities to assimilate Catholic teaching and practice into their lives and will be encouraged to participate in the celebration of the sacraments, especially the eucharist as the most perfect act of community worship. When the academic community includes members of other churches, ecclesial communities, or religions, their initiatives for reflection and prayer in accordance with their own beliefs are to be respected.

40. Those involved in pastoral ministry will encourage teachers and students to become more aware of their responsibility towards those who are suffering physically or spiritually. Following the example of Christ, they will be particularly attentive to the poorest and to those who suffer economic, social, cultural, or religious injustice. This responsibility begins within the academic community, but it also finds application beyond it.

41. Pastoral ministry is an indispensable means by which Catholic students can, in fulfillment of their baptism, be prepared for active participation in the life of the church; it can assist in developing and nurturing the value of marriage and family life, fostering vocations to the priesthood and religious life, stimulating the Christian commitment of the laity, and imbuing every activity with the spirit of the Gospel. Close cooperation between pastoral ministry in a Catholic university and the other activities within the local church, under the guidance or with the approval of the diocesan bishop, will contribute to their mutual growth.

42. Various associations or movements of spiritual and apostolic life, especially those developed specifically for students, can be of great assistance in developing the pastoral aspects of university life.[35]

3. Cultural Dialogue

43. By its very nature, a university develops culture through its research, helps to transmit the local culture to each succeeding generation through its teaching, and assists cultural activities through its educational services. It is open to all human experience and is ready to dialogue with and learn from any culture. A Catholic university shares in this, offering the rich experience of the church's own culture. In addition, a Catholic university, aware that human culture is open to revelation and transcendence, is also a primary and privileged place for a fruitful dialogue between the Gospel and culture.

44. Through this dialogue a Catholic university assists the church, enabling it to come to a better knowledge of diverse cultures, discern their positive and negative aspects, to receive their authentically human contributions, and to develop means by which it can make the faith better understood by men and women of a particular culture.[36] While it is true that the Gospel cannot be identified with any particular culture and transcends all cultures, it is also true that "the kingdom which the Gospel proclaims is lived by men and women who are profoundly linked to a culture, and the building up of the kingdom cannot avoid borrowing the elements of human culture or cultures."[37] "A faith that places itself on the margin of what is human, of what is therefore culture, would be a faith unfaithful to the fullness of what the word of God manifests and reveals, a decapitated faith, worse still, a faith in the process of self-annihilation."[38]

45. A Catholic university must become more attentive to the cultures of the world of today, and to the various cultural traditions existing within the church in a way that will promote a continuous and profitable dialogue between the Gospel and modern society. Among the criteria that characterize the values of

a culture are above all, the meaning of the human person, his or her liberty, dignity, sense of responsibility, and openness to the transcendent. To a respect for persons is joined the preeminent value of the family, the primary unit of every human culture.

Catholic universities will seek to discern and evaluate both the aspirations and the contradictions of modern culture, in order to make it more suited to the total development of individuals and peoples. In particular, it is recommended that by means of appropriate studies, the impact of modern technology and especially of the mass media on persons, the family, and the institutions and whole of modern culture be studied deeply. Traditional cultures are to be defended in their identity, helping them to receive modern values without sacrificing their own heritage, which is a wealth for the whole of the human family. Universities, situated within the ambience of these cultures, will seek to harmonize local cultures with the positive contributions of modern cultures.

46. An area that particularly interests a Catholic university is the dialogue between Christian thought and the modern sciences. This task requires persons particularly well versed in the individual disciplines and who are at the same time adequately prepared theologically, and who are capable of confronting epistemological questions at the level of the relationship between faith and reason. Such dialogue concerns the natural sciences as much as the human sciences which posit new and complex philosophical and ethical problems. The Christian researcher should demonstrate the way in which human intelligence is enriched by the higher truth that comes from the Gospel: "The intelligence is never diminished, rather, it is stimulated and reinforced by that interior fount of deep understanding that is the word of God, and by the hierarchy of values that results from it. . . . In its unique manner, the Catholic university helps to manifest the superiority of the spirit, that can never, without the risk of losing its very self, be placed at the service of something other than the search for truth."[39]

47. Besides cultural dialogue, a Catholic university, in accordance with its specific ends, and keeping in mind the various religious-cultural contexts, following the directives promulgated by competent ecclesiastical authority, can offer a contribution to ecumenical dialogue. It does so to further the search for unity among all Christians. In interreligious dialogue it will assist in discerning the spiritual values that are present in the different religions.

4. Evangelization

48. The primary mission of the church is to preach the Gospel in such a way that a relationship between faith and life is established in each individual and in the

socio-cultural context in which individuals live and act and communicate with one another. Evangelization means "bringing the good news into all the strata of humanity, and through its influence transforming humanity from within and making it new.... It is a question not only of preaching the Gospel in ever wider geographic areas or to ever greater numbers of people, but also of affecting and, as it were, upsetting, through the power of the Gospel, humanity's criteria of judgment, determining values, points of interest, lines of thought, sources of inspiration, and models of life, which are in contrast with the word of God and the plan of salvation."[40]

49. By its very nature, each Catholic university makes an important contribution to the church's work of evangelization. It is a living institutional witness to Christ and his message, so vitally important in cultures marked by secularism, or where Christ and his message are still virtually unknown. Moreover, all the basic academic activities of a Catholic university are connected with and in harmony with the evangelizing mission of the church: research carried out in the light of the Christian message which puts new human discoveries at the service of individuals and society; education offered in a faith-context that forms men and women capable of rational and critical judgment and conscious of the transcendent dignity of the human person; professional training that incorporates ethical values and a sense of service to individuals and to society; the dialogue with culture that makes the faith better understood, and the theological research that translates the faith into contemporary language. "Precisely because it is more and more conscious of its salvific mission in this world, the church wants to have these centers closely connected with it; it wants to have them present and operative in spreading the authentic message of Christ."[41]

II. GENERAL NORMS

ARTICLE 1. THE NATURE OF THESE GENERAL NORMS

1. These general norms are based on, and are a further development of, the Code of Canon Law[42] and the complementary church legislation, without prejudice to the right of the Holy See to intervene should this become necessary. They are valid for all Catholic universities and other Catholic institutes of higher studies throughout the world.

2. The general norms are to be applied concretely at the local and regional levels by episcopal conferences and other assemblies of Catholic hierarchy[43] in

conformity with the Code of Canon Law and complementary church legislation, taking into account the statutes of each university or institute and, as far
as possible and appropriate, civil law. After review by the Holy See,[44] these local
or regional "ordinances" will be valid for all Catholic universities and other
Catholic institutes of higher studies in the region, except for ecclesiastical universities and faculties. These latter institutions, including ecclesiastical faculties
which are part of a Catholic university, are governed by the norms of the apostolic constitution *Sapientia Christiana*.[45]

3. A university established or approved by the Holy See, by an episcopal conference or another assembly of Catholic hierarchy, or by a diocesan bishop is to
incorporate these general norms and their local regional applications into its
governing documents, and conform its existing statutes both to the general
norms and to their applications, and submit them for approval to the competent ecclesiastical authority. It is contemplated that other Catholic universities, that is, those not established or approved in any of the above ways, with the
agreement of the local ecclesiastical authority, will make their own the general
norms and their local and regional applications, internalizing them into their
governing documents, and, as far as possible, will conform their existing statutes
both to these general norms and to their applications.

Article 2. The Nature of a Catholic University

1. A Catholic university, like every university, is a community of scholars representing various branches of human knowledge. It is dedicated to research,
to teaching, and to various kinds of service in accordance with its cultural
mission.

2. A Catholic university, as Catholic, informs and carries out its research,
teaching, and all other activities with Catholic ideals, principles and attitudes.
It is linked with the church either by a formal, constitutive and statutory bond
or by reason of an institutional commitment made by those responsible for it.

3. Every Catholic university is to make known its Catholic identity, either in
a mission statement or in some other appropriate public document, unless authorized otherwise by the competent ecclesiastical authority. The university, particularly through its structure and its regulations, is to provide means which will
guarantee the expression and the preservation of this identity in a manner consistent with Section 2.

4. Catholic teaching and discipline are to influence all university activities,
while the freedom of conscience of each person is to be fully respected.[46] Any

official action or commitment of the university is to be in accord with its Catholic identity.

5. A Catholic university possesses the autonomy necessary to develop its distinctive identity and pursue its proper mission. Freedom in research and teaching is recognized and respected according to the principles and methods of each individual discipline, so long as the rights of the individual and of the community are preserved within the confines of the truth and the common good.[47]

ARTICLE 3. THE ESTABLISHMENT OF A CATHOLIC UNIVERSITY

1. A Catholic university may be established or approved by the Holy See, by an episcopal conference or another assembly of Catholic hierarchy, or by a diocesan bishop.

2. With the consent of the diocesan bishop, a Catholic university may also be established by a religious institute or other public juridical person.

3. A Catholic university may also be established by other ecclesiastical or lay persons; such a university may refer to itself as a Catholic university only with the consent of the competent ecclesiastical authority, in accordance with the conditions upon which both parties shall agree.[48]

4. In the cases of Sections 1 and 2, the statutes must be approved by the competent ecclesiastical authority.

ARTICLE 4. THE UNIVERSITY COMMUNITY

1. The responsibility for maintaining and strengthening the Catholic identity of the university rests primarily with the university itself. While this responsibility is entrusted principally to university authorities (including, when the positions exist, the chancellor and/or a board of trustees or equivalent body), it is shared in varying degrees by all members of the university community, and therefore calls for the recruitment of adequate university personnel, especially teachers and administrators, who are both willing and able to promote that identity. The identity of a Catholic university is essentially linked to the quality of its teachers and to respect for Catholic doctrine. It is the responsibility of the competent authority to watch over these two fundamental needs in accordance with what is indicated in canon law.[49]

2. All teachers and all administrators, at the time of their appointment, are to be informed about the Catholic identity of the institution and its im-

plications, and about their responsibility to promote, or at least to respect, that identity.

3. In ways appropriate to the different academic disciplines, all Catholic teachers are to be faithful to, and all other teachers are to respect, Catholic doctrine and morals in their research and teaching. In particular, Catholic theologians, aware that they fulfill a mandate received from the church, are to be faithful to the magisterium of the church as the authentic interpreter of sacred Scripture and sacred tradition.[50]

4. Those university teachers and administrators who belong to other churches, ecclesial communities, or religions, as well as those who profess no religious belief, and also all students, are to recognize and respect the distinctive Catholic identity of the university. In order not to endanger the Catholic identity of the university or institute of studies, the number of non-Catholic teachers should not be allowed to constitute a majority within the institution, which is and must remain Catholic.

5. The education of students is to combine academic and professional development with formation in moral and religious principles and the social teachings of the church; the program of studies for each of the various professions is to include an appropriate ethical formation in that profession. Courses in Catholic doctrine are to be made available to all students.[51]

ARTICLE 5. THE CATHOLIC UNIVERSITY WITHIN THE CHURCH

1. Every Catholic university is to maintain communion with the universal church and the Holy See; it is to be in close communion with the local church and in particular with the diocesan bishops of the region or nation in which it is located. In ways consistent with its nature as a university, a Catholic university will contribute to the church's work of evangelization.

2. Each bishop has a responsibility to promote the welfare of the Catholic universities in his diocese and has the right and duty to watch over the preservation and strengthening of their Catholic character. If problems should arise concerning this Catholic character, the local bishop is to take the initiatives necessary to resolve the matter, working with the competent university authorities in accordance with established procedures[52] and, if necessary, with the help of the Holy See.

3. Periodically, each Catholic university to which Article 3, Section 1 and 2 refers is to communicate relevant information about the university and its activities to the competent ecclesiastical authority. Other Catholic universities

are to communicate this information to the bishop of the diocese in which the principal seat of the institution is located.

Article 6. Pastoral Ministry

1. A Catholic university is to promote the pastoral care of all members of the university community, and to be especially attentive to the spiritual development of those who are Catholics. Priority is to be given to those means which will facilitate the integration of human and professional education with religious values in the light of Catholic doctrine, in order to unite intellectual learning with the religious dimension of life.

2. A sufficient number of qualified people—priests, religious, and lay persons—are to be appointed to provide pastoral ministry for the university community, carried on in harmony and cooperation with the pastoral activities of the local church under the guidance or with the approval of the diocesan bishop. All members of the university community are to be invited to assist the work of pastoral ministry, and to collaborate in its activities.

Article 7. Cooperation

1. In order better to confront the complex problems facing modern society, and in order to strengthen the Catholic identity of the institutions, regional, national, and international cooperation is to be promoted in research, teaching, and other university activities among all Catholic universities, including ecclesiastical universities and faculties.[53] Such cooperation is also to be promoted between Catholic universities and other universities, and with other research and educational institutions, both private and governmental.

2. Catholic universities will, when possible and in accord with Catholic principles and doctrine, cooperate with government programs and the programs of other national and international organizations on behalf of justice, development, and progress.

TRANSITIONAL NORMS

Article 8

The present constitution will come into effect on the first day of the academic year 1991.

ARTICLE 9

The application of the constitution is committed to the Congregation for Catholic Education, which has the duty to promulgate the necessary directives that will serve toward that end.

ARTICLE 10

It will be the competence of the Congregation for Catholic Education, when with the passage of time circumstances require it, to propose changes to be made in the present constitution in order that it may be adapted continuously to the needs of Catholic universities.

ARTICLE 11

Any particular laws or customs presently in effect that are contrary to this constitution are abolished. Also, any privileges granted up to this day by the Holy See whether to physical or moral persons that are contrary to this present constitution are abolished.

CONCLUSION

The mission that the church, with great hope, entrusts to Catholic universities holds a cultural and religious meaning of vital importance because it concerns the very future of humanity. The renewal requested to Catholic universities will make them better able to respond to the task of bringing the message of Christ to man, to society, to various cultures: "Every human reality, both individual and social, has been liberated by Christ: persons, as well as the activities of men and women, of which culture is the highest and incarnate expression. The salvific action of the church on cultures is achieved, first of all, by means of persons, families and educators. . . . Jesus Christ, our Savior, offers his light and his hope to all those who promote the sciences, the arts, letters, and the numerous fields developed by modern culture. Therefore, all the sons and daughters of the church should become aware of their mission and discover how the strength of the Gospel can penetrate and regenerate the mentalities and dominant values that inspire individual cultures, as well as the opinions and mental attitudes that are derived from it."[54]

It is with fervent hope that I address this document to all the men and women engaged in various ways in the significant mission of Catholic higher education.

Beloved brothers and sisters, my encouragement and my trust go with you in your weighty daily task that becomes ever more important, more urgent, and necessary on behalf of evangelization for the future of culture and of all cultures. The church and the world have great need of your witness and of your capable, free, and responsible contribution.

Given in Rome, at Saint Peter's, on August 15, the Solemnity of the Assumption of the Blessed Virgin Mary into heaven, in the year 1990, the twelfth of the pontificate.

Pope John Paul II

NOTES

1. Cf. The letter of Pope Alexander IV to the University of Paris, April 14, 1255, Introduction, *Bullarum Diplomatrum . . .* , vol. 3, (Turin 1858), p. 602.

2. St. Augustine, *Confessions,* X, xxiii, 33, "In fact, the blessed life consists in *the joy that comes from the truth,* since this joy comes from you who are truth, God my light, salvation of my face, my God," *Patrologia Latina* 32, pp. 793–794. Cf. St. Thomas Aquinas, *De Malo,* IX, 1: "It is actually natural to man to strive for knowledge of the truth."

3. John Paul II, Discourse to the Catholic Institute of Paris, June 1, 1980: *Insegnamenti di Giovanni Paolo II,* vol. 3/1 (1980), p. 1581.

4. John Paul II, Discourse to the Cardinals, Nov. 10, 1979: *Insegnamenti di Giovanni Paolo II,* vol. 2/2 (1979), p. 1096; cf. Discourse to UNESCO, Paris, June 2, 1980: *Acta Apostolicae Sedis* 72 (1980), pp. 735–752.

5. Cf. John Paul II, Discourse to the University of Coimbra, May 15, 1982: *Insegnamenti di Giovanni Paolo II,* vol. 5/2 (1982), p. 1692.

6. Paul VI, Allocution to Representatives of States, October 4, 1965: *Insegnamenti di Paolo VI,* vol. 3 (1965), p. 508.

7. Cardinal John Henry Newman, *The Idea of a University* (London: Longmans, Green and Company, 1931), p. XI.

8. *Jn.* 14:6.

9. Cf. St. Augustine, *Sterm.* 43, 9: PL 38, 258. Cf. also St. Anselm, *Proslogion,* Ch. I: PL 158, p. 227.

10. Cf. John Paul II, Allocution to the International Congress on Catholic Universities, April 25, 1989, no. 3: *AAS* 18 (1989), p. 1218.

11. Ibid., *Sapientia Christiana,* Apostolic Constitution Concerning the Ecclesiastical Universities and Faculties, April 15, 1979: *AAS* 17 (1979), pp. 469–521.

12. Vatican Council II, Declaration on Catholic Education *(Gravissimum Educationis),* 10: *AAS* 58 (1966), p. 737.

13. *Mt.* 13:52.

14. Cf. *The Magna Carta of the European Universities,* Bologna, Italy, September 18, 1988, "Fundamental Principles."

15. Cf. Vatican Council II, Pastoral Constitution on the Church in the Modern World *(Gaudium et Spes)*, 59: *AAS* 58 (1966), p. 1080; *Gravissimum Educationis*, 10: *AAS* 58 (1966), p. 737. *Institutional autonomy* means that the governance of an academic institution is and remains internal to the institution; *academic freedom* is the guarantee given to those involved in teaching and research that, within their specific specialized branch of knowledge and according to the methods proper to that specific area, they may search for the truth wherever analysis and evidence lead them, and may teach and publish the results of this search, keeping in mind the cited criteria, that is, safeguarding the rights of the individual and of society within the confines of the truth and the common good.

16. There is a two-fold notion of *culture* used in the document: the *humanistic* and the *socio-historical.* "The word *culture* in its general sense indicates all those factors by which man refines and unfolds his manifold spiritual and bodily qualities. It means his effort to bring the world itself under his control by his knowledge and his labor. It includes the fact that by improving customs and institutions he renders social life more human both within the family and in the civic community. Finally, it is a feature of culture that throughout the course of time man expresses, communicates, and conserves in his works great spiritual experiences and desires, so that these may be of advantage to the progress of many, even of the whole human family. Hence it follows that human culture necessarily has a historical and social aspect and that the word culture often takes on a sociological and ethnological sense" *Gaudium et Spes*, 53.

17. "The Catholic University in the Modern World," final document of the Second International Congress of Delegates of Catholic Universities, Rome, Nov. 20–29, 1972, sec. 1.

18. Ibid.

19. John Paul II, Allocution to the International Congress of Catholic Universities. Cf. also *Gaudium et Spes*, 61. Cardinal Newman observes that a university "professes to assign to each study which it receives, its proper place and its just boundaries; to define the rights, to establish the mutual relations and to effect the intercommunion of one and all" (*The Idea of a University*, p. 457).

20. *Gaudium et Spes*, 36. To a group of scientists I pointed out that "while reason and faith surely represents two distinct orders of knowledge, each autonomous with regard to its own methods, the two must finally converge in the discovery of a single whole reality which has its origin in God" (John Paul II, Address at the Meeting on Galileo, May 9, 1983, no. 3: *AAS* 75 [1983], p. 690).

21. John Paul II, Address at UNESCO, 22. The last part of the quotation uses words directed to the Pontifical Academy of Sciences, Nov. 10, 1979: *Insegnamenti di Giovanni Paolo II*, vol. 2/2 (1979), p. 1109.

22. Cf. *Gravissimum Educationis*, 10.

23. *Gaudium et Spes*, 59. Cardinal Newman describes the ideal to be sought in this way: "A habit of mind is formed which lasts through life, of which the attributes are freedom, equitableness, calmness, moderation, and wisdom" (*The Idea of a University*, pp. 101–102).

24. John Paul II, apostolic exhortation *Christifideles Laici*, Dec. 30, 1988, no. 44: *AAS* 81 (1989), p. 479.

25. Vatican Council II, Dogmatic Constitution on the Church (*Lumen Gentium*), 31: *AAS* 57 (1965), pp. 37–38. Cf. Decree on the Apostolate of the Laity (*Apostolican Actuositatem*), passim: *AAS* 58 (1966), pp. 837 ff. Cf. also *Gaudium et Spes*, 43.

26. Cf. ibid., Declaration on Religious Liberty *(Dignitatis Humanae)*, 2: *AAS* 58 (1966), pp. 930–931.

27. John Paul II, Address to Leaders of Catholic Higher Education, Xavier University of Louisiana, September 12, 1987, no. 4: *AAS* 80 (1988), p. 764.

28. *Gaudium et Spes*, 59.

29. Cf. Vatican Council II, Dogmatic Constitution on Divine Revelation *(Dei Verbum)*, nos. 8–10: *AAS* 58 (1966), pp. 820–822.

30. Cf. *Lumen Gentium*, 25.

31. Cf. Congregation for the Doctrine of the Faith, Instruction on the Ecclesial Vocation of the Theologian, May 24, 1990.

32. Cf. John Paul II, encyclical *Sollicitudo Rei Socialis*, 27–34: *AAS* 80 (1988), pp. 547–560.

33. Paul VI, encyclical *Populorum Progressio*, 1: *AAS* 59 (1967), p. 257.

34. "Therefore, in that there has been a pleasing multiplication of centers of higher learning, it has become apparent that it would be opportune for the faculty and the alumni to unite in common association which, working in reciprocal understanding and close collaboration, and based upon the authority of the supreme pontiff, as father and university doctor, they might more efficaciously spread and extend the light of Christ" (Pius XII, apostolic letter *Catholicas Studiorum Universitates*, with which the International Federation of Catholic Universities was established: *AAS* 42 [1950], p. 386).

35. The Code of Canon Law indicates the general responsibility of the bishop toward university students: "The diocesan bishop is to have serious pastoral concern for students by erecting a parish for them or by assigning a priest for this purpose on a stable basis, he is also to provide for Catholic university centers at universities, even non-Catholic ones, to give assistance, especially spiritual to young people" (Canon 813).

36. "Living in various circumstances during the course of time, the church, too has used in her preaching the discoveries of different cultures to spread and explain the message of Christ to all nations, to probe it and more deeply understand it, and to give it better expression in liturgical celebrations and in the life of the diversified community of the faithful" (*Gaudium et Spes*, 58).

37. Paul VI, apostolic exhortation *Evangelii Nuntiandi*, 20: *AAS* 68 (1976), p. 18. Cf. *Gaudium et Spes*, 58.

38. John Paul II, Address to Intellectuals, Students, and University Personnel, July 5, 1986, n. 3: *AAS* 79 (1987), p. 99. Also *Gaudium et Spes*, 58.

39. Paul VI, Address to Delegates of the International Federation of Catholic Universities, Nov. 27, 1972: *AAS* 46 (1972), p. 770.

40. Paul VI, *Evangelii Nuntiandi*, 18 ff.

41. Paul VI, Address to Presidents and Rectors of the Universities of the Society of Jesus, August 6, 1975, no. 2: *AAS* 67 (1975), p. 553. Speaking to the participants of the International Congress on Catholic Universities, April 25, 1989, I added (no. 5): "Within a Catholic university the evangelical mission of the church and the mission of research and teaching become interrelated and coordinated."

42. Cf. in particular the chapter of the code: "Catholic Universities and Other Institutes of Higher Studies" (Canon 807–814).

43. Episcopal conferences were established in the Latin rite. Other rites have other assemblies of Catholic hierarchy.

44. Cf. Canon 455.2.

45. Cf. *Sapientia Christiana*. Ecclesiastical universities and faculties are those that have the right to confer academic degrees by the authority of the Holy See.

46. Cf. *Dignitatis Humanae*, 2.

47. Cf. *Gaudium et Spes*, 57 and 59; *Gravissimum Educationis*, 10.

48. Both the establishment of such a university and the conditions by which it may refer to itself as a Catholic university are to be in accordance with the prescription issued by the Holy See, episcopal conference, or other assembly of Catholic hierarchy.

49. Canon 810 of the Code of Canon Law specifies the responsibility of the competent authorities in this area: Section 1: "It is the responsibility of the authority who is competent in accord with the statutes to provide for the appointment of teachers to Catholic universities who, besides their scientific and pedagogical suitability, are also outstanding in their integrity of doctrine and probity of life; when those requisite qualities are lacking they are to be removed from their positions in accord with the procedure set forth in the statutes. Section 2: The conference of bishops and the diocesan bishops concerned have the duty and right of being vigilant that in these universities the principles of Catholic doctrine are faithfully observed." Cf. also Article 5.2 ahead in these norms.

50. *Lumen Gentium*, 25; *Dei Verbum*, 8–10; cf. Canon 812: "It is necessary that those who teach theological disciplines in any institute of higher studies have a mandate from the competent ecclesiastical authority."

51. Cf. Canon 811.2.

52. For universities to which Article 3, Secs. 1 and 2 refer, these procedures are to be established in the university statutes approved by the ecclesiastical authority; for other Catholic universities, they are to be determined by episcopal conferences or other assemblies of Catholic hierarchy.

53. Cf. Canon 820. Cf. also *Sapientia Christiana*, "norms of application," Article 49.

54. John Paul II, Address to the Pontifical Council for Culture, Jan. 13, 1989, no. 2: *AAS* 81 (1989), pp. 857–858.

2 | Letter to Presidents of Catholic Colleges and Universities from Archbishop Daniel E. Pilarczyk

December 15, 1990

Dear ————

The Apostolic Constitution of Pope John Paul II on Catholic Higher Education, "Ex Corde Ecclesiae" gives Episcopal Conferences the responsibility of applying its general norms to local and regional levels.

I am pleased to announce that the following persons have accepted the invitation of the National Conference of Catholic Bishops to review the Constitution and aid in its implementation: Cardinal James Hickey of Washington, Archbishop Oscar Lipscomb of Mobile, Archbishop Adam Maida of Detroit, Archbishop Francis Schulte of New Orleans, Bishop James Griffin of Columbus, Bishop John Leibrecht of Springfield–Cape Girardeau, Bishop James Malone of Youngstown, Doctor Dorothy McKenna Brown of Rosemont College, Reverend William Byron, S.J. of the Catholic University of America, Brother Raymond Fitz, S.M. of the University of Dayton, Doctor Norman Francis of Xavier University, Sister Karen Kennelly, C.S.J. of Mount Saint Mary's College, Reverend Edward Malloy, C.S.C. of the University of Notre Dame, Reverend J. Donald Monan, S.J. of Boston College, and Doctor Matthew Quinn of Carroll College.

The Committee to implement the apostolic constitution will be assisted by the following resource persons: Sister Sharon Euart, RSM, Sister Alice Gallin, OSU, Reverend Charles Hagan, Mr. John Liekweg, Monsignor Frederick McManus, and Sister Lourdes Sheehan, RSM. The Committee will begin to meet

From the College of New Rochelle Archives, president's office files.

shortly after the beginning of the New Year. You will receive further updates on the work of the Committee.

I am grateful for your interest in this important initiative of our Conference.

Fraternally yours in Christ,

Most Reverend Daniel E. Pilarczyk
Archbishop of Cincinnati
President, NCCB/USCC

3 | Directives to Assist in the Formulation
of the Ordinances for the Apostolic
Constitution *Ex Corde Ecclesiae*

Congregation for Catholic Education

January 21, 1991

A. INTRODUCTION

1. These Directives of the Congregation for Catholic Education are to assist the
    Episcopal Conferences and other Assemblies of Catholic Hierarchy in draw-
    ing up the concrete applications (Ordinances) of the General Norms of the
    Apostolic Constitution "Ex Corde Ecclesiae", in accordance with General
    Norms, Article 1, §2 of that Constitution. The formulation of these Directives
    is a fulfillment of Transitional Norms, Article 9 of the same Constitution. As
    in the Constitution itself (cf. General Norms, Article 1, §1), so also in these
    Directives and in the Ordinances to be formulated, "Catholic University" in-
    cludes all other Catholic Institutions of Higher Studies (except Ecclesiastical
    Universities and Faculties, which are governed by the norms of the Apostolic
    Constitution "Sapientia Christiana", cf. General Norms Article 1, §2).
2. The background, the content, and the spirit of the Apostolic Constitution
    are to guide the drawing up of the Ordinances.
3. The Ordinances are to make the contents of the seven articles of the Gen-
    eral Norms concrete at the local and regional levels. This means that they
    are to specify the ways in which the General Norms are to be applied in the
    local context, not merely repeat the General Norms.
4. Episcopal Conferences and other Assemblies of Catholic Hierarchy are en-
    couraged to seek the collaborative assistance of the Catholic Universities in
    their respective countries in drawing up the Ordinances.

From the author's files.

B. DIRECTIVES

The basic elements which should appear in the Ordinances applying the Apostolic Constitution to local and regional circumstances are these:

1. In accord with Article 1, §§1, 2, and 3 of the General Norms, a listing of the different types of Catholic Universities and other Catholic Institutes of Higher Studies to be found in the region or country and the exact nature of the relationship of each type with the Church and with ecclesiastical authorities. On the basis of this listing, each Catholic institution should be asked to specify the category to which it belongs and the conditions under which it has received the consent of competent ecclesiastical Authority (cf. General Norms, Article 3, §3).

2. The essential elements to be contained in a mission statement or some other appropriate public document, by means of which the Catholic institution is to make known its Catholic identity (cf. General Norms, Article 2, §3).

3. The conditions under which a University established by private persons, ecclesiastical or lay, can be considered a Catholic University (cf. General Norms, 3, §3 and note 48).

4. The rights and duties pertaining to:
   a. the Episcopal Conference or other Assemblies of Catholic Hierarchy;
   b. the Bishop in whose diocese the Catholic University is located (cf. General Norms, Article 5, §2, CIC 810, §2);
   c. the Religious Institute which established the University, or which is responsible for it, or to which it is entrusted;
   d. the University itself and its authorities (cf. General Norms, Article 4, §1), including where the positions exist, the Chancellor and/or a Board of Trustees or equivalent body.

5. Appropriate procedures by which:
   a. to ensure the recruitment of teachers and administrative personnel willing and able to promote the institution's Catholic identity (cf. General Norms, Article 4, §1);
   b. at the time of their appointment, teachers and administrative personnel are to be informed about the Catholic identity of the institution and its implications (cf. General Norms, Article 4, §2);
   c. those who are Catholics will promote that identity, and those who are not Catholics will at least respect it (*ibid.*);
   d. those who teach theology will receive a mandate from the competent ecclesiastical authority (cf. Article 4, §3; CIC, 812);

   e. problems can be resolved (mandated by General Norms, Article 5, §2 and note 52);

   f. relevant information about the University and its activities are communicated to the competent ecclesiastical authority or the Bishop of the diocese (cf. General Norms, Article 5, §3).

6. Means to promote the teaching of theology in Catholic Universities (cf. CIC, 811; General Norms, Article 1, §2).

7. Means to ensure:

   a. that the education of students combines academic and professional development with formation in moral and religious principles and the social teachings of the Church;

   b. appropriate ethical formation in each of the professional studies;

   c. that courses in Catholic doctrine are available to all students (cf. General Norms, Article 4, §5).

8. Means to ensure that Pastoral Ministry for the University community is sufficiently cared for (cf. General Norms, Article 5, CIC; 813).

C. THE PROCESS TO BE FOLLOWED

1. After the Ordinances have been formulated by an Episcopal Conference or other Assembly of Catholic Hierarchy, they are to be sent to the Congregation for Catholic Education, which has been given the responsibility of reviewing them and declaring whether they conform to the Apostolic Constitution (cf. General Norms, Article 1, §2).

2. After the Ordinances have been reviewed by the Holy See, the Universities are to incorporate both the General Norms and the Ordinances into their Statutes or other documents of governance. The Universities referred to in the General Norms, Article 3, §§1, 2, and 4 are then to submit these to the competent ecclesiastical authority for approbation. For those Universities referred to in the General Norms, Article 3, §3 and note 48 it should be ascertained that the conditions under which they received the consent of the competent ecclesiastical authority are fulfilled.

3. The Apostolic Constitution comes into effect on the first day of the academic year 1991 (cf. Transitional Norms, Article 8). Episcopal Conferences and other Assemblies of Catholic Hierarchy should present their Ordinances to the Congregation for Catholic Education before 1 March 1992.

4 | "Mandate" in the Context of *Ex Corde Ecclesiae*: A Theologian's Reflections

Lisa Sowle Cahill

Presented to the Implementation Committee, September 9 –10, 1992

A recent survey on Catholic identity, conducted by Fordham University, yields the not surprising finding that while a bare majority of bishops (51%) see control of the hiring of theology faculty in Catholic universities and colleges as outside their role, 92% of higher education respondents would agree.[1] This discrepancy goes a long way toward explaining the need for this committee on "Ex Corde Ecclesiae," and also highlights the delicacy of its task. My own contribution to the discussion will be theological. I will aim to put the notion of "mandate"—a term with a primarily juridical function—in a broader theological context. In doing so, I will also indicate how the individual theologian and the theological community might respond to the prospect of defining theology's relation to the episcopacy primarily in terms of a "mandate."

My fundamental view is that there are two different interpretations of the bishop-theologian relationship appearing in papal statements and official documents such as "Ex Corde Ecclesiae." One envisions that relationship in a reciprocal, cooperative way, and one in a hierarchical, legal way. Theologians are much more encouraged in their work within the church when bishops are sympathetic to the former approach, and indeed it is a question whether the later one is compatible with a spirit of trust. The term "mandate" is usually associated with the juridical approach, because of its place in canon law. However, mandate can also be interpreted in the context of a *communio* between bishops and theologians. The community-centered interpretation may be conducive to a more flexible, progressive, and positive understanding of how bishops recognize theologians

From the author's files. Printed by permission of Lisa Sowle Cahill.

than that denoted by mandate as direct individual certification or cancellation of the theological function. In developing an argument in favor of the communally oriented interpretation of mandate, I will rely on the distinction between the theological and pastoral roles, on the variety of language in "Ex Corde Ecclesiae," on "Doctrinal Responsibilities" (an NCCB document to which the U.S. bishops have already given their approval), on Sharon Euart's distinction between mission and mandate, on biblical models of church as community, and on the effects on the theological community of different episcopal stances toward it.

A theological perspective on "mandate" may begin, then, by noting that there are at least two contrasting construals of the bishop-theologian relationship which may guide the discussion of mandate. One proceeds from canon law and views persons either in juridical terms or in relationship to a hierarchical structure. The other addresses Church as a community in which persons and groups have complementary functions. According to the first paradigm, the relationship is a structural one, realized via institutionalized procedures by which the episcopacy directly certifies theologians. The legal context highlights juridical processes by which an institution exercises control over its identity, prerogatives and members, even by negative sanctions. This interpretation is implied by placing the "mandate" as a requirement of canon law. According to a second paradigm, the bishop-theologian relationship is embedded in a larger community of religious identity, where theologians and bishops fulfill respective scholarly and pastoral functions. This view of the bishop-theologian relation gives more emphasis to the shared commitments, loyalty, and respect which give community its personal meaning—granting that large and extensive communities must also be sustained by institutional structures. Although it is part of the pastoral function of the bishop to reprove or exclude unacceptable theological proposals, the means of accomplishing this go beyond the revocation of a juridically granted mandate.[2] Legitimate episcopal care for authentic doctrine is perhaps even more effectively obtained through means which attend to the quality of community, than by more pointed but essentially restrictive measures.

In the present essay, I shall develop the second of these contexts—the communal—as especially important in comprehending the place of theology in the Church. Two aspects of the theological enterprise are crucial to the bishop-theologian relationship in such a context. First, theology is inquiry rather than catechesis. It is a branch of scholarship, a field of study appropriately conducted within the university; and it is precisely as scholarly inquiry that theology contributes to the community. Second, church as community (*koinonia, communio*) of Christian faith and life is a reality in which bishops, Catholic institutions of higher learning, and theologians all participate by fulfilling discrete but complementary roles. Development of the first aspect, which places theology within the academy, involves reference to academic freedom; the second, which locates theology in the church as community, will examine the notion of "mandate" via a comparison of biblical models of church with a recent CDF letter on *communio*.

I. THE CATHOLIC UNIVERSITY AND THEOLOGY

In "Ex Corde Ecclesiae," John Paul II alludes to his personal enrichment by the university's "ardent search for truth" and its commitment to "think rigorously" as well as to "act rightly" (no. 2).[3] He continues, "a Catholic university is distinguished by its free search for the whole truth about nature, man and God," and commends the "universal humanism" of Catholic education (no. 4), which permits "impartial" (no. 5) research of truth "without fear, but rather with enthusiasm" (no. 4).

Traditionally, the possibility of attaining theological and moral truths through intellectual and scientific work has been very important to Roman Catholicism. This note is sounded in the pope's affirmation of the unity of all truth, and of faith and reason (no. 17). Developing Anselm's and Augustine's theme of "faith seeking understanding," Catholicism since Aquinas and the medieval universities has envisioned theology as a part of the "sacred teaching" (*sacra doctrina*) which begins with God's self-revelation, and also as a kind of science. While theology presumes faith and begins from revelation, it is still an academic discipline alongside philosophy.[4] "Ex Corde Ecclesiae" picks up this theme: "Theology has its legitimate place in the university alongside other disciplines. It has proper principles and methods which define it as a branch of knowledge" (no. 29). In the contemporary university, theology is a discipline carried out among colleagues motivated by the "ultimate questions" about God, humanity, life and death. In the Catholic university, these questions are pursued on the basis of a shared dedication to the Roman Catholic tradition of Christianity as a secure bearer of insight into these realities. The mode in or method by which theology interacts with the tradition is constituted by intellectual inquiry, critical argument, and reliance upon the many related scholarly disciplines which are the university's distinctive resources.

In contrast, the bishop's work may be described in the words of James T. McHugh, Bishop of Camden NJ, as a "responsib[ility] to proclaim the faith, preserve the faith, and encourage the development of a faith perspective in all his people." His role "is primarily a pastoral role."[5] This view is confirmed in

"Doctrinal Responsibilities," a set of guidelines worked out through the cooperation of the Canon Law Society of America, the Catholic Theological Society
of America, and the Committee on Doctrine of the NCCB, and approved by the
bishops at their June, 1989, meeting at Seton Hall University. According to this
document, "bishops have the pastoral duty in the name of Christ to proclaim
the word of God with authority, to teach the truth of the faith and to maintain
the authentic interpretation of the word of God as it has been handed down
in the course of history. . . ." The theologian, on the other hand, is "the Catholic
who seeks to mediate through the discipline of scholarship, between a living
faith and the culture it is called to transform." Therefore, theologians "serve the
Gospel . . . through their scholarly work," but "they are not primarily preachers or catechists."[6] Examples of the bishop's work are "authoritative teaching
and pastoral leadership," while theologians engage in "ethical reflection, theological education and research."[7]

Clearly, theology as scholarship is different from catechesis and doctrinal
proclamation. As a consequence, the relation of the bishop to doctrine (and its
teachers) may be different from his relation to theology. In her history of *missio* and *mandatum* in canon law, Sharon Euart alludes to this distinction in her
clarification of the use of the term "mandatum" in canon 812. Essentially, she
makes the argument that, if one reads this canon in the light of Vatican II's Decree on the Apostolate of the Laity, it implies a looser supervisory role of the
hierarchy in relation to theology than to the teaching of doctrine. The distinction is key, not for the legitimacy of the hierarchy's concern for the teaching of
theology, but for the form in which that concern receives expression.

The Decree on the Apostolate of the Laity, article 24, uses the word *man-
daturm* to refer to some forms of the apostolate of the laity which are joined to
that of the hierarchy, but which retain relative autonomy; it also uses the term
missio to refer to other activities of the laity which are "entrusted" by the hierarchy, and "which are more closely connected with the pastoral duties of the
hierarchy, such as the teaching of Christian doctrine."[8] In the words of the Decree, the "mandate" is "a procedure of the hierarchy" by which it "joins" some
form of the laity's activity, under the condition that "the proper nature and individuality of each apostolate must be preserved, and the laity must not be de-
prived of the possibility of acting on their own accord." By contrast, the word
"mission" is used to designate entrusted functions (including "the teaching of
Christian doctrine") which "are fully subject to higher ecclesiastical direction
in the performance of such work" (no. 24).

The use of the word *mandatum* in canon 812 suggests that the work to which
reference is being made—theology—differs from teaching doctrine, by vir-

tue of a less close and non derivative relation to the bishop. Unlike the teaching of doctrine (requiring a *missio*), the "theological disciplines" are not "entrusted" to the laity by the individual bishops, and, it follows, not necessarily delegated or governed by the latter. Theology is work proper to the laity (often done by clerics, but not as a direct function of ordination), carried out in "communion" with the hierarchy, but not requiring the same degree of "ecclesiastical direction." (Even on this interpretation, however, at least according to canon law, "some authorization, approval or recognition from ecclesiastical authority is needed for those who teach theological disciplines in Catholic colleges and universities."[9] The nature of the "recognition" which the episcopacy might best give theology will be addressed further under the topic of community.)

The work and purpose of theology are also addressed in "Ex Corde Ecclesiae." When one compares the document's picture of theology with its ideals for the university, one appreciates the President of Fordham's suspicion that "the language in *Ex Corde Ecclesiae* in several instances is carefully constructed to paper over very different perspectives. . . ."[10] The constitution envisions that theology is "faithful to Scripture, tradition and the church's magisterium," and so will foster awareness of "Gospel principles" (no. 20); theologians seek to understand and "effectively" communicate "revelation as transmitted in Scripture and tradition and in the church's magisterium" (no. 29). Now a theologian could hardly disagree either with the proposition that the subject matter of theology comes from Scripture and tradition, the same subject matter which the magisterium seeks to transmit; or that it is important to foster in the Catholic university "Gospel principles." The issue is rather that emphasis in the task of *theology* has swung away from scholarship to what more properly might be called proclamation or catechesis, that is, toward a task which is more doctrinal and pastoral. This is all the more evident in the document's description of teaching theology, not as induction into the scholar's sources, methods, and criteria for seeking truth, but as "formation in moral and religious principles;" and its insistence that "[c]ourses in Catholic doctrine are to be made available to all students" (Article 4.5). However, in the contemporary university, theology is respected as a scholarly discipline, not as aimed *primarily* at the personal religious and moral formation of students (which may be a very legitimate and desirable secondary effect). Theology cannot be reduced to catechesis or religious formation or preaching. These all have their place in the Catholic university, but they are not the specific function of the theology faculty. In the field of theology, scholarly inquiry is first, and is indeed the spring out of which a deepening of faith and religious identity often flow.

At least in North America, a phrase which is symbolic of the scholarly and academic nature of intellectual inquiry in the university is "academic freedom." This phrase, reminiscent of the Western political emphasis on "freedom of speech" and "freedom of religion" as civil liberties, can often carry an individualistic and libertarian connotation. For this reason, I am not absolutely committed to it as an expression of theology's contribution to Catholic life, whether intellectual or ecclesial. However, one thing the notion does accomplish is to affirm the status of theology as a fully and integrally functioning member of the university community, that is, as a legitimate field of academic research. Since "academic freedom" appears favorably in "Ex Corde Ecclesiae," it is useful to examine the nuances which are there given it (no. 29 and footnote 15). The important thing is that, while those who teach and do research may adhere to the methods of their specialization and "search for the truth wherever analysis and evidence lead them," as well as "teach and publish the results of this search," this enterprise is carried out in the service of "the truth and the common good" (footnote 15). In the document, academic research takes on the additional role of fulfilling the good of the community—presumably, the community in both its academic and ecclesial senses.

How are this communal good and the discovery of truth best served? A social concept, academic freedom specifies the dialogue and dialectical expansion of viewpoint requisite to intellectual advancement. It indicates the collegial process of thesis, antithesis, refinement, and reformulation or synthesis, which is constitutive of research itself. In other words, theology is an academic discipline with a place in the university, not as doctrinal definition, preaching or catechesis, but as scholarly investigation of those things affirmed in Scripture and tradition. Theology's investigation is both fully free and fully accountable to the criteria of intellectual honesty, coherence, and rigor. This is its distinctive contribution to the common good of the Church. The Roman Catholic presupposition of faith and reason's compatibility make the Catholic university especially hospitable to the integrity of the theological enterprise.

II. BISHOPS, UNIVERSITIES AND THEOLOGIANS IN COMMUNITY

As does the description of the theological task, the portrayal of the relation between local ordinary and university theology receives a somewhat ambiguous treatment in *Ex Corde Ecclesiae*. On the one hand, "close personal and pastoral relationships" are commended to university and church authorities, relations "characterized by mutual trust, close and consistent cooperation and continuing dialogue" (no. 28). But on the other hand, in the crucial passage, "Catholic theologians, aware that they fulfill a mandate received from the church, are to be faithful to the magisterium of the church as the authentic interpreter of sacred Scripture and sacred tradition" (Article 4.3). It is evident that juridical procedures for granting and revoking such a mandate may be an issue, especially as indicated by canon 812.

Another canon cited in this context by "Ex Corde Ecclesiae" is 810, which assigns to bishops the duty of "being vigilant" toward the university's observance of "Catholic doctrine." While the English verb connotes a police function likely to be unappealing to pastors and presidents alike, even the canonical uses of the word "watchfulness" are susceptible to the more benign meaning of "avoiding danger." Avoidance is certainly a more attractive prospect than punitive intervention after the fact, and the question may now become how that avoidance is best and most positively accomplished. Especially since theology faculties are not directly dedicated to the promulgation of "doctrine," but rather to the study of theology, the establishment of a community of trust and free dialogue between the theological and the pastoral roles, unafraid of mutual criticism, could be a means of avoiding either doctrinal danger or theological confrontation, in accord with "Ex Corde Ecclesiae," no. 28 (calling for trust, cooperation, and dialogue). As the pope stated over a decade ago,

> The magisterium and theology have two different tasks to perform. That is why neither can be reduced to the other. Yet they serve the one whole. But precisely on account of this configuration they must remain in consultation with one another.[11]

Certainly "consultation" suggests a relationship of mutual respect and cooperation, and requires the kind of community in which it can become a reality.

In my view, the fostering of genuine community between universities and local ordinaries (and the bishops' conference), and between theologians and bishops, is the crucial issue, and without it, no amount of canon law loopholing or noose-tying will resolve the proper function of theological inquiry in the North American church. It is notable that the one direct mention of the mandate in the constitution on universities appears to regard theologians as *already* recognizing and fulfilling a mandate received from "the church," and to present the magisterium not in a juridical role, but as "authentic interpreter" of Scripture and tradition. This language, especially keeping in mind the distinction of doctrinal and theological functions, permits a wider construal of the theologian's vocation within the community, of the magisterium's role in conveying the essence of Scripture and tradition, and of mandate. It seems not to require that the local ordinary be involved directly in certifying individual theologians, or that a faithful theologian will give unquestioning assent to all proposals of the ordinary magisterium, even when they make no claim to infallibility. As I will clarify further with some examples at the end of this paper, theologians are most encouraged by a sense that personal interest and support are extended to them by the episcopal representatives of the church. A juridical approach to theological conformity undermines the work of theology and the morale of theologians.

Moreover, it should be recognized that most theologians have a sense of integrity which would prohibit easy acquiescence to episcopal demands which the theological community or the individual theologian considered inimical to the welfare of the church or the coherence of the theological enterprise. It is with a great deal of personal pain that theologians submit even to investigations which call into question their loyalty to Catholic tradition by defining the acceptable parameters of study with great narrowness. For many it would be a matter of character and principle to hold fast to the development of Catholic teaching as they most truly see it, rather than to yield under threat of administrative and economic reprisals. In the words of "Doctrinal Responsibilities," the implementation of the constitution on Catholic universities ought not "presuppose a situation of tension or envisage adversarial relations between bishops and theologians in the United States, as if the rights of one had to be protected against the other." Instead, it ought "to encourage increased communication and collaboration between bishops and theologians, to forestall disputes and if such disputes arise to promote their resolution for the good of the faithful."[12]

The broader context for the bishop-theologian relation is supported by comparing *koinonia* in the early church with a recent Vatican document on *communio*. I realize that the discussion of the latter term has recently referred to the relation between the universal church and the local churches, or even to that between the Vatican and local episcopal conferences. Yet the way *communio* is envisioned in general is quite pertinent to the relations at other levels. Indeed, according to the CDF's recent letter, this concept may be "the key to ecclesiology" (no. 3).[13]

The Vatican letter of last June emphasizes that, although the universal church may validly be seen as a communion of churches, the unity of the church in the institutional sense must not be threatened. The universal church is neither simply the aggregate of particular churches, nor a "federation" of them. The document begins by acknowledging that Bible and tradition envision the church as having both vertical and horizontal dimensions (no. 3). It also cites the formula of *Lumen Gentium*: *"The church in and formed out of the churches (ecclesia in et ex ecclesiis)"* (no. 9). However, it immediately qualifies this formula with the later insistence of John Paul II that it is "inseparable" from its opposite: *"the churches in and formed out of the church (ecclesiae in et ex ecclesia)"* (no. 9).

Inseparable though the two may be, the Vatican's recent letter quite clearly magnifies the latter, even attributing to the universal church the character of a Platonic, pre-existing model which is both "ontologically and temporally prior to every individual particular church" (no. 9). "From the church, which in its origins and its first manifestation is universal, have arisen the different local churches as particular expressions of the one unique church of Jesus Christ" (no. 10). On the agenda of this document is also the reinforcement of a unified and hierarchical episcopacy, reflecting the priority of the universal church, and the derivative nature of local churches. "As the very idea of the body of the churches calls for the existence of a church that is head of the churches, which is precisely the church of Rome . . . , so too the unity of the episcopate involves the existence of a bishop who is head of the body or college of bishops, namely the Roman pontiff" (no. 12).

This reading of church as ordered derivation from a pre-existing model may be complemented by some New Testament alternatives. A diversity of church models characterized Christianity in the era immediately after the deaths of the first apostles, the era in which most of the New Testament was probably written. Raymond E. Brown outlines several such models in *The Churches the Apostles Left Behind*,[14] analyzing each in terms of strengths and weaknesses. These churches vary in terms of importance of centralized structure versus dynamic flexibility, even, for instance, in traditions all deriving from Paul (the Pastoral Epistles, Colossians and Ephesians, Luke/Acts) which would have understood themselves to be in *koinonia* (communion) with each other.[15]

One community strongly emphasizing structure is that which produced the Pastoral Epistles, and its strength is "impressive stability and solid continuity . . . designed to preserve the apostolic heritage."[16] The authors of the pastorals direct their warnings against teachers of deceptive new ideas, men who love controversies! The faithful are to be submissive to authorities, and the purveyors of innovations to be stopped from teaching (1 Tim 1:13). "They must be silenced, for they are upsetting whole households by teaching for dishonest profit what they have no right to teach" (Titus 1:11). "In the Pastorals, then, we have the ancestor of the theology of a deposit of doctrine, and such ecclesiastical developments as the approval of professors, imprimaturs, an index of forbidden books, and supervised church presses. . . ."[17] The danger here, as Brown sees it, is that measures assumed in moments of crisis become "a consistent way of life," taken out of context, and formed into "a universal and unconditioned policy."[18] We may distinguish further between those measures that move to constrain "before" from those that act "after" the fact of a conflict. The mandate juridically understood is an instance of the former, whereas an episcopal statement about the unsuitability of a certain position would be the latter. The first type of measure is much more far-reaching and makes juridical control a *sine qua non* of the very undertaking of theology, while the second type reserves it to the rare crisis situation. To subject theological inquiry to doctrinal and canonical strictures from the outset would almost inevitably have a crippling effect on its achievements. As Brown concludes, "[a]t certain times the greatest peril facing a well-ordered institutional church is not the peril of new ideas but the peril of no ideas. The community described in the Pastorals would be perfectly safe if no one thought any other ideas than those handed down."[19]

A different model appears in the letters indisputably attributable to Paul, such as Corinthians and Galatians. Here "church" refers most often to local communities ("the church of God which is in Corinth," "the churches of Galatia," "in every church"), lending credence to the idea that, in the NT at least, Christian identity as church did indeed spring historically from conversion experiences within local communities and households, united around faith in the one Jesus Christ, which then communicated with one another. Colossians and Ephesians, later letters in the Pauline "school," take Paul's emphasis on body, and transform it into an ideal image of church as a corporate entity. However, the stress is not on the institutional identity of church, but on the body of Christ as a growing community united by love (cf. Col 1:17–18; Christ himself, not an ideal church -type [*sic*], is "before all things," the head of the church, and the source of its unity). Brown, noting that any church must become institutionalized if it lasts long enough and attracts a large membership, still comments that people do not love institutions as such and rarely give themselves for them; it is institutions which exist to serve the people. "But if the church is loved in a personalized relationship, it becomes a cause that attracts generosity from generation to generation."[20]

As Brown himself concludes in the book, a study of NT ecclesiologies demonstrates a pluralism that is instructive for the church. No one model is fully adequate, but always stands to be complemented by another. The NT is not a monolithic blueprint for theology, ethics, or church order. Its very diversity has enabled the church to adapt historically to various challenges and contexts, drawing on themes or images which are useful at the time in encouraging faithfulness to the gospel. But the NT itself provides four "gospels" and several other expressions of Christian witness besides. The historical church may also go back to these to renew its own identity, and to take its lead not only from their content, but from the very fact of their diversity.

By now, I suspect it is apparent how I intend to connect this glance at NT ecclesiology with the above discussion of "mandate." The very notion of requiring of theologians a mandate from ecclesiastical authorities is part and parcel of an institutionally oriented, strongly structured, "top-down" ecclesiology. Proper attention to church structure is no doubt necessary. But a one-sided emphasis on structure and authority will result in a dead church, unless enlivened by the spirit of love and community witnessed by Paul himself and by some of his later followers. Indeed, I would say that unless a community of trust exists first, not only does the institutional arm of the Church lack true Christian "authority," as essentially an ability to command respect on the basis of a recognizable representation of Christ. Even worse, there could be no genuine mandate for theologians in light of the common good, no possibility of their being called by and affirmed in the community to carry out their special vocation of reflection and teaching. We recall that the theologian's task is not first and foremost to preach or teach doctrine, but to investigate intellectually and in the company of scholars the implications of the biblical and doctrinal symbols. His or her mandate derives from the confidence of the community, as represented or crystalized in the bishop, rather than as created by him. This confidence is placed in the peculiar theological task of scholarship as valuable in its own right and as making its distinctive contribution to the church through its own proper methods and criteria.

For some of these reasons, I want to move beyond one solution to the "mandate" problem, mentioned in Sharon Euart's paper, and often identified with Ladislas Orsy. This solution is that the episcopacy deal with theologians directly in conferring the mandate, leaving the process outside the governance structure and hiring procedures of the university. This solution is sometimes supported by the argument that, since institutions with a civil charter are not juridical persons under the law, any obligations imposed by canon law can apply only to persons employed by such institutions, but not to the institutions as such (or to their representative officers). However, since the mandate requirement of canon 812 and of "Ex Corde Ecclesiae" refers directly to theologians, not to universities, the solution in question need not depend on the preceding thesis. The solution may hold some attractiveness to university presidents, since it would allow them to leave the implementation of the mandate to individual bishops. Bishops would then approach individual faculty, who in turn would decide their level of cooperation. By this solution, universities also extend significant support to theologians, since they would not necessarily make employment contingent on the mandate. Yet the interpretation still reflects the top-down juridical model of church-theologian relationship, defines the problem in terms of a legal code, and leaves unresolved the essential meaning of *communio* and the question of how best to foster it. A more radical response, both theological and practical, is called for.

Certainly, the best response is a positive one. What is most needed is not juridical investigations at the margins which exacerbate conflict which has already occurred, leading to an atmosphere of hostility and fear, but basic community-building in advance of the confrontations we all desire to avoid. (The need for those charged with the pastoral care of the church to take a stand against some unacceptable theological positions, and perhaps to deal explicitly with the mandate issue which has already proceeded from the institutional church, will be raised again below.) When I speak of community-building, I have in mind very concrete initiatives which would give bishops and theologians greater exposure to one another in productive contexts. Four examples:

1) *Theological consultation initiated by the bishops' conference.* Efforts such as this one by departments of the USCC to bring theologians into the conversation. In June, I attended a symposium at Notre Dame for the NCCB Marriage and Family Life Committee, in which the topic of discussion was the "domestic church." This small and informal meeting of bishops, theologians, and pastoral ministers expanded horizons by showing all participants aspects of the question—whether practical or theoretical—which might be shaping the agendas of others, but which were new to their own outlook. For instance, I learned the value of "domestic church" in the black and hispanic communities. This image encourages families with their struggles and successes in living Christianity out of particular cultural traditions. I also was able to clarify to other participants the nervousness of some theologians about whether "domestic church" is really aimed at greater ecclesiastical control over family life; and I was gratified to see that the bishop members of the group were primarily concerned with pastoral issues of including families within the church's work and demonstrating that the church is behind them.

2) *Commission of Bishops and Scholars.* In 1987, the Committee on Doctrine and the Joint Commission of Catholic Learned Societies and Scholars (composed of representatives from about eight professional societies, and chaired by the CTSA representative, Donald Buggert, O. Carm.) formed a "Commission of Bishops and Scholars," which in turn has begun to sponsor a series of

colloquies for bishops and scholars in a given area. To take just one instance, the third colloquy, on "Contemporary Theological and Pastoral Significance of the Notion of Reception," was held in Mundelein IL in 1990, and was attended by 13 bishops, 17 scholars, and six speakers. Comments on the evaluation forms testified to lack of pressure or intimidation; honest and open as well as enjoyable dialogue; tremendous group spirit and rapport; and added, "It was a great experience to have such open discussion with the bishops"; and "We learned so much from each other."

3) The Catholic Theological Society of America. As you know, this is a North American professional society, committees of which have previously addressed issues of mutual concern to bishops and theologians, and which has even consulted with the episcopacy. We also have several bishop members. The untapped potential of the CTSA is to serve as a relatively nonthreatening setting where bishops could achieve exposure to current theological and ethical discussions, and establish personal relationships with theologians. Absolute agreement among our members on theological and moral issues would be an impossible goal for the CTSA, and one not even to be desired. But disagreements do not undermine our common commitment to the church, or our ability to interact in a collegial manner. There is no reason why bishops could not be included in this cordial spirit! It is the custom for the CTSA President Elect, who plans the annual convention, to issue local bishops a personal invitation to attend. A greater response, and even a national response, to the theological forum we offer would be very heartening for us.

Each year, the bishop of the city in which we meet is invited to offer words of welcome at our opening session, and we have invariably received a gracious response from the bishop or his delegate. This year, Donald Wuerl of Pittsburgh spoke of the mutually enhancing relationship between practical pastoral experience and the theological enterprise, commending institutions of higher learning for the contribution they make to the ongoing proclamation of the gospel. His mere presence, and even more his obvious efforts to establish a positive relationship with our members, were immensely appreciated.

I must also mention the quite remarkable occasion in 1989 when John May addressed us in St. Louis, and on which he argued also from the *communio* between bishops and theologians. Without making any specific concessions to so-called "dissenting" theological positions, he expressed his conviction of the faithfulness and good will of theologians working to articulate Catholic faith more adequately in intellectual terms. Most importantly, he reasserted the appreciation which the NCCB has for Catholic theologians in this country and repudiated attempts to divide bishops from theologians by means of sweeping but indirect accusations against the latter as leading a benighted charge into heterodoxy and schism. Permit me to quote.

> I think the church in the United States suffers from too many anxious, warning voices that would divide the bishops against the theologians. . . . The real situation, in the experience of the vast majority of the bishops, is . . . one of a healthy, sound, 'developing cooperation.' . . . We must not let these attacks destroy the communio in which we live nor allow ungrounded and ungovernable suspicions to descend like a fog over the church in the United States. In spite of all this negativity and prophecies of gloom, we together must 'make every effort to preserve the unity which has the Spirit as its origin and peace as its binding force' (Eph. 4:3). In this way, and only in this way, can we build up the church together in love and theological wisdom for the glory of God.[21]

May received a prolonged and resounding ovation from his theological audience.

4) Expanded theological and social interaction. The last example is a proposal rather than a reality, one mentioned hopefully to me by Bishop James McHugh. He suggested that bishops get together with theologians more regularly and frequently, both on a consultative and on an informal basis, especially when there is a college or colleges in the diocese. A dinner together at the bishop's invitation might be an occasion to look at issues of mutual concern, and to discover areas of common outlook rather than focusing on points of disagreement. Or a university might provide a forum for several bishops to attend a theological colloquium, e.g., on the Universal Catechism, on Catholic feminist theology, on a bioethical topic, or on a recently released encyclical. In such ways, alliances could be formed and trustful working relationships established. In line with John May's comments to the CTSA, such relationships do not necessarily demand conformity of viewpoint on every single particular matter.

Finally, I want to observe (discreetly donning my moral theologian's hat) that, generally speaking, bishops and Catholic theologians are quite similar in their basic theological and moral commitments. Although we Catholics spend an inordinate amount of time drawing up battle lines between "liberals/ proportionalists" and "conservatives/reactionaries," the fact of the matter is that, on a scale of one to ten, the great majority of Catholic theologians and bishops are fighting for turf all within about three notches of the right end of the spectrum, as compared to the rest of the culture. *There is much more that unites us than separates us.* This is a point bearing reaffirmation and further discussion.

In my view, a renewed *communio* among the theologians and the pastors of the church could work toward strengthening the witness and credibility of Catholic moral values in a culture in desperate need of a sense of direction on some of the very issues that have torn internally and so painfully at our own community. We need to identify and recover our common ground—much larger than the small plot sprouting thorny hedges that divide! With a united front, seeded with conviction and watered by mutual generosity, we can put together a much more edifying apologetics than the defensiveness grown from infighting, condemnations, and counterreactions.

When all is said and done, we will no doubt be left with gaps and frictions between church as community and as institution; and between the theologian/scholar and the bishop/pastor. These are inevitably the product of identities and roles which overlap while not completely meshing. For instance, the theologian's niche as "scholar" cannot realistically be divided by an impermeable barrier from other areas of church life, including the doctrinal, pastoral, practical moral, and catechetical. Nor should it be. "Ivory tower" theology would be isolated and useless in relation to the larger life of the church. Similarly, as Bishop Wuerl told the CTSA, moral and pastoral practice feeds back into the reflective moment and creates a stronger theological analysis. Resulting tensions between theological scholarship and religious and moral practice are the natural outcome of the struggle to be as "one body" while still remaining individual and differentiated in role and standpoint. The NT model of churches (and charisms) may reassure us that such tensions need not be settled once and for all and that the balance may swing legitimately between the poles of theology and practice, of institution and personal community, and tradition and creativity or critique.

Finally, we come full circle to two practical questions which the existence of "Ex Corde Ecclesiae" presses on us: the granting of mandates to theologians and the correction of unacceptable theological positions. On the first issue, I can only recommend envisioning the mandate more generally in relation to the *communio* we have been discussing, rather in accord with the narrowest interpretation of canon law. Is not the legal framework, after all, secondary, limited, and insufficient as a guide to the unity of Roman Catholicism? As I have indicated above, the language of "Ex Corde Ecclesiae" itself permits a shift to the communal orientation, and that language ought to be exploited. The document gives its essential definition of the relation of bishop to university in terms of trust and collaboration. It presents the mandate in terms of an ongoing function of the theologian within the community. The notion of a "joining" (Decree on the Laity) or of a "communion" between the distinct functions of theologian and bishop seems far more appropriate an heuristic device here than that of delegated function. The mandate should be understood more in terms of an ongoing relationship of assumed cooperation than of specific accreditation, a relation which could be mutually "recognized" by bishops and theologians through a less formal and more continuous process.

Second, although I would see pluralism of theory and liveliness of scholarly interaction as the best way of pruning out dead or deformed theological branches, there will undoubtedly come times when a bishop feels the obligation to distance a theological position from the collection of those that are helpful for the refinement of doctrine and the encouragement of common life. This is part of the identity formation of and by the church as community. I can only surmise, however, that both the specific accreditation in advance of theological research and teaching, and the muffling of dissident voices via the revocation of mandates, will have a counterproductive effect. Juridical measures are frequently employed precisely when the magisterium's positions lack the theological argumentation, the pastoral witness, and the confirmation in the life of the faithful to make them persuasive in their own right. In such instances, what appears at least to outside observers to amount to the harassment of theologians, often in secret and fixed on a predetermined outcome, can become a source of scandal. In other words, it does little to attract onlookers to the Church's moral positions as illustrating a communal experience of Christ for which 1 Corinthians 13 could serve in any way as the norm.

It is encouraging to realize that a preferable alternative has been devised through a process of consultation among theologians and bishops, and has received positive recognition from Cardinal Ratzinger subsequent to a consultation in Rome with U.S. bishops.[22] "Doctrinal Responsibilities" provides for the promotion of cooperation and informal dialogue, especially through personal contacts among bishops and theologians. But it also foresees instances in which "doctrinal disputes" may arise in dioceses. In such cases, a "formal doctrinal dialogue" may be initiated if agreed upon by both parties. Such a dialogue would be open and direct, preferably include face-to-face discussion between the participants, and would be confirmed at several stages by written progress reports, signed by both parties. Both would have access to records, to theological experts, to personal advisors, and to a facilitator. If no agreement is reached at the end of the process, several options are available, including an agreement to disagree; a call for further theological study; an expansion of dialogue from the regional to national level; the issuing of a "doctrinal monitum, i.e., a clear warning of danger to the faith in what is being taught"; a public declaration of the error of a position; or other qualified classification of a position in relation to Catholic tradition. Although the guidelines allow for unspecified "further administration action," they also remind their audience that the "best response to bad teaching is good teaching."[23]

The "formal" dialogue process presumably would be used sparingly, would be carried out in consultation with reputable and judicious theologians with solid professional reputations, and would avoid resort to coercive or legalist measures against the individual concerned. The effectiveness of the option chosen at the end of such a process would depend on a rationale which is both intellectually coherent as theology, and compelling as an expression of the local community's experience of Christian identity. Condemnations not backed by convincing reasons result in the impression, widespread within the Catholic community as elsewhere, that Catholic theological and especially moral positions are simply based on "papal infallibility" (thought to cover everything), and have no intrinsic merits to commend them. One's willingness to accept them therefore depends on one's ability to identify with an essentially sectarian church which sacrifices relevance to the dilemmas of modern life to the desire to have a clear-cut if separatist identity. This is not the center of the Catholic tradition, and does little to serve the role of the Church in political, economic, and cultural affairs.

I conclude with the personal realization that theological reflections about ideal relations within an ideal community may lack immediate pragmatic worth in resolving the pointed issue of how university presidents, bishops, and theologians can work together to translate an official document into a workable, fair, and even inspirational policy. But I trust that placing the concept of "mandate" in an expanded hermeneutical context will stimulate the imagining of practical alternatives by those to whom it falls to carry out this task. Certainly one alternative is further exploration of the significance and character of the bishops' recognition of the ecclesial role of theologians as a precondition for defining more precisely the ways in which a "mandate" could be used to do so. It would be valuable, for instance, to study dioceses in which constructive cooperation has been pursued according to the above episcopally approved guidelines, and in which the foregoing process of formal dialogue has subsequently been applied in problematic cases. Such a review would no doubt provide valuable insights into the nature of the *communio* between bishops and theologians and into the most fruitful measures to encourage and sustain it.

Lisa Sowle Cahill
Professor of Theology, Boston College
President, Catholic Theological Society of America

NOTES

1. Joseph A. O'Hare, S.J., "Catholic Institutional Identity in Higher Education," in Msgr. Charles J. Fahey and Mary Ann Lewis, eds., *The Future of Catholic Institutional Ministries: A Continuing Conversation* (New York: Third Age Center, Fordham University, 1992) 93.

2. See "Doctrinal Responsibilities: Approaches to Promoting Cooperation and Resolving Misunderstandings Between Bishops and Theologians," *Origins* 19/7 (1989) 97–110, especially Part III, "A Possibility for Formal Doctrinal Dialogue."

3. All citations of this document are taken from "Ex Corde Ecclesiae," The Apostolic Constitution on Catholic Universities, *Origins* 20/17 (October 4, 1990) 266–76.

4. Francis Schussler Fiorenza, "Systematic Theology: Tasks and Methods," in Francis Schussler Fiorenza and John P. Galvin, eds., *Systematic Theology: Roman Catholic Perspectives, volume I* (Minneapolis: Augsburg Fortress, 1991) 22.

5. Personal letter to the author, May 21, 1992.

6. "Doctrinal Responsibilities," 100–101. In his weekly general audience of June 24, the pope also remarked on the value of constructive criticism in the Church, mentioning Catherine of Siena.

7. Ibid., 105.

8. Sharon Euart, RSM, *Church State Implications in the United States of Canon 812 of the 1983 Code of Canon Law,* "Chapter One: History of the Canon: From Canonical Mission to Mandate," 21. Euart points out that the term mandate has been used back as far as the 1917 code, and that it carries a variety of meanings, which she does not aim to settle conclusively. Rather, she clarifies one possible direction in which an interpretation of the term might proceed.

9. Ibid., 30.

10. O'Hare, "Catholic Institutional Identity, 92.

11. John Paul II. *L'Osservatore Romano* (English), Dec. 15, 1980, 17; as cited in "Doctrinal Responsibilities," n. 8.

12. "Doctrinal Responsibilities," 99.

13. Congregation for the Doctrine of the Faith, "Some Aspects of the Church Understood as Communion," *Origins* (June 24, 1992) 108–112.

14. (New York/Ramsey: Paulist Press, 1984).

15. Ibid., 22.

16. Ibid., 37.

17. Ibid., 38.

18. Ibid., 39.

19. Ibid., 40.

20. Ibid., 54.

21. John L. May, "Address of Welcome," *CTSA Proceedings* 44 (1989)189, 191, 192.

22. "Doctrinal Responsibilities" evolved over a seven-year period and underwent repeated revisions. In March, 1989, Archbishop Oscar H. Lipscomb, chairman of the Committee on Doctrine, accompanied officers of the NCCB to Rome to confer with the CDF on the results. Afterwards, Ratzinger expressed by letter his appreciation for the meeting, and concluded: "At this time, it (the congregation) can only express its satisfaction with the way in which the bishops' conference has chosen to deal with this matter." (See *Origins* sidebar on "Doctrinal Responsibilities," 19/7.)

23. "Doctrinal Responsibilities," 108.

5 | Some Theological Reflections on Canon 812

Joseph A. Komonchak
Presented to the Implementation Committee,
September 9–10, 1992

I will not discuss the possible canonical differences between the mandate required in Canon 812 and a canonical mission, and simply take them both to refer to some sort of needed ecclesiastical authorization for someone to teach Catholic theology, an authorization that is apparently expected also to have some juridical consequences.

Before I enter into a theological reflection on the *mandatum docendi* required by canon 812, I wish to note that the discussion, as I am familiar with it, includes both matters of principle and interpretations of past and present situations. Thus, on the one hand, there is both a principled concern for integral and faithful communication of the Church's constitutive faith and for the authority of the bishop's role in supervising it and the view that these values have been threatened and are threatened today by certain developments in the Church in general and in Catholic colleges in particular. On the other hand, a concern in principle for the autonomy of Catholic colleges and for the academic freedom of theologians within them is accompanied by the memory and fear of abuses of ecclesiastical power. It is of some importance to keep these two levels of concern distinct and perhaps also not to allow the practical questions to remain merely tacit, if only to recognize that the passions this debate can manifest are largely inspired by differing interpretations of the Church's present situation and can prevent an agreement that might be possible on the level of principle.

From the author's files. Printed by permission of Joseph A. Komonchak.

That said, I will discuss successively: (1) the Church's central task of communicating the faith, (2) the role of the theologian within it, (3) his relationship to the magisterium, and (4) the specific requirement of a *mandatum docendi.*

COMMUNICATING THE FAITH

The faith—here understood as a body of truths that spell out the implications of the life, ministry, teachings, death and resurrection of Jesus for our understanding of God, the world, and ourselves—is both constitutive of the Church—makes it the distinct social body that it is—and the basic contribution it makes to the redemption of human history. In short, without the faith, the Church is not the Church and Christ's Word no longer influences human history.

If the Church is first of all, at least genetically, the *congregatio fidelium,* then the communication of the faith is the first and most basic of all its activities. The gathered community in one generation is the *creatura Verbi, Ecclesia ex auditu,* the child born of an earlier generation's communication of the Word of Christ and of the reception of the Holy Spirit by which alone one can say that "Jesus is Lord." The generative event of the Church is the process of communication and appropriation reflected at the beginning of the First Epistle of St. John: "What we have seen and heard we proclaim to you, so that you may have communion with us, and our communion is with the Father and with his Son, Jesus Christ" (1 Jn 1:3). This event at once generates the *koinonia* that is the Church's essential reality and fulfills Christ's final commissioning of the disciples: "Go, teach all nations" (Mt 28:19). Everything else in the Church rests upon this primary moment and constitutive event.

Koinonia in the apostolic preaching is a specific reality; that is, it is not a vague feeling, but a body of truths that spell out the implications of the Christ-event. Concern for the integrity and purity of the faith is visible in New Testament writings as varied as the Gospels of Matthew and of John, the Acts of the Apostles, Paul's Epistles to the Corinthians and the Galatians, the Pastoral Epistles, and the Epistles of John. And this concern for orthodoxy—"right-thinking"—has marked the Church ever since, most visibly in the ecumenical councils from Nicaea to Vatican II.

The Church communicates its vital faith in many ways: by the basic announcement of the Gospel, by catechesis, by formal magisterial statements, in its worship and devotions, through the witness and example of exemplary Christian lives, etc. This whole vast process is what Vatican II meant by the living and active Tradition of the Church: "What was handed on by the Apostles comprises everything that serves to make the People of God live their lives in holiness and increase their faith, and it is in this way that the Church in its doctrine, life and worship perpetuates and transmits to every generation all that it itself is, all that it believes" (*Dei verbum*, 8).

Since apostolic times, the first duty of pastoral leaders in the Church has been to proclaim the Gospel, to defend it from attack, and to apply its light and power to new generations and situations. The over-seeing (*episcopê*) of the communication of the faith in and by the whole Church is a basic and essential part of the episcopal office. In other words, the task that a Paul, say, carried out in his own lifetime vis-à-vis his own churches falls upon those who have succeeded to his ministry: here the important NT texts are Acts 20:18–24 and the Pastoral Epistles. Leadership over the Church entails leadership over the constitutive and generative process of the communication and appropriation of the faith.

But this communication is a responsibility that falls upon all members of the Church, clergy, laity, and religious, as an implication of their basic calling. As the Council put it:

> By its very nature, the Christian vocation is also a vocation to the apostolate. As in the organism of a living body, no member plays a purely passive role but shares at once in the life of the body and in its activity, so also in the Body of Christ that is the Church, the whole body "with the proper functioning of every part brings about the body's growth" (Eph 4:16). Such unity and solidarity exist among the members of this body (see Eph 4:16) that a member that does not contribute to the growth of the body in his own measure must be considered useless both to the Church and to himself (*Apostolicam actuositatem*, 2).

> On all Christians, therefore, falls the noble task of working to see that the divine message of salvation is known and accepted by all people everywhere (*Ibid.*, 3; see Lumen *gentium*, 33).

According to the Council (*Ibid.*, 3), this "right and duty to be apostles," to spread the Gospel, has two basic foundations. The first is sacramental: it is grounded in baptism and confirmation and nourished by the eucharist. But besides this common basis, there is another: the special gifts the Spirit gives to each Christian for the exercise of the apostolate. The Council stresses the point:

> From the reception of these charisms, even the most ordinary ones, there arises for each of the faithful the right and duty to exercise them in the

Church and in the world for the good of men and the building-up of the Church, in the freedom of the Holy Spirit who "blows where he will" (Jn 3:8), and at the same time in communion with his brothers in Christ, and especially with his pastors, whose role it is to pass judgement on the authenticity and orderly exercise of these gifts, not indeed to extinguish the Spirit but to test all and to keep what is good (see 1 Th 5:12, 19, 21).

This basic teaching of the Council seems to me to be particularly important for our discussion. The Council made *the whole Church* the primary sign and instrument of Christ's revelation and redemption, to contribute to which is a right and duty of all Christians in general as an implication of their sacramental initiation and of each Christian in virtue of special gifts of the Spirit. This empowerment for ministry occurs within a hierarchically ordered community, but it comes immediately from God and differs from other types of authorization that may depend on explicit authorization (mission or mandate) by hierarchical authority.

It is over this living and differentiated communion of believer-apostles that the pastoral leaders preside in order to ensure its unity, fidelity and effectiveness. But if the bishop *presides* within this body, he first lives there himself. His ministerial rights and duties themselves presuppose his own initiation into the life of the body; and the special gifts that he receives in virtue of his ordination, important as they are, exist alongside other gifts of which the Spirit of God himself is the author. If the Council recalls the bishop's right to evaluate the gifts, it warns him against the danger of quenching the Spirit. St. Paul's words come to mind: "The eye cannot say to the hand, 'I do not need you,' nor again the head to the feet, 'I do not need you'" (1 Co 12:21).

The Council thus insists on all the elements that need to be taken into account: unity of mission and diversity of ministry (see *AA* 2), sacramental communion and charismatic variety, freedom and communion, authority and discernment.

THE ROLE OF THE THEOLOGIAN

Immediately after invoking the variety of special gifts through which the Spirit equips the People of God to carry out its prophetical function in the world, the recent "Instruction on the Ecclesial Vocation of the Theologian" went on to say: "Among the vocations awakened in this way by the Spirit in the Church is that of the theologian" (#5–6, see also #40: "their own proper charisms").[1]

This seems to me an important statement for situating the place and role of the theologian in the Church. It obviously presupposes that the theologian is a sacramentally initiated Christian, but it does not ground his vocation there but in a special calling deriving from special gifts of the Spirit. The theologian's vocation, then, is not mediated sacramentally nor does it originate from ecclesiastical authorization: it is charismatically based. As such, it can be numbered among those special gifts that ground a right and duty to be exercised in freedom and in communion of which the Council spoke in *AA* 3.

The Council itself made the point when, in one of its very rare references to theologians, it said: "For the proper exercise of this role, the faithful, both clerical and lay, should be accorded a lawful freedom of inquiry, of thought, and of humbly and courageously expressing their views in whatever branch of study they are expert" (*Gaudium et spes*, 62). This was a particular application of a principle the Council had articulated more generally in *Lumen gentium*, 37: "In proportion to their knowledge, competence, and pre-eminence, lay people have the right—indeed sometimes also the duty—to make known their views on matters that concern the good of the Church." The new Code of Canon Law generalized this statement into one of the fundamental rights and obligations of all the faithful, adding to it, however, the words: "to the sacred Pastors and, while preserving the integrity of faith and morals and respect for the Pastors and considering the common good and the dignity of persons, to make them known to the rest of the faithful" (*CIC*, c. 212:3).

As I am taking the term in this discussion, to be a theologian requires one to share in the faith and in the communion of the Church; but if this general, sacramentally mediated and hierarchically ordered communion is necessary, it is not sufficient to make one a theologian. Special gifts are needed—the intelligence, knowledge, skills in research and scholarship—that enable one to undertake a critical and scientific understanding, defence, and communication of the faith.

As the same Instruction points out, the theologian's task, like that of the apostolate in general, is both ecclesial—addressing "the inner life of the People of God"—and cultural—engaged in a "missionary vocation" in the world. Theology is a dimension of that "contemplation and study of believers who ponder these things in their hearts (see Lk 2:19, 51)" (*DV,* 8) through which an unseeing faith seeks understanding and love desires "a better knowledge of the beloved" (*Instruction*, 7). At the same time, and inseparably, theology mediates between the Gospel and contemporary culture, whether on behalf of believers themselves, who by their faith are not removed from their culture, or as the effort "to give an explanation to anyone who asks you for a reason for your hope" (1 Pt 3:15).

The matrix of the theologian's work is the faith and life of the Church, outside of which he ceases to be a Catholic theologian. His task is only one of the ways in which the Church carries out its mission in the world, and theologians may occasionally need to be reminded of Paul's question to the Corinthians: "Are all teachers?" (1 Co 12:29). As everyone else in the Church, the theologian is the heir of a faith handed on since the Apostles in the living community of the Church and authoritatively expressed and defended in creeds and in magisterial statements. without this insertion into the traditional faith of the Church, the theologian has nothing with which to confront the vital intellectual problems posed by contemporary culture.

This first and most important meaning of the theologian's relation to the Church grounds any others that may arise in virtue of special authorization by mission or mandate. One can be a Catholic theologian without such formal authorization—in fact the great majority of Catholic theologians in the past and today have not had one nor would the authority of the better ones have been increased by having had it. I also agree with Avery Dulles that to say that a theologian with such authorization teaches "in the name of the Church" is ambiguous "since it tends to obscure the distinction between the role of bishops, who can by their teaching publicly commit the Church, and that of theologians, who cannot."[2] It may even be dangerous because it may be understood to give a theologian a formal authority, whereas the proper authority of a theologian is demonstrated competency and achievement.

THEOLOGY AND THE MAGISTERIUM

This ecclesial reference is the context in which to raise the narrower question of the theologian's relation to the Church's magisterium. In his presentation of his Congregation's recent Instruction on theologians, Cardinal Ratzinger noted that it did not begin "from the dualism between magisterium and theology, but in the context of a triangular relationship: People of God as bearer of the sense of faith and as the place common to all in the ensemble of faith, magisterium, and theology." The ecclesial character of theology, in other words, is not reducible to its relation to the magisterium. The Cardinal was very clear about the point:

> Theology is not simply and exclusively an auxiliary function of the magisterium. It must not limit itself to gathering arguments for what the magisterium affirms. In such a case magisterium and theology would come close

to being an ideology for which it is only a matter of acquiring and maintaining power.[3]

The great theologians of the past and the present have thought within the magisterially mediated communion of the faith, but their work has never been simply commentary on magisterial statements. For one thing, such statements are only one of the ways in which the faith has been expressed, and the Council insisted that the magisterial task is subordinate to the primary articulations of the faith in the Scriptures and Tradition. It is the latter that are supposed to be the primary source from which the theologian draws.

Secondly, theology engages its task at the frontiers between the Church and contemporary culture, and this has often and still often requires the raising and answering of questions on which the magisterium has not spoken and may not yet be able to speak. What the Tradition amply illustrates in figures from Augustine to John Courtney Murray was acknowledged at the Council when it gave the example of how biblical scholarship can help the Church's judgement to mature (*DV,* 12). The exercise of the official magisterium requires theological judgement, and the bearers of that task, popes and bishops, are not provided by ordination with sources of the faith or with intellectual and spiritual insights that render the normal procedures of theological investigation and reflection unnecessary. Theology, then, as Pope Paul VI noted, is an intrinsic dimension of the exercise of the magisterium. Without theological scholarship, the magisterium itself is incapable of fulfilling its distinct task. The relationship between the magisterium—specific popes and bishops—and theologians, then, is not one in which the latter are simply dependent on the former.

That said, it remains that the judgements of the magisterium are also a criterion for the theologian's exercise of his role. It is, of course, a differentiated criterion, as we all learned in our theological courses where our textbooks carefully distinguished between the various degrees to which the Church had committed itself to various "theses." One of the contributions of the recent Instruction on theologians is the admission of these various levels of magisterial commitment and the corresponding variety of responses expected from believers and theologians. These range from dogmatic definitions to primarily disciplinary measures that are in the nature of warnings about "unsafe" teachings. After the unconditional response expected to definitions of faith and to "definitive" teachings on other matters, the Instruction recalls the Council's teaching on the "religious submission of mind and will" expected to be given to what commonly are called exercises of the Church's "ordinary" magisterium. The Instruction would appear to interpret this *obsequium religiosum* in terms of "the willingness to submit loyally to the teaching of the magisterium on matters per se not irreformable" (#24), a "fundamental openness loyally to accept the teaching of the magisterium as is fitting for every believer by reason of the obedience of faith" (#29). I am inclined to agree with Avery Dulles that "the implication seems to be that *obsequium,* while inclining a person to assent, need not in every case result in actual assent."[4]

The furor over the Instruction's identification of "dissent" with politically motivated public defiance caused many people to overlook the fact that this is the first Roman magisterial text to acknowledge that theologians may responsibly find themselves unable to accept a teaching of the non-irreformable magisterium and to discuss what they are to do in this case (#25–31). Cardinal Ratzinger introduces this section in the following way:

> The document does not pass over in silence the fact that even under the most favorable conditions tensions can exist—tensions which can be fruitful, however, if they are faced by both sides with a recognition of the inner correlation of their roles. The text also offers different forms of binding which arise from different levels of magisterial teaching. It states—perhaps for the first time with this clarity—that there are decisions of the magisterium that cannot be the last word on a subject as such, but are a substantial anchorage in the problem and are first and foremost an expression of pastoral prudence, a sort of provisional disposition. Their core remains valid, but the individual details influenced by the circumstances at the time may need further rectification. In this regard one can refer to the statements of the Popes of the last century on religious freedom as well as to the anti-modernist decisions at the beginning of this century, especially the decisions of the Biblical Commission at the time. As a warning-cry against hasty and superficial adaptations, they remain fully justified. . . . But the details of the determinations of their contents were later superceded once they had carried out their pastoral duty at a particular moment *(Oss. Rom.).*

In his joint-interview with Cardinal König, Cardinal Ratzinger, after again citing the examples of the Church's response to nineteenth-century liberalism and of the Biblical Commission's decrees, commented:

> In the course of the magisterium's historical development, we find decisions— this needs to be said—that, while exercises of authority, were really abuses of it. The closer a statement is to the nucleus of divine revelation the more trustworthy it is. The farther it is from it, entering a new territory and involving

itself in the turmoil of everyday life, the more problematic it becomes. In the future it will be necessary for the magisterium to follow a rule of prudence: carefully to weigh how far it can go and not to lose sight of the different degrees of certainty.[5]

In the face of magisterial judgements that are not "the last word on a subject," the Instruction admits the possible legitimacy of a theologian's disagreement. While it speaks only of his revealing his difficulties to the magisterial authorities, several commentators have argued that discussion of these difficulties in "scholarly journals, professional societies, seminars, and the like" is not excluded,[6] and this position is confirmed in the U.S. Bishops' recent document, vetted by the Congregation for the Doctrine of the Faith, on the teaching role of the diocesan bishop.

The Instruction's frank admission of "contingent and conjectural elements" and of "deficiencies" in magisterial interventions ("Pastors and their advisers have not always taken into immediate account every aspect or the entire complexity of a question") and of the fact that only the passage of time may enable one "to distinguish between what is necessary and what is contingent" or between "true assertions and others that were not sure" (*Instruction*, #24), is also a long-overdue acknowledgement that relations between magisterium and theologians are more complex than they are made to appear when communion with the Church under the magisterium is simply equated with submission at every moment to every sort of decree.

I bring up these matters because they seem to me fundamental for a discussion of the question of ecclesiastical authorization of theologians that wishes to take all the elements of the problem into account. Things would be very clear if the Church and theologians within it always faced an infallible statement each time the magisterium speaks. The difficulties arise when one recognizes that infallible statements are extremely rare, that individual magisterial statements can be not only imprudent and inopportune but mistaken, that even when correct they may contain "deficiencies," "assertions that are not sure," and "contingent" elements alongside the needed ones. In other words, a process of discernment (today often discussed as "reception") takes place within the whole Church in response to a magisterial statement, and it has classically been thought to be one of the roles of the theologian by his critical reflection and scholarship to assist in what the Instruction calls the "filtering," which it also recognizes can take some time, by which the permanently valid elements of a statement are distinguished from the contingent.

To disagree with the teaching presented in such a magisterial text, to point out the difficulties, to argue another case are not necessarily signs that a theologian is violating the rule the Instruction set out: "the willingness to submit loyally to the teaching of the magisterium on matters per se not irreformable." In such a case, theological disagreement contributes to the process by which the Church is led to a fuller, clearer, surer judgement. Certainly, that process would be much delayed if all forms of public disagreement were disallowed.

All this is relevant to the question of an ecclesiastical mandate to teach, particularly if one suspects that in most cases the primary criterion for granting is likely to be a theologian's fidelity to the Church's magisterium. What should count as "fidelity" is a highly differentiated reality, and the danger that it will be over-simplified is not unreal, which is what leads me to my last section.

THE MANDATE TO TEACH

The requirement of a *mandatum docendi* is a new element in the Church's legislation with regard to higher education. It almost certainly has been proposed in order to reassert and to guarantee episcopal supervision in that dimension of the Church's essential task of transmitting and defending the faith. That it should be thought necessary today, I believe, does not merely reflect a certain perennial temptation to juridicize all relationships within the Church, but also two developments in the post-conciliar Church. First, some people appear to believe that the real, but rather informal, relations that used to prevail between Catholic colleges and bishops have proven inadequate in recent decades. Before the Council colleges considered themselves Catholic and were considered so by others not primarily because of direct episcopal control over them, but because of a common and commonly perceived commitment to the communication of the Catholic vision. If tensions arose, they tended to be handled informally, and episcopal supervision was taken for granted as part of the meaning of being a Catholic institution. Various institutional developments since the Council have led to formal statements of the legal (civilly, that is) independence of these institutions, a development in many cases prompted by civil requirements for public financial assistance. It is this development that underlies the question of the relationship between the *mandatum docendi* and a Catholic college's institutional autonomy.

Secondly, several well-publicized cases have arisen in which people teaching in faculties of theology have been thought to have departed in various degrees from official Catholic teaching. Complaints have been registered from many sides that teachers who were supposed to be communicating Catholic teaching had by their publications and other public activities and even in their teaching made it clear that they do not agree with one or another point of Catholic doctrine. This appeared to many people to be a problem that needed to be addressed, and the requirement of an official mandate from ecclesiastical authority was proposed as a solution. From now on, the logic seems to be, only those who have manifested fidelity to the Church's magisterium would be granted the mandate, and this formal authorization could, on the other hand, be withdrawn if a teacher ceased to manifest it in the course of his academic career. The clear implication seems to be, although it is not formally stated in the Code, that the college should not hire someone who did not have the mandate and that it should dismiss him if he violated its conditions. It is this development that underlies the question of the relationship between the *mandatum docendi* and a Catholic teacher's academic freedom.

Now I hope that I have indicated sufficiently above that I do maintain that a bishop's office includes *episcopê* over the transmission of the faith. I even regard it as his first and most important task. I include within that task the right and duty of a bishop to pass judgement and, if necessary, to make it public, on whether or not a theologian is teaching in communion and fidelity with the Church's faith.

But it is important to note that the bishop is not the only one with rights and duties within the Church. As we saw above and as the new Code has dramatically illustrated for the first time (cc. 208–223), all Christians have certain rights and duties within the Church, and I take it to be respect for them that leads the Code to retain as a fundamental norm of interpretation that laws that inflict penalties or restrict rights are to be interpreted strictly (c. 18). I also take it that canon 812 is one of the laws that requires such strict interpretation.

We face, then, conflict, or at least tension, between two sets of rights and duties. On the one hand, there are the rights and duties of the bishop, which may also be understood as designed to protect the rights and duties of the Church itself and of its members to receive the faith integrally and faithfully. On the other hand, there are the sacramentally and charismatically grounded rights and duties of the theologian, some of them implications of his right and duty to participate in the Church's mission, including its evangelizing mission, some of them necessary requirements of critical and scientific work. (I will leave to others with more background in this area a consideration of the rights and duties of institutions within the Church such as Catholic colleges.)

The problem as I see it is that while canon 812's mandate to teach is designed to ensure the first set of rights and duties—so that academic abuses may be prevented or addressed—, it offers no equivalent legal assurance that the rights of teachers of theology will be protected. This reflects a general problem in the new Code. While canon 221 states that Christians have a right to vindicate and defend their rights before a competent ecclesiastical forum, the Code does not include measures for the resolution of disputes administratively on a local level. This legal imbalance is at the heart of our problem.

If theologians are asked to acknowledge the rights and duties of the bishop with respect to the transmission of the faith, it is only right that bishops acknowledge the rights and duties of theologians. If the former are to be given juridical articulation and protection in canon 812, the latter ought also to be articulated and protected in any possible implementation of the canon.

It is not basically concern that Catholic colleges adopt certain widely shared interpretations of academic freedom that inspires the fears or suspicions of Catholic theologians with regard to canon 812, but rather a concern that rights and duties that are intrinsic to the theological task and that are stated both in Council and in Code be respected. And this concern is all the more urgent because this whole discussion takes place against the background of a painful history, particularly in the last two centuries, in which these rights and duties have not been respected by Roman or by local episcopal authority.

If I may cite someone whom no one will ever accuse of indulging in "the anti-Roman affect," Hans Urs von Balthasar has a long paragraph in which he describes the effects on the Church of Rome's inability to "adapt her spiritual horizon to the radical changes brought about by the French Revolution and particularly by German Idealism and its incalculable consequences":

> Hence, fear expressed itself in conservative defensiveness toward the "outside" (the "Syllabus") and by mistrust turned inward. This fear, nourished by an insufferable, sycophantic and informer spirit, manifested itself in consistent rejection (practically without exception) of all Catholic attempts to meet the modern intellectual world with empathy and dialogue. In an earlier time, the Inquisition prepared stakes for the burning of heretics; now it methodically burned that Catholic spirit which was attempting, in continuity with the Church Fathers and even with High Scholasticism (in its dialogue with Islam and Judaism), to make contact with the spirit of the new age. This brought about an atmosphere of terror, an artificial, paralyzing quiet. But embers continued to glow under the ashes. A long list of

unnecessary human tragedies attested to the uneasy and unclarified relationship between theology and the Magisterium. This sickness had three crises: the first was around the time of the "Syllabus" (1866 *[sic]*), the longest and most important was that of Modernism, which outwardly was put down by the encyclical *Pascendi* (1907); and finally, as epilogue, the false alarm concerning the *Nouvelle Théologie* to which *Humani generis* (1953 *[sic]*) intended to put an end. The secret proceedings of the Holy Office—denounced by Cardinal Frings at Vatican II as infringing all natural rights guaranteed to the human person—and the associated practice of cowardly denunciations, poisoned the intellectual atmosphere of the Church for more than a century. It required almost superhuman spiritual heroism on the part of individuals if they were not to become embittered. This is well illustrated by citing only four names (and there were many others) whose bearers narrowly escaped condemnation: Newman, Blondel, de Lubac, Teilhard.[7]

This is a harsh indictment, telling a story whose pain can only be lessened if we learn from it and do not continue it or repeat it. Von Balthasar is talking not only about the "corpses" of traditionalists and rationalists strewn across the pages of Denzinger, whose condemnation might have been justified, but also of the tragedy that "many an intellect which should have been encouraged to find such a path [forward] was in fact disheartened, intimidated or embittered." These "unnecessary human tragedies" were permitted and sometimes even caused by the highest Church authorities. Rome, he says, "could deliver hard blows to those who departed from the center line but was unable to contribute much that was constructive toward solving the problems presented by the times."[8]

Now the point at issue here is not simply the rights and duties of individuals, although these also ought to be considered something sacred within the Church, but also the consequences this atmosphere and these actions had on the Church itself, on its ability to meet the challenges of a new age, on its capacity to serve as a redemptive instrument of Christ in the modern world. It was the integrity and force of the Church's redemptive presence that were compromised by the actions of the Magisterium. Was the Church's relation to modern political freedoms more helped or hindered by the condemnation of Lamennais and by the suspicions cast upon Montalembert? Was the Church more helped or hindered by the fact that Newman spent most of his Catholic life under local and Roman suspicion because of his views on the development of doctrine, on the laity, on the temporal power, on the psychology of faith? Was it more helped or hindered by an action that not only condemned a Loisy but constricted a Lagrange, a Duchesne, a Batiffol? Who was a more faithful and effective translator of Thomas Aquinas to the modern world, the Garrigou-Lagrange who assisted the Holy Office or the Blondel or de Lubac who suffered for years under his, and its, suspicions? Who more perceptively anticipated the orientations of the Council and of the present pontificate, Congar and Chenu or Gagnebet, Boyer and Tromp? Closer to home, who more acutely and effectively addressed "the spiritual crisis in the temporal order," John Courtney Murray or Cardinal Ottaviani and his American cohorts, Joseph Clifford Fenton and Francis Connell, who for nearly twenty years actively sought a public repudiation of Murray's views and had to be content that, under privately communicated pressure, he ceased publishing views that became part of the common teaching of the Church only ten years later?

These examples, which are not exhaustive, illustrate what is at stake in the question we are addressing. It is not only individual rights and duties that are at issue, but the degree to which and the effectiveness with which *the Church,* that whole vast, differentiated community of believers, accomplishes its redemptive task in the world. That the pope has universal and the bishop local responsibility for the inspiration, coordination and direction of this task is not debatable, but they do not undertake the task alone, theirs is not even necessarily the most important or the most effective element in it, and they have made and can make mistakes in undertaking it. Some of these mistakes have involved and can involve real injustices to individuals, have caused and can cause real damage to the Church's redemptive effectiveness.

A Code of Canon Law exists in order to serve the life and mission of the Church. The new Code includes provisions designed to ensure the whole Church's fidelity to the Gospel by which it lives and also to defend the rights and duties of all Christians without which the Church is not faithful to the Gospel and cannot effectively communicate it to the world. Canon 812 can be understood as a measure taken to try to ensure that fidelity and to defend certain of the rights and duties that embody it. But it does not ensure them all. As written, it is much more concerned about real and possible abuses of the theologian's rights and freedom than it is about real and possible abuses of the rights of ecclesiastical authority. For this reason it cannot be considered an adequate response to the general or particular problem it was designed to meet, and to implement it without safeguards that recognize other dimensions of the general and particular problem runs the risk of doing more harm than good to the life and work of the Church.

Part of my reason for that final judgement is that I have been closely acquainted with three different cases at Catholic University involving the granting of tenure, two of them requiring the *missio canonica*. (In addition, I will simply mention that I was once myself the object of anonymous measures taken to prevent me from accepting the post of scholar-in-residence at the North American College.) It is my judgement that in all the cases there was no legitimate ground for raising questions about the ability of the three candidates to teach Catholic theology. None of the positions questioned violated the norms of communion with the faith and life of the Church. If all three cases were resolved happily, to my mind, it was in good part because (a) the final decision rested with the whole Board of Trustees and not with a single bishop, (b) a process was initiated in order to clarify the problems, and (c) the candidates could call to their assistance a number of qualified defenders.

But suppose that one of these candidates had been applying for tenure at another Catholic college in a diocese whose bishop disagreed with some of their positions and so refused to grant a mandate to teach. Does the professor have a right to know the objections raised? Will he be given an opportunity to explain his positions or to defend their compatibility with the Church's teachings? Does he have a right to ask for such an opportunity? What assurances will he have that the bishop will not make his own personal opinions on a disputed matter the criterion of his decision?

Or suppose that after having taught at the college for some time, the professor publishes an opinion that the bishop disagrees with, and the bishop withdraws the mandate to teach. Or suppose that a new bishop comes in to the diocese and decides that his predecessor was mistaken in giving the mandate in the first place and moves to withdraw it. Will the professor be told of the reasons for this decision and be given an opportunity to explain and defend his views? Does the professor have a right to ask for such an opportunity? What assurances will there be that justice is done to all persons and all values that are at stake?

I think that these questions and, surely, others like them, need to be asked, and that until they are answered in the form of clear personal and procedural commitments on the part of bishops, that the implementation of canon 812 will be a one-sided solution to the problem. The bishop's rights will be secured, but not the theologian's. But if, as I was taught, rights and duties are correlatives, then the bishop's rights are conditioned by his duty to respect the rights of others. And, within the Church, theologians, too, have rights.

Joseph A. Komonchak
School of Religion and Religious Education
The Catholic University of America

NOTES

1. The Instruction is published in *Origins,* 20 (July 5, 1990), 117–26; for commentaries, see Joseph A. Komonchak, "The Magisterium and Theologians," *Chicago Studies,* 29 (1990), 307–29; Avery Dulles, "The Magisterium and Theological Dissent," in *The Craft of Theology: From Symbol to System* (New York: Crossroad, 1992), 105–18; Francis Sullivan, "The Theologian's Ecclesial Vocation and the 1990 CDF Instruction," *Theological Studies,* 52 (1991), 51–68.

2. Dulles, *The Craft of Theology,* 170.

3. I have translated these remarks from the Italian edition of *Osservatore Romano* and note that the English edition of these remarks of the Cardinal at his June 26, 1990 press conference differs. The Cardinal repeated his comment in his joint-interview with Cardinal König: ". . . a theology based solely on the magisterium of the Pope would be a mistake. The teachings of the Pope do not substitute for theology"; "Franz König and Joseph Ratzinger, "Perché amiamo questa Chiesa," *Jesus,* 14 (May 1992) 53.

4. See Avery Dulles, *The Craft of Theology: From Symbol to System* (New York: Crossroad, 1992) 110–11.

5. "Perché amiamo questa Chiesa," *Jesus,* 56.

6. See Dulles, *The Craft of Theology,* 114.

7. Hans Urs von Balthasar, *The Office of Peter and the Structure of the Church* (San Francisco: Ignatius Press, 1986) 260, where in a footnote with reference to the practice of the Holy Office he cites Lamennais' complaint: "I shall never understand a form of justice where the accused is not informed of the accusation, without investigation, without debate, without any defense. So monstrous a judicial proceeding would be revolting even in Turkey."

8. Ibid., 260–61.

6 | The Mandate to Teach and the Ecclesiology of Communion

Avery Dulles, S.J.

Presented to the Implementation Committee,
September 9–10, 1992

With the prior understanding that the "mandate" mentioned by canon 812 of the Code of Canon Law has already been examined from the canonical aspect, I shall attempt in this paper to address the issues within a theological framework and especially in relation to an ecclesiology of communion.

The life of the Christian is essentially corporate. Christ delivered the good news of the gospel to the community of disciples, under the collegial leadership of Peter and the other apostles. The Holy Spirit was poured forth on the gathered community, and is promised to the Church as a whole as the ground of its indefectibility. Any individual can lapse from the faith, but the Church as a whole will persevere to the end.[1]

THE CHURCH AS COMMUNION

The Church may be viewed under one aspect as a communion, a mystery of divine life shared by human beings, who are brought close to one another by being brought close to God. Summarizing what the early Christians understood by *communio*, one authority writes:

> Its content could perhaps be best described in the following terms: *Communio* is the bond that united the bishops and the faithful, the bishops among themselves, and the faithful among themselves, a bond that was both

From the author's files. Printed by permission of Avery Dulles, S.J.

effected and at the same time made manifest by eucharistic communion. *Communio* very often means simply the Church itself.[2]

Communio is a rich and complex concept having many analogous forms of realization. In some respects it is invisible: it depends on interior spiritual gifts, including sanctifying grace and the infused theological virtues (faith, hope, and charity). But the Church is not and cannot be a merely invisible reality. It comes to visibility through doctrinal, sacramental, and juridical bonds, including the profession of the apostolic faith, participation in the Church's sacramental life, and submission to the hierarchical authorities.

The Congregation for the Doctrine of the Faith, in its recent letter to the bishops of the Catholic Church, "Some Aspects of the Church Understood as Communion,"[3] emphasizes the inseparability between two dimensions, the vertical dimension of communion with God and the horizontal dimension of communion with fellow human beings. It is by means of "the visible communion in the teaching of the apostles, in the sacraments, and in the hierarchical order" that Christ carries out in history his prophetic, priestly, and royal functions. "This link between the invisible and the visible elements of ecclesial communion constitutes the Church as the sacrament of salvation" (no. 4).

The hierarchical magisterium, succeeding to the authority of the Twelve, has the right and the duty to safeguard the integrity of the faith and to see to its correct and effective transmission from generation to generation. The bishops are the officially qualified and authoritative teachers of the faith. They teach the faith in communion with one another and with the successor of Peter, the bishop of Rome. In order to teach with the authority of Christ, the bishop must be in "hierarchical communion" with the episcopal college and its visible head.[4] As stated in the Prefatory Note of Explanation presented at Vatican Council II, *communio* is to be "understood not of a certain vague feeling but of an *organic reality* which demands a juridical form, and is simultaneously animated by charity."[5] Hierarchical communion is the mutuality that obtains among bishops who are members of the episcopal college, capable of joining in collegial actions pertaining to doctrine and ecclesiastical governance. A fully collegial action is one emanating from the entire college together with its head.

Each particular church has its own bishop as a visible source and foundation of its own inner unity and of communion with the universal Church. Since the bishop is joined by hierarchical communion with the bishop of Rome and the other members of the college, the mystery of the total Church is in a sense interior to each particular church. There is a "mutual interiority between the universal Church and the particular church."[6] As the United States bishops recently declared, the diocesan bishop "teaches as the authoritative voice of the local church in which the universal church is rendered present in a particular place."[7]

Ecclesial communion, however, is broader than merely hierarchical communion. It is shared by all members of the Church, and establishes rights and duties among all. "The Christian faithful are bound by an obligation, even in their own patterns of activity, always to maintain communion with the Church" (canon 209, #1). They must continually seek to be "of one heart and one mind" (Acts 4:32), devoting themselves "to the teaching of the apostles and to communal life, to the breaking of bread and to the prayers" (Acts 2:42).

Communio should not be understood in merely passive or static terms. It makes all the faithful participate in the threefold *munus* of Christ as priest, prophet, and ruler (canon 204; cf. LG 31); it makes them coresponsible for promoting the growth and sanctification of the Church (canon 210; cf. LG 33, 40); and, in summary form, "to work so that the divine message of salvation may increasingly reach the whole of humankind in every age and in every land" (canon 211; cf. LG 33). Whatever may have been thought in the past, the Church since Vatican II may no longer be seen as a society in which only the clergy are active, with the laity passively receiving what is handed out to them from above. All members of the Church participate actively according to their respective roles and vocations.

THEOLOGY AS AN ECCLESIAL VOCATION

Among the many callings and charisms that God bestows for the benefit of the Church, one must recognize those of studying and teaching Christian doctrine. Theology, in current usage, generally means a methodical effort to reflect on the grounds, content, and implications of the Church's corporate faith, with a view to clearer intellectual understanding. Like other charisms, theology is bestowed for the building up of the body of Christ in unity and love (cf. 1 Cor 14:26).

The qualifications needed for the practice of theology are both spiritual and intellectual. Like the call to apostolic activity, theology is a connatural outgrowth of faith itself. "Revelation in fact penetrates human reason, elevates it and calls it to give an account of itself (cf. 1 Pt 3:15). . . . The service of doctrine, implying as it does the believer's search for an understanding of the faith, i.e., theology, is therefore something indispensable to the Church."[8] "The theologian's work thus responds to a dynamism found in the faith itself" (Instr., 7).

Any believer, clerical or lay, may receive the vocation to become a theologian, and may fulfill this vocation provided that he or she acquires the necessary competence. Vatican II encouraged lay people to enter the theological field in greater numbers, adding that "the faithful, whether clerical or lay, have a just freedom of inquiry, of thought, and of expression to disclose their mind humbly and courageously in matters in which they are competent" (GS 62). Canon law recognizes the right of the laity to deepen their knowledge of the sacred sciences (canon 229, #2) and to express their opinions freely about matters in which they are expert, while observing due respect *(obsequium)* for the magisterium of the Church (canon 218).

Theology, however, is not a purely individual matter. Since the Church, as stated above, is the primary bearer of faith, the theologian must adhere to the faith of the Church. Normally the theologian must be a participant, "dwelling in" the Church as the community of faith, for without this lived relationship the theologian could not be a reliable interpreter of the meaning and importance of the Christian formulas and symbols.

Since the hierarchical magisterium has the right and duty to formulate the doctrine of the Church and to exercise vigilance over the teaching done by others, theologians have an indispensable and essential relationship to the bishops. The role of theology "is to pursue in a particular way an ever deeper understanding of the word of God found in the inspired Scriptures and handed on in communion with the magisterium, which has been charged with the responsibility of preserving the deposit of the faith" (Instr., 6). "The theologian, if he is to be faithful to his role of service to the truth, must take into account the proper mission of the magisterium and collaborate with it" (Instr., 20).

It has become almost trite to say that the relations between theology and the hierarchical magisterium are reciprocal (Instr., 21). Neither can perform its task in a satisfactory way without reliance on the other. By their study and reflection theologians, like exegetes, can help to mature the judgment of the Church and thus prepare the way for official doctrinal pronouncements (cf. DV 12). The scholarly output of theologians, however, must be guided by the magisterium, which presents the content of faith in a sound and reliable manner, warning against misinterpretations of Scripture and tradition. When theologians deviate from sound teaching, they must expect to be corrected by the magisterium, which has the exclusive power to interpret the word of God with public authority, exercised in the name of Christ (Instr., 13; cf. DV 10 and 12).

The teaching of the bishops, therefore, is not simply external to theology. Any theologian who refused to operate under the direction and vigilance of the magisterium, and to offer his or her conclusions for the judgment of the magisterium, would thereby cease to be a Catholic theologian. Theology always stands to benefit from a living relationship with the magisterium, and conversely the magisterium benefits from a living relationship to the theological schools. In the issuance of conciliar and other documents, the bishops normally call upon the advice and assistance of theologians to ensure that the doctrine is stated in accord with the findings of scholarly research.

Theology, then, operates in multiple relationships of communion. In solidarity with the whole Church as linked together by the college of bishops, theologians are also in communion with other theologians who share the same presuppositions of faith. Although Catholic theologians may enjoy a large degree of communion with those who are not Catholic, they are united among themselves by even closer bonds. They stand in a doctrinal or theological communion with other Catholic theologians who work under the aegis of the same hierarchy and within the framework of the inherited body of Catholic doctrine.

Since any Christian with the necessary skills is entitled to reflect on the faith, no delegation or empowerment from the hierarchy is needed for a believer to become a theologian. Nor is any special act of the hierarchical teachers needed to establish the relationship of communion between theologians and themselves. Theology by its very nature is a service offered to the hierarchy and to the whole Church. Whether the theologian does or does not have a canonical mission or mandate, the Holy See and the bishops have a power of vigilance and exercise disciplinary and canonical control over theologians when they fall into doctrinal errors. The bishops are always able to issue particular precepts forbidding the theologians to preach or to publish, or requiring them to retract errors. They can, for grave reasons, impose canonical penalties extending all the way to excommunication.

CANONICAL MISSION AND THE MANDATE TO TEACH

In the light of these preliminaries, we must now ask about the significance of the "canonical mission" and "mandate" that are sometimes conferred upon particular theologians. Following the precedent set by Pius XI in his apostolic constitution, *Deus scientiarum Dominus* (1931), the Congregation for Catholic Education, in the Norms appended to the Apostolic Constitution *Sapientia christiana* (1979), required a canonical mission for certain teachers in ecclesiastical universities and faculties.

It declared:

Article 27, #1 – Those who teach disciplines concerning faith or morals must receive, after making their profession of faith, a canonical mission from the

Chancellor or his delegate, for they do not teach on their own authority but by virtue of a mission they have received from the Church. The other teachers must receive permission to teach (*venia docendi*) from the Chancellor or his delegate.

The 1983 revision of the Code of Canon Law does not, in the finished text, refer to a "canonical mission" to teach theological disciplines. But in two canons it speaks explicitly of a "mandate" to teach:

Canon 229, #3 – ... Lay persons are capable of receiving from legitimate ecclesiastical authority a mandate to teach the sacred sciences.

Canon 812 – It is necessary that those who teach theological disciplines in any institute of higher studies have a mandate from the competent ecclesiastical authority.

Canon 812 appears in a chapter devoted to Catholic universities. In the following chapter, dealing with ecclesiastical universities and faculties, it is said that several canons concerning Catholic universities, including canon 812, apply also to ecclesiastical universities and faculties. Thus it is not clear from the Code itself that there is a real difference between the canonical mission of *Sapientia christiana* and the mandate of canon 812.

The apostolic constitution *Ex corde Ecclesiae*, prescribing norms for non-ecclesiastical universities and faculties, in a footnote, quotes canon 812 requiring a mandate for teachers of the theological disciplines.[9] From the context it seems that this requirement is not restricted to universities established and governed by the Holy See, by bishops, or by religious orders, but that it applies to all Catholic universities, including those established by the free initiative of lay persons without ecclesiastical charter. Some interpreters of the Code believe that canon 812 applies also to teachers in *secular* institutions, both public and private.[10] Most interpreters, however, on the ground that canon 812 appears in a chapter on Catholic universities and institutions of higher education, limit the applicability to teachers in *Catholic* institutions. In view of the fact that a strict interpretation is to be made of canons that impose burdens, the latter interpretation would seem preferable. All agree that the canon does not apply to non-Catholic teachers, in view of canon 11, which exempts non-Catholics from purely ecclesiastical laws.

In order to discuss the significance of the mandate it will be necessary first to ask whether it differs from the canonical mission, and if so, how. That some difference exists, at least in the mind of the drafters of the Code, is evident from the fact that in earlier drafts what is now called a mandate had been called a canonical mission. In a *Relatio* issued to explain this change in 1981, the Code Commission explained: "It seemed more opportune to use language referring to a mandate instead of a canonical mission, which in this case in not fully equated with a true canonical mission."[11] Thus the mandate was seen as something less than a canonical mission.

In the discussion of Catholic Action at Vatican II, a distinction was made between a "mission" and a "mandate." Article 3 of the Decree on the Apostolate of the Laity explains that the laity, having been brought into the Mystical Body of Christ by baptism, and been strengthened by the power of the Spirit in confirmation, are assigned to the apostolate by the Lord himself. Article 20 goes on to explain that in Catholic Action lay people, while continuing to act in a manner proper to themselves, collaborate with the hierarchy for the apostolic goals of the Church. The hierarchy may even authorize this collaboration by an explicit mandate.

Article 24 delves more deeply into the meaning of this mandate. By means of a mandate the ecclesiastical authorities may select certain apostolic works directly concerned with spiritual ends, promote them, and assume responsibility for them. The hierarchy thereby unites these works more closely with its own apostolic function, while preserving the nature of the lay apostolate and its distinction from that of the hierarchy, so that the capacity of the laity to act on their own accord is not lost.

The same article speaks of a "mission" as distinct from a mandate. The mission will be given for functions closely connected with their hierarchy's own pastoral office, such as teaching Christian doctrine, certain liturgical actions, and the care of souls. "In virtue of this mission, lay people are fully subject to the direction of the ecclesiastical superior in the exercise of these functions." The implication is that the mandate is given for functions less intimately connected with the specific functions of the hierarchy, and that it leaves greater scope for the free initiative of the laity.

Commentaries on these texts generally point out that a mission enables the laity to participate in what would ordinarily be the apostolate proper to the hierarchy, whereas a mandate simply recognizes that the spiritual apostolate of a lay group is in accord with the apostolic aims and priorities of the hierarchy.[12] Although the Decree on the Apostolate of the Laity does not speak explicitly of a "canonical" mission, what it says about mission converges with the council's understanding of "canonical mission," as may be gleaned from texts such as

AG 17 (dealing with the canonical mission of catechists), PO 7 (dealing with the ministries entrusted to priests) and LG 24 (dealing with the canonical mission whereby specific tasks are assigned to bishops by the pope).

This explanation of the distinction between canonical mission and mandate sheds some light on the passages quoted above from *Sapientia christiana* and the revised Code. In the General Norms appended to *Sapientia christiana* (art. 27) we are told that to teach in an ecclesiastical faculty gives powers that do not pertain to the theologian as such. The assignment enables the teachers to speak "by virtue of the mission they have received from the Church." Thus they are considered to have a certain authority in communicating Catholic doctrine, even though they do not enjoy the prerogatives of the hierarchy in judging, establishing, and promulgating doctrine.

The mandate referred to in the Code, it would appear, gives no power to share in the authentic teaching power of the hierarchy. Teachers with a mandate still do so as private persons, and not in the name of another. In the judgment of one canon lawyer:

> He who teaches in virtue of a "mandate" continues to exercise his own personal responsibility as a [member of the] Christian faithful, because the mandate does not communicate any sharing in the authentic power of teaching, nor any particular function within the Christian community. It simply is an official attestation from the hierarchical superior that the one teaching is a Catholic in communion with the Church, whereas in the content of his teaching there is nothing to contradict this good standing.[13]

Although I find this interpretation convincing, I am aware that some authorities disagree. Commenting on canon 812, one canonist remarks:

> The implication of even the amended wording is clear. The right to teach theology in a formal academic setting rests not only on one's faith commitment and scholarly expertise but on hierarchical deputation as well. In this way, the theologian-teacher officially exercises the *munus docendi* on behalf of the church. This hierarchical concept suggests that one teaches theology as an agent commissioned by the church's juridically recognized leaders.[14]

If this latter interpretation is correct, it becomes more difficult to maintain the distinction between the communication of church doctrine and theology as the kind of free and open search for truth and understanding described, for example, in the "Instruction on the Ecclesial Vocation of the Theologian" (Instr. 12 and passim). This point may be of some importance in connection with issues of accreditation and eligibility for funding in a pluralistic society, as will be seen below.

MANDATE AND COMMUNION

Several authors use the term "communion" in connection with the mandate. John J. Strynkowski, writing before the publication of the revised Code, spoke in general terms of "canonical mission" and "mandate," without distinguishing very sharply between them. Both, he maintained, are expressions of communion. Of the former he wrote:

> Canonical mission could thus be seen as the expression of the authority which the theologian enjoys not only on the basis of his competence, but also because he exercises the responsibility of theological understanding which is necessary for the Church within the context of ecclesial communion. . . . It is a sign that the theologian is an essential and necessary part of the Church and that the Church is an essential and necessary source and context of his work.[15]

Of the mandate Strynkowski wrote: "The theologian is what he is by virtue of his gifts through baptism and the Spirit, and of his competence. Mandate is an expression of the fact that he is necessary to the Church and the Church necessary to him. It is a sign of the communion among bishops, theologians, and the rest of the Church."[16]

Robert P. Deeley, while making a sharper distinction between canonical mission and mandate, interprets mandate in much the same way as Strynkowski. For him it is not a nomination, approbation, or empowerment, since the laity have a right as baptized believers to pursue theological inquiry and to express their findings. He then adds:

> More positively, the request for a mandate can be seen as an acknowledgement that one wishes to teach in communion with the Church. The granting of the mandate by the competent ecclesiastical authority is an acknowledgement that a person is so teaching. It is an attestation that there is nothing objectionable concerning faith or morals in what is taught.[17]

Deeley goes on to say that the mandate for teachers is in some ways equivalent to the *nihil obstat* given to a book by a censor. The censor's approval is not a positive endorsement of the content but simply a recognition that there is nothing objectionable concerning faith or morals in what the person is teaching in the theological area.[18]

Deeley confesses that his interpretation of the meaning of mandate (which in substance agrees with the interpretations of Strynkowski and Urrutia) runs against a common understanding of the term "mandate," which frequently connotes "acting in the name of another." But this objection does not seem fatal since, as he points out, the term "mandate" was used in AA 24 without any connotation of agency.[19] Francis Sullivan, like Urrutia, Strynkowski, and Deeley, rejects the idea that the ecclesial ministry to teach theology involves agency. In response to Alesandro he writes: "I do not see any reason why 'working in communion with' and 'under the authority of the hierarchy' has to mean 'working as delegated by' or 'by mandate of' the hierarchy."[20]

While the concept of teaching in communion with the bishops is surely helpful, it has not as yet been clarified to the point where one can speak of a common interpretation. For this reason anyone seeking to obtain or give the mandate may be in some doubt as to exactly what is required to qualify for receiving this recognition. There is a risk that different bishops or conferences might understand the mandate in very different ways, thus defeating the purpose of the law. If the meaning of the mandate is not spelled out with some degree of clarity, the denial or withdrawal of the mandate could in some cases involve a real injustice, unduly damaging the reputation and possibly the livelihood of a theologian who by other standards would deserve to receive the mandate.

Following certain suggestions in Deeley's article, one might distinguish between the positive and the negative requirements. Positively, it may be said that those receiving the mandate must acknowledge that their service of teaching associates them closely with the hierarchical magisterium, which is responsible for the integral and pure transmission of the faith. This solidarity between university professors of theology and the bishops has sometimes been overlooked either by theologians who have positioned themselves critically against the hierarchy or by members of the hierarchy who have looked on theology as unnecessary or detrimental to the apostolate. The Holy See, in the recent documents we have examined, is calling for a shared sense of responsibility between bishops and theologians. If the two functions do not support each other, the transmission of the faith to new generations is impeded. The concept of communion requires that theologians consciously operate within the Catholic tradition and recognize the authority of the hierarchy to make authoritative judgments about what may and may not be held in the Church.

Negatively, the mandate implies that a theologian is not seen as deviating from the doctrinal standards of the Catholic Church. The creedal statements and dogmas of the Church must be upheld, and the noninfallible pronouncements of the magisterium must, in general, be accepted as reliable. As explained in the "Instruction on the Ecclesial Vocation of the Theologian," the theologian is not reduced to a mechanical and uncritical repetition of the official formulations of doctrine. Attention must be paid to rigorous critical standards (Instr. 9). "It can happen that a theologian may, according to the case, raise questions regarding the timeliness, the form or even the contents of magisterial interventions" (Instr., 24). Occasional tensions that do not spring from hostility can be a positive stimulus toward the development and clarification of doctrine (Instr., 25).

Finally it should be mentioned that the conditions for receiving a mandate should not be confused with those required for a canonical mission. If the change of wording in the revised Code has any meaning (as the Commission evidently felt that it did), a distinction should be made between the conditions required for each. Since the mandate, as here interpreted, does not make the recipient a participant in the functions of the hierarchical magisterium, it could be given to some theologians who might not qualify for receiving a canonical mission to teach in an ecclesiastical faculty.

THE RESPONSIBILITIES OF UNIVERSITIES

The concept of communion is applicable not only to theologians but also, in some sense, to universities themselves. "Every Catholic university is to maintain communion with the universal Church and the Holy See; it is to be in close communion with the local church and in particular with the diocesan bishops of the region or nation in which it is located" (General Norms, Art. 5).

Difficult as it is to spell out the precise meaning of communion in the case of the individual theologian, it is still more difficult to apply the concept to colleges, universities, and other institutions of higher learning. For one thing, such institutions have no soul. They cannot be in a state of grace; they cannot have the virtue of faith or have any interior convictions.

An institution such as a diocese or parish, which performs certain essential functions of the Church, can be in external communion if its ministries are recognized as conforming to the requirements of orthodoxy and canon law. Educational institutions do not belong in the same way to the formal structures of the Church, but they can be church-related in various ways. Three categories of university are recognized in *Ex corde Ecclesiae* (General Norms, art. 3, #3):

1. Those established or approved by the Holy See, by an episcopal conference, or the diocesan bishop.
2. Those established by a religious institute or other public juridical person.
3. Those established by some other agency, including a group of laity.

The article does not touch on the complicated question of what happens in the case where a university originally established by a religious order or congregation is turned over to the direction of a predominantly lay board of trustees, so that the religious institute can no longer exercise effective control. If the transfer of authority is recognized in canon law as a valid alienation, such a university has probably moved from the second to the third category.

Universities of the first category may be described as juridical persons in canon law; those of the second are controlled by juridical persons; those of the third category are usually described as having no status in the public law of the Church. Yet every Catholic university, according to *Ex corde Ecclesiae*, "has a relationship to the Church that is essential to its institutional identity" (no. 27) and is required "to make known its Catholic identity either in a mission statement or in some other appropriate public document, unless authorized otherwise by the competent ecclesiastical authority."[21] The Catholic character of the university may also be implicit in certain institutional actions such as calling itself Catholic or joining associations such as the Association of Catholic Colleges and Universities or the International Federation of Catholic Universities.

To use the name "Catholic," universities require the approval of competent ecclesiastical authority. To obtain such approval, the universities must conform to the prescriptions of the Holy See, the episcopal conference, and other hierarchical agencies.[22] One prescription of *Ex corde Ecclesiae,* as we have seen, is that universities of all three categories maintain communion with the Church.

Universities of the first category are required to incorporate the provisions of *Ex corde Ecclesiae* into their governing documents and statutes, submitting these to the competent ecclesiastical authority. It is contemplated that other Catholic universities (those of the second and third categories) will internalize these norms into their governing documents and as far as possible align their statutes with the norms.[23]

The apostolic constitution does not directly place on the universities any obligation to implement canon 812, but it does require, in accord with canon 810,

that those responsible for the appointment of teachers see to it that those selected are distinguished for their integrity of doctrine.[24] Bishops likewise are to
watch over the preservation and strengthening of the Catholic character of the
universities in their dioceses.[25] Procedures for strengthening the Catholic character of universities in the third category are to be determined by episcopal conferences and other assemblies of the Catholic hierarchy.[26]

The apostolic constitution avoids saying that conformity with canon 812
should be a condition of employment of teachers in the theological fields. It is
conceivable, however, that a conference of bishops might prescribe that this be
done. To judge from preliminary reactions, the majority of Catholic universities
in the United States and Canada would consider any such prescription detrimental to their apostolate. Many hold that to make the mandate a requirement
for employment of certain teachers would be an unwarranted extension of the
canon and of the apostolic constitution; that it would be unenforceable under
civil law, or that it would do severe damage to the financial, legal, and academic
standing of the universities.[27] It could also lead to administrative problems, of
which administrators could speak with an authority that is lacking to the present author.

It would seem that if the bishops decide to go ahead with the implementation of canon 812 in the United States, they might prefer to begin by granting
the mandate to individuals who apply for it or manifest willingness to receive it.
Some smaller colleges and universities of a strongly Catholic orientation might
voluntarily take the step of requiring the mandate of all teachers joining their
theology department. Other universities, faced with greater demands for pluralism by reason of their traditions, statutes, or constituencies, will presumably
wish to move more slowly.

Differences of view about the implementation of canon 812 should not be
allowed to prevent the rich and varied forms of communion envisaged by *Ex
corde Ecclesiae.* The great value of this apostolic constitution, in the eyes of many,
is to have gotten beyond a merely canonical approach to the idea of communion
between Catholic universities and the Church. It emphasized the service that
universities can render through reflection on the faith, dispassionate inquiry
into truth, and skillful analysis of the problems of society and culture in the
light of the gospel. These functions can best be carried out in lively relations
between university and the community of faith, involving the bishops in their
role as pastors. For the most part, these relations are not reducible to juridical
factors. Unless cooperation is pursued in a broader context, the juridical problems will possibly defy solution.

NOTES

1. The points made in this paragraph are taken from Avery Dulles, *The Craft of Theology: From Symbol to System* (New York: Crossroad, 1992), esp. 8.

2. Ludwig Hertling, *Communio: Church and Papacy in Early Christianity* (Chicago: Loyola University, 1972), 16.

3. Congregation for the Doctrine of the Faith, "Some Aspects . . . ," May 28, 1992; translation in *Origins* 22 (June 25, 1992): 108–12.

4. Vatican II, LG 21; cf. U.S. Bishops, "The Teaching Mission of the Diocesan Bishop," *Origins* 21 (Jan. 2, 1992): 473–92, at 480.

5. Walter M. Abbott, ed., *The Documents of Vatican II* (New York: America Press, 1966), 99.

6. CDF, "Some Aspects," no. 13.

7. U.S. Bishops, "Teaching Mission," 480.

8. Congregation for the Doctrine of the Faith, "Instruction on the Ecclesial Vocation of the Theologian"; *Origins* 29 (July 5, 1990): 117–26; no. 1. This document will hereafter be abbreviated "Instr."

9. *Ex corde Ecclesiae*, General Norms, art. 4, #3, and footnote 50; *Origins* 20 (Oct. 4, 1990): 265–76, at 274 and 276.

10. Robert P. Deeley, "Canon 812: The Mandate for Those Who Teach Theology: An Interpretation," *Proceedings of the Canon Law Society of America, Fiftieth Annual Convention* (1989): 70–85, at 83–84. For a contrary view see Sharon A. Euart, *Church State Implications in the United States of Canon 812 of the 1983 Code of Canon Law* (J.C.D. Dissertation, The Catholic University of America, 1988), chapter 2; in privately distributed excerpt, 36–37.

11. *Relatio* (Rome: Typis Polyglottis Vaticanis, 1981), 183; reproduced in *Communicationes* (1983): 57–109.

12. Ferdinand Klostermann, "Decree on the Apostolate of the Laity" in *Commentary on the Documents of Vatican II*, ed. by Herbert Vorgrimler (New York: Herder and Herder, 1969), 3:273–404, at 382. Cf. Deeley, "An Interpretation of Canon 812," 74–75.

13. Francisco Javier Urrutia, "Ecclesiastical Universities and Faculties (Canons 815–821)," *Studia canonica* 23 (1989): 459–69, at 468.

14. John A. Alesandro, "The Rights and Responsibilities of Theologians: A Canonical Perspective," in *Cooperation between Theologians and the Ecclesiastical Magisterium*, ed. Leo J. O'Donovan (Washington, D.C.: Canon Law Society of America and the Catholic University of America, 1982), 76–116, at 107.

15. John J. Strynkowski, "Theological Pluralism and Canonical Mandate," *The Jurist* 42 (1982): 524–33, at 532–33.

16. Ibid., 533.

17. Deeley, "An Interpretation of Canon 812," 80.

18. Ibid., 81.

19. Ibid.

20. Francis A. Sullivan, *Magisterium* (New York: Paulist, 1983), 196–204; quotation from 202.

21. *Ex corde Ecclesiae*, General Norms, art. 2, #3.

22. Ibid., art. 3, #3, and note 48.

23. Ibid., art. 1, #3.

24. Ibid., note 49.

25. Ibid., General Norms, Art. 5, #2.

26. Ibid., note 52.

27. From the perspective of federal law see Sharon A. Euart, "Implications of Canon 812 for Federal Constitutionality of Government Aid to Catholic Colleges and Universities," *Jurist* 50 (1990) 167–97. Her concluding paragraph reads, in part (p. 197): "In the light of the potentially disqualifying characteristics articulated by the federal district court in the *Bubb* case, it is entirely possible that requiring ecclesiastical authorization of those who would teach compulsory theology courses would be viewed by the courts as an imposition of religious restrictions on how or what the faculty may teach, bespeaking a close relationship of the institution to the sponsoring body, and evidencing indoctrination of religious values as a principal purpose of the institution. Such findings could well result in a determination of pervasive sectarianism sufficient to rule out the constitutional permissibility of government funding of the institutions."

7 | Letter from Bishop John Leibrecht

December 30, 1992

Dear Bishops and Presidents:

Pope John Paul II released his Apostolic Constitution "Ex Corde Ecclesiae" on Catholic colleges and universities on September 25, 1990. General norms in the Constitution are "to be applied concretely at the local and regional levels by episcopal conferences."

To that purpose the president of the U.S. bishops' conference, Archbishop Daniel Pilarczyk, appointed a committee to implement the Apostolic Constitution. Committee members are:

Dr. Dorothy McKenna Brown	Rosemont College (past pres.)
Rev. William Byron, S.J.	Catholic University of America (past pres.)
Brother Raymond Fitz, S.M.	University of Dayton
Dr. Norman C. Francis Xavier	University of Louisiana
Most Rev. James A. Griffin	Bishop of Columbus
James Cardinal Hickey	Archbishop of Washington
Sister Karen M. Kennelly, CSJ	Mount St. Mary's College
Most Rev. John J. Leibrecht	Bishop of Springfield–Cape Girardeau
Most Rev. Oscar Lipscomb	Archbishop of Mobile
Most Rev. Adam J. Maida	Archbishop of Detroit
Most Rev. James W. Malone	Bishop of Youngstown
Rev. Edward A. Malloy, CSC	University of Notre Dame
Rev. J. Donald Monan, SJ	Boston College
Dr. Matthew Quinn	Carroll College
Most Rev. Francis B. Schulte	Archbishop of New Orleans

From the author's files.

Resource persons to the Committee are Sister Alice Gallin, former executive director of the Association of Catholic Colleges and Universities, and Msgr. Frederick McManus of the Catholic University of America.

Staff from NCCB/USCC assisting the Committee are Sharon Euart, RSM, associate general secretary; John Leikweg, associate general counsel; Rev. Charles Hagan, representative for higher education and campus ministry; Lourdes Sheehan, RSM, USCC secretary of education.

The Ex Corde Ecclesiae Committee has been meeting since February, 1991 and, within the next few months, will have a draft of the regional ordinances called for by the Apostolic Constitution.

I write at this time to indicate that as soon as the draft becomes available, it will be sent to you with the encouragement of Cardinal Laghi, Prefect of the Congregation for Catholic Education, for your review and comments. Consultation will be with all bishops and presidents of Catholic colleges and universities. Within the institutions of higher education, presidents will review the draft with appropriate parties. Bishops and presidents in the diocese are encouraged to discuss the draft with one another.

More detail on the consultation process will be forwarded with the draft itself when it is mailed to you.

After consultation as outlined above, the Ex Corde Ecclesiae Committee will submit ordinances for the United States to the full assembly of bishops. After action by that body, ordinances will be submitted to the Holy See.

I write at this time simply to alert you to the consultation with you which will take place several months from now. It may be timely to begin thinking in a preliminary way about those with whom you might wish to consult.

If there is any question at this time, please call Father Charles Hagan (202) 541-3165 or me (417) 866-0841.

With every best wish, I am,

Sincerely in Christ,

Most Rev. John J. Leibrecht
Chair, Ex Corde Ecclesiae Committee

8 | Memo from Bishop John Leibrecht

March 18, 1993

TO: College and University Presidents
           of the Ex Corde Ecclesiae Committee
FROM: Bishop John Leibrecht, Chair
RE: Voting

At our last meeting on January 29, a discussion arose about voting procedures within the Committee. I said the matter would be clarified before our meeting March 26.

You received a copy of Sister Sharon Euart's helpful memorandum on voting. The memorandum stated that the "final draft document to go before the (Conference of) Bishops is reserved to the bishop members of the committee." It also said that "developing a draft document (for consultation) during committee meetings can be determined by the committee itself."

On this latter point the bishops of the committee, appointed as members by Archbishop Pilarczyk to be assisted by college and university presidents as consultants, had a conference phone call last week on the topic of voting. I write to share the consensus of that conversation.

The final wording of the documents both to the college and university communities for consultation, and to the National Conference of Catholic Bishops after the consultation, shall be voted on only by bishops. On the document sent for consultation to colleges and universities, a vote both of the bishop members and the consultant presidents will be individually noted on each of the ordinances. In their recent conference phone call, the bishops felt that most notations of votes by bishops and presidents on ordinances would show a common ground.

From the author's files.

In view of the above clarification, the March 26 meeting will begin by recording two votes, one of bishops and one of presidents, on ordinances 1 through 5. Before the vote on ordinance 2, we will re-visit two matters: (1) whether to change "ideals" to "principles" and (2) whether to add an additional statement to the wording as it stands now. On ordinance 3, we will re-visit whether to delete the phrase "seek to." After recording votes by number and not by name of bishops and presidents on the first five ordinances, we will immediately begin discussion and voting on other ordinances beginning with ordinance 6.

I hope that having addressed voting procedures between our January and March meetings will prove helpful and time-saving. Any questions regarding this memorandum I'll be happy to address at our meeting.

Many thanks for all you contribute to the important work before us!

cc: Bishop Members

9 | Draft of Ordinances and Questionnaire from Bishop John Leibrecht

May 4, 1993

DATE: May 4, 1993
TO: Archbishops and Bishops
          Presidents of Catholic Colleges and Universities
FROM: Bishop John Leibrecht

In 1990, the president of the National Conference of Catholic Bishops, Archbishop Daniel Pilarczyk, appointed a Committee to Implement the Apostolic Constitution *Ex corde Ecclesiae* promulgated by Pope John Paul II that same year. The Committee of seven bishops is assisted by eight Catholic college and university presidents as consultors. Several resource persons also take part in the Committee's deliberations. The task of the Committee, in response to the Apostolic Constitution itself, is to begin the process of drawing up national ordinances by applying the Constitution's general norms to the United States.

The enclosed draft of ordinances is sent as part of a national consultation with bishops and presidents of Catholic colleges and universities. All bishops in the United States are invited to submit recommendations on the enclosed draft, especially if there are Catholic colleges and universities in their arch/dioceses. They are asked to consult with any advisors they believe helpful. Presidents are invited to consult with their boards, faculties and others associated with their colleges and universities. Where applicable, they are asked to seek comments from provincials of religious communities which sponsor their institutions.

The Committee sending this draft of ordinances strongly recommends that bishops and presidents in each diocese meet together in order to benefit from one another's insights before comments are sent back to the Committee. Some

From the author's files.

123

bishops and presidents may want to make joint recommendations in addition to individual ones. The Association of Catholic Colleges and Universities has offered to facilitate regional opportunities for dialogue between bishops and presidents.

The draft text is from the bishop members of the Committee. Presidents and resource people participated fully in all discussions prior to the bishops' decisions about the text of the draft. On some matters during discussion, bishops and presidents agreed—both about what particular issues should be addressed in the ordinances for the United States and the wording of individual ordinances. In some cases, bishops and presidents found themselves unanimously with opposing views on a particular proposal. In some discussions neither the bishops nor presidents were, among themselves, unanimous in their opinions. Votes among the bishops were unanimous on the ordinances finally presented in the accompanying draft.

This draft is also being sent for comment to Catholic learned societies in the United States.

After recommendations have been received, the *Ex corde Ecclesiae* Implementation Committee will draw up a revised document to be considered by the full assembly of the National Conference of Catholic Bishops. After NCCB action, the document will be sent for review to the Apostolic See.

If there are any questions, please feel free to contact me (417/866-0841) or Father Charles Hagan (202/541-3134), who staffs the Committee. In the name of the entire Committee, I sincerely thank you for your time and your recommendations.

The enclosed evaluation form is meant to be of assistance in making your recommendations.

Your recommendations to the Committee are due no later than December 31, 1993.

Please return them to:

Bishop John J. Leibrecht, Chair
Ex corde Ecclesiae Implementation Committee
National Conference of Catholic Bishops
3211 4th Street, NE
Washington, D.C. 20017-1194

Committee Members

His Eminence, James Cardinal Hickey
Most Rev. James A. Griffin
Most Rev. John J. Leibrecht
Most Rev. Oscar Lipscomb
Most Rev. Adam J. Maida
Most Rev. James W. Malone
Most Rev. Francis B. Schulte

Resource Persons

Rev. Msgr. Frederick R. McManus
Alice Gallin, O.S.U.
Mr. Benito Lopez

Consultors

Dr. Dorothy McKenna Brown
Reverend William Byron, S.J.
Brother Raymond Fitz, S.M.
Dr. Norman C. Francis
Karen M. Kennelly, C.S.J.
Reverend Edward A. Malloy, C.S.C.
Reverend J. Donald Monan, S.J.
Dr. Matthew Quinn

NCCB/USCC Staff

Sharon Euart, R.S.M.
John Liekweg
Reverend Charles Hagan
Lourdes Sheehan, R.S.M.

PROPOSED ORDINANCES FOR CATHOLIC COLLEGES AND UNIVERSITIES IN THE UNITED STATES

PART ONE: INTRODUCTION

In the Introduction to his Apostolic Constitution _Ex corde Ecclesiae_ (August 15, 1990), His Holiness Pope John Paul II says, "I desire to share with everyone my profound respect for Catholic Universities" [No. 2]. He notes that the Catholic university shares with every other university that _"gaudium de veritate"_, so precious to Saint Augustine, which is that joy of searching for, discovering and communicating truth in every field of knowledge." But the Catholic university, according to the Holy Father, also has the "privileged task" to unite two orders of reality that too often remain unconnected and "frequently tend to be placed in opposition as though they were antithetical," namely, the orders of faith ("the certainty of already knowing the fount of truth") and reason ("the search for truth") [No. 1].

The "honor and responsibility," as Pope John Paul II puts it, of the Catholic university is to "consecrate itself without reserve to the cause of truth" [No. 4]. And in doing so, the Holy Father says, the Catholic college or university is serving both the dignity of the human person and the good of the Church.

"If it is the responsibility of every university to search . . . for meaning," observes the Pope, "a Catholic university is called in a particular way to respond to this need: its Christian inspiration enables it to include the moral, spiritual and religious dimension in its research, and to evaluate the attainments of science and technology in the perspective of the totality of the human person" [No. 7].

Ex corde Ecclesiae identifies four characteristics that "necessarily" belong to research conducted by a Catholic university: "(a) the search for and integration of knowledge, (b) a dialogue between faith and reason, (c) an ethical concern, and (d) a theological perspective" [No. 15].

Of particular interest to the Catholic university, writes the Pope, "is the dialogue between Christian thought and the modern sciences. This task requires persons particularly well versed in the individual disciplines who are at the same time adequately prepared theologically, and who are capable of confronting epistemological questions at the level of the relationship between faith and reason" [No. 46]. The apostolic constitution recalls for its readers the purpose of Catholic higher education as articulated in the Second Vatican Council's declaration on Christian education: that "the Christian mind may achieve as it were, a public, persistent and universal presence in the whole enterprise of advancing higher culture . . ." [No. 9].

According to *Ex corde Ecclesiae*, "the objective of a Catholic university is to assure in an institutional manner a Christian presence in a university world confronting the great problems of society and culture" [No. 13]. Hence, the Holy Father regards the work of Catholic colleges and universities as "irreplaceable" [No. 10] in the life of the Church. He concludes the apostolic constitution by saying to Catholic college and university educators: "The Church and the world have great need of your witness and of your capable, free, and responsible contribution."

The purpose of the following ordinances is to provide implementation guidelines that embody both the vision and the spirit of *Ex corde Ecclesiae*. These ordinances do not apply to ecclesiastical faculties, which are governed by the Apostolic Constitution *Sapientia Christiana* (1979), but they do apply to all the rest of the remarkable set of Catholic institutions of higher learning in the United

States to which Pope John Paul II looks for their "capable, free, and responsible contribution" to the future of both church and culture.

PART TWO: ORDINANCES

The ordinances on Catholic higher education for the dioceses of the United States are complementary to and in harmony with Canons 807–814 of the Code of Canon Law and the general norms of the Apostolic Constitution *Ex corde Ecclesiae* (part II), both of which in their entirety are part of the universal law of the Church.

1. Catholic colleges and universities are those which, through their governing boards, freely commit themselves to the Christian message as it comes to us through the Catholic church, and together with the bishops, seek to preserve and foster their Catholic character and mission.

2. Catholic colleges and universities are to identify themselves as belonging to one of the descriptive categories on the list appended to these ordinances (see Appendix) and include the appropriate identification in their governing documents [Gen. Norms, 1:3] or statements of mission [Gen. Norms, 2:3].

3. Periodically, and at least every ten years, each Catholic college or university is to undertake an internal review of the congruence of its research program [Nos. 7, 15, 18, 45], course of instruction [Nos. 16, 17, 19, 20], and service activity [Nos. 21, 31, 32, 34, 36, 37, 38] with the ideals and principles expressed in *Ex corde Ecclesiae* [Gen. Norms 2 and 5].

4. As a manifestation of their common desire to maintain the Catholic identity of the college/university, institutional authorities and the diocesan bishop, according to their own proper roles, will seek to promote the teaching of Catholic theological disciplines in communion with the church [Gen. Norms 4:3].

5. The mandate granted to those who teach theology in Catholic colleges and universities should be understood as recognition by the competent ecclesiastical authority of a Catholic professor's suitability to teach theological disciplines [Gen. Norms, 4:3].

6. Catholic professors of theological disciplines are to be advised by academic officials of the Church's expectation that they request the mandate from the competent ecclesiastical authority, normally the diocesan bishop or his delegate (cf. Canon 812). Accordingly, the bishop is to invite the Catholic professor to request the mandate and, after appropriate review, the bishop is to respond to the request.

7. If a dispute arises between the competent ecclesiastical authority and a Catholic college or university, or individuals or groups within such institutions, it is to be resolved according to procedures that respect the rights of persons in the church (for example, Canons 208–223, 224–231, and 273–289), the autonomy of the academic institution (I, n. 12; II, art. 2, par. 5; art. 5, par. 2), and the responsibility of church authorities (I, nn. 28–29; II art. 4, par. 1; art. 5 par. 2) to assist in the preservation of the institution's Catholic identity. Such procedures are also to follow the principles and, to the extent applicable, the procedures of the documents of the National Conference of Catholic Bishops *On Due Process* (1972) in administrative matters and *Doctrinal Responsibilities* (1989) in matters of differences in doctrine.
8. Governing Boards, in appropriate collaboration with the administration of the college/university, should provide for an adequately staffed campus ministry program and suitable liturgical and sacramental opportunities under the moderation of the local bishop [Gen. Norms 6: 1–2].

The ordinances, as particular law for the dioceses of the United States, become effective at the beginning of the academic year following their enactment by the National Conference of Catholic Bishops and communication from the Congregation for Catholic Education that they have been reviewed by the Apostolic See (Gen. Norms, 1:2).

APPENDIX

Descriptive Categories of Catholic Colleges and Universities

1. Ecclesiastical Faculties/Universities.
2. Canonically Established (by the Holy See).
3. Established by a Diocese:
   a) governed by a board of trustees with some powers reserved to the diocese; or
   b) independent governing board with no powers reserved to the diocese.
4. Established by a Religious Community:
   a) governed by a board of trustees with some powers reserved to the religious community; or
   b) independent governing board with no powers reserved to the religious community.

5. Established by other ecclesiastical or lay initiative:
    a) governed by a board of trustees with some powers reserved to the founding entity; or
    b) independent governing board with no powers reserved.

Institutions in this fifth category may call themselves "Catholic" by consent of the competent ecclesiastical authority.

QUESTIONNAIRE

Please Respond to the Following Questions

Using the scale below, indicate your position on the following: (Please put the number that best responds to your answer on the line next to the question.)

9 8	7 6 5 4 3	2 1
Strongly Agree	Agree Disagree	Strongly Disagree

1. _____ Introduction

2.   Ordinances:

_____ Ordinance One

_____ Ordinance Two

_____ Ordinance Three

_____ Ordinance Four

_____ Ordinance Five

_____ Ordinance Six

_____ Ordinance Seven

_____ Ordinance Eight

3. _____ Appendix

4. How well does the Introduction apply the Apostolic Constitution *Ex corde Ecclesiae* to the Catholic colleges and universities in the United States? (Please check one)

a. _____ Perfectly

b. _____ Very well

c. _____ Fairly well

d. _____ Not well

5. How well do the Ordinances apply the Apostolic Constitution *Ex corde Ecclesiae* to Catholic colleges and universities in the United States? (Please check one)

a. _____ Perfectly

b. _____ Very well

c. _____ Fairly well

d. _____ Not well

6. Can you locate your institution(s) in the Appendix within the categories therein described? (Please check one) (To be answered by college presidents and bishops with Catholic colleges or universities in the diocese).

a. _____ Yes

b. _____ No

If no, please indicate what is needed.

7. Please indicate other matters, if any, which should be treated in the Introduction.

8. Please indicate additional matters, if any, which should be treated within the section on Ordinances.

9. What recommendations, if any, do you have on any specific ordinance(s) in this draft?

10. Additional comments. (Use the other side of this questionnaire or attach a separately signed letter.)

10 | Some Initial Reflections from a Canon Law Perspective on the Proposed Ordinances for Catholic Higher Education

James H. Provost

Submitted by Ben J. Lopez, Executive Director of ACCU, to the Implementation Committee, September 8, 1993

FOR: Presidents of Catholic Colleges
and Universities in the United States
FROM: Ben J. Lopez
DATE: September 8, 1993
RE: Proposed Ordinances for the United States:
Reflections by James H. Provost

As you are aware, Bishop John Leibrecht has invited all Catholic bishops and the presidents of all Catholic colleges and universities in the United States to comment on the proposed ordinances offered by the bishop-members of the NCCB committee for the implementation of *Ex Corde Ecclesiae* in the United States. Comments must be received by the end of this year.

To assist you in developing your response to this invitation, ACCU is sponsoring regional meetings. To further assist you, I enclose, with permission, a copy of an unpublished critique of the proposed ordinances by (Rev.) James H. Provost, associate professor of canon law, The Catholic University of America, the author of "A Canonical Commentary on *Ex Corde Ecclesiae*," in *Catholic Universities in Church and Society, A Dialogue on "Ex Corde Ecclesiae,"* p. 105, Georgetown University Press (1993).

From the author's files. Printed by permission of James H. Provost.

SOME INITIAL REFLECTIONS FROM A CANON LAW PERSPECTIVE ON THE PROPOSED ORDINANCES FOR CATHOLIC HIGHER EDUCATION

John Paul II issued the apostolic constitution *Ex corde Ecclesiae* as a sort of 'magna carta' for Catholic universities.[1] One of the key features of the document is its commitment to subsidiarity in the area of Catholic higher education. This is expressed particularly in the protection of the proper autonomy of each Catholic college or university, particularly in terms of respecting their statutes (cf. *Ex corde Ecclesiae,* nn. 12 and 37), and in the provision for *ordinationes* to be issued by bishops' conferences to adapt the provisions of *Ex corde Ecclesiae* to the conditions of Catholic higher education in their respective territories (*Ex corde Ecclesiae,* art. 1, §2).

On May 4, 1993 Bishop John Leibrecht circulated to the archbishops and bishops of the United States, and to the presidents of Calholic colleges and universities, a draft of ordinances which are being considered for possible adoption for the United States by the National Conference of Catholic Bishops. Comments and recommendations were requested no later than December 31, 1993.

The following comments are developed from the perspective of canon law, only one of the many perspectives which need to be taken into consideration in the drafting and implementation of the proposed *ordinationes.* These comments are offered in the interest of being of service to the archbishops and bishops of the United States, and to officials of American Catholic higher education, as they discuss the draft ordinances.

1. NATURE OF THE "ORDINANCES"

The "Proposed Ordinances" have been drafted by a committee of the National Conference of Catholic Bishops, the canonical episcopal conference for the United States, and it is anticipated that a finalized version will be adopted by the usual vote of the conference's members. The document is clearly intended to fulfill the requirement of *Ex corde Ecclesiae* (art. 1, §2) that episcopal conferences develop *ordinationes* for their country.

The proposed text anticipates that they will be "reviewed" by the Apostolic See. This appears to accept the inaccurate rendering of *inspectionem* in the official Latin text by "reviewed" in the English translation, a regrettable lapse in the "Proposed Ordinances" given the technical meaning of the terms involved.[2] This is all the more unfortunate in that it may cloud the canonical nature of the ordinances themselves.

The *ordinationes* of which *Ex corde Ecclesiae* speaks appear to be instructions from a canon law point of view. In promulgating *Ex corde Ecclesiae* and its accompanying norms, the pope saw fit to distinguish the *ordinationes* from general decrees (c. 29) or general executory decrees (c. 31). He did this by requiring only "inspection" rather than "review" prior to their taking effect (art. 1, §2), and he did not require that they be promulgated. Both general decrees and general executory decrees of episcopal conferences must receive the *recognitio* of the Apostolic See (c. 455, §2), and must be promulgated (cc. 29 and 31, §2). Since neither are required for the *ordinationes,* they appear to fit the category of instruction (c. 34).

Instructions are binding documents; they are to be obeyed. They "clarify the prescriptions of laws and elaborate on and determine an approach to be followed in implementing them" (c. 34, §1). In the case at hand, *Ex corde Ecclesiae* as an apostolic constitution is universal law; the *ordinationes* are instructions clarifying the prescriptions of *Ex corde Ecclesiae* and determining the approach to be followed to implement them within the territory of the episcopal conference.

Instructions differ from general executory decrees in that they are "given for the use of those persons whose concern it is to see that the laws are implemented" (c. 34, §1). The ordinances proposed for the United States apply to bishops and to officials of Catholic institutions of higher education, and so fit the nature of an instruction.

The ordinances, as an instruction, "oblige" bishops and officials of Catholic higher education "in the implementation of the laws" (c. 34, §l). However, "regulations found in instructions do not derogate from laws, and if any of them cannot be reconciled with the prescriptions of laws, they lack all force" (c. 34, §2; cf. *Ex corde Ecclesiae,* art. 1, §2). That is, if there is any question on whether an ordinance goes beyond what is authorized for the bishops to command, the provisions of the law (i.e., *Ex corde Ecclesiae*) are to resolve the question. There still remains the question of to what extent an instruction can impose new obligations beyond the law (*praeler legem*).

The purpose for the ordinances, then, is to apply the Church's legislation to local and regional situations. Because they must respect the statutes of the institutions as well as the general law of the Church (art. 1, §2), their most important function ought to be in establishing standards adapted to the area and setting up procedures for their implementation. The "Proposed Ordinances" can be evaluated in this light.

2. IDENTIFYING CATHOLIC UNIVERSITIES

The Introduction to the "Proposed Ordinances" focuses on what the apostolic constitution states about the research dimension of what a Catholic university does, but it passes over in silence what a Catholic university is. The focus of the Introduction is on the relationship between faith and reason in the research function of the university.

This is a significant standard, but is it sufficient for the situation in the United States, where many Catholic colleges focus primarily on the teaching and service dimensions of what a Catholic university does? A more balanced approach would be to reaffirm as a standard the four key characteristics which *Ex corde Ecclesiae* (n. 13) identifies as constituting a Catholic university, then to reaffirm the importance of teaching and service as well as research in American Catholic colleges and universities, and finally to address the relationship of faith and reason, the witness of Catholic higher education within the academic world in the United States, and the service of these Catholic institutions in contemporary American society.

The situation is not much better in the ordinances themselves. The first ordinance collapses the carefully nuanced approach of *Ex corde Ecclesiae* and presents two elements as the standard for determining what universities are Catholic: (1) the free commitment by governing boards (which is only one of the elements in *Ex corde Ecclesiae*—art. 2. §2), and (2) seeking "together with the bishops . . . to preserve and foster their Catholic character and mission." In the apostolic constitution, the role of bishops in fostering the Catholic character and mission of Catholic universities is not presented as integral to the identity of Calholic universities, but as flowing from the place of these institutions in the Church (cf. art. 5, §2).

To what extent can the standards in the *ordinationes* go beyond the central elements identifying a Catholic university as found in the apostolic constitution? If they do, to what extent are these added elements normative in determining the Catholic identity of institutions within the ambit of the episcopal conference? For example, if a bishop fails to work "to preserve and foster the Catholic character and mission" (Ord. 1) of a Catholic college or university within his diocese, does the institution cease to be Catholic? To lose Catholic identity because of episcopal neglect would be contrary to the very purpose of *Ex corde Ecclesiae.* On the other hand, if the institution's authorities and the bishop disagree over the best means to foster its Catholic character and mission, does their failure "to work together" (Ord. 1) at this time suspend the university's Catholic identity?

If the document needs to say anything about the Catholic identity of universities beyond what is already stated in the apostolic constitution, the proposed ordinance should respect the papal document's careful distinctions and nuances.[3] A more fitting ordinance might be simply to reaffirm that the standards for what constitutes an institution of Catholic higher education in the United States are those set in *Ex corde Ecclesiae.*

3. CLASSIFICATION OF CATHOLIC UNIVERSITIES

Ex corde Ecclesiae has two systems for classifying Catholic higher education. The first system applies to institutions *already in existence* (art. 1, §3):

(1) those established by the Holy See, an episcopal conference, or diocesan bishop;
(2) all others.

The second system applies to the *founding of new universities* (art. 3):

(1) established by the Holy See, an episcopal conference, or diocesan bishop;
(2) established by a public juridic person, including a religious institute;
(3) all others.

In an appendix the "Proposed Ordinances" have developed an entirely different set of descriptive categories, which are to be used by "Catholic colleges and universities . . . to identify themselves" (Ord. 2).

The first of the classifications in the Appendix (ecclesiastical faculties and universities) is not covered by the "Proposed Ordinances," as the last paragraph of the Introduction makes clear. It would appear to be included in the appendix only for the sake of completeness.

The second category, "Canonically Established (by the Holy See)," raises certain problems. First, it could mean only those institutions which have been *established* by the Apostolic See, and not those which may have subsequently been *approved* by the Apostolic See. Yet *Ex corde Ecclesiae* includes both establishment and approval by the Holy See in such a category (art. 1, §3; art. 3, 1). Second, it is not only the Apostolic See which can establish a university "canonically." To establish something canonically is to establish it in keeping with the provisions of canon law. A decree of the episcopal conference can establish something canonically, as can a decree of the diocesan bishop. Such decrees could erect entities as public juridic persons (or as "moral persons" under the 1917 code), or they could erect them as church institutions without specific reference to a juridic status. All of this is "canonical," for it is done in virtue of the authority possessed by bishops and their conferences according to canon law. This is why *Ex corde Ecclesiae* groups all these institutions into the same category, whether currently existing or yet to be founded. The standard set by this category in the Appendix needs to be revised in keeping with the apostolic constitution itself.

The third category gives some indication of the origin of the distinctions among the descriptive categories. It subdivides those established by a diocese into those "with some powers reserved to the diocese," and those with "no powers reserved to the diocese." This is a distinction drawn from American civil law. It is not clear why the distinctions are made in a canonical document such as the "Proposed Ordinances" of the episcopal conference. Moreover the distinctions are not presented as standards, nor do they seem to have any practical application in any of the proposed ordinances.

Canonically, institutions erected by a diocesan bishop may be distinguished, for example, into (1) those which remain diocesan; (2) those which were set up as an independent institution, even though founded by the diocese; (3) those which have been canonically "alienated" from the diocese but retain a Catholic identity (e.g., they were taken over by a religious institute, by an association of the faithful, or by individuals who run them as Catholic institutions); and (4) those which have been secularized (even if not taken over by the state). This is also true of institutions established by a "Religious Community," to which the fourth category applies the same subdivisions as those applied to dioceses.

In keeping with both the code (c. 808: *etsi reapse catholica*) and *Ex corde Ecclesiae* (art. 2, §2), although the founding group may no longer retain even "reserved powers," the institution may still be "really Catholic." It is not clear, therefore, how the distinctions in the descriptive categories apply to the concerns addressed by the bishops' document.

A fifth category, similarly subdivided according to the question of "reserved powers," is for those "established by other ecclesiastical or lay initiative." Related to this category is a statement which amounts to another proposed ordinance at the conclusion of the descriptive categories in the Appendix. Aside from the anomalous location of a new ordinance in the Appendix rather than in the body of the "Proposed Ordinances" themselves, this statement repeats *Ex corde Ecclesiae*'s requirement for newly formed universities to obtain the consent of competent ecclesiastical authority in order to call themselves "Catholic"; i.e., to *refer* to themselves this way (art. 3, §3). But the statement does not include any standards to be met before competent authority will grant such approval (as *Ex corde Ecclesiae* encouraged be done in episcopal conference *ordinationes;* cf. note 48 to art. 3, §3), nor does it provide the procedures to be followed for this. Moreover, the wording gives the impression this requirement applies to existing institutions, which is not the case in *Ex corde Ecclesiae* (where it only applies to those yet to be established).

It may not be necessary for Ordinance 2 to say anything more than is already clearly required in the norms of the apostolic constitution regarding a public statement of Catholic identity. If it is, it does not seem that the incorporation of one of the appendix's descriptive categories into the governing documents or mission statement would be very helpful, given the difficulties associated with the classification list and the fact that they serve no evident purpose in providing for Catholic identity in higher education. Instead, Ordinance 2 might more appropriately be modified to a straightforward affirmation of the requirement of a public commitment to Catholic identity, and specify that it be in one of the documents which are typical of Catholic higher education in the United States ("governing documents" or "statements of mission"— Ord. 2).

4. PERIODIC EVALUATION

A time-honored practice in American higher education is the self-study associated with accreditation. In calling for a periodic review of the institution's performance in research, teaching, and service activity from the perspective of its Catholic identity, the bishops are adopting this American practice and provide for a procedure to assist Catholic universities to meet their responsibilities under *Ex corde Ecclesiae.* Ordinance 3 provides a helpful process, and clearly indicates the standards to be applied during the process. It might be even clearer if this requirement were explicitly related to the existing self-study process.

5. THEOLOGICAL DISCIPLINES

Three of the eight proposed ordinances deal with the teaching of theology and theologians. Ordinance 4 reaffirms the respective competencies of the institution's authorities and the diocesan bishop in promoting the teaching of Catholic theological disciplines in communion with the Church. It does this without spelling out the standards to determine their respective roles nor does it provide procedures for their coordination. The only reference in the ordinance is to article 4, §3 of *Ex corde Ecclesiae*, which does not shed much light on this issue. It would be more helpful to cite article 4, §1, which provides a better explanation of the respective roles in general and also contains the text of canon 810 in a note; this canon is even more specific about the respective roles of the institution and the bishop.

Ordinance 5 addresses the mandate to teach. It characterizes the mandate as a recognition of a theologian's "suitability to teach theological disciplines." This is a helpful start; it provides a description of the mandate which does not attempt to turn it into a "mission" or other empowerment by the bishop. What "suitability" means, however, is not particularly clear. For example, it may be within the bishop's competence to judge suitability in terms of one's standing in the Church's communion, but it may be beyond his competence to judge one's suitability in instructional method. The ordinance fails to provide standards which would assure fairness throughout the country on this question, it does not provide a procedure for a bishop to follow in determining whether to grant the mandate, and it does not resolve the question of portability. It may be that these issues are too sensitive among the bishops themselves at this time for the ordinance to be able to do this, although models do exist (e.g., from the German episcopal conference).

Ordinance 6 is sensitive to the fact that the mandate applies to the theologian, not to the institution. It calls for academic officials to remind Catholic professors of theological disciplines to request the mandate, but it leaves the actual initiative up to the individual professor. It also calls for the bishop to invite the professor to request the mandate, but again leaves the actual initiative up to the individual. The sensitivity evident in this approach is encouraging.

The ordinance, however, does not set standards for the "appropriate review" the bishop is to conduct. This is not helped by the failure to establish standards in the previous ordinance as well. Nor are the procedures for this review spelled out.

The ordinance uses the technical term "professor." This is a narrower description of the position than the code uses (where the generic "those who teach" is used in c. 812). It may be appropriate to restrict the mandate to those who have reached professorial rank, although that does not seem the intent of the code or *Ex corde Ecclesiae,* again raising the question of how binding a provision of the ordinances may be if it differs from the general law.

In using the language of invitation, Ordinance 6 does not provide much help in determining what course of action to take if a professor of theology fails to respond to the invitation to seek the mandate. Standards and procedures applicable to this situation may eventually have to be developed.

6. DISPUTE RESOLUTION

Ordinance 7 sets the standards to be observed in resolving any disputes between competent ecclesiastical authority and a Catholic institution of higher education. These include respect for the rights of persons, the institution's proper autonomy, and the responsibility of church authorities to assist in preserving the institution's Catholic identity. It also suggests that existing NCCB procedures be applied— *On Due Process* for administrative matters, and *Doctrinal Responsibilities* for doctrinal matters. These procedures can be helpful.

The two NCCB documents, however, are not binding on the bishops, and were adopted as guides or aids to be used to the extent a bishop decides to use them. *Ex corde Ecclesiae* (art. 5, §2, and note 52) calls for procedures to be established either in the statutes of institutions which receive approval from competent ecclesiastical authority, or by the episcopal conference. Although Ordinance 7 calls for procedures to be used in resolving disputes, it does not establish any; even in recommending the optional NCCB procedures, it qualifies this with "to the extent applicable." The weakness of this ordinance may become apparent when it has to be used in situations where more than optional possibilities are needed.

7. CAMPUS MINISTRY

Ordinance 8 properly locates the basic responsibility for campus ministry within the university. However, it makes this a matter for the governing board. The specificity of locating this responsibility within the governing board may fail to show proper respect for the statutes of the various Catholic institutions of higher education, some of which may have located this responsibility elsewhere within their structure.

8. FINAL COMMENT

It is very difficult to draft a suitable set of standards and procedures for the many issues involved in Catholic higher education which the bishops have attempted to address. The proposed ordinances reflect this difficulty. While they do provide helpful standards and even procedures in some matters, in their present form they provide little help to bishops or university administrators in addressing many of the complexities of maintaining Catholic identity today. The role of the faculty is not addressed, nor that of the wider Catholic or academic community; standards and procedures which might provide some sense of fair treatment for theologians nationally are missing; even the introduction of American civil law concepts is without practical purpose, and appears to neglect the richer sense of Catholic identity within the code which itself reflects Vatican II's teachings.

In the past the NCCB has benefited from the initiative and collaboration of scholars in many fields for the drafting of various documents, including *On Due Process* and *Doctrinal Responsibilities*. That experience may provide a model for continued work on the standards and procedures appropriate to Catholic higher education in the United States. The proposed ordinances, even in a revised form, may have to serve as an interim document until a more interdisciplinary and reflective process can develop standards and procedures truly adapted to the local and regional situation.

James H. Provost, J.C.D.
The Catholic University of America

NOTES

1. John Paul II, apostolic constitution *Ex corde Ecclesiae,* August 15, 1990: *AAS* 82 (1990) 1475–1509; see nn. 8 and 9: 1480.
2. For a more complete discussion of this issue, see James H. Provost, "A Canonical Commentary on *Ex Corde Ecclesiae,*" in *Catholic Universities in Church and Society: A Dialogue on "Ex Corde Ecclesiae"* (Washington, D.C.: Georgetown University Press, 1993).
3. See ibid. for a canonical analysis of these nuances and distinctions.

11 | Theologians and the Mandate to Teach

Sister Sharon Euart, R.S.M.

When the revised Code of Canon Law was promulgated by Pope John Paul II on Jan. 25, 1983, it contained a chapter not found in the previous code, titled "Catholic Universities and Other Institutes of Higher Studies." Among the eight canons in this chapter is Canon 812, which prescribes: "They who teach theological disciplines in any institute of higher studies should have a mandate from the competent ecclesiastical authority."[1]

Canon 812 is a new canon. There was no parallel in the 1917 code requiring ecclesiastical authorization for teachers of theology in institutes of higher education. Nor is there evidence of such a requirement in the teachings of the Second Vatican Council. The intent of Canon 812 is to uphold the orthodoxy of church teaching. The requirement of the mandate represents a juridical response to a potential danger to the faith and an effort to protect and defend the rights of the faithful and the good of the church. The consequences of the application of this new canon to Catholic colleges and universities in the United States has been a source of apprehension and concern to educators, theologians, and canon and civil lawyers since the norm was first proposed in 1977.

The requirement of the mandate is also referred to in Article 4.3 of the general norms of *Ex Corde Ecclesiae,* the apostolic constitution on Catholic higher education promulgated by Pope John Paul II in August 1990.[2] The long-awaited apostolic constitution is a strong affirmation of the value and importance of Catholic colleges and universities and a welcome call to renewal and a re-examination of Catholic higher education in light of the Gospel and culture. *Ex Corde Ecclesiae,* at the same time, poses challenges about Catholic identity, institutional autonomy and the relationship between theologians and bishops that are best addressed through ongoing cooperation and dialogue between

From the author's files; published in *Origins* 23, no. 27 (December 16, 1993). Printed by permission of Sharon Euart, R.S.M.

bishops and representatives of Catholic colleges and universities. The incorporation of the requirement of Canon 812 in *Ex Corde Ecclesiae,* namely that Catholic teachers of theological disciplines obtain a mandate from competent ecclesiastical authority, has probably evoked more debate and discussion, generated
more fears and suspicion on the part of theologians and university officials, and
raised more concerns and complexities than any other requirement in the apostolic constitution.

In my comments this evening I wish to address the requirement of the mandate for theology teachers in four parts: first, a brief review of the historical development of Canon 812; second, the distinction between mandate and canonical mission; third, the implementation of *Ex Corde Ecclesiae* and the implications
of the mandate vis-a-vis the relationship between bishops and theologians; and
fourth, procedures for applying the mandate in Catholic colleges and universities in the United States.

HISTORICAL DEVELOPMENT OF CANON 812

The requirement of ecclesiastical authorization for teachers of theology first
appeared in the 1977 draft of proposed canons for Book III of the revised Code
of Canon Law. Opposition to the proposed norm was particularly strong in the
United States and Canada. Educators, theologians, canonists and members of
the episcopacy urged that the proposed canon be deleted. Those opposing the
proposed canon viewed it as (1) requiring the intrusion of external ecclesiastical authority into the operation of Catholic colleges and universities; (2) having a "chilling and stifling" effect on theological investigation; and (3) having
the potential for placing in jeopardy the future of academic accreditation and
public financial assistance for such institutions.[3]

When the 1980 schema of the new code was published, the canon remained
unchanged. Opposition to the proposed canon continued in the United States
and Canada. Once again educators, canonists and bishops called for its deletion in the revised law.

During the 1981 plenary session of the Pontifical Commission for the Revision of the Code, several textual changes were introduced into the canon, the
most significant of which involved the substitution of the term *mandate* for
the previously used *canonical mission* to describe the required ecclesiastical authorization.[4]

The report *(relatio)* of the 1981 plenary session noted that Cardinal G. Em-
mett Carter of Toronto had suggested that the canon be omitted since the

requirement of a "canonical mission" could endanger the relationship between Catholic colleges and the civil government. It also reported that then-
Archbishop Joseph Bernardin of the United States had intervened on behalf of
American educators, canonists and bishops suggesting that "canonical mission"
was not necessary since concern for surveillance over Catholic orthodoxy in
institutions of higher learning was "sufficiently provided for" in the two prior
canons (Canons 765 and 766, later Canons 810.2, 811.1).[5]

While these suggestions to omit the canon were not accepted, the text was
amended to read that "those who teach theological disciplines in any institute
of higher studies are to have a mandate from the competent ecclesiastical authority." The reason for the textual change from canonical mission to mandate
was stated as follows: "It seemed opportune to insert language concerning a
mandate instead of canonical mission, which in this case is not fully equated
with a true canonical mission."[6] No explanation was offered as to why *canonical mission* in this context would not be a "true canonical mission."

Despite the textual changes, opposition to the proposed canon remained
strong among American educators, canonists and bishops. The mere existence
of the canon continued to be a source of concern. Whether the norm required
a mandate or canonical mission was considered, in one sense, irrelevant. What
mattered most was that the requirement involved an intrusion by external ecclesiastical authority into the governance of Catholic colleges and universities, an intervention which was seen to present potential obstacles to theological investigation and to future accreditation and government funding of these
institutions.

In 1982, a delegation of representatives from the Association of Catholic Colleges and Universities and a representative of the American hierarchy (Bishop
James Malone of Youngstown, Ohio) appealed personally to Pope John Paul II
urging the deletion of the canon. Noting the potential for legal and financial
problems which the proposed canon presented for American Catholic colleges
and universities, the delegation requested that the canon not be included in the
revised code but that other, nonjuridical, means of maintaining and strengthening the relationship between Catholic institutions of higher learning and
church authorities be sought.

When the Code of Canon Law was promulgated on Jan. 25, 1983, the proposed canon became Canon 812, unchanged from the text as amended in the
relatio of 1981 and as presented to Pope John Paul II in 1982. Concern over the
application of the canon to Catholic colleges and universities in the United
States did not end with the promulgation of the code. Rather, the inclusion of
Canon 812 in the revised law has intensified the need to examine the meaning

of the new norm and its significance for Catholic higher education in the United States.

In 1990 Pope John Paul II promulgated the long-awaited apostolic constitution on Catholic colleges and universities, *Ex Corde Ecclesiae*. The constitution requires episcopal conferences to apply concretely the norms of the constitution at the local and national levels (Article 1.2). It is this task of making the norms applicable to the United States that a committee of bishops, with the assistance of Catholic college presidents, has been studying and developing over the past two years. Among the draft "ordinances" currently proposed for implementation in the United States are two regarding the granting of the canonical mandate to Catholic teachers of theological disciplines in Catholic colleges and universities.[7]

CANONICAL MISSION AND MANDATE

In order to discuss the significance of the mandate of Canon 812, its incorporation in *Ex Corde Ecclesiae* and its implementation in the United States, it is helpful to determine whether or not it differs from canonical mission and if so, how. That some difference exists would appear evident from the fact that in earlier drafts what is now called a *mandate* had been called a *canonical mission*. Some light might be shed on why the term *canonical mission* had been incorporated in the earlier drafts, why it was later thought not to be opportune and why *mandate* was considered to be more suitable, by a brief review of past usage of the terms *canonical mission* and *mandate*.

The notion of canonical mission *(missio canonica)* as applied to teaching in the church is rooted in conciliar legislation of the Middle Ages concerning requirements for preaching. For example, Lucius III, at the Council of Verona in 1184, condemned those who "presumed to preach" without "having been sent [*non missi*] by the Holy See or a local bishop."[8] Similar condemnations were issued against positions that denied the necessity of ecclesiastical authorization for preaching by the Fourth Lateran Council, the Council of Constance and the Council of Trent.[9] This conciliar legislation seems to have relied on the Letter of Paul to the Romans, in which the author states, "But how shall they call on him in whom they believe unless they have heard of him? And how can they hear unless there is someone to preach? And how can men preach unless they are sent?" In so doing, the conciliar documents appear to have juridicized the biblical notion of "being sent" to preach the Word of God.

Later in the 19th century, canonical mission was applied more broadly to all public religious instruction with the federalization of schools and universities in Germany. The church required all teachers of theology, at whatever level of teaching, to have an ecclesiastical (canonical) mission from the bishop to ensure freedom from state intervention in the teaching of theology.

In the 1917 code the term *missio canonica* was used to denote the principal means of acquiring the power of jurisdiction, a power that could only be exercised by clergy. In the writings of many commentators on the 1917 code, however, it was also applied to liturgical preaching and to the entire ministry of teaching, including catechetical teaching as well as preaching. The basis of this usage was Canon 1328, which did not use the term *missio canonica;* it used simply the term *missio* to describe the authorization needed for the ministry of preaching.[10] The placement of Canon 1328 in the 1917 code and the organization of the section in which the canon appeared supported the opinion that the required authorization called for in the canons applied to the broader ministry of teaching, including catechetical teaching as well as preaching.[11]

Although Canon 1328 did not use the term *missio canonica,* many commentators interpreted the term *missio* in the canon to mean *missio canonica.* Much of the debate around the authorization of Canon 1328 focused on the dispute over the relationship of ecclesiastical magisterium to the power of jurisdiction, namely whether or not ecclesiastical jurisdiction included the power to teach as well as the power to govern.[12] In recognizing the applicability of Canon 1328 to the entire ministry of ecclesiastical teaching, commentators on the 1917 code had to grapple with the practical application of the *missio* to laypersons. For most, it was not a canonical mission in the strict sense of participation in the church's power of jurisdiction, since only clergy were capable of such power. It could more precisely be called a *mandate* or an *assignment* from ecclesiastical authority. As a "mandate without jurisdiction," such a "commission" was not an ecclesiastical office, but rather an appointment of a layperson by competent ecclesiastical authority to perform a special function.

In light of this canonical history, it might be argued that the roots of the mandate of Canon 812 include the *missio* of Canon 1328 of the 1917 code as it was understood to be some form of ecclesiastical authorization distinct from the *missio canonica* of the same code.

In 1931 the requirement of a canonical mission for some public ecclesiastical teaching became an explicit part of the universal law in the norms governing ecclesiastical faculties and universities.[13] Article 21 of the apostolic constitution *Deus Scientiarum Dominus* listed five requirements for faculty selection, the fifth of which required that each professor "receive a canonical mission for teaching from the chancellor after having obtained the *nihil obstat* from the Holy See. A second reference to canonical mission was found in Article 22, which authorized the chancellor to withdraw the canonical mission where a professor had been shown to have departed from doctrinal integrity.[14]

In 1979, Pope John Paul II promulgated the apostolic constitution *Sapientia Christiana,* replacing the previous norms regulating ecclesiastical faculties and universities.[15] *Sapientia Christiana* retains the requirement of a canonical mission for teachers of disciplines related to faith and morals; other teachers require "permission" to teach *(venia docendi).*

While the term *missio canonica* had been incorporated into the early drafts of Canon 812, the reason for its inclusion does not appear in the published legislative history of the canon. It would seem reasonable that the drafters of Canon 812, intending to uphold the integrity of Catholic doctrine by requiring ecclesiastical authorization for the teaching of theology in institutes of higher studies, introduced a term whose past usage could be said to lend legitimacy to such a contemporary application.

When it was later determined that the *missio canonica* was not opportune terminology, the drafters were not suggesting that ecclesiastical authorization was unnecessary. Rather, the deletion of *missio canonica* simply reflected concern over the nature of the authorization required for public ecclesiastical teaching. Since the *missio canonica* was not considered to be "fully equated with a true canonical mission," its deletion in the final version and its replacement with *mandatum* seem related to the association of *missio canonica* with jurisdiction and to yet-unresolved questions concerning lay participation in the power of governance in the church.

In the preparation of the Second Vatican Council's Decree on the Apostolate of the Laity, the council fathers discussed the distinction between *mandatum* and *missio canonica.*[16] In Article 24 of the decree the council set forth different grades or types of relationship between the lay apostolate and the hierarchy, beginning with the more remote relationships and moving to closer relationships in which the laity are fully subject to hierarchical direction. In so doing, the council taught that there are certain forms of the apostolate of the laity which the hierarchy joins more closely to its own apostolic endeavors without, however, depriving the apostolate of the laity of its own nature, individuality and initiative. This act of joining some forms of the apostolate of the laity to that of the hierarchy is called a *mandatum.*

The same article then speaks of another form of cooperative relationship between laity and hierarchy in which the hierarchy "entrusts" to the laity some functions which are more closely connected with the pastoral duties of the hierarchy such as the teaching of Christian doctrine, certain liturgical actions and the care of souls.[17] The term *missio* is used here to describe those "entrusted" functions that are fully subject to hierarchical direction.

The distinction between *missio* and *mandatum* in Article 24 has been used by some to explain Canon 812. Although this distinction may provide some insight into the meaning of the *mandatum* of Canon 812, the distinction is not all that clear. From the earliest discussions of the Preparatory Commission on the Apostolate of the Laity it was obvious that no real clarity existed in regard to the notion of mandate. The concept was confused with both the notion of canonical mission and with other juridical meanings of mandate. The Conciliar Commission for the Apostolate of the Laity made further attempts to clarify the distinction between canonical mission and mandate by appending lengthy explanatory notes to the 1963 schema.[18] One of the explanatory notes enumerated the areas of the apostolate requiring a *missio canonica*, which included teaching Christian doctrine in a public manner.[19]

The conciliar commission prepared another draft of the text in 1964 which became the basis for discussion at the third session of the council in October 1964. Criticism of the text was strong among the council fathers, although it came from differing viewpoints. The final text of the decree in September 1965 contained no changes in the distinction between *mandatum* and *missio*. Further clarity in the application of the two notions was lost as a result of the commission's decision to delete the accompanying explanatory notes.

What does seem clear from the promulgated decree is that the council considered mission and mandate to be two distinct concepts. *Mission* connotes entrusting to the laity certain tasks and certain offices which are considered to be proper to the hierarchy but which require neither the power of orders nor the power of jurisdiction for their lawful exercise. *Mandate,* on the other hand, refers to those apostolic activities which remain activities proper to the laity in virtue of baptism, but which at times are joined more closely to the apostolic responsibility of the bishop. When acting pursuant to a mandate, a layperson acts, it would seem, on his or her own and in communion with the bishop, but not in the name of the bishop or the church hierarchy.

The use of *mandatum* in Canon 812 suggests that the teaching of theological disciplines differs from the teaching of Christian doctrine by virtue of a less close relationship to the hierarchy. Unlike the teaching of Christian doctrine, which according to the conciliar decree requires a *missio*, the teaching of "theological disciplines" is not "entrusted" to the laity by the hierarchy, but is considered to be work proper to the laity (as well as to clergy), carried out in communion with the hierarchy, but not requiring the same degree of ecclesiastical recognition.

At the present time there does not seem to be a common interpretation of the distinction between *mandatum* and *missio canonica* nor is there a common understanding of the precise meaning of the mandate of Canon 812. Some suggest the terms are interchangeable, while others note they are not equivalent. Some interpretations include understanding the *mandatum* as hierarchical deputation or agency,[20] a commission to teach,[21] a disciplinary matter[22] and an expression of communion between theologian and hierarchy.[23] What is common to the various interpretations is that some ecclesiastical authorization is required for those who teach theological disciplines in Catholic colleges and universities.

Based on the canonical history of the notions of *missio canonica* and *mandatum*, it seems to me that the two concepts are distinct and that the change from canonical mission to mandate in Canon 812 is not without significance. It would seem, too, that the meaning of the term *mandatum* set forth in the Decree on the Apostolate of the Laity signifies a relationship between bishops and theologians in which the teaching of theology is carried out in communion with the hierarchy and in a manner that acknowledges the proper role of bishops and theologians. Such an understanding of mandate would seem to contribute to a more effective implementation of Canon 812 and the norms of *Ex Corde Ecclesiae.*

RELATIONSHIP BETWEEN BISHOPS AND THEOLOGIANS

An important context for interpreting the mandate is the notion of *communio* between bishops and theologians whereby bishops promote, assist and protect Catholic universities. This community-centered framework may be conducive to a more flexible and positive understanding of the relationship between bishops and theologians than that denoted by mandate as a direct certification of an individual theologian. The church as a community *(communio)* of Christian faith and life is a reality in which bishops, Catholic institutions of higher education and theologians all participate in fulfilling distinct but complementary roles. The Catholic university arises then as a differentiated institution within the whole ecclesial communion.[24]

Ex Corde Ecclesiae affirms the distinctive role of the Catholic university in the church in acknowledging that "it [the Catholic university] possesses the institutional autonomy necessary to perform its functions" (No. 12) and "guarantees its members academic freedom, so long as the rights of the individual person and the community be preserved within the confines of the truth and the common good" (No. 12, Article 2.5). In the area of theology, *Ex Corde Ecclesiae* further acknowledges that "theologians enjoy this same [academic] freedom so long as they are faithful" to the "principles and methods which define theology as a branch of knowledge" (No. 19). In seeking to understand faith,[25] theologians respond with respect for the authority of the pope and bishops and assent to Catholic doctrine in accord with the level of authority with which it is taught. Therefore, dialogue between bishops and theologians is indispensable to the guarantee of institutional autonomy and academic freedom, on the one hand, and respect for church authority and loyal assent, on the other.

A set of guidelines for promoting cooperation and resolving misunderstandings between bishops and theologians was developed in cooperation with the bishops' Committee on Doctrine, the Canon Law Society of America and the Catholic Theological Society of America and approved by the bishops in June 1989.

This document, titled "Doctrinal Responsibilities,"[26] describes the bishop's role as primarily a "pastoral duty in the name of Christ to proclaim the word of God with authority, to teach the truth of faith and to maintain the authentic interpretation of the word of God as it has been handed down in history." The theologian, on the other hand, is a Catholic "who seeks to mediate through the discipline of scholarship, between a living faith and the culture it is called to transform." Theologians "serve the Gospel . . . through scholarly work," but they are not "primarily preachers or catechists." The bishop's work is "authoritative teaching and pastoral leadership" while theologians engage in "ethical reflection, theological education and research."[27]

Theology as scholarship, then, would seem to differ from catechesis and doctrinal proclamation. As a consequence, the relationship of a bishop to doctrine and its teachers may be different from his relationship to theology and its teachers. This proposition is supported, I believe, by the conciliar discussions on the distinction between mandate and canonical mission in the Decree on the Apostolate of the Laity, which seem to suggest a less close supervisory role for the bishop in relation to theology than to the teaching of doctrine. The distinction is important relative to the form through which the hierarchy expresses its concern for the teaching of theology in the practical order.

A relationship between bishops and university theologians that is characterized by mutual trust, cooperation, a shared sense of responsibility and community is crucial to the proper functioning of theology in the church in this country. If the mandate is viewed simply as a juridical mechanism for theological uniformity and conformity, the work of theology and the morale of theologians may well be undermined. On the other hand, if there exists a community of trust and dialogue between theologians and bishops or at least an effort at building such a community, the work of theology will be enhanced and the challenges associated with the mandate may be minimized.

PROCEDURES FOR GRANTING, WITHDRAWAL OR DENIAL OF THE MANDATE

One of the more significant challenges flowing from the implementation of the apostolic constitution *Ex Corde Ecclesiae* concerns the mandate for theologians. Lack of a common interpretation of the meaning of the mandate suggests a need for clarity on precisely what is required on the part of a Catholic theologian to receive a mandate from ecclesiastical authority and, at the same time, a determination of the conditions under which the mandate may be denied or withdrawn by church authority. This *lacuna* strongly suggests the necessity of establishing mutually acceptable standards and procedures for the granting, withdrawal or denial of the mandate which would ensure fairness in their application throughout the country.

Early last summer the proposed draft ordinances for the application of *Ex Corde Ecclesiae* in the dioceses of the United States were sent out for consultation among bishops, Catholic college presidents, faculties and boards. The purpose of the ordinances is to apply the church's legislation, that is, the norms of *Ex Corde Ecclesiae,* to local and regional situations. Because they are to respect the statutes of the institutions as well as the general law of the church (Article 1.2), the most important function of the ordinances ought to be in establishing standards adapted to the local situation and in setting up procedures for their implementation.

One of the proposed ordinances (No. 5) describes the mandate of Article 4.3 as "recognition by competent ecclesiastical authority of a Catholic professor's suitability to teach theological disciplines." While this understanding of the mandate is certainly consistent with the meaning of Canon 812, questions about its application may arise. For example, what does *suitability* mean? What determines one's suitability? Is it academic credentials, teaching experience, probity of life, orthodoxy of the theologian's writings, one's intention to teach in accord with the magisterium? While a bishop may certainly be competent to judge suitability in regard to one's standing in the church, all bishops may not be equally competent to judge one's suitability in pedagogy. Moreover, on what basis can a Catholic theologian be denied the mandate? Under what conditions can it be withdrawn? Is the mandate portable?[28] Answers to questions such as these will be necessary if relations between bishops and theologians are to be "characterized by mutual trust, close and consistent cooperation and continuing dialogue" (*Ex Corde Ecclesiae*, 28).

What then should be considered, from a canonical perspective, in developing standards and procedures to address these concerns? Canon 812 is a legal norm. It involves a right-and-duty situation,[29] namely, the granting, withdrawal or denial of a mandate for teachers of theology. The requirement of a mandate is in the nature of a restriction on the rights of those engaged in sacred disciplines to freedom of inquiry and prudent expression, a right recognized in Canon 218 of the 1983 code.[30]

In addition to Canon 218, two other canons also affirm basic ecclesial rights of the Christian faithful. The first is Canon 211, which affirms the duty and right of the faithful to participate in the spreading of the Gospel;[31] the second is Canon 216, which acknowledges the right of the faithful, in accord with each one's state and condition, to promote and support apostolic undertakings of their own initiative.[32]

As a restriction on the free exercise of rights, Canon 812 is to be interpreted strictly, that is, as narrowly as is consistent with the ordinary meaning of the words (Canon 18). Consequently, wherever Canon 812 is susceptible to differing interpretations, the stricter or narrower interpretation should be given.

In addition to the canons that provide a frame of reference for interpreting Canon 812, there are other relevant canons that afford an important framework for applying the canon. Canon 812, for example, also exists in the context of the basic human right to one's good reputation, a right recognized in Canon 221, which states that one's reputation is not to be unlawfully damaged.[33] Any procedure for the application of Canon 812, therefore, should be sensitive to foreseeable effects upon the reputation of those involved. Finally, Canon 221 provides juridical protection of rights, stating that the Christian faithful have a right to vindicate or defend their rights before a competent forum in the church.[34] Although Canon 812 lays down no procedure for the granting, withdrawal or denial of a mandate, canon law does afford recourse for wrongful, arbitrary action.

A sound understanding and interpretation of the meaning of the mandate should be made in light of such rights as are enumerated in these canons, and any application of the mandate should be careful not to ignore or infringe upon these same rights. Any procedure for the application of the mandate must respect the rights of both theologians and bishops. As teachers of the faith, bishops are to provide episcopal supervision over the transmission of the faith and to safeguard the integrity of Catholic teaching.[35] When the right of the bishop to protect the rights of the church and its members to receive the faith integrally and faithfully is in tension with the rights of the theologian enumerated above, mutual trust, cooperation and dialogue are placed in jeopardy unless a just and equitable resolution is sought.

In this context, the guidelines enumerated in "Doctrinal Responsibilities" provide an important framework for implementation of the mandate of Article 4.3 of the general norms of *Ex Corde Ecclesiae*. The apostolic constitution ought not to "presuppose a situation of tension or envisage adversarial relations between bishops and theologians in the United States, as if the rights of one had to be protected against the other." Rather, it ought "to encourage increased communication and collaboration between bishops and theologians, to forestall disputes and, if such disputes arise, to promote their resolution for the good of the faithful."

Should disputes arise concerning the granting, withdrawal or denial of the mandate, it is important that agreed upon procedures be established for the resolution of such conflicts. Whether this procedure is based on the formal dialogue outlined in "Doctrinal Responsibilities" or the steps enumerated in "On Due Process"[36] for administrative matters or adapted from a procedure established in a particular diocese for dispute resolution, the manner in which it is carried out should respect the rights of all concerned—the bishop, the theologian, the college or university, and the Christian faithful.

CONCLUSION

As I noted at the beginning of my comments, the inclusion of the requirement of the mandate in the apostolic constitution *Ex Corde Ecclesiae* has intensified fears and heightened concerns of centralization in the church. The greater danger at this time, however, may be to view the mandate outside the broader context of the central call of *Ex Corde Ecclesiae,* namely a concrete affirmation of the Catholic university as a bridge between the Gospel and culture. To overlook the positive contribution the apostolic constitution makes to the role of the Catholic university in the life of the church and society and to the idea of communion between Catholic universities and the church would be to miss an essential and invaluable message about the university's Catholic identity and the service it can render through reflection on the faith, inquiry into truth and analysis of the problems of society in light of the Gospel. It's a message that we all should hear.

NOTES

1. All translations of the 1983 Code of Canon Law are taken from *The Code of Canon Law, Latin-English Edition* (Washington, D.C.: Canon Law Society of America, 1983).

2. John Paul II, apostolic constitution *Ex Corde Ecclesiae*, Aug. 15, 1990, *Acta Apostolicae Sedis* 82 (1990) 1475–1509. General norms, Article 4.3 speaks of "Catholic theologians, aware that they fulfill a mandate received from the church, are to be faithful to the magisterium of the church as the authentic interpreter of Sacred Scripture and sacred tradition."

3. Other reasons for opposing the promulgation of Canon 812 included: its potential for conflict with teachers' unions, the administrative burden it might be for some bishops and the fact that the canon was unnecessary in that its purpose was already being accomplished within institutions of higher education and is adequately covered in Canon 810. See James A. Coriden, "Book III; The Teaching Office of the Church," in J. Coriden et al., eds., *The Code of Canon Law: A Text and Commentary* (Mahwah, N.J.: Paulist Press, 1985) 575.

4. Pontifical Commission for the Revision of the Code of Canon Law, *Relatio* (Vatican City: Vatican Polyglot Press, 1981) 183.

5. Ibid.

6. Ibid., p. 184.

7. See "Memorandum to Archbishops and Bishops, Presidents of Catholic Colleges and Universities from Bishop John Leibrecht, Proposed Ordinances for Catholic Colleges and Universities in the United States," May 4, 1993, reprinted in John P. Langan, SJ, ed., *Catholic Universities in Church and Society: A Dialogue on Ex Corde Ecclesiae* (Washington, D.C.: Georgetown University Press, 1993) 258: Ordinance 5. "The mandate granted to those who teach theology in Catholic colleges and universities should be understood as recognition by the competent ecclesiastical authority of a Catholic professor's suitability to teach theological disciplines [Norms, 4:3]." Ordinance 6. "Catholic professors of theological disciplines are to be advised by academic officials of the church's expectation that they request the mandate from the competent ecclesiastical authority, normally the diocesan bishop or his delegate (cf. Canon 812). Accordingly, the bishop is to invite the Catholic professor to request the mandate and, after appropriate review, the bishop is to respond to the request."

8. *"Qui vel prohibiti vel non missi, praeter auctoritatem ab Apostolica Sede vel episcopo loci susceptam publice vel privatim praedicare praesumpserint."* Canon 9, X *De Haereticis*, V. 7.

9. See Canon 13, X *De Haereticis*, V. 7; Martin V, *Inter Cunctas*, Feb. 22, 1418, Art. 14; Council of Trent, Session XXIII, *De Ecclesiastica Hierarchia et Ordinatione*, Canon 7.

10. 1917 code, Canon 1328: *"Nemini ministerium praedicationis licet exercere, nisi a legitimo superiore missionem receperit, facultate peculiariter data, vel officio collato, cui ex sacris canonibus praedicandi munus inhaereat."*

11. Title XX of the 1917 code was titled *"De Divina Verbi Praedicatione."* The title contained three chapters: *"De Catechetica Institutione," "De Sacris Concionibus"* and *"De Sacris Missionibus."* It would seem that the term *praedicatione* in the heading of Title XX, which could be understood to connote preaching in the strict liturgical sense, should rather be understood in the broader sense of "teaching" so as to include each of the chapters of the title, namely catechetical instruction as well as *de sacris concionibus,*

which concerned preaching in the strict liturgical sense. For a similar opinion, see Heinrich Flatten, *"Missio Canonica,"* in Theodor Filthaut and Josef A. Jungmann, eds., *Verkundigung und Glaube. Festschrift fur Franz X. Arnold* (Freiburg-Br.: Herder, 1958) 134, fn. 36.

12. See, for example, E. F. Regatillo, *Institutiones Iuris Canonici,* (1961) No. 178; F. X. Wernz and P. Vidal, *Ius Canonicum* 2 (1935) No. 48; A. Vermeersch and J. Creusen, *Epitome Iuris Canonici* 2 (1940) No. 656; P. M. Conte a Coronata, *Institutiones Iuris Canonici* (1947) No. 168.

13. Pius XI, apostolic constitution *Deus Scientiarum Dominus,* May 24, 1931, *Acta Apostolicae Sedis* 23 (1931) 251, Art. 21, No. 5. [*Acta Apostolicae Sedis* referred to hereafter as AAS.]

14.. Ibid., Art. 22.

15. John Paul II, apostolic constitution *Sapientia Christiana,* April 15, 1979, AAS 71 (1979) 469–499, Art. 27.1.

16. *Apostolicam Actuositatem,* Nov. 18, 1965, AAS 58 (1966) 837–864, Art. 24.

17. Ibid., 857.

18. Archives of the Second Vatican Ecumenical Council, *Acta Synodalia Sacrosancti Concilii Oecumenici Vaticani* II, III/4 (Rome: Vatican Polyglot Press, 1974) 677–678.

19. Ibid., 681.

20. John A. Alesandro, "The Rights and Responsibilities of Theologians: A Canonical Perspective," in *Cooperation Between Theologians and Ecclesiastical Magisterium,* ed. Leo J. O'Donovan, SJ (Washington, D.C.: Canon Law Society of America, 1982) 107.

21. Ladislas Orsy, "The Mandate to Teach Theological Disciplines: On Canon 812 of the New Code," *Theological Studies* 44 (1983) 480–481.

22. James A. Coriden, "Book III: The Teaching Office of the Church," in Coriden, *The Code of Canon Law: A Text and Commentary,* 576.

23. John Strynkowski, "Theological Pluralism and Canonical Mandate," *The Jurist* 42 (1982) 532–33; Robert P. Deeley, "Canon 812: The Mandate for Those Who Teach Theology: An Interpretation," *Proceedings of the Canon Law Society of America* 50 (1989) 80.

24. Joseph A. Komonchak, "The Catholic University in the Church," in Langan, 42.

25. Congregation for the Doctrine of the Faith, Instruction on the Ecclesial Vocation of the Theologian *Donum Veritatis* (May 24, 1990), 6 AAS 82 (1990) 1552.

26. National Conference of Catholic Bishops, "Doctrinal Responsibilities: Approaches to Promoting Cooperation and Resolving Misunderstandings Between Bishops and Theologians" (Washington, D.C.: U.S. Catholic Conference Publications, 1989) 100–101.

27. Ibid., 105.

28. James H. Provost, "A Canonical Commentary on *Ex Corde Ecclesiae,*" in Langan, 124.

29. Orsy, 480.

30. Canon 218: "Those who are engaged in the sacred disciplines enjoy a lawful freedom of inquiry and of prudently expressing their opinions on matters in which they have expertise, while observing a due respect for the magisterium of the church."

31. Canon 211: "All the Christian faithful have the duty and right to work so that the divine message of salvation may increasingly reach the whole of humankind in every age and in every land."

32. Canon 216: "All the Christian faithful, since they participate in the mission of the church, have the right to promote or to sustain apostolic action by their own undertak-

ings in accord with each one's state and condition; however, no undertaking shall assume the name Catholic unless the consent of competent ecclesiastical authority is given."

33. Canon 220: "No one is permitted to damage unlawfully the good reputation which another person enjoys nor to violate the right of another person to protect his or her own privacy."

34. Canon 221.1: "The Christian faithful can legitimately vindicate and defend the rights which they enjoy in the church before a competent ecclesiastical court in accord with the norm of law."

35. Canon 753: "Although they do not enjoy infallible teaching authority, the bishops in communion with the head and members of the college, whether as individuals or gathered in conferences of bishops or in particular councils, are authentic teachers and instructors of the faith for the faithful entrusted to their care; the faithful must adhere to the authentic teaching of their own bishops with a sense of religious respect."

36. National Conference of Catholic Bishops, "On Due Process" (Washington, D.C.: USCC Publications, 1972).

12 | The Rights of Religious Academic Communities

Douglas Laycock

Controversy continues over the right of governments and of academic associations to enforce the full secular scope of academic freedom at religiously affiliated universities. On many issues, but especially on this one, I am struck by the extraordinary gulf in understanding between most secular academics and most seriously religious citizens, including seriously religious academics. Sitting in the middle and talking to both sides, I have the sense that religious academics have some understanding of the secularists, maybe because they are exposed to so many more of them. But I also have the sense that many of the secularists have no understanding whatever of the believers.

I. THE ROLE OF RELIGIOUS UNIVERSITIES

Two aspects of most believers' religious commitments are central to the role of religiously affiliated universities, and Judge Noonan's article in this issue of THE JOURNAL OF COLLEGE AND UNIVERSITY LAW touches on both of them.[1] First, for most believers, part of the individual exercise of religion is to form and join in communities of faith exercising the same religion. I do not think it matters whether we conceive of religious exercise as a group right or an individual right. I think it is both, as Judge Noonan has said. But even if one conceives of it only as an individual right, part of that individual right is the right to form a religious community.

Second, most serious believers believe that the religious aspects of their lives cannot be segregated or isolated from the other aspects of their lives. They be-

From *The Journal of College and University Law* 20, no. 1 (Summer 1993): 15–41. Printed in full by permission of the National Association of College and University Attorneys. All rights reserved.

lieve that their religious commitments are relevant to their other roles. They reject the model of religion as something private, reserved for Sunday morning or Friday night, and irrelevant to the rest of the week.

Thomas Shaffer[2] and others[3] have created a serious literature on what it means to be a Christian lawyer or a Christian law teacher. It is a sophisticated and nuanced literature. Of course there are religious polemicists and absolutists, but little of this literature is in that genre. Most religious law teachers recognize that their roles sometimes conflict—that they owe duties to students, colleagues, clients, and employers, many of whom do not share their religious commitments. If there is an absolutist position in this debate, it is the position of many secular academics that every institution must follow exactly the same rules with no exceptions, however minor.

The combined effect of the commitment to religious communities and the commitment to integrate religion with all aspects of life is that some of the religious individuals in academia will be attracted to religiously affiliated institutions of higher education. That is true for law teachers as well as for faculty in other disciplines. Their religion is important to their understanding of law, to their conduct as lawyers, and to their conduct as law teachers. Given the opportunity, many religious law teachers would pursue that interaction in a like-minded community.

It follows that schools such as Brigham Young, Notre Dame, Baylor, Pepperdine, Valparaiso, and Cardozo are, in significant part, exercises of religion. Each of them is a faith community in pursuit of a common project. The nature of that community is both religious and academic, and the balance between the two commitments is both delicate and precarious. If the school becomes wholly religious, it will lose its academic standing, and if it becomes wholly academic, it will no longer be religious. The difficulty of maintaining the balance is illustrated by the very large number of American schools that have failed to maintain the balance. Examples include Harvard, Yale, Chicago, Northwestern, Vanderbilt, Boston University, and Southern Methodist. Some of these schools retain vestiges of their original religious commitment, perhaps more than an outside observer can see, but none of them appear to remain religious institutions in any sense that affects the daily lives of students and faculty. There are other religious universities that are not so obviously secularized but seem well along the way, where some students and faculty complain that the religious element has become too attenuated.[4]

But a few institutions have successfully maintained a community that is both seriously religious and seriously academic. I want to provide some feel for the role that these institutions play in the lives of religious academics. To do that, I will do something that is not my usual style, but is the style of other legal academics these days. I will tell some stories about the importance of these communities to individuals. Some of the stories involve law professors; some involve professors in other disciplines.

I will start with another discipline. This professor is a blue-chip All-America scholar. She publishes prize-winning books. She is a member of the most exclusive research association in her discipline. She advises the federal government at the highest levels in her discipline. She wins teaching awards. She has held important administrative positions and served on key committees; she is trusted and respected by her colleagues. She has obviously belied the prediction of her dissertation supervisor, who told her that she could not be good in her academic discipline and also be a good Catholic.

She is at an elite public institution, but she often wishes she were at Notre Dame. Notre Dame is quite respectable in her field, but not so prestigious as the school where she is now. But she says:

> When I'm at Notre Dame, I'm a whole person again. When I'm at Notre Dame, I don't have to suppress the most important part of my life and conceal it from my colleagues. When I'm at Notre Dame, there is a community that I'm comfortable with and that I can relate to.

If Notre Dame made an offer, and if she were not tied down by family obligations, she would sacrifice the prestige and move in a minute.

My second story deals with another highly successful teacher and scholar, an Episcopalian teaching at an elite public law school. Episcopalians are not a denomination usually thought to be alienated from elite American culture. Episcopalians are sometimes derided by conservatives as not religious enough to count.[5] This law teacher once said to me:

> I get so tired of the pervasive commitment to secularism in this place. There are things you cannot say. There are things that make perfect sense to say at church that make no sense to say in this law school—that no one *would* say in this law school.

The third and fourth stories involve the same analogy. I have heard it twice, from sources in different parts of the country; I suspect it has circulated widely among religious academics. One of my sources is an evangelical Protestant teaching at a non-elite religious law school, who quotes a friend teaching in some unidentified state law school. The friend contemplates what would happen if he were ever to say in a faculty meeting, "This is a difficult issue. Let's meet again in two days. I want to pray about this before I vote." My other source is a member of a small Protestant denomination, who teaches in another discipline at an elite private school. He describes the reaction when he actually did say, in a seminar on ethical issues, that Christian theologians had said something about the issue under discussion.

The law professor imagining the reaction, and the other professor reporting the actual reaction, both use the same analogy. "It would be (It was) as though I had farted." The only response to such inappropriate behavior is to silently ignore it, and to go on as if nothing had happened.

Three of these stories are about concealment—about hiding a central part of one's identity from scholarly colleagues. They are like the stories of gays and lesbians who are still in the closet. The last story—the professor who spoke up at the ethics seminar—is a story of coming out of the closet. The response did not make him glad that he had come out. These stories help illustrate the unadorned conclusion of a fifth informant, a scholar with two Ivy League degrees who is now teaching at a school with strong religious commitments. He says one reason for joining that faculty was that, given what he wanted to work on, his academic freedom would be better protected there than at any secular school of comparable quality.[6]

All these informants are people who feel the need for the kind of combined religious and academic community that only a place like Brigham Young or Baylor or Notre Dame or Cardozo can provide. There are very few of those places left. The ones that remain cannot survive without careful nurturing of the balance between their religious commitments and their academic commitments. A larger number of small undergraduate colleges have maintained serious religious and academic teaching commitments, without much in the way of research programs or academic prestige, and we have data on the practices of these schools.[7] They perform a valuable function, but they are usually not an option for scholars committed to research.

II. CONSTITUTIONALLY PROTECTED LIMITS ON ACADEMIC FREEDOM

Much of the nurturing of a religious university's dual commitments will be informal. It will be social and communal. It will be wholly consistent with the most rigorous understanding of academic freedom. But at least some of that nurturing must depart from the conceptions of academic freedom that we apply in secular institutions.

At the very least, these schools must indulge a hiring preference. They must be free to take into account their need to maintain the necessary core of Catholic faculty or Mormon faculty or whatever. Given the realities of the teaching market, they will get plenty of applications from non-Catholics, from non-Mormons, from people who are not attracted to the institution but want some teaching job somewhere. Some of these applicants, if hired, will be committed to changing the institution, committed to turning Notre Dame or Baylor into Northwestern or Vanderbilt. The institution has to be able to take account of the religious part of its needs at the hiring stage.

The problem is not that religious ideas cannot survive in competition with secular ideas.[8] Religious ideas have always seemed compellingly true to some and incomprehensible to others, and that is unlikely to change. The religious minority among academics is in no danger of disappearing. But religious universities cannot survive if the religious individuals are scattered randomly among all the faculties. To gather a critical mass of religious academics in a single community, the institution must take account of religious commitment in hiring. At least as of fifteen years ago, most religiously affiliated colleges and universities reported religious preferences in hiring for at least some faculty positions, and nearly half reported such preferences for all faculty positions.[9]

Limitations on the academic freedom of incumbent faculty are far more controversial both within and without religious universities, and for that reason they are rarely imposed, especially in institutions that take their academic commitments seriously. But all religiously affiliated institutions must have the constitutional right to interfere with the academic freedom of their incumbent faculty. The rare cases in which it is thought necessary to exercise this right usually arise in theology departments; I do not know a single example that has actually arisen in a law school. There is an actual dispute in law schools over codes of moral behavior, triggered when the Association of American Law Schools repealed the religious exemption from the ban on discrimination on the basis of sexual orientation.[10] But even this so far appears to be a passionate argument over principle and policy; I know of no disputes over actual application of the competing principles.

Even so, genuine academic-freedom controversies are at least imaginable, even in law schools and even with respect to teaching and writing that is clearly within the usual scope of academic freedom. There may be issues of intense religious commitment and deep symbolic importance, with respect to which the self-definition of the community requires unanimity or at least acquiescence among faculty and administrators. With respect to these few issues, a faculty member who actively disagrees will have to move elsewhere. For example, I do not think we can expect, in the name of academic freedom, that a faculty member at Notre Dame can litigate law-reform abortion cases on the pro-choice side. It is entirely appropriate for academics to be involved in the abortion issue on either side. But it is also entirely appropriate for Notre Dame to say that its faculty cannot use Notre Dame as a platform for abortion rights, or commit Notre Dame's name and facilities to pro-choice activism. I suspect that Cardozo would face similar problems of institutional identity if it had a faculty member writing that the Holocaust was a legitimate response to provocation or disloyalty.

In the extreme case, a religious university must have the legal right to discharge such a faculty member, even one with tenure. Obviously, such a discharge imposes hardship on the faculty member, and the institution would be aware of that. It is nearly as obvious that such a discharge imposes serious costs on the institution. An institution that wants any respect for the academic part of its mission will be extraordinarily reluctant to restrict the academic freedom of its faculty. Both faculty and administration must know that they will pay an enormous price in terms of the respect of their peers at other institutions, and in terms of their capacity to recruit new faculty. Catholic University will pay for years in the academic marketplace for its decision to restrict Father Curran's teaching.[11] There are enormous incentives not to impose any sanction likely to come to public notice.

If, notwithstanding these costs, Notre Dame were to decide that as a matter of self-definition, as a matter of keeping faith with parents who want a Catholic education for their children, or for whatever reasons that might arise within the Notre Dame community—if Notre Dame were to decide that it simply cannot retain a faculty member leading the pro-choice movement, the state and the larger academic community would have to respect Notre Dame's right to act on that decision. I do not know what Notre Dame would actually decide in such a case; I am confident only that there would be sharp debate within the Notre Dame community. Most religious universities proclaim their commitment to academic freedom, but if in the extreme case they found it necessary to make an exception for religious reasons, the Free Exercise Clause should protect them. If an academically respectable school denies or revokes tenure over a religious issue, the very fact that a good school would do it is powerful evidence that the issue is of supreme importance to the school. I would defend their right to do it, just as I defended Catholic University's right to act in the case of Father Curran.[12]

When I say the religious university has a right to discharge in these situations, I mean that legislatures, judges, administrative agencies, and accreditation authorities are constitutionally precluded from imposing sanctions on the institution, or ordering reinstatement of the faculty member, or awarding compensation to the faculty member, on the basis of any alleged duty imposed on the institution from the outside. The only sanction I would permit is a suit for breach of contract if the institution had entered into a contract that was clearly written to be enforced in a secular court.[13]

I have been told that it is an extreme position to say that Notre Dame could fire a tenured faculty member. But that comment simply highlights the gulf between secular and religious understandings of religious institutions. The extreme position is to say that Notre Dame can be forced by legal sanction to retain and support the work of a faculty member leading the pro-choice movement, or that Catholic University could be forced to retain and support the work of a dissident theologian. The Constitution protects the free exercise of religion from state interference; it does not protect the right of religious dissenters to use the name and facilities of religious institutions.

The examples I have offered do not exhaust the possible conflicts between religious values and academic or other important secular values. If religious universities are free to discipline or exclude sexually active gays and lesbians, as religious law schools contend in their current dispute with the AALS, why can they not forbid interracial dating or exclude African-Americans altogether? Fortunately, very few universities with religious affiliations, and none with both religious affiliations and even a pretense to intellectual quality, claim a right to discriminate on the basis of race or sex. We have a real issue with respect to sexual orientation at a small number of seriously religious high-quality schools. But I know of no issue at such schools with respect to race or sex.

We may have the problem at fringe schools. What should we do about it? If the school is a religious institution, and if religious institutions can discriminate on the basis of religion or sexual morality, then does it follow that they can act on their religious commitments with respect to anything else, even including discrimination on the basis of race? I have argued that they can, so long as they remain pervasively religious enclaves and do not take over a significant part of the function of public education.[14] But that is not the law, there is no apparent support for changing the law, and it is clear that we can distinguish race from homosexuality in defensible ways if we choose to do so.

The Supreme Court said in *Bob Jones University v. United States* that the interest in racial equality in education is a compelling interest that overrides any free-exercise right.[15] That was before the Court largely repealed the Free Exercise Clause in *Employment Division v. Smith*.[16] The nation can choose to accept the holding in *Bob Jones* and put race in a special category. As a polity we may want to say that race is special even for free-exercise issues, because race in this country has a special history, because we suspect that many religious claims about race are insincere anyway, and because even sincere beliefs in racial discrimination are less central to most religious traditions than theology or sexual morality. If that is what the polity believes, we can draw a line and explain it in terms of compelling interest, as the Supreme Court did in *Bob Jones*.[17] The line would even be a bright line: the Free Exercise Clause does not protect racial discrimination in educational institutions. Period.

Religious limitations on academic freedom may also have implications for teaching. Could a religious law school direct that certain cases not be taught, or that they be taught in certain ways? I am reluctant to say that a school could direct that cases not be taught, because withholding information that is part of a professional education moves the school into the realm of educational malpractice much more quickly than adhering to a religious worldview. Moreover, I cannot imagine any religious law school doing so, however weak or strong it might be academically. Religiously committed law schools have every reason not to let their students be surprised by a "bad" case the first time someone cites it against them.

But let us assume the unimaginable, that a religious law school has a short list of cases that its faculty is forbidden to assign. So what? There is no case that the accreditation authorities require every law student in America to be taught, and I doubt there is any case that every law student in America actually is taught. I graduated from The University of Chicago Law School without being assigned to read *Marbury v. Madison*,[18] *Hawkins v. McGee*,[19] or *Pierson v. Post*.[20] The University of Texas Law School is about to begin graduating one hundred students per year to whom *Marbury* was never assigned;[21] it has long graduated a substantial number to whom *Roe v. Wade* was never assigned.[22]

If an idiosyncratic instructor omits a case that most of us think is central to a course, the conventional wisdom is to defend the instructor's academic freedom. The conventional wisdom does not change much if the instructor is teaching the only section of a required course. Colleagues might intervene in a sufficiently extreme case, but the accreditation authorities would not. If an individual instructor can withhold the case from the whole student body without attracting the attention of the accreditation authorities, it is hard to see why a religious law school cannot do so as a matter of institutional policy.

I think it far easier to conclude that a religious school could direct that certain cases be taught in particular ways that reflect the school's religious commitments. For example, a religious law school could direct its faculty that, when they teach *Roe v. Wade*, they have to teach that the sponsoring church believes the case is wrong, and they have to make sure their students understand the arguments supporting that belief. Teaching that *Roe* is wrong is not like teaching that the earth is flat; it is not merely a religious view; it is not a view inconsistent with a professional education. Having the institution rather than individual faculty make pedagogical choices is not in my view a good way to run a law school, but I would not withhold accreditation.

My standard for withholding accreditation for religiously-motivated policies is pretty simple. The standard should not be whether these religious law schools, because of their religious commitments, have departed from the norms we uphold for most of our institutions. The standard should be: have these schools departed in such a way that the education actually delivered is worse than that delivered at the worst secular law school that is currently accredited?

There were audible gasps in the room when I said that to an audience of officials of academic associations. Those gasps are significant. The gaspers know that we are not talking about quality of education in any of these disputes. The gaspers know that many of these religious schools have a long way to fall before their legal education would be at all comparable to that of the worst secular schools already accredited. There are a lot of weak schools, schools without adequate resources, schools that lose most of the good applicants to stronger competitors, schools that for whatever reason cannot deliver a legal education the accreditors consider excellent, or that cannot even meet all the formal accreditation standards. But the reasons for their failure are secular, and academics tend to be tolerant of secular failings. Perhaps more important, the authorities believe that these schools are incapable of substantial improvement, at least in the short term. If compliance is impossible, then coercion to comply is futile, and it would be impractical to disaccredit all the schools in such situations.

But academics are not so tolerant of religious institutions. More important, the authorities believe that religious schools could comply by making what seems to the authorities only a modest departure from religious commitments. Because compliance is physically possible, coercion seems feasible. So it has seemed to religious persecutors through the ages. But if the authorities are coercing religious schools to abandon their religious commitments, they must have a compelling governmental interest.[23] I do not think they can begin to argue about a plausible compelling interest until the quality of education falls below that of the weakest secular schools.

What the authorities say, sometimes explicitly and always in effect, is that the religious schools have to compromise, i.e., that they have to compromise their religious commitments. They can keep their religious commitment so long as it does not interfere with our secular standards, but they cannot depart from our secular standards in any way. That is no compromise at all. The secular authorities will compromise by letting religious schools exist if they submit to all the secular authorities' demands.

The compromise already in place, which the secular side should happily accept, is that the secular side controls 97% or so of the institutions. Can the three percent have some existence of their own? Can the three percent strike their own balance of religious and academic commitments? Or is the secular model so absolutist that it cannot tolerate a three percent minority with a different solution? That is the issue.

In these debates about academic freedom in religious institutions, I sense from many on the secular side hostility to the very nature of these institutions. Hostility is frequently expressed with respect to the two commitments with which I began, the commitments to religious community and to integration of religion with the whole person. The secular regulator often says something like: "Of course I respect your religious liberty, but this is not a religious institution. This is a law school." Such a regulator rejects the claim that there can be such a thing as a religious law school, and therefore implicitly rejects the view that religion can be integrated with the rest of one's life in a communal enterprise.

These rejections of basic religious commitments are often corollaries of what is not spoken, which is a tendency to reject religious faith outright as an incomprehensible survival of superstition.[24] But let us give our hypothetical regulator the benefit of the doubt and assume that she genuinely is not hostile to religion in what she conceives to be its proper place. She simply believes that controlling a law school is not the proper place. She says in complete good faith that you can practice your religion, but not communally and at the same time integrated with your work as a legal scholar. That is equivalent to saying: "You cannot practice your religion as you understand it. Rather, you can practice it only as I think I would understand it, if I understood it at all." That is not much of a concession to the free exercise of religion.[25]

Secular academics are obviously free to disagree about the benefits of maintaining institutions that are both religious and academic. The AALS and the American Association of University Professors are entirely within their rights to issue statements regretting the limitations on academic freedom at religious universities, and alerting potential students and faculty to those limitations. They can put the warning in terms that are respectful and tolerant, or vociferous and hostile, or even vicious and hateful. They too are entitled to the full protections of the First Amendment.

I would not suggest that they minimize their fundamental policy disagree-ment with religious limitations on academic freedom, or any of their other dis-agreements with religion. Those disagreements are important. But I think they would do well to put their disagreements in as tolerant and nonjudgmental a fashion as possible. One of the things we should have learned from the history of religious conflict is that however vigorous our religious disagreements, it is important to the welfare of the whole society that we contain those disagree-ments, that we respect other religious traditions even when we disagree, and even when we are trying to limit what we perceive to be the pernicious conse-quences of some of those traditions. Intense condemnation of religious minori-ties flares quickly into persecution, even in this country.[26]

My legal claim is only that it is unlawful to go beyond statements of disap-proval and invoke the power of the state to coerce compliance to secular norms of academic freedom. If a religious school were to be threatened with disaccred-itation because of its religious preference in hiring, or because it shut down the abortion-rights clinic, the threat would violate the Constitution. Even under *Smith*, this should be a hybrid right, involving the institution's rights of free ex-ercise, free speech, and religious education of the young.[27] I agree with Judge Noonan that we should not have to talk about it as a hybrid. But at the moment, that is the way legal doctrine requires it to be argued.

Even if the religious university's claim were not a hybrid claim and *Smith* de-prived the religious schools of all constitutional protection, that should not free the AALS or the AAUP to coerce religious schools. Religious liberty as under-stood by the AALS or the AAUP should not be limited to religious liberty as un-derstood by Justice Scalia or Chief Justice Rehnquist.[28] The AALS and the AAUP do not take the Supreme Court's word for any other form of liberty. They do not believe that free-speech rights for public employees are properly limited by *Connick v. Myers*[29] to matters "of public concern."[30] And if the Supreme Court were ever to say, as the Eleventh Circuit recently said in *Bishop v. Aranov*,[31] that academic freedom in the public-university classroom is not a First Amendment right at all, because faculty are just agents of the state, the AAUP and the AALS would not accept that for a minute. We are equally obliged to make up our own minds about a proper conception of religious liberty. Moreover, our views on religious liberty should not be distorted by our views on religion. A central point of religious liberty is to reduce the effect of disagreements about religion.

Once the religious commitments of the individuals who form religiously affiliated law schools are understood, it follows that those law schools are an ex-ercise of religion, and that the operation of those schools is within the proper

scope of religious liberty for the religious-academic communities that constitute them. The academic community should respect religious liberty even if the
Supreme Court does not force it to do so.

III. THE PROBLEM OF NOTICE

Even for readers who accept everything I have said, an important collateral issue
remains. Do religious universities have either a legal or moral duty to warn potential faculty of religious restrictions on academic freedom?

In its 1940 Statement of Principles, the AAUP recognized that religious commitments might require limitations on academic freedom, but it insisted that
these limitations should be fully disclosed in advance.[32] Subsequent AAUP statements have attempted to interpret away this exception, which is commonly referred to as the "limitations clause." A 1970 interpretation asserted that "[m]ost
church-related institutions no longer need or desire the departure from the principle of academic freedom implied in the 1940 Statement, and we do not now
endorse such a departure."[33] A 1988 subcommittee announced that institutions
that invoke the limitations clause forfeit "the moral right to proclaim themselves as authentic seats of higher learning."[34] The full committee on academic
freedom rejected this report, and voted instead that invoking the clause "does
not relieve an institution of its obligation to afford academic freedom as called
for in the 1940 Statement."[35] In subsequent commentary, the committee's chair
reported his view that this report held schools invoking the limitations clause
to the same standards of full academic freedom as any school not invoking the
clause, but that a majority of his committee described the report as a tautology
that begged all questions.[36] Michael McConnell reads recent AAUP reports cen-
suring religious institutions as de facto repudiation of the limitations clause
and of any recognition of the needs of religious universities, whatever the ambiguity of the AAUP's formal statements.[37]

Whatever its view of the merits of the limitations clause, the AAUP presumably still believes that religious schools that limit academic freedom should
disclose in advance. Ironically, by purporting to expel from the academic community any school that invokes the limitations clause, or to deprive schools of
any benefit even when they invoke it, the AAUP ensures that few academically
serious universities will ever disclose potential limits on academic freedom.
The most notable exception is Brigham Young, which has recently completed a
courageous effort to state as carefully as possible the limitations on academic

freedom necessary to its mission.[38] Smaller, less prestigious colleges are more likely to state formal limits on academic freedom,[39] but there is reason to believe that most of these statements are general and conclusory.[40]

The academic pressure against real disclosure is unfortunate, because it is clear that disclosure is better than nondisclosure. If an academic institution departs from the usual norms of academic freedom, prospective faculty have a strong interest in knowing that fact before they commit a part of their life to the institution. Relocation is always costly, and especially so in an age of two-career families. Full disclosure should be encouraged by statements that respect rather than deride the dual aspirations of religious universities.

But disclosure will never be easy, for the quite legitimate reason that the university's response to hard cases cannot be known in advance, and for the less attractive human reason that the faculty has strong incentives to dissemble. All faculties in a recruiting mode paint the best possible picture of their institution. When a departmental faculty at a religious university is recruiting a "hot" secular prospect, and the prospect asks if the institution's religious commitments are ever a problem for the faculty, there is great temptation to assure him that religious commitments will never affect him or make any demands on him. If religious demands are enforced only by social sanction and not by formal rules, the recruiters may convince themselves that they are not really demands at all, because dissenters are formally free to ignore them. But such recruiters would be lying to themselves and to the prospect; a new colleague who resents the informal religious demands will have an immediate sense of grievance.

Written rules and formal policies are easier to disclose, but they are likely to be vague and uninformative, and they may be neglected in the recruiting process. Even specific formal rules may go undisclosed if they seem routine and insignificant to the institution and the recruiting faculty members. But this is a serious mistake, because such rules may loom large to outsiders. An example comes from a recent incident at a university that asks all candidates for faculty appointment to disclose their religious affiliation. A candidate who declined to answer was hired as an assistant professor, and no representative of the university pressed the issue. But the university later insisted that disclosure of religious affiliation was an absolute prerequisite to tenure. For a faculty member with a principled objection to making that disclosure to an employer, this was an unconscionable entrapment. From the victim's perspective, the university lured people in by ignoring the rule, and then sprung it on them at tenure time, when they were maximally vulnerable.

Both administration and faculty at religiously affiliated institutions should disclose all formal policies and describe the informal atmosphere as honestly as possible. Egregious misrepresentations or failures to disclose might stop the institution from enforcing the misrepresented or undisclosed rules. But courts should be slow to reach this conclusion, both because it requires a holding that the institution waived its constitutional rights, and because faculty and administrators seeking to secularize the institution, or to increase its independence from the sponsoring church, have both motive and opportunity to attempt to waive the institution's rights without authority.[41]

The most important reason disclosure is necessarily limited is that the institution cannot decide what to do about the hard cases until they arise. This limitation inheres both in the religious university's self-understanding and in the standard secular critique of religious universities. It is often suggested that the academic conception of truth is inconsistent with a religious conception of truth, because the academy requires an objectivity about all possible truth claims, and this universal objectivity is inconsistent with any religious claim of revealed truth.

Certainly there is sometimes a tension between academic and religious conceptions of truth. An absolutist conception of either is inconsistent with preservation of the other. But the religious schools are committed to synthesizing the two and to preserving the essence of both. Such a synthesis may require some internal compromises at those schools. Many academics may not want such explicit compromises at their own schools (although most of them regularly make implicit compromises with the conventional wisdom at their institutions). But whatever the difficulties of synthesizing two conceptions of truth, that is what the religious schools are striving to do.

To say that the two conceptions are fully inconsistent and that there is no possibility of synthesis is to say that the religious schools are trying to do an impossible thing. It is to say that there can be no such thing as a religious university that does not entirely subordinate its religious commitments to its academic commitments. Secular bodies sometimes say exactly that.[42]

The more accurate response is to recognize that these universities are striving for a difficult synthesis, and the more tolerant response is to let them strive for it. Precisely because they are striving for a goal that is never fully defined, they cannot disclose in advance the details of their possible limitations on academic freedom. They share many of the same goals and ideals of academic freedom as the secular schools, but they also maintain a competing commitment. The effort to synthesize these commitments requires discussion and sometimes bitter debate within the institution and its sponsoring church. But this is an internal discussion; it need not be an external discussion and it should not be a search for compromise with outsiders. How the religious university ultimately resolves the occasional conflict between its dual commitments is not the legitimate concern of outsiders. And it may be that the most these schools can disclose is to say something like: "This is what we are striving to do. This is the way that we approach the world. We can usually reconcile our religious and our academic commitments. But sometimes, on really important issues, we may decide that our religious commitments may have to prevail."

The Brigham Young Statement is probably as full a disclosure as can reasonably be achieved. There are ten pages of explanation and context for the ultimate standards, an explanation of the University's academic and religious commitments, a clear statement that individual academic freedom is "broad" and "presumptive" while restrictions are "exceptional and limited."[43] But the Statement could not avoid ultimate reliance on standards of degree and of subjective states of mind. Brigham Young claims the right to limit faculty behavior or expression that "*seriously* and *adversely* affects the University mission or the Church,"[44] or in another formulation, that "offer[s] *compelling* threats to BYU's mission or the Church."[45] Examples include expression in public or with students that "contradicts or opposes, rather than analyzes or discusses, *fundamental* Church doctrine or policy," or that "*deliberately* attacks or derides the Church or its general leaders."[46] An important safeguard of the Brigham Young policy is a requirement of fair warning: "A faculty member shall not be found in violation of the academic freedom standards unless the faculty member can *fairly* be considered aware that the expression violates the standards."[47] But even this may depend on states of mind and matters of degree.

At any school of any quality, the religious commitment will not lead to discipline or discharge of a tenured faculty member unless the issue is of extraordinary importance to the institution. On issues that are so central to the religious mission that a school of any quality will be moved to discharge, the discharged faculty member will not be unfairly surprised. Charles Curran could not reasonably have been surprised when he was told that he could not continue to attack the Church's teaching on sexual morality from his position as a professor of theology at Catholic University of America. He could not know the exact point at which he would provoke the University to discharge him; the University could not know that either. But he knew or should have known from the beginning that he was testing the limits and running serious risks.

CONCLUSION

For the state or academic associations to protect academic freedom at religious universities would require a secular intrusion into the central deliberative processes of a religious institution. To decide what innovations a religious tradition can and cannot tolerate is to decide the future content of the faith. It is of the essence of religious liberty that such decisions be made by the religious community, and never by secular authority. Religious limitations on academic freedom may be wise or foolish, and they may be administered well or badly. The questions raised by such limitations are the subject of serious debate within religious universities. That is where the debate should be conducted, and the Constitution should protect whatever answers emerge.

NOTES

[The author is] Alice McKean Young Regents Chair in Law and Associate Dean for Research, The University of Texas Law School. This article was first presented at Tulane Law School's Conference on Academic Freedom and Legal Education, April 4, 1992. The examples are therefore set in law school contexts, but the principles would be the same in any discipline. The article benefitted from many insightful questions and comments at that conference, some of which I have attempted to paragraphse in text. I am also grateful to Edward Gaffney and Linda Mullenix for comments on an earlier draft.

Cole Durham and James Gordon provided the recent Statement on Academic Freedom at Brigham Young University, reprinted with BYU's permission as an Appendix to this article. Both this article and the BYU Statement emphasize the dual commitments of religious universities of academic and religious missions. The BYU committee had completed its work before it learned of this article, and I had substantially completed the article before I learned of their Statement. But intellectual priority is not in doubt: I have learned what I know about the commitments of religious academics by talking to religious academics at many schools over a period of years. I take more personal credit or responsibility for my argument that constitutional law and academic associations should respect the religious liberty of the institutions that religious academics create.

1. John T. Noonan, *Religious Law Schools and the First Amendment,* 19 J.C. & U.L. 43 (1993).

2. *See* THOMAS L. SHAFFER, FAITH AND THE PROFESSIONS (1987); THOMAS L. SHAFFER, ON BEING A CHRISTIAN AND A LAWYER (1980); Thomas L. Shaffer, *Should a Christian Lawyer Serve the Guilty?,* 23 GA. L. REV. 1021 (1989); Thomas L. Shaffer, *Christian Lawyer Stories and American Legal Ethics,* 33 MERCER L. REV. 877 (1982); Thomas L. Shaffer, *Christian Theories of Professional Responsibility,* 48 S. CAL. L. REV. 721 (1975).

3. *See* Thomas E. Baker & Timothy W. Floyd, *The Role of Religious Convictions in the Teaching of Law Students,* 17 J. LEGAL PROFESSION—(forthcoming 1992); Edward

McGlynn Gaffney, Jr., *The Gospel in the Law: The Jurisprudence of Pastor Neuhaus,* 14 VAL. U. L. REV. 15 (1979); Rex E. Lee, *The Role of the Religious Law School,* 30 VILL. L. REV. 1175 (1985); John T. Noonan, *A Catholic Law School,* 67 NOTRE DAME L. REV. 1037 (1992); Thomas L. Shaffer & Robert E. Rodes, Jr., *A Catholic Theology for Roman Catholic Law Schools,* 14 U. DAYTON L. REV. 5 (1988). The Shaffer & Rodes article is accompanied by brief responses from James L. Heft, Richard B. Saphire, and Susan Brenner. For shorter essays on these themes, by academics and practicing lawyers, pick up almost any issue of the *Christian Legal Society Quarterly.*

4. On the problems of preserving both religious and scholarly commitments throughout the institution, *see* James Tunstead Burtchaell, *The Decline and Fall of the Christian College (II),* 13 FIRST THINGS 30 (May 1991); James Tunstead Burtchaell, *The Decline and Fall of the Christian College,* 12 FIRST THINGS 16 (Apr. 1991); Lee, *supra* note 3, at 1175; David W. Lutz, *Can Notre Dame Be Saved?,* 19 FIRST THINGS 35 (Jan. 1992); George M. Marsden, *The Soul of the American University,* 9 FIRST THINGS 34 (Jan. 1991); Leonard J. Nelson, III, *God and Man in the Catholic Law School,* 26 CATH. LAW. 172 (1981). For essays on the secularization of both public and church-affiliated institutions, *see* THE SECULARIZATION OF THE ACADEMY (George M. Marsden & Bradley J. Longfield, eds., 1993).

5. *See* Richard Brookhiser, *Are There Episcopalians in Fox Holes? What in Heaven's Name Is Happening to the Episcopal Church?,* NATIONAL REVIEW, July 29, 1991, at 24.

6. *Cf.* Bishop v. Aranov, 926 F.2d 1066 (11th Cir. 1991), cert. denied, 112 S. Ct. 3026 (1992) (university forbade "1) the interjection of religious beliefs and/or preferences during instructional time periods, and 2) the optional classes where a 'Christian Perspective' of an academic topic is delivered." *Id.* at 1069). A survey of very small evangelical colleges affiliated with the Christian College Coalition also found a widespread view that "freedom for faculty members to view data within Christian assumptions and to witness (noncoercively) to Christian commitments" would be restricted at many secular institutions of higher education. Barry L. Callen, Faculty Academic Freedom in Member Institutions of the Christian College Coalition 135 (1983) (Unpublished, D. Ed. dissertation, Indiana University).

7. *See* EDWARD MCGLYNN GAFFNEY, JR. & PHILIP R. MOOTS, GOVERNMENT AND CAMPUS: FEDERAL REGULATION OF RELIGIOUSLY AFFILIATED HIGHER EDUCATION 8–10 (1982). Gaffney & Moots report a 1978 survey of religiously affiliated colleges and universities. The survey was sent to 801 schools, of whom 226 responded, from which sixteen seminaries and bible colleges were eliminated. Thus, the data reflect the responses of 210 schools offering education in secular subjects. Only twenty-eight of these schools had more than 3000 students, and only six of those had more than 7500 students. Other data from this survey is reported *infra* notes 9 and 39.

8. *See* Judith Jarvis Thomson and Matthew W. Finkin, *Academic Freedom and Church Related Higher Education: A Reply to Professor McConnell,* FREEDOM AND TENURE IN THE ACADEMY 419, 421 (William W. Van Alstyne, ed.) (1993), for this misunderstanding of the need for limitations on academic freedom. The article to which Thompson and Finkin are replying was quite clear that its principal concern about survival of religious institutions was the risk of random distribution of faculty among institutions. Michael W. McConnell, *Academic Freedom in Religious Colleges and Universities,* 53 LAW & CONTEMP. PROBS. No. 3 at 303, 313 (Summer 1990).

9. GAFFNEY & MOOTS, *supra* note 7, at 34.

10. *See* Ass'n Am. Law Schools Exec. Comm. Reg. 6–17 (available from the Association). For earlier examples, *see* Carl S. Hawkins, *Accreditation of Church-Related Law Schools*, 32 J. LEGAL EDUC. 172, 174–75, 179–81 (1982); Sanford H. Kadish, *Church-Related Law Schools: Academic Values and Deference to Religion*, 32 J. LEGAL EDUC. 161, 163, 169 (1982).

11. For accounts of this controversy, *see The Catholic University of America*, 75 Academe No. 5 at 27 (Sept.–Oct. 1989); for the legal resolution, *see* Curran v. Catholic University, No. 1562–87 (D.C. Sup'r Ct. 1989).

12. Douglas Laycock & Susan E. Waelbroeck, *Academic Freedom and the Free Exercise of Religion*, 66 TEX. L. REV. 1455 (1988).

13. This distinction is elaborated *id.* at 1467–73. The distinction between outside regulation and internal contract follows from a more basic point that I may have assumed without sufficient elaboration. Michael McConnell did elaborate the point, in an unpublished response to Thomson & Finkin, *supra* note 8:

> Professors Thomson and Finkin concede the value of religiously distinctive institutions of higher learning, but deny that "it conduces to the common good that they continue to exist at the cost of using coercion." (Citing *id.* at 423, 425–26, 429.) But who is coercing whom? A religious college is a voluntary institution, formed by like-minded scholars, benefactors, and students for the pursuit of knowledge within a particular tradition of thought. No one coerces anyone to join. Internal enforcement of the rules of a voluntary association is not "coercion." It more closely resembles freedom of contract.

14. Douglas Laycock, *Tax Exemption for Racially Discriminatory Religious Discriminatory Schools*, 60 TEX. L. REV. 259 (1982).

15. 461 U.S. 574, 602–04, 103 S. Ct. 2017 (1983).

16. 494 U.S. 872, 110 S. Ct. 1595 (1990). For criticism of *Smith*, *see* James D. Gordon III, *Free Exercise on the Mountaintop*, 79 CAL. L. REV. 91 (1991); Michael W. McConnell, *Free Exercise Revisionism and the Smith Decision*, 57 U. CHI. L. REV. 1109 (1990); Douglas Laycock, *The Remnants of Free Exercise*, 1990 SUP. CT. REV. 1. For a defense of *Smith's* holding (but not of the opinion), *see* William P. Marshall, *In Defense of Smith and Free Exercise Revisionism*, 58 U. CHI. L. REV. 308 (1991). *See also* Michael W. McConnell, *A Response to Professor Marshall*, 58 U. CHI. L. REV. 329 (1991).

17. I do not mean to imply that religious centrality is a threshold to any protection of free exercise. But I do believe that the compelling interest test is a form of balancing, with the scales tilted heavily against the government, and that the centrality of a religious practice is relevant to the balance. Laycock, *supra* note 16, at 31–33. What the compelling interest test should require is that the government interest in regulating religion compellingly outweigh the resulting burden on religion, whatever the magnitude of that burden.

18. 5 U.S. (1 Cranch) 137 (1803). *Marbury* was a staple of Constitutional Law I; my classmates who took the course spent seven weeks on it—on a quarter system where class lasted only ten weeks. But I took Constitutional Law II and III and skipped Constitutional Law I. No constitutional law course was required at Chicago.

19. 146 A. 641 (N.H. 1929). This case appeared in the casebook used at Chicago in 1970, but the damages issue that is the staple introduction to Contracts had been edited out. FRIEDRICH KESSLER & GRANT GILMORE, CONTRACTS: CASES AND MATERIALS 111–12 (2d ed. 1970). To the best of my recollection, the part that remained was not assigned.

20. 3 Cai. R. 175 (N.Y. Sup. Ct. 1805). This staple of first-year property casebooks is not mentioned in the casebook used at Chicago in 1970. ALLISON DUNHAM, MODERN REAL ESTATE TRANSACTIONS: CASES AND MATERIALS (2d ed. 1958). I learned nothing of personal property, takings, or future interests; I was later shocked to learn that first-year students at Texas and many other law schools learn nothing of mortgages or the recording system.

21. My colleague Sanford Levinson has decided not to assign *Marbury* in his section of Constitutional Law I. The hundred students randomly assigned to his section are unlikely to read the case elsewhere in the curriculum.

22. Roe v. Wade, 410 U.S. 113, 93 S. Ct. 705 (1973), is taught by two of the six faculty who most often teach the five sections of Constitutional Law I. All students must elect an additional constitutional law course, but many options are available. Students who elect a course in free speech or equal protection are unlikely to encounter *Roe* unless they got it in Constitutional Law I. I assume that *Roe* was the principal example Professor Hodes had in mind when he first asked this question about omitting cases for religious reasons.

23. Even after Employment Div., Or. Dep't of Human Res. v. Smith, 494 U.S. 872, 110 S. Ct. 1595 (1990). *See infra* note 27 and accompanying text.

24. *See*, e.g., Suzanna Sherry, *Outlaw Blues*, 87 MICH. L. REV. 1418, 1427 (1989) (reviewing MARK TUSHNET, RED, WHITE, AND BLUE: A CRITICAL ANALYSIS OF CONSTITUTIONAL LAW (1988)) ("divine revelation and biblical literalism are irrational superstitious nonsense"); Tony Pasquarello, *Humanism's Thorn: The Case of the Bright Believers*, 13 FREE INQUIRY 1 at 38, 39 (Winter 1992/93) ("And there lies our dilemma—that nasty set of incompatible propositions: 1. There are bright believers. 2. Bright people don't believe nonsense. 3. Traditional theism is nonsense.").

25. For an example of this sort of argument, *see* Thompson & Finkin, *supra* note 8, at 425 n.23 (arguing that *no* religious community needs colleges and universities, because *some* religious communities do not have them).

26. *See* Laycock, *supra* note 16, at 59–68.

27. *See* Employment Div., Or. Dep't of Human Res. v. Smith, 494 U.S. 872, 881–82, 10 S. Ct. 1595, 1600 (1990); *cf.* People v. DeJorge, 1993 Westlaw 206470, *3 + n.27 (Mich. May 25, 1993) (finding hybrid free-exercise right to educate children at home with uncertified teachers).

28. The argument that the AAUP should take the Supreme Court's word for the scope of religious liberty is made in Thompson & Finkin, *supra* note 8, at 425.

29. 461 U.S. 138, 103 S. Ct. 1684 (1983). For criticism of the case and its application to academic freedom, *see* Matthew W. Finkin, *Intramural Speech, Academic Freedom, and the First Amendment*, 66 TEX. L. REV. 1323 (1988).

30. For general analysis and criticism of the public concern doctrine, *see* Cynthia L. Estlund, *Speech on Matters of Public Concern: The Perils of an Emerging First Amendment category*, 59 GEO. WASH. L. REV. 1 (1990).

31. 926 F.2d 1066 (11th Cir. 1991), cert. denied, 112 S. Ct. 3026 (1992).

32. American Ass'n of Univ. Professors & Association of Am. Colleges, Statement of Principles on Academic Freedom and Tenure (1940), in AMERICAN ASS'N OF UNIV. PROFESSORS, POLICY DOCUMENTS & REPORTS 3 (1990) ("Limitations of academic freedom because of religious or other aims of the institution should be clearly stated in writing at the time of the appointment."). This important document is reprinted in

53 LAW & CONTEMP. PROBS. No. 3 at 407 (Summer 1990) (Appendix B to Symposium on *Freedom and Tenure in the Academy: The Fiftieth Anniversary of the 1940 Statement of Principles*).

33. American Ass'n of Univ. Professors, 1970 Interpretive Comments, in Policies, Documents & Reports, *supra* note 32, at 6. This statement about the desires of church-related schools was written by Professor Sanford Kadish, who never taught in such a school and admitted that he had not consulted broadly with the leadership of such schools. Conversation between Sanford Kadish and Edward McGlynn Gaffney, summarized in letter from Gaffney to Douglas Laycock, December 20, 1992 (copy on file with author). Not surprisingly, small evangelical colleges disagree with Kadish's generalization. Callen, *supra* note 6, at 134–35.

34. Subcommittee of Committee A, *The "Limitations" Clause in the 1940 Statement of Principles,* 74 Academe No. 5 at 52, 55 (Sept.–Oct. 1988)

35. *Report of Committee A 1988–89,* 75 Academe No. 5 at 49, 54 (Sept.–Oct. 1988).

36. *Id.*

37. McConnell, *supra* note 8, at 311.

38. Statement on Academic Freedom at Brigham Young University (1992) (reprinted as Appendix to this Article).

39. About a third of the mostly-small church-affiliated colleges responding to a 1978 survey reported that a clause of their faculty employment contracts requires adherence to or respect for the beliefs or values taught by the affiliated church. PHILIP R. MOOTS & EDWARD McGLYNN GAFFNEY, JR., CHURCH AND CAMPUS: LEGAL ISSUES IN RELIGIOUSLY AFFILIATED HIGHER EDUCATION 73–74 (1979). Seven of the 210 schools had had occasion to enforce one of these clauses in the previous five years (1973–78). *Id.* Neither of the books based on this study describes these seven disputes. For a brief description of the survey, *see supra* note 7.

A 1983 survey of twenty-five small evangelical colleges found that eighteen had formal statements guaranteeing academic freedom, but that in all eighteen, "freedom was limited to some degree by the religious commitments central to the distinctive nature of these colleges." Callen, *supra* note 6, at 134. Callen concluded that the remaining schools had similar policies but no formal statements. A survey of 1327 full-time faculty at these schools, with 1024 usable responses, found a mean response that the school's published policies were halfway between "somewhat" and "very much" "adequate to clarify for faculty what religious viewpoints and classroom procedures are considered acceptable by the administration." *Id.* at General Report of Statistics, item 11. These faculty reported that between "none" and "very few" "faculty members have been treated unjustly by this college in matters related to academic freedom" "in recent years," and that between "very few" and a "large minority" of those cases "began primarily as a conflict" over religious commitments. *Id.* items 15–16. It is not clear what these faculty members would consider "unjust." They reported that protecting "the right of faculty members to present unpopular or controversial ideas in the classroom" was a goal of "medium importance" at their college, but that it should be a goal of medium to high importance (mean of 3.62, with standard deviation of .95, where 3 is medium and 4 is high). The strongest response on any question to these faculty was to the question, "[H]ow important is it that *every* full-time faculty member believe the central teachings of historic Christianity?" The mean response was 4.40, where 4 is "very much" and 5 is "completely." *Id.* item 6.

40. Conversation with Professor James Gordon, January 18, 1993, reporting his unpublished research as a member of the committee that drafted the Brigham Young Statement, *supra* note 38.

41. Both points are discussed in Laycock & Waelbroeck, *supra* note 12, at 1470–73.

42. *See* the AAUP subcommittee statement quoted in text at note 34; *Honor Society Rejects Membership Bid*, CHRON. OF HIGHER EDUC. A4 (June 3, 1992) (reporting that the honorary society Phi Beta Kappa has rejected Brigham Young for membership, and that the society apparently demands that BYU renounce even the barest creedal statement that education should emphasize salvation through Christ). Both the AAUP subcommittee statement and Phi Beta Kappa's exclusion of Brigham Young were within the rights of these private organizations. But I believe that each organization behaved inappropriately, intolerantly, and counterproductively.

43. BYU Statement, *infra* at 41.

44. *Id.* at 40 (some emphasis added).

45. *Id.* at 41 (emphasis added).

46. *Id.* at 40 (emphasis added).

47. *Id.* at 41 (emphasis added).

APPENDIX

STATEMENT ON ACADEMIC FREEDOM AT BRIGHAM YOUNG UNIVERSITY

PREFACE: At Brigham Young University, faculty and students are enjoined to "seek learning . . . by study and also by faith" (D&C 88:118). This integration of truth lies at the heart of BYU's institutional mission.[1] As a religiously distinctive university, BYU opens up a space in the academic world in which its faculty and students can pursue knowledge in light of the restored gospel as taught by The Church of Jesus Christ of Latter-day Saints. For those who have embraced the gospel, BYU offers an especially rich and full kind of academic freedom. To seek knowledge in the light of revealed truth is, for believers, to be free indeed.

The freedom to form religiously distinctive intellectual communities is protected not only by the principle of religious freedom but also by long-established principles of academic freedom.[2] The BYU community embraces traditional freedoms of study, inquiry, and debate, together with the special responsibilities implicit in the University's religious mission. These include the duty to exemplify charity and virtue, to nurture faith, and to endeavor to teach all subjects with the Spirit of the Lord.

This document articulates in clear but general terms how BYU's unique religious mission relates to principles of academic freedom. BYU regards the following approach not as narrowing the scope of freedom but as *enabling* greater (or at least different) and much prized freedoms.

I. INDIVIDUAL AND INSTITUTIONAL ACADEMIC FREEDOM AT BYU: The concept of academic freedom at BYU is grounded in a distinction, often blurred but vital and historically based, between *individual* and *institutional* academic freedom.[3] These two facets of academic freedom have been described as "the freedom of the individual scholar to teach and research without interference" and "the freedom of the academic institution from outside control."[4] Both individual and institutional academic freedom are necessary to maintain the unique intellectual climate of BYU. What follows is an attempt to define why both individual and institutional academic freedom are valuable at BYU and how they must be protected.

A. INDIVIDUAL FREEDOM: Individual freedom lies at the core of both religious and academic life. Freedom of thought, belief, inquiry, and expression are crucial no less to the sacred than to the secular quest for truth. Historically, in fact, freedom of conscience and freedom of intellect form a common root, from which grow both religious and academic freedom. It is no wonder then that both the Church and the academy affirm the need for individual freedom—the Church through the doctrine of individual "agency," the academy through the concept of individual academic freedom.

1. INDIVIDUAL AGENCY: The Church teaches that "moral agency" (which encompasses freedom and accountability) is basic to the nature and purpose of mortality (see 2 Ne 2:26, D&C 93:30–31; D&C 101:77–78). In LDS theology, individual freedom is essential to intellectual and spiritual growth. Every Latter-day Saint is enjoined to know truth for himself or herself. We claim it as our privilege to seek wisdom, like the Prophet Joseph Smith, for ourselves. Teachers and institutions play a crucial role in making truth available and discoverable. But neither testimony, nor righteousness, nor genuine understanding is possible unless it is freely discovered and voluntarily embraced.

2. INDIVIDUAL ACADEMIC FREEDOM: Perhaps no condition is as important to creating a university as is the freedom of the individual faculty member "to teach and research without interference,"[5] to ask hard questions, to subject answers to rigorous examination, and to engage in scholarship and creative work. The academy depends on untrammelled inquiry to discover, test, and transmit knowledge. This includes the traditional right to publish or present the results of original research in the reputable scholarly literature and professional conferences of one's academic discipline. Although all universities place some restraints on individual academic freedom, every institution that qualifies for the title of university allows ample room for genuine exploration of diverse ideas.

3. INTEGRATION OF INDIVIDUAL AGENCY AND ACADEMIC FREEDOM: Latter-day Saint scholars are thus doubly engaged to learn truth for themselves because both the Church and the academy bid them undertake a personal quest for knowledge. BYU aspires to be a host for this integrated search for truth by offering a unique enclave of inquiry, where teachers and students may seek learning "by study and also by faith" (D&C 88:118; cf. "The Mission of Brigham Young University").

4. SCOPE OF INTEGRATION: Because the gospel encompasses all truth and affirms the full range of human modes of knowing, the scope of integration for LDS scholars is, in principle, as wide as truth itself. Brigham Young eloquently articulated this gospel-based aspiration, proclaiming "it is our duty and calling . . . to reject every error . . . to gather up all the truths in the world pertaining to life and salvation, to the gospel we preach . . . to the sciences, and to philosophy, wherever it may be found in every nation, kindred, tongue, and people."[6]

Similarly, modern revelation instructs Latter-day Saints to learn:

Of things both in heaven and in the earth, and under the earth; things which have been, things which are, things which must shortly come to pass; things which are at home, things which are abroad; the wars and perplexities of the nations, and the judgments which are on the land; and a knowledge also of countries and of kingdoms. (D&C 88:79)

Further, Latter-day Saints believe, as an article of faith, "all that God has revealed, all that He does now reveal, and . . . that He will yet reveal many great and important things" (9th Article of Faith), and they are encouraged to use all their faculties—including heart, mind, and spirit—in their quest for truth (cf. D&C 4:2; 9:7–9).

5. SUMMARY: At BYU, individual academic freedom is based not only on a belief (shared by all universities) in the value of free inquiry, but also on the gospel principle that humans are moral agents who should seek knowledge in the sacred as well as in the secular, by the heart and spirit as well as by the mind, and in continuing revelation as well as in the written word of God. BYU students and their parents are entitled to expect an educational experience that reflects this aspiration.

B. INSTITUTIONAL ACADEMIC FREEDOM:

1. BYU'S MISSION: BYU has always defined itself as an openly and distinctively LDS university. BYU is wholly owned by the Church, which provides the University's principal source of funding from the tithing funds paid to the Church by its members. BYU draws its faculty and students principally from Church members. Everyone who works and studies at BYU subscribes to an Honor Code in order that the University may "provide a university education in an atmosphere consistent with the ideals and principles of the Church."[7] New faculty are interviewed by Church General Authorities as a condition of employment, and Church members are subsequently expected, as part of their university citizenship, to "live lives of loyalty to the restored gospel."[8] Faculty of other faiths agree to respect the LDS nature of the University and its mission, while the University in turn respects their religious convictions.

Thus BYU defines itself as having a unique religious mission and as pursuing knowledge in a climate of belief. This model of education differs clearly and consciously from public university models that embody a separation of church and state. It is not expected that the faculty will agree on every point of doctrine, much less on the issues in the academic disciplines that divide faculties in any university. It *is* expected, however, that a spirit of Christian charity and common faith in the gospel will unite even those with wide differences and that questions will be raised in ways that seek to strengthen rather than undermine faith. It is also expected that faculty members will be sensitive to the difference between matters that are appropriate for public discussion and those that are better discussed in private. In short, BYU defines itself as an intellectual community of faithful Latter-day Saints, and those sympathetic to their convictions, who pursue knowledge from the baseline of religious belief.

2. DEFINITION OF INSTITUTIONAL ACADEMIC FREEDOM: BYU claims the right to maintain this identity by the appropriate exercise of its institutional academic freedom. "Institutional academic freedom" is the term used to express the privilege of universities to pursue their distinctive missions. This concept harks back to well-established early definitions of academic freedom that sought to guarantee institutional autonomy. The concept of institutional academic freedom is tacitly sanctioned in AAUP and NASC limitation clauses referred to in the Preface. It is also implicit in principles and practices of other church-related universities.[9] BYU likewise affirms that its relationship to The Church of Jesus Christ of Latter-day Saints is essential to its unique institutional identity.[10]

3. BENEFITS OF INSTITUTIONAL FREEDOM: The religious university constitutes an endangered species in today's academic ecosystem.[11] To force religious institutions to comply with narrowly secular definitions of academic freedom is to further imperil the survival of these distinctive intellectual communities. There are at least three reasons why the institutional academic freedom of religious institutions should be protected: to maintain institutional pluralism, to be consistent with the antidogmatic principles of academic freedom, and to safeguard religious freedom.[12] Each argument is sufficiently important to bear brief summary:

* *Pluralism:* Religious colleges and universities contribute to our diverse "ethical, cultural, and intellectual life."[13] Few enough to pose no threat of sectarian domination, religious institutions provide important alternatives to prevailing secular modes of thought. This "makes them better able to resist the popular currents of majoritarian culture and thus to preserve the seeds of dissent and alternative understandings that may later be welcomed by the wider society."[14] Furthermore, to impose a definition of academic freedom that disallows creedal and philosophical considerations "is to randomize every faculty with respect to creed and philosophy. This increases diversity within each faculty, but it eliminates the diversity among faculties."[15]

* *Antidogmatism:* Academic freedom is grounded in the Enlightenment's opposition to dogmatism; it presupposes that truth is discovered not through reve-

lation but rationally, through the "clash of competitive ideas." "But this idea, too, must be subject to testing."[16] Historically, the most thorough challenge to narrowly rationalist methodologies has come from religion. Religion offers venerable alternative theories of knowledge by presupposing that truth is eternal, that it is only partly knowable through reason alone, and that human reason must be tested against divine revelation. President J. Reuben Clark, Jr., stated that one "cannot rationalize the things of the spirit, because first, the things of the spirit are not sufficiently known and comprehended, and secondly, because finite mind and reason cannot comprehend nor explain infinite wisdom and ultimate truth."[17] It is simply inconsistent with the antidogmatic principles of academic freedom not to permit its own premises about knowledge to be tested against such claims as these. "It is important that a principle born of opposition to dogmatism not itself become dogmatic and authoritarian."[18]

* *Religious Freedom:* Religiously distinctive colleges and universities are "an important means by which religious faiths can preserve and transmit their teachings from one generation to the next, particularly nonmainstream religions whose differences from the predominant academic culture are so substantial that they risk annihilation if they cannot retain a degree of separation."[19] This right to religious freedom should "override whatever exiguous benefit to society might be achieved by forcing religiously distinctive institutions to conform to secular academic freedom."[20]

4. ABUSES OF INSTITUTIONAL FREEDOM: Institutional academic freedom, important for *any* college or university, is indispensable for institutions with distinct religious missions. Nevertheless, institutional freedom is a prerogative that, if regarded as absolute, would invite abuse. Therefore, academic freedom must include not only the institution's freedom to claim a religious identity but also the individual's freedom to ask genuine, even difficult questions. Learning can be unsettling. There is no such thing as risk-free genuine education, just as according to LDS theology there is no risk-free earthly experience. At any religious university, including at BYU, there always will be the possibility of friction between individual and institutional academic freedom.

There is no way to eliminate these tensions altogether, except by eliminating the claims of one kind of freedom or the other. But to do so would result in a net loss to the Church, the University, and to the family of universities to which BYU belongs. To eliminate BYU's right to define and preserve its institutional identity would threaten to transform BYU into a university like any other. At the same time, to override the very concept of individual academic freedom would threaten the vitality of BYU as a university. Either move would lessen the value of

BYU to its faculty and students, to the Church, and to the academic community at large. Therefore, the task is to establish principles and procedures that help minimize conflict and that guide the Board of Trustees, faculty, and administration through differences that may arise.

II. RELATIONSHIP BETWEEN INDIVIDUAL AND INSTITUTIONAL ACADEMIC FREEDOM:

A. NEITHER FREEDOM IS UNLIMITED: Neither individual nor institutional academic freedom can be unlimited. The reasons for this have been suggested already. To elaborate:

1. LIMITS ON INDIVIDUAL ACADEMIC FREEDOM: There can be no unlimited individual academic freedom. Were there no constraints on individual academic freedom, religious universities could converge toward a secular model and lose their distinctive character, thus diminishing pluralism in academia. Furthermore, absolute individual freedom would place the individual faculty member effectively in charge of defining institutional purpose, thereby infringing on prerogatives that traditionally belong to boards, administrations, and faculty councils. Such arrogation of authority is particularly intolerable when the disagreement concerns Church doctrine, on which BYU's Board of Trustees claims the right to convey prophetic counsel. Yet even secular universities, whose boards claim no special religious authority, do not empower individual faculty members with absolute individual freedom relative to the University mission. For example, universities have censured professors for racist, anti-Semitic, or otherwise offensive expression. In addition, state universities have prohibited the advocacy of religious values to protect a separation of church and state. Every university places some limitations on individual academic freedom.[21]

2. LIMITS ON INSTITUTIONAL ACADEMIC FREEDOM: Neither can there be unlimited institutional academic freedom. If institutional freedom were limitless, BYU could cease to be a genuine university, devoid of the exploratory environment vital to intellectual endeavor and with little room for disagreement and questioning. At BYU, the Church enjoys a special, deeply appreciated relation to the University, but its relation is not simply that of employer to employee—for a university faculty constitutes a special kind of employee. While each faculty member is fully accountable to the University, he or she also works in a space that is open to inquiry, discovery, and discussion. Any limitations in this space must be narrowly drawn so as not to impede the robust interchange of ideas, because the Board and administration wish to set policy for an institution that legitimately may be called a university.

B. REASONABLE LIMITATIONS: It follows that the exercise of individual and institutional academic freedom must be a matter of reasonable limitations. In general, at BYU a limitation is reasonable when the faculty behavior or expression *seriously and adversely affects* the University mission or the Church.[22] Examples would include expression with students or in public that:

1. contradicts or opposes, rather than analyzes or discusses, fundamental Church doctrine or policy; .
2. deliberately attacks or derides the Church or its general leaders; or
3. violates the Honor Code because the expression is dishonest, illegal, unchaste, profane, or unduly disrespectful of others.

Reasonable limits are based on careful consideration of what lies at the heart of the interests of the Church and the mission of the University. A faculty member shall not be found in violation of the academic freedom standards unless the faculty member can fairly be considered aware that the expression violates the standards.

These principles shall be interpreted and applied with persuasion, gentleness, meekness, kindness, and love unfeigned—in the spirit of D&C 121:41–44—and through established procedures that include faculty review. The ultimate responsibility to determine harm to the University mission or the Church, however, remains vested in the University's governing bodies—including the University president and central administration and, finally, the Board of Trustees.

C. SYNTHESIS: Reasonable limitations mediate the competing claims of individual and institutional academic freedom. In practice, instances in which limitations are invoked against individual faculty conduct or expression are few and infrequent. This is because:

1. INDIVIDUAL ACADEMIC FREEDOM IS PRESUMPTIVE, WHILE INSTITUTIONAL INTERVENTION IS EXCEPTIONAL: Individual freedom of expression is broad, presumptive, and essentially unrestrained except for matters that seriously and adversely affect the University mission or the Church. By contrast, institutional intervention is exceptional and limited to cases the University's governing bodies deem to offer compelling threats to BYU's mission or the Church. The Board and administration most effectively exercise their freedom to preserve BYU's institutional identity by setting general policies.

2. UNIVERSITY POSTURE IS ONE OF TRUST: The faculty is entrusted with broad individual academic freedom to pursue truth according to the methodologies and assumptions that characterize scholarship in various disciplines. This trust necessarily encompasses the freedom to discuss and advocate

controversial and unpopular ideas. However, the Board and administration reserve the right to designate, in exceptional cases, restrictions upon expression and behavior that, in their judgment, seriously and adversely affect BYU's mission or the Church.

3. FACULTY POSTURE IS ONE OF LOYALTY: Faculty members, for their part, agree to be loyal university citizens according to the guidelines set forth in the BYU Handbook. It is expected that the faculty will strive to contribute to the unique mission of BYU. This expectation, which aims at the fulfillment of University aspirations rather than merely at the absence of serious harm, properly figures in advancement and continuing status decisions.

4. TONE OF THE BYU COMMUNITY IS CHARITABLE: The faculty, administration, and the Board should work together in a spirit of love, trust, and goodwill. The faculty rightly assumes its work is presumptively free from restraint, but at the same time it assumes an obligation of dealing with sensitive issues sensitively and with a civility that becomes believers. BYU rightly expects LDS faculty to be faithful to, and other faculty to be respectful of, the Church and BYU's mission. Thus both the University's governing bodies and the faculty obligate themselves to use their respective academic freedom responsibly, within the context of a commitment to the gospel. As Elder B. H. Roberts said, "In essentials let there be unity; in non-essentials, liberty; and in all things, charity."[23]

CONCLUSION: It is the intent of Brigham Young University to reaffirm hereby its identity as a unique kind of university—an LDS university. BYU intends to nourish a community of believing scholars, where students and teachers, guided by the gospel, freely join together to seek truth in charity and virtue. For those who embrace the gospel, BYU offers a far richer and more complete kind of academic freedom than is possible in secular universities because to seek knowledge in the light of revealed truth is, for believers, to be free indeed.

NOTES TO APPENDIX

1. *See* the Mission of Brigham Young University in the *BYU General Bulletin* or University Electronic Handbook.

2. Both the American Association of University Professors (AAUP) and the Northwest Association of Schools and Colleges (NASC) have traditionally provided for special treatment of academic freedom issues in religious institutions, whose existence contributes to genuine pluralism in an overwhelmingly secular modern academia. The

AAUP's "1940 Statement of Principles on Academic Freedom and Tenure" provides that "limitations of academic freedom because of religious or other aims of the institution should be clearly stated in writing at the time of appointment" (*AAUP, Policy Documents & Reports* [Washington, D.C.: 1990], 3). Similarly, the NASC *Accreditation Handbook* "allows 'reasonable limitations on freedom of inquiry or expression which are dictated by institutional purpose' as long as they are 'published candidly.'" (1988 ed), 9–10; see also 133.

3. See Michael W. McConnell, "Academic Freedom in Religious Colleges and Universities," 53 Law and Contemporary Problems 53.3 (1990): 303–24; David M. Rabban, "A Functional Analysis of 'Individual' and 'Institutional' Academic Freedom under the First Amendment," the Law and Contemporary Problems 53.3 (1990): 227–301.

4. McConnell, "Academic Freedom," 305.

5. Ibid.

6. *Journal of Discourses* (Liverpool: Amasa Lyman, 1860), 7:283–84.

7. *See* policy on Honor Code, University Electronic Handbook.

8. Faculty Rank and Status: Professorial Policy, Policy and Procedures Section, University Electronic Handbook (rev. 1 June 1992), sec. 3.0.

9. For example, the Catholic church's major statement on academic freedom in Catholic universities, *Ex Corde Ecelesiae,* affirms, among other things, that "every Catholic university, without ceasing to be a university, has a relationship to the church that is essential to its institutional identity" (John Paul II, "Apostolic Constitution on Catholic Universities), [Ex Corde Ecclesiae]," paragraph 27 [1990]).

10. For a discussion of "The Greater Institutional Academic Freedom of Private Universities," see Rabban, "A Functional Analysis," 266–71.

11. See, for example, several articles appearing in *First Things*: James Nuechterlein, "The Death of Religious Higher Education (January 1991): 7–8; George M. Marsden, "The Soul of the American University" (January 1991): 34–47; James Tunstead Burtchaell, "The Decline and Fall of the Christian College" (April 1991): 16–29 and (May 1991): 30–38; David W. Lutz, "Can Notre Dame Be Saved" (January 1992): 35–40.

12. See McConnell, "Academic Freedom," 311–18.

13. Ibid., 312.

14. Ibid.

15. Ibid., 313. Similarly, Rabban argues that private universities may be granted greater latitude to establish educational policies than state institutions because "The resulting pluralism within the academic world . . . may provide more tolerance for diverse and unpopular views than a rule that would subject all universities to the commitment to diversity of thought that the first amendment imposes on public ones" ("A Functional Analysis," 268–69).

16. McConnell, "Academic Freedom," 313.

17. J. Reuben Clark, Jr., "The Charted Course of the Church in Education," in *Messages of the First Presidency,* ed. James R. Clark (Salt Lake City: Bookcraft, 1975).

18. McConnell, "Academic Freedom," 314.

19. Ibid., 316.

20. Ibid.

21. As George S. Worgul, Jr., states in the "Editor's Preface" to *Issues in Academic Freedom* (Pittsburgh: Duquesne Univ. Press, 1992): "'academic freedom' at any university— whether public, private, church-related or church-sponsored—is never unlimited or

absolute. Every university has an identity and mission to which it must adhere. . . . Freedom is always a situated freedom and a responsible freedom" (viii–ix).

22. This document does not address policies, common to all universities, that govern the orderly maintenance of the institution, the disruption of classes, or the university endorsement of personal actions. This document speaks only to limitations arising from BYU's mission.

23. Conference Reports, Oct. 1912, 30. The source of Roberts's citation is the Latin maxim, *"In necessariis unitas, in non-necessariis* (or, *dubiis*) *libertas, in utrisque* (or, *omnibus*) *caritas"* (see Philip Schaff, *History of the Christian Church,* 2nd ed. [New York: Scribners, 1915], 6:650–53).

13 | *Ex Corde Ecclesiae* and American
Catholic Higher Education:
A Quandary or an Opportunity?

Charles H. Wilson

American Catholic universities, confronted with the need to take some action in light of the promulgation of *Ex Corde Ecclesiae*,[1] find themselves caught between the proverbial rock and the hard place—between the Scylla of adapting to an important church pronouncement on higher education and the Charybdis of maintaining their secular standing and aspirations within the larger higher education community. How that quandary is resolved is probably the most important issue that American Catholic universities face in the waning years of the 20th century. The issue exists in several contexts and on several levels, and its resolution will undoubtedly chart the course that American Catholic universities will follow well into the next century.

The focus of this paper is on the implications of *Ex Corde Ecclesiae* for American Catholic colleges and universities under civil law. But even that limited focus is multidimensional. On one level is the problem of the eligibility of American Catholic colleges and universities and their students to continue to participate in public aid programs. On another level is their status in the American community of institutions of higher education, including compliance with accreditation standards. On a third level are the relationships between the American Catholic colleges and universities and their various constituencies, including most particularly their faculties. In some ways, all three issues are interrelated. I shall examine each of those levels of civil law concern separately below. First, however, I shall review briefly the provisions of *Ex Corde Ecclesiae* that can give rise to civil law concerns.

From *Current Issues in Catholic Higher Education* 14, no. 1 (Winter 1994): 5–15.

I. THE APOSTOLIC CONSTITUTION AND
THE LOCAL ADAPTATIONS

On August 15, 1990, the Feast of the Assumption, Pope John Paul II promulgated *Ex Corde Ecclesiae*, an apostolic constitution for Catholic universities around the world. It is the first apostolic constitution that the Holy See has issued that is applicable to non-ecclesiastical Catholic universities.[2] That document was the product of years of drafting, redrafting and controversy. As the controversy coalesced toward the end of the drafting process, the focus was not so much on any new provisions of the apostolic constitution as on certain provisions of the Code of Canon Law that *Ex Corde Ecclesiae* specifically incorporates by reference.

In 1983, the church issued a total revision of the 1917 Code of Canon Law. The provision of the new Code that raised the greatest concerns among the leadership of American Catholic higher education is Canon 812, which provides: "It is necessary that those who teach theological disciplines in any institute of higher studies have a mandate from the competent ecclesiastical authority." The leaders of Catholic higher education in this country repeatedly expressed the concerns that Canon 812 could unduly restrict the academic freedom of Catholic theologians in the academy and, equally significant, could allow ecclesiastical authorities external to Catholic universities to make judgments on the academic competence of Catholic theologians on university faculties.[3] Despite those expressions of concern, the mandate requirement of Canon 812 became a part of the new Code of Canon Law.

The second controversial provision of the new Code, Canon 810, provoked less discussion but is potentially more far-reaching. Section 1 of Canon 810 provides as follows:

> It is the responsibility of the authority who is competent in accordance with the statutes to provide for the appointment of teachers at Catholic universities who besides their scientific and pedagogical suitability are also outstanding in their integrity of doctrine and probity of life; when those requisite qualities are lacking they are to be removed from the positions in accord with the procedure set forth in the statutes.

The concerns raised by this provision are both obvious and ominous. If implemented at American Catholic universities, this provision could lead to disciplinary actions against Catholic professors[4] who are not totally faithful to Catholic doctrine in their teaching and in their personal conduct.

Canon 810 has a second section that raises different concerns. That section provides:

> The conference of bishops and the diocesan bishops concerned have the duty and right of being vigilant that in these universities the principles of Catholic doctrine are faithfully observed.

While that provision is decidedly vague in specifying how the bishops should exercise their vigilance, it is unambiguous in authorizing persons external to the Catholic universities—the bishops—to intervene and act if questions arise about doctrinal integrity at those institutions.

(Apart from the provisions of the Code of Canon Law, *Ex Corde Ecclesiae* provides an independent basis for bishops to involve themselves in the internal affairs of Catholic universities. Section 2 of article 5 of the general norms decrees that bishops have a "responsibility" to promote the welfare of Catholic universities and "the right and duty to watch over the preservation and strengthening of their Catholic character." That section then provides:

> If problems should arise concerning this Catholic character, the local bishop is to take the initiatives necessary to resolve the matter, working with the competent university authorities in accordance with established procedures and, if necessary, with the help of the Holy See.

Again, the circumstances that would warrant intercession by a bishop are not delineated, but the authority to intercede could not be stated more clearly.)

While Canons 810 and 812 have been a source of apprehension among these concerned about American Catholic higher education, there is no recorded instance of those canons being applied at or against any Catholic college or university in this country. Indeed, in the immediate aftermath of the promulgation of the new Code of Canon Law, much of the discussion about Canon 812 concerned whether its mandate requirement applied at all to American Catholic universities and their theology faculties. *Ex Corde Ecclesiae* would seem to have put an end to that debate.

The first sentence of the general norms of *Ex Corde Ecclesiae* provides:

> These general norms are based on, and are a further development of, the Code of Canon Law and the complementary Church legislation, without

prejudice to the right of the Holy See to intervene should this become necessary.[5]

The reference to the Code of Canon Law in that sentence is accompanied by a footnote that reads: "Cf. in particular the Chapter of the Code: 'Catholic Universities and Other Institutes of Higher Studies' (CIC can. 807–814)." Thus, if *Ex Corde Ecclesiae* is applicable to American Catholic colleges and universities, a matter that no one seriously disputes, then Canons 810 and 812 are also made applicable by the specific reference to them in the general norms.[6]

The extent to which *Ex Corde Ecclesiae* and Canons 810 and 812 are applicable to particular American Catholic universities, however, is somewhat clouded by a further provision of the general norms that draws distinctions between the types of Catholic universities and by the status of American Catholic institutions under civil law.

Article 1, section 3 of the general norms seeks to delineate the scope of the applicability of the general norms to particular types of Catholic colleges and universities. The first sentence of that section states that a university established by the Holy See, an episcopal conference or a diocesan bishop "is to incorporate these General Norms . . . into its governing documents and conform its existing statutes . . . to the general norms. . . ."[7] That language would seem to obligate the types of Catholic universities described to conform to the general norms. By contrast, the second sentence of that section states that, as to "other Catholic universities, . . . [i]t is contemplated that [they] will make their own the General Norms[,] . . . internalizing them into governing documents, and, as far as possible, will conform their existing statutes . . . to these General Norms. . . ."[8] The contrast between the mandatory language of the first sentence and the less than mandatory language of the second sentence suggests that "other Catholic universities" should have some latitude in deciding whether to adopt and be bound by the general norms.

The status of American Catholic colleges and universities under civil law also bears upon the question of the binding effect of *Ex Corde Ecclesiae*. Colleges and universities in this country gain their standing as "legal persons" under civil law through the act of incorporation. By incorporating under the laws of the jurisdiction in which they are located, American colleges and universities obtain all the rights, privileges and obligations of all other "persons" in society. One of those "rights" is the right to direct their own affairs, subject only to the laws of the jurisdiction of incorporation and of the federal government that apply to all like "persons" in society.

Typically, the act of incorporation vests the governance of an institution of higher education in a board of trustees or board of directors. That governing board alone establishes the rules of conduct by which the institution operates. Apart from applicable state and federal laws, only the rules and regulations promulgated by an institution's governing board legally bind the institution. Rules of conduct issued by an external entity, whether it be the Holy See or the American Association of University Professors, cannot be applicable to a duly incorporated American college or university unless its governing board agrees to be bound by them. This fact of corporate existence under civil law establishes an institution's "legal autonomy."[9]

Whether, as a practical matter, an American Catholic university can exercise its autonomy under civil law to the extent of embracing *Ex Corde Ecclesiae* less than fully and enthusiastically and remain in the good graces of the church is problematic. The general norms instruct every Catholic university to "make known its Catholic identity" and to "provide means which will guarantee the expression and preservation of this identity" (art. 2, § 3). In addition, the general norms vest in each bishop the "responsibility to promote the welfare of the Catholic universities in his diocese" and "the right and duty to watch over the preservation and strengthening of their Catholic character." The general norms further provide that, "[i]f problems should arise concerning this Catholic character, the local bishop is to take the initiatives necessary to resolve the matter" (art. 5, § 2). Whether a Catholic university's failure to adopt and implement *Ex Corde Ecclesiae* to the satisfaction of the local ordinary, a prerogative that it has under civil law, would prompt or require the ordinary's intercession is an unresolved quandary posed by the apostolic constitution.

One of the persistent criticisms of the early drafts of *Ex Corde Ecclesiae* was that the document failed to give adequate consideration to the local conditions in which Catholic universities necessarily operate. To meet that criticism, the final document requires that

> [t]he general norms are to be applied concretely at the local and regional levels by episcopal conferences and other assemblies of Catholic hierarchy. . . , taking into account the statutes of each university or institute and, as far as possible and appropriate, civil law (art. 1, § 2).

That provision of the general norms also requires that local or regional "ordinances" adopted to implement *Ex Corde Ecclesiae* be approved by the Holy See and then be considered "valid" for all Catholic universities and institutes subject to the apostolic constitution. Responding to that mandate, the National Conference of Catholic Bishops created a committee, headed by Bishop John Leibrecht, to consult with the leaders of American Catholic higher education and to draft the ordinances mandated by *Ex Corde Ecclesiae*. That committee's draft ordinances were issued on May 4, 1993, and circulated for comment.

The draft ordinances are brief, only eight in number, and they address issues that most concerned the American Catholic higher education community while the drafts of the apostolic constitution were being debated and discussed. The first ordinance delineates as Catholic colleges and universities those which, "through their governing boards, freely commit themselves to the Christian message as it comes to us through the Catholic Church, and together with the bishops, seek to preserve and foster their Catholic character and mission." The reference to the institutions' governing boards and acknowledgement that the institutions must "freely commit" themselves to the status of being Catholic would seem to be a recognition that, under civil law, *Ex Corde Ecclesiae* cannot be imposed on an American Catholic college or university without the consent of its governing board.

The second ordinance requires Catholic colleges and universities to identify themselves as fitting one of several descriptive categories appended to the draft ordinances[10] and to include that identification in their governing documents or statements of mission. The third ordinance requires each Catholic college and university to undertake "periodically, and at least every ten years," an internal review of "the congruence of its research program, course of instruction, and service activity with the ideals and principles expressed in *Ex Corde Ecclesiae*." The reference to ten years would seem to be designed to allow the institution to conduct the required internal review at the same time that it prepares for periodic reaccreditation by the regional accrediting associations.

The next three ordinances address the mandate requirement of Canon 812. The fourth ordinance directs institutional authorities to promote the teaching of Catholic theological disciplines in communion with the church "[a]s a manifestation of their common desire to maintain the Catholic identity" of the institution. The fifth ordinance defines the mandate of Canon 812 as "recognition by the competent ecclesiastical authority of a Catholic professor's suitability to teach theological disciplines." The sixth ordinance identifies the diocesan bishop or his delegate as the "competent ecclesiastical authority" who issues the mandate to Catholic theologians. That ordinance also attempts to make the mandate a matter to be resolved between the professor, or prospective professor, and the ordinary rather than between the professor and authorities at the college or university. Thus, academic officials are required only to advise teachers of theological disciplines of "the Church's expectation that they request the mandate" from the local bishop or his delegate. In addition, the bishop is "to invite the Catholic professor to request the mandate and, after appropriate review, the bishop is to respond to the request."

The significance of those three ordinances is what they do not say. For example, neither the ordinances nor the general norms of *Ex Corde Ecclesiae* the ordinances amplify stipulates the qualifications a Catholic teacher of theology must possess to obtain the mandate. Moreover, the ordinances are silent on whether, consistent with *Ex Corde Ecclesiae,* a Catholic university may hire or retain a theology professor who is denied the mandate by the local ordinary.

The ordinances do anticipate, however, that neither they nor the apostolic constitution, by their terms, will put to rest all of the disagreements that surfaced during the drafting stages of *Ex Corde Ecclesiae.* The seventh ordinance refers to disputes that might arise "between the competent ecclesiastical authority and a Catholic college or university, or individuals or groups within such institutions." The ordinance provides that such disputes are

> to be resolved according to procedures that respect the rights of persons in the church . . . , the autonomy of the academic institution . . . , and the responsibility of church authorities . . . to assist in the preservation of the institution's Catholic identity.

The ordinance further provides that the procedures are also "to follow the principles and, to the extent applicable, the procedures" set forth in two documents issued by the National Conference of Catholic Bishops: *On Due Process* (1972), for administrative matters, and *Doctrinal Responsibilities* (1989), for matters relating to differences in doctrine.

The language of the seventh ordinance makes that provision applicable to problems or disputes about the Catholic character of an institution, as that concept is set forth in section 2 of article 5 of the general norms of *Ex Corde Ecclesiae.* The reference in the seventh ordinance to the NCCB document on *Doctrinal Responsibilities* would seem to make that ordinance applicable to disagreements that arise over the decision of an ordinary to grant or withhold the mandate prescribed by Canon 812. The subtitle of *Doctrinal Responsibilities* is "Approaches to Promoting Cooperation and Resolving Misunderstandings between Bishops and Theologians."

The draft ordinances issued and circulated by the NCCB committee are moderate in their scope.[11] They attempt to clarify the mandate requirement of Canon 812, a matter that has been the object of considerable discussion since the adoption of the new Code of Canon Law. They take due recognition of American civil law and urge Catholic colleges and universities, through their governing boards, to commit themselves "freely" to the principles embodied in *Ex Corde Ecclesiae*. And, through the proposed seventh ordinance, the committee expresses its hope that disagreements about the future course of Catholic higher education in this country be resolved through the processes of dialogue and conciliation. Only time can determine whether the bishops' objectives will be realized.

What is predictable at this stage of the evolution of the apostolic constitution is that the express terms of the general norms of *Ex Corde Ecclesiae* will have repercussions for American Catholic colleges and universities under civil law. To explore those potential repercussions, I shall assume that American Catholic colleges and universities that choose to adhere to *Ex Corde Ecclesiae* and the ordinances of the American bishops will do so without modifying those documents in any substantial way.[12] Whether the governing boards of those institutions will want to embrace *Ex Corde Ecclesiae* in its entirety or in some modified form is a decision only they can make. My purpose is provide those who must make such decisions the information they should have to act in an informed way.

II. ELIGIBILITY FOR PUBLIC AID PROGRAMS

For better or worse, the financial welfare of American Catholic colleges and universities has become dependent on the ability of those institutions and their students to continue to be eligible for funds from federal and state programs that benefit higher education generally. Catholic institutions share with other independent colleges and universities the burden of convincing Congress and state legislatures that, as a matter of sound public policy, they should share in that portion of the public fisc that is allocated to higher education. At the state level, particularly, there is a pronounced bias in favor of public universities.[13]

Catholic institutions, along with other independent colleges and universities that have religious affiliations, face an additional hurdle in the continuing struggle to participate equitably in public funding programs: federal and state constitutional provisions that restrict the power of government to act in a way that benefits, or appears to benefit, religion. It is in this arena that *Ex Corde Ecclesiae* could have a profound impact. At this time, the federal constitutional principles that restrict public aid to church-affiliated institutions are more settled than the principles that apply under various state constitutions.

A. THE ESTABLISHMENT CLAUSE OF THE FIRST AMENDMENT

Catholic colleges and universities have been consistently successful in lawsuits challenging their eligibility under the Establishment Clause of the First Amendment[14] to participate in public aid programs. By contrast, Catholic parochial schools have lost most of the significant cases under the Establishment Clause contesting their right and the right of their students to benefit from public aid programs. The different outcomes are a direct result of how courts perceive the impact of religion on the academic programs of church-related colleges, on the one hand, and of Catholic parochial schools, on the other hand.

The most significant college-level cases are *Tilton v. Richardson*[15] and *Roemer v. Board of Public Works*.[16] Both decisions, by the narrowest of margins,[17] upheld the right of Catholic colleges to participate in the institutional aid programs challenged in those cases. In reaching those results, the Supreme Court emphasized certain characteristics of the defendant colleges that reflected the interaction of their religious orientations with their academic programs. Those characteristics were as follows: (1) the colleges did not discriminate on religious grounds in faculty hiring and student admissions;[18] (2) although the colleges required their students to take courses in theology or religious studies, those courses were taught as academic disciplines and not to proselytize the Catholic faith;[19] (3) the colleges made no effort in any aspect of their curricula to proselytize religious doctrine; (4) the colleges did not require their students to attend religious worship; and (5) the colleges adhered to accepted standards of academic freedom.

The Supreme Court also noted that the colleges in the two cases were operated by Catholic religious organizations and had faculties that were predominantly Catholic. But neither of those factors was constitutionally disabling. Rather, the Court concluded in *Tilton* that the Catholic colleges before it were "institutions with an admittedly religious function but whose predominant higher education mission is to provide their students with a secular education."[20]

The portrait of Catholic parochial schools[21] that emerges from Supreme Court decisions is quite different. The Court has constructed a "profile" of pervasively sectarian schools to describe Catholic parochial schools. The seven to ten elements of that profile are the obverse of *Tilton/Roemer* characteristics. Painting with a broad brush, the Court has described Catholic parochial schools as "schools in which education is an integral part of the dominant sectarian mission and in which an atmosphere dedicated to the advancement of religious belief is constantly maintained."[22] Based on this and similar descriptions, the Court has ruled in case after case that public aid programs that benefit Catholic parochial schools or their students impermissibly advanced religion or created the potential for excessive government entanglement with religion.[23]

For Catholic universities concerned about their continued eligibility for public aid programs, the issue presented by *Ex Corde Ecclesiae* is whether institutions that adopt it will be perceived by the courts as having a more intense religious orientation than the colleges described in *Tilton/Roemer* and whether the perception of such an orientation will affect the eligibility determination. One difficulty in answering that question is that the Supreme Court has never considered the constitutionality of an institutional aid program in a case in which the church-affiliated colleges have deviated from the *Tilton/Roemer* model. Only one federal court, a three-judge district court in Kansas, has examined colleges that did not conform to the *Tilton/Roemer* model, and it ruled that a single deviation from that model, such as compulsory chapel attendance or an affirmation of church doctrine as a condition to graduating, was sufficient to render a college ineligible for public aid.[24] Because that case was not appealed, we do not know whether the Supreme Court would have agreed with that reasoning.[25] Thus, attempting to project how a Catholic university's adoption of *Ex Corde Ecclesiae* might affect a court's assessment of its eligibility for public funds is necessarily speculative.

Nevertheless, it is fair to examine how a court employing the *Tilton/Roemer* criteria might view a Catholic university that adopts the apostolic constitution. Canon 812, which is incorporated by reference in *Ex Corde Ecclesiae*, imposes the mandate requirement on Catholic theologians at Catholic universities.[26]

A court could conclude that the mandate requirement arose from the church's desire to maintain orthodoxy on theological faculties at its universities and that the threat of withholding or withdrawing the mandate for not observing orthodoxy would inhibit the academic freedom of Catholic theologians. A court that took such a view of the mandate requirement would be hard pressed to find that the required theology courses at institutions that adopt *Ex Code Ecclesiae* are taught as academic disciplines and not to indoctrinate the Catholic faith or that the institutions are characterized by an atmosphere of academic freedom.

Comparable concerns can arise from Canon 810, which is also incorporated into *Ex Corde Ecclesiae*.[27] That canon would appear to require Catholic universities to remove from teaching positions Catholics who do not exhibit integrity of doctrine and probity of life. On its face, Canon 810 applies to all Catholic faculty members, irrespective of their academic disciplines, and extends to how they conduct their personal lives. Thus, that canon could, at least in theory, lead to the discharge of a physics professor who is a Catholic and who divorces and remarries without obtaining an annulment of the first marriage.[28] Many Catholic parochial schools reserve in their contracts the right to discharge elementary school teachers who engage in such conduct. Accordingly, a court considering the public aid eligibility of a Catholic university that adopts *Ex Corde Ecclesiae* and that thus reserves the right to discipline faculty members under section 1 of Canon 810 might consider such an institution closer to the parochial school model than to the *Tilton/Roemer* model.

Finally, article 5, section 2, of the general norms of *Ex Corde Ecclesiae*, combined with section 2 of Canon 810, confers on local bishops broad powers of supervision over Catholic universities to assure that they remain faithful to their Catholic character. The Supreme Court in *Roemer* was not concerned that ordinaries and members of religious orders served on the governing boards of Catholic universities. But membership on governing boards makes religious internal to the institution and presumably subject to the same fiduciary obligations as other board members.[29] Whether the Court would be as sanguine about the intervention in university affairs by religious authorities considered external to the institution is problematic.[30]

This analysis notwithstanding, I would conclude that a Catholic university that adopts *Ex Corde Ecclesiae* does not, from that act alone, face a serious risk of traditional litigation[31] challenging its constitutional eligibility for public aid. The last of the important cases challenging institutional aid that benefits Catholic colleges was *Roemer,* which the Supreme Court decided more than seventeen years ago. By affirming the general principle that church-affiliated institutions of higher education can, consistent with the strictures of the Establishment Clause, constitutionally participate in public aid programs, the Supreme Court left those opposed to that principle the prospect of prevailing in such cases only if they can establish that particular church-affiliated colleges receiving public funds are "pervasively sectarian." That no significant college aid cases have been litigated since *Roemer* suggests that the difficulties of proving such a claim have been sufficiently onerous to discourage further challenges. It is fair to ask whether the mere adoption of the apostolic constitution, which remains uncertain in its scope and applicability, by a Catholic university would be sufficient to induce the organizations that traditionally challenge the participation of church-affiliated colleges in public aid programs to get back into the quagmire of Establishment Clause litigation.

Moreover, the current emphasis in college-level public aid programs is on student aid. And the Supreme Court has twice ruled that students attending even pervasively sectarian colleges can, consistent with the Establishment Clause, participate in student aid programs.[32]

B. State Constitutional Restrictions

The Establishment Clause of the First Amendment is only one of the constitutional hurdles that church-affiliated colleges can face in their quest to participate in educational aid programs enacted by state legislatures. Most state constitutions contain clauses that prohibit public aid to religion or to religious institutions, and many of these state constitutional provisions are far more restrictive than the Establishment Clause.

For example, in 1961, the Oregon Supreme Court ruled that providing free textbooks to students in Catholic parochial schools in the state violated a state constitutional provision that prohibited state funds from being used to benefit religious institutions.[33] Several years later, the United States Supreme Court ruled that a similar textbook program enacted by the New York legislature did not violate the Establishment Clause.[34]

The case that most dramatically illustrates the different results that can be reached under the federal and state constitutions involved a challenge to a State of Washington program that provided tuition benefits to blind persons. Mr. Witters, who was blind, sued when the responsible administrative agency denied him benefits because he attended a Bible college. The agency had relied on a Washington state constitutional provision that it had construed to prohibit the use of state funds to aid in "religious" training. When the case reached the Washington Supreme Court, the agency defended its actions by arguing that both the state and federal constitutions prohibited the aid that Mr. Witters was seeking. The Washington Supreme Court ruled that it was not necessary to reach the state constitutional issue because the type aid Mr. Witters was seeking violated the Establishment Clause of the First Amendment.[35]

The United States Supreme Court agreed to hear the case and reversed.[36] The Supreme Court's reasoning draws a critical distinction between institutional aid and student aid for purposes of Establishment Clause analysis. The Court ruled that the state was aiding only students who met religiously neutral eligibility criteria (the petitioner was legally blind) and that the fact that the state-provided tuition assistance was paid to a Bible college or other pervasively sectarian institution was the result of that recipient's decision and not the decision of a state agency.[37]

The Court remanded the case to the Washington Supreme Court, and that court then ruled that the state program in question violated the Washington constitution.[38] The United States Supreme Court declined to review that second decision of the state court[39] since it has no authority to revise the interpretation of a state constitution by a state's highest court. Thus, after years of litigation, Mr. Witters was left without the tuition benefits he would have received had he chosen to attend a college without a religious orientation.

It is not possible to generalize about the difficulties that might lurk in particular state constitutions. Catholic colleges and universities can only be advised that decisions under any state constitutional provisions relating to aid to religion or religious institutions should be checked if there is any concern about an institution's continued eligibility for state aid under a state constitution if it adopts *Ex Corde Ecclesiae.*

III. ACCREDITATION

Adoption of *Ex Corde Ecclesiae* by Catholic colleges and universities could also affect their eligibility for accreditation or reaccreditation. I refer to the type of accreditation that is conferred by regional accrediting associations, such as the Middle States Association of Colleges and Schools (hereinafter referred to as "Middle States"). Strictly speaking, accreditation is not a civil law issue since the regional accrediting associations are private entities and not agencies or agents of government.[40] However, most public aid programs limit participation to institutions that are accredited or to students who attend accredited institutions. Thus, the ability to be accredited is integral to the whole question of a university's ability to participate in public aid programs.

For many institutions, however, the question of regional accreditation implicates broader concerns. Such accreditation is a matter of considerable prestige, a sort of seal of approval and acknowledgement that the institution is part of the mainstream of American higher education. Since Catholic colleges and universities do more than engage in religious education and activities, a fact acknowledged and applauded by *Ex Corde Ecclesiae,* regional accreditation confirms that an institution is succeeding in its pursuit of excellence within the American higher education community.

Regional accreditation is a form of self-regulation within the academic community. It is an evaluative process that seeks to determine whether a particular institution meets certain standards of academic quality. The core of the accrediting process is the institution's own self-study in which it sets forth its mission and its goals and objectives for its academic program and related activities. The institution is then evaluated according to how well it is achieving its goals and objectives in light of its resources and the needs of its constituents.

For the most part, the accrediting process measures how well an institution is achieving its own stated goals rather than its conformity to certain externally imposed criteria.

However, regional accrediting associations do establish certain basic criteria to which all institutions seeking accreditation must conform, For example, a university that offers graduate degrees in the physical sciences is expected to have library resources of sufficient size and quality to support those programs. Such an institution cannot define for itself what library resources are adequate if an objective assessment would conclude that those resources are inadequate.

Two important accrediting criteria—institutional integrity and autonomy, and academic freedom—are implicated by *Ex Corde Ecclesiae*. The standards of accreditation published by Middle States explain the concept of institutional integrity and autonomy as follows:

> The maintenance and exercise of institutional integrity presupposes appropriate autonomy and freedom. The freedom to examine data, to question assumptions, to be guided by evidence, to teach what one knows, to be a scholar. Similarly, autonomy is the freedom that allows an institution to get on with its essential work. A college must be morally responsible but, even when church-related, it is not a religion or a church. Those within an institution have as a first concern evidence and truth rather than particular judgments of institutional benefactors, public or social pressure groups or religious or political factions.

I would expect regional accrediting associations to view *Ex Corde Ecclesiae* as impinging on institutional integrity and autonomy at American Catholic colleges and universities. That document has been issued by an entity external to those institutions, the Holy See, and that document purports to establish grounds for a Catholic university's discipline of its faculty that the institution itself might not establish and to define the appropriate scope of academic inquiry in theology and other disciplines where the integrity of church doctrine is involved.

The Middle States' standards of accreditation define academic freedom as follows:

> It gives one the right and implies the obligation as a scholar to examine all data and question every assumption. It debars one from preconceived conclusions. It obliges teachers to present all information fairly because it asserts

the student's right to know the facts. To restrict the availability or limit the presentation of data or opinions, even those that may be completely erroneous, is to deny academic freedom.

No reach is required to anticipate how accrediting associations will view the potential impact of *Ex Corde Ecclesiae* on academic freedom at Catholic colleges and universities.[41] The provisions of Canons 810 and 812 that *Ex Corde Ecclesiae* incorporates would seem to restrict the data or opinions a professor can present in courses that touch upon matters taught by the Catholic Church as doctrine and, thus, restrict academic freedom as so defined. Moreover, a factor inherent in the concept of academic freedom in this country is that a professor's competence should be judged solely by his academic peers and not by persons external to the academy. To the extent that Canons 810 and 812 give bishops an implicit role in policing Catholic universities for doctrinal orthodoxy, they conflict with this aspect of academic freedom.

That the governing board of a Catholic university freely adopts *Ex Corde Ecclesiae* may not shield the institution from criticism from accrediting agencies. In 1988, the Southern Association of Colleges and Schools issued a report highly critical of the Southeastern Baptist Theological Seminary because of what it viewed as the improper intrusion of the institution's board of trustees into its academic affairs. In particular, the accrediting agency charged that the board of trustees had taken a number of questionable actions to require that biblical inerrancy and no other approach to scriptural interpretation be taught at the seminary. To many Southern Baptists, biblical inerrancy is the equivalent of doctrinal orthodoxy.

No one can say for certain that the adoption of *Ex Corde Ecclesiae* by a Catholic college or university will jeopardize its accreditation. A wide variety of factors are examined during the accrediting process, and it is difficult to identify any one or two factors that will be determinative. Moreover, the accrediting process is not adversarial in nature. If an accrediting agency identifies potential problems during the accrediting visit, it will point out those problems in a preliminary report and ask the institution for an explanation. This give and take process generally allows an institution to demonstrate that the perception of a problem does not conform to institutional realities. Nevertheless, even if the adoption of the apostolic constitution by a Catholic university does not cause it to lose or fail to achieve accreditation, the impact of that document on the academic integrity of the institution would certainly be scrutinized during the accrediting process.

IV. THE IMPACT OF *EX CORDE ECCLESIAE* ON FACULTY, STUDENTS AND OTHERS AT CATHOLIC UNIVERSITIES

An American Catholic university's adoption of *Ex Corde Ecclesiae* can also affect its legal relationships with its faculty and students, and with others who claim an interest in its fidelity to its mission as a Catholic institution.

Under civil law, a private university's relationship with its faculty (and its students) is contractual in nature. Under custom and usage in American higher education,[42] the terms of the contractual relationship between a university and its faculty members are contained not only in the formal contract document executed between the university and a professor but also in the faculty handbook.[43] To the extent that a Catholic university's adoption of *Ex Corde Ecclesiae* alters the terms of the contractual relationship between the university and members of its faculty, the institution's faculty handbook must be modified accordingly. It is not sufficient, for purposes of civil law, that the university publicize the governing board's action in adopting the apostolic constitution or incorporate the essential terms of that papal document into its mission statement. The contractual documents that set forth the rights and obligations of faculty members must be revised to reflect any changes in those rights and obligations brought about by the adoption of *Ex Corde Ecclesiae*. If such revisions are not made, the institution will not be able to invoke the terms of the apostolic constitution to defend any of its actions that are challenged in court by a faculty member.

One area in which a clarification of contract obligations would be necessary relates to the mandate requirement of Canon 812. While the draft ordinances issued by the American bishops make clear that the mandate requirement is a matter to be resolved between the Catholic theologian and the ordinary, the clear intent of Canon 812 and article 4, section 3 of the general norms of *Ex Corde Ecclesiae* is that Catholic theologians at Catholic universities should possess the mandate. Thus, in addition to informing a Catholic theologian of the mandate requirement and how the mandate is to be obtained, the university that adopts the apostolic constitution must also spell out what action, if any, the university will take if the ordinary denies the mandate at the hiring stage or withdraws the mandate after the theologian becomes a member of the faculty. Absent such notice, the university will find it difficult to prevail in subsequent litigation if it refuses to hire an otherwise qualified theologian because the mandate was denied or fires a theologian whose mandate is withdrawn.

The notice issues concerning the mandate are rather simple compared to those presented by section 1 of Canon 810 if a Catholic university chooses to rely on the provisions of that section as a basis for disciplining a faculty member. The first problem is defining adequately "integrity of doctrine" as it pertains to how faculty members carry out their teaching and research responsibilities in the various disciplines and what conduct conflicts with the "probity of life" language of the canon. The institution would also have to examine its academic freedom statement and make appropriate revisions to conform the statement to the definitions of activities proscribed by section 1 of Canon 810.[44]

Problems of a different magnitude implicate a Catholic university's efforts to comply with the requirement of article 4, section 4 of the general norms that requires that "the number of non-Catholic teachers should not be allowed to constitute a majority within the institution" so that its "Catholic identity" can be maintained. Complying with that requirement could put an American Catholic university on a collision course with federal and state anti-discrimination laws. For example, Title VII of the Civil Rights Act of 1964 prohibits employers from refusing to hire or firing anyone because, *inter alia,* of religion.[45] Efforts to maintain a Catholic-majority faculty could conflict with the provision.

Title VII does contain an exemption for religious educational institutions.[46] The exemption applies "with respect to the employment of individuals of a particular religion to perform work connected with the carrying on by such . . . educational institution . . . of its activities." Title VII provides further that

> it shall not be an unlawful employment practice for a school, college, university, or other educational institution or institution of learning to hire and employ employees of a particular religion if such school, college, university, or other educational institution or institution of learning is, in whole or substantial part, owned, supported, controlled, or managed by a particular religion or by a particular religious corporation, association, or society, or if the curriculum of such school, college, university, or other educational institution or institution of learning is directed toward the propagation of a particular religion.[47]

Whether a Catholic university should avail itself of the Title VII exemptions to comply with the majority Catholic faculty requirement of *Ex Corde Ecclesiae* is a matter that should be given considerable thought.

First, for positions such as those in the institution's campus ministry program, another Title VII exemption permits the use of religion as a hiring criterion.[48] Religion need only be a "bona fide occupational qualification" to satisfy that exemption, and staffing a campus ministry office with clergy or religious of particular denominations to meet the religious needs of various members of the student body meets that requirement Second, where a person's religion may appear to be the basis for a hiring decision, other reasons may be successfully advanced to support the decision.

For example, the Supreme Court in the *Roemer* case indicated, without disapproval, that the hiring decisions for the theology departments at the four defendant colleges were made on the basis of religion, 426 U.S. at 757.[49] In addition, the Court in that case also noted without disapproval that the decisions of some of the defendant colleges to hire members of the sponsoring religious orders for faculty positions rather than lay persons had an economic, rather than a religious, motivation, *Id.* at 757. Because the members of the religious orders contributed their services, the colleges saved money by hiring them.

I have deliberately chosen to refer to these aspects of the *Roemer* decision because of a crucial element that a Catholic university should consider before deciding to invoke the Title VII exemption to comply with the Catholic majority requirement of *Ex Corde Ecclesiae*. Because of the wording of the exemption, a Catholic university that invokes it may say something about itself that it does not intend: that it has the characteristics of a "pervasively sectarian" institution that is ineligible for public funds. Thus, the civil law issues surrounding the question of employment discrimination that may inhere in complying with *Ex Corde Ecclesiae* can also implicate the broader question of an institution's participation in public aid programs.[50]

Unintended consequences may also attach to contract disputes that may arise between a Catholic university that adopts *Ex Corde Ecclesiae* and its faculty. I have previously noted that the organizations that have traditionally challenged public aid programs that benefit church-affiliated colleges have stayed out of the litigation battles in recent years.[51] However, faculty members who file lawsuits to challenge any disciplinary action taken against them pursuant to *Ex Corde Ecclesiae* can, in addition to their normal breach of contract claims, assert that a university's adoption of the apostolic constitution renders it ineligible for public aid.[52] Even students who sue their institutions for perceived injustices can try to put the institution's eligibility for public funds at issue.[53]

Wholly apart from civil law disputes, Catholic universities that adopt *Ex Corde Ecclesiae* may face other challenges to their actions. The dispute mechanism established by the seventh ordinance issued by the American bishops for implementing the apostolic constitution is available for undifferentiated disputes that may arise between "the competent ecclesiastical authority and a Catholic college or university, or individuals or groups within such institutions." That mechanism would seem to be available to resolve "problems . . .

concerning the Catholic character" of such institutions, as referred to in article 5, section 2 of the general norms of *Ex Corde Ecclesiae*.[54]

Two years ago, a group described by the media as "conservative Catholics" petitioned James Cardinal Hickey, the Archbishop of Washington, DC, to revoke the canonical status of Georgetown University because the institution had agreed to provide funding and other campus privileges to a pro-abortion student organization.[55] Cardinal Hickey declined to intercede in the dispute because, since Georgetown had obtained its canonical status from the Holy See, he had no jurisdiction. However, should such a dispute arise in the future at a Catholic university that adopts the apostolic constitution, those opposing the institution could well invoke the dispute resolution mechanism proposed by the American bishops. While the outcome may be no different, the very existence of a forum for adjudicating such disputes may attract them.[56]

What I have described is just a brief survey of the types of civil law issues that could arise between Catholic universities that adopt *Ex Corde Ecclesiae* and their various constituencies.[57] As American Catholic universities and their governing boards undertake an examination of the apostolic constitution and its ramifications, they should be aware of these potential consequences.

CONCLUSION

The title of this paper suggests that *Ex Corde Ecclesiae* presents American Catholic colleges with both an "opportunity" and a "quandary." The "opportunity" is presented by both the pope's introduction and Part I, which is entitled "Identity and Mission." The pope's introduction and Part I contain insightful observations about the appropriate scope of academic freedom in a Catholic university, the relationship between faith and reason in the university setting, and the service that a Catholic university can provide to the church and to society. These are all issues that have concerned Catholic educators over the years, and the apostolic constitution provides a context and a framework for re-examining those important issues.

The "quandary" is posed by the general norms in Part II of the apostolic constitution and the potential they present for conflict with the civil law rights and obligations of American Catholic colleges and universities. Viewed in isolation, some of the potential conflicts presented by the general norms—such as the ability of a Catholic university and its students to remain eligible for public aid while the institution identifies itself with *Ex Corde Ecclesiae*—are difficult enough. But, when those issues are combined with a university's desire to

embrace the philosophy and educational policy articulated in the pope's introduction and Part I, the task facing American Catholic colleges and universities
is formidable. Those who confront that task should pray that they have been
endowed with sufficient faith and reason to accomplish it.

NOTES

1. Portions of this paper have been adapted by the author from two papers he pre-
viously delivered on the subject of *Ex Corde Ecclesiae*: "American Catholic Universities
and *Ex Corde Ecclesiae*—A Matter of Choice Under Civil Law," in *Catholic Universities in
Church & Society: A Dialogue on "Ex Corde Ecclesiae,"* pp. 176–86 (J.P. Langan, ed.;
Georgetown University Press); *Ex Corde Ecclesiae: The New Apostolic Constitution for
Catholic Universities,* 34 Cath. Lawyer 17 (1991).

2. In 1979, the Holy See issued *Sapientia Christiana,* an apostolic constitution applicable to ecclesiastical universities and faculties that confer academic degrees by authority
of the Holy See. See *Ex Corde Ecclesiae,* general norms art. 1, § 2.

3. The brevity of Canon 812 masks a complexity of canon law issues that continue
to be discussed and debated. For example, see James H. Provost, "A Canonical Commentary on *Ex Corde Ecclesiae,*" in *Catholic Universities in Church and Society: A Dialogue on
"Ex Corde Ecclesiae,"* pp. 105, 121–24 and authorities cited in n. 44 (J.P. Langan, ed.;
Georgetown University Press, 1993).

4. The provisions of section 1 of Canon 810 apply only to faculty members who are
Catholic, because the Code of Canon Law cannot restrict or affect the conduct of persons of other religious faiths. Similarly, the provisions of Canon 812 apply only to those
theologians at Catholic universities who profess the Catholic faith.

5. *Ex Corde Ecclesiae,* general norms, art. 1, § 1 (hereinafter cited as "general norms").

6. In fact, both Canon 810 and Canon 812 are specifically referenced in article 4 of
the general norms in footnotes that quote each of those canonical provisions. See general norms, art. 4, § 1 (n. 49) & § 3 (n. 50). Moreover, in the draft ordinances that a committee of the National Conference of Catholic Bishops issued on May 4, 1993, the committee states: "The[se] ordinances on Catholic higher education for the dioceses of the
United States are complementary to and in harmony with Canons 807–814 of the Code
of Canon Law and the general norms of the Apostolic Constitution *Ex Corde Ecclesiae*
(part II), both of which in their entirety are part of the universal law of the Church."

7. In the United States, this sentence would appear to be applicable only to The
Catholic University of America, which was established by the American bishops with
the approval of the Holy See, and to the several diocesan colleges.

8. In the United States, the "other Catholic universities" would principally be those
that were founded by religious orders and that, to one degree or another, continue to be
sponsored by those orders.

9. The consequences of an institution's legal autonomy with respect to *Ex Corde Ec-
clesiae* are examined in detail in Charles H. Wilson, "American Catholic Universities and
Ex Corde Ecclesiae—A Matter of Choice Under Civil Law," in *Catholic Universities in
Church and Society: A Dialogue on "Ex Corde Ecclesiae,"* pp. 176–86 (J.P. Langan, ed.;
Georgetown University Press, 1993).

10. The categories are: (1) Ecclesiastical faculties/universities; (2) Canonically established (by the Holy See); (3) Established by a diocese, and governed by a board of trustees with some powers reserved to the diocese, or with an independent governing board with no powers reserved to the diocese; (4) Established by a religious community, and governed by a board of trustees with some powers reserved to the religious community, or with an independent governing board and no powers reserved to the religious community; and (5) Established by other ecclesiastical or lay initiative, and governed by a board of trustees with some power reserved to the founding entity, or with a governing board with no powers reserved. Institutions in the fifth category may call themselves Catholic only by the consent of "the competent ecclesiastical authority."

11. The eighth ordinance, which is not discussed in the text of this article, provides: "Governing Boards, in appropriate collaboration with the administration of the college/university, should provide for an adequately staffed campus ministry program and suitable liturgical and sacramental opportunities under the moderation of the local bishop."

12. Such an assumption is necessary for rational analysis. However, the very fact that American Catholic colleges and universities cannot, under civil law, be bound by the apostolic constitution without affirmative action by their governing boards suggests that those boards can ameliorate some of the anticipated civil law repercussions by modifying the basic document. But that exercise can be undertaken only if the full potential ramifications of the apostolic constitution, as issued by the Holy See, are examined under the light of American civil law.

13. That bias is understandable since the public institutions of higher education in the states are creatures of the very legislative bodies that allocate public money to higher education. Since the federal government maintains no system of public universities of its own (the military academies being the exception), federal programs that benefit higher education tend to treat public and independent institutions equitably.

14. U.S. Constitution, Amend. 1: "Congress shall make no law respecting an establishment of religion. . . ."

15. 403 U.S. 672 (1971).

16. 426 U.S. 736 (1976).

17. In *Tilton,* the defendant Catholic colleges prevailed by a five to four vote. In *Roemer,* three justices joined the plurality opinion, two justices concurred and four justices dissented.

18. This characteristic raises questions about one of the general norms of *Ex Corde Ecclesiae.* Article 4, section 4 recognizes that persons other than those who profess the Catholic faith will occupy teaching and administrative positions at a Catholic university. That section states that such persons "are to recognize and respect the distinctive Catholic identity of the university." That provision should create no problems under civil law. The same, however, cannot be said of the second sentence of that section, which provides: "In order not to endanger the Catholic identity of the university or institute of higher studies, the number of non-Catholic teachers should not be allowed to constitute a majority within the institution, which is and must remain Catholic." Universities that wish to maintain the nondiscrimination stance of the *Tilton/Roemer* profile may have difficulty complying with that provision of the general norms. Moreover, as will be discussed below, the Catholic majority requirement of article 4, section 4 can create problems under federal and state anti-discrimination laws.

19. This criterion finds its source in *Tilton* alone. In *Roemer,* the trial court professed to be unable to determine, based on the evidence presented, whether the required theology courses were taught without the purpose of religious indoctrination. The Supreme Court ruled that gap in the trial court's findings was not inconsistent with its conclusion that the defendant Catholic colleges were not pervasively sectarian (426 U.S. at 758 n. 21).

20. 403 U.S. at 687.

21. The term "parochial schools" denotes Catholic schools at the elementary and secondary level. The cases do not draw any distinctions among the various types of Catholic schools, such as parish elementary schools, diocesan high schools, schools at various grade levels sponsored by religious orders, or private Catholic schools with varying affiliations. For purposes of the Supreme Court's constitutional analysis, all Catholic educational institutions below the college level are treated identically.

22. *Mule v. Pittenger,* 421 U.S. 349, 371 (1975).

23. E.g. *School District of Grand Rapids v. Ball,* 473 U.S. 373 (1985); *Aguilar v. Felton,* 463 U.S. 402 (1985); *Meek v. Piltenger,* 421 U.S. 349 (1975); *Committee for Public Education v. Nyquist,* 413 U.S. 756 (1973); *Lemon v. Kurtzman,* 403 U.S. 602 (1971). For a recent contrary decision upholding particularized aid to a disabled student in a Catholic high school, see *Zobrest v. Catalina Foothills School Dist.,* 113 S. Ct. 2462 (June 18, 1993). This decision, standing alone, does not necessarily signal a change for Catholic parochial schools in the course of adjudication that began with the *Lemon* decision in 1971.

24. *Americans United v. Bubb,* 379 F. Supp. 872 (D. Kan 1974).

25. We do know, however, that Justice White, who cast the decisive vote for the federal program challenged in *Tilton,* would not have tolerated certain departures from the *Tilton/Roemer* model. In a separate opinion in which he concurred in the *Tilton* result but dissented from the decision in *Lemon v. Kurtzman, supra,* Justice White stated that he would hold unconstitutional any aid extended to an educational institution that restricted the entry of students on religious (or racial) grounds or that required all students to receive instruction in the tenets of a particular faith. 403 U.S. at 671 n. 2. However, Justice White's retirement from the Supreme Court and the changed makeup of the Court since the *Roemer* case was decided make it impossible to guess how the present Court would treat a church-affiliated college that did not possess the essential *Tilton/Roemer* characteristics.

26. General norms, art. 1, § 1; art. 4, § 3.

27. General norms, art. 1, § 1; art. 4, § 3.

28. This hypothetical is not fanciful. Several years ago, the Catholic University of Puerto Rico fired a member of its English department who had married without obtaining an annulment of her first marriage. For an account of that controversy, see P. Burling & G. Moffatt, "Notes from the Other Side of the Wall: A University Counsel's Reflections on Potential Interactions between the Civil Law and the Apostolic Constitution," in *Catholic Universities in Church and Society: A Dialogue on "Ex Corde Ecclesiae,"* pp. 153, 160–61 (J. P. Langan, ed.; Georgetown University Press, 1993).

29. Indeed, in an old and seldom cited decision, the Supreme Court ruled that the fact that the board of trustees of a Catholic hospital was composed solely of members of the hospital's sponsoring religious order did not transform that hospital into a sectarian institution. *Bradfield v. Roberts,* 175 U.S. 291 (1899). That case involved an Establishment Clause challenge to a congressional appropriation for the construction of an isolation ward at Providence Hospital in the District of Columbia. In dismissing the constitu-

tional claim, the Court said the plaintiff's allegations about the composition of the hospital's governing board "do not change the legal character of the institution or render it on that account a religious or sectarian body. Assuming that the hospital is a private eleemosynary corporation, the fact that its members . . . are members of a monastic order or sisterhood of the Roman Catholic Church, and further the fact that the hospital is conducted under the auspices of said church, are wholly immaterial" to a determination of "the legal character of the hospital" 175 U.S. at 298–99. Several years later, the Supreme Court used that analysis to rule that Georgetown University, the oldest Catholic institution of higher education in the United States, was not a "sectarian" institution. *Speer v. Colbert,* 200 U.S. 130, 143–44 (1906).

30. Those challenging the constitutional eligibility of Catholic colleges and universities to participate in public aid programs would find further ammunition in Pope John Paul II's most recent encyclical, *Veritatis Splendor.* In discussing the duty of the pontiff and his fellow bishops to "be vigilant that the word of God is faithfully taught," the encyclical states: "A particular responsibility is incumbent upon bishops with regard to Catholic institutions. Whether these are agencies for the pastoral care of the family or for social work, or institutions dedicated to teaching or health care, bishops can canonically erect and recognize these structures and delegate certain responsibilities to them. Nevertheless, bishops are never relieved of their own personal obligations. It falls to them, in communion with the Holy See, both to grant the title *Catholic* to church-related schools, universities, health-care facilities and counseling services, and, in the case of a serious failure to live up to that title, to take it away" *Veritatis Splendor,* 116 (Aug. 6, 1993). This passage of the encyclical, it can be argued, is evidence of the intention of the Holy See, through the bishops, to police Catholic universities to assure their adherence to doctrinal orthodoxy.

31. By "traditional litigation," I mean the type of lawsuit that the Catholic colleges and universities faced in *Tilton* and *Roemer.* The nominal plaintiffs in those cases were taxpayers complaining that their tax funds were being expended in violation of constitutional limitations. But the real forces behind the cases were organizations, such as the American Jewish Congress and Americans United for Separation of Church and State, for which opposition to public aid to church-related education is central to their agendas. The interest of such organizations in college-level aid programs waned after the *Roemer* decision

32. See *Witters v. Washington Dep't of Services to the Blind,* 474 U.S. 481 (1986); *Americans United v. Blanton,* 433 F. Supp. 97 (M.D. Tenn.), aff'd, 434 U.S. 803 (1977).

33. *Dickman v. School District No. 62C,* 232 Or. 238, 366 P.2d 533 (1961).

34. *Board of Education v. Allen,* 392 U.S. 236 (1968).

35. *Witters v. Washington Comm'n for the Blind,* 689 P.2d 53 (Wash. 1984).

36. *Witters v. Washington Dep't of Services for the Blind,* 474 U.S. 481 (1986).

37. Nine years earlier, the Supreme Court had acknowledged the constitutional difference between institutional and student aid programs by its summary affirmance of the decision by a three judge district court involving a Tennessee student aid program. See *Americans United v. Blanton,* 433 F. Supp. 97 (M.D. Tenn.), aff'd, 434 U.S. 803 (1977). The *Witters* decision is the first one in which the Court articulated its own reasons for drawing the constitutional distinction.

38. *Witters v. State Comm'n for the Blind,* 771 P.2d 1119 (Wash. 1989).

39. 110 S. Ct. 147 (1989).

40. See *Marjorie Webster Junior College, Inc. v. Middle States Ass'n of Colleges & Secondary Schools, Inc.*, 432 F.2d 650 (D.C. Cir.), cert. den., 400 U.S. 965 (1970).

41. A recent article by a prominent commentator on the religion clauses of the First Amendment about the issue of academic freedom in religious academic communities, including law schools, offers some interesting insights. See D. Laycock, "The Rights of Religious Academic Communities", 20 *J. of Coll. & Univ. Law* 15 (1993). Professor Laycock notes, for example:

> In these debates about academic freedom in religious institutions, I sense from many on the secular side hostility to the very nature of these institutions. Hostility is frequently expressed with respect to the two commitments [of religious institutions], the commitments to religious community and to integration of religion with the whole person. The secular regulator often says something like: 'Of course I respect your religious liberty, but this is not a religious institution. This is a law school.' Such a regulator rejects the claim that there can be such a thing as a religious law school, and therefore implicitly rejects the view that religion can be integrated with the rest of one's life in a communal enterprise" *Id.* at 26.

42. In its analysis of the terms of the contractual relationship between a university and its faculty, an American court will examine the customs and practices of the university. See, e.g., *Howard University v. Best*, 484 A.2d 958, 967 (D.C. 1984).

43. See, e.g., *McConnell v. Howard University*, 818 F.2d 58, 62–63 (D.C. Cir. 1987). Similarly, the terms of a university's contract with its students can be found in any student handbook and comparable documents, as well as pertinent sections of the institution's catalog or bulletin.

44. One commentary notes that some issues that might arguably fall within the "probity of life" criteria—such as a married Catholic faculty member having an affair with a student—could be dealt with through existing prohibitions against "conduct unbecoming" or "acts of moral turpitude." P. Burling & G. Moffatt, *supra* note 28, at pp. 159–62. But other conduct arguably proscribed by Canon 810, such as divorce and remarriage by a Catholic faculty member or the marriage of a priest faculty member without a dispensation from his vows, cannot be so easily finessed.

45. 42 U.S.C. § 2000e-2.

46. 42 U.S.C. § 2000e-1.

47. 42 U.S.C. § 2000c-2(c)(2).

48. 42 U.S.C. § 2000e-2(e)(1).

49. The Court in *Roemer* was evaluating whether the colleges were too religious in their orientation to receive public funds. It was not ruling on a Title VII challenge to the institutions' hiring policies, and it is not possible to read into its ruling any implication of how it would treat such challenge. But there is at least an arguable basis for contending that the religious affiliation of a person hired for a theology department is a bona fide occupational qualification within the meaning of the Title VII exemption for that purpose.

50. It is fair to ask whether maintaining a faculty a majority of whose members are Catholic is essential to maintaining the Catholic "character" of a university. John T. Noonan, Jr., makes a persuasive case that none of the "special features" of a religiously committed college "is possible without a community of believers" and that "[a] Catholic law school does not exist unless a substantial number of the faculty are in fact committed Catholics." J. T. Noonan, Jr., "Religious Law Schools and the First Amendment," 20 *J. of*

Coll. & Univ. Law 43, 45 (1993). But it does not necessarily follow that a majority of the faculty is a necessary critical mass to have a community of believers that will preserve an institution's religious commitment. Even Judge Noonan does not advocate that active membership in the sponsoring church be a condition of continued employment or that the sanction of losing one's job be the way to maintain an institution's Catholic identity, *Id.* Depending on circumstances, attraction and affinity may be more effective than discriminatory hiring policies in sustaining a university's Catholic character.

51. See note 3D, *supra*, and accompanying text.

52. For a case in which a faculty member unhappy with his contract challenged a Catholic university's eligibility for public aid, see *Broderick v. Catholic University*, 530 F.2d 1035 (D.C. Cir. 1976).

53. Such a claim was made by the students who sued Georgetown University under the District of Columbia's Human Rights Act for its refusal to grant official university recognition to two student gay groups. *Gay Rights Coalition v. Georgetown University*, 536 A.2d 1 (1987). The students claimed that, because the university invoked the Free Exercise Clause of the First Amendment to defend its right not to recognize the gay organizations, the university was necessarily too religious to qualify for the receipt of public funds. The court did not give serious consideration to that claim, but the claim did have to be defended.

54. Reports of disputes at two different Catholic universities that appeared two weeks apart in one publication involved alumni dissatisfaction with issues relating to the "Catholic character" of those institutions. One report involved a religious studies professor at the University of Detroit Mercy who published a book contending that Mary, the mother of Jesus, was not a virgin but was a woman who had been raped. The report said that complaints about the professor and her book had been directed to Detroit Archbishop Adam J. Maida and that some alumni had canceled their contributions to the university. "A Scholar's Conclusion About Mary Stirs Ire," *Chronicle of Higher Education*, October 6, 1993, p. B5. The University of St. Thomas in St. Paul, MN, attracted attention when it included in a library display a poster of Margaret Sanger, an advocate of birth control. An alumnus complained that such a poster was inappropriate at a Catholic institution, and a local bishop asked that it be removed. The university's president declined to remove the poster. "Catholic University Defends Poster of Sanger," *Chronicle of Higher Education*, October 20, 1993, p. A4. One wonders if alumni unhappy with such events could invoke the procedures in the seventh ordinance and have a formal adjudication of their complaints.

55. An account of this incident can be found in P. Burling & G. Moffat, *supra* note 28, at p. 165.

56. One is reminded of the line from the movie, *The Field of Dreams*: "Build it and they will come."

57. For a more detailed examination of the issues that might arise with respect to faculty members and students, see P. Burling & G. Moffatt, *supra* note 28.

14 | Letter to Bishop John Leibrecht from Author Hughes, Chair of ACCU, with the Synthesis of Five Regional Meetings Held by ACCU

November 10, 1993

In response to your invitation to comment on the draft of the proposed ordinances for the implementation of *Ex Corde Ecclesiae* in the United States, the Association of Catholic Colleges and Universities organized five regional meetings where representatives of our member institutions could discuss together their reactions to the draft. For your information, I am enclosing a summary of the principal concerns that emerged at these meetings.

Many participants in our discussions, particularly those who had been delegates to the April 1989 meeting in the Vatican, were puzzled and disappointed by the lack of any specific reference to the particular history and circumstances of Catholic higher education in the United States. It was their understanding and ours that the decision in 1989 to leave the development of specific applications to regional conferences of bishops grew out of an appreciation of the different cultural and legal environments in which Catholic colleges and universities existed around the world. One universal document could not address these different situations successfully. We expected, then, that these ordinances would address the special circumstances, legal and academic, of higher education in the United States. Instead, the introduction and the eight ordinances remain very abstract and could apply to Catholic institutions in any part of the world.

The introduction to the ordinances, for example, would seem an appropriate place to briefly describe the changes in governance that have taken place over the last 25 years in our American Catholic colleges and universities.

From *Origins* 23, no. 35 (February 17, 1994): 610–614.

Typically, our institutions are governed by independent, self-perpetuating boards of trustees, where the majority of the members of the board are lay people. This development has brought many benefits, including eligibility for public funding and status with accreditation associations.

At the same time, we are aware of the history of many Protestant colleges and universities in the United States that began in the 19th century as church-sponsored institutions, then moved through a period of laicization and independence from denominational control to become thoroughly secularized institutions today. While we recognize the weight of this historical precedent and are not complacent about the dangers confronting Catholic colleges and universities, we are committed, however, to the Catholic identity of our institutions and do not believe that our present mode of governance means an erosion of that identity.

For this reason, we welcomed the publication of *Ex Corde Ecclesiae* and, in particular, its assertion that "even when they do not enter directly into the internal governance of the university, bishops should be seen not as external agents but as participants in the life of the Catholic university" (No. 28). We understood this to mean that, in a spirit of ecclesial communion rather than juridical control, our colleges and universities should work closely with our bishops in promoting the service to the church that Catholic institutions of higher education can provide. For Catholic universities in the United States, where typically bishops do not enter into the internal governance of the institution, the challenge of *Ex Corde Ecclesiae* is to find ways of strengthening our relationship with the church without compromising a mode of governance that has assured the institutional autonomy and academic freedom of our institutions.

From a pragmatic standpoint, the mode of governance that has become typical of Catholic colleges and universities in the United States is, in our judgment, far more congenial to the legal and cultural environment in which we live and work. The results have been beneficial not only for our institutions but also for the church. If local bishops were to intervene in the hiring or firing of faculty, for example, they would become legally vulnerable to the charges of discrimination that are a common occurrence in our very litigious society. There can be, and often is, very lively and mutually beneficial communication between our universities and their local bishops without any compromise to the independence of the institution. We believe the ordinances should be designed to encourage and expand such relationships.

It is our consensus, then, that in their present form the proposed ordinances do not offer constructive assistance in dealing with the real problems we confront and, instead, could create new problems for our institutions and our bishops.

We appreciate the invitation to offer our candid comments on the present draft, and we look forward to working with you in the development of regional norms for *Ex Corde Ecclesiae* that would better reflect the distinctive history and challenges of Catholic colleges and universities in the United States.

SYNTHESIS OF FIVE REGIONAL MEETINGS
(prepared by Benito Lopez, Jr., Executive Director, ACCU)

During September 1993, the Association of Catholic Colleges and Universities sponsored five regional meetings on an introductory statement and eight ordinances circulated for comment and proposed by the bishop members of the National Conference of Catholic Bishops' committee for the review and implementation of *Ex Corde Ecclesiae* in the United States as the instruments for the regional application in the United States of the general norms in Part 2 of the apostolic constitution. The presidents of all American Catholic colleges and universities were invited to attend one of these meetings and to bring others, including bishops, who might be expected to contribute to the conversation. The purpose of each meeting was to afford each participant the opportunity to inform his/her thinking with the views expressed by others.

A total of four bishops and 178 representatives from 103 institutions attended these conferences. The institutional participants, who accurately reflected the broad range of Catholic colleges and universities in the United States, were predominantly presidents, but included as well theologians, other faculty and administrators.

The conferences were held at Fordham University, N.Y., on the 27th of September, Neumann College, Pa., on the 30th, St. Louis University, Mo., on the 21st, University of San Francisco, Calif., on the 17th, and University of St. Thomas, Minn., on the 16th. ACCU is grateful for the generosity and hospitality extended by the presidents of these host institutions.

At each of the five conferences the text of *Ex Corde Ecclesiae* was highly praised as a teaching document; in fact, it was suggested that Catholic colleges and universities should "make their own" the vision, goals, aspirations and challenges articulated in the text of *Ex Corde Ecclesiae* and measure their Catholic identity by their continuous striving to fulfill its promise. (References in this synthesis to the text of *Ex Corde Ecclesiae* are to Part 1.)

On the other hand, the reaction to the introductory statement and ordinances proposed by the bishop-members was almost invariably negative, due largely to the failure in both to acknowledge and accommodate the unique characteristics of the environment in which the American Catholic colleges and universities operate.

A synthesis of the comments made in the five regional meetings follows. It has been compiled from the notes produced by one or more appointed recorders at each meeting and the recollections of the executive director of ACCU, who participated in all five conferences. To the extent possible, they have been merged in the cause of brevity without knowingly distorting any particular point of view.

General Comments

The proposed ordinances fail to fill the expectations arising out of the Rome 1989 consultation.

While some of the problems with the texts of the proposed ordinances can be traced to the language of the general norms in Part 2 of *Ex Corde Ecclesiae,* the introductory statement and ordinances circulated by the bishop members seem to ignore the strong sense of the Rome 1989 consultation that the interpretation of the general norms would be left to the discretion of the regional bishops' conferences. The decision to leave more specific regulations to the determination of the regional bishops' conferences was in response to the belief of the delegates to the International Conference on Higher Education that the Vatican could not legislate for institutions that existed in so many different cultural and legal environments. Against this background, it is disappointing that neither the introductory statement nor the proposed ordinances issued by the bishop members make reference to the distinctive circumstances in the United States that have affected the development of American Catholic colleges and universities.

Relationships that allow the hierarchy to intervene in the internal affairs of Catholic colleges and universities are incompatible with the traditions of American higher education.

Ex Corde Ecclesiae provides for many constructive contributions on the part of bishops. However, one should not misread the sentence in Part 1, Paragraph 28, of that document: "Even when they do not enter directly into the internal governance of the university, bishops 'should be seen not as external agents but as participants in the life of the Catholic university.'" In the United States, bishops do not typically enter into the governance of Catholic colleges and universities.

There is widespread concern about how the ordinances will be applied to the colleges and universities, how application of the ordinances will change the relationships of the Catholic colleges and universities with their bishops and whether these new relationships can be accommodated without jeopardizing the standing of these institutions in the higher education community in the United States, their eligibility for accreditation, their compliance with federal and state laws and regulations, and their continuing eligibility and that of their students for desperately needed federal and state funding.

There is fear for the effect of the ordinances on the interior life of the institutions. Will they be at risk legally for actions initiated by bishops? Will their public images be tarnished by external intrusion on institutional autonomy and governance? Will recruitment of faculty be affected? Will they lose their best Catholic theology and philosophy faculty to other institutions? Will they be forced by circumstances to forgo their recognition as Catholic in order to be truly both university and Catholic? Will there be a litmus test for Catholic colleges and universities? Will the test differ from diocese to diocese? Will these institutions be competing with each other for the title *Catholic?* If they lose their autonomy, can they continue to be of service to the church? Continue to be places where the church does its thinking? Can we not reshape the conversation in terms of *communio:* working toward common objectives rather than defining control?

Many have worked hard to cause *Ex Corde Ecclesiae* to be written in such a way that it would be acceptable to those involved in Catholic higher education in the United States. The proposed ordinances seem to undermine the progress made in the apostolic constitution. There is doubt that the ordinances might go through an evolutionary process much as *Ex Corde Ecclesiae* did.

Concern for orthodoxy must be addressed without diminishing the hard-won respect for American Catholic colleges and universities.

Application of the ordinances could carry the American Catholic colleges and universities back to the 1950s, when our institutions were more homogeneous and operated outside the mainstream of higher education in the United States.

In the view of the leadership of the American Catholic colleges and universities, the proposed ordinances do not address the problems confronting their institutions and might instead create new ones. These administrators can relate to the text of *Ex Corde Ecclesiae,* but, for them, the proposed ordinances have an air of unreality about them.

The proposed ordinances are overreaching and lack clarity.

In some instances the proposed ordinances appear to legislate beyond the stated intentions of the general norms, as in Ordinances 1, 2 and 6. Generally, the ordinances are seen as unclear or vague. One expects to find these characteristics in a document developed by a committee representing divergent views. Indeed, precision might raise more serious issues. However, many believe there must be enough clarity to facilitate fair and consistent implementation throughout the country.

Where do we go from here?

It is hard to identify a response to the introductory statement and ordinances proposed by the bishop members. Some believe the process should begin again. Others hold that such an action would not be helpful since the process is flawed; the implementation committee can meet only infrequently and lacks geographical distribution, particularly among the bishop members.

A revision of the introductory statement to address the specific circumstances that define the situation of Catholic colleges and universities in the United States would be helpful, particularly if it reflected the findings of Martin J. Stamm's study of the governance structures of American Catholic colleges and universities as they have evolved over the last 25 years into predominantly lay boards led by lay chairpersons. (The study was published in the summer 1993 issue of Current Issues in Catholic Higher Education.)

The issues will be resolved by dialogue and inspiration, not laws.

There is a critical need for genuine dialogue between the American hierarchy and those who lead the Catholic colleges and universities, free of preconceptions and characterized by trust. Such an atmosphere could lead to creative solutions that respect both the necessary autonomy of American Catholic colleges and universities in the context of the traditions of American higher education and the obligations of NCCB to respond to its own mandate from the Congregation for Catholic Education and the Holy See. Catholic colleges and universities do wish to be authentically Catholic, to serve the church and its mission. These institutions cannot do so if they are constrained to live in confrontation with their local bishops or under threat of being denied the title *Catholic*.

The dialogue must engage the theologians.

The partners to this dialogue must meaningfully engage the theological community. Many members of this scholarly and dedicated group consider (for better or worse) that they, their work and their careers, dedicated to the service of the church and their college or university, are vulnerable and jeopardized by the proposed ordinances.

The Vatican must be persuaded to accommodate to the legal and cultural norms of American higher education.

NCCB, individual bishops and American Catholic institutions must continue to make repeated interventions with the Congregation for Catholic Education and the Holy See to stress the consequences of the application of the general norms of *Ex Corde Ecclesiae* and the proposed ordinances in the United States, stressing the potential for damage to the effectiveness of the American Catholic colleges and universities, both as university and as Catholic, and the potential liabilities to which such application could expose the bishops and the institutions under U.S. law.

Specific Comments

Introductory Statement

The language in the first paragraph of the introductory statement (paraphrasing the last clause of the first paragraph of the introduction to *Ex Corde Ecclesiae*) that contrasts the order of faith as "the certainty of already knowing the fount of truth" with reason as "the search for truth" could appear to be antithetical to the intellectual life of a college or university. The notion of theology as faith seeking understanding is a recurrent theme in the Catholic tradition and suggests a very different relationship between faith and reason. The language in this paragraph needs to be revised.

Further, the statement fails to stress teaching as the central mission of most American Catholic colleges and universities.

Ordinance 1

There is general discontent about the language of this ordinance. Reasons include the parity it suggests between the roles of those responsible for the internal governance of the institution and the bishop as well as the narrow relationship with the church that it describes, a relationship that in reality touches the whole church in the largest meaning of that word. The bishop's role has traditionally been seen as benign surveillance, not as partnership with the governing body.

In this connection, the advisability of having the bishop as a trustee was raised. In fact, since no individual member of an independent board of trustees has any authority to act for the board or the institution, the bishop's presence on the board would not add to his individual authority. Specifically, he would have no authority as a trustee to enforce any ordinance without the approval of the board of trustees acting as a body.

The suggestion was made to replace this ordinance with one that would identify the Catholic nature of the institution by its continuous striving to fulfill the promise of *Ex Corde Ecclesiae*.

Ordinance 2

The requirement that each institution identify itself in one of the categories listed in Appendix A to the ordinances is questioned. (The list appears to respond to the first of a number of directives issued by the Congregation for Catholic Education "to assist the episcopal conferences and other assemblies of Catholic hierarchy in drawing up the concrete applications (ordinances) of the general norms of the apostolic constitution *Ex Corde Ecclesiae,* in accordance with General Norms, Article 1, Section 2 of that constitution." However, the requirements articulated in the first directive are an extension, rather than an interpretation, of the general norms.)

The list seems far more restrictive than necessary to accommodate either the division in Article 1, No. 3 of the norms of *Ex Corde Ecclesiae* between those institutions that were ecclesiastically founded and all others, or the division in Article 2, No. 2 of the norms to determine whether an institution "is linked with the church . . . by a formal, constitutive and statutory bond [presumably a bond reflected in its institutional statutes], or by reason of an institutional commitment made by those responsible for it." It was recalled that during the Rome consultation in 1989 this formulation, in the minds of many, resolved a troublesome issue by providing room for Catholic institutions that would be independent of ecclesiastical jurisdiction in the formal sense and yet be truly Catholic. The appendix to the ordinances, however, defines five categories of Catholic colleges and universities, differentiates those in each category further by relationship to authority, and requires that those in the fifth category seek the consent of the competent ecclesiastical authority in order to call themselves Catholic. Such detail is inconsistent with the intention behind these broad divisions, particularly since the fifth category is defined only in Article 3 of the general norms, which applies only to Catholic colleges and universities founded in the future.

There is a strong consensus that this ordinance was unnecessary and troublesome and should be eliminated. A more positive set of ordinances would encourage greater cooperation and communication between bishops and the Catholic colleges and universities.

Ordinance 3

Unease was expressed concerning the use of the periodic evaluation. The regional accrediting agencies in the United States jealously protect their member institutions from external interference and constraints; even the semblance of a threat to academic freedom or institutional autonomy would raise questions regarding accreditation. Imprecise language, e.g., "congruence" was also cited as a problem. Internalizing the process as a part of an already existing self-evaluation program, the results of which are routinely shared with multiple constituencies, including the local bishop, might be a solution.

Ordinance 4

This ordinance links the institutional authorities of a Catholic college or university and its diocesan bishop with "a common desire" to maintain the Catholic identity of the college or university without articulating the essential elements of that identity or a process for exploring it. While the ordinance recognizes the differentiated roles of the institutional authorities and the local bishop, it is unclear how these complementary roles intersect.

The meaning of "the teaching of Catholic theological disciplines" was suggested to be moot because current pedagogy exposes students early to the methodology appropriate to the theological disciplines.

Ordinances 5 and 6

Representatives of almost all the colleges and universities had great difficulty with these ordinances and the one that follows them. Problems include imprecise language (e.g. the first sentence of Ordinance 6 indicates the bishop is not always the competent ecclesiastical authority while the second indicates that the bishop is always responsible for conferring the mandate), lack of protection from inconsistent application, portability of the mandate and incompatibility of the mandate with the cultural and legal framework of American higher education. The hortatory, encouraging tone of *Ex Corde Ecclesiae* is jolted by this juridical intervention into the academic community and its effect on the ability of the American Catholic colleges and universities to carry out the mission assigned to them in the apostolic constitution. The proposed ordinances, if enforced, will do more to secularize these institutions than any of the challenges they are now taking bold steps to confront. Enforcement will once again marginalize the church in American culture.

Questions raised include the following: Who are included in the term *professor?* What studies are included in the "theological disciplines"? What does *suitability* mean? Is the "competent ecclesiastical authority" necessarily competent to judge the competence of a theologian to teach? What happens if the theologian does not seek the mandate? If the mandate is denied or later withdrawn? Can due process be assured when the documents and procedures suggested in Ordinance 7 are not binding on the competent ecclesiastical authority? Does the competent ecclesiastical authority risk legal liability when he intervenes in the affairs of an American Catholic college or university governed by an independent board of trustees? What would be the legal, accreditational and governmental funding consequences to the subject college or university and (if accreditation is threatened) its students?

Representatives of smaller Catholic institutions expressed the fear that these ordinances could pose particular difficulties for these institutions where the local bishop might be more likely to intervene in the affairs of the institution. (Recent incidents indicate that fear may be well-founded.) The requirement of the mandate results in other negative consequences. For example, much as the fair-employment-practices laws have made it difficult for employers to terminate or to decide not to promote protected employees for poor performance in borderline circumstances, theologians who choose not to seek the mandate and later are legally dismissed or denied tenure for unsatisfactory performance may sue for damages by alleging the action taken was really for failure to seek the mandate.

It was observed at one meeting that it is unlikely that most bishops would want to deal with the mandate. Irony was seen in the use of a tactic intended to ensure authenticity in the teaching of Catholic theological disciplines in an environment free of governmental intervention should now be used to impose limits on Catholic theological exploration in an environment in which there exists no such governmental threat and in which Catholic theology has flourished. A likely result could be to accelerate the move, already in progress, of Catholic theologians to other independent and state-supported colleges and universities, some of which have strong theology departments.

The possibility that the bishop could delegate the authority to grant the mandate to someone in the institution was discussed. However, the effect would be to have someone on the campus acting in the name of the bishop and therefore answerable to him, in effect representing an external authority on the campus.

Great concern was voiced about the uncertainty surrounding the way in which an individual bishop will interpret the text. Few take refuge in the absence of a requirement that the mandate be a condition of employment.

Concern was expressed for the purpose of these ordinances: Is it to ensure authentic Catholic teaching? To gain control over lay theologians? To control dissent on campus? There are extensive legal protections under civil law for the rights of individuals in these situations. The bishops must be made aware of the legal consequences of their actions to the institution and possibly to the bishops themselves.

The principle of subsidiarity, regularly praised in the church, may yield a more promising result. The relevant issues are appropriate responsibilities of the governing structure of the institution and the local bishop. These two interested parties must strive for a complementary relationship. Solution of issues as they arise should grow from the supportive and trusting relationships the two parties attain and the sensitivity they share for the boundaries within which solutions must be found.

Ordinance 7

There is widespread concern that the procedures outlined would not operate to protect the rights of persons in the church, the autonomy of the academic institutions and the responsibilities of church authorities. In this connection it was noted that the documents and procedures referred to are not binding on the bishops. Moreover, because these processes are not developed in accordance with the internal governance requirements of the institutions, they are flawed. In any event, they would have to meet the due process standards of American law.

Ordinance 8

While governing boards are ultimately responsible for the governance of their institutions, they do not engage directly in the operations of these institutions. It is therefore unusual to assign more than oversight responsibility to these boards. The development of the campus ministry and liturgical opportunities rests with the institutional administration, subject to the board's oversight. The bishop has a legitimate interest in the appropriateness of the liturgical and sacramental opportunities made available to the campus community. However, the local bishop customarily does not exercise control over the very wide variety of programs offered through the campus ministry apostolate.

Conclusion

ACCU and the American Catholic colleges are anxious to pursue solutions to the problems articulated herein. These institutions have the capacity and the will to make a necessary and valuable contribution to the life of the church and its interaction with the secular culture. We are confident that in an atmosphere of mutual trust and understanding the Holy Spirit will guide us in our search for relationships that inspire us to work together in the service of the church rather than those that separate us and lead to confrontation.

15 | Address of Bishop John Leibrecht, Annual ACCU Meeting

February 2, 1994

The bishops of the *Ex Corde Ecclesiae* implementation committee are deeply grateful for the invitation to spend time with you today in dialogue. We express our thanks to Dr. Author Hughes and Ben Lopez for sending us the summary report of the five regional meetings which the Association of Catholic Colleges and Universities sponsored last September on the first draft of *Ex Corde Ecclesiae* ordinances for the United States.

My purpose here is to offer a brief background from the perspective of the bishops' committee for our dialogue today. I will submit several assumptions which I think most U.S. bishops have in approaching the implementation of *Ex Corde Ecclesiae.* Then I will list several guidelines which the committee employed in developing ordinances.

First, the assumptions of most bishops:

1. The bishops of the United States recognize and truly appreciate the great asset which Catholic colleges and universities are to the church and this nation. The lives both of the church and our country are significantly enriched by Catholic colleges and universities.
2. Bishops realize that the funding and maintaining of most Catholic colleges and universities are the result of the foresight and labors of many religious communities of men and women as well as talented and dedicated lay people. Acknowledging the proud history of Catholic colleges and universities in the United States, the bishops want to look to the future with you so that a clear Catholic identity is maintained within U.S. higher education. With you, bishops know that forces toward secularization are real and not imagined.

From *Origins* 23, no. 35 (February 17, 1994): 605, 607–608.

They know the history in this country of religiously sponsored institutions of higher education which evolved into being fully secularized. The impactful presence of Catholic colleges and universities, as Catholic, bishops see as a real need for the future.

3. U.S. bishops believe that *Ex Corde Ecclesiae* offers a vision to Catholic higher education which is generally welcomed by Catholic colleges and universities in the United States.

4. The bishops trust the vision of *Ex Corde Ecclesiae* for Catholic higher education and know that they have the responsibility of implementing its norms given in Part 2 of the document. Those norms call for "ordinances," and the bishops responsible for developing them desire a process of consultation with appropriate parties.

5. The basic relationship of bishops to Catholic colleges and universities should remain informal and dialogic in nature. No ordinances will replace the good that can be accomplished by ongoing personal relationships between the local bishop and Catholic colleges and universities.

6. *Ex Corde Ecclesiae* clearly states that the bishop is not related to the internal governance of the Catholic college or university. Rather, *Ex Corde Ecclesiae* describes bishops as "participants in the life of the Catholic college or university" (No. 28). The first draft of Ordinances 1 and 4, for instance, although their wording clearly needs improvement, intends to recognize the proper roles of governing bodies, institutional authorities and the diocesan bishop. That same thing is true for Ordinance 8, which addresses the need for campus ministry programs and sacramental life.

7. The relationship of the bishop to the Catholic college or university is one of communion and not control. Ordinances, therefore, are in service to communion. Communion, we know, does not simply happen but needs some structure. Proper structure can enhance communion. That is the elusive but desired goal of ordinances. The fact that ordinances have a legal nature need not be seen in a negative light.

8. The bishops, knowing that Catholic colleges and universities have relationships with agencies such as accrediting associations, the American Association of University Professors and athletic associations such as the National Collegiate Athletic Association, assume that their relationship can also be present without interference in the internal governance of the institution.

9. The ordinances developed for the United States must respect an educational environment which values academic freedom and institutional autonomy.

10. The diocesan bishop has a special role in guarding authentic Catholic teaching and practice. Every Catholic, individually and institutionally, also has responsibilities toward authentic Catholic teaching and practice, but the role of the bishop is unique. He is obliged to fulfill that role in a variety of ways within all Catholic life.

11. Internal procedures in Catholic higher education for addressing unauthentic Catholic teaching and practice are too little known; some bishops question if such procedures are effective.

12. The bishops assume that the mandate, requested by *Ex Corde Ecclesiae* and Canon 812, is the most difficult matter to implement. Ordinances 5 and 6 pertain to the mandate and, to no one's surprise, have received the most comment and the severest criticism. The bishops' implementation committee struggled to find a way of implementing the mandate while respecting academic freedom and institutional autonomy. Inadequately worded and with many unresolved questions, Ordinances 5 and 6 were written with certain provisions in mind: (a) the mandate is not a part of the hiring or firing procedure because that process belongs to the institution; (b) the mandate is not addressed directly to the institution but to the individual professor; (c) the mandate creates a direct relationship between the bishop and a professor. The bishops of the implementation committee know they need much assistance on this topic of the mandate.

Now I would like to offer a few guidelines which the bishops of the implementation committee are keeping in mind during their work:

1. The number of ordinances should be limited. While addressing the need for implementation responsibly, the bishops have taken fewer rather than many ordinances as their goal.

2. The committee recognizes that the ordinances must eventually prove acceptable to the full body of U.S. bishops and to Catholic colleges and universities in the United States. Between and within those groupings, differences of opinion exist. The committee also recognizes that the ordinances must be acceptable to the Holy See.

3. Local implementation is preferred to national, so that the great diversities among dioceses and institutions of Catholic higher education might be respected. The regional meetings of ACCU criticized the first draft of ordinances for being unclear and vague. That seems a legitimate critique. The intention of the committee, however, is to have ordinances general enough

to allow for local application. For instance, Ordinance 3 calls for an internal review of the principles of *Ex Corde Ecclesiae* at least every 10 years in each Catholic college and university. Some institutions may want such a review as part of the self-study done by accrediting associations; some institutions may think other times are better. Another example is seen in Ordinance 7, which deals with processes to resolve disputes. Rightly or wrongly, the committee is of the mind that such processes should be locally drafted in order to fit local circumstances and proposed several resources which may or may not be used.

4. The committee believes that after experience with the promulgated ordinances a review should take place and the ordinances amended as needed.

The question before us then is, What are the proper relationships between U.S. Catholic colleges and universities and diocesan bishops? The ACCU paper, summarizing the first critique of the proposed ordinances, concluded by saying that Catholic colleges and universities want to participate in that "search for relationships." I hope our time together today helps in that search.

16 | Report on the Implementation Committee's Work

April 11, 1994

TO: Archbishops and Bishops
             Presidents of Catholic Colleges and Universities
             Religious Communities of Men and Women
             Catholic Learned Societies
FROM: Most Reverend John J. Leibrecht
DATE: April 11, 1994

I write to report on the outcome of the most recent meeting of the *Ex corde Ecclesiae* Implementation Committee. Over 200 responses from bishops, presidents, learned societies and other groups were received as a result of the Committee's request for comments made in a May 4, 1993 letter. Many thanks to all respondents! Much of the Committee's time at its March meeting was devoted to summarizing and analyzing the suggestions and critiques we received.

In view of what the Committee received and heard, the following steps will be taken:

(1) Time will be given to additional dialogue among bishops, presidents and others involved in U.S. Catholic higher education.
(2) As the Committee continues to respond to its charge of developing ordinances for submission to the full assembly of U.S. bishops, it will invite additional experts to assist in its work.
(3) Private funding is being sought for a full-time project director to work with the Implementation Committee.

From the author's files.

The Committee will have its next meeting after its effort to engage a project director has been resolved. That position, if realized, will have many responsibilities toward dialogue in order to promote mutual understanding in implementing *Ex corde Ecclesiae.*

Further information will be sent to you as it becomes available.

Again, many thanks to all who are participating in addressing the important matters before us.

17 | The Church's Presence in the University and in University Culture

Vatican Congregation for Catholic Education and the Pontifical Councils for the Laity and for Culture

May 22, 1994

FOREWORD

NATURE, AIM AND INTENDED READERS

The university and, more widely, university culture, constitute a reality of decisive importance. In this field vital questions are at stake and profound cultural changes present new challenges. The church owes it to herself to advert to them in her mission of proclaiming the Gospel.[1]

In the course of their *ad limina* visits, many bishops have expressed their desire to find help in meeting new and serious problems that are rapidly emerging and for which those responsible are at times unprepared. The usual pastoral methods often prove ineffective and even the most zealous are discouraged. Various dioceses and bishops' conferences have undertaken pastoral reflection and action that already provide elements of response. Religious communities and apostolic movements are also approaching with fresh generosity the new challenges of university pastoral action.

For a sharing of these initiatives and a global assessment of the situation, the Congregation for Catholic Education, the Pontifical Council for the Laity and the Pontifical Council for Culture undertook a new consultation of the bishops' conferences, of religious institutes and of various ecclesial bodies and movements. A first synthesis of the replies was presented on Oct. 28, 1987, to the Synod of Bishops on the vocation and mission of the laity in the church

From *Origins* 24, no. 5 (June 16, 1994): 74–80.

and in the world.[2] This documentation has been enriched in many meetings and also by the reactions of the institutions concerned to the published text and by the publication of studies and research on the action of Christians in the university world.

It has been possible in this way to ascertain a number of facts, to formulate questions in precise terms and to indicate certain guidelines on the basis of the apostolic experience of people involved in the university world.

The present document, drawing attention to the more significant questions and initiatives, is intended as an instrument for study and action at the service of the particular churches. It is addressed in the first place to the episcopal conference and, in a special way, to bishops who are directly concerned due to the presence in their dioceses of universities or institutes of higher studies. But the facts and the orientations presented here are intended, at the same time, for all those who take part in university pastoral action under the guidance of the bishops: priests, lay people, religious institutes, ecclesial movements. The suggestions made for the new evangelization are meant to inspire deeper reflection on the part of all those concerned and a renewal of pastoral action.

An Urgent Need

The university was in its earliest stages one of the most significant expressions of the church's pastoral concern. Its birth was linked to the development of the schools set up in the Middle Ages by the bishops of the great episcopal sees. If the vicissitudes of history have led the *universitas magistrorum et scholarium* to become more and more autonomous, the church nevertheless continues to nourish the same concern that gave rise to this institution.[3] The church's presence in the university is not, in fact, a task that would remain, as it were, external to the mission of proclaiming the faith. "The synthesis between culture and faith is a necessity not only for culture, but also for faith. . . . A faith that does not become culture is a faith that is not fully received, not entirely thought through and faithfully lived."[4] The faith that the church proclaims is a *fides quaerens intellectum* that must penetrate the human intellect and heart, that must be thought out in order to be lived. The church's presence cannot, therefore, be limited to a cultural and scientific contribution: It must offer a real opportunity for encountering Christ.

Concretely, the church's presence and mission in the university culture take varied and complementary forms. In the first place, there is the task of giving support to the Catholics engaged in the life of the university as professors, students, researchers or nonacademic staff. The church is concerned with proclaiming the Gospel to all those within the university to whom it is still unknown and who are ready to receive it in freedom. Her action also takes the form of sincere dialogue and loyal cooperation with all members of the university community who are concerned for the cultural development of the human person and of all the people involved.

This approach requires pastoral workers to see the university as a specific environment with its own problems. The success of their commitment depends, indeed, to a great extent on the relations they establish with this milieu and which at times are still only embryonic. University pastoral action often remains in fact on the fringe of ordinary pastoral action. The whole Christian community must therefore become aware of its pastoral and missionary responsibility in relation to the university milieu.

I. SITUATION OF THE UNIVERSITY

In the space of half a century, the university as institution has undergone a notable transformation. One cannot generalize, however, about the features of this transformation in all countries. Such changes do not apply equally to all the academic centers of a single region. Each university is marked by its historical, cultural, social, economic and political context. This great variety calls for careful adaptation in the forms that the church's presence will take.

1. In many countries, especially in certain developed countries, after the confrontation of the years '68–'70 and the institutional crisis that threw the university into a certain confusion, several trends, both positive and negative, emerged. Clashes and crises, and in particular the collapse of ideologies and utopias that were once dominant, have left deep marks. The university that was formerly reserved for the privileged has become wide open for the vast public, both in its initial teaching and through continuing education.

This is a significant feature of the democratization of social and cultural life. In many cases, students have come in such numbers that the infrastructures, the services and even traditional teaching methods can prove inadequate. In certain cultural contexts, moreover, various factors have brought about crucial changes in the position of the teaching staff. Between isolation and collegiality, diverse professional commitments and family life, they see a decline in their academic and social status, their authority and their security.

The concrete situation of the students is also a cause of anxiety. Structures are often lacking for welcoming and supporting them and for community life. Many of them, transplanted far from their family to a strange town, suffer from loneliness. In addition, contact with the professors is often limited, and the students find themselves without guidance in face of problems of adjustment which they are unable to solve. At times they have to enter an environment marked by the influence of attitudes of a sociopolitical kind and by the claim to unlimited freedom in all fields of research and scientific experimentation.

Finally, in some cases the young university students are confronted with the prevalence of a relativistic liberalism, a scientific positivism and a certain pessimism caused by the insecurity of professional prospects in the current economic crisis.

2. Elsewhere the university has lost part of its prestige. The proliferation of universities and their specialization have created a situation of great disparity. Some enjoy unquestioned prestige, while others are barely able to offer a mediocre standard of teaching. The university no longer has a monopoly of research in fields where specialized institutes and research centers, both private and public, achieve excellence. These institutes and centers are part, in any case, of a specific cultural context of the "university culture" that generates a characteristic *forma mentis* or mind-set: the importance attached to the force of reasoned argument, the development of a critical spirit, a high level of compartmentalized information and little capacity for synthesis, even within specific sectors.

3. Living in this changing culture with a desire for truth and an attitude of service in conformity with the Christian ideal has at times become difficult. In the past, becoming a student, and even more so a professor, was everywhere an unquestionable social promotion. Today the context of university studies is often marked by new difficulties of a material or moral order that rapidly become human and spiritual problems with unforeseeable consequences.

4. In many countries, the university meets with great difficulties in the effort for renewal that is constantly required by the evolution of society, the development of new sectors of knowledge, the demands of economies in crisis. Society aspires to a university that will meet its specific needs starting from employment for all. In this way, the industrial world is having a notable impact on the university with its specific demands for rapid and reliable technical services. This "professionalization," with its undeniable benefits, does not always go together with a "university" formation in a sense of values, in professional ethics and in an approach to other disciplines as a complement to the necessary specialization.

5. In contrast to the professionalization of some institutes, many faculties, especially of arts, philosophy, political science and law, often limit themselves

to providing a generic formation in their own discipline, without reference to possible professional outlets for their students. In many countries of medium development, government authorities use the universities as "parking areas" to reduce the tensions caused by unemployment among the youth.

6. Another inescapable fact emerges: Whereas the university, by vocation, has a primary role to play in the development of culture, it is exposed in many countries to two opposing risks: either passively to submit to the dominant cultural influences or to become marginal in relation to them. It is difficult to face these situations because the university often ceases to be a "community of students and teachers in search of truth," becoming a mere "instrument" in the hands of the state and of the dominant economic forces. The only aim is then to assure the technical and professional training of specialists, without giving to education of the person the central place it has by right. Moreover—and this is not without grave consequence—many students attend the university without finding there a human formation that would help them toward the necessary discernment about the meaning of life, and about the bases and development of values and ideals; they live in a state of uncertainty, with the added burden of anxiety for their future.

7. In countries which were or still are subjected to a materialistic and atheistic ideology, research and teaching have been permeated by this ideology, especially in the fields of the human sciences of philosophy and history. As a result, even in some countries that have passed through radical changes on the political level there is not yet sufficient freedom of thought to discern, where necessary, the dominant trends and to perceive the relativistic liberalism that is often concealed within them. A certain skepticism begins to arise concerning the very idea of truth.

8. Everywhere one notices great diversification in the fields of knowledge. The different disciplines have succeeded in defining their specific field of investigation and truth claims, and in recognizing the legitimate complexity and the diversity of their methods. There is a danger, becoming more and more evident, that research workers, teachers and students will close themselves within their specific field of knowledge, seeing only a fragment of reality.

9. In some disciplines, there is emerging a new positivism, with no ethical reference: science for the sake of science. Utilitarian formation takes precedence over integral humanism, tending to neglect the needs and expectations of persons, to censure or stifle the most basic questions of personal and social existence. The development of scientific techniques in the fields of biology, communications and automation raises new and crucial ethical questions. The more

human beings become capable of mastering nature, the more they depend on technology, the more they need to protect their own freedom. This raises new questions about the approaches and the epistemological criteria of the different disciplines.

10. The skepticism and indifference engendered by the prevailing secularism exist together with a new and ill-defined searching of a religious kind. In the climate of uncertainty that characterizes the intellectual horizon of teachers and students, the university at times provides a context for the development of aggressive nationalistic behavior. But in some situations, the climate of confrontation gives way to conformism.

11. The development of university education "at a distance" or *tele-education* (correspondence, audiovisual techniques, etc.) makes information more widely accessible; but the personal contact between teacher and student is in danger of disappearing, together with the human formation bound up with this indispensable relationship. Some mixed forms are a judicious combination of tele-education and occasional contacts between teacher and student; this could be a good way of developing university formation.

12. Interuniversity and international cooperation shows real progress. The more developed academic centers can help the less advanced; this is at times, but not always, to the advantage of the latter. The major universities can, indeed, exercise a certain technical and even ideological "domination" beyond their national frontiers, to the detriment of the less-favored countries.

13. The place women are taking in the university and the general widening of access to university studies already constitute a well-established tradition in some countries. Elsewhere they come as a new development, offering an exceptional opportunity for renewal and an enrichment of university life.

14. The central role of universities in development programs brings with it a tension between the pursuit of the new culture engendered by modernity and the safeguard and promotion of traditional cultures. In responding to its vocation, however, the university lacks a guiding idea, an anchor for its multiple activities. This is at the root of the present crisis of identity and purpose in an institution that, of its nature, is directed toward the search for truth. The chaos of thought and the poverty of basic criteria sterilize the process that should produce educational proposals capable of meeting the new problems. In spite of its imperfections, by vocation the university with the other institutions of higher education remains a privileged place for the development of knowledge and formation, and plays a fundamental role in preparing leaders for the society of the 21st century.

15. A renewed pastoral effort. The presence of Catholics in the university is, in itself, a question and a hope for the church. In many countries this presence is indeed, at one and the same time, numerically impressive and relatively modest in its effect. Too many teachers and students consider their faith a strictly private affair or do not perceive the impact their university life has on their Christian existence. Their presence in the university seems like a parenthesis in their life of faith. Some, among them even priests or religious, in the name of university autonomy, go so far as to refrain from any explicit witness to their faith. Others use this autonomy to spread doctrines contrary to the church's teaching. This situation is aggravated by the lack of theologians with competence in the scientific and technical fields, and of professors specialized in the sciences who have a good theological formation. Obviously, this calls for a renewed awareness, leading to a new pastoral effort. Moreover, while appreciating the praiseworthy initiatives undertaken in various places, one cannot fail to see that the Christian presence often seems limited to isolated groups, sporadic initiatives, the occasional witness of well-known personalities and the action of one or another movement.

II. PRESENCE OF THE CHURCH IN THE UNIVERSITY AND UNIVERSITY CULTURE

1. Presence in University Structures

Sent by Christ to all human beings of every culture, the church tries to share with them the good news of salvation. Having received through Christ the revealed truth about God and humankind, she has the mission to provide, through her message of truth, an opening for authentic freedom. Founded on the mandate received from Christ, she seeks to cast light on cultural values and expressions to correct and purify them, where necessary, in the light of faith in order to bring them to their fullness of meaning.[5]

Within the university, the church's pastoral action, in its rich complexity, has in the first place a subjective aspect: the evangelization of people. From this point of view the church enters into dialogue with real people: men and women, professors, students, staff and, through them, with the cultural trends that characterize this milieu. But one cannot forget the objective aspect: the dialogue between faith and the different disciplines of knowledge. In the context of the university the appearance of new cultural trends is, indeed, closely linked to the great questions concerning humanity: the value of the human person, the meaning of human existence and action, and especially conscience and freedom. At this level Catholic intellectuals should give priority to promoting a renewed and vital synthesis between faith and culture.

The church must not forget that her action is carried out in the particular situation of each university center and that her presence in the university is a service rendered to the people concerned in their twofold dimension: personal and social. The type of presence is therefore different in each country, which bears the marks of its historical, cultural, religious and legislative tradition. In particular, where the legislation permits, the church cannot forsake her institutional action within the university. She seeks to support and foster the teaching of theology wherever possible. At the institutional level the university chaplaincy has a special importance on the campus. By offering a wide range of both doctrinal and spiritual formation, it constitutes, in fact, an important source for the proclamation of the Gospel. Through the stimulus and awareness given through the chaplaincy, university pastoral action can hope to achieve its aim, that is, to create within the university environment a Christian community and a missionary faith commitment.

Religious orders and congregations bring a specific presence to the universities. By the wealth and diversity of their charism—especially their educational charism—they contribute to the Christian formation of teachers and students. In their pastoral options, these religious communities that are much in demand for primary and secondary education should take into consideration what is at stake in their presence within higher education; they should be careful not to draw back in any way under pretext of entrusting to others the mission corresponding to their vocation.

To be accepted and influential, the church's institutional presence in university culture must be of good quality. Often there is a lack of personnel, or at times of the necessary financial resources. This situation calls for creativity and an adequate pastoral effort.

2. The Catholic University

Among the different institutional forms of the church's presence in the university world, emphasis must be placed on the Catholic university, itself an institution of the church.

The existence of a large number of Catholic universities—differing greatly according to regions and countries, from a large number to a total absence—is in itself a richness and an essential factor of the church's presence within university culture. However, this investment does not always produce the fruit for which one might legitimately hope.

Important indications for the specific role of the Catholic university were given in the apostolic constitution *Ex Corde Ecclesiae,* published Aug. 15, 1990. The constitution points out that the institutional identity of the Catholic university depends on its realizing together its characteristics as *university* and as *Catholic.* It only achieves its full identity when, at one and the same time, it gives proof of being rigorously serious as a member of the international community of knowledge and expresses its Catholic identity through an explicit link with the church, at both local and universal levels—an identity which marks concretely the life, the services and the programs of the university community. In this way, by its very existence, the Catholic university achieves its aim of guaranteeing, in an institutional form, a Christian presence in the university world. From this stems its specific mission, characterized by several inseparable features.

In order to carry out its function in relation to the church and to society, the Catholic university must study the grave problems of the day and propose solutions that express the religious and ethical values proper to a Christian vision of the human person.

Next comes university pastoral action in the strict sense. In this respect, the challenges the Catholic university has to meet are not substantially different from those confronting other academic centers. However, we should stress that an academic institution which defines itself as Catholic is committed to university pastoral action at the same depth as the goals it sets for itself: the integral formation of the people, men and women, who in the academic context are called to active participation in the life of society and of the church.

A further aspect of the mission of the Catholic university is, finally, a commitment to dialogue between faith and culture, and the development of a culture rooted in faith. Even in this regard, if there must be concern for the development of a culture in harmony with faith wherever baptized persons are involved in the life of the university, this is still more urgent in the context of the Catholic university, called to become in a special way a significant interlocutor of the academic, cultural and scientific world.

Clearly the church's concern for the university—in the direct service of people and the evangelization of culture—necessarily has a point of reference in the Catholic university. The growing demand for a qualified presence of baptized people in university culture becomes, in this way, a call to the whole church to become more and more aware of the specific vocation of the Catholic university and to facilitate its development as an effective instrument of the church's evangelizing mission.

3. Fruitful Initiatives Already Implemented

In response to the demands of university culture, many local churches have taken appropriate action in various ways:

1. Appointment by the bishops' conference of university chaplains with an ad hoc formation, a specific status and adequate support.

2. Creation, for university pastoral action, of diversified diocesan teams that show the specific responsibility of the laity and the diocesan character of these apostolic units.

3. First steps in a pastoral approach to university rectors/presidents and faculty professors, whose milieu is often dominated by technical and professional concerns.

4. Action taken for the setting up of "departments of religious sciences," capable of opening up new horizons for teachers and students, and compatible with the mission of the church. In these departments Catholics should play a prominent role, especially when faculties of theology are lacking in the university structures.

5. Institution of regular courses on morals and professional ethics in specialized institutes and centers of higher education.

6. Support for dynamic ecclesial movements. University pastoral action achieves better results when it is based on groups or movements and associations—at times, few in number but of high quality—that have the support of the dioceses and bishops' conferences.

7. Stimulus for a university pastoral action that is not limited to a general and undifferentiated pastoral action for youth, but which takes as its starting point the fact that many young people are deeply influenced by the university environment. It is there, to a great extent, that they have their encounter with Christ and bear their witness as Christians. The aim is therefore to educate and accompany the young people, enabling them to live in faith the concrete reality of their milieu and their own activities and commitments.

8. Facilitating dialogue between theologians, philosophers and scientists for a profound renewal of attitudes and to create new and fruitful relations between Christian faith, theology, philosophy and the sciences in their concrete search for truth. Experience shows that university people, priests and especially lay people are in the forefront in maintaining and promoting cultural debate on the great questions regarding humanity, science, society and the new challenges for the human spirit. It is for Catholic teachers and their associations, in particular, to promote interdisciplinary initiatives and cultural encounters inside and outside the university, combining critical method and confidence

in reason, in order to bring face to face in the language of the different cultures metaphysical and scientific positions and the affirmations of faith.

III. PASTORAL SUGGESTIONS AND GUIDELINES

1. Pastoral Suggestions from Local Churches

1. A consultation conducted by the ad hoc episcopal commissions would make it possible to have a better idea of the different initiatives for university pastoral action and for the presence of Christians in the university, and to prepare guidelines to support fruitful apostolic undertakings and to promote those seen to be necessary.

2. The setting up of a national commission for questions related to the university and to culture would help the local churches to share their experiences and their capabilities. It would be for the commission to sponsor a program of activities, reflection and meetings on evangelization and culture, intended for the seminaries and the formation centers for religious and laity; one section would be devoted explicitly to university culture.

3. At the diocesan level, in university towns, it would be good to encourage the setting up of a specialized commission composed of priests and Catholic university people, teachers and students. The aim would be to provide useful indications for university pastoral action and for the activity of Christians in the fields of education and research. The commission would be a help to the bishop in the exercise of his specific mission of promoting and confirming the various initiatives in the diocese and facilitating contact with national or international initiatives. By virtue of his pastoral task at the service of his church, the diocesan bishop bears the first responsibility for the presence and pastoral action of the church in the state universities as well as in the Catholic universities and other private institutions.

4. At the parish level, it would be desirable for the Christian communities — priests, religious and lay faithful — to pay greater attention to students and teachers, and also to the apostolate of the university chaplaincies. The parish is of its nature a community, within which fruitful relationships can be established for a more effective service of the Gospel. It plays a considerable role through its capacity to welcome people, especially when it facilitates the setting up and functioning of student hostels and university residences. The success of the evangelization of the university and of university culture depends to a great extent on the commitment of the whole local church.

5. The university parish is, in some places, an institution more necessary than ever. It supposes the presence of one or more priests with a good preparation for this specific apostolate. The parish is unique as a milieu for communication with all the variety of the academic world. It makes possible relations with people from the fields of culture, art and science; at the same time it allows the church to penetrate into this complex milieu. As a place of meeting and of Christian reflection and formation, it opens to young people the doors of a church hitherto unknown or misunderstood, and opens the church up to the students, their questions and their apostolic dynamism. As a privileged place for the liturgical celebration of the sacraments, it is above all the place of the eucharist, heart of every Christian community, source and summit of every apostolate.

6. Wherever possible, university pastoral action should create or intensify relations between Catholic universities or faculties and all other university milieus in varied forms of collaboration.

7. The present situation is an urgent call to organize the formation of qualified pastoral workers within parishes and Catholic movements and associations. It urgently demands the implementation of a long-term strategy, for cultural and theological formation requires appropriate preparation. Concretely, many dioceses are not in a position to set up and carry out a formation of this kind at university level. This demand can be met by sharing the resources of dioceses, specialized religious institutes and lay groups.

8. In every situation the presence of the church must be seen as a *plantatio* (planting) of the Christian community in the university milieu through witness, proclamation of the Gospel and service of charity. This presence will mean growth for the *Christifideles* (faithful) and a help in approaching those who are far from Jesus Christ. In this perspective, it seems important to develop and promote:

—A catechetical pedagogy characterized by a sense of community, offering a variety of proposals, the possibility of differentiated itineraries and responses to the real needs of concrete persons.
—A pedagogy of personal guidance: welcome, availability and friendship, interpersonal relationships, discernment of the circumstances in which students are living and concrete means for their improvement.
—A pedagogy for the deepening of faith and spiritual life, rooted in the word of God, shared in depth through sacramental and liturgical life.

9. Finally, the presence of the church in the university calls for a common witness of Christians. This ecumenical witness, inseparable from the missionary

dimension, is an important contribution to Christian unity. Without prejudice to the pastoral care of the Catholic faithful, ecumenical collaboration will take the forms and respect the limits established by the church. It supposes an adequate formation and will be particularly fruitful in the study of social questions, and, in general, of all questions related to humankind, to the meaning of human existence and activity.[6]

2. DEVELOPING THE APOSTOLATE OF THE LAITY, ESPECIALLY OF TEACHERS

"The Christian vocation is, of its nature, a vocation to the apostolate."[7] This statement of the Second Vatican Council, when applied to university pastoral action, is a resounding challenge to responsibility for Catholic teachers, intellectuals and students. The apostolic commitment of the faithful is a sign of vitality and spiritual progress for the whole church.

Developing in university people this consciousness of the duty of apostolate is consistent with the pastoral orientations of Vatican II. At the heart of the university community, faith becomes in this way a radiating source of new life and of genuinely Christian culture. The lay faithful enjoy a legitimate autonomy in the exercise of their specific apostolic vocation. Pastors are invited not only to recognize this specificity but to give it warm support. This apostolate starts and develops from professional relationships, common cultural interests and the sharing of daily life in the different sectors of university activity. The individual apostolate of Catholic lay people is "the starting point and condition of the whole lay apostolate, even in its organized expression, and admits of no substitute."[8] Nevertheless, it remains necessary and urgent for the Catholics present in the university to give a witness of communion and unity. In this respect, the ecclesial movements are particularly valuable.

Catholic teachers play a fundamental role for the church's presence in university culture. In certain cases, their quality and generosity can even make up for imperfections in the structures. The apostolic commitment of the Catholic teacher who gives priority to respect and service for individuals — colleagues and students — offers the witness of the "new man, always ready to render an account to anyone who asks for the hope that is in him, and to do it with courtesy and respect" (cf. 1 Pt. 3:15–16). The university is certainly a limited sector of society, but qualitatively its influence is in greater proportion to its quantitative dimension. By contrast, however, even the figure of the Catholic intellectual seems to have almost disappeared from certain university contexts where the students feel painfully the lack of genuine mentors whose constant presence and availability would provide a "companionship" of high quality.

This witness of the Catholic teacher certainly does not consist in filling disciplines that are being taught with religious subject matter. Rather it means opening up the horizon to the ultimate and fundamental questions, with the stimulating generosity of an active presence for the often inarticulate demands of young minds in search of points of reference and certainties, of guidance and purpose. Their life tomorrow in society depends on this. Even more do the church and the university expect from priests teaching in the university a high standard of competence and a sincere ecclesial communion.

Unity grows in diversity, resisting the temptation to unify and formalize activities. The variety of apostolic initiatives and resources, far from opposing ecclesial unity, requires and enriches it. Pastors who take into account the legitimate characteristics of the university spirit: diversity and spontaneity, respect for personal freedom and responsibility, resistance to any attempt at imposing uniformity.

Catholic movements or groups should be encouraged to multiply and to grow; but it is important also to recognize and to vitalize associations of the Catholic laity that boast a long and fruitful tradition of university apostolate. The apostolate, exercised by lay people, is fruitful to the extent that it is ecclesial. The criteria for evaluation of the different commitments include doctrinal consistency with Catholic identity, together with an exemplary moral and professional standard, ensuring the radiating authenticity of the lay apostolate, of which spiritual life is the guarantee.

Conclusion

Among the immense fields of apostolate and action for which the church is responsible, university culture is one of the most promising, but also one of the most difficult. This particular milieu has so great an influence on the social and cultural life of nations, and on it depends to a great extent the future of the church and that of society. Within it the church maintains an apostolic presence and action at both the institutional and the personal levels, with specific cooperation of priests and lay people, administrative staff, teachers and students.

Consultation and meetings with many bishops and university people have shown the importance of cooperation between the different ecclesial bodies concerned. The Congregation for Catholic Education, the Pontifical Council for the Laity and the Pontifical Council for Culture express again their readiness to facilitate exchanges and to promote meetings at the level of bishops' conferences, Catholic international organizations and of commissions for teaching, education and culture acting in this particular field.

Service of the individuals involved in the university, and through them service of society, the presence of the church in the university milieu enters into the process of inculturation of the faith as a requirement of evangelization. On the threshold of a new millennium, of which university culture will be a major component, the duty of proclaiming the Gospel becomes more urgent. It calls for faith communities able to transmit the good news to all those who are formed, who teach and who exercise their activity in the context of university culture. The urgency of this apostolic commitment is great, for the university is one of the most fruitful centers for the creation of culture.

"Fully aware of a pastoral urgency that calls for an absolutely special concern for culture . . . the church calls upon the faithful to be present, as signs of courage and intellectual creativity, in the privileged places of culture, that is, the world of education—school and university—and places of scientific and technological research, the areas of artistic creativity and work in the humanities. Such a presence is destined not only for the recognition and possible purification of the elements that critically burden existing culture, but also for the elevation of these cultures through the riches which have their source in the Gospel and the Christian faith."[9]

Vatican City, Pentecost, May 22, 1994.

> Cardinal Pio Laghi,
> Prefect, Congregation for Catholic Education;
> Cardinal Eduardo Pironio,
> President, Pontifical Council for the Laity;
> Cardinal Paul Poupard,
> President, Pontifical Council for Culture.

NOTES

1. This pastoral concern is evidenced in the church's magisterium, for example in the addresses to university people of Pope John Paul II (cf. Giovanni Paulo II: *Discorsi alle Universita,* Camerino 1991). Of particular significance was the pope's address of March 8, 1982, for a work session on university apostolate with the clergy of Rome (cf. *L'Osservatore Romano,* English edition, May 3, 1982, pp. 6–7).

2. This synthesis, presented by Cardinal Paul Poupard on behalf of the three dicasteries, was published March 25, 1988, and reproduced in several languages (cf. *Origins,* Vol. 18, No. 7, June 30, 1988, 109–112; *La Documentation Catholique,* June 19, 1988, 623–628; *Ecclesia,* July 23, 1988, 1105–1110; *La Civilta Cattolica,* May 21, 1988, N. 3310, 364–374.

3. Cf. John Paul II, *Ex Corde Ecclesiae,* Aug. 15, 1990, No. 1.

4. John Paul II, letter instituting the Pontifical Council for Culture, May 20, 1982, *AAS,* 74 (1983), 683–688.

5. Cf. John Paul II, encyclical *Veritatis Splendor,* 30–31.

6. Cf. Pontifical Council for Promoting Christian Unity, *Ecumenical Directory,* 1993, Nos. 211–216.

7. Vatican Council II, *Apostolicam Actuositatem,* 2.

8. Ibid., 16.

9. John Paul II, *Christifideles Laici,* Dec. 30, 1988, No. 44.

18 | Request for Dialogue and Questions for Reflection

July 8, 1994

TO: Bishops and Presidents
Learned Societies/Experts
FROM: Bishop John J. Leibrecht
RE: *Ex Corde Ecclesiae*
DATE: July 8, 1994

I write to ask that, in accord with the continuing work of the *Ex corde Ecclesiae* Implementation Committee, further dialogue take place between Catholic colleges, universities and bishops. Enclosed are themes which may be of assistance. Additional themes will probably be addressed during individual dialogues around the country. Learned societies and experts may participate in such dialogues or send their observations and recommendations directly to the Implementation Committee.

The plan is to have a dialogue on the enclosed themes in the Fall of 1994 and another, in the Spring of 1995, on the topic of the mandate and related matters. The Committee invites and welcomes comments from all dialogue participants as it continues its task of developing ordinances to implement *Ex corde Ecclesiae*. The U.S. bishops will devote time to ordinances, based upon *Ex corde Ecclesiae*, at their national meeting in November, 1995.

Please send your comments and recommendations from this Fall dialogue to the attention of the *Ex corde Ecclesiae* Implementation Committee at the National Conference of Catholic Bishops in Washington, D.C. by December 10, 1994.

At the time of this writing, the process of retaining a Project Director to assist the Implementation Committee is well under way. As soon as the Director is selected, information will be sent to you. If you would like to invite the

From the author's files.

Project Director to be present for your dialogue, please send the invitation to the NCCB address.

Theme:	CATHOLIC IDENTITY
Reflection:	A Catholic college or university, by institutional commitment, brings to its task the inspiration and light of the Christian message. *Ex corde Ecclesiae* addresses the nature and objectives of Catholic identity in paragraphs 12–20. In paragraph 13 the document lists four essential characteristics of a Catholic college or university.
Personal Reflection:	
Questions:	How are the determinants of the Catholic character of the local college or university addressed by administrators? the board? the academic community? bishops? others?
	Who is involved in determining the Catholic character of the college or university?
Theme:	COMMUNIO
Reflection:	*Communio* is a rich and complex concept having many analogous forms of realization. In the early church, *communio* was seen as the bond that united bishops and faithful, the bishops among themselves, and the faithful among themselves. In particular, the notion of *communio* involves the development of trust between the bishops and those who are responsible for administration and teaching in Catholic colleges and universities.
Personal Reflection:	
Questions:	How is the concept *communio* between the local bishop and the Catholic college or university within the diocese expressed in the Apostolic Constitution *Ex corde Ecclesiae*?

How is *communio* realized in the relationship between bishops and Catholic universities/colleges and between bishops and theologians?

How does *Ex corde Ecclesiae* view the relationship between faith and scholarship?

How can Catholic colleges and universities be assisted in their efforts to recruit faculty who evidence "an attained integration between faith and life and between professional competence and Christian wisdom".

What are the principal obstacles to *communio* at present?

What can be done to overcome them?

Theme: RELATING FAITH AND CULTURE

Reflection: One important recent phenomenon on Catholic college and university campuses in the United States is the effort of faculty, administrators and students to address the issue of evangelizing the culture as part of the mission of the institution.

Personal Reflection:

Questions: What form is the effort to evangelize the culture taking today? Who on campus is involved?

How is this effort to evangelize the culture related to the local church?

How is this effort to evangelize the culture related to *Ex corde Ecclesiae*?

What are some structures that might be supportive of this effort to evangelize the culture? What are some obstacles?

Theme:	PASTORAL MINISTRY ON CAMPUS
Reflection:	*Ex corde Ecclesiae* underscores the importance of pastoral ministry on campus that "promotes the pastoral care of all members of the university community" by providing for "a sufficient number of qualified people—priests, religious, and lay persons" for the ministry of facilitating "the integration of human and professional education with religious values in light of the Catholic doctrine".
Personal Reflection:	What are the various dimensions of pastoral ministry on campus?
	Who is responsible for providing an adequately staffed pastoral ministry on campus?
	What is the relationship between campus pastoral ministry and the local church?
	What is the relationship between campus ministry and the academic community? Between campus ministry and administration? And the bishop?
Theme:	THE RELATIONSHIP BETWEEN THE DIOCESAN BISHOP AND THE CATHOLIC COLLEGE OR UNIVERSITY WITHIN THE DIOCESE.
Reflections:	*Ex corde Ecclesiae* directs that "every Catholic university . . . is to be in close communion with the local church and in particular with the diocesan bishops of the region or nation in which it is located". The Apostolic Constitution suggests further that "each bishop has a responsibility to promote the welfare of the Catholic universities in his diocese and has the right and duty to watch over the preservation and strengthening of their Catholic character".
	Furthermore, *Ex corde Ecclesiae* suggests that "if problems should arise concerning this Catholic character,

the local bishop is to take the initiatives necessary to resolve the matter, working with the competent university authorities in accordance with established procedures and, if necessary, with the help of the Holy See".

Personal Reflection: What mechanisms exist for dialogue between the local bishops and Catholic colleges or universities in the diocese?

Identify some of the important issues in the dialogue between the local bishop and a college or university in his diocese.

How does the local bishop "promote the welfare" of Catholic colleges or universities in his diocese?

What mechanisms exist now for the resolution of disputes and how could they be better utilized?

Theme: LEGAL ISSUES INVOLVED IN THE IMPLEMENTATION OF *EX CORDE ECCLESIAE*

Reflection: A number of civil law implications for institutions and dioceses have emerged as a result of the discussion on the implementation of *Ex corde Ecclesiae.* These issues need to be further specified and addressed by those familiar with college and university law.

Personal Reflection:

Questions: What are the implications of any set of ordinances, for public funding to institutions and to students, when they are internalized by action of the appropriate university authorities?

What are some legal issues that need to be considered in the implementation of *Ex corde Ecclesiae* from the perspective of your institution?

19 | Evangelization and the Catholic University: A Reflection from the Board of the Association of Catholic Colleges and Universities

August 17, 1994

INTRODUCTION

(1) These reflections are divided into four parts: first, a clarification of the meaning of the word "evangelization" for Catholics; second, a brief exposition of the various meanings of the word "evangelization" as it is used by *Ex corde Ecclesiae*; third, *Ex corde*'s description of the unique contribution a Catholic university makes to the Church's mission of evangelization; and fourth, in the light of all the above, a brief response to the discussion questions provided by the *Ex corde Ecclesiae* Implementation Committee.

I. EVANGELIZATION AND NORTH AMERICAN CULTURE

(2) Until the early seventies, the word evangelization was used mainly by Protestant evangelicals and fundamentalists, and was typically understood as an aggressive style of presenting the Gospel to all who were not yet personally converted to Jesus. From the early eighties to the present, this intense activity has made extensive use of television, through which animated preachers, supported by witness talks of the newly converted, have made an urgent case for complete conversion as the condition for personal salvation. Today, North American Catholics, in general, will not think of their preachers as "evangelizers." Catholics seem more at home with those who "give sermons," who "witness" to their

From the author's files.

faith, and who just live the Christian life or give good example. For Catholics, a broader view of sanctification involves not only preaching but, perhaps still more, liturgical rituals and the sacramental life. Moreover, for Catholics, the life of faith involves more than personal conversion; for many, it involves the transformation of communities and the critique of culture, or, to be more precise about the United States, the critique of its many diverse cultures—a clarification that should be kept in mind throughout these reflections. In a word, the Catholic Church has developed a rich and multi-faceted understanding of the process of evangelization.

II. *EX CORDE ECCLESIAE* AND EVANGELIZATION

(3) At the very end of the Apostolic Constitution, *Ex corde Ecclesiae,* Pope John Paul II outlines in two paragraphs a rich notion of evangelization as it should be taken up by the Catholic university. He speaks (Art. 49) of the Catholic university's contribution to the Church's primary mission: "to preach the Gospel in such a way that a relationship between faith and life is established in each individual and in the socio-cultural context in which individuals live and act and communicate with one another" (Art. 48). Evangelization affects, therefore, not only individuals, but the communities in which they live. In fact, the radical nature of the Gospel leads inevitably, at times, to a confrontation with those aspects of peoples' lives and their culture, "upsetting . . . humanity's criteria of judgement, determining values, points of interest, lines of thought, sources of inspiration and models of life, which are in contrast with the word of God and the plan of salvation" (Art. 48, citing Pope Paul VI's *Evangelii Nuntiandi,* 18 ff.).

(4) But the process of evangelizing people and culture is not merely a matter of confronting that which opposes the Gospel; it is also a matter of benefiting from the good elements that all cultures possess. In particular, Article 44 of *Ex corde* explains that the Catholic university assists the Church by enabling it to come to a better knowledge of diverse cultures, to "discern their positive and negative aspects, and to develop means by which it can make the faith better understood. . . ." Moreover, it adds that the Gospel is lived by people "who are profoundly linked to a culture, and the building up of the kingdom cannot avoid borrowing the elements of human culture or cultures" (again, citing Pope Paul's *Evangelii Nuntiandi*). The Constitution then cites John Paul II's striking comments to the intellectuals, students, and university personnel at Medellin in 1986:

A faith that places itself on the margin of what is human, of what is there-fore culture, would be a faith unfaithful to the fullness of what the word of God manifests and reveals, a decapitated faith, worse still, a faith in the pro-cess of self-annihilation.

These quotations from *Ex corde* indicate that the full Catholic understanding of evangelization includes multiple dimensions, both personal and communal, both critical and appreciative of the cultures in which it takes place. The process of sharing the faith is complex, requires patient discernment, and calls for neither the complete denunciation nor the full approval of any culture.

III. THE UNIQUE ROLE OF THE CATHOLIC UNIVERSITY

(5) *Ex corde Ecclesiae* develops a rich appreciation of the nature of a university. As its very first paragraph puts it, the university "has always been recognized as an incomparable center of creativity and dissemination of knowledge for the good of humanity" (Art. 1). Its fourth paragraph speaks of "a kind of universal humanism," by which "a Catholic university is completely dedicated to the re-search of all aspects of truth in their essential connection with the supreme Truth, who is God." As a consequence, a university must pursue "every path of knowledge." Especially important is the assistance the university can offer the Church in understanding and influencing the nature and direction of modern science (see Articles 7, 45 and 46).

(6) Finally, *Ex corde* stresses that the Church believes in "the intrinsic value of knowledge and research" (Art. 15). Realizing that all truth is ultimately one, that the truth is the only sure road to freedom, and that Jesus is the Truth, the Church sees an intimate relationship between research for the truth and com-ing to know who God is. The Catholic university is well positioned to empha-size neglected aspects of evangelization, especially the intimate relationship between a serious intellectual life and a mature Christian faith, and the nec-essary relationship between the communities of inquiry and the communities of belief.

(7) After an introduction of eleven articles, the body of the remainder of the Constitution is divided between (a) the identity of a Catholic university (Articles 12−29), and (b) the mission of service of a Catholic university (Ar-ticles 30−49). Article 15 lists four essential characteristics that every Catholic university must have:

1. the search for an integration of knowledge,
2. a dialogue between faith and reason,
3. an ethical concern, and
4. a theological perspective.

Article 30 introduces the unique role of the Catholic university by distinguishing between what a university itself does and what a Catholic university does:

> The basic mission of a university is a continuous quest for truth through its research, and the preservation and communication of knowledge for the good of society. A Catholic university participates in this mission with its own specific characteristics and purposes.

(8) And what are the specific characteristics and purposes of a Catholic university? They are (1) service to Church and society; (2) pastoral ministry; (3) cultural dialogue; (4) and evangelization. What is not clear is the exact relationship between the four essential characteristics that Article 15 states each Catholic university must have, and four "specific characteristics and purposes" that describe the mission of service extended by a Catholic university. It may well be the case that the Constitution's listing of the four "essential characteristics" is not necessarily exhaustive, especially given the great diversity of our actual institutions.

(9) In any event, at the heart of each of the four special purposes of the Catholic university is the existential uniting of two orders of reality: "the search for truth and the certainty of already knowing the fount of truth" (Art. 1). The firm belief that all truth, ultimately, is one, and that through faith we know the fount of truth, does not remove our necessarily limited grasp of the truth nor exempt us from the continual struggle to integrate our diverse perceptions of truth. In recent years, members of the scientific community have become increasingly aware of how their measurements are often only approximations; and for centuries, Christians, even when we look through the eyes of faith, only see, so St. Paul reminds us, through a glass darkly.

(10) Among these four special characteristics of a Catholic university are not only pastoral ministry and evangelization, but also service and cultural dialogue. How can the latter two be essential parts of the way a Catholic university enters into the process of evangelization? It may be helpful here to recall the famous statement of the document entitled "Justice in the World," issued by the 1971 World Synod of Bishops:

Action on behalf of justice and participation in the transformation of the world fully appear to us as a constitutive dimension of the preaching of the Gospel, or, in other words, of the Church's mission for the redemption of the human race and its liberation from every oppressive situation.

Since 1971, serious theological analyses and criticism of this Synod statement have helped us avoid promoting a sort of social Gospel for the Catholic Church. Keeping in mind such criticism, the Synod's more inclusive understanding of evangelization, nonetheless, makes it more possible to see how the following research themes, which are an integral part of so many research programs at our Catholic universities, can be thought of as a part of the university's efforts at evangelization:

> ... the dignity of human life, the promotion of justice for all, the quality of personal and family life, the protection of nature, the search for peace and political stability, a more just sharing in the world's resources, and a new economic and political order that will better serve the human community at a national and international level (Art. 32).

All professors, including those who are not Catholic but nonetheless respect the Catholic character of the university (Art. 27), can be committed to such research. For the Christian believer, such research seeks to understand the dignity of the human person, that is, to develop "a true Christian anthropology, founded on the person of Christ" (Art. 33). At the same time, what Christian anthropology affirms, guided by the mystery of the incarnation, is of importance to more than believers, since the full sense of Christ, who is the head of a community, embraces the whole human family. Such efforts constitute part of the unique contribution of the Catholic university to the mission of the Church at large.

(11) The cultural dialogue, which is open to all human experience, focuses, again, according to *Ex corde,* on such matters as

> the meaning of the human person, his or her liberty, dignity, sense of responsibility, and openness to the transcendent. To a respect for persons is joined the preeminent value of the family, the primary unit of every human culture (Art. 45).

As noted earlier, Article 45 singles out as an area of particular interest modern science, which raises complex questions about the relationship between faith and reason, and requires not only a knowledge of theology, but also a deep grasp of modern science, along with its epistemological questions.

(12) *Ex Corde* describes pastoral ministry as the integration of religious and moral principles with academic study and non-academic activities through prayer, sacraments, and various forms of religious outreach. In its treatment of pastoral ministry, the Apostolic Constitution recognizes that some members of our university communities may not share our faith and that pastoral ministry must be provided in a way that respects their beliefs.

(13) In summary then, when *Ex corde* develops the unique role of the Catholic university, it specifies a wide range of intellectual and religious efforts that requires that we presuppose a broad understanding of "evangelization." While the Catholic university undertakes the direct pastoral ministry of preaching and the sacraments in much the same way as the Church might do so throughout the world, it, nonetheless, makes a unique contribution to the process of evangelization, broadly understood, by its work of research, teaching, and dialoguing with all facets of modern culture.

IV. RESPONSES TO DISCUSSION QUESTIONS POSED BY THE *EX CORDE ECCLESIAE* IMPLEMENTATION COMMITTEE

(14) The Association of Catholic Colleges and Universities is currently in the midst of a major study of its member institutions, asking, among other things, how they are promoting the dialogue between faith and culture, for which *Ex Corde* calls. While it is too soon to report now on the data being collected, we have learned that some colleges have established special interdisciplinary centers for the dialogue; others have organized lecture series; still others have developed curricula that take up the very themes emphasized in *Ex Corde*. These efforts involve virtually everyone on the campuses, certainly first the faculty and the administration, but also the students and staff. These efforts vary greatly, a not surprising finding given how greatly our schools themselves vary (in this country)—from valuable small colleges to large research universities. The complexity of the latter, their professional schools and specialized doctoral programs, constitute an audience which, if we are to address them effectively, will require especially thoughtful and demanding dialogue.

(15) One of the most common ways these efforts relate to the Church is the participation of Catholic faculty and staff in the parishes located near the college or the university. Frequently faculty are asked to speak at parishes, and members

of various parishes often come to campuses for lectures, or for continuing education or even graduate programs. In addition, many of our institutions serve the Church far beyond the local Church to assist the Church nationally and even internationally.

(16) Obstacles to evangelization are many. Article 18 of *Ex corde* describes effectively the vision needed to overcome obstacles typical in our culture:

> It is essential that we be convinced of the priority of the ethical over the technical, of the primacy of the person over things, of the superiority of the spirit over matter. The cause of the human person will only be served if knowledge is joined to conscience.

And since none of us lives apart from our culture, each of us has to deal with the challenge of making sure that that which is most important actually guides us in our research and teaching. To the extent that our colleges and universities are able to articulate such a vision, and then win the support of the university community in the effort to realize that vision, that community ensures that the structures that are supportive are in place and sustained. Such structures make it more likely that individuals supportive of the unique mission of the institution are hired, that promotion and tenure activities are not unrelated to the unique mission of the institution, and that budget decisions buttress visibly the centrality of the dialogue between faith and culture.

February 1, 1995

Bishop John Leibrecht:

The last 30 years have seen many changes in Catholic colleges and universities.
Enrollments increased dramatically so that now over 600,000 students, almost
two-thirds of them full time, participate in Catholic higher education. Governance shifted in many cases from religious communities to boards which include lay men and women. The ratio of religious to lay faculty moved toward a
significant lay majority. Catholic colleges and universities are perceived today,
more than 30 years ago, as mainstream and academically solid.

What will Catholic colleges and universities be like years from now? That
question is occasioned, in part, by *Ex Corde Ecclesiae* in which Pope John Paul II
gives his vision of Catholic higher education for the future. In particular, the
pope wants colleges and universities to continue specifically as Catholic. That
same hope is shared, I am sure, by all of us at this annual meeting of the Association of Catholic Colleges and Universities.

Many of us here this morning will not be participating in Catholic higher
education 30 years from now. New generations of presidents, trustees, deans
and faculty members will replace us and one another between now and then.

Is there anything that can be done now to ensure Catholic identity 30 years
from now? *Ex Corde Ecclesiae* offers us a timely opportunity to impact Catholic
higher education as we look ahead. Without deliberate action, some of our institutions may drift away from an effective religious dimension.

From *Origins* 24, no. 35 (February 16, 1995): 577, 579–580, 580–582.

Some colleges and universities in this nation identified decades ago as Protestant no longer have a perceptible presence of religious values affecting their institutional lives. Those colleges did not lose their religious identity suddenly. Rather, change resulted from a gradual process which involved successive presidencies, new trustees and different faculties. My belief, and that of the *Ex Corde Ecclesiae* implementation committee, is that we have a unique opportunity of ensuring the Catholic identity of our institutions for the future.

Today I would like to report on three of the themes which the *Ex Corde Ecclesiae* implementation committee suggested to presidents and bishops for dialogue in the fall of 1994. Catholic identity, the relationship of faith and culture, and pastoral ministry on campus are three clearly interrelated themes. (Bishop James Malone will speak in a few moments about other themes from the dialogue.)

Dialogues between bishops and representatives of Catholic colleges and universities will take place this coming spring on the canonical mandate about teaching theological disciplines and related matters. Materials for those discussions will be sent to you within the next two weeks.

The implementation committee clearly heard the concerns expressed regarding the first draft of ordinances sent to you in May 1993. Those ordinances have been taken off the table. New ordinances, in a new format, will be sent for review after the implementation committee studies the reports from the dialogues held this academic year between bishops and representatives of Catholic colleges and universities.

Ex Corde Ecclesiae refers to four characteristics of a college or university which identifies itself as Catholic. It has a Christian inspiration of the university community as well as of individuals; it reflects on human knowledge in the light of faith; it remains faithful to the Christian message as it comes to us through the church; and has an institutional commitment to service. These are not the only possible characteristics, but Pope John Paul II identifies them as central. While common among all Catholic institutions of higher education, these characteristics take form in diverse ways depending upon the size, programs, geography, faculty, student body and other variables at each institution.

The general norms of *Ex Corde Ecclesiae* indicate that the college or university itself is the agent responsible for Catholic identity (General Norms, 4.1). Within the institution, that responsibility is to be shared by the board of trustees, the president, deans and faculty. The bishop's role is to promote and assist the preservation of Catholic identity (No. 28). *Ex Corde Ecclesiae* states (No. 22) that the relationship of the Catholic college and university to the church is essential for its identity. The Catholic university is linked to the church by a statutory bond or an institutional commitment (General Norms, 2.2).

Early dialogue reports from around the country indicate that at some colleges and universities a person or team has been appointed to promote Catholic identity. In some institutions, the founding religious community remains the primary agent responsible for Catholic identity. Such individuals and teams are similar to mission-effectiveness personnel in Catholic medical centers.

One ordinance suggested more than a year ago by the *Ex Corde Ecclesiae* implementation committee called for a review of Catholic identity every 10 years. Such a review could, for instance, be part of an accrediting association self-study or done at another time. Further consultation on this matter will be helpful.

The relationship between faith and culture is a second theme from the recent dialogue. *Ex Corde Ecclesiae* asks that the university help the church understand the positive and negative aspects of various cultures (No. 44). The church looks to the college and university to lead the dialogue between Christian thought and the sciences (No. 46). Religion offers insights for reflection on human life, justice, family life, the environment and nature, peace and political stability (No. 32). *Ex Corde Ecclesiae* also asks that Catholic colleges and universities promote ecumenical dialogue.

One dialogue report doubted that objective judgments called for by the pope's apostolic constitution are possible. Such a statement, it seems to me, invites further conversation. The pope believes that a faith which places itself on the margin of culture is "a faith in the process of self-annihilation" (No. 44).

In any effort to relate faith to culture, it would not be correct to assume that all Catholic faculty are well-informed about the Catholic faith. Because of their academic credentials and a familiarity with Catholicism, faculty who are not Catholic can definitely play an important role in relating faith to culture. One dialogue report suggested that an effort among all Catholic colleges and universities to develop better interviewing procedures for the hiring process might be helpful.

Several dialogue reports indicated that assisting students to relate faith to culture has become difficult because of religious illiteracy among many students, including Catholic students. How might that situation be addressed? How might a relationship between faith and culture be addressed in the case of students who are not Catholic?

A third theme from the recent dialogues was pastoral ministry. *Ex Corde Ecclesiae* describes this ministry as integrating religious and moral principles with academic study and nonacademic activities (No. 38). Pastoral ministry involves both faculty and students, especially those who are Catholics (General Norms, 6.1).

Comments which the implementation committee has received on this theme have been brief. The main challenge is to integrate pastoral ministry with the entire life of the college or university. Several reports indicated that pastoral ministry sometimes seems to be separated from the rest of life on campus, particularly its academic programs. Many fine pastoral ministry programs exist, but they can benefit from additional attention.

Now I would like to invite Bishop Malone to share some thoughts with you about the two themes of *communio* and the relationship of the bishop to the Catholic college and university. When he completes his remarks, we will have a conversation with you on any matters suggested by the dialogue themes. I have asked Father Terrence Toland, project director of the implementation committee, to participate with Bishop Malone and myself in our discussions.

Bishop James Malone:

Since the last time we were together a year ago, a decision was made to extend the time frame of our deliberations in the United States on the implementation of *Ex Corde Ecclesiae.*

At our bishops' 1994 November meeting I recall two bishop members who asked for more time—Cardinal Anthony Bevilacqua of Philadelphia and Bishop John D'Arcy of Fort Wayne–South Bend, Ind.

More important, I think, we also began an expanded process of consultation and dialogue between the bishops and Catholic higher education people back in their own hometowns, expanded both in content and in participation—that means, for example, that participants in many dialogues included presidents, sponsoring religious communities, faculty members and trustees.

The focus and purpose of these local dialogues across the country is to discover what is the common ground which we all can use as a basis for developing a program of implementing *Ex Corde Ecclesiae*: an implementation that is faithful to both *Ex Corde Ecclesiae* and to the experience of U.S. Catholic higher education.

Before moving to the two items which I am briefly to talk about, I do want to say that our latest meeting last week, the meeting of the implementation committee composed of some bishops and some eight consultants, college and university presidents, was an upbeat meeting for me. Others remarked on it as well as our meeting ended, including Father Don Monan and Sister Karen Kennelly.

When the daylong meeting came to a close, I boarded my plane for Ohio with a lighter heart and with renewed enthusiasm for the ultimate success of our efforts to implement *Ex Corde* together.

In that connection, I remind you that the two topics for this current ACCU session are, Where are we now and where are we going?

Where are we now? I think we are moving forward together, talking to each other, respecting one another. On *Ex Corde,* I think we are further along the road we need to walk than we were a year ago. The time we are spending together—bishops and Catholic higher education people—is paying dividends.

Last evening, at one reception, in conversation with Father Monk Malloy and Professor Vincent Hanssens of the Catholic University of Louvain, I was reassured to hear Professor Hanssens say, "Like you in the United States, so also we in Belgium need time to get acquainted, we university people and our bishops; and then we can move forward on our *Ex Corde* topics."

But even as I repeat that remark to this audience, I hurry to add that I know that many of you in leadership posts at our Catholic colleges and universities have already put a lot of your time and energy into dialogue and bridge building to many of your publics. But at this point of our *Ex Corde* dialogue, I earnestly ask that together we keep on with dialogue despite your fatigue and *deja vu.* Do not let other demands get in the way. Take advantage of this opportunity to dialogue on *Ex Corde.* Give it time.

And also, our program today asks, Where are we going, we bishops and you Catholic higher education leaders?

As I shall say again later in these remarks, I think we are going to find some new insights on the topic of *communio* which can help us get a better grasp on our mutual responsibilities, we bishops and you academic leaders, in this endeavor.

Of great help to us all will be Father Terry Toland, SJ, the new staff person of our implementation committee. Father Toland is experienced, insightful, hardworking, encouraging and humorous. He has related well to bishops and presidents on our committee and to many local people in the dioceses and academic communities which he has visited.

Now in the few minutes I have today I would like to do two things. First, I would like to re-present to you some newer insights on *communio* that emerged from my reading of the reports that were submitted from your discussions. I was especially impressed with the rich promise of the *communio* idea as it was lifted up in some of your reports. And then, second, I will offer some reflections that flow from what I heard you saying in those same reports.

First, then, *communio.* In a sense, Bishop John Leibrecht anticipated some of what has now transpired in the dialogues. He wrote last summer that *communio* is a "rich and complex concept having many analogous forms of realization." In the responses which I read, I found that many of your responses held that same notion about *communio.* You suggested that it is the manner in which we understand *communio* that will guide or even determine the way in which we will approach the relationship between Catholic colleges and universities and the pastoral office of bishop, the "personal and pastoral" relationship importantly described in Paragraph 28 of the *Ex Corde* document.

I was particularly helped by one analysis which gave me a new insight about *communio*. This analysis pointed out that the popular understanding of *communio* presumes that the word *communio* is a combination of the words *common* and *unity,* with the emphasis on unity rather than on commonality. This is said to be the usual understanding of *communio*. But then this newer analysis went on to propose that the real root of *communio* is not *unio* (union), but rather the root is *munus* (office, function or duty): *com-munus*. The focus is on shared responsibility, shared duties, *com-munus*.

The Latin *communis* indeed means "shared, common, general." In community, we are about common functions, common duties and common offices. The source of this common life is the unity that flows from our participating in the life of the triune God. I suggest we link this common life to the underlying reason for the "mutual respect" noted in that same Paragraph 28.

In this expansive understanding of *communio,* there is suggested also a reciprocity which ought to exist between us who share common responsibilities. This newer notion moves us to say that the church does not belong to the bishops nor does the church belong to the colleges and universities. Similarly, colleges and universities are not an instrument of the hierarchy nor do these institutions themselves exist as independent, self-defining entities. This newer notion of *communio* is theological, speaking to us about a reciprocity rather than a notion of *communio* that is institutional or sociological. In this new approach we can think in religious or theological categories about our relationships as presidents and bishops.

Thus we do not think about *communio* in canonical or jurisdictional language, which reflects a narrower understanding of *communio*. On the other hand, this theological or religious mindset of *communio* can envision a unity that allows for an appropriate plurality.

Now it seems to me that flowing from this expanded perspective of *communio* as meaning "shared duties" is the proposal that our own best context for carrying forward such an understanding is one of dialogue between bishops and colleges and universities. I would describe it as a dialogue that would avoid suspicion and mistrust between us, a dialogue that would be motivated by a search for what is mutual and common between us.

Such dialogue would involve us bishops and Catholic higher education people in an openness to learning as well as encourage us in an expression of the bonds that tie us together, university people and bishops. Again, we can think of Paragraph 28, which speaks of continuing dialogue.

Now to my second point: my reflection on your reports to our implementation committee about your dialogues at your home places.

1. Briefly stated, as regards your reports, I was impressed by their content, encouraged by their candor and reassured that most participants considered their time on them well-spent.

2. For myself, I am convinced that the time we are now giving to our dialogues is preparing us for more and better dialogue in days ahead. By our talking together, we are not, I think, merely marking time. Rather, I am persuaded that we are moving forward together toward goals which *Ex Corde* offers to us.

3. At the same time, I want to be realistic about the obstacles to our dialogue. Obstacles exist on both sides, and they must be acknowledged and addressed.

Perhaps the greatest obstacle we face is in deciding how we can move from the level of "*communio* theory" to that of "*communio* practice": Here we are without any clear guideposts. In a sense we are in a creative process when it comes to applying the *communio* theory. This will be our challenge in the next phase of our discussions.

We bishops and Catholic higher education people will have to discuss in concrete terms how do we live out our mutual participation in the life and mission of the church. For example, how does the bishop respect the distinctive way in which a Catholic college or university fulfills its unique pastoral role; how does the institution experience its legitimate autonomy and its integral responsibilities within the larger community that is the church? And also, how does a college and university respect the "presiding and overseeing" role of the diocesan bishop, who is the visible source of unity of the community of faith that is a local church and, as such, is present to and participates in the life of the college or university community?

Obviously these are questions to be pursued. As bishops, we cannot come here today and give answers. It is important, however, that we all realize that together, as bishops and leaders in Catholic higher education, we must move on to some conclusion, however provisional. The purpose of the dialogue process we have entered upon is to develop a clear sense of direction so that, with fidelity and integrity, we together can respond to the expectations that come to us from the one who exercises the Petrine ministry which binds us together as a universal community of faith.

In conclusion, dear friends, I am confident that through honest labor and renewed openness to the promptings of the Holy Spirit we can move toward these outcomes.

21 | Questions for Spring 1995 Dialogues

February 10, 1995

TO: Bishops, Presidents,
Learned Societies, Sponsoring Religious Bodies
FROM: Bishop John J. Leibrecht
DATE: 10 February 1995
ON: *Ex corde Ecclesiae* Spring 1995 Dialogues

The *Ex Corde Ecclesiae* Implementation Committee meeting, 27 January 1995, reviewed reports from the Fall 1994 dialogues of bishops and representatives of Catholic colleges and universities. Many thanks to all who participated in these dialogues and forwarded summaries of their discussions. Brief commentaries on the themes and reports of the Fall 1994 dialogues, presented by Bishop James Malone and myself at the annual meeting of the Association of Catholic Colleges and Universities two weeks ago, are available in *Origins* (16 February 1995).

Enclosed are several suggested questions for the Spring 1995 dialogues relative to the Mandate (Canon 812) cited in *Ex corde Ecclesiae*. The Implementation Committee suggests that the focus of the dialogues be on the goals of the Canon, the values it seeks, and specific ways to achieve those goals and values in the context of contemporary American higher education.

Some values identified in *Ex corde Ecclesiae*, for example, are as follows:

Catholic theology, taught in a manner faithful to Scripture, Tradition, and the Church's Magisterium, provides an awareness of the Gospel principles which will enrich the meaning of human life and give it a new dignity. (Part I, #20)

Theology has its legitimate place in the University alongside other disciplines. It has proper principles and methods which define it as a branch of

From the author's files.

knowledge. Theologians enjoy this same freedom so long as they are faithful to these principles and methods.

Bishops should encourage the creative work of theologians. They serve the Church through research done in a way that respects theological method. They seek to understand better, further develop and more effectively communicate the meaning of Christian Revelation as transmitted in Scripture and Tradition.

EX CORDE ECCLESIAE

SUGGESTED QUESTIONS FOR THE SPRING 1995 DIALOGUES

The Implementation Committee of *Ex corde Ecclesiae* affirms and respects the integrity of the established, peer-generated processes by which Catholic colleges and universities hire faculty, including members of the theology/religious studies departments. The expectation is that the Catholic institution seeks effective and qualified staff who are committed to the Catholic tradition or, if the applicants are not Catholic, respectful of that tradition.

1. How does your current program in theology/religious studies achieve the values/goals mentioned in *Ex corde Ecclesiae*?
2. What do you see as needed in your program for a better achievement of those goals and values?
3. How do you envision hiring faculty committed to such goals? How can you facilitate the present faculty members' consideration of them?
4. Are there existing opportunities for inter-disciplinary discussions where theological traditions can be explored by faculty from many disciplines and be related to their own areas of research and teaching? Can some be created?
5. *EcE* #48 calls attention to a meaning of "evangelization" which has special significance to the academic community. How can a Catholic college or university go about "bringing the Good News into all strata of humanity, and through its influence transforming humanity from within . . . "? How can a Catholic college or university "affect and upset humanity's criteria of judgment, determining values, points of interest, lines of thought, sources of inspiration and models of life, which are in contrast with the Word of God and the plan of salvation"?

22 | Draft of "*Ex Corde Ecclesiae*: An Application to the United States" with Accompanying Documents

August 25, 1995

(*EcE*-doc A)
Covering Letter

DATE: August 25, 1995
TO: Bishops, Presidents, Learned Societies,
          Sponsoring Religious Communities
FROM: Bishop John J. Leibrecht
ON: *Ex corde Ecclesiae*

Thanks to all of you who have communicated with the *Ex corde Ecclesiae* Implementation Committee this past year. Your comments and recommendations have been considered by the Committee as it responds to its charge of preparing for the bishops of the United States a proposal which implements the apostolic constitution.

The enclosed paper, "*Ex corde Ecclesiae: An Application to the United States*," is the latest effort of the Committee to place *Ex corde Ecclesiae* within the context of our nation. The Committee requests that bishops and college/university representatives, including trustees and faculty, meet together to discuss the paper. No written reports are asked of dialogue participants, but anyone who would like to write to the Committee is encouraged to do so (*Ex corde Ecclesiae* Implementation Committee, 3211 Fourth Street, NE, Washington, D.C. 20017-1194). Also enclosed are "*Background I*" (history), "*Background II-A*" (comments

From the author's files.

on draft document), and *Background II-B* (a canonical rationale—canon 812) which might be useful in the discussion.

Dialogues should be completed prior to the November 13, 1995, meeting of the National Conference of Catholic Bishops where, pending approval by the Administrative Board, time will be available for discussion of the enclosed *"Application"* paper. Dialogues before mid-November, therefore, could be very helpful to the bishops at their annual meeting.

The Committee is not asking the bishops of NCCB for approval of the enclosed paper at this November's meeting, but is asking for discussion and guidance for a revision which will then be presented for action and approval at a 1996 NCCB meeting. Prior to that 1996 meeting, bishops will again be asked to meet with college/university representatives. After a vote by the national assembly of bishops, the document implementing *Ex corde Ecclesiae* in the United States will be sent to the Congregation for Catholic Education for final canonical recognition.

If there is any question about the above procedure or time line, please call Reverend Terrence Toland SJ, Project Director for the *Ex corde Ecclesiae* Implementation Committee (202-541-3017) or myself (417-866-0841). We will be happy to assist.

(*EcE*-doc B)

DRAFT FOR DISCUSSION

EX CORDE ECCLESIAE

AN APPLICATION TO THE UNITED STATES

Catholic colleges and universities are participants in both the life of the Church and the higher education enterprise of the United States. As such, they "are called to continuous renewal, both as 'Universities' and as 'Catholic.'"[1] This twofold relationship is described in the 22 May 1994 joint document of the Congregation for Catholic Education and the Pontifical Councils for the Laity and for Culture which states that the Catholic university achieves its purpose when

> ... it gives proof of being rigorously serious as a member of the international community of knowledge and expresses its Catholic identity through an explicit link with the Church, at both local and universal levels—an identity which marks concretely the life, the services and the programs of the university community. In this way, by its very existence, the Catholic university achieves its aim of guaranteeing, in institutional form, a Christian presence in the university world. . . .[2]

This relationship is clarified through dialogue which includes faculty, students, staff, academic officers, trustees, and sponsoring religious communities of the educational institutions. The bishop and his collaborators in the local church are integral parties in this dialogue.

The Catholic college or university is related to the entire ecclesial community,[3] to the legal and civil context,[4] and to the higher education academy.[5] We are directing special attention to the relationship between the institutions and church authorities. *Ex corde Ecclesiae* itself provides a useful framework to address this specific relationship:

> Bishops have a particular responsibility to promote Catholic Universities, and especially to promote and assist in the preservation and strengthening of their Catholic identity, including the protection of their Catholic identity in relation to civil authorities. This will be achieved more effectively if close and pastoral relationships exist between University and Church authorities, characterized by *mutual trust, close and consistent cooperation and continuing dialogue.* Even when they do not enter directly into the internal government of the University, Bishops "should be seen not as external agents but as participants in the life of the Catholic University" (italics added).[6]

Each of these three elements in the pastoral relationship of bishops with Catholic colleges and universities warrants attention.

I. Mutual trust between university and church authorities

A. Mutual trust goes beyond the personalities of those involved in the relationship. The trust is grounded in a shared baptismal belief in the implications, secular and religious, which are identified in Scripture concerning the mystery of the Incarnation: God the creator, who works even until now; God the incarnate redeemer, who is the Way and the Truth and the Life; and God the Paraclete, the Holy Spirit whom the Father sends. In the spirit of *communio,* the relationship between college/university and church authorities is based on these shared beliefs and is fostered by mutual listening, collaboration which respects differing responsibilities and gifts, and by a solidarity which mutually recognizes official and statutory limitations, as well as responsibilities.

B. From this it follows:

1. that the institution's relationship to the Church, in accord with the principles of *Ex corde Ecclesiae,* should be affirmed by the institution through public acknowledgment of its Catholic identity in official documentation (e.g., in its mission statement);
2. that the institution, following its own procedures in the hiring and retention of professionally qualified faculty and staff, seeks individuals who are committed to the Catholic tradition or, if the applicants are not Catholic, aware and respectful of that tradition;
3. that, aware of the contributions made by theologians to Church and academy, the local bishop in accord with his ecclesial responsibility, in circumstances where he questions whether or not an individual theologian is presenting authentic Catholic teaching, shall follow procedures of due process (as noted next in #4) and take appropriate action;
4. that *Doctrinal Responsibilities: Approaches to Promoting Cooperation and Resolving Misunderstandings Between Bishops and Theologians,* approved and published by the National Conference of Catholic Bishops, 17 June 1989, is adopted as the appropriate procedure to assure due process to both bishop and theologian.

II. Close and consistent cooperation between university/college and church authorities

A. Collaborating to integrate faith with life is a necessary part of the "close personal and pastoral relationships"[7] to which colleges/universities and bishops aspire. Many cooperative programs, related to Gospel outreach, already flourish throughout the country. It is highly desirable that issues concerning social justice and the needs of the poor be identified, studied, and programmed jointly by representatives of both the educational institution and Church authorities.

Allocation of personnel and money to assure the special contributions of campus ministry is required. As a concern of the whole Church, and in view of the presence on campus of persons of other religious traditions, ecumenical and interreligious relationships should be fostered with sensitivity.

B. From this it follows:

1. that an institutional plan (which includes, but is not restricted to, campus ministry) be in place to encourage on-campus awareness of ways to be of service to the Church,[8] including contributions to the mission of evangelization,[9] service to the poor, social justice initiatives, and ecumenical and interreligious activities;
2. that provision be made cooperatively for adequately staffed campus ministry programs, including opportunities for the sacraments and other liturgical celebrations.[10]

III. Continuing dialogue among college/university representatives and church authorities

A. Dialogues occasioned by *Ex corde Ecclesiae* are graced moments characterized by (a) a manifest openness to a further analysis and local appropriation of Catholic identity, (b) an appreciation of the positive contributions which campus-wide conversations make, and (c) a conviction that conversation can develop and sustain relationships. A need exists for continued attention and commitment to the far-reaching implications—curricular, staffing, programming—of major themes within *Ex corde Ecclesiae*. These include Catholic identity, *communio,* relating faith and culture, pastoral outreach, the new evangelization, and relationship to the Church.

B. From this it follows:

1. that a mutual commitment to regular dialogues, according to local needs and circumstances, be honored by institution and diocese;
2. that periodically, every Catholic college/university undertake an internal review of the congruence of its course of instruction, its service activity, and its research programs with the ideals and principles expressed in *Ex corde Ecclesiae*;
3. that the National Conference of Catholic Bishops, through an appropriate committee structure, continue its dialogue with the Association of Catholic Colleges and Universities.

The bishops of the United States, in offering this application of *Ex corde Ec-clesiae,* join in sentiments expressed by Pope John Paul II:

I turn to the whole Church, convinced that Catholic Universities are essen-tial to her growth and to the development of Christian culture and human progress. For this reason, the entire ecclesial community is invited to give its support to Catholic Institutions of higher education and to assist them in their process of development and renewal. . . .[11]

NOTES

1. *Ex corde Ecclesiae,* Introduction, #7.

2. "The Church's Presence in the University and in University Culture," *Origins,* 16 June 1994, II, #2.

3. *Ex corde Ecclesiae,* Introduction, #11.

4. Ibid., Part II, 1, #2.

5. Ibid., Part I, #12.

6. Ibid., Part 1, #28. The citation at the end is from John Paul II, Address to Leaders of Catholic Higher Education, Xavier University of Louisiana, U.S.A., 12 September 1987, n. 4: *AAS* 80 (1988), p. 764.

7. Ibid., Part I, #28.

8. Ibid., #38 ff.

9. Ibid., #48–49.

10. Ibid., Part II, 6, #2.

11. Ibid., #11.

(*EcE*-doc C)
BACKGROUND I: HISTORY

EX CORDE ECCLESIAE

SOME HISTORY

Two questions receive repeated attention in Catholic higher education: (1) What does it mean to be a college or university? and (2) What does it mean for that institution to be Catholic? The 1990 papal document on Catholic universities, *Ex corde Ecclesiae,* was part of this inquiry.

The Second Vatican Council, 1963–1965, noted that higher education, secular and Catholic, contributes to the well-being both of society and the community of believers who are citizens of this world and the City of God. The Council's document, the *Pastoral Constitution on the Church in the Modern World (Gaudium et Spes)* "affirms the legitimate autonomy of human culture and especially of the sciences," but notes that there are "many links between the message of salvation and human culture" (cf. #57–62). In its *Declaration on Christian Education (Gravissimum Educationis,* #10), the Council encourages students "to shoulder society's heavier burdens and to witness the faith to the world."

The importance of Catholic higher education to the Church in the United States has been affirmed in several ways. In 1974, a joint committee of U.S. bishops and Catholic college/university presidents was established to provide a forum for support and the exchange of information. Pope John Paul II spoke of his high regard for Catholic higher education at The Catholic University of America in October 1979, and again at Xavier University of Louisiana in September 1987. The bishops of the United States issued a pastoral letter, *Higher Education and the Pastoral Mission of the Church* in 1980.

In the introduction of his 1990 Apostolic Constitution on Catholic higher education, Pope John Paul II recalled that the historical origin of the university is traced back to the Church, to the "heart of the Church." Building upon that long-standing relationship between university and Church, the Pope offers his vision of the identity and mission of the Catholic college or university, as Catholic. Developed after consultation with leadership from Catholic higher education, *Ex corde Ecclesiae* and its General Norms are "to be applied concretely at the local and regional levels by episcopal conferences . . . taking into account the statutes of each university or institute and, as far as possible and appropriate, civil law." (*Ex corde Ecclesiae,* Part II, Article 1, {2})

In 1991 [December 15, 1990; see Doc. 2] the president of the National Conference of Catholic Bishops in the United States, Archbishop Daniel Pilarczyk, established a committee of seven bishops and eleven consultants, eight of whom were Catholic college and university presidents. The committee's task was to develop a process for implementing *Ex corde Ecclesiae* in the United States.

For information on how these questions have been addressed over the past three decades, for the story of "times of startling changes, significant soul-searching, and extraordinary maturing," see *American Catholic Higher Education: Essential Documents, 1967–1990,* edited by Alice Gallin, O.S.U., University of Notre Dame Press, Notre Dame, Indiana, 1992. A briefer study was provided by Phillip Gleason, 'The American Background of *Ex corde Ecclesiae,* A Historical Perspective," an essay included in *Catholic Universities in Church and Society and Ex corde Ecclesiae,* edited by John P. Langan, S.J., Georgetown University Press, Washington, D.C., 1993.

Those applying the papal document to Catholic higher education in the United States recognize the significant diversity among these institutions in size, history, location and changing constituencies. They recognize, too, that in their relationships to State and Church and Academy, U.S. Catholic colleges and universities are also distinct, if not unique, in the international academic community.

(*EcE*-doc D)

BACKGROUND II-A

COMMENTS ON DRAFT DOCUMENT

FROM: Bishop John J. Leibrecht

A few comments may be helpful regarding the draft document, "*Ex corde Ecclesiae*: An Application to the United States." Each comment below refers to a corresponding numbered statement in the three sections beginning "From this it follows."

I. Mutual trust between college/university and church authorities

> NB: as a response to the application of the purpose and value of canon 812, these four points should be viewed as a whole.

"From this it follows:"

1) This provision involves more than simply identifying the college or university as Catholic. In identifying the institution as Catholic, some means should be provided for addressing Catholic identity. Some colleges and universities, for instance, have informed our Implementation Committee about mission-effectiveness staff whose continuing responsibility is to promote the Catholic identity of the institution. Such staff persons

serve the entire institution which, as a totality, has the responsibility for Catholic identity.

2) Responsibility for Catholic identity is with the institution. Its own internal procedures should effectively promote the Catholic nature of the college or university.

3) This statement addresses Canon 812. My mailing to you of February 10, 1995, included an article from the September 1994 issue of the *Newsletter* of the Canon Law Society of Great Britain and Ireland. Bishop John Jukes, OFM Conv., is one of several who have proposed this view of Canon 812. For the position of our *Ex corde Ecclesiae* Implementation Committee, see the attached *"Background II-B* A Canonical Rationale: Canon 812."

4) The document, *Doctrinal Responsibilities,* was approved in 1989 for use by those bishops who wanted to use it as a guide. This provision in the draft document for discussion would, in effect, establish that already approved document as the accepted due process procedure.

II. Close and consistent cooperation between university/college and church authorities

"From this it follows:"

1) The sections cited on "Pastoral Ministry" and "Evangelization" in *Ex corde Ecclesiae* form the reference points for this particular statement.

2) Campus ministry is a pastoral aspect of college and university life, including sacramental and other liturgical celebrations, in which cooperation between the local bishop and the university is especially important.

III. Continuing dialogue among college/university representatives and church authorities

"From this it follows:"

1) No particular definition is made of the word "regular" in this statement. Its interpretation should be made locally. The statement does, however, call for calendar commitments to on-going dialogues.

2) Some colleges and universities will associate such an internal review with what they normally do at the time of accrediting association reviews. It is possible to have what is called for in this statement at another time than that. "Periodically" is not specified but should be locally decided.

3) Dialogues over the years between the ACCU and bishops have been productive for all concerned. This statement would establish a specific mechanism for on-going dialogue between the two.

In the name of the Implementation Committee, I thank all of you for your
interest and help in taking these next steps and providing the comments and
recommendations needed for a next revision. Little by little, the focus will be
shifting from the Implementation Committee to individual bishops and college and university representatives in their arch/dioceses. It will also become
more focused on the full assembly of bishops in their national meetings. Dialogues between bishops and representatives of Catholic higher education, in
the months ahead, will prove especially helpful.

Thank you.

JJL:kas

(*EcE*-doc E)

BACKGROUND II-B

A CANONICAL RATIONALE: CANON 812

The concrete application of the norms of *Ex corde Ecclesiae* in the United States,
while in conformity with the Code of Canon Law, complementary Church legislation, and the statutes of each Catholic college or university, will of necessity
take into consideration the particular circumstances of Catholic higher education in our country. During the many months of consultation and discussion
on the apostolic constitution and its implementation in the United States, the
matter of canon 812 and its provision of ecclesiastical authorization (a *mandatum*) for Catholic teachers of theology in institutions of higher education
continued to raise concerns among bishops, educators, theologians, canon and
civil lawyers.

The *Ex corde Ecclesiae* Implementation Committee has listened. We have
spent many hours in study and discussion looking for the best means of preserving the value that underlies canon 812, namely, safeguarding the orthodoxy

of church teaching within Catholic colleges and universities. We believe, however, that canon 812 and the mandate should not be viewed outside the broader context of the central call of *Ex corde Ecclesiae,* that is, to fulfill a Catholic mission and identity. The canon must be seen as integral to the apostolic constitution's concrete affirmation of the Catholic college and university as a bridge between the Gospel and culture.

In this context we believe that the local application of the norms of *Ex corde Ecclesiae* must take into consideration the long history of Catholic higher education in the United States and the uniqueness of the some 230 Catholic colleges and universities in this country. At the same time, such applications must safeguard church teaching for the people of God while guaranteeing institutional autonomy and academic freedom, on the one hand, and respect for church authority and loyal assent, on the other. We believe, too, that dialogue between bishops and theologians is indispensable to the guarantee of these values.

To achieve this balance we are convinced that the values inherent in canon 812 are best realized through a non-juridical application of the *mandatum,* that is, through the institution of processes and procedures that can be viewed as fulfilling the purpose of canon 812 while respecting established standards of Catholic higher education. *The four points contained in section I, B, of the Implementation Committee's draft document for discussion should be viewed as a whole, for the totality of these points constitutes its response to the application of the value and purpose of canon 812.*

23 | Response from the Cardinal Newman Society for the Preservation of Catholic Higher Education

November 1, 1995

Cardinal Newman Society
for the Preservation of Catholic Higher Education
November 1, 1995
Feast of All Saints

Most Rev. John Leibrecht
Ex corde Ecclesiae Implementation Committee
National Conference of Catholic Bishops
3211 4th Street, NE
Washington, DC 20017-1194

Your Excellency:

It is with honest sincerity that we applaud the efforts of the Implementation Committee in its recent draft of ordinances to fulfill a mandate expressed in *Ex corde Ecclesiae.*

Indeed we are well aware of how complex the dialogue process has been. There are a myriad of representatives from each area of Catholic higher education all involved in the dialogue. Therefore we praise your efforts to take all voices in account and urge you to continue to seek new ways to ensure the future strength of Catholic higher education.

From the author's files.

There are a number of concerns we wish to bring to your attention. In particular we believe that the proposed ordinances fail to adequately address existing pro-abortion and homosexual activism, dissident theologians, administrators and faculty members who oppose Church teachings, and a general disregard for the teaching authority of the Magisterium at Catholic colleges and universities nationwide.

Specifically we believe that the new draft of ordinances fails to address the most urgent needs of Catholic higher education, including the following:

- **Ensuring that theological educators are faithful to the Magisterium of the Church.**
  The ordinances reject implementation of the requirement in Canon 812 and *Ex corde Ecclesiae,* that teachers of theology must obtain a mandate from the local bishop or other suitable "ecclesiastical authority". Instead, the Committee inappropriately assumes the authority to create a substitute to Canon Law that is intended only to "preserve the value that underlies" that Law. The purpose of the ordinances is to implement *Ex corde Ecclesiae* and Canon Law, not to rewrite the Law. The Committee's substitute is a weak method for ensuring "due process" after a dispute has already occurred between a bishop and a theologian.
- **Providing an authentically Catholic perspective in the teaching of all academic disciplines.**
  The broad language of the ordinances undermines the specific requirement of *Ex corde Ecclesiae* that non-Catholics may not constitute a majority of an institution's faculty. No process is offered to resolve concerns about teachers in disciplines other than theology. The ordinances do not forbid institutions from claiming a policy of nondiscrimination with regard to religious beliefs, a claim that exposes institutions with hiring preferences for Catholics to civil litigation.
- **Guaranteeing that "Catholic ideals, attitudes and principles penetrate and inform university activities in accordance with the proper nature and autonomy of these activities."** *(Ex corde Ecclesiae)*
  The ordinances do not address concerns about institutions that support, financially or otherwise, or provide facilities to advocates of views that are contrary to Catholic teachings. Student activities are not addressed by the "internal review" required of each institution. In addition, the ordinances do not address concerns about dormitory living and campus activities that foster promiscuous activity and views that are contrary to Catholic

teachings. Campus policies and services are not addressed by the "internal review" required of each institution.

- **Providing for Catholic chaplaincy services, including evangelization and opportunities to receive the sacraments, in a manner that is in accordance with Church norms.**
  The ordinances fail to clarify that campus ministry staff must not only be adequate in number, but must also be faithful Catholics who minister within the context of Catholic teachings and in accordance with the Church's liturgical norms.

- **Preventing the dilution of the institutions' Catholic identity due to misguided policies affecting non-Catholics.**
  The ordinances fail to distinguish between undue discrimination against non-Catholics and appropriate efforts to maintain a Catholic identity by hiring Catholic personnel, recruiting Catholic students, and refusing to provide institutional support for non-Catholic beliefs. A prohibition is needed against institutionally supported religious services, evangelization, course work, and campus events which promote non-Catholic beliefs or present such beliefs outside the context of Catholic teachings. Support includes the use of campus facilities, institutional funds, or other services provided by the institution.

- **Ensuring that any future dialogue on Catholic higher education includes students, faculty, alumni, and trustees of American Catholic institutions.**
  The introduction to the ordinances rightly calls for a dialogue "which includes faculty, students, staff, academic officers, trustees, and sponsoring religious communities of the educational institutions," as well as "the bishop and his collaborators". Nevertheless, the dialogue that has been conducted for the past several years has been restricted primarily to the bishops and college and university administrators. The single ordinance referring to a continuing dialogue (Article III, B-3) includes only the Association of Catholic Colleges and Universities (ACCU) in this dialogue. We are concerned that the ACCU does not include several of the most faithful Catholic institutions among its members, and the ACCU has demonstrated a strong reluctance to implement *Ex corde Ecclesiae* in the United States.

We humbly submit these considerations to aid the discussion on the ordinances at the November NCCB meeting and we urge you and your fellow bishops to insist that the full vision of *Ex corde Ecclesiae* be implemented for the future of Catholic higher education.

Please let us know if we can assist you further.

May God bless you for your service to the Church and keep in strength and wisdom.

> Sincerely,
> Patrick J. Reilly
> Executive Director

24 | Draft of "*Ex Corde Ecclesiae*: An Application to the United States"

February 23, 1996

TO:	Bishops, College/University Presidents, Learned Societies, Religious Community Sponsors
FROM:	Bishop John J. Leibrecht Chair, Ex corde Ecclesiae Implementation Committee
DATE:	23 February 1996
ON:	revised draft, "Ex corde Ecclesiae, An Application to the United States"

When the first draft of [the Application of] "*Ex corde Ecclesiae*" was mailed on 25 August 1995, you were invited to forward suggestions to the Implementation Committee. At the Committee meeting on 26 January 1996, every proposed revision without exception was carefully considered. This included the suggestions made during the floor discussion at the meeting in November 1995 of the National Conference of Catholic Bishops. The attached draft under date of 2/23/96 incorporates the proposals accepted by the Committee at its meeting last month. New wording is italicized in this revised text.

In decisions about proposed revisions, the Committee members kept in mind that the Apostolic Constitution itself is the primary text offering guidance for the future. Building on the pastoral relationships between colleges/universities and Church authorities about which the Holy Father speaks of in #28 of *Ex corde Ecclesiae,* the enclosed document proposes to structure the three components of relationship-building which are noted in that same paragraph.

All concerned, especially those who have not yet had dialogues on the application document for the United States, are encouraged to do so during the next few months of this Spring academic semester. These conversations will be

From the author's files.

helpful to the bishops who will be discussing this revised document at the NCCB meeting on 20–23 June 1996. The Implementation Committee will welcome and review all suggestions at its meeting the last week of June.

A newly revised document for implementing *Ex corde Ecclesiae* in the United States will be sent to you late this summer. Dialogues on that draft during the 1996 Fall semester will precede a vote by the full assembly of bishops at its 11–14 November meeting this year.

As in the past, the *EcE* Project Director, Reverend Terrence Toland SJ, will be happy to be with you for your local dialogues or to respond to any questions you might have. His telephone number at the NCCB/USCC: 202–541–3017.

Thanks to all for your continuing cooperation in the work of the *Ex corde Ecclesiae* Implementation Committee.

2/23/96

(NOTE: 8/25/95—ORIGINAL DRAFT; 2/23/96—FIRST REVISION;
CHANGES APPROVED BY
IMPLEMENTATION COMMITTEE ARE ITALICIZED)
DRAFT FOR DISCUSSION

EX CORDE ECCLESIAE

AN APPLICATION TO THE UNITED STATES

Catholic colleges and universities are participants in both the life of the Church and the higher education enterprise of the United States. As such, they "are called to continuous renewal, both as 'Universities' and as 'Catholic.'"[1] This twofold relationship is described in the 22 May 1994 joint document of the Congregation for Catholic Education and the Pontifical Councils for the Laity and for Culture which states that the Catholic university achieves its purpose when

. . . it gives proof of being rigorously serious as a member of the international community of knowledge and expresses its Catholic identity through an explicit link with the Church, at both local and universal levels—an identity which marks concretely the life, the services and the programs of the university community. In this way, by its very existence, the Catholic university achieves its aim of guaranteeing, in institutional form, a Christian presence in the university world. . . .[2]

This relationship is clarified through dialogue which includes faculty *of all disciplines,* students, staff, academic officers, trustees, and sponsoring religious communities of the educational institutions. The bishop and his collaborators in the local church are integral parties in this dialogue.

The Catholic college or university is related to the entire ecclesial community,[3] to the *broader society,*[4] as well as to the higher education academy.[5] We are directing special attention to the relationship between the institutions and church authorities. Ex corde Ecclesiae itself provides a useful framework to address this specific relationship:

> Bishops have a particular responsibility to promote Catholic Universities, and especially to promote and assist in the preservation and strengthening of their Catholic identity, including the protection of their Catholic identity in relation to civil authorities. This will be achieved more effectively if close and pastoral relationships exist between University and Church authorities, characterized by *mutual trust, close and consistent cooperation and continuing dialogue.* Even when they do not enter directly into the internal government of the University, Bishops "should be seen not as external agents but as participants in the life of the Catholic University" (italics added).[6]

Each of these three elements in the pastoral relationship of bishops with Catholic colleges and universities warrants attention.

I. Mutual trust between university and church authorities

A. Mutual trust goes beyond the personalities of those involved in the relationship. The trust is grounded in a shared baptismal belief in the *truths that* are *found* in Scripture concerning the mystery of the Incarnation: God the creator, who works even until now; God the incarnate redeemer, who is the Way and the Truth and the Life; and God the Paraclete, the Holy Spirit whom the Father sends. In the spirit of communio, the relationship of trust between college/ university and church authorities, based on these shared beliefs *with secular and religious implications,* is fostered by mutual listening, by collaboration that respects differing responsibilities and gifts, and by a solidarity that mutually recognizes respective statutory limitations and responsibilities.

B. From this it follows:

1. that the institution's relationship to the Church, in accord with the principles of <u>Ex corde Ecclesiae,</u> should be affirmed by the institution through public acknowledgment of its Catholic identity in official documentation (e.g., in its mission statement);

2. *that, when appropriate, bishops acknowledge publicly the service of Catholic colleges/universities to the Church, and support the Catholic identity of the institutions if this identity is unjustifiably challenged;*

3. that the institution, following its own procedures in the hiring and retention of professionally qualified faculty and staff, seeks individuals who are committed to the Catholic tradition or, if not Catholic, who are aware and respectful of that tradition;

4. that, aware of the contributions made by theologians to Church and academy, the local bishop in accord with his ecclesial responsibility, in circumstances where he questions whether or not an individual theologian is presenting authentic Catholic teaching, shall follow *established procedures* (as noted next in #5) and take appropriate action;

5. that <u>Doctrinal Responsibilities: Approaches to Promoting Cooperation and Resolving Misunderstandings Between Bishops and Theologians,</u> approved and published by the National Conference of Catholic Bishops, 17 June 1989, is adopted as the appropriate procedure to assure *a process acceptable to* both bishop and *teacher.*

II. Close and consistent cooperation between university/college and church authorities

A. Collaborating to integrate faith with life is a necessary part of the "close personal and pastoral relationships"[7] to which colleges/universities and bishops aspire. *Within their academic mission of teaching and research, in ways appropriate to their own histories and constituencies, institutions offer courses in Catholic theology that are taught in accord with the best scholarship and the authentic teaching authority of the Church.*

Many cooperative programs, related to Gospel outreach, already flourish throughout the country. It is highly desirable that issues concerning social justice and the needs of the poor continue to be identified, studied, and pro-grammed jointly by representatives of both the educational institution and Church authorities.

Allocation of personnel and money to assure the special contributions of campus ministry is required. As a concern of the whole Church, and in view of the presence on campus of persons of other religious traditions, ecumenical and interreligious relationships should be fostered with sensitivity.

B. From this it follows:

1. that *a plan for fulfilling its institutional mission as Catholic* be in place which encourages on-campus awareness of ways *to grow in understanding of the faith and* to be of service to the Church,[8] *and which addresses intellectual and pastoral* contributions to the mission of evangelization,[9] service to the poor, social justice initiatives, and ecumenical and interreligious activities;
2. that provision be made cooperatively for adequately staffed campus min-istry programs, including opportunities for the sacraments and other litur-gical celebrations.[10]

III. Continuing dialogue among college/university representatives and church authorities

A. Dialogues occasioned by <u>Ex corde Ecclesiae</u> are graced moments charac-terized by (a) a manifest openness to a further analysis and local appropriation of Catholic identity, (b) an appreciation of the positive contributions which campus-wide conversations make, and (c) a conviction that conversation can de-velop and sustain relationships. A need exists for continued attention and com-mitment to the far-reaching implications—curricular, staffing, programming—of major themes within <u>Ex corde Ecclesiae</u>. These include Catholic identity, <u>communio</u>, relating faith and culture, pastoral outreach, the new evangelization, and relationship to the Church.

B. From this it follows:

1. that a mutual commitment to regular dialogues, according to local needs and circumstances, be honored by institution and diocese;
2. that periodically, every Catholic college/university undertake an internal re-view of the congruence of its *mission statement,* its courses of instruction, its service activity, and its research programs with the ideals and principles expressed in <u>Ex corde Ecclesiae</u>;

3. that the National Conference of Catholic Bishops, through an appropriate committee structure, continue its dialogue with the Association of Catholic Colleges and Universities.

The bishops of the United States, in offering this application of <u>Ex corde Ecclesiae</u>, join in sentiments expressed by Pope John Paul II:

I turn to the whole Church, convinced that Catholic Universities are essential to her growth and to the development of Christian culture and human progress. For this reason, the entire ecclesial community is invited to give its support to Catholic Institutions of higher education and to assist them in their process of development and renewal. . . .[11]

NOTES

1. *Ex corde Ecclesiae,* Introduction, #7.
2. "The Church's Presence in the University and in University Culture," *Origins,* 16 June 1994, II, #2.
3. *Ex corde Ecclesiae,* Introduction, #11.
4. Ibid., Part II, #2.
5. Ibid., Part I, #12.
6. Ibid., Part I, #28. The citation at the end is from John Paul II, Address to Leaders of Catholic Higher Education, Xavier University of Louisiana, U.S.A., 12 September 1987, n. 4: *AAS* 80 (1988), p. 764.
7. Ibid., Part I, #28.
8. Ibid., #38 ff.
9. Ibid., #48–49.
10. Ibid., Part II, 6, #2.
11. Ibid., #11.

25 | Opening Comments by Bishop John Leibrecht, NCCB Meeting

June 20, 1996

Bishop Pilla, thanks very much to you and to the administrative board for this opportunity to continue the discussion on *Ex corde Ecclesiae*. Recall that our meeting last November ended when there were still some bishops who wanted to speak and so we sought this additional time today. I also want to thank the bishops who have corresponded with the Implementation Committee since our November meeting. Before hearing comments and suggestions from the floor, I'd like to make a few opening remarks.

What will be happening after today? Our Committee will meet next week to go over both what we hear today and everything we've received since last November. Then, we'll send to you a new draft for dialogues this fall with your institutions. We hope to have a vote on that draft at our November meeting and, depending upon what happens there, we may or may not be in a position to forward a document to the Holy See. It is this timeline on which we are proceding.

The intention of our Committee is to give you a document that really is pastoral in its approach. I cannot emphasize that enough. Some of the more positive reactions we have heard, not only from yourselves but also from the institutions, come because this pastoral mode is being picked up.

In following a pastoral approach, our Committee believes we are following the lead of our Holy Father. In *Ex corde Ecclesiae,* he encourages "personal and pastoral relationships" between the Catholic institutions of higher education and church authority. Personal and pastoral—that's what has been evident these past months and last few years in all the dialogues around the country. We think the quality of a pastoral approach is very important and hope that, whatever our final document may be, we keep that tone in mind.

From the author's files.

A pastoral approach applies to everything that has to do with Catholic identity and Catholic mission. There are many aspects, many elements, to what makes a college or university Catholic. We bishops have a role in looking at all of that.

One of the items within that broader picture of Catholic identity and mission is Canon 812. I would like to take just a few minutes to share with you the development of thinking within the Committee over our five years of work. I hope that sharing the evaluation of our own thinking might be helpful and give context to our conversations today.

In May of 1993, we sent out our first draft of ordinances and one of the ordinances dealt with Canon 812. In that proposal, we tried to come up with something which took many factors into view. For instance, *Ex corde Eccelsiae* tells us that the bishop is to be a participant in the life of the university but is not to be involved in its internal government. That must be kept in mind. The Committee also knew that the institutions have autonomy and that professors have academic freedom. *Ex corde Ecclesiae* specifically refers to those two factors. It is the university and college which hires and dismisses any of its staff. The Committee tried to keep all of these things in mind and come up with something that would, in effect, be a kind of certification for those who are involved in what *Ex corde Ecclesiae* calls the theological disciplines. In the Committee document of May, 1993, an ordinance stated: "When a professor is to be hired, the college or university should inform that person that the church expects that he or she have a mandate." The institution was in a role of *informing* the professor. The second step in this proposed ordinance was that the bishop would invite the professor to seek a *mandate* from him. That proposed ordinance of May, 1993, was sent out to all of you, Catholic institutions of higher education, learned societies, and others.

If you will recall, there was a great concern about the proposed ordinance not only from the institutions, but from many bishops. The theme heard by the Committee was: "That approach is going to create more problems than it solves; it is not the way to go."

Our Committee met again after hearing from you and made several conclusions: one was that implementing Canon 812 by a certificate process would potentially create all kinds of divisions—divisions between the institutions themselves, divisions within the theological departments, possibly divisions between the institutions and bishops. Not all concluded that; but it was a clear and consistent theme. The Committee heard that a process of certification as licensing is potentially very divisive.

The second conclusion we made was that we could not "fix" the proposed ordinance—do something to it that would make it more acceptable and better. We had to look for some new way other than the one than we had proposed.

What would that new way be? First of all, we talked about seeking an indult. But as the Committee worked we said no, we don't want to seek an indult, we want to implement Canon 812 in some way within our own tradition of higher education in the United States.

As we looked for a new way, we went to the General Norms (article 4, paragraph 3). That particular General Norm states that "Catholic theologians" are "to be faithful to the magisterium of the church." At the end of that article is the footnote which names several documents to confer; one of which is Canon 812. That's how Canon 812 specifically comes into *Ex corde Ecclesiae,* in a footnote, but the footnote is to a Norm which states that Catholic theologians must be faithful to the magisterium of the church. Our Committee asked how that Norm could be implemented? If we can implement the intent of that Norm, then at the same time we'll be addressing Canon 812. How can the goal of that particular Norm be fulfilled by other than a process of certification?

In the next draft we sent to you, the Committee put together several things that we thought would implement Canon 812 in this country. It basically said two things:

First, the institution itself had to be aware of and responsible for its hiring of professors who would be faithful to the magisterium. The institution itself sees to it that the department or school of theology is really functioning in a way that helps it remain faithful to the magisterium. The institution has a responsibility to see to it that the magisterium is respected by professors in hiring and its work of teaching and research.

Secondly, we said that if something goes wrong, the bishop needs to step in with a procedure agreed to by everyone whereby the bishop can address problems. That was the approach. Some of you said that approach could work. Some of you were concerned that we were really not implementing 812. The Committee knows it's difficult to keep in mind all the various factors, regarding the appropriate role of bishops and how Catholic higher education functions in this country, and produce a plan consistent with our hopes.

Look to the responsibilities of the institution and remind them of their responsibilities. If that doesn't work well in a particular situation, then the bishop has to have a process or procedure to address the matter in a successful way.

Canon 812 is still the neuralgic issue before the Committee. There are many other considerations, as you all know, to having an institution be Catholic in its identity and its mission—many other items. Catholic identity and mission are not identified with Canon 812 only. That's too narrow, but it and its goal of orthodoxy in theological disciplines are obviously a very important and special part of the broader issue of identity and mission in Catholic higher education.

The Committee, therefore, progressed from a proposal for certification to locating a more conscious responsibility in the institution and a pastoral oversight role for the bishop when there are problems. Some will agree with that thinking, some are concerned that it does not adequately address the situation.

In the last Committee meeting, we took the concerns we heard about Canon 812 into consideration. We talked about them and, basically, come back to say that what we present to you now is still fairly much what we presented last November. We want to hear more, but we think that the proposal we tried first in May of 1993, a certification process, as many said, would create more problems than it would solve. We will have to give additional attention to this issue.

Before opening to the floor for comments, I want to cite two resources that might be helpful. "Contending with Modernity, Catholic Higher Education in the Twentieth Century" is a recent book written by Professor Philip Gleason of the University of Notre Dame. It is published by Oxford University Press. "Contending with Modernity" is a history of how Catholic universities and colleges in the past have tried to react to new and changing situations. It offers a good context for our discussions.

The second resource I want to mention comes from the Holy Father's Encyclical *Ut Unum Sint*. He writes in one section about dialogue—ecumenical dialogue—but addresses the values of dialogue itself. He does so in an encouraging way, showing the importance of dialogue in the life of the church. The specific reference I draw your attention to in *Ut Unum Sint* is paragraphs 28–39 with their four sections: what is ecumenical dialogue, creating local structures for dialogue, dialogue as an examination of conscience and dialogue as a means of resolving differences. Even though the document is directed to the ecumenical effort, the Holy Father's general comments about dialogue in the church are quite good.

Bishop Pilla, if we can now receive suggestions and questions for the floor, I'll appreciate that.

26 | Draft of "*Ex Corde Ecclesiae*: An Application to the United States"

August 2, 1996

TO:	Bishops, Presidents, Learned Societies, and Sponsoring Religious Communities
FROM:	Most Reverend John J. Leibrecht, Chair, *Ex corde Ecclesiae* Implementation Committee
DATE:	August 2, 1996
ON:	Application to the United States of *Ex corde Ecclesiae*

Enclosed is the latest draft of a document implementing Pope John Paul II's apostolic constitution *Ex corde Ecclesiae.* The draft provides an opportunity for your comments and recommendations prior to a discussion and vote on it by bishops during their national meeting November 11–14, 1996.

What you find in underlined boldface in this draft are changes from the draft previously sent to you August 25, 1995.

Because the intent of the *Ex corde Ecclesiae* Implementation Committee is to present this text for a vote this coming November, usual procedures of the NCCB/USCC preliminary to a vote will be followed. Bishops will have the opportunity of presenting amendments to this draft. The Implementation Committee will address each recommended amendment and then a vote by all bishops will take place.

Comments and recommendations at this point in time, in light of the above procedures, should be made to local ordinaries rather than to the Implementation Committee. This can be done through personal dialogues or in other appropriate ways.

Our committee's project director, the Reverend Terrence Toland, S.J., is available to participate in dialogues. He can be contacted at 202-541-3017. Many people have told me how his presence proved very helpful.

From the author's files.

In the name of the Implementation Committee, I thank all of you who have helped bring implementing *Ex corde Ecclesiae* to this point. Committee members are: His Eminence James Cardinal Hickey; His Eminence Adam J. Maida; Most Reverend Oscar H. Lipscomb; Most Reverend Francis B. Schulte; Most Reverend James A. Griffin; Most Reverend John J. Leibrecht. A member of the committee who now serves as consultant is Most Reverend James W. Malone.

Again, many thanks for your help.

Enclosure

2 AUGUST 1996

PRENOTE: On August 15, 1990, Pope John Paul II issued an apostolic constitution on Catholic higher education entitled *Ex corde Ecclesiae*. Addressing the identity and mission of Catholic colleges and universities, the apostolic constitution also included General Norms designed to help fulfill its vision. The General Norms are to be applied concretely by episcopal conferences taking into account the status of each college and university and, as far as possible and appropriate, civil law. The following document makes that application to the United States in a manner which complements, and does not repeat, the themes and ideals of *Ex corde Ecclesiae* itself.

EX CORDE ECCLESIAE

AN APPLICATION TO THE UNITED STATES

Catholic colleges and universities are participants in both the life of the Church and the higher education enterprise of the United States. As such, they "are called to continuous renewal, both as 'Universities' and as 'Catholic.'"[1] This twofold relationship is described in the 22 May 1994 joint document of the Congregation for Catholic Education and the Pontifical Councils for the Laity and for Culture which states that the Catholic university achieves its purpose when

> . . . it gives proof of being rigorously serious as a member of the international community of knowledge and expresses its Catholic identity through an explicit link with the Church, at both local and universal levels—an identity which marks concretely the life, the services and the programs of the university community. In this way, by its very existence, the Catholic university achieves its aim of guaranteeing, in institutional form, a Christian presence in the university world. . . .[2]

This relationship is clarified through dialogue which includes faculty **of all disciplines,** students, staff, academic officers, trustees, and sponsoring religious communities of the educational institutions, **all of whom share responsibility for the character of Catholic higher education.** The bishop and his collaborators in the local church are integral parties in this dialogue.

The Catholic college or university is related to the entire ecclesial community,[3] to the **broader society,**[4] as well as to the higher education academy.[5] We are directing special attention to the relationship between the institutions and church authorities. *Ex corde Ecclesiae* itself provides a useful framework to address this specific relationship:

> Bishops have a particular responsibility to promote Catholic Universities, and especially to promote and assist in the preservation and strengthening of their Catholic identity, including the protection of their Catholic identity in relation to civil authorities. This will be achieved more effectively if close personal and pastoral relationships exist between University and Church authorities, characterized by *mutual trust, close and consistent cooperation and continuing dialogue.* Even when they do not enter directly into the internal government of the University, Bishops "should be seen not as external agents but as participants in the life of the Catholic University" (underlining added).[6]

Each of these elements in the pastoral relationship of bishops with Catholic colleges and universities warrants attention.

I. Mutual trust between university and church authorities

A. Mutual trust goes beyond the personalities of those involved in the relationship. The trust is grounded in a shared baptismal belief in the **truths that** are **found** in Scripture concerning the mystery of the Incarnation: God the creator, who works even until now; God the incarnate redeemer, who is the Way and the Truth and the Life; and God the Paraclete, the Holy Spirit whom the Father sends. In the spirit of *communio,* the relationship of trust between college/university and church authorities, based on these shared beliefs **with secular and religious implications,** is fostered by mutual listening, by collaboration that respects differing responsibilities and gifts, and by a solidarity that mutually recognizes respective statutory limitations and responsibilities.

B. From this it follows:

1. that the institution's relationship to the Church, in accord with the principles of *Ex corde Ecclesiae,* should be affirmed by the institution through public acknowledgment of its Catholic identity in official documentation (e.g., in its mission statement);
2. **that, when appropriate, bishops acknowledge publicly the service of Catholic colleges/universities to the Church, and support the Catholic identity of the institutions if this identity is unjustifiably challenged;**
3. that the institution, following its own procedures in the hiring and retention of professionally qualified faculty and staff, **makes serious effort to seek** individuals who are committed to the Catholic tradition or, if not Catholic, who are aware and respectful of that tradition;
4. that, aware of the contributions made by theologians to Church and academy, the local bishop in accord with his ecclesial responsibility, in circumstances where he questions whether or not an individual theologian is presenting authentic Catholic teaching, shall follow **established procedures** (as noted next in #5) and take appropriate action;
5. that *Doctrinal Responsibilities: Approaches to Promoting Cooperation and Resolving Misunderstandings Between Bishops and Theologians,* approved and published by the National Conference of Catholic Bishops, 17 June 1989, is adopted as the appropriate procedure to assure **a process acceptable to** both bishop and **teacher.**

II. Close and consistent cooperation between university/college and church authorities

A. Collaborating to integrate faith with life is a necessary part of the "close personal and pastoral relationships"[7] to which colleges/universities and bishops aspire. **Within their academic mission of teaching and research, in ways**

appropriate to their own constituencies and histories, including their sponsorship by religious communities, institutions offer courses in Catholic theology taught in accord with the best scholarship and the authentic teaching authority of the Church.

Many cooperative programs, related to Gospel outreach, already flourish throughout the country. It is highly desirable that issues concerning social justice and the needs of the poor continue to be identified, studied, and programmed jointly by representatives of both the educational institution and Church authorities.

Allocation of personnel and money to assure the special contributions of campus ministry is required. As a concern of the whole Church, and in view of the presence on campus of persons of other religious traditions, ecumenical and interreligious relationships should be fostered with sensitivity.

B. From this it follows:

1. that **a plan for fulfilling its institutional mission as Catholic** be in place which encourages on-campus awareness of ways **to grow in understanding and practice of the faith and** to be of service to the Church,[8] **and which addresses intellectual and pastoral** contributions to the mission of evangelization,[9] service to the poor, social justice initiatives, and ecumenical and interreligious activities;
2. that provision be made cooperatively for adequately staffed campus ministry programs, including opportunities for the sacraments and other liturgical celebrations.[10]

III. Continuing dialogue among college/university representatives and church authorities

A. Dialogues occasioned by *Ex corde Ecclesiae* are graced moments characterized by (a) a manifest openness to a further analysis and local appropriation of Catholic identity, (b) an appreciation of the positive contributions which campus-wide conversations make, and (c) a conviction that conversation can develop and sustain relationships. A need exists for continued attention and commitment to the far-reaching implications—curricular, staffing, programming—of major themes within *Ex corde Ecclesiae.* These include Catholic identity, *communio,* relating faith and culture, pastoral outreach, the new evangelization, and relationship to the Church.

B. From this it follows:

1. that a mutual commitment to regular dialogues, according to local needs and circumstances, be honored by institution and diocese;
2. that periodically, every Catholic college/university undertake an internal review of the congruence of its **mission statement,** its courses of instruction, its service activity, and its research programs with the ideals and principles expressed in *Ex corde Ecclesiae*;
3. that the National Conference of Catholic Bishops, through an appropriate committee structure, continue its dialogue with the Association of Catholic Colleges and Universities **regarding application of the ideals and principles expressed in *Ex corde Ecclesiae*.**

The bishops of the United States, in offering this application of *Ex corde Ecclesiae*, join in sentiments expressed by Pope John Paul II:

I turn to the whole Church, convinced that Catholic Universities are essential to her growth and to the development of Christian culture and human progress. For this reason, the entire ecclesial community is invited to give its support to Catholic Institutions of higher education and to assist them in their process of development and renewal. . . .[11]

NOTES

1. *Ex corde Ecclesiae,* Introduction, #7.
2. "The Church's Presence in the University and in University Culture," *Origins,* 16 June 1994, II, #2.
3. *Ex corde Ecclesiae,* Introduction, #11.
4. Ibid., Part II, #2.
5. Ibid., Part I, #12.
6. Ibid., Part I, #28. The citation at the end is from John Paul II, Address to Leaders of Catholic Higher Education, Xavier University of Louisiana, U.S.A., 12 September 1987, n. 4: *AAS* 80 (1988), p. 764.
7. Ibid., Part I, #28.
8. Ibid., #38 ff.
9. Ibid., #48–49.
10. Ibid., Part II, 6, #2.
11. Ibid, #11.

27 | Response and Alternative Ordinances from the Fellowship of Catholic Scholars

September 25, 1996

FELLOWSHIP OF CATHOLIC SCHOLARS
RESPONSE TO DRAFT [Sent to all U.S. Bishops]
September 25, 1996

Gerard V. Bradley
President

Your Excellency:

I write to you about the future of Catholic higher education in the United States. This letter is being sent to all the bishops of the United States.

The Fellowship of Catholic Scholars has followed with interest the work of the bishops' Implementation Committee for *Ex Corde Ecclesiae* on Catholic universities. What now seems evident to the interested observer is that, even after several years of work and consultations with some of the current leaders of Catholic higher education, we seem no closer to the adoption in the United States of the local higher education Ordinances required by the current law of the universal Church (ECE, II 1 § 2).

In particular, the paper presented to the bishops at their meeting in November, 1995, and discussed further at the bishops' meeting in June, 1996, as a "non-juridical application" of *Ex Corde Ecclesiae,* actually seems to move the Church away from the adoption of any higher education Ordinances, suggesting that the law of the universal Church pertaining to Catholic colleges and universities does not necessarily apply in the United States. This impression was confirmed

From the author's files.

by what we understand to be the Implementation Committee's plan to submit for a vote at the bishops' meeting on November 11–14 substantially the same paper entitled "*Ex Corde Ecclesiae*: An Application to the United States."

The Fellowship of Catholic Scholars believes that higher education Ordinances based on *Ex Corde Ecclesiae* can and should be adopted for the United States. To show that such Ordinances are possible and doable in this country, the Board of Directors of the Fellowship recently appointed a committee composed of some representative and knowledgeable people in higher education chaired by a former U.S. Assistant Secretary of Education. This special committee of the Fellowship produced a set of "Suggested Ordinances for Catholic Colleges and Universities in the United States." The Board of Directors of the Fellowship, whose members are listed below, approved these ordinances at its meeting in Saint Louis, Missouri, on September 20.

I hope that these Suggested Ordinances, prefaced with a brief explanatory discussion of the overall problem of Catholic higher education today, will be helpful to the bishops as they consider the status and future of Catholic higher education in the United States. The Fellowship stands ready to assist the bishops in any way through the considerable knowledge and expertise on this topic to be found among the membership.

Sincerely,

Gerard V. Bradley
Professor of Law
University of Notre Dame;
and President,
Fellowship of Catholic Scholars

BOARD OF DIRECTORS
FELLOWSHIP OF CATHOLIC SCHOLARS

PRESIDENT
Prof. Gerard V. Bradley

PRESIDENT EMERITUS
Rev. Msgr. George A. Kelly
St. John's University (retired)

VICE PRESIDENT
Rev. Joseph Fessio
Ignatius Press

EXECUTIVE SECRETARY/TREASURER
Dr. Jude Dougherty
Catholic University of America

SUGGESTED ORDINANCES FOR CATHOLIC COLLEGES AND UNIVERSITIES IN THE UNITED STATES

Prepared by the Fellowship of Catholic Scholars

DISCUSSION OF THE QUESTION

A great deal has been said about the difficulties of the application of Pope John Paul II's Apostolic Constitution *Ex Corde Ecclesiae* on Catholic universities in this country, particularly the application of Canon 812 of the Code of Canon

Law, which requires that teachers in theological disciplines have a mandate from competent ecclesiastical authority. This is held by some to constitute an unwarranted "outside" interference in the institutional autonomy of a university, and this in turn is said to be unacceptable by current United States academic and university standards and practice.

The real difficulties supposedly posed for American Catholic institutions by Canon 812, however, have surely been greatly exaggerated. For one thing, American universities regularly and routinely accept many requirements imposed from "outside"—requirements established by local, state, and federal governments, by accrediting associations, by foundations and other funding entities or donors, by professional associations in fields such as engineering, law, nursing, the sciences, and so on. American universities think nothing at all of accepting these requirements constantly imposed on them from "outside"; it is standard practice, in fact.

Only when the subject is theology and the outside entity is the Church, apparently, does the question of outside "interference" in the governance of Catholic higher education institutions normally even get raised. Yet the very data of Catholic theology as a science necessarily contain within themselves the teaching of the Church's Magisterium; Catholic theology fails both academically and professionally if it does not accept this; Catholic institutions undermine their own necessary foundation when they try to pretend that they can do Catholic theology independently of the Church.

In any case, according to *Ex Corde Ecclesiae,* it is not the primary responsibility of the Church or the bishops to insure that teachers in theological disciplines in Catholic colleges and universities have the proper "credentials" or "accreditation" from the proper "professional" association (in this case, the Church). This is not an "outside" function at all. It is the proximate, "on-hands" responsibility of the institution which wishes to be designated and recognized as "Catholic" itself to insure that its teachers in the theological disciplines have the requisite mandate to teach from proper Church authority. Although the bishops have "oversight," *Ex Corde Ecclesiae* clearly places the first responsibility on the institution itself (ECE, 4 §§ 1–5).

Thus, a good deal of the discussion that has taken place regarding actual or potential outside Church interference in institutional autonomy and academic freedom has simply been misplaced. The real question is: does the institution wish to be Catholic or not? If it does, it is incumbent upon the institution itself to take the necessary steps to meet the Church's conditions for being Catholic, that is, *inter alia,* to recruit and retain theologians who really are Catholic theologians. This is not something the institution has to do because the Church or the bishops say so; it is something the institution has to do if it is really going to be a Catholic institution.

In any case, a much more fundamental question than whether Catholic university teachers in the theological disciplines are or should be subject to ecclesiastical oversight regarding their authenticity as Catholic teachers is the question of whether *institutions* wishing to call themselves Catholic could ever be truly such while declaring their independence as a practical matter from the universal law of the Church. The fundamental question is not whether Canon 812 applies to Catholic universities in the United States but whether the Code of Canon Law itself applies to them.

It is not clear whether there is any other field or sector in the life of the Church other than higher education where the bishops are, in effect, "negotiating" with the subjects of Canon Law as to whether or not it applies to them. This appears to be a situation without precedent. Are there any other "nonjuridical applications" of the law of the universal Church being proposed or discussed besides the one being discussed for Catholic higher education in the United States?

The Church, after years of careful study and wide consultations with academics and educators, especially with those in the United States, has decided upon certain wholly legitimate conditions and requirements which must now, with the promulgation of *Ex Corde Ecclesiae,* be met by a university or college in order to be entitled to call itself a Catholic institution. It would seem that the refusal of an institution to accept these legitimate Church conditions and requirements really amounts to a practical declaration on the institution's part that it does not really wish to be Catholic.

The problem thus is not, and never has been, a question of possible outside Church "control" of higher education institutions, and the issue should therefore not be discussed in these terms. Rather, it is for higher education institutions themselves to decide whether or not they wish to be Catholic. If so, then they have an obligation to adhere to and implement on their campuses what the Church now officially says in *Ex Corde Ecclesiae* a Catholic university is.

No matter how sincerely many leaders of Catholic higher education in this country may have believed, or may still believe, that the extensive secularization of Catholic institutions that has taken place since the Land O'Lakes statement in 1967 represents a legitimate interpretation of the renewal called for by Vatican Council II, the promulgation of *Ex Corde Ecclesiae* in 1990 now definitively establishes that this secularization went too far. The time has come for some of the current leaders of Catholic higher education to recognize that, if they wish their institutions to continue to be considered Catholic, some of the missteps of the fairly recent past now have to be retraced.

The legitimate professionalization sought by many Catholic institutions following Vatican II often contained unstated and perhaps unexamined presuppositions taken from modern secularism which must now, in the light of *Ex Corde Ecclesiae*, be re-examined and, in some cases, modified, if these schools wish to remain Catholic.

The secularizing changes of recent years cannot be considered as sacrosanct and irreversible; whether a particular change that was made may still remain in place under *Ex Corde Ecclesiae*, or whether it might have to be modified in the light of that document's requirements, or even reversed, has to be a legitimate subject for discussion in the dialogue currently going on over Catholic higher education. The indisputable fact is that *Ex Corde Ecclesiae* does now represent the law of the universal Church with respect to Catholic higher education, and it cannot simply be bypassed or ignored.

It is understandable, of course, that the bishops of the United States should be concerned that no harsh or sudden action on their part might be the cause of an open, irreparable break between the Church and some institutions still thought to be Catholic, or still calling themselves Catholic, even while they are apparently reluctant to implement *Ex Corde Ecclesiae*. It is also desirable that the Catholic faithful be spared further public controversies and even scandals over the conditions on some Catholic campuses.

The bishops should accordingly not act in an abrupt or authoritarian way that would perhaps cause immediate formal breaks with the Church on the part of certain institutions; nor should episcopal action be taken in such a way as to precipitate the departure of some institutions from the official ranks of schools still bearing the Catholic name. These outcomes should be avoided if at all possible. Many of the changes made on Catholic campuses which may now need to be revisited in light of *Ex Corde Ecclesiae* were no doubt originally made with no specific intent to contravene Catholic doctrine or governance; but rather were made because they seemed to be the thing to do at the time.

In order to allow institutions maximum maneuvering room which in turn allows them to revisit and rethink their true situations in the light of the firm requirements of *Ex Corde Ecclesiae*, it would not even seem to be necessary, at least for the moment, to establish any fixed timetable for requiring the norms of the Apostolic Constitution to come into full force on all American Catholic campuses.

What does appear to be necessary, though is for the American hierarchy to put in place a set of Ordinances based en *Ex Corde Ecclesiae* that do clearly and firmly set forth the expectations and requirements of what it means to be a Catholic university in the United States as we move into the twenty-first century. Ordinances based on the pope's Apostolic Constitution should therefore be approved and promulgated by the bishops without attempting to seek the "agreement" of those subject to them, namely the current Catholic college presidents. Appropriate Ordinances should be enacted independently of the current leaders of Catholic higher education institutions, who have already been consulted at length and indeed exhaustively, with few or no tangible results.

The promulgation of Ordinances enacted by the bishops' conference will provide a definite and definitive statement of what not a few Catholic colleges and universities will then have to begin to endeavor to return to, however carefully and in stages—if they wish to continue to merit the name and status of "Catholic."

In particular, it is hard to see how the Association of Catholic Colleges and Universities (ACCU) can even be allowed to go on using the name, if the organization is not willing to accept ECE local Ordinances when lawfully promulgated by the bishops of the United States. These Ordinances would seem to represent the position the Church is strictly obliged to take now that *Ex Corde Ecclesiae* has been issued; they also, surely, constitute the renewed goal towards which Catholic higher education institutions would then have to return.

Putting in place such a set of authentic local Ordinances based on *Ex Corde Ecclesiae* would not only provide a statement of what the Catholic university in the United States must henceforth be; it would, and not incidentally, encourage many elements already present within many institutions (faculty, administrators, trustees, benefactors, etc.) desirous of not losing their Catholic identity and affiliation to begin to act to help move their institutions back towards authentic Catholicity. The policy of "dialoguing" chiefly with the current leadership of the ACCU would seem to provide those elements already known to oppose the implementation of *Ex Corde Ecclesiae* with a veto over any possible movement out of our current higher education impasse; as long as "non-juridical applications" go on being seriously discussed, schools have no incentive even to begin to consider what might be entailed in returning to the Catholic fold in a real sense.

"The Church has the right to erect and supervise universities . . ." (*Codex Iuris Canonis*, Canon 807). The recurring claim over the past generation by some of the leaders of Catholic higher education that the American higher education system does not recognize Church-affiliated institutions as universities in the true sense is a false claim and has never been anything but a false claim. Universities governed by independent, self-perpetuating boards of trustees, as most of our Catholic institutions now are governed, are entirely free to elect and implement a firm religious affiliation; nor is their accreditation and, for the most part, public funding as well, in any way affected by such a religious affiliation (as some Catholic institutions have erroneously tried to claim in the past).

What this latter claim amounts to is a practical—as well as a unilateral—abrogation by these same Catholic higher education leaders of the First Amendment rights of Catholic Americans generally to establish and maintain universities in this country as we see fit, according to the tenets of our faith.

But the present generation of Catholic higher education leaders does not have the right to abrogate the First Amendment rights of Catholic Americans, any more than they have the right to hold the Catholic higher education of the future hostage to their present short-sighted views. Neither does the bishops' conference have the right to do these things for that matter. The fact is that the Church *does* have the right to erect and supervise truly Catholic universities under current United States law, and the Church should in any case be insisting upon this. The judgment in the case of *Curran v. the Catholic University of America,* for example, confirmed what was already pretty clear in the case law anyway, namely, that the dire consequences once predicted if Catholic colleges ever violated American-style "academic freedom" were almost wholly groundless.

Moreover, any Catholic university which now does move to implement fully the norms of *Ex Corde Ecclesiae* will lose very little if any of the public aid it is now receiving (except perhaps for a relatively small amount of some state aid in a few states). U.S. government aid to higher education has never been contingent upon secularization, as has sometimes been falsely claimed, but rather simply upon successful accreditation by recognized accrediting agencies. Over 90 percent of all government aid to higher education in any case comes in the form of student financial assistance which, as everyone acquainted with the various G. I. Bills of Rights since World War II knows, flows impartially to students in all institutions, those which are religiously affiliated as well as those which are secular; and the right of students even in wholly "sectarian" institutions to receive government student financial assistance has been specifically upheld by the U.S. Supreme Court as recently as the 1980s.

In short, there exist no real external obstacles to the full implementation of *Ex Corde Ecclesiae* in the United States. If it is not currently being implemented, this is because some apparently do not want to implement it. However, they cannot really pretend to be under any external constraint in the matter. Thus, it is time to begin orienting those institutions that wish to continue being "Catholic" institutions back towards the goal of implementing the current higher education norms that are indisputably required by Church law. No matter what the present difficulties might be, no matter how long it may take, it is time to begin the process.

In order to assist in this much desired process, the Fellowship of Catholic scholars asked a committee composed of some of our academic members chaired by a former U.S. Assistant Secretary of Education (for postsecondary education) to draft a set of "Suggested Ordinances for Catholic Colleges and Universities in the United States." This set of draft suggested Ordinances follows and has been approved by the Board of Directors of the Fellowship.

It is to be hoped that the bishops will find in these draft suggested Ordinances ideas and suggestions, if not actual language, that will assist in the preparation of official higher education Ordinances based on *Ex Corde Ecclesiae* for the United States. It is also to be hoped that, once a suitable set of Ordinances has been approved and promulgated by the bishops' conference, the great majority of colleges and universities still bearing the name of "Catholic" in this country will see the wisdom of rallying to these Ordinances and beginning the various implementation of them on their campuses.

Even with suitable Ordinances in place, nothing will prevent the bishops' conference, as well as, especially, the individual bishop, from exercising great patience and understanding with regard to the many practical difficulties faced by some Catholic colleges and universities attempting to move out of the present difficult situation in which Catholic higher education currently finds itself in this country. But proper Ordinances do need to be put in place regardless of what today's higher education leaders think or say about them. The following Suggested Ordinances show the kind of thing that can and should be enacted in this country by the National Conference of Catholic Bishops.

INTRODUCTION

"Born from the heart of the Church," Pope John Paul II's Apostolic Constitution on Catholic Universities *Ex Corde Ecclesiae* states, "a Catholic university is located in that course of tradition which may be traced back to the very origin of the university as an institution. . . By vocation the *universitas magistrorum et scholarium* is dedicated to research, to teaching, and to the education of students . . . With every other university, it shares in that *gaudium de veritate,* so precious to St. Augustine, which is the joy of searching for, discovering, and communicating truth in every field of knowledge."[1]

"A Catholic university is distinguished by its free search for the whole truth about nature, man, and God," this Apostolic Constitution on universities aptly continues. "The present age is in urgent need of this kind of disinterested service, namely, of *proclaiming the meaning of truth*, that fundamental value without which freedom, justice, and human dignity are extinguished."[2]

According to *Ex Corde Ecclesiae*, "every Catholic university, as *Catholic*, must have the following *essential characteristics*:

"1. A Christian inspiration not only of individuals but of the university community as such;

"2. A continuing reflection in the light of the Catholic faith upon the growing treasury of human knowledge, to which it seeks to contribute by its own research;

"3. Fidelity to the Christian message as it comes to us through the Church; and

"4. An institutional commitment to the service of the People of God and of the human family in their pilgrimage to the transcendent goal which gives meaning to life."[3]

Thus, "in the light of these four characteristics, it is evident that besides the teaching, research, and services common to all universities, a Catholic university, *by institutional commitment,* brings to its task the inspiration and light of the *Christian message.* In a Catholic university . . . Catholic ideals, attitudes, and principles penetrate and inform university activities in accordance with the proper nature and autonomy of these activities."[4]

"A Catholic university pursues its objectives through its formation of an authentic human community animated by the spirit of Christ. The source of its unity springs from a common dedication to the truth, a common vision of the dignity of the human person and, ultimately, the person and message of Christ, which gives the institution its distinctive character. As a result of this inspiration, the community is animated by a spirit of freedom and charity; it is characterized by mutual respect, sincere dialogue, and protection of the rights of individuals."[5]

"Every Catholic university, without ceasing to be a university, has a relationship to the Church that is essential to its institutional identity. As such, it participates most directly in the life of the local Church in which it is situated; at the same time, because it is an academic institution and therefore part of the international community of scholarship and inquiry, each institution participates in and contributes to the life and the relationship to the Church . . . One consequence of its essential relationship to the Church is that the *institutional* fidelity of the university to the Christian message includes a recognition of and adherence to the teaching authority of the Church in matters of faith and morals. Catholic members of the university are called to a personal fidelity to the Church and all that implies. Non-Catholic members are required to respect the Catholic character of the university, while the university in turn respects their religious liberty."[6]

"Bishops have a particular responsibility to promote Catholic universities, and especially to promote and assist in the preservation and strengthening of their Catholic identity, including the protection of their Catholic identity into civil authorities . . . Even when they do not enter directly into the internal governance of the university, bishops 'should not be seen as external agents but as participants in the life of the Catholic university.'"[7]

However, since the Church accepts "the legitimate autonomy of human culture and especially of the sciences," the Church also "recognizes the academic freedom of scholars in each discipline in accordance with its own principles and proper method, and within the confines of truth and the common good."[8] The Church also recognizes that a Catholic university "possesses that institutional autonomy necessary to perform its functions effectively."[9]

"'Institutional autonomy' means that the governance of an academic institution is and remains internal to the institution; 'academic freedom' is the guarantee given to those involved in teaching and research that, within their specific specialized branch of knowledge and according to the methods proper to that specific area, they may search for the truth wherever analysis and evidence lead them, and may teach and publish the results of this search, keeping in mind the cited criteria, that is, safeguarding the rights of the individual and of society within the confines of truth and the common good."[10]

"Theology has its legitimate place in the university alongside other disciplines. It has the proper principles and methods which define it as a branch of knowledge . . . Bishops should encourage the creative work of the theologians. They serve the Church through research done in a way that respects theological method. They seek to understand better, further develop, and more effectively communicate the meaning of Christian revelation as transmitted in Scripture and Tradition and in the Church's Magisterium . . . At the same time, since theology seeks an understanding of revealed truth whose authentic interpretation is entrusted to the bishops of the Church, it is intrinsic to the principles and methods of their research and teaching in the academic discipline that theologians respect the authority of the bishops and assent to Catholic doctrine according to the degree of authority with which it is taught. Because of their interrelated roles, dialogue between bishops and theologians is essential."[11]

"The basic mission of a university is a continuous quest for truth through its research, and the preservation and communication of knowledge for the good of society. The Catholic university participates in this mission with its own specific characteristics and mission."[12]

In summary, a Catholic university is called to be "a living *institutional* witness to Christ and his message, so vitally important in cultures marked by secularism, or where Christ and his message are virtually unknown. Moreover, all the basic academic activities of a Catholic university are connected with and in harmony with the evangelizing mission of the Church: research carried out in the light of the Christian message which puts new human discoveries at the service of individuals and society; education offered in a faith context that forms men and women capable of rational and critical judgment and conscious of the transcendent dignity of the human person; professional training that incorporates ethical values and a sense of service to individuals and to society; the dialogue with culture that makes faith better understood; and the theological research that translates the truth into contemporary language."[13]

The purpose of the following Ordinances is to provide for the implementation of *Ex Corde Ecclesiae* in the United States. These Ordinances apply to all Catholic universities and other Catholic institutions of higher studies in the United States as a condition of the institution's ability to describe itself publicly as "Catholic": "No university may bear the title or name *Catholic university* without the consent of the competent ecclesiastical authority."[14]

These Ordinances do not apply to ecclesiastical universities and faculties with authority to confer academic degrees by the authority of the Holy See; these institutions and faculties are governed by the Apostolic Constitution *Sapientia Christiana*.[15]

These Ordinances are complementary to and in harmony with Canons 807–814 of the Code of Canon Law and with the General Norms of *Ex Corde Ecclesiae* itself (Part II), both of which in their entirety are part of the universal law of the Church.

SUGGESTED ORDINANCES

Ordinance #1: In order to employ the designation "Catholic," a university must insure that the General Norms of the Apostolic Constitution *Ex Corde Ecclesiae* are incorporated into its operative statutes and governing documents such as its Articles of Incorporation, Mission Statement, Constitution and By-Laws, Faculty and Student Handbooks, etc.; in particular, its Catholic identity must be clearly stated in a Mission Statement or other appropriate public document.[16]

Ordinance #2: The Catholic university's Mission Statement and other governing documents must be submitted for approval to the competent ecclesiastical authority, normally the diocesan bishop of the place where the institution is located.[17]

Ordinance #3: Periodically and at least every ten years, every approved Catholic college or university is to undertake an internal review of the congruence of its research program (## 7, 15, 18, 45), course of instruction (## 16, 17, 19, 20), service activity (## 21, 31, 32, 36, 37), and campus policies and practices (## 21, 22, 32, 33, 38, 39) with the norms and principles of *Ex Corde Ecclesiae*; the results of this review are to be submitted to competent ecclesiastical authority, normally the diocesan bishop, for continued recognition and approval as an institution of higher education entitled to employ the term "Catholic" in its name.[18]

Ordinance #4: The responsibility for maintaining the Catholic identity of the university rests with the institution itself, including especially its officers and board of directors/trustees, but also including its teachers and administrators; recruitment and engagement of them should accordingly be made with this as one of the principal ends in view.[19]

Ordinance #5: A Catholic university must insure through its administrative and personnel policies and practices, as well as in the contracts it enters into, that its teachers who are Catholic are required to be publicly faithful to, and all other teachers are required publicly to respect, Catholic doctrine and morals in their teaching and research; and that the Catholic identity of the institution is not to be jeopardized by allowing non-Catholic teachers to constitute a majority within the institution.[20] A Catholic university accordingly may *not* publicly advertise or claim that it does not discriminate on the basis of *religion* or *creed*.

Ordinance #6: Employment contracts must specify that public expression of dissent from or lack of respect for authentic Catholic teaching, as declared by the Magisterium of the Church, as well as public acts or a lifestyle that are immoral according to that same teaching, may constitute grounds for contract termination.[21] Institutions should have written procedures for adjudicating such cases which provide for appropriate due process rights and reasonable appeals.

Ordinance #7: Students at a Catholic university must receive formation in moral and religious principles and in the moral and social teaching of the Church. In addition to academic and professional education, courses in the ethics of the professions should be included where applicable. Courses in Catholic doctrine are to be available to all.[22]

Ordinance #8: Every Catholic college or university should have faculty, or at least a chair, of Catholic theology.[23] Theology should be taught in the light of the perennial philosophy, relying on the Church's "philosophical patrimony which is forever valid."[24]

Ordinance #9: Theology teachers fulfill a mandate received from the Church and therefore are to be faithful to the Magisterium of the Church as the authentic interpreter of Sacred Scripture and Sacred Tradition; it is the responsibility of the institution to insure that teachers in the theological disciplines comply with this requirement, including through the incorporation of appropriate language in employment contracts.[25]

Ordinance #10: If a dispute arises between the competent ecclesiastical authority and a Catholic college or university, or individuals or groups within a Catholic college or university, it is to be resolved according to procedures that respect the rights of persons in the Church (e.g., CIC, Canons 208–223, 224–231, and 273–289), the institutional autonomy of the institution (ECE I, 12; II, 2 § 5; II, 5 § 2), and the responsibility of Church authorities (ECE I, nn.28–29; II, 4 § 1; II, 5 § 2) to assist in the preservation of the institution's Catholic identity.

Ordinance #11: Governing boards, in appropriate collaboration with the administration of the college/university and the diocesan bishop, should provide for an adequately staffed campus ministry program and suitable liturgical and sacramental opportunities offered in accordance with the church's liturgical and sacramental norms.[26]

Ordinance #12: Catholic teaching and discipline are to influence all university activities, including sponsorship or support of extracurricular activities by students or faculty, provision of campus facilities or services, administration of student residence halls, etc.; no action sponsored or permitted on campus should be allowed to violate the institution's Catholic character; however, the freedom of conscience of each person is to be respected in accordance with the principles of Vatican Council II's Declaration on Religious Freedom *Dignitatis Humanae.*[27]

Note: These "Suggested Ordinances" were approved by the Board of Directors of the Fellowship of Catholic Scholars on September 21, 1996; they were prepared for the Fellowship by an FCS *Ex Corde Ecclesiae* Committee consisting of the following:

Chairman:
The Honorable Kenneth D. Whitehead
Former U.S. Assistant Secretary of Education (for Postsecondary Education)

Members:
Dr. Jude P. Dougherty, Dean, School of Philosophy
The Catholic University of America

Dr. Robert P. George, Department of Politics
Princeton University

Rev. Msgr. George A. Kelly
St. John's University (retired)

Dr. Kenneth L. Schmitz
John Paul II Institute

NOTES

1. Pope John Paul II, Apostolic Constitution *Ex Corde Ecclesiae* on Catholic Universities, August 15, 1990, #1.

2. *Ibid.,* #4.

3. *Ibid.,* #13, quoting "The Catholic University in the Modern World," final document of the Second International Congress of Delegates of Catholic Universities, Rome, November 20–29, 1972.

4. *Ibid.,* #14, quoting the same document.

5. *Ibid.,* #21.

6. *Ibid.,* #27, referring to Vatican Council II's Declaration on Religious Liberty *Dignitatis Humanae* in the last sentence.

7. *Ibid., 28,* quoting in the last sentence Pope John Paul II's "Address to Leaders of the Catholic Higher Education," Xavier University of Louisiana, September 12, 1987.

8. *Ibid.,* #29.

9. *Ibid.,* #12.

10. *Ibid.,* Note #15.

11. *Ibid.,* #29, referring both to Vatican II's *Dei Verbum* ##8–10 and *Lumen Gentium* #25.

12. *Ibid.,* #30.

13. *Ibid.,* #49.

14. Codex Iuris Canonis, Canon 808.

15. Apostolic Constitution *Sapientia Christiana,* AAS 71 (1979), pp. 469–521.

16. *Ex corde Ecclesiae,* Part II, General Norms, Article 1 § 3 and 2 § 3.

17. *Ibid.,* 1 § 3.

18. *Ibid.,* 5 § 3.

19. *Ibid.,* 4 § 1 and 4 § 2.

20. *Ibid.,* 4 § 3 and 4 § 4.

21. *Ibid.,* 4 § 1; CIC, Canon 810.

22. *Ibid.,* 4 § 5; CIC, Canon 811 § 2.

23. *Ibid.,* Part I, 19; CIC, Canon 811 § 1.

24. Vatican Council II, *Optatam Totius,* #14.

25. *Ibid.,* Part II, 4 § 3; CIC, Canon 812.

26. *Ibid.,* 6 §§ 1–2; CIC, Canon 813.

27. *Ibid.,* 2 § 4, quoting Vatican II's *Dignitatis Humanae* in the last clause; also CIC, Canon 810.

28 | *Ex Corde Ecclesiae*: An Application to the United States

Approved by NCCB, November 13, 1996

Prenote. On Aug. 15, 1990, Pope John Paul II issued an apostolic constitution on Catholic higher education titled *Ex Corde Ecclesiae*. Addressing the identity and mission of Catholic colleges and universities, the apostolic constitution also included general norms designed to help fulfill its vision. The general norms are to be applied concretely by episcopal conferences, taking into account the status of each college and university and, as far as possible and appropriate, civil law. The following document makes that application to the United States in a manner which complements, and does not repeat, the themes and ideals of *Ex Corde Ecclesiae* itself. This document should be read in conjunction with the general norms.

Catholic colleges and universities are participants in both the life of the church and the higher education enterprise of the United States. As such, they "are called to continuous renewal, both as 'universities' and as 'Catholic.'"[1] This twofold relationship is described in the May 22, 1994, joint document of the Congregation for Catholic Education and the pontifical councils for the Laity and for Culture which states that the Catholic university achieves its purpose when:

"It gives proof of being rigorously serious as a member of the international community of knowledge and expresses its Catholic identity through an explicit link with the church at both local and universal levels—an identity which marks concretely the life, the services and the programs of the university community. In this way, by its very existence, the Catholic university achieves its aim of guaranteeing, in institutional form, a Christian presence in the university world."[2]

This relationship is clarified through dialogue which includes faculty of all disciplines, students, staff, academic and other administrative officers, trustees

From *Origins* 26, no. 24 (November 28, 1996): 382–384.

and sponsoring religious communities of the educational institutions, all of whom share responsibility for the character of Catholic higher education. The bishop and his collaborators in the local church are integral parties in this dialogue.

The Catholic college or university is related to the entire ecclesial community,[3] to the broader society,[4] as well as to the higher education academy.[5] We are directing special attention to the relationship between the institutions and church authorities. *Ex Corde Ecclesiae* itself provides a useful framework to address this specific relationship:

"Bishops have a particular responsibility to promote Catholic universities, and especially to promote and assist in the preservation and strengthening of their Catholic identity, including the protection of their Catholic identity in relation to civil authorities. This will be achieved more effectively if close personal and pastoral relationships exist between university and church authorities, characterized by *mutual trust, close and consistent cooperation and continuing dialogue.* Even when they do not enter directly into the internal government of the university, bishops 'should be seen not as external agents but as participants in the life of the Catholic university'" [emphasis added].[6]

Each of these elements in the pastoral relationship of bishops with Catholic colleges and universities warrants attention.

I. Mutual Trust Between University and Church Authorities

A. Mutual trust goes beyond the personalities of those involved in the relationship. The trust is grounded in a shared baptismal belief in the truths that are rooted in Scripture and tradition as interpreted by the church concerning the mystery of the Trinity: God the Father and creator, who works even until now; God the Son and incarnate redeemer, who is the way and the truth and the life; and God the Holy Spirit, the Paraclete, whom the Father sends. In the spirit of *communio,* the relationship of trust between college/university and church authorities, based on these shared beliefs with their secular and religious implications, is fostered by mutual listening, by collaboration that respects differing responsibilities and gifts, and by a solidarity that mutually recognizes respective statutory limitations and responsibilities.

B. From this it follows:

1. That the institution's relationship to the church, in accord with the principles of *Ex Corde Ecclesiae,* be affirmed by the institution through public

acknowledgment of its Catholic identity in official documentation (e.g., in its mission statement).

2. That, when appropriate, bishops acknowledge publicly the service of Catholic colleges/universities to the church, and support the Catholic identity of the institutions if this identity is unjustifiably challenged.

3. That the institution, following its own procedures in the hiring and retention of professionally qualified faculty and staff, makes serious effort to appoint individuals who are committed to the Catholic faith tradition or, if not Catholic, who are aware and respectful of that faith tradition.

4. That the institution, aware of the contributions made by theologians to church and academy, expects them to present authentic Catholic teaching.

5. That the local bishop, aware of these contributions and in accord with his ecclesial responsibility, in circumstances where he questions whether or not an individual theologian is presenting authentic Catholic teaching, follows established procedures (as noted next in No. 6) and takes appropriate action.[7]

6. That "Doctrinal Responsibilities: Approaches to Promoting Cooperation and Resolving Misunderstandings Between Bishops and Theologians," approved and published by the National Conference of Catholic Bishops, June 17, 1989, is adopted as the appropriate procedure to assure a process acceptable to both bishop and faculty member.

II. Close and Consistent Cooperation Between University/College and Church Authorities

A. Collaborating to integrate faith with life is a necessary part of the "close personal and pastoral relationships"[8] to which colleges/universities and bishops aspire. Within their academic mission of teaching and research, in ways appropriate to their own constituencies and histories, including their sponsorship by religious communities, institutions offer courses in Catholic theology that reflect current scholarship and are in accord with the authentic teaching of the church.

Many cooperative programs, related to Gospel outreach, already flourish throughout the country. It is highly desirable that representatives of both educational institutions and church authorities jointly identify, study and pursue solutions to issues concerning social justice and the needs of the poor.

Allocation of personnel and money to assure the special contributions of campus ministry is required. In view of the presence on campus of persons of other religious traditions, it is a concern of the whole church that ecumenical and interreligious relationships should be fostered with sensitivity.

B. From this it follows:

1. That the institution has a plan for fulfilling its mission as Catholic which develops the Catholic intellectual tradition, encourages ways to grow in the practice of the faith and be of service to the church.[9] The plan also addresses intellectual and pastoral contributions to the mission of evangelization,[10] service to the poor, social justice initiatives, and ecumenical and interreligious activities.
2. That provision is made cooperatively for adequately staffed campus ministry programs, including opportunities for the sacraments and other liturgical celebrations.[11]

III. Continuing Dialogue Among College/University Representatives and Church Authorities

A. Dialogues occasioned by *Ex Corde Ecclesiae* are graced moments characterized by (a) a manifest openness to a further analysis and local appropriation of Catholic identity, (b) an appreciation of the positive contributions which campuswide conversations make and (c) a conviction that conversation can develop and sustain relationships. A need exists for continued attention and commitment to the far-reaching implications—curricular, staffing, programming—of major themes within *Ex Corde Ecclesiae.* These include Catholic identity, *communio,* relating faith and culture, pastoral outreach, the new evangelization, and relationship to the church.

B. From this it follows:

1. That a mutual commitment to regular dialogues to achieve the goals of *Ex Corde Ecclesiae,* according to local needs and circumstances, is honored by institution and diocese.
2. That periodically every Catholic college/university undertakes an internal review of the congruence of its mission statement, its courses of instruction, its service activity and its research programs with the ideals and principles expressed in *Ex Corde Ecclesiae.*
3. That the National Conference of Catholic Bishops, through an appropriate committee structure, continues its dialogue with the Association of Catholic

Colleges and Universities regarding application of the ideals and principles expressed in *Ex Corde Ecclesiae.*

The bishops of the United States, in offering this application of *Ex Corde Ecclesiae,* join in sentiments expressed by Pope John Paul II:

"I turn to the whole church, convinced that Catholic universities are essential to her growth and to the development of Christian culture and human progress. For this reason, the entire ecclesial community is invited to give its support to Catholic institutions of higher education and to assist them in their process of development and renewal."[12]

NOTES

1. *Ex Corde Ecclesiae,* Introduction, 7.
2. "The Church's Presence in the University and in University Culture," *Origins,* June 16, 1994, II, 2.
3. *Ex Corde Ecclesiae,* Introduction, 11.
4. Ibid., Part II, 2.
5. Ibid., Part I, 12.
6. Ibid., Part I, 28. The citation at the end is from John Paul II, Address to Leaders of Catholic Higher Education, Xavier University, New Orleans, La., Sept. 12, 1987, No. 4: *AAS* 80 (1988), p. 764.
7. The mandate of Canon 812 will be the subject of further study by the NCCB.
8. *Ex Corde Ecclesiae,* Part I, 28.
9. Ibid., 38 ff.
10. Ibid., 48–49.
11. Ibid., Part II, 6, 2.
12. Ibid., 11.

29 | Response of the Congregation for Catholic Education to "*Ex Corde Ecclesiae*: An Application to the United States"

April 23, 1997

His Excellency
Most Reverend Anthony M. Pilla
Bishop of Cleveland
President, NCCB/USCC
Washington, D.C.

Your Excellency,

In response to your kind letter of 25 November 1996 and in accordance with what this Congregation wrote to you on 10 January 1997, we have concluded the study of the "Ordinances" for the application in the United States of the Apostolic Constitution, "Ex Corde Ecclesiae", titled: Ex Corde Ecclesiae: An Application to the United States.

We have been kept very well informed both by the successive Presidents of the Bishops' Conference and by Bishop Leibrecht of the many stages of this work and of the numerous and delicate questions which the project gave rise to in the context of the United States University system. For this we are most grateful. We have tried not to lose sight of all of these factors in our own study of the text.

We are pleased to communicate that now that the study of this first draft has been completed, the Congregation has prepared some observations which it asks to have taken into consideration in the preparation of a second draft.

Allow us to say further that the request on the part of the Congregation for more than one draft of a Conference's "Ordinances" is normal rather than exceptional. The reason for this is one shared by the Bishops' Conference and the

From the author's files.

Congregation, namely, to have the best possible instrument, in the light of the Holy Father's Apostolic Constitution, for the promotion of our Universities as university and as Catholic.

Your letter correctly seeks the "recognitio" of the Holy See in accordance with CIC can. 455 § 2. We would call your attention, in particular, to "General Observation" 3 § 2 where the procedure for the "recognitio", in the case of the "Ordinances" is described in detail.

This Congregation now requests that a second draft of the "Ordinances" be drawn up, in the light of the enclosed observations, with a view to our being able to give it our approval and send it then to the Congregation for Bishops, which is competent for the "recognitio".

We ask that you extend to Bishop Leibrecht and his episcopal colleagues on the committee and to the commission of University Presidents as well as to the other experts who labored over this document the profound gratitude of the Congregation.

It is obvious that we remain always disposed for any further clarifications, either by way of correspondence or in personal meetings.

With the hope soon to have a draft of the "Ordinances" to be put into effect in the United States, where the Catholic Universities are both numerous and important, we take the occasion to express sentiments of high esteem and best wishes.

Sincerely in Christ,
Pio Cardinal Laghi

CONGREGATION FOR CATHOLIC EDUCATION
SOME OBSERVATIONS ON THE TEXT
"Ex Corde Ecclesiae:
An Application to the United States"

A. GENERAL OBSERVATIONS

1. The Congregation deeply appreciates the efforts and time which the Bishops' Conference, Bishop Leibrecht's committee and the body of University Presidents

and others have given to the drafting of this document ("ORDINANCES"). It is aware of the careful organization of the working groups and of the number of opinions of learned societies and others, requested, or spontaneously proposed, that have been studied by the committee. It is aware as well of the complexities of the university situation in the United states that had to be taken into consideration.

2. Account is taken of the importance of the ecclesiological elements referred to, which are at the basis of the Catholic University, and, consequently, of the theme of mutual trust between university and Church authorities, called for by "Ex Corde Ecclesiae" and stressed in the Bishops' document. This is one of the attitudes which may have been less obvious in the past and which should mark a new era in the place given to—and the role performed by—the Catholic University within the Church, for the good of the Church and for the good of society.

3. The Congregation notes that the document, while having, in some places, a certain legal tone, lacks, in some other instances, the necessary juridical elements for an effective functioning institutionally of Catholic Universities as university and as Catholic in all aspects of their organization, life and activity and, therefore, it could happen that this document would not be helpful for those possible cases where tensions, crises or problems require such a juridical instrument for their resolution. It will be pointed out in the "particular observations" below the places where these juridical elements are to be introduced, in a second draft, in accordance with art. 1 § 2 of the "General Norms" of the Apostolic Constitution. Likewise reference will be made in the "particular observations" to the places where "The Directives to Assist in the Formulation of the Ordinances for the Apostolic Constitution 'Ex Corde Ecclesiae'" (Congregation for Catholic Education, January 21, 1991) need to be given further implementation than that which has already been done by the text submitted.

As an indication that the "Ordinances" are to have true juridical character, it should be pointed out that the "review" of them by the Holy See (Cf. "General Norms" art 1 § 2) is the "recognitio" spoken of in CIC can. 455 § 2 (Cf. note 44), which is required for all general decrees of a Bishops' Conference. In accordance with the Apostolic Constitution "Pastor Bonus" (art. 82) that "recognitio" is the competence of the Congregation of Bishops, to which this Congregation will send the final draft of the "Ordinances" after its own approval of them. The Congregation of Bishops seeks the opinion as well of the Pontifical Council for the Interpretation of Legislative Texts. At the end of that procedure the Congregation of Bishops will communicate to the Bishops'

Conference when the "recognitio" of the Holy See has been given to the legislation in question.

4. The Congregation notes that the structure of the "Ordinances" differs from what is proposed in the "General Norms" art. 1 § 2 where it is stated: "The General Norms are to be applied concretely at the local and regional levels . . ." The structure of the text submitted seems, instead, to be that of a series of applications of N. 28, with reference—to be sure—to other aspects of the Apostolic Constitution and the "General Norms". Without minimizing the importance of N. 28, this structure hinders, at times, a more direct stating of some of the essential elements called for by the article of the "General Norms" mentioned above, namely, that all of the "General Norms" are to be applied locally, and by the "Directives" of the Congregation of January 21, 1991. The Congregation recommends that this structure be examined again with a view to achieving this more direct stating of the essential elements required in a document of local application.

B. PARTICULAR OBSERVATIONS

1. Prenote: in place of the last two sentences, it should read as follows: "The following document, while recognizing that the Apostolic Constitution "Ex Corde Ecclesiae" and its "General Norms" are to be observed as the academic legislation of the Church, seeks to apply these in the context of the United States".

2. The material preceding letter "B" (page 3) constitutes, in general, a quite helpful preamble, underlining, as it does, the spirit called for by N. 28, even if it does not take fully into account some of the other ecclesiological elements of the Constitution.

3. With regard to page 2 para. 2, it should be noted that every Catholic University has a relationship to the Church that is essential to its institutional identity (N. 27 and art. 5 "General Norms"). In this light the paragraph in question should read, regarding what follows: "'Ex Corde Ecclesiae' provides one of the ecclesiological principles to address . . ."

4. Page 3 B 1, line 3 after the words "in its mission statement", there should be added something about the essential elements of a mission statement that are to be listed (Cf. "Directives", B 2).

5. With regard to page 4 N. 3 line 2, in place of "makes serious efforts to appoint", it should read: "shall ensure the appointment of" in order to respect art. 4 § § 1 and 2 of "the General Norms". Mention should also be made about in-

forming such persons of the Catholic identity of the Institution and its impli-cations, and about their responsibility to promote, or at least, to respect that identity. Here too the provisions of footnote 49 (based on CIC can. 810) should find their place.

6. Page 4 before # 5 there should be added the idea: that the local Bishop has a responsibility to promote the welfare of the Catholic Universities in his diocese and has the right and the duty to watch over the preservation and strengthening of their Catholic character. ("General Norms" art. 5 § 2).

7. Page 4 ##5 and 6: the Congregation would make two observations at this point.

a. The Congregation takes note with satisfaction that the plenary session of the Bishops' Conference voted to study further the question of the mandate of CIC can. 812. We hope that a solution will soon be found so as to have a full ap-plication of the canon incorporated into a second draft of the "Ordinances".

b. Regarding the document "*Doctrinal Responsibilities: Approaches to Pro-moting Cooperation and Resolving Misunderstandings Between Bishops and Theologians*". Without entering into a consideration of its various merits in other circumstances, the Congregation wishes to point out that this docu-ment differs from the mandate, in that, among other things, it does not ad-dress the situation of the teacher of theology at the moment of his appoint-ment to this function and the relationship between teaching theology and the Church. The mandate, on the other hand, has this positive dimension: "In par-ticular, Catholic theologians, aware that they fulfill a mandate received from the Church, are to be faithful to the Magisterium of the Church as the authen-tic interpreter of Sacred Scripture and Sacred Tradition" ("General Norms" art. 4 § 3).

Concerning the same document, "Doctrinal Responsibilities . . .", and pre-scinding from its valuable elements with regard to procedure and respect for the persons involved, it does not seem to facilitate the exercise of the rights and duties of the local Bishop when problems arise, a procedure such as is called for by "General Norms" art. 5 § 2.

8. Page 5 B 1 line 1, add: communicates and before "develops".

9. Page 6 B 2 line 3, read: "the ideals, principles and norms".

10. Page 6 B 3 line three: same as previous comment.

11. Attentive to the various roles of Religious Institutes in the Catholic Uni-versities and Colleges, and in accordance with the "Directives of the Congrega-tion", B 4 c mention should be made of these Religious Institutes along the lines of N. 25 of the Apostolic Constitution.

12. In light of the particular importance which the Board of Trustees hold in so many Catholic Colleges and Universities in the United States, their responsibility for maintaining and strengthening the Catholic identity of the University should be given some place in the "Ordinances" (cf. "General Norms" art. 4 § 1 and "Directives of the Congregation" B 4 d).

Rome, 23 April 1997

30 | Letter from Bishop Anthony M. Pilla to Bishop John Leibrecht

May 6, 1997

Most Reverend John J. Leibrecht
Bishop of Springfield–Cape Girardeau
601 South Jefferson Avenue
Springfield, MO 65806

Dear Bishop Leibrecht:

During our recent visit to the Congregation for Catholic Education in Rome, Cardinal Laghi presented me with a response to our request for a *recognitio* for the Pastoral Application of *Ex Corde Ecclesiae.*

After reading the response from the Congregation, you will understand why I am now asking you to reconvene the *Ad hoc* Committee on *Ex Corde Ecclesiae* to address those items cited in the Congregation's document.

I have greatly appreciated all that has been done, the time and energy expended and the outstanding work of the *Ad hoc* Committee but must sincerely ask for the Committee to reconvene as soon as possible.

With prayerful best wishes, I am

Sincerely yours in Christ,

Most Reverend Anthony M. Pilla
Bishop of Cleveland
President, NCCB/USCC

From the author's files.

31 | Report of Bishop John Leibrecht to the Implementation Committee, May 23, 1997

DATE: May 23, 1997
TO: *Ex Corde Ecclesiae* Implementation Committee
FROM: Most Rev. John J. Leibrecht

Enclosed is a copy of the letter from Cardinal Pio Laghi to Bishop Pilla regarding the implementation document which the National Conference of Catholic Bishops sent to the Congregation for Catholic Education in late 1996. Also enclosed are four pages of "observations" from the Congregation for Catholic Education. We will address this material at a meeting of our committee, the date for which will be set at a later time.

The newly established Subcommittee, chaired by Cardinal Bevilacqua, will be making recommendations to us on two matters: appropriate use of canonical language where necessary and comments on Canon 812. When it seems that the Subcommittee is coming close to finishing its report to us, I will be in contact with you to set a date for our meeting. That date will be set as far ahead as possible because of the crowded calendars everyone has.

The enclosed papers from the Congregation for Catholic Education will be the topic of the meeting which several of us episcopal members are having with Cardinal Laghi and his staff in Rome on June 26.

As the new Subcommittee does its work, Cardinal Maida will be able to bring to the committee the thinking developed over our years of working together in designing an implementation document. I also indicated to Cardinal Bevilacqua that if I could be helpful in any way by providing information to the Subcommittee, I would be happy to do so.

Thanks for all you have already done and for helping to resolve our present situation as we seek a recognitio!

Enclosures

From the author's files.

32 | Report on June Meeting in Rome

July 3, 1997

TO: Bishops, College/University Presidents, Learned Societies,
          Religious Community Sponsors
DATE: 3 July 1997
FROM: Most Reverend John J. Leibrecht
          Chair, *Ex corde Ecclesiae* Implementation Committee

In his recent letter to Bishop Anthony Pilla, President of NCCB/USCC, offering observations on the implementation of *Ex corde Ecclesiae* in the United States, Pio Cardinal Laghi, Prefect of the Congregation for Catholic Education, wrote that he was "always disposed for any further clarification, either by way of correspondence or in personal meetings." In my most recent memorandum to you (23 May 1997), I indicated that several bishops from NCCB's Implementation Committee would meet in Rome with Cardinal Laghi and his staff. That meeting took place 26 June.

The meeting was helpful to all participants. Bishops from the Implementation Committee indicated that certain observations from the Congregation seemed as though they could readily be incorporated into the next document in ways which would help perfect it. The bishops also said that some observations from the Congregation need further study and reflection. The greatest amount of time was devoted to a discussion of Canon 812.

Discussions at the meeting, not always leading to a conclusion, helped set directions for the next phase of work.

Since many of the Congregation's observations are of a juridical nature, Bishop Pilla has appointed a subcommittee chaired by Anthony Cardinal Bevilacqua to give special attention to the Congregation's proposed emendations.

From the author's files.

The subcommittee hopes to have at least a preliminary report to the NCCB Implementation Committee by early Fall.

Both the Congregation for Catholic Education and the bishops' Implementation Committee agree that the next document should be developed for vote by the full assembly of bishops, and forwarded to the Congregation for Catholic Education and then to the Congregation for Bishops for a "recognitio," as soon as possible.

Present for the 26 June meeting in Rome from the NCCB Implementation Committee were James Cardinal Hickey, Adam Cardinal Maida, Archbishop Francis Schulte and myself, with two priests from the NCCB/USCC staff, Msgr. Thomas McDade and Reverend Terrence Toland, S.J.

Permit me to repeat the suggestion in my 23 May memo to you that discussions of *Ex corde Ecclesiae,* the apostolic constitution itself, serve as the focus of continuing contacts between bishops and representatives of Catholic colleges and universities. The vision in that document can be constructively addressed even as the work on its U.S. implementation continues.

Additional information should be forthcoming in the Fall.

33 | Preliminary Subcommittee Report on *"Ex Corde Ecclesiae*: An Application to the United States"

July 15–16, 1997

A. GENERAL STRUCTURE OF THE DOCUMENT: A TWO-PART APPROACH

In analyzing the Congregation's observations, the subcommittee has come to the conclusion that the entire Application can substantially be retained as a theological-pastoral *Introduction* to which will be attached an addendum of *Particular Norms*. The subcommittee's reasons for recommending this two-part approach are the following:

1. The Congregation considers the Application as drafted a good basis for particular ordinances.
2. Since the conference of bishops has already voted favorably on the wording of the Application, its retention as the theological and pastoral context for the particular norms should pave the way for the acceptance of the revised document.
3. This approach (theological-pastoral section, juridical section) is a common style of the Roman Curia. For example, the third draft of the Canadian ordinances adopts this approach.
4. The addition of a section on particular norms will satisfy the Congregation's request for the incorporation of "necessary juridical elements."

B. SUBCOMMITTEE TASKS

- The subcommittee has divided up its responsibilities into three projects:
    1. **Preparation of the particular norms.** These particular norms, while juridical in nature, should reflect the pastoral style and tone of the

From the author's files.

Application. Bishop Thomas Doran and Bishop Raymond Burke will develop the initial draft of the norms (except for norms pertaining to Canons 812 and 810 and *Doctrinal Responsibilities*).

2. **The proper role of *Doctrinal Responsibilities* throughout the document (both the Introduction and the Particular Norms).** This addresses the Congregation's "Particular Observation 7b." Cardinal Maida will develop the initial draft in collaboration with Msgr. Alesandro.

3. **The canonical mandate (c. 812).** This addresses the Congregation's "Particular Observation 7a." At this point, the subcommittee feels that a key to the understanding and application of canon 812 can be found in the theological concept of *communio*. It may be possible to develop various options for the canonical mandate suitable for the varying situations represented by different Catholic colleges and universities. Cardinal Bevilacqua will develop the initial draft in collaboration with Msgr. Alesandro.

- Msgr. Alesandro will serve as the final draftsman of the subcommittee's work in order to develop a unified and harmonious style.
- The subcommittee is sensitive to the fact that the development of a draft with additional juridical elements cannot be accomplished in a vacuum. Before the document is finalized, informal and discreet consultation must take place to ensure its acceptability.
- When the subcommittee's draft reaches a certain stage, consultation should include a discussion with the presidents of Catholic colleges and universities currently serving as consultants to the *Ex corde Ecclesiae* committee. Consultation should also take place with other representatives of Catholic colleges and universities who have made observations and comments on the Application. The subcommittee may recommend informal and discreet consultation with other parties. (Cf. *Directives* A, 4.)

———

EX CORDE ECCLESIAE

PRELIMINARY REVISIONS OF THE APPLICATION IN RESPONSE TO THE CONGREGATION'S OBSERVATIONS

PARTICULAR OBSERVATION #1

Prenote: In place of the last two sentences, it should read as follows: "The following document, while recognizing that the Apostolic Constitution "Ex Corde

Ecclesiae" and its "General Norms" are to be observed as the academic legislation of the Church, seeks to apply these in the context of the United States."

Subcommittee: Page 1, Prenote
    The last two sentences should read:
        "The following document, while recognizing that the Apostolic Constitution "Ex Corde Ecclesiae" and its "General Norms" are to be observed as the academic legislation of the Church, seeks to apply these through particular legislation for the Roman Catholic Church in the United States."

PARTICULAR OBSERVATION #2

The material preceding letter "B" constitutes, in general, a quite helpful preamble, underlining, as it does, the spirit called for by N. 28, even if it does not take fully into account some of the other ecclesiological elements of the Constitution.

Subcommittee: Pages 1–3
    The first two-and-a-half pages of the Application (until page 3, line 11) are considered an appropriate part of the Introduction. The subcommittee feels that this section can easily be incorporated as an integral part of the Introduction to be followed by Particular Norms.
    The Congregation mentions the need to take account of "other ecclesiological elements" of the Constitution. The subcommittee feels that the final revision of the Introduction will highlight other ecclesiological elements as a context for the particular norms that follow.

PARTICULAR OBSERVATION #3

With regard to page 2, para. 2, it should be noted that every Catholic University has a relationship to the Church that is essential to its institutional identity (N. 27 and art. 5 "General Norms"). In this light the paragraph in question should read, regarding what follows: "'Ex Corde Ecclesiae' provides one of the ecclesiological principles to address . . ."

Subcommittee: Page 2, lines 8–9
    The sentence should read: "*Ex Corde Ecclesiae* provides one of the ecclesiological principles to address this specific relationship."

PARTICULAR OBSERVATION #4

Page 3 B1, line 3 after the words "in its mission statement," there should be added something about the essential elements of a mission statement that are to be listed (Cf. "Directives" §2).

Subcommittee: Page 3, line 16

The listing of essential elements of a mission statement can more properly be incorporated in the section on particular norms.

PARTICULAR OBSERVATION #5

With regard to page 4 N. 3 line 2, in place of "makes serious efforts to appoint," it should read: "shall ensure the appointment of" in order to respect art. 4 §§ 1 and 2 of the "General Norms." Mention should also be made about informing such persons of the Catholic identity of the Institution and its implications, and about their responsibility to promote, or at least, to respect that identity. Here too the provisions of footnote 49 (based on CIC can. 810) should find their place.

Subcommittee: Page 3, lines 20–23

Paragraph 3 should read as follows:

"3. that the institution, following its own procedures in the hiring and retention of professionally qualified faculty and staff, recruits and appoints individuals who are committed to the Catholic faith tradition or, if not Catholic, who are aware and respectful of that faith tradition."

The subcommittee recommends that the second and third parts of observation #5 (concerning Catholic identity and footnote 49 of the Constitution [c. 810]) be incorporated in the section on particular norms

PARTICULAR OBSERVATION #6

Page 4 before #5 there should be added the idea: that the local Bishop has a responsibility to promote the welfare of the Catholic Universities in his diocese and has the right and the duty to watch over the preservation and strengthening of their Catholic character ("General Norms" art. 5 §2).

Subcommittee: Page 4, line 26

Accept the Congregation's wording as is.

Insert: "that the local Bishop has a responsibility to promote the welfare of the Catholic Universities in his diocese and has the right and the duty to watch over the preservation and strengthening of their Catholic character ("General Norms" art. 5, §2)."

PARTICULAR OBSERVATION #7A

The Congregation take note with satisfaction that the plenary session of the Bishops' Conference voted to study further the question of the mandate of CIC Can. 812. We hope that a solution will soon be found so as to have a full application of the canon incorporated into a second draft of the "Ordinances."

Subcommittee: Page 3, lines 26 to Page 4, line 6
  The subcommittee is studying canon 812 separately and will make additional recommendations at a later time.

PARTICULAR OBSERVATION #7B
Regarding the document *"Doctrinal Responsibilities: Approaches to Promoting Cooperation and Resolving Misunderstandings Between Bishops and Theologians."* Without entering into a consideration of its various merits in other circumstances, the Congregation wishes to point out that this document differs from the mandate, in that, among other things, it does not address the situation of the teacher of theology at the moment of his appointment to this function and the relationship between teaching theology and the Church. The mandate, on the other hand, has this positive dimension: "In particular, Catholic theologians, aware that they fulfill a mandate received from the Church, are to be faithful to the Magisterium of the Church as the authentic interpreter of Sacred Scripture and Sacred Tradition" ("General Norms" art. 4 §3).

Subcommittee: Page 3, line 26 to Page 4, line 6
  The subcommittee is studying the references to *Doctrinal Responsibilities* separately and will make additional recommendations at a later time.

PARTICULAR OBSERVATION #8
Page 5 B 1 line 1, add: communicates and before "develops."

Subcommittee: Page 5, lines 1–2
  Accept the Congregation's wording as is.
    "1. that the institution has a plan for fulfilling its mission as Catholic which communicates and develops the Catholic intellectual tradition. . . ."

PARTICULAR OBSERVATION #9
Page 6 B 2 line 3, read: "the ideals, principles and norms."

Subcommittee: Page 6, lines 2–3
  Accept the Congregation's wording as is.
    ". . .and its research program with the ideals, principles and norms expressed in *Ex Corde Ecclesiae*;"

PARTICULAR OBSERVATION #10
Page 6 B 3 line 3, read: "the ideals, principles and norms."

Subcommittee: Page 6, lines 6–7

Accept the Congregation's wording as is.

"...regarding application of the ideals, principles and norms expressed in *Ex Corde Ecclesiae*;"

PARTICULAR OBSERVATION #11

Attentive to the various roles of Religious Institutes in the Catholic Universities and Colleges, and in accordance with the "Directives of the Congregation," B 4 c, mention should be made of these Religious Institutes along the lines of N. 25 of the Apostolic Constitution.

Subcommittee:

The subcommittee recommends that this reference be included in the section on particular norms.

PARTICULAR OBSERVATION #12

In light of the particular importance which the Board of Trustees holds in so many Catholic Colleges and Universities in the United States, their responsibility for maintaining and strengthening the Catholic identity of the University should be given some place in the "Ordinances" (Cf. "General Norms" art. 4, §1 and "Directives of the Congregation" B4d)

Subcommittee:

The subcommittee recommends that this observation be incorporated in the section on particular norms. It is likely that there will be additional references in the section on particular norms to the role of boards of trustees.

34 | Response for the Implementation Committee to Cardinal Bevilacqua

August 21, 1997

His Eminence
Anthony Cardinal Bevilacqua
Archdiocese of Philadelphia
222 N. 17th Street
Philadelphia, PA 19103-1299

Your Eminence:

I write in response to your letter of August 1, 1997 which sought direction from the *Ex Corde Ecclesiae* Implementation Committee for the work of your Subcommittee. Many thanks for helping us revise our implementation document as requested by the Holy See.

Today, the Implementation Committee had a conference call to discuss the two questions posed in your August 1 letter. You asked first: Does the *Ex Corde Ecclesiae* Committee agree with the two-fold approach recommended by the Subcommittee? The answer is yes. We believe it is a positive way of approaching the task ahead and provides a good hypothesis for what needs to be accomplished. It is too early to know a final outcome, of course, but the Implementation Committee is grateful for this particular suggestion in addressing the concerns of the Holy See.

Your second question was: Does the *Ex Corde Ecclesiae* Committee agree with the suggested revisions contained in the document, "Preliminary Revisions of the Application"? If so, does it wish the Subcommittee to prepare a draft of the Introduction? The Implementation Committee recommends that the suggested revisions be incorporated at this time for a more thorough examination at a later time. The Committee welcomes preparation of a draft of the Introduction by the Subcommittee for the sake of consistency between the Introduction and the Particular Norms. The Implementation Committee agrees with the Subcommittee's position that minimum revision is desirable, but that having a single author (possibly, Monsignor Alesandro) offer a draft of both the Introduction and the Particular Norms would be of great assistance to the future work of the Implementation Committee. As canonical matters are addressed, the hope is that the entire document will still have a clearly pastoral tone.

The Implementation Committee hopes it might be able to meet with you and your Subcommittee members this Fall as soon as you have a draft available. That would be the next step after your draft is completed, namely, the meeting of the Implementation Committee with you and your Subcommittee. Following that meeting, we could outline the next steps in consulting others.

The Implementation Committee sees as realistic the possibility of presenting the revised application document for *Ex Corde Ecclesiae* to the body of bishops at its June, 1998 meeting.

I'll give you a call on Thursday, August 28, to respond to any questions which this letter may have left unanswered. If after receiving the letter, you would like to call me before that time, please do so.

Again, Your Eminence, many thanks to you and all your associates for assisting us in preparing a document for vote by the National Conference of Catholic Bishops.

Gratefully in Christ,

Most Rev. John J. Leibrecht
Bishop of Springfield-Cape Girardeau

cc: *Ex Corde Ecclesiae* Implementation Committee Members

35 | Draft of *"Ex Co[...]* An Application[...] September 27, [...] from Bishop J[...]

DATE: October 15, 1998

TO: Presidents on the *Ex corde Ecclesiae* Implementation
Committee Resource Persons on the *Ex corde Ecclesiae*
Implementation Committee

FROM: Most Rev. John J. Leibrecht

In a conference call on October 15, the bishops of the Implementation Committee decided, for several reasons, to send the Subcommittee Draft *as is* without any additions. As you can see from the enclosed material, the draft is being sent to all bishops, presidents of Catholic colleges and universities, sponsoring religious communities and learned societies.

The hope is that at least a few bishops and representatives of Catholic colleges and universities might meet before the November 16–19 national assembly of bishops in Washington, D.C. so that their discussions can be reported from the floor. Because time is so short, however, most such discussions will take place sometime later.

In the name of the bishops of the Implementation Committee, I again want to thank you for your work with us. We look forward to further consultations with you as the Implementation Committee addresses the content of a draft to be submitted in the future for a vote by the assembly of bishops.

If there is any question now, just let me know.

Enclosure

From the author's files.

DATE: October 15, 1998
TO: Bishops
          Presidents of Catholic Colleges and Universities
          Sponsoring Religious Communities
          Learned Societies
FROM: Bishop John J. Leibrecht, Chair
          Ex corde Ecclesiae Implementation Committee

As you will recall, the National Conference of Catholic Bishops on November 13, 1996 at its national assembly in Washington, D.C. approved an Application of *Ex corde Ecclesiae* for the United States. The proposed Application was sent to the Holy See. In a letter of April 23, 1997 the Congregation for Catholic Education indicated that a "second draft" was needed from the U.S. bishops which would be a "juridical instrument" having norms for the United States which "have a true juridical character."

In view of the Congregation's requirement that the Application of *Ex corde Ecclesiae* have "juridical elements," the NCCB Implementation Committee requested Bishop Anthony Pilla, President of NCCB/USCC, to appoint a Subcommittee of canon lawyers to assist it. The Subcommittee was established, chaired by Cardinal Anthony Bevilacqua, with a membership of four bishops and a priest, all canon lawyers.

The Implementation Committee asked the Subcommittee to draw up a document organized into two parts: Part I would contain theological and pastoral considerations and Part II particular norms. In the enclosed document, Part I is basically the wording of the Application passed by the U.S. bishops in November, 1996. It contains additional sections on the concepts of Communion (II) and Catholic identity (VII). Norms from the former Application have been included with the new norms in Part Two.

The Implementation Committee asks for discussions of the enclosed Subcommittee draft between bishops and representatives of Catholic colleges and universities in which representatives of sponsoring religious communities also participate. If any bishops and representatives of Catholic higher education are able to schedule such meetings prior to the NCCB/USCC meeting November 16–19, reports on those discussions would be welcomed as part of the discussion of *Ex corde Ecclesiae* which will be taking place at that meeting.

Learned societies are invited to forward to bishops any comments they would like to make.

The effort continues to develop an Application of *Ex corde Ecclesiae* for the United States which meets the hopes of bishops, institutes of Catholic higher education and the Holy See. Accomplishing that is particularly challenging. Study and discussion of the enclosed document is an important step towards arriving at the goal set before us.

Although Part Two of the enclosed document contains some juridical language which at times can be unfamiliar, the discussions requested above can provide the opportunity to clarify its substance and intent.

Many thanks for reviewing the Subcommittee's draft and communicating with the appropriate people in your (arch)diocese! May the Lord guide us!

Enclosure

EX CORDE ECCLESIAE

AN APPLICATION TO THE UNITED STATES

PART ONE: THEOLOGICAL AND PASTORAL PRINCIPLES

I. Introduction

On August 15, 1990, Pope John Paul II issued an apostolic constitution on Catholic higher education entitled *Ex corde Ecclesiae*.[1] The Apostolic Constitution described the identity and mission of Catholic colleges and universities and provided General Norms to help fulfill its vision. The General Norms are to be applied concretely by episcopal conferences, taking into account the status of each college and university and, as far as possible and appropriate, civil law.

This document, while recognizing that the Apostolic Constitution *Ex corde Ecclesiae* and its General Norms are to be observed as the academic legislation of the Church, applies these through particular norms for the Roman Catholic Church in the United States.

II. The Ecclesiological Concept of Communion

The Church is made up of individual faithful and communities linked with one another through many active ecclesial relationships. A true understanding of these dynamic relationships flows from the faith-conviction that the Tri-une God, through the incarnate Son, Jesus Christ, has revealed His desire to incorporate all of us into the life of the Trinity. It is in the Church, by the in-dwelling of the Holy Spirit, that this relationship of all persons and commu-nities with the Triune God takes place. This body of dynamic relationships held together by the unity of faith is aptly described in the theological concept of communion.[2]

From an ecclesial perspective, the dynamic of communion unites on a deeper and more productive level the various communities in the Church through which so much of her mission of salvation is carried out. More specifically, the ecclesiology of communion furnishes the basis for the collaborative relation-ships between the hierarchy and Catholic universities called for by *Ex corde Ecclesiae*: "Every Catholic University is to maintain communion with the uni-versal Church and the Holy See; it is to be in close communion with the local Church and in particular with the diocesan bishops of the region or the nation in which it is located."[3] The Catholic university is a vital institution in the com-munion of the Church and makes an important contribution to the Church's work of evangelization.[4]

The richness of communion illuminates the ecclesial relationship that unites the distinct, and yet complementary, teaching roles of bishops and Catholic universities. In the light of communion, the teaching responsibilities of the hi-erarchy and of the Catholic universities retain their distinctive autonomous nature and goal but are joined as activities contributing to the fulfillment of the Church's universal teaching mission. The communion of the teaching functions of the bishops and of the Catholic universities centers on the relationship be-tween the bishops' right and obligation to communicate and safeguard the in-tegrity of Church doctrine and the right and obligation of Catholic universities to investigate, analyze and communicate truths freely in communion with the magisterium. Furthermore, the communion between the bishop and the teacher of theology furnishes the basis for the proper understanding and application of the mandate of Canon 812.[5] The mandate simply attests that the Catholic teacher of the theological disciplines carries out his or her task in communion with the Church.

The communion of all the faithful, communities and structures with the Tri-une God and with one another is a theological reality expressing the will of God. It is in understanding and living this communion that bishops and Catholic universities most effectively collaborate to fulfill their proper mission within the Church. In carrying out this mission, the Catholic university is uniquely situated in the search for truth to serve not only the people of God but the entire human family "in their pilgrimage to the transcendent goal which gives meaning to life."[6]

III. The Catholic University's Twofold Relationship

Catholic universities[7] are participants in both the life of the Church and the higher education enterprise of the United States. As such, they "are called to continuous renewal, both as 'universities' and as 'Catholic.'"[8] This twofold relationship is described in the May 22, 1994 joint document of the Congregation for Catholic Education and the Pontifical Councils for the Laity and for Culture, which states that the Catholic university achieves its purpose when

> . . . it gives proof of being rigorously serious as a member of the international community of knowledge and expresses its Catholic identity through an explicit link with the Church, at both local and universal levels — an identity which marks concretely the life, the services and the programs of the university community. In this way, by its very existence, the Catholic university achieves its aim of guaranteeing, in institutional form, a Christian presence in the university world . . .[9]

This relationship is clarified through dialogue that includes faculty of all disciplines, students, staff, academic and other administrative officers, trustees, and sponsoring religious communities of the educational institutions, all of whom share responsibility for the character of Catholic higher education. The bishop and his collaborators in the local Church are integral parties in this dialogue.

The Catholic university is related to the entire ecclesial community,[10] to the broader society,[11] as well as to the higher education academy.[12] We are directing special attention to the relationship between the institutions and Church authorities. *Ex corde Ecclesiae* provides one of the ecclesiological principles to address this specific relationship.

> Bishops have a particular responsibility to promote Catholic Universities, and especially to promote and assist in the preservation and strengthening of their Catholic identity, including the protection of their Catholic identity in relation to civil authorities. This will be achieved more effectively if close personal and pastoral relationships exist between University and Church authorities, characterized by *mutual trust, close and consistent cooperation and continuing dialogue*. Even when they do not enter directly into the internal

government of the University, bishops "should be seen not as external agents but as participants in the life of the Catholic University." [italics added][13]

Each of these elements in the pastoral relationship of bishops with Catholic universities warrants attention.

IV. Mutual Trust between University and Church Authorities

Mutual trust goes beyond the personalities of those involved in the relationship. The trust is grounded in a shared baptismal belief in the truths that are rooted in Scripture and Tradition, as interpreted by the Church, concerning the mystery of the Trinity: God the Father and Creator, who works even until now; God the Son and incarnate Redeemer, who is the Way and the Truth and the Life; and God the Holy Spirit, the Paraclete, whom the Father and Son send. In the spirit of *communio,* the relationship of trust between university and Church authorities, based on these shared beliefs with their secular and religious implications, is fostered by mutual listening, by collaboration that respects differing responsibilities and gifts, and by a solidarity that mutually recognizes respective statutory limitations and responsibilities.

V. Close and Consistent Cooperation between University and Church Authorities

Collaborating to integrate faith with life is a necessary part of the "close personal and pastoral relationships"[14] to which universities and bishops aspire. Within their academic mission of teaching and research, in ways appropriate to their own constituencies and histories, including their sponsorship by religious communities, institutions offer courses in Catholic theology that reflect current scholarship and are in accord with the authentic teaching of the Church.

Many cooperative programs, related to Gospel outreach, already flourish throughout the country. It is highly desirable that representatives of both educational institutions and Church authorities jointly identify, study, and pursue solutions to issues concerning social justice, human life and the needs of the poor.

Allocations of personnel and money to assure the special contributions of campus ministry are required. In view of the presence on campus of persons of other religious traditions, it is a concern of the whole Church that ecumenical and inter-religious relationships should be fostered with sensitivity.

VI. *Continuing Dialogue among University Representatives and Church Authorities*

Dialogues occasioned by *Ex corde Ecclesiae* are graced moments characterized by

1. a manifest openness to a further analysis and local appropriation of Catholic identity;
2. an appreciation of the positive contributions that campus-wide conversations make; and
3. a conviction that conversation can develop and sustain relationships.

A need exists for continued attention and commitment to the far-reaching implications—curricular, staffing, programming—of major themes within *Ex corde Ecclesiae.* These include Catholic identity, *communio,* relating faith and culture, pastoral outreach, the New Evangelization, and relationship to the Church.

VII. *Catholic Identity*

In 1979, Pope John Paul II, in an address to the Catholic academic community at The Catholic University of America, stressed the importance of the Catholic character of Catholic institutions of higher learning:

> Every university or college is qualified by a specified mode of being. Yours is the qualification of being Catholic, of affirming God, his revelation and the Catholic Church as the guardian and interpreter of that revelation. The term 'Catholic' will never be a mere label either added or dropped according to the pressures of varying factors.[15]

Catholic universities should excel in theological education, prayer and liturgy, and works of charity. These religious activities, however, do not alone make a university "Catholic." *Ex corde Ecclesiae* highlights four distinctive characteristics that are essential for Catholic identity:

1. Christian inspiration in individuals and the university community;
2. Reflection and research on human knowledge in the light of the Catholic faith;

3. Fidelity to the Christian message in conformity with the magisterium of the Church;
4. Institutional commitment to the service of others."[16]

In order to maintain and safeguard its Catholic identity, every Catholic university should set out clearly in its statutes or mission statement or in some other internal document its Catholic character and make every effort to enhance its communion with the hierarchy so that through their relationship they may assist each other to accomplish their mission.

In a secular world the strong Catholic identity of our institutes of higher learning is an invaluable instrument of grace witnessing to the relationship of truth and reason, the call of the revealed Word, and the authentic meaning of human life. "The present age is in urgent need of this kind of disinterested service, namely of proclaiming the meaning of truth, that fundamental value without which freedom, justice and human dignity are extinguished."[17]

VIII. Conclusion

The bishops of the United States, in offering this application of *Ex corde Ecclesiae,* join in sentiments expressed by Pope John Paul II:

> I turn to the whole Church, convinced that Catholic universities are essential to her growth and to the development of Christian culture and human progress. For this reason, the entire ecclesial community is invited to give its support to Catholic institutions of higher education and to assist them in their process of development and renewal . . .[18]

PART TWO: PARTICULAR NORMS

Art. 1. The Nature of the Particular Norms

1. These particular norms are based on and apply the Code of Canon Law, the general norms of *Ex corde Ecclesiae,* and complementary Church legislation.[19] They are applicable to all Catholic colleges, universities and institutions of higher learning within the territory encompassed by the National

Conference of Catholic Bishops, contrary particular laws, customs or privileges notwithstanding.[20]

2. Catholic universities are to observe the general norms of *Ex corde Ecclesiae* and the following particular norms as they apply to their individual institutions, taking into account their own statutes and, as far as possible and appropriate, relevant provisions of applicable federal and state law, regulations and procedures.

   a) Those established or approved by the Holy See, by the NCCB, by a group of diocesan bishops or by an individual diocesan bishop and those established by a public juridic person, such as a religious institute, are to incorporate, by reference and in other appropriate ways, the general and particular norms into their governing documents and conform their existing statutes to such norms. Within five years of the effective date of these particular norms, they are to submit the aforesaid incorporation for review and approval to the university's competent ecclesiastical authority.

   b) Other Catholic universities are to make the general and particular norms their own, include them in the university's official documentation by reference and in other appropriate ways, and, as much as possible, conform their existing statutes to such norms. These steps to ensure their Catholic identity are to be carried out in agreement with the diocesan bishop of the place where the seat of the university is situated.[21]

3. Those establishing or sponsoring a Catholic university have an obligation to make certain that they will be able to carry out their canonical duties in a way acceptable under relevant provisions of applicable federal and state law, regulations and procedures, reserving to themselves, insofar as possible, such powers as to enable them to preserve and strengthen the Catholic identity of the university.[22]

Art. 2. *The Nature of a Catholic University*

1. A Catholic university enjoys institutional autonomy, which must be respected and promoted by all, so that it may effectively carry out its mission of freely searching for all truth.[23]

2. Academic freedom is an essential component of a Catholic university. The university should take steps to ensure that all professors are accorded "a lawful freedom of inquiry and of thought, and of freedom to express their minds humbly and courageously about those matters in which they enjoy competence."[24] In particular, "[t]hose who are engaged in the sacred disciplines enjoy a lawful freedom of inquiry and of prudently expressing their

opinions on matters in which they have expertise, while observing a due respect [*debito obsequio*] for the magisterium of the Church."[25]

3. With due regard for the common good and the need to safeguard and promote the integrity and unity of the faith, the diocesan bishop has the duty to recognize and promote the rightful academic freedom of professors in Catholic universities in their search for truth.[26]

4. Recognizing the dignity of the human person, a Catholic university, in promoting its own Catholic identity and fostering Catholic teaching and discipline, must respect the religious liberty of every individual, a right with which each is endowed by nature.[27]

5. A responsibility of every Catholic university is to affirm its essential characteristics, in accord with the principles of *Ex corde Ecclesiae,* through public acknowledgment in its mission statement and/or its other official documentation of its canonical status[28] and its commitment to the elements of Catholic identity, including but not limited to the following:[29]

   a) Commitment to be faithful to the teachings of the Catholic Church;

   b) Commitment to Catholic ideals, principles and attitudes in carrying out research, teaching and all other university activities, including activities of officially-recognized student and faculty organizations and associations, and with due regard for academic freedom and the conscience of every individual;[30]

   c) Commitment to serve others, particularly the poor, underprivileged and vulnerable members of society;

   d) Commitment of witness of the Catholic faith by Roman Catholic teachers and administrators, especially those teaching the theological disciplines, and acknowledgment and respect on the part of non-Catholic teachers and administrators of the university's Catholic identity and mission;

   e) Commitment to provide courses for students on Catholic moral and religious principles and their application to critical issues such as human life and social justice;

   f) Commitment to care pastorally for the students, faculty, administration and staff;

   g) Commitment to provide personal services (health care, counseling and guidance) to students, as well as administration and faculty, in conformity with the Church's ethical and religious teaching and directives.

6. The university (in particular, the trustees, administration, and faculty) should take practical steps to implement its mission statement in order to foster and strengthen at every level its Catholic nature and character.[31]

Art. 3. The Establishment of a Catholic University

1. A Catholic university may be established, or an existing university approved, by the Holy See, the National Conference of Catholic Bishops, or an individual diocesan bishop or group of diocesan bishops. It may also be established by a religious institute or some other public juridic person, or by individual Catholics, acting singly or in association.[32]
2. At the time of its establishment the university should see to it that its canonical status is identified, including the ecclesiastical authority by which it has been established or approved or to which it otherwise relates.[33]

Art. 4. The University Community

1. The responsibility for safeguarding and strengthening the Catholic identity of the university rests primarily with the university itself. All the members of the university community are called to participate in this important task in accordance with their specific roles: the board of trustees, the administration and staff, the faculty, and the students.[34]
2. *The Board of Trustees*
    a) As much as possible, the majority of the board should be faithful Catholics—clergy, religious or lay.
    b) Each member of the board must be committed to the mission statement of the university.
    c) The board should develop practical ways of relating to and collaborating with the local bishop and diocesan agencies on matters of mutual concern.[35]
    d) The board should analyze ecclesiastical documents on higher education, such as *Ex corde Ecclesiae* and these particular norms, and develop ways of implementing them in the structure and life of the university.
    e) The board should see to it that the university periodically undertakes an internal review of the congruence of its mission statement, its courses of instruction, its research program, and its service activity with the ideals, principles and norms expressed in *Ex corde Ecclesiae*.
3. *Administration and Staff*
    a) The university president should be a faithful Catholic.[36]
    b) The administration should inform faculty and staff at the time of their appointment regarding the Catholic identity, mission and religious practices of the university and encourage them to participate, to the degree possible, in the spiritual life of the university.

   c) The administration should support the pastoral ministry of the university.

   d) The administration should be in dialogue with the local bishop about ways of promoting Catholic identity and the contribution that the university can make to the life of the Church in the area.

4. *Faculty*

   a) In accordance with its procedures for the hiring and retention of professionally qualified faculty and relevant provisions of applicable federal and state law, regulations and procedures, the university should recruit and appoint faithful Catholics as professors so that, as much as possible, those committed to the witness of the faith will constitute a majority of the faculty. Professors who are not Catholic are expected to be aware and respectful of the Catholic faith tradition.

   b) To the extent possible, the faculty, especially those who are Catholic, should participate in the religious life and activities of the university. Lectures on Catholic teaching should be made available on a regular basis to members of the administration and faculty.

   c) All professors, especially those teaching the theological disciplines, are expected to exhibit not only academic competence but integrity of doctrine and good character.[37] When these qualities are found to be lacking, the university statutes are to specify the competent authority and the process to be followed to remedy the situation.[38]

   d) Catholic theology should be taught in every Catholic university, and, if possible, a department or chair of Catholic theology should be established. Academic events should be organized on a regular basis to address theological issues, especially those relative to the various disciplines taught in the university.[39]

   e) Both the university and the bishops, aware of the contributions made by theologians to Church and academy, have a right to expect them to present authentic Catholic teaching. Catholic professors of the theological disciplines, insofar as they fulfill an ecclesial mandate obtained from a competent ecclesiastical authority, have a corresponding duty to be faithful to the Church's magisterium as the authoritative interpreter of Sacred Scripture and Sacred Tradition.

   f) Catholics who teach the theological disciplines in a Catholic university are required to have a mandate granted by competent ecclesiastical authority.[40]

      1) The mandate is fundamentally an acknowledgment by Church authority that a Catholic professor of a theological discipline teaches within the full communion of the Catholic Church. The acknowledg-

ment recognizes that he or she is a faithful Catholic, an active member of the Church's communion who teaches a theological discipline as a special ministry within the Church community.

2) The mandate recognizes the professor's commitment and responsibility to teach authentic Catholic doctrine and to refrain from putting forth as Catholic teaching anything contrary to the Church's magisterium.

3) The mandate should not be construed as an appointment, authorization, delegation or approbation of one's teaching by Church authorities. Those who have received a mandate teach in their own name in virtue of their Christian initiation and their academic and professional competence, not in the name of the Bishop or of the Church's magisterium.[41]

4) The following procedure is given to facilitate the process of requesting and granting the mandate.

   (a) The competent ecclesiastical authority to grant the mandate is the bishop of the diocese in which the Catholic university is located; he may grant the mandate personally or through a delegate.

   (b) The attestation or declaration of the professor that he or she will teach in communion with the Church can be expressed by the profession of faith and oath of fidelity or in any other reasonable manner acceptable to the one granting the mandate.

   (c) Without prejudice to the rights of the local bishop, a mandate, once granted, remains in effect wherever and as long as the professor teaches unless and until withdrawn by competent ecclesiastical authority.

   (d) The mandate should be given in writing to provide the most secure manner of demonstrating the fulfillment of canon 812.[42]

   (e) The mandate can be denied or removed. In either case, reasons for such an act should be given in writing so that the person who deems his or her rights to have been injured may seek recourse.[43]

   (f) In matters relating to the mandate, the university should maintain close contacts with the local diocesan bishop.

5. *Students.* With due regard for the principles of religious liberty and freedom of conscience, students should have the opportunity to be educated in the Church's moral and religious principles and social teachings and to participate in the life of faith.[44]

   a) Catholic students have a right to receive from a university instruction in authentic Catholic doctrine and practice, especially from those who teach the theological disciplines. They also have a right to be provided with opportunities to practice the faith through participation in Mass, the sacraments, religious devotions and other authentic forms of Catholic spirituality.

b) Courses in Catholic doctrine and practice should be made available to all students.

c) Catholic teaching should have a place, appropriate to the subject matter, in the various disciplines taught in the university.[45] Students should be provided with adequate instruction on professional ethics and moral issues related to their profession.

d) In accordance with the Church's teaching on the family, the university should relate to its students within the context of their individual situations, developing programs to foster and support family life.

Art. 5. *The Catholic University within the Church*

1. The Universal Church:
   a) The university shall develop and maintain a plan for fulfilling its mission as Catholic that communicates and develops the Catholic intellectual tradition, is of service to the Church and society, and encourages the members of the university community to grow in the practice of the faith.[46]
   b) The university plan should address intellectual and pastoral contributions to the mission of evangelization,[47] service to the poor, social justice initiatives, and ecumenical and inter-religious activities.

2. The Local Church
   a) In accordance with Church teaching and canon law, the local Bishop has a responsibility to promote the welfare of the Catholic universities in his diocese and to watch over the preservation and strengthening of their Catholic character.[48]
   b) Bishops should, when appropriate, acknowledge publicly the service of Catholic universities to the Church and support the institution's Catholic identity if it is unjustifiably challenged.
   c) Diocesan and university authorities should commit themselves mutually to regular dialogues to achieve the goals of *Ex corde Ecclesiae* according to local needs and circumstances.
      1) University authorities and the local diocesan bishop should develop practical methods of collaboration that are harmonious with the university's structure and statutes.[49]

2) Similar forms of collaboration should also exist between the university and the religious institute to which it is related by establishment or tradition.[50]

d) *Doctrinal Responsibilities: Approaches to Promoting Cooperation and Resolving Misunderstandings between Bishops and Theologians,* approved and published by the National Conference of Catholic Bishops, June 17, 1989, can serve as a useful guide for bishops, professors of the theological disciplines and administrators of universities to promote informal cooperation and collaboration in the Church's teaching mission and the faithful observance within Catholic universities of the principles of Catholic doctrine.

e) Disputes about Church doctrine should be resolved, whenever possible, in an informal manner. At times, the resolution of such matters may benefit from formal doctrinal dialogue as proposed by *Doctrinal Responsibilities* and adapted by the parties in question.[51]

f) When such disputes are not resolved within the limits of informal or formal dialogue, they should be addressed in a timely manner by the competent ecclesiastical authority through appropriate doctrinal and administrative actions, taking into account the requirements of the common good and the rights of the individuals and institutions involved.

g) The National Conference of Catholic Bishops, through an appropriate committee structure, should continue to dialogue and collaborate with the Catholic academic community and its representative associations about ways of safeguarding and promoting the ideals, principles and norms expressed in *Ex corde Ecclesiae.*

Art. 6. Pastoral Ministry

1. The diocesan bishop has overall responsibility for the pastoral care of the university's students, faculty, administration and staff.
2. The university, in cooperation with the diocesan bishop, shall make provision for effective campus ministry programs, including the sacraments, other liturgical celebrations, and opportunities for prayer and spiritual reflection.[52]
3. When selecting pastoral ministers—priests, deacons, religious and lay persons—to carry on the work of campus ministry, the university authorities should work closely with the diocesan bishop and interested religious institutes. Priests and deacons must enjoy pastoral facilities from the local ordinary in order to exercise their ministry on campus.

4. With due regard for religious liberty and freedom of conscience, the university, in cooperation with the diocesan bishop, should collaborate in ecumenical and interfaith efforts to care for the pastoral needs of students, faculty and other university personnel who are not Catholic.

5. In these pastoral efforts, the university and the diocesan bishop should take account of the prescriptions and recommendations issued by the Holy See and the guidance and pastoral statements of the National Conference of Catholic Bishops.[53]

Art. 7. Cooperation

1. Catholic universities should commit themselves to cooperate in a special way with other Catholic universities, institutions and professional associations, in the United States and abroad, in order to build up the entire Catholic academic community.[54]

2. In collaborating with governmental agencies, regional associations, and other universities, whether public or private, Catholic universities should give corporate witness to and promote the Church's social teaching and its moral principles in areas such as the fostering of peace and justice, respect for all human life, the eradication of poverty and unjust discrimination, the development of all peoples and the growth of human culture.[55]

NOTES

1. Pope John Paul II, Apostolic Constitution on Catholic Universities *Ex corde Ecclesiae,* August 15, 1990, *AAS* 82 (1990) pp. 1475–1509. English translation: *Origins,* CNS Documentary Service, October 4, 1990 [cited throughout the remainder of this document as *ECE*].

2. *See* Vatican Council II, Dogmatic Constitution on the Church *(Lumen Gentium)* 4, 7, 9–29 (Chapter II: the People of God) and *passim;* Congregation for the Doctrine of the Faith, "Letter to the Bishops of the Catholic Church on Some Aspects of the Church Understood as Communion," *Origins,* 22 (1992), 108–112; *Catechism of the Catholic Church,* nn. 787–801 and *passim;* 1985 Extraordinary Synod of Bishops, "A Message to the People of God," *Origins* 15 (1985), 441–444, and "The Final Report," *Origins* 15 (1985), 444–450.

3. *ECE,* II, Art. 5, §1.

4. *ECE,* I, n. 49.

5. "It is necessary that those who teach theological disciplines in any institute of higher studies have a mandate from the competent ecclesiastical authority." (c. 812)

6. *ECE,* I, 13, quoting from "The Catholic University in the Modern World," the final document of the Second International Congress of Delegates of Catholic Universities, Rome, Nov. 20–29, 1972, Sec. 1.

7. For purposes of stylistic simplicity this document, in both the "Preamble" and "Particular Norms," uses the word "university" as a generic term to include universities, colleges and other institutions of higher learning.

8. *ECE,* Introduction, n. 7.

9. "The Church's Presence in the University and in University Culture," II, §2, *Origins,* June 16, 1994, 74–80.

10. *ECE,* I, nn. 27–29, 31.

11. *Ibid.,* I, nn. 32–37.

12. *Ibid.,* I, nn. 12, 37; II, Art. 7, §§1–2.

13. *Ibid.,* I, n. 28. The citation at the end is from John Paul II, *Address to Leaders of Catholic Higher Education,* Xavier University of Louisiana, U.S.A., 12 September 1987, n. 4: *AAS* 80 (1988) 164.

14. *ECE,* I, n. 28.

15. Pope John Paul II, *Address* "Ad prope et exstantes sedes Studiorum Universitatis Catholicae profectus hanc allocutionem fecit ad moderatores et doctores eiusdem Athenaei atque ad legatos Collegiorum Universitatumque Catholicarum totius Nationis," October 6, 1979, *AAS* 71:13 (1979) 1260.

16. *ECE,* I, n. 13.

17. *ECE,* I, n. 4.

18. *Ibid.,* Introduction, n. 11.

19. *See ECE,* II, Art. 1, §§1&2.

20. *ECE,* II, Art. 11: "Any particular laws or customs presently in effect that are contrary to this constitution are abolished. Also, any privileges granted up to this day by the Holy See whether to physical or moral persons that are contrary to this present constitution are abolished." These Particular Norms are not applicable to ecclesiastical universities and faculties insofar as they are governed by *Sapientia Christiana.*

21. Cf. *ECE,* Art. 1, §3.

22. *See* canon 807 and *ECE,* Art. 3; Congregation for Catholic Education, *Directives to Assist in the Formulation of the Ordinances for the Apostolic Constitution "Ex corde Ecclesiae,"* not dated [Jan. 21, 1991; see Doc. 3], n. B1.

23. *Institutional autonomy* means that governance of an academic institution is and remains internal to the institution itself. *See ECE,* I, n. 12 and footnote 15; Vatican Council II, Pastoral Constitution on the Church in the Modern World *(Gaudium et Spes)* 59; Declaration on Catholic Education *(Gravissimum educationis)* 10.

24. Vatican Council II, Church in the Modern World *(Gaudium et Spes)* 62. A university's commitment to Catholic ideals, principles and attitudes is not only consistent with academic freedom and the integrity of secular subjects, it requires "[f]reedom in research and teaching" and respect for "the principles and methods of each individual discipline." *ECE,* II, Art. 2, §5.

25. C. 218.

26. *See ECE,* II, Art. 2, §5.

27. The purpose of a Catholic university is education. Though thoroughly imbued with Christian inspiration, the university's Catholic identity should in no way

be construed as an excuse for religious indoctrination or proselytization. *See* Vatican Council II, Declaration on Religious Liberty *(Dignitatis humanae)* 2–4.

28. *See* footnote 33 for a listing of canonical categories.

29. "[E]very Catholic university, as Catholic, must have the following essential characteristics:

'1. A Christian inspiration not only of individuals but of the university community as such.

'2. A continuing reflection in the light of the Catholic faith upon the growing treasury of human knowledge, to which it seeks to contribute by its own research.

'3. Fidelity to the Christian message as it comes to us through the Church.

'4. An institutional commitment to the service of the people of God and of the human family in their pilgrimage to the transcendent goal which gives meaning to life.'"

ECE, I, n. 13 [quoting "The Catholic University in the Modern World," the final document of the Second International Congress of Delegates of Catholic Universities, Rome, Nov. 20–29, 1972, Sec.1].

30. *See ECE,* II, Art. 2, §§4–5.

31. In this regard, the university may wish to establish a "mission effectiveness committee" or some other appropriate structure to develop methods by which Catholics may promote the university's Catholic identity and those who are not Catholic may acknowledge and respect this identity.

32. *ECE,* II, Art. 3, §§1–3. Note that, under Canon 322, private associations of the faithful can acquire juridic personality by the issuance of a formal decree of competent ecclesiastical authority (§1) and approval of their statutes, retaining, all the while, their private character (§2).

33. A Catholic university may be established by various ecclesiastical authorities or entities (e.g., the Holy See) or by individual Catholics. Moreover, the university may be erected as a self-standing public juridic person or it may be simply a complex "activity" or "apostolate" of a public juridic person. The following alternatives outline different categories that describe a Catholic university from the canonical perspective:

(a) *The university as an apostolate of the Holy See.* The Holy See may erect a university or approve an already-established university as an apostolate of the Holy See itself. Such universities, which are sometimes granted the title of "pontifical," are erected or approved by a decree of the Holy See and their statutes must be approved by the Holy See. The "competent ecclesiastical authority" to which such universities are related is the Holy See through the Congregation for Catholic Education.

(b) *The university as an apostolate of the National Conference of Catholic Bishops.* An episcopal conference has the right to erect a university or approve an already-established university as an apostolate of the conference itself through the issuance of a decree and approval of its statutes. The "competent ecclesiastical authority" to which such a university is related is the National Conference of Catholic Bishops.

(c) *The university as an apostolate of a diocesan bishop or a group of diocesan bishops.* Diocesan bishops, acting individually or jointly, have the right to erect a university or approve an already-established university as a diocesan or inter-diocesan apostolate through the issuance of a decree and approval of its statutes. The "com-

petent ecclesiastical authority" to which such a university is related is the individual diocesan bishop or the group of diocesan bishops establishing or approving it.

(d) *The university as an apostolate of a public juridic person.* A university may be established or approved as an apostolate of a public juridic person (such as a religious institute). In such cases the consent of the bishop of the diocese in which
the seat of the university is situated (or of a group of bishops, the NCCB or the
Holy See) and approval of its statutes are required. Such a university relates to the
public juridic person that established or approved it and to the diocesan bishop
(or group of bishops, the NCCB or the Holy See) as its "competent ecclesiastical
authority."

(e) *The university as a public juridic person.* A university may itself be erected as a public association of the faithful or some other type of public juridic person *(universitas rerum* or *universitas personarum).* Such juridic personality requires the issuance
of a decree of erection and approval of the statutes by the Holy See, the National
Conference of Catholic Bishops, or an individual or group of diocesan bishops.

(f) *The university established by individuals.* Individual Catholics may found a university or convert an existing university into a Catholic institution without its being
established or approved by the Holy See, the National Conference of Catholic
Bishops, individual diocesan bishops or a public juridic person. Nonetheless, in
accordance with canon 808, such a university may refer to itself as Catholic only
with the consent of the competent ecclesiastical authority.

34. *ECE,* II, Art. 4. §1. In these norms the phrases "board of trustees," "president" and
"administration" are used to denote the highest bodies of governance within the university's corporate and operational structure. If, in an individual case, the university's governance uses a different structure or other titles, the norms should be applied accordingly.

35. In individual situations, it may be possible and appropriate to invite the diocesan
bishop or his delegate to be a member of the board itself. In other cases, arranging periodic meetings to address the university's Catholic identity and mission may prove more
practical and effective.

36. Upon assuming the office of president for the first time, a Catholic should take the
prescribed profession of faith and oath of fidelity (*See* c. 833, §7; *AAS* 81 [1989] 104–106,
1169). When a candidate who is not a Catholic is being considered for appointment as
president of a Catholic university, the university should consult with the competent ecclesiastical authority about the matter. In all cases, the president is expected to uphold the
university's Catholic identity and to respect and promote Catholic principles and ideals.

37. The Church's expectation of "integrity of doctrine" should not be misconstrued
to imply that a Catholic university's task is to indoctrinate or proselytize its students. Educational integrity requires that the teaching of secular subjects be measured by the professional standards applicable and appropriate to the individual disciplines. *See* above
footnotes 24 and 27.

38. C. 810, §1.

39. *Gravissimum educationis* 10.

40. C. 812 and *ECE,* II, Art. 4, §3. "Mandate" is a technical term referring to the juridical expression of the ecclesial relationship of communion that exists between the Church
and the Catholic teacher of a theological discipline in the Catholic university. This special relationship is the basis for the requirement in canon law that Catholics teaching the

theological disciplines take the prescribed profession of faith and oath of fidelity at the start of their term (c. 833, §7; *AAS* 81 [1989] 104–106, 1169). The phrase "theological disciplines" refers to several areas of teaching: sacred scripture; dogmatic theology; moral theology; pastoral theology; canon law; liturgy; and Church history (c. 252, §3).

41. The prescription of canon 812 is grounded in the right and responsibility of bishops to safeguard the faithful teaching of Catholic doctrine to the people of God and to assure the authentic presentation of the Church's magisterium. Those with such a mandate are not agents of the magisterium; they teach in their own name, not in the name of the bishop. Nonetheless, they are not separate from the Church's teaching mission. Responding to their baptismal call, their ecclesial task is to teach, write and research for the benefit of the Church and within its communion. The mandate is essentially the recognition of an ecclesial relationship between the professor and the Church (*See* canon 229, §3).

Moreover, it is not the responsibility of a Catholic university to seek the mandate; this is a personal obligation of each professor. If a particular professor lacks a mandate and continues to teach a theological discipline, the university must determine what further action may be taken in accordance with its own mission and statutes (cf. canon 810, §l).

42. Administrative acts in external forum must be in writing (c. 37).

43. *See* canons 1732–1739.

44. In *Gravissimum educationis* 10, the Vatican Council expressed the hope that students in Catholic institutions of higher learning will become "truly outstanding in learning, ready to shoulder society's heavier burdens and to witness the faith to the world."

45. *See* above footnotes 27 and 37.

46. *See ECE,* I, n. 38 *ff.* and footnote 44.

47. *See ECE,* I, nn. 48–49.

48. *See ECE,* II, Art. 5, §2.

49. The following are some suggestions for collaboration:

- Arranging for the diocesan bishop or his delegate to be involved in the university's governance, perhaps through representation on the board of trustees or in some other appropriate manner.
- Sharing the university's annual report with the diocesan bishop, especially in regard to matters affecting Catholic identity.
- Scheduling regular pastoral visits to the university on the part of the diocesan bishop.
- Collaborating on works of evangelization.
- Conducting dialogues on matters of doctrine and pastoral practice.
- Resolving issues affecting the university's Catholic identity in accordance with established procedures. (*See ECE,* II, Art. 5, §2 and *ECE* footnote 52.)
- Participating together in ecumenical and inter-religious endeavors.
- Contributing to the diocesan process of formulating the quinquennial report to the Holy See.

50. The following are some suggestions for collaboration:

- Arranging for members of the religious institute to be involved in the university's governance, perhaps through representation on the board of trustees.
- Sharing the university's annual report with the religious institute, especially in regard to matters affecting Catholic identity and the religious institute's charism.
- Scheduling regular pastoral visits to the university on the part of the religious institute's leadership and involving the members of the institute in campus ministry.

- Collaborating on evangelization and on the special works of the religious institute.
- Conducting dialogues on matters of doctrine and pastoral practice and on the development of spirituality in accordance with the religious institute's charism.
- Resolving issues affecting the university's Catholic identity in accordance with established procedures. (*See ECE,* II, Art. 5, §2 and *ECE* footnote 52.)
- Participating together in ecumenical and inter-religious endeavors.
- Contributing together in the diocesan process of formulating the quinquennial report to the Holy See.

51. See National Conference of Catholic Bishops, *Doctrinal Responsibilities: Approaches to Promoting Cooperation and Resolving Misunderstandings between Bishops and Theologians,* June 17, 1989, Washington, D.C.: USCC, III, C, pp. 16–22.

52. *See ECE,* II, Art. 6, §2.

53. *See* National Conference of Catholic Bishops, "Sons and Daughters of the Light: A Pastoral Plan for Ministry with Young Adults," *Origins,* November 28, 1996, 384–402, especially 398–401; "Letter to College Students," *Origins,* December 7, 1995, 429–430; *Empowered by the Spirit,* Washington, D.C.: USCC, 1985.

54. *See ECE,* I, n. 35.

55. See ECE, I, nn. 32–35.

36 | Draft of "*Ex Corde Ecclesiae*: An Application to the United States" Submitted to the NCCB General Meeting

November 16–19, 1998

EX CORDE ECCLESIAE IMPLEMENTATION COMMITTEE
(Subcommittee Draft)
Discussion: *Ex Corde Ecclesiae*: An Application to the United States
NCCB/USCC GENERAL MEETING
November 16–19, 1998
Washington, D.C.

EX CORDE ECCLESIAE IMPLEMENTATION COMMITTEE

MEMBERS: Most Rev. John J. Leibrecht (Chair), Most Rev. James A. Griffin, James Cardinal Hickey, Most Rev. Oscar Lipscomb, Adam Cardinal Maida, Most Rev. James W. Malone (Consultant), Most Rev. Francis B. Schulte. PRESIDENT CONSULTANTS: Dr. Dorothy McKenna Brown, Reverend William J. Byron, S.J., Brother Raymond L. Fitz, S.M., Dr. Norman C. Francis, Sister Karen M. Kennelly, C.S.J., Reverend Edward A. Malloy, C.S.C., Reverend J. Donald Monan, S.J., Dr. Matthew J. Quinn. RESOURCE PERSONS: Sister Sharon Euart, R.S.M., Dr. Monika Hellwig, Rev. Msgr. Thomas J. McDade, Rev. Msgr. Frederick McManus. PROJECT DIRECTOR: Reverend Terrence Toland, S.J.

Anthony Cardinal Bevilacqua (Chair), Bishop Raymond Burke, Bishop Thomas Doran, Adam Cardinal Maida (who is also on the Implementation Committee) and Rev. Msgr. John Alesandro are members of the Subcommittee specially appointed to assist the Implementation Committee.

From the author's files.

The Implementation Committee met with the special Subcommittee on 28 January 1998 and again on 28 August 1998. Based on questions, comments and suggestions made at these meetings, as well as written comments by the legal counsel of the NCCB, the Subcommittee completed the enclosed draft dated 27 September 1998. This document is attached. Consistent with past practice, this document is also being mailed to the presidents of all the USA Catholic colleges and universities, officers of learned societies and sponsoring religious communities, all of whom are asked to communicate their reflections to local Ordinaries.

The Implementation Committee is presenting the Subcommittee's draft for discussion by the body of bishops at the coming meeting of the Conference this November 1998. Although the time is short, it is hoped that some of the bishops will have taken the opportunity to discuss the document with local college and university personnel. It will be valuable for the national body of bishops to hear local reflections. No vote is scheduled at this meeting.

> Most Reverend John J. Leibrecht
> Chair, *Ex corde Ecclesiae* Implementation Committee
> October 1998

EX CORDE ECCLESIAE

AN APPLICATION TO THE UNITED STATES

PART ONE: THEOLOGICAL AND PASTORAL PRINCIPLES

I. Introduction

On August 15, 1990, Pope John Paul II issued an apostolic constitution on Catholic higher education entitled *Ex corde Ecclesiae*.[1] The Apostolic Constitution described the identity and mission of Catholic colleges and universities and provided General Norms to help fulfill its vision. The General Norms are to be applied concretely by episcopal conferences, taking into account the status of each college and university and, as far as possible and appropriate, civil law.

This document, while recognizing that the Apostolic Constitution *Ex corde Ecclesiae* and its General Norms are to be observed as the academic legislation of the Church, applies these through particular norms for the Roman Catholic Church in the United States.

II. *The Ecclesiological Concept of Communion*

The Church is made up of individual faithful and communities linked with one another through many active ecclesial relationships. A true understanding of these dynamic relationships flows from the faith-conviction that the Triune God, through the incarnate Son, Jesus Christ, has revealed His desire to incorporate all of us into the life of the Trinity. It is in the Church, by the indwelling of the Holy Spirit, that this relationship of all persons and communities with the Triune God takes place. This body of dynamic relationships held together by the unity of faith is aptly described in the theological concept of communion.[2]

From an ecclesial perspective, the dynamic of communion unites on a deeper and more productive level the various communities in the Church through which so much of her mission of salvation is carried out. More specifically, the ecclesiology of communion furnishes the basis for the collaborative relationships between the hierarchy and Catholic universities called for by *Ex corde Ecclesiae*: "Every Catholic University is to maintain communion with the universal Church and the Holy See; it is to be in close communion with the local Church and in particular with the diocesan bishops of the region or the nation in which it is located."[3] The Catholic university is a vital institution in the communion of the Church and makes an important contribution to the Church's work of evangelization.[4]

The richness of communion illuminates the ecclesial relationship that unites the distinct, and yet complementary, teaching roles of bishops and Catholic universities. In the light of communion, the teaching responsibilities of the hierarchy and of the Catholic universities retain their distinctive autonomous nature and goal but are joined as activities contributing to the fulfillment of the Church's universal teaching mission. The communion of the teaching functions of the bishops and of the Catholic universities centers on the relationship between the bishops' right and obligation to communicate and safeguard the integrity of Church doctrine and the right and obligation of Catholic universities to investigate, analyze and communicate truths freely in communion with the magisterium. Furthermore, the communion between the bishop and the teacher of theology furnishes the basis for the proper understanding and application of the mandate of Canon 812.[5] The mandate simply attests that the Catholic teacher of the theological disciplines carries out his or her task in communion with the Church.

The communion of all the faithful, communities and structures with the Triune God and with one another is a theological reality expressing the will of God. It is in understanding and living this communion that bishops and Catholic universities most effectively collaborate to fulfill their proper mission within the Church. In carrying out this mission, the Catholic university is uniquely situated in the search for truth to serve not only the people of God but the entire human family "in their pilgrimage to the transcendent goal which gives meaning to life."[6]

III. The Catholic University's Twofold Relationship

Catholic universities[7] are participants in both the life of the Church and the higher education enterprise of the United States. As such, they "are called to continuous renewal, both as 'universities' and as 'Catholic.'"[8] This twofold relationship is described in the May 22, 1994 joint document of the Congregation for Catholic Education and the Pontifical Councils for the Laity and for Culture, which states that the Catholic university achieves its purpose when

> . . . it gives proof of being rigorously serious as a member of the international community of knowledge and expresses its Catholic identity through an explicit link with the Church, at both local and universal levels—an identity which marks concretely the life, the services and the programs of the university community. In this way, by its very existence, the Catholic university achieves its aim of guaranteeing, in institutional form, a Christian presence in the university world . . .[9]

This relationship is clarified through dialogue that includes faculty of all disciplines, students, staff, academic and other administrative officers, trustees, and sponsoring religious communities of the educational institutions, all of whom share responsibility for the character of Catholic higher education. The bishop and his collaborators in the local Church are integral parties in this dialogue.

The Catholic university is related to the entire ecclesial community,[10] to the broader society,[11] as well as to the higher education academy.[12] We are directing special attention to the relationship between the institutions and Church authorities. *Ex corde Ecclesiae* provides one of the ecclesiological principles to address this specific relationship.

Bishops have a particular responsibility to promote Catholic Universities, and especially to promote and assist in the preservation and strengthening of their Catholic identity. including the protection of their Catholic identity in relation to civil authorities. This will be achieved more effectively if close personal and pastoral relationships exist between University and Church authorities, characterized by *mutual trust, close and consistent cooperation and continuing dialogue.* Even when they do not enter directly into the internal government of the University. Bishops "should be seen not as external agents but as participants in the life of the Catholic University." [italics added][13]

Each of these elements in the pastoral relationship of bishops with Catholic universities warrants attention.

IV. *Mutual Trust between University and Church Authorities*

Mutual trust goes beyond the personalities of those involved in the relationship. The trust is grounded in a shared baptismal belief in the truths that are rooted in Scripture and Tradition, as interpreted by the Church, concerning the mystery of the Trinity: God the Father and Creator, who works even until now; God the Son and incarnate Redeemer, who is the Way and the Truth and the Life; and God the Holy Spirit, the Paraclete, whom the Father and Son send. In the spirit of *communio,* the relationship of trust between university and Church authorities, based on these shared beliefs with their secular and religious implications, is fostered by mutual listening, by collaboration that respects differing responsibilities and gifts, and by a solidarity that mutually recognizes respective statutory limitations and responsibilities.

V. *Close and Consistent Cooperation between University and Church Authorities*

Collaborating to integrate faith with life is a necessary part of the "close personal and pastoral relationships"[14] to which universities and bishops aspire. Within their academic mission of teaching and research, in ways appropriate to their own constituencies and histories, including their sponsorship by religious communities, institutions offer courses in Catholic theology that reflect current scholarship and are in accord with the authentic teaching of the Church.

Many cooperative programs, related to Gospel outreach, already flourish throughout the country. It is highly desirable that representatives of both educational institutions and Church authorities jointly identify, study, and pursue so-lutions to issues concerning social justice, human life and the needs of the poor.

Allocations of personnel and money to assure the special contributions of campus ministry are required. In view of the presence on campus of persons of other religious traditions, it is a concern of the whole Church that ecumenical and interreligious relationships should be fostered with sensitivity.

VI. *Continuing Dialogue among University Representatives and Church Authorities*

Dialogues occasioned by *Ex corde Ecclesiae* are graced moments characterized by

1. a manifest openness to a further analysis and local appropriation of Catholic identity;
2. an appreciation of the positive contributions that campus-wide conversations make; and
3. a conviction that conversation can develop and sustain relationships.

A need exists for continued attention and commitment to the far-reaching implications—curricular, staffing, programming—of major themes within *Ex corde Ecclesiae.* These include Catholic identity, *communio,* relating faith and culture, pastoral outreach, the New Evangelization, and relationship to the Church.

VII. *Catholic Identity*

In 1979, Pope John Paul II, in an address to the Catholic academic community at The Catholic University of America, stressed the importance of the Catholic character of Catholic institutions of higher learning:

> Every university or college is qualified by a specified mode of being. Yours is the qualification of being Catholic, of affirming God, his revelation and the Catholic Church as the guardian and interpreter of that revelation. The term 'Catholic' will never be a mere label either added or dropped according to the pressures of varying factors.[15]

Catholic universities should excel in theological education, prayer and liturgy, and works of charity. These religious activities, however, do not alone make a university "Catholic." *Ex corde Ecclesiae* highlights four distinctive characteristics that are essential for Catholic identity:

1. Christian inspiration in individuals and the university community;
2. Reflection and research on human knowledge in the light of the Catholic faith;
3. Fidelity to the Christian message in conformity with the magisterium of the Church;
4. Institutional commitment to the service of others.[16]

In order to maintain and safeguard its Catholic identity, every Catholic university should set out clearly in its statutes or mission statement or in some other internal document its Catholic character and make every effort to enhance its communion with the hierarchy so that through their relationship they may assist each other to accomplish their mission.

In a secular world the strong Catholic identity of our institutes of higher learning is an invaluable instrument of grace witnessing to the relationship of truth and reason, the call of the revealed Word, and the authentic meaning of human life. "The present age is in urgent need of this kind of disinterested service, namely of proclaiming the meaning of truth, that fundamental value without which freedom, justice and human dignity are extinguished."[17]

VIII. Conclusion

The bishops of the United States, in offering this application of *Ex corde Ecclesiae*, join in sentiments expressed by Pope John Paul II:

> I turn to the whole Church, convinced that Catholic universities are essential to her growth and to the development of Christian culture and human progress. For this reason, the entire ecclesial community is invited to give its support to Catholic institutions of higher education and to assist them in their process of development and renewal . . .[18]

Part Two: Particular Norms

Art. 1. The Nature of the Particular Norms

1. These particular norms are based on and apply the Code of Canon Law, the general norms of *Ex corde Ecclesiae*, and complementary Church legislation.[19] They are applicable to all Catholic colleges, universities and institu-

tions of higher learning within the territory encompassed by the National Conference of Catholic Bishops, contrary particular laws, customs or privileges notwithstanding.[20]

2. Catholic universities are to observe the general norms of *Ex corde Ecclesiae* and the following particular norms as they apply to their individual institutions, taking into account their own statutes and, as far as possible and appropriate, relevant provisions of applicable federal and state law, regulations and procedures.

   a) Those established or approved by the Holy See, by the NCCB, by a group of diocesan bishops or by an individual diocesan bishop and those established by a public juridic person, such as a religious institute, are to incorporate, by reference and in other appropriate ways, the general and particular norms into their governing documents and conform their existing statutes to such norms. Within five years of the effective date of these particular norms, they are to submit the aforesaid incorporation for review and approval to the university's competent ecclesiastical authority.

   b) Other Catholic universities are to make the general and particular norms their own, include them in the university's official documentation by reference and in other appropriate ways, and, as much as possible, conform their existing statutes to such norms. These steps to ensure their Catholic identity are to be carried out in agreement with the diocesan bishop of the place where the seat of the university is situated.[21]

3. Those establishing or sponsoring a Catholic university have an obligation to make certain that they will be able to carry out their canonical duties in a way acceptable under relevant provisions of applicable federal and state law, regulations and procedures, reserving to themselves, insofar as possible, such powers as to enable them to preserve and strengthen the Catholic identity of the university.[22]

Art. 2. *The Nature of a Catholic University*

1. A Catholic university enjoys institutional autonomy, which must be respected and promoted by all, so that it may effectively carry out its mission of freely searching for all truth.[23]

2. Academic freedom is an essential component of a Catholic university. The university should take steps to ensure that all professors are accorded "a lawful freedom of inquiry and of thought, and of freedom to express their minds humbly and courageously about those matters in which they enjoy competence."[24] In particular, "[t]hose who are engaged in the sacred disciplines

enjoy a lawful freedom of inquiry and of prudently expressing their opinions on matters in which they have expertise, while observing a due respect [*debito obsequio*] for the magisterium of the Church."[25]

3. With due regard for the common good and the need to safeguard and promote the integrity and unity of the faith, the diocesan bishop has the duty to recognize and promote the rightful academic freedom of professors in Catholic universities in their search for truth.[26]

4. Recognizing the dignity of the human person, a Catholic university, in promoting its own Catholic identity and fostering Catholic teaching and discipline, must respect the religious liberty of every individual, a right with which each is endowed by nature.[27]

5. A responsibility of every Catholic university is to affirm its essential characteristics, in accord with the principles of *Ex corde Ecclesiae*, through public acknowledgment in its mission statement and/or its other official documentation of its canonical status[28] and its commitment to the elements of Catholic identity, including but not limited to the following:[29]

   a) Commitment to be faithful to the teachings of the Catholic Church;

   b) Commitment to Catholic ideals, principles and attitudes in carrying out research, teaching and all other university activities, including activities of officially-recognized student and faculty organizations and associations, and with due regard for academic freedom and the conscience of every individual;[30]

   c) Commitment to serve others, particularly the poor, underprivileged and vulnerable members of society;

   d) Commitment of witness of the Catholic faith by Roman Catholic teachers and administrators, especially those teaching the theological disciplines, and acknowledgment and respect on the part of non-Catholic teachers and administrators of the university's Catholic identity and mission;

   e) Commitment to provide courses for students on Catholic moral and religious principles and their application to critical issues such as human life and social justice;

   f) Commitment to care pastorally for the students, faculty, administration and staff;

   g) Commitment to provide personal services (health care, counseling and guidance) to students, as well as administration and faculty, in conformity with the Church's ethical and religious teaching and directives.

6. The university (in particular, the trustees, administration, and faculty) should take practical steps to implement its mission statement in order to foster and strengthen at every level its Catholic nature and character.[31]

Art. 3. The Establishment of a Catholic University

1. A Catholic university may be established, or an existing university approved, by the Holy See, the National Conference of Catholic Bishops, or an individual diocesan bishop or group of diocesan bishops. It may also be established by a religious institute or some other public juridic person, or by individual Catholics, acting singly or in association.[32]
2. At the time of its establishment the university should see to it that its canonical status is identified, including the ecclesiastical authority by which it has been established or approved or to which it otherwise relates.[33]

Art. 4. The University Community

1. The responsibility for safeguarding and strengthening the Catholic identity of the university rests primarily with the university itself. All the members of the university community are called to participate in this important task in accordance with their specific roles: the board of trustees, the administration and staff, the faculty, and the students.[34]
2. *The Board of Trustees*
   a) As much as possible, the majority of the board should be faithful Catholics — clergy, religious or lay.
   b) Each member of the board must be committed to the mission statement of the university.
   c) The board should develop practical ways of relating to and collaborating with the local bishop and diocesan agencies on matters of mutual concern.[35]
   d) The board should analyze ecclesiastical documents on higher education, such as *Ex corde Ecclesiae* and these particular norms, and develop ways of implementing them in the structure and life of the university.
   e) The board should see to it that the university periodically undertakes an internal review of the congruence of its mission statement, its courses of instruction, its research program, and its service activity with the ideals, principles and norms expressed in *Ex corde Ecclesiae*.
3. *Administration and Staff*
   a) The university president should be a faithful Catholic.[36]
   b) The administration should inform faculty and staff at the time of their appointment regarding the Catholic identity, mission and religious practices of the university and encourage them to participate, to the degree possible, in the spiritual life of the university.

c) The administration should support the pastoral ministry of the university.

d) The administration should be in dialogue with the local bishop about ways of promoting Catholic identity and the contribution that the university can make to the life of the Church in the area.

4. *Faculty*

a) In accordance with its procedures for the hiring and retention of professionally qualified faculty and relevant provisions of applicable federal and state law, regulations and procedures, the university should recruit and appoint faithful Catholics as professors so that, as much as possible, those committed to the witness of the faith will constitute a majority of the faculty. Professors who are not Catholic are expected to be aware and respectful of the Catholic faith tradition.

b) To the extent possible, the faculty, especially those who are Catholic, should participate in the religious life and activities of the university. Lectures on Catholic teaching should be made available on a regular basis to members of the administration and faculty.

c) All professors, especially those teaching the theological disciplines, are expected to exhibit not only academic competence but integrity of doctrine and good character.[37] When these qualities are found to be lacking, the university statutes are to specify the competent authority and the process to be followed to remedy the situation.[38]

d) Catholic theology should be taught in every Catholic university, and, if possible, a department or chair of Catholic theology should be established. Academic events should be organized on a regular basis to address theological issues, especially those relative to the various disciplines taught in the university.[39]

e) Both the university and the bishops, aware of the contributions made by theologians to Church and academy, have a right to expect them to present authentic Catholic teaching. Catholic professors of the theological disciplines, insofar as they fulfill an ecclesial mandate obtained from a competent ecclesiastical authority, have a corresponding duty to be faithful to the Church's magisterium as the authoritative interpreter of Sacred Scripture and Sacred Tradition.

f) Catholics who teach the theological disciplines in a Catholic university are required to have a mandate granted by competent ecclesiastical authority.[40]

1) The mandate is fundamentally an acknowledgment by Church authority that a Catholic professor of a theological discipline teaches within the full communion of the Catholic Church. The acknowledg-

ment recognizes that he or she is a faithful Catholic, an active member of the Church's communion who teaches a theological discipline as a special ministry within the Church community.

2) The mandate recognizes the professor's commitment and responsibility to teach authentic Catholic doctrine and to refrain from putting forth as Catholic teaching anything contrary to the Church's magisterium.

3) The mandate should not be construed as an appointment, authorization, delegation or approbation of one's teaching by Church authorities. Those who have received a mandate teach in their own name in virtue of their Christian initiation and their academic and professional competence, not in the name of the Bishop or of the Church's magisterium.[41]

4) The following procedure is given to facilitate the process of requesting and granting the mandate.

   (a) The competent ecclesiastical authority to grant the mandate is the bishop of the diocese in which the Catholic university is located; he may grant the mandate personally or through a delegate.

   (b) The attestation or declaration of the professor that he or she will teach in communion with the Church can be expressed by the profession of faith and oath of fidelity or in any other reasonable manner acceptable to the one granting the mandate.

   (c) Without prejudice to the rights of the local bishop, a mandate, once granted, remains in effect wherever and as long as the professor teaches unless and until withdrawn by competent ecclesiastical authority.

   (d) The mandate should be given in writing to provide the most secure manner of demonstrating the fulfillment of canon 812.[42]

   (e) The mandate can be denied or removed. In either case, reasons for such an act should be given in writing so that the person who deems his or her rights to have been injured may seek recourse.[43]

   (f) In matters relating to the mandate, the university should maintain close contacts with the local diocesan bishop.

5. *Students.* With due regard for the principles of religious liberty and freedom of conscience, students should have the opportunity to be educated in the Church's moral and religious principles and social teachings and to participate in the life of faith.[44]

   a) Catholic students have a right to receive from a university instruction in authentic Catholic doctrine and practice, especially from those who teach the theological disciplines. They also have a right to be provided with opportunities to practice the faith through participation in Mass, the sacraments, religious devotions and other authentic forms of Catholic spirituality.

b) Courses in Catholic doctrine and practice should be made available to all students.

c) Catholic teaching should have a place, appropriate to the subject matter, in the various disciplines taught in the university.[45] Students should be provided with adequate instruction on professional ethics and moral issues related to their profession.

d) In accordance with the Church's teaching on the family, the university should relate to its students within the context of their individual situations, developing programs to foster and support family life.

Art. 5. The Catholic University within the Church

1. The Universal Church:

a) The university shall develop and maintain a plan for fulfilling its mission as Catholic that communicates and develops the Catholic intellectual tradition, is of service to the Church and society, and encourages the members of the university community to grow in the practice of the faith.[46]

b) The university plan should address intellectual and pastoral contributions to the mission of evangelization,[47] service to the poor, social justice initiatives, and ecumenical and inter-religious activities.

2. The Local Church

a) In accordance with Church teaching and canon law, the local Bishop has a responsibility to promote the welfare of the Catholic universities in his diocese and to watch over the preservation and strengthening of their Catholic character.[48]

b) Bishops should, when appropriate, acknowledge publicly the service of Catholic universities to the Church and support the institution's Catholic identity if it is unjustifiably challenged.

c) Diocesan and university authorities should commit themselves mutually to regular dialogues to achieve the goals of Ex corde Ecclesiae according to local needs and circumstances.

1) University authorities and the local diocesan bishop should develop practical methods of collaboration that are harmonious with the university's structure and statutes.[49]

2) Similar forms of collaboration should also exist between the university and the religious institute to which it is related by establishment or tradition.[50]

a) *Doctrinal Responsibilities: Approaches to Promoting Cooperation and Resolving Misunderstandings between Bishops and Theologians,* approved and published by the National Conference of Catholic Bishops, June 17, 1989, can serve as a useful guide for bishops, professors of the theological disciplines and administrators of universities to promote informal cooperation and collaboration in the Church's teaching mission and the faithful observance within Catholic universities of the principles of Catholic doctrine.

b) Disputes about Church doctrine should be resolved, whenever possible, in an informal manner. At times, the resolution of such matters may benefit from formal doctrinal dialogue as proposed by *Doctrinal Responsibilities* and adapted by the parties in question.[51]

c) When such disputes are not resolved within the limits of informal or formal dialogue, they should be addressed in a timely manner by the competent ecclesiastical authority through appropriate doctrinal and administrative actions, taking into account the requirements of the common good and the rights of the individuals and institutions involved.

d) The National Conference of Catholic Bishops, through an appropriate committee structure, should continue to dialogue and collaborate with the Catholic academic community and its representative associations about ways of safeguarding and promoting the ideals, principles and norms expressed in *Ex corde Ecclesiae.*

Art. 6. Pastoral Ministry

1. The diocesan bishop has overall responsibility for the pastoral care of the university's students, faculty, administration and staff.

2. The university, in cooperation with the diocesan bishop, shall make provision for effective campus ministry programs, including the sacraments, other liturgical celebrations, and opportunities for prayer and spiritual reflection.[52]

3. When selecting pastoral ministers—priests, deacons, religious and lay persons—to carry on the work of campus ministry, the university authorities should work closely with the diocesan bishop and interested religious institutes. Priests and deacons must enjoy pastoral facilities from the local ordinary in order to exercise their ministry on campus.

4. With due regard for religious liberty and freedom of conscience, the university, in cooperation with the diocesan bishop, should collaborate in ecumenical and interfaith efforts to care for the pastoral needs of students, faculty and other university personnel who are not Catholic.
5. In these pastoral efforts, the university and the diocesan bishop should take account of the prescriptions and recommendations issued by the Holy See and the guidance and pastoral statements of the National Conference of Catholic Bishops.[53]

Art. 7.   *Cooperation*

1. Catholic universities should commit themselves to cooperate in a special way with other Catholic universities, institutions and professional associations, in the United States and abroad, in order to build up the entire Catholic academic community.[54]
2. In collaborating with governmental agencies, regional associations, and other universities, whether public or private, Catholic universities should give corporate witness to and promote the Church's social teaching and its moral principles in areas such as the fostering of peace and justice, respect for all human life, the eradication of poverty and unjust discrimination, the development of all peoples and the growth of human culture.[55]

NOTES

1. Pope John Paul II, Apostolic Constitution on Catholic Universities *Ex corde Ecclesiae,* August 15, 1990, *AAS* 82 (1990) pp. 1475–1509. English translation: *Origins,* CNS Documentary Service, October 4, 1990 [cited throughout the remainder of this document as *ECE*].

2. *See* Vatican Council II, Dogmatic Constitution on the Church (*Lumen Gentium*) 4, 7, 9–29 (Chapter II: the People of God) and *passim;* Congregation for the Doctrine of the Faith, "Letter to the Bishops of the Catholic Church on Some Aspects of the Church Understood as Communion," *Origins,* 22 (1992), 108–112; *Catechism of the Catholic Church,* nn. 787–801 and *passim;* 1985 Extraordinary Synod of Bishops, "A Message to the People of God," *Origins* 15 (1985), 441–444, and "The Final Report," *Origins* 15 (1985), 444–450.

3. *ECE,* II, Art. 5, §1.

4. *ECE,* I, n. 49.

5. "It is necessary that those who teach theological disciplines in any institute of higher studies have a mandate from the competent ecclesiastical authority." (c. 812)

6. *ECE*, I, 13, quoting from "The Catholic University in the Modern World," the final document of the Second International Congress of Delegates of Catholic Universities, Rome, Nov. 20–29, 1972, Sec. 1.

7. For purposes of stylistic simplicity this document, in both the "Preamble" and "Particular Norms," uses the word "university" as a generic term to include universities, colleges and other institutions of higher learning.

8. *ECE*, Introduction, n. 7.

9. "The Church's Presence in the University and in University Culture," II, §2, *Origins*, June 16, 1994, 74–80.

10. *ECE*, I, nn. 27–29, 31.

11. *Ibid.*, I, nn. 32–37.

12. *Ibid.*, I, nn. 12, 37; II, Art. 7, §§1–2.

13. *Ibid.*, I, n. 28. The citation at the end is from John Paul II, *Address to Leaders of Catholic Higher Education*, Xavier University of Louisiana, U.S.A., 12 September 1987, n. 4: *AAS* 80 (1988) 764.

14. *ECE*, I, n. 28.

15. Pope John Paul II, *Address* "Ad prope et exstantes sedes Studiorum Universitatis Catholicae profectus hanc allocutionem fecit ad moderatores et doctores eiusdem Athenaei atque ad legatos Collegiorum Universitatumque Catholicarum totius Nationis," October 6, 1979, *AAS* 71:13 (1979) 1260.

16. *ECE*, I, n. 13.

17. *ECE*, I, n. 4.

18. *Ibid.*, Introduction, n. 11.

19. *See ECE*, II, Art. 1, §§1&2.

20. *ECE*, II, Art. 11: "Any particular laws or customs presently in effect that are contrary to this constitution are abolished. Also, any privileges granted up to this day by the Holy See whether to physical or moral persons that are contrary to this present constitution are abolished." These Particular Norms are not applicable to ecclesiastical universities and faculties insofar as they are governed by *Sapientia Christiana*.

21. Cf. *ECE*, Art. 1, §3.

22. *See* canon 807 and *ECE*, Art. 3; Congregation for Catholic Education, *Directives to Assist in the Formulation of the Ordinances for the Apostolic Constitution "Ex corde Ecclesiae,"* not dated [Jan. 21, 1991; see Doc. 3], n. B1.

23. *Institutional autonomy* means that governance of an academic institution is and remains internal to the institution itself. *See ECE*, I, n. 12 and footnote 15; Vatican Council II, Pastoral Constitution on the Church in the Modern World *(Gaudium et Spes)* 59; Declaration on Catholic Education *(Gravissimum educationis)* 10.

24. Vatican Council II, Church in the Modern World *(Gaudium et Spes)* 62. A university's commitment to Catholic ideals, principles and attitudes is not only consistent with academic freedom and the integrity of secular subjects, it requires "[f]reedom in research and teaching" and respect for "the principles and methods of each individual discipline." *ECE*, II, Art. 2, §5.

25. C. 218.

26. *See ECE*, II, Art. 2, §5.

27. The purpose of a Catholic university is education. Though thoroughly imbued with Christian inspiration, the university's Catholic identity should in no way be

construed as an excuse for religious indoctrination or proselytization. *See* Vatican Council II, Declaration on Religious Liberty (*Dignitatis humanae*) 2–4.

28. *See* footnote 33 for a listing of canonical categories.

29. "[E]very Catholic university, as Catholic, must have the following essential characteristics:

'1. A Christian inspiration not only of individuals but of the university community as such.

'2. A continuing reflection in the light of the Catholic faith upon the growing treasury of human knowledge, to which it seeks to contribute by its own research.

'3. Fidelity to the Christian message as it comes to us through the Church.

'4. An institutional commitment to the service of the people of God and of the human family in their pilgrimage to the transcendent goal which gives meaning to life.'"

ECE, I, n. 13 [quoting "The Catholic University in the Modern World," the final document of the Second International Congress of Delegates of Catholic Universities, Rome, Nov. 20–29, 1972, Sec. 1].

30. *See ECE,* II, Art. 2, §§4–5.

31. In this regard, the university may wish to establish a "mission effectiveness committee" or some other appropriate structure to develop methods by which Catholics may promote the university's Catholic identity and those who are not Catholic may acknowledge and respect this identity.

32. *ECE,* II, Art. 3, §§1–3. Note that, under Canon 322, private associations of the faithful can acquire juridic personality by the issuance of a formal decree of competent ecclesiastical authority (§1) and approval of their statutes, retaining, all the while, their private character (§2).

33. A Catholic university may be established by various ecclesiastical authorities or entities (e.g., the Holy See) or by individual Catholics. Moreover, the university may be erected as a self-standing public juridic person or it may be simply a complex "activity" or "apostolate" of a public juridic person. The following alternatives outline different categories that describe a Catholic university from the canonical perspective:

(a) *The university as an apostolate of the Holy See.* The Holy See may erect a university or approve an already-established university as an apostolate of the Holy See itself. Such universities, which are sometimes granted the title of "pontifical," are erected or approved by a decree of the Holy See and their statutes must be approved by the Holy See. The "competent ecclesiastical authority" to which such universities are related is the Holy See through the Congregation for Catholic Education.

(b) *The university as an apostolate of the National Conference of Catholic Bishops.* An episcopal conference has the right to erect a university or approve an already-established university as an apostolate of the conference itself through the issuance of a decree and approval of its statutes. The "competent ecclesiastical authority" to which such a university is related is the National Conference of Catholic Bishops.

(c) *The university as an apostolate of a diocesan bishop or a group of diocesan bishops.* Diocesan bishops, acting individually or jointly, have the right to erect a university or approve an already-established university as a diocesan or inter-diocesan apostolate through the issuance of a decree and approval of its statutes. The "competent ecclesiastical authority" to which such a university is related is the individual diocesan bishop or the group of diocesan bishops establishing or approving it.

(d) *The university as an apostolate of a public juridic person.* A university may be established or approved as an apostolate of a public juridic person (such as a religious institute). In such cases the consent of the bishop of the diocese in which the seat of the university is situated (or of a group of bishops, the NCCB or the Holy See) and approval of its statutes are required. Such a university relates to the public juridic person that established or approved it and to the diocesan bishop (or group of bishops, the NCCB or the Holy See) as its "competent ecclesiastical authority."

(e) *The university as a public juridic person.* A university may itself be erected as a public association of the faithful or some other type of public juridic person *(universitas rerum* or *universitas personarum).* Such juridic personality requires the issuance of a decree of erection and approval of the statutes by the Holy See, the National Conference of Catholic Bishops, or an individual or group of diocesan bishops.

(f) *The university established by individuals.* Individual Catholics may found a university or convert an existing university into a Catholic institution without its being established or approved by the Holy See, the National Conference of Catholic Bishops, individual diocesan bishops or a public juridic person. Nonetheless, in accordance with canon 808, such a university may refer to itself as Catholic only with the consent of the competent ecclesiastical authority.

34.   *ECE*, II, Art. 4. §1. In these norms the phrases "board of trustees," "president" and "administration" are used to denote the highest bodies of governance within the university's corporate and operational structure. If, in an individual case, the university's governance uses a different structure or other titles, the norms should be applied accordingly.

35.   In individual situations, it may be possible and appropriate to invite the diocesan bishop or his delegate to be a member of the board itself. In other cases, arranging periodic meetings to address the university's Catholic identity and mission may prove more practical and effective.

36.   Upon assuming the office of president for the first time, a Catholic should take the prescribed profession of faith and oath of fidelity (*See* c. 833, §7; *AAS* 81 [1989] 104–106, 1169). When a candidate who is not a Catholic is being considered for appointment as president of a Catholic university, the university should consult with the competent ecclesiastical authority about the matter. In all cases, the president is expected to uphold the university's Catholic identity and to respect and promote Catholic principles and ideals.

37.   The Church's expectation of "integrity of doctrine" should not be misconstrued to imply that a Catholic university's task is to indoctrinate or proselytize its students. Educational integrity requires that the teaching of secular subjects be measured by the professional standards applicable and appropriate to the individual disciplines. *See* above footnotes 24 and 27.

38.   C. 810, §1.

39.   *Gravissimum educationis* 10.

40.   C. 812 and *ECE*, II, Art. 4, §3. "Mandate" is a technical term referring to the juridical expression of the ecclesial relationship of communion that exists between the Church and the Catholic teacher of a theological discipline in the Catholic university. This special relationship is the basis for the requirement in canon law that Catholics teaching the theological disciplines take the prescribed profession of faith and oath of fidelity at the start of their term (c. 833, §7; *AAS* 81 [1989] 104–106. 1169). The phrase "theological

disciplines" refers to several areas of teaching: sacred scripture; dogmatic theology; moral theology; pastoral theology; canon law; liturgy; and Church history (c. 252, §3).

41. The prescription of canon 812 is grounded in the right and responsibility of bishops to safeguard the faithful teaching of Catholic doctrine to the people of God and to assure the authentic presentation of the Church's magisterium. Those with such a mandate are not agents of the magisterium; they teach in their own name, not in the name of the bishop. Nonetheless, they are not separate from the Church's teaching mission. Responding to their baptismal call, their ecclesial task is to teach, write and research for the benefit of the Church and within its communion. The mandate is essentially the recognition of an ecclesial relationship between the professor and the Church (*See* canon 229, §3).

Moreover, it is not the responsibility of a Catholic university to seek the mandate; this is a personal obligation of each professor. If a particular professor lacks a mandate and continues to teach a theological discipline, the university must determine what further action may be taken in accordance with its own mission and statutes (cf. canon 810, §l).

42. Administrative acts in external forum must be in writing (c. 37).

43. *See* canons 1732–1739.

44. In *Gravissimum educationis* 10, the Vatican Council expressed the hope that students in Catholic institutions of higher learning will become "truly outstanding in learning, ready to shoulder society's heavier burdens and to witness the faith to the world."

45. *See* above footnotes 27 and 37.

46. *See ECE,* I, n. 38 *ff.* and footnote 44.

47. *See ECE,* I, nn. 48–49.

48. *See ECE,* II, Art. 5, §2.

49. The following are some suggestions for collaboration:
Arranging for the diocesan bishop or his delegate to be involved in the university's governance, perhaps through representation on the board of trustees or in some other appropriate manner.

- Sharing the university's annual report with the diocesan bishop, especially in regard to matters affecting Catholic identity.
- Scheduling regular pastoral visits to the university on the part of the diocesan bishop.
- Collaborating on works of evangelization.
- Conducting dialogues on matters of doctrine and pastoral practice.
- Resolving issues affecting the university's Catholic identity in accordance with established procedures. (*See ECE,* II, Art. 5, §2 and *ECE* footnote 52.)
- Participating together in ecumenical and inter-religious endeavors.
- Contributing to the diocesan process of formulating the quinquennial report to the Holy See.

50. The following are some suggestions for collaboration:

- Arranging for members of the religious institute to be involved in the university's governance, perhaps through representation on the board of trustees.
- Sharing the university's annual report with the religious institute, especially in regard to matters affecting Catholic identity and the religious institute's charism.
- Scheduling regular pastoral visits to the university on the part of the religious institute's leadership and involving the members of the institute in campus ministry.
- Collaborating on evangelization and on the special works of the religious institute.

- Conducting dialogues on matters of doctrine and pastoral practice and on the development of spirituality in accordance with the religious institute's charism.
- Resolving issues affecting the university's Catholic identity in accordance with established procedures. (*See ECE,* II, Art. 5, §2 and *ECE* footnote 52.)
- Participating together in ecumenical and inter-religious endeavors.
- Contributing together in the diocesan process of formulating the quinquennial report to the Holy See.

51. *See* National Conference of Catholic Bishops, *Doctrinal Responsibilities: Approaches to Promoting Cooperation and Resolving Misunderstandings between Bishops and Theologians,* June 17, 1989, Washington, D.C.: USCC, III, C, pp. 16–22.

52. *See ECE,* II, Art. 6, §2.

53. *See* National Conference of Catholic Bishops, "Sons and Daughters of the Light: A Pastoral Plan for Ministry with Young Adults," *Origins,* November 28, 1996, 384–402, especially 398–401; "Letter to College Students," *Origins,* December 7, 1995, 429–430; *Empowered by the Spirit,* Washington, D.C.: USCC, 1985.

54. *See ECE,* I, n. 35.

55. *See ECE,* I, nn. 32–35.

37 | ACCU Alternative Proposals

Submitted to the Implementation Committee
April 28, 1999

In response to the invitation to comment on the sub-committee draft of 1998, ACCU respectfully submits to the implementation committee the following suggestions:

I.

To leave the text of the 1996 document already passed by the NCCB intact, appending to it proposed structures to ensure the practical realization of what is listed in the General Norms of the Apostolic Constitution itself.

The rights and responsibilities which form the juridical framework are set out below (part III), following exactly the order and content of the General Norms, without adding further rules or regulations from other sources.

II.

In formulating the suggestions that follow, we are mindful:

that the Apostolic Constitution itself requires that the *norms given therein should be adapted* by the bishops' conferences to the circumstances in each country; that in the case of the United States the Catholic institutions are governed by state charters and civil laws; that fiduciary responsibility for the financial and general well being of the institutions is vested by civil law in the boards of trustees; that there are conditions to qualify for the public funds needed for the very survival of the institutions; that the institutions are subject to criteria for

From the author's files.

accreditation established by the regional accrediting associations; and that there are other academic requirements and expectations related to the universities and colleges of the United States;

that ECE II, Art. 1, 3 requires incorporation of the General Norms and the regional application into the governing documents only in the case of institutions established or approved by the Holy See, an episcopal conference, another assembly of Catholic hierarchy or a diocesan bishop, and that the great majority of our US Catholic institutions do not fall into this category;

that Canon 810. No. 2 adequately provides for the bishops' right and duty of vigilance that principles of Catholic doctrine are faithfully observed in the Catholic universities.

III.

We suggest the following structures as a juridical framework:

1.

It is understood that the general norms are to be applied concretely by the episcopal conference, adapted to take into account existing university and college statutes and other constraints and demands of civil law and customary academic organization. (ECE II, Art. 1, 1 & 2)

2.

Recognizing that the US Catholic institutions are incorporated under civil law with charters from the States or the Congress, are governed by boards with fiduciary responsibilities under the civil law, and in most cases depend for their continued existence on conditions of eligibility for public funding, each institution shall clearly state its identity in its documents, following the norms for this as far as possible. (ECE II, Art. 1, 3)

3.

Institutions not linked with the Church by a formal, constitutive and statutory bond shall make clear their relationship with the Church by the institutional commitment expressed by those responsible for the institution. This commitment includes Catholic ideals, principles and attitudes in the carrying out of research, teaching, ministry and other activities. (ECE II, Art. 2, 1 & 2)

4.

Each institution is to set out the practical implications of its Catholic identity in a mission statement or equivalent document. (ECE II, Art. 2, 3)

5.

Acknowledging that both the faculty and the student body on most Catholic campuses include members of various religious backgrounds and affiliations, those responsible for each institution shall make its Catholic principles clear in institutional structure, strategic planning and financial allocation, while respecting individual freedom of conscience and academic standards of research and teaching. (ECE II, Art. 2, 4 & 5)

6.

Any university or college to be established in the future shall call itself Catholic only with the consent of the local ordinary or other competent ecclesiastical authority. (ECE II, Art. 3)

7.

Each Catholic university or college is to include in its hiring process and orientation a clear explanation to all candidates of the Catholic character of the institution and the expectation that the mission of the institution will be respected and fostered. Reference may be made to the mission statement or other document, which sets the matter forth in more detail. (ECE II, Art. 4, 2)

8.

The administration has the immediate responsibility to see that the principles and values of a Catholic institution are respected by all. In particular, those who teach Catholic theology should do so in fidelity to the magisterium. It is understood that both positive and speculative theology have always had a rightful place in the Catholic tradition, that there is a difference between catechesis and theology, and that it is the function of a university to conduct research and critical reflection. All shall, however, be mindful of the age and degree of maturity of the students in each class when raising new and critical issues. (ECE II, Art. 4, 1 & 3)

9.

Each university and college is to make all reasonable efforts to attract faculty members who are both fully competent in their field and committed to maintaining the specific Catholic identity of the institution. Sustained efforts should be made to engage and develop persons in leadership positions who are able and willing to promote and sustain the Catholic character of the institution. (ECE II, Art. 4, 4)

10.
It is the responsibility of those who determine curricula of instruction to ensure that all undergraduate students, but especially Catholic students, are offered the opportunity to study not only religious questions in a general or ecumenical context, but also Catholic doctrinal, sacramental and moral theology, including the social teaching of the church. While respecting freedom of conscience and the religiously varied composition of the student body, those responsible should exert every effort to make these courses attractive, academically excellent and readily available to all. Those responsible for professional schools and departments shall ensure that appropriate courses in ethics are integral to the professional programs. (ECE II, Art. 4, 5)

11.
To enhance communion with the universal Church and the Holy See, each Catholic university or college should be alert to current documents of the Holy See and arrange public lectures, colloquia or seminars from time to time at which the teaching in these documents can be presented and discussed. The same attention should be paid to pastoral letters of the US bishops' conference. To strengthen communion with the local church, each institution shall invite the local ordinary to the campus from time to time to engage in formal or informal dialogue with administration, faculty and students. All these initiatives will contribute to the broader dialogue between faith and culture. (ECE II, Art. 5, 1)

12.
The local ordinary and the president of each institution shall structure an appropriate periodic dialogue concerning the state and activities of the institution, especially as to its Catholic character.

13.
If at any time there are problems that touch on the Catholic character of the institution, these should be resolved as far as possible between the president and the local ordinary. If they cannot be resolved in this way, either party may refer the matter to the NCCB/ACCU Bishops and Presidents Committee. (ECE II, Art. 5, 2 & 3)

14.

Each institution shall ensure that adequate pastoral care is provided for all its members, especially those who are Catholic, and that those who are charged with this are competent to assist faculty and students to integrate professional and intellectual life with religious faith. (ECE II, Art. 6, 1)

15.

The pastoral care of the university community shall be conducted in cooperation with the local church. Both faculty and students shall be encouraged to be active in their home parishes. Liturgies on campus shall be celebrated according to the norms of the church. (ECE II, Art. 6, 2)

16.

Catholic colleges and universities of the US shall collaborate to the best of their ability among themselves, with institutions overseas, and with governmental and non-governmental organizations on behalf of peace, justice and development for the poorer populations of the world. The research universities more especially shall promote collaboration in research and service for the betterment of the human situation on a global scale. (ECE II, Art. 7, 1 & 2).

38 | Response from the Catholic Biblical
Association, the Catholic Theological
Society of America, and the College
Theology Society

April 23, 1999

The Most Reverend John J. Leibrecht, D.D., Ph.D.
Chairman
Ad Hoc Committee for the Implementation of Ex Corde Ecclesiae
The Catholic Center
601 South Jefferson Avenue
Springfield, MO 65806-3143

Dear Bishop Leibrecht:

The learned societies we represent: the Catholic Biblical Association, the Catholic Theological Society of America and the College Theology Society, whose members teach at Catholic colleges and universities in the United States, have been following the efforts of the Ex Corde Ecclesiae Implementation Committee with the greatest of interest and most profound concern. (We understand that the Canon Law Society of America, since it will be addressing the specifically canonical issues involved, will be sending a separate letter.) We were exceedingly heartened by the implementation norms passed so overwhelmingly by the National Conference of Catholic Bishops in 1996. This document was the product of the mutual efforts of the hierarchy and the Catholic higher education community. It ably testified to a deep concern both for Catholic identity and respect for standards and practices in American higher education. We shared your disappointment when this document failed to receive approval by the Holy See.

From the author's files.

A significant level of trust, cooperation and mutual respect has been established between the bishops and the academic community in developing the 1996 document. We believe that the approach of the 1998 subcommittee draft, currently under consideration by your committee, would militate against that level of trust and respect. Rather than enhance Catholic identity, the implementation of these norms would significantly erode the Catholic identity of many institutions. Many Catholic colleges and universities would find their application simply unworkable in the American setting and could face significant civil litigation with the probable loss of the level of state funding necessary for their continued existence. Further, Catholic scholars will find employment within institutions governed by these norms to be unnecessarily onerous and their academic credibility doubted. They probably would frequently choose employment in non-Catholic private or state run institutions. Gifted Catholic doctoral students for similar reasons would also gravitate to non-Catholic institutions.

In response to your request for comment on the subcommittee draft of 1998, we endorse wholeheartedly the suggestions of the Association of Catholic Colleges and Universities presidents, namely:

1. To preserve the previously approved 1996 document.
2. To append to that document structures to ensure the practical realization of the goals of Ex Corde Ecclesiae in Catholic institutions in the United States.
3. To follow exactly the order and content of the general norms of Ex Corde Ecclesiae without adding further rules or regulations from other sources.

We urge your acceptance of the fourteen structures of implementation recommended by the ACCU.

Sincerely,

Michael L. Barre, S.S.   Robert J. Schreiter, C.PP.S.   Theresa Moser, R.S.C.J.
President, CBA   President, CTSA   President, CTS

39 | Report by the Board of Governors of the Canon Law Society of America to the Implementation Committee

April 30, 1999

BACKGROUND OF THIS REPORT

In his memorandum of January 8, 1999, Bishop John J. Leibrecht, chair of the NCCB *Ex corde Ecclesiae* Implementation Committee, invited the CLSA to offer comments and recommendations on the *Subcommittee Draft* by May 1, 1999. At its January, 1999 meeting, the CLSA Board of Governors identified a number of canonists who may be competent to offer reflections on the *Draft*, and directed the CLSA Vice-President/President-Elect to contact those canonists and to synthesize their reflections. The BOG reviewed the individual reflections (attached) and the synthesis (which is this report). All these are respectfully presented to the NCCB *Ex corde Ecclesiae* Implementation Committee.

PRESUMPTIONS

The NCCB approved an *Application of "Ex corde Ecclesiae" for the United States* at its national assembly on November 13, 1996. The Congregation for Catholic Education replied on April 23, 1997 that a second draft was necessary which would be a "juridic instrument" having norms for the United States which would "have a true juridic nature."

We acknowledge that the *Application* is concerned with *how* to adopt the more general norms of *ECE* (and certainly not, as some others would argue, with *whether* those norms should be adopted). This CLSA report focuses on

From the author's files.

the canonical legislation contained in the *Draft* and offers comments and recommendations from that perspective.

COMMENTS AND RECOMMENDATIONS
[see text of draft Doc. #36]

Part One

I, p. 1, lines 17–20—Change to read:

> This document applies these General Norms through particular norms for
> the Roman Catholic Church in the United States.

The revision is concise and more accurate (since "the academic legislation of the
Church" includes *ECE*, cc. 807–814, and complementary legislation).

II, p. 2, lines 13–26—Should something be included here (or elsewhere) that the
diocesan bishop is the "moderator of the entire ministry of the word" (c. 756,
§ 2)? While there is a *communio* between the bishop and the Catholic university (teachers of theology), there is not a parity. Indeed, the proclamation of
the gospel has been especially entrusted to the Roman Pontiff and the college
of bishops (c. 756, § 1) and not so immediately to others (including universities, theologians, teachers, etc.).

V, p. 4, lines 36–37—Change to read:

> . . . institutions offer courses in Catholic theology that reflect the authentic
> teaching of the Church and that reflect current scholarship.

The primary focus of the theology courses should be the authentic teaching of
the Church. The recommended reversed order bespeaks this.

Part Two

Art. 1, p. 7, fn. 19—Add:

> These particular norms do not replace cc. 807–814 of the Code of Canon
> Law, nor do they cover all the matter contained in these canons or other
> relevant canons throughout the code.

Art. 1, 2, p. 7, lines 23–24—Who is "the university's competent authority"? It seems the matter concerns the power of governance (not precisely the *munus docendi*); if this is correct, then would the competent ecclesiastical authority sometimes be the major superior of clerical institute of pontifical right? A more precise determination would be welcomed.

Art. 2, 2, p. 8, lines 14–17—The new CLSA translation of c. 218 says:

> Can. 218—Those engaged in the sacred disciplines have a just freedom of inquiry and of expressing their opinion prudently on those matters in which they possess expertise, while observing the submission due to the magisterium of the Church.

Art. 2, 3, p. 8, lines 19–21—Change to read:

> . . . the diocesan bishop has the duty to recognize and promote the rightful academic freedom of professors in Catholic universities in their search for truth, as long as the rights of the individuals and of the community are preserved.

This reflects completely the sentiment of *ECE* II, 2, 5.

Art. 3. fn. 33, pp. 10–11—Is there any reason to distinguish in the *norms* these six different categories of Catholic universities? Do the *norms* apply in the same way to each?

Art. 3. fn. 33, (d), p. 11—Detail more precisely how a university which is an apostolate of a public juridic person relates both to that juridic person **and** to the diocesan bishop (or a group of bishops, the NCCB or the Holy See) as its "competent ecclesiastical authority."

Art. 4, 2, a, p. 11, lines 9–10—The term *faithful Catholic* (throughout the *Draft*) may be made more precise. The term is not found in *ECE*. Perhaps the term should be replaced by

> Catholics who lead a life in harmony with the faith (c. 874, § 1, n. 3)—and/or—Catholics not bound by any canonical penalty legitimately imposed or declared (see c. 874, § 1, n. 4).

Art. 4, 4, a), p. 12, lines 27–28—Change to read:

> so that, as much as possible, those who are faithful to Catholic doctrine and morals in the research and teaching will constitute the majority of the faculty.

This reflects the language of *ECE* II, 4, 3.

Art. 4, p. 12, fn. 36—Explain that the *president* of a Catholic university is called its *rector* in c. 833, n. 7.

Art. 4, 4, b), p. 13, line 5—Clarify if *Catholic teaching* means *Catholic doctrine* (rather than *Catholic pedagogical method*). The term *teaching* is ambiguous.

Art. 4, 4, c), p. 13, lines 7–8—Change to read:

> All professors [...] are expected to exhibit . . .

Canon 810, § 1 does not distinguish between teachers of theological disciplines and other teachers. *ECE,* however, does expect Catholic theologians to be faithful to the magisterium of the Church as the authentic interpreter of sacred Scripture and sacred tradition. (*ECE,* II, 4, 3)

Art. 4, 4, c), p. 13, lines 8–9—Change to read:

> . . . are expected to exhibit not only academic competence but also are to respect Catholic doctrine and morals in their research and teaching.

This reflects more precisely *ECE,* II, 4, 3. It also would allow the *Draft* to eliminate fn. 37.

Thus, lines 7–9 may be reformulated:

> All professors are expected to exhibit not only academic competence but also are to respect Catholic doctrine and morals in their research and teaching. In particular, Catholic theologians, aware that they fulfill a mandate received from the church, are to be faithful to the magisterium of the church as the authentic interpreter of sacred Scripture and sacred tradition.

Art. 4, 4, fn. 40, p. 13—The footnote may wish to add that c. 812 expects those who teach theological disciplines in *any* university to receive the mandate—not just those who teach in a *Catholic* university.

Art. 4, 4, f), pp. 13–14—The *Draft* may wish to provide more detail about the mandate: the process of granting, refusing, renewing, and removing it. Also, the grant of the mandate is situated within the content of *communio*. What is signified vis-a-vis this *communio* when a mandate is refused or removed? *Communio* is a concept with great significance in canon law.

Art. 4, 4, f), 1, lines 3–7, p. 14—It seems this sentence (concerning probity of life) applies to any Catholic teacher (c. 810, § 1), including those who teach theology with the mandate. Is repeating this requirement here redundant (since it applies to all Catholic teachers) or not (since among those Catholic teachers to whom this applies are the theologians)? Should the specifics of the *mandate* be the more precise focus here—knowing that general requirements for all Catholic teachers exist elsewhere—or not?

Art. 6, 3, lines 16–17, p. 18—Do the pastoral faculties come from the local ordinary only? Can they be granted by the major religious superior to his clerics on behalf of those students who live day and night at the university? Maybe the phrase would read:

> . . . must enjoy the appropriate pastoral faculties in order to exercise their ministry on campus.

Art. 7, lines 29–30, p. 18—Change to read:

> . . . other Catholic universities, ecclesiastical universities and faculties, institutions and professional associations, . . .

This addition is helpful and reminds that *ECE* is not about ecclesiastical universities and faculties.

40 | *Ex Corde Ecclesiae*: An Application to the United States

Approved by NCCB

November 17, 1999

INTRODUCTION

Catholic higher education in the United States has a unique history. The opening of Georgetown in 1789 and subsequent growth into 230 Catholic colleges and universities is a remarkable achievement for the church and the United States.

Catholic colleges and universities are related to the ecclesial community, to the higher education enterprise of the United States and to the broader society. Founded and developed principally by religious communities of women and men, they now involve lay administrators, professors and trustees who are Catholic and not Catholic—all committed to the vision of Catholic higher education.

Catholic colleges and universities, where culture and faith intersect, bring diversity to American higher education. Diversity is present among the institutions themselves: two-year colleges and graduate-program universities; liberal arts colleges and research universities; schools for the professions and schools for technical education.

To all participating in Catholic higher education, the bishops of the United States express their admiration and sincere gratitude, knowing that both the nation and ecclesial community are affected by their commitments and talents. Bishops want to maintain, preserve and guarantee the Catholic identity of Catholic higher education, a responsibility they share in various ways with sponsoring religious communities, boards of trustees, university administration, faculty and staff.

From *Origins* 29, no. 25 (December 1, 1999): 402–409.

PART 1: THEOLOGICAL AND PASTORAL PRINCIPLES

I. Ex Corde Ecclesiae

On Aug. 15, 1990, Pope John Paul II issued an apostolic constitution on Catholic higher education titled *Ex Corde Ecclesiae*.[1] The apostolic constitution described the identity and mission of Catholic colleges and universities and provided general norms to help fulfill its vision.

The general norms are to be applied concretely by episcopal conferences, taking into account the status of each college and university and, as far as possible and appropriate, civil law. Accordingly, recognizing that the apostolic constitution *Ex Corde Ecclesiae* is normative for the church throughout the world, this document seeks to apply its principles and norms to the Catholic colleges and universities in the United States.

II. The Ecclesiological Concept of Communion

The church is made up of individual faithful and communities linked with one another through many active ecclesial relationships. A true understanding of these dynamic relationships flows from the faith conviction that God the Father, through his incarnate Son, Jesus Christ, has revealed his desire to incorporate all people into the life of the Trinity. It is in the church, through the indwelling of the Holy Spirit, that this relationship of all persons and communities with the triune God takes place. This body of dynamic relationships held together by the unity of faith is aptly described in the theological concept of *communion*.[2]

The dynamic of communion unites on a deeper and more productive level the various communities in the church through which so much of her mission of salvation, and consequently human progress, is carried out. More specifically, ecclesial communion furnishes the basis for the collaborative relationships between the hierarchy and Catholic universities contemplated in *Ex Corde Ecclesiae*: "Every Catholic university is to maintain communion with the universal church and the Holy See; it is to be in close communion with the local church and in particular with the diocesan bishops of the region or the nation in which it is located."[3] The Catholic university is a vital institution in the communion of the church and is "a primary and privileged place for a fruitful dialogue between the Gospel and culture."[4]

The richness of communion illuminates the ecclesial relationship that unites the distinct, and yet complementary, teaching roles of bishops and Catholic universities. In the light of communion, the teaching responsibilities of the hierarchy and of the Catholic universities retain their distinctive autonomous nature and goal, but are joined as complementary activities contributing to the fulfillment of the church's universal teaching mission. The communion of the church embraces both the pastoral work of bishops and the academic work of Catholic universities, thus linking the bishops' right and obligation to communicate and safeguard the integrity of church doctrine with the right and obligation of Catholic universities to investigate, analyze and communicate all truth freely.

The communion of all the faithful with the triune God and with one another is a theological reality expressing the will of God. It is by understanding and living this communion that bishops and Catholic universities can most effectively collaborate to fulfill their proper mission within the church. In carrying out its mission to search for truth the Catholic university is uniquely situated to serve not only the people of God but the entire human family "in their pilgrimage to the transcendent goal which gives meaning to life."[5]

III. The Catholic University's Twofold Relationship

Catholic universities are participants in the life of the universal church, the local church, the higher education community of the United States and the civic community. As such, they "are called to continuous renewal, both as 'universities' and as 'Catholic.'"[6] This twofold relationship is described in the May 22, 1994, joint document of the Congregation for Catholic Education and the pontifical councils for the Laity and for Culture, which states that the Catholic university achieves its purpose when "it gives proof of being rigorously serious as a member of the international community of knowledge and expresses its Catholic identity through an explicit link with the church, at both local and universal levels—an identity which marks concretely the life, the services and the programs of the university community. In this way, by its very existence, the Catholic university achieves its aim of guaranteeing in institutional form a Christian presence in the university world."[7]

One of the ways this relationship is clarified and maintained is through dialogue that includes faculty of all disciplines, students, staff, academic and other administrative officers, trustees and sponsoring religious communities of the educational institutions, all of whom share responsibility for the character of Catholic higher education. The bishop and his collaborators in the local church are integral parties in this dialogue.

The Catholic university is related to the local and universal ecclesial community[8] as well as to the broader society[9] and the higher education academy.[10] In this document we are directing special attention to the relationship between universities and church authorities. *Ex Corde Ecclesiae* provides one of the ecclesiological principles to address this specific relationship.

"Bishops have a particular responsibility to promote Catholic universities and especially to promote and assist in the preservation and strengthening of their Catholic identity, including the protection of their Catholic identity in relation to civil authorities. This will be achieved more effectively if close personal and pastoral relationships exist between university and church authorities, characterized by *mutual trust, close and consistent cooperation and continuing dialogue*. Even though they do not enter directly into the internal government of the university, bishops 'should be seen not as external agents but as participants in the life of the Catholic university'" [italics added].[11]

Each of these elements in the pastoral relationship of bishops with Catholic universities warrants attention.

IV. Mutual Trust Between University and Church Authorities

Mutual trust goes beyond the personalities of those involved in the relationship. The trust is grounded in a shared baptismal belief in the truths that are rooted in Scripture and tradition, as interpreted by the church concerning the mystery of the Trinity: God the Father and Creator, who works even until now, God the Son and incarnate Redeemer, who is the way and the truth and the life; and God the Holy Spirit, the Paraclete, whom the Father and Son send. In the spirit of *communio*, the relationship of trust between university and church authorities, based on these shared beliefs with their secular and religious implications, is fostered by mutual listening, by collaboration that respects differing responsibilities and gifts, and by a solidarity that mutually recognizes respective statutory limitations and responsibilities.

V. Close and Consistent Cooperation Between University and Church Authorities

Collaborating to integrate faith with life is a necessary part of the "close personal and pastoral relationships"[12] to which universities and bishops are called. Within their academic mission of teaching and research, in ways appropriate to their own constituencies and histories, including their sponsorship by religious communities, institutions offer courses in Catholic theology that reflect current scholarship and are in accord with the authentic teaching of the church.

Many cooperative programs, related to Gospel outreach, already flourish throughout the country. It is highly desirable that representatives of both educational institutions and church authorities jointly identify, study and pursue solutions to issues concerning social justice, human life and the needs of the poor.

Allocation of personnel and money to assure the special contributions of campus ministry is indispensable. In view of the presence on campus of persons of other religious traditions, it is a concern of the whole church that ecumenical and interreligious relationships should be fostered with sensitivity.

A structure and strategy to ensure ongoing dialogue and cooperation should be established by university and church authorities.

VI. Continuing Dialogue Among University Representatives and Church Authorities

Dialogues occasioned by *Ex Corde Ecclesiae* are graced moments characterized by:

—A manifest openness to a further analysis and local appropriation of Catholic identity;

—An appreciation of the positive contributions that campuswide conversations make; and

—A conviction that conversation can develop and sustain relationships.

A need exists for continued attention and commitment to the far-reaching implications—curricular, staffing, programming—of major themes within *Ex Corde Ecclesiae.* These include Catholic identity, *communio,* relating faith and culture, pastoral outreach, the new evangelization and relationship to the church.

VII. Catholic Identity

Catholic identity lies at the heart of *Ex Corde Ecclesiae.* In 1979, Pope John Paul II, in an address to the Catholic academic community at The Catholic University of America, stressed the importance of the Catholic character of Catholic institutions of higher learning:

"Every university or college is qualified by a specified mode of being. Yours is the qualification of being Catholic, of affirming God, his revelation and the Catholic Church as the guardian and interpreter of that revelation. The term

Catholic will never be a mere label, either added or dropped according to the pressures of varying factors."[13]

Catholic universities, in addition to their academic commitments to secular goals and programs, should excel in theological education, prayer and liturgy, and works of charity. These religious activities, however, do not alone make a university "Catholic." *Ex Corde Ecclesiae* highlights four distinctive characteristics that are essential for Catholic identity:

— Christian inspiration in individuals and the university community.

— Reflection and research on human knowledge in the light of the Catholic faith.

— Fidelity to the Christian message in conformity with the magisterium of the church.

— Institutional commitment to the service of others.[14]

Catholic universities cherish their Catholic tradition, and in many cases, the special charisms of the religious communities that founded them. In the United States they enjoyed the freedom to incorporate these religious values into their academic mission. The principles of *Ex Corde Ecclesiae* afford them an opportunity to re-examine their origin and renew their way of living out this precious heritage.

Catholic universities enjoy institutional autonomy: As academic institutions, their governance "is and remains internal to the institution."[15] In order to maintain and safeguard their freely chosen Catholic identity, it is important for Catholic universities to set out clearly in their official documentation their Catholic character and to implement in practical terms their commitment to the essential elements of Catholic identity, including the following:

— Commitment to be faithful to the teachings of the Catholic Church.

— Commitment to Catholic ideals, principles and attitudes in carrying out research, teaching and all other university activities, including: activities of officially recognized student and faculty organizations and associations, and with due regard for academic freedom and the conscience of every individual.[16]

— Commitment to serve others, particularly the poor, underprivileged and vulnerable members of society.

— Commitment of witness of the Catholic faith by Catholic administrators and teachers, especially those teaching the theological disciplines, and acknowledgment and respect on the part of non-Catholic teachers and administrators of the university's Catholic identity and mission.

— Commitment to provide courses for students on Catholic moral and religious principles and their application to critical areas such as human life and other issues of social justice.

—Commitment to care pastorally for the students, faculty, administration and staff.

—Commitment to provide personal services (health care, counseling and guidance) to students, as well as administration and faculty, in conformity with the church's ethical and religious teaching and directives.

—Commitment to create a campus culture and environment that are expressive and supportive of a Catholic way of life.

Catholic universities should make every effort to enhance their communion with the hierarchy so that through this special relationship they may assist each other to accomplish the mission to which they are mutually committed.

In a secular world the strong Catholic identity of our institutes of higher learning is invaluable in witnessing to the relationship of truth and reason, the call of the revealed word and the authentic meaning of human life. "The present age is in urgent need of this kind of disinterested service, namely of proclaiming the meaning of truth, that fundamental value without which freedom, justice and human dignity are extinguished."[17]

PART 2: PARTICULAR NORMS

The chief purpose of the following norms is to assist Catholic colleges and universities in their internal process of reviewing their Catholic identity and clarifying their essential mission and goals. They are intended to provide practical guidance to those committed to the enterprise of Catholic higher education as they seek to implement the theological and pastoral principles of *Ex Corde Ecclesiae.* Accordingly, the norms follow the basic outline of the general norms found in *Ex Corde Ecclesiae* and provide concrete steps that will facilitate the implementation of the Holy Father's document in the context of the relevant sections of the Code of Canon Law and complementary church legislation.[18]

Article 1. The Nature of the Particular Norms

1. These particular norms are applicable to all Catholic colleges, universities and institutions of higher learning within the territory encompassed by the National Conference of Catholic Bishops, contrary particular laws, customs or privileges notwithstanding.[19]

2. Catholic universities are to observe the general norms of *Ex Corde Ecclesiae* and the following particular norms as they apply to their individual institutions, taking into account their own statutes and, as far as possible and ap-

propriate, relevant provisions of applicable federal and state law, regulations and procedures.

a) Those universities established or approved by the Holy See, by the NCCB, by other hierarchical assemblies or by individual diocesan bishops are to incorporate, by reference and in other appropriate ways, the general and particular norms into their governing documents and conform their existing statutes to such norms. Within five years of the effective date of these particular norms, Catholic universities are to submit the aforesaid incorporation for review and affirmation to the university's competent ecclesiastical authority.

b) Other Catholic universities are to make the general and particular norms their own, include them in the university's official documentation by reference and in other appropriate ways and, as much as possible, conform their existing statutes to such norms. These steps to ensure their Catholic identity are to be carried out in agreement with the diocesan bishop of the place where the seat of the university is situated.[20]

c) Changes in statutes of universities established by the hierarchy, religious institutes or other public juridic persons that substantially affect the nature, mission or Catholic identity of the university require the approval of competent ecclesiastical authority.[21]

3. Those establishing or sponsoring a Catholic university have an obligation to make certain that they will be able to carry out their canonical duties in a way acceptable under relevant provisions of applicable federal and state law, regulations and procedures.[22]

Article 2. The Nature of a Catholic University

1. The purpose of a Catholic university is education and academic research proper to the disciplines of the university. Since it enjoys the institutional autonomy appropriate to an academic institution, its governance is and remains internal to the institution itself. This fundamental purpose and institutional autonomy must be respected and promoted by all, so that the university may effectively carry out its mission of freely searching for all truth.[23]

2. Academic freedom is an essential component of a Catholic university. The university should take steps to ensure that all professors are accorded "a lawful freedom of inquiry and of thought, and of freedom to express their minds humbly and courageously about those matters in which they enjoy competence."[24] In particular, "[t]hose who are engaged in the sacred disciplines enjoy a lawful freedom of inquiry and of prudently expressing their opinions on

matters in which they have expertise, while observing the submission *[obsequio]* due to the magisterium of the church."[25]

3. With due regard for the common good and the need to safeguard and promote the integrity and unity of the faith, the diocesan bishop has the duty to recognize and promote the rightful academic freedom of professors in Catholic universities in their search for truth.[26]

4. Recognizing the dignity of the human person, a Catholic university, in promoting its own Catholic identity and fostering Catholic teaching and discipline, must respect the religious liberty of every individual, a right with which each is endowed by nature.[27]

5. A responsibility of every Catholic university is to affirm its essential characteristics, in accord with the principles of *Ex Corde Ecclesiae,* through public acknowledgment in its mission statement and/or its other official documentation of its canonical status[28] and its commitment to the practical implications of its Catholic identity, including but not limited to those specified in Part I, Section VII of this document.

6. The university (in particular, the trustees, administration and faculty) should take practical steps to implement its mission statement in order to foster and strengthen its Catholic nature and character.[29]

Article 3. The Establishment of a Catholic University

1. A Catholic university may be established, or an existing university approved, by the Holy See, the National Conference of Catholic Bishops, other hierarchical assemblies or individual diocesan bishops. It may also be established by a religious institute or some other public juridic person, or by individual Catholics, acting singly or in association, with proper ecclesiastical approval.[30]

2. At the time of its establishment the university should see to it that its canonical status is identified, including the ecclesiastical authority by which it has been established or approved or to which it otherwise relates.[31]

3. The statutes of Catholic universities established by hierarchical authority or by religious institutes or other public juridic persons must be approved by competent ecclesiastical authority.[32]

4. No university may assume the title *Catholic* without the consent of the local ordinary or other competent ecclesiastical authority.[33]

Article 4. The University Community

1. The responsibility for safeguarding and strengthening the Catholic identity of the university rests primarily with the university itself. All the members of the

university community are called to participate in this important task in accordance with their specific roles: the sponsoring religious community, the board of trustees, the administration and staff, the faculty and the students.[34] Men and women of other religious faiths than Catholic on the board of trustees, on the faculty and in other positions can make a valuable contribution to the university. Their presence affords the opportunity for all to learn and benefit from each other. The university should welcome them as full partners in the campus community.

2. The Board of Trustees

a) Each member of the board must be committed to the practical implications of the university's Catholic identity as set forth in its mission statement or equivalent document.

b) To the extent possible, the majority of the board should be Catholics committed to the church.

c) The board should develop effective ways of relating to and collaborating with the local bishop and diocesan agencies on matters of mutual concern.[35]

d) The board should analyze ecclesiastical documents on higher education such as *Ex Corde Ecclesiae* and these particular norms and develop specific ways of implementing them appropriate to the structure and life of the university.

e) The board should see to it that the university periodically undertakes an internal review of the congruence of its mission statement, its courses of instruction, its research program and its service activity with the ideals, principles and norms expressed in *Ex Corde Ecclesiae*.

3. Administration and Staff

a) The university president should be a Catholic.[36]

b) The administration should inform faculty and staff at the time of their appointment regarding the Catholic identity, mission and religious practices of the university and encourage them to participate, to the degree possible, in the spiritual life of the university.

c) The administration should be in dialogue with the local bishop about ways of promoting Catholic identity and the contribution that the university can make to the life of the church in the area.

4. Faculty

a) In accordance with its procedures for the hiring and retention of professionally qualified faculty and relevant provisions of applicable federal and state law, regulations and procedures, the university should strive to recruit and appoint

Catholics as professors so that, to the extent possible, those committed to the witness of the faith will constitute a majority of the faculty. All professors are expected to be aware of and committed to the Catholic mission and identity of their institutions.

b) All professors are expected to exhibit not only academic competence and good character but also respect for Catholic doctrine.[37] When these qualities are found to be lacking, the university statutes are to specify the competent authority and the process to be followed to remedy the situation.[38]

c) Catholic theology should be taught in every Catholic university, and if possible, a department or chair of Catholic theology should be established. Academic events should be organized on a regular basis to address theological issues, especially those relative to the various disciplines taught in the university.[39]

d) Both the university and the bishops, aware of the contributions made by theologians to church and academy, have a right to expect them to present authentic Catholic teaching. Catholic professors of the theological disciplines have a corresponding duty to be faithful to the church's magisterium as the authoritative interpreter of sacred Scripture and sacred tradition.

e) Catholics who teach the theological disciplines in a Catholic university are required to have a *mandatum* granted by competent ecclesiastical authority.[40]

1) The *mandatum* is fundamentally an acknowledgment by church authority that a Catholic professor of a theological discipline is a teacher within the full communion of the Catholic Church.

2) The *mandatum* should not be construed as an appointment, authorization, delegation or approbation of one's teaching by church authorities. Those who have received a *mandatum* teach in their own name in virtue of their baptism and their academic and professional competence, not in the name of the bishop or of the church's magisterium.[41]

3) The *mandatum* recognizes the professor's commitment and responsibility to teach authentic Catholic doctrine and to refrain from putting forth as Catholic teaching anything contrary to the church's magisterium.

4) The following procedure is given to facilitate, as of the effective date of this application, the process of requesting and granting the *mandatum*. Following the approval of the application, a detailed procedure will be developed outlining the process of requesting and granting (or withdrawing) the *mandatum*.

(a) The competent ecclesiastical authority to grant the *mandatum* is the bishop of the diocese in which the Catholic university is located; he may grant the *mandatum* personally or through a delegate.[42]

(b) Without prejudice to the rights of the local bishop, a *mandatum*, once granted, remains in effect wherever and as long as the professor teaches unless and until withdrawn by competent ecclesiastical authority.

(c) The *mandatum* should be given in writing. The reasons for denying or removing a *mandatum* should also be in writing.[43]

5. Students

With due regard for the principles of religious liberty and freedom of conscience, students should have the opportunity to be educated in the church's moral and religious principles and social teachings and to participate in the life of faith.[44]

a) Catholic students have a right to receive from a university instruction in authentic Catholic doctrine and practice, especially from those who teach the theological disciplines. They also have a right to be provided with opportunities to practice the faith through participation in Mass, the sacraments, religious devotions and other authentic forms of Catholic spirituality.

b) Courses in Catholic doctrine and practice should be made available to all students.

c) Catholic teaching should have a place, if appropriate to the subject matter, in the various disciplines taught in the university.[45] Students should be provided with adequate instruction on professional ethics and moral issues related to their profession and the secular disciplines.

Article 5. The Catholic University in the Church

1. The Universal Church

a) The university shall develop and maintain a plan for fulfilling its mission that communicates and develops the Catholic intellectual tradition, is of service to the church and society, and encourages the members of the university community to grow in the practice of the faith.[46]

b) The university plan should address intellectual and pastoral contributions to the mission of communicating Gospel values,[47] service to the poor, social justice initiatives, and ecumenical and interreligious activities.

2. The Local Church

a) In accordance with church teaching and canon law, the local bishop has a responsibility to promote the welfare of the Catholic universities in his diocese and to watch over the preservation and strengthening of their Catholic character.[48]

b) Bishops should, when appropriate, acknowledge publicly the service of Catholic universities to the church and support the institution's Catholic identity if it is unjustifiably challenged.

c) Diocesan and university authorities should commit themselves mutually to regular dialogues to achieve the goals of *Ex Corde Ecclesiae* according to local needs and circumstances.

d) University authorities and the local diocesan bishop should develop practical methods of collaboration that are harmonious with the university's structure and statutes. Similar forms of collaboration should also exist between the university and the religious institute to which it is related by establishment or tradition.[49]

e) "Doctrinal Responsibilities: Approaches to Promoting Cooperation and Resolving Misunderstandings Between Bishops and Theologians," approved and published by the National Conference of Catholic Bishops, June 17, 1989, can serve as a useful guide for diocesan bishops, professors of the theological disciplines and administrators of universities to promote informal cooperation and collaboration in the church's teaching mission and the faithful observance within Catholic universities of the principles of Catholic doctrine.

f) Disputes about church doctrine should be resolved, whenever possible, in an informal manner. At times the resolution of such matters may benefit from formal doctrinal dialogue as proposed by "Doctrinal Responsibilities" and adapted by the parties in question.[50]

g) The NCCB, through an appropriate committee structure, should continue to dialogue and collaborate with the Catholic academic community and its representative associations about ways of safeguarding and promoting the ideals, principles and norms expressed in *Ex Corde Ecclesiae.*

Article 6. Pastoral Ministry

1. The diocesan bishop has overall responsibility for the pastoral care of the university's students, faculty, administration and staff.

2. The university, in cooperation with the diocesan bishop, shall make provision for effective campus ministry programs, including the celebration of the sacraments, especially the eucharist and penance, other liturgical celebrations, and opportunities for prayer and spiritual reflection.[51]

3. When selecting pastoral ministers—priests, deacons, religious and laypersons—to carry on the work of campus ministry, the university authorities should work closely with the diocesan bishop and interested religious institutes. Without prejudice to the provision of Canon 969, §2, priests and deacons

must enjoy pastoral faculties from the local ordinary in order to exercise their ministry on campus.

4. With due regard for religious liberty and freedom of conscience, the university, in cooperation with the diocesan bishop, should collaborate in ecumenical and interfaith efforts to care for the pastoral needs of students, faculty and other university personnel who are not Catholic.

5. In these pastoral efforts, the university and the diocesan bishop should take account of the prescriptions and recommendations issued by the Holy See and the guidance and pastoral statements of the NCCB.[52]

Article 7. Cooperation

1. Catholic universities should commit themselves to cooperate in a special way with other Catholic universities, institutions and professional associations in the United States and abroad, in order to build up the entire Catholic academic comminty.[53]

2. In collaborating with governmental agencies, regional associations and other universities, whether public or private, Catholic universities should give corporate witness to and promote the church's social teaching and its moral principles in areas such as the fostering of peace and justice, respect for all human life, the eradication of poverty and unjust discrimination, the development of all peoples and the growth of human culture.[54]

CONCLUSION

This application will become effective one year after its *recognitio* by the Holy See.

During the five years following the effective date of this application, the NCCB in collaboration with representatives of Catholic universities, should develop a mutually agreeable process to review and evaluate the implementation of *Ex Corde Ecclesiae* and this application, particularly regarding the nature, mission and Catholic identity of the universities.

Ten years after the effective date of this application, the NCCB will review this application of *Ex Corde Ecclesiae* for the United States.

The bishops of the United States, in offering this application of *Ex Corde Ecclesiae,* join in sentiments expressed by Pope John Paul II:

"I turn to the whole church, convinced that Catholic universities are essential to her growth and to the development of Christian culture and human progress. For this reason, the entire ecclesial community is invited to give its support to Catholic institutions of higher education and to assist them in their process of development and renewal."[55]

NOTES

1. Pope John Paul II, Apostolic Constitution on Catholic Universities *Ex Corde Ecclesiae,* Aug. 15, 1990, *Acta Apostolicae Sedis* 82 (1990) pp. 1475–1509. English translation: *Origins,* CNS Documentary Service, Oct. 4, 1990 [cited throughout the remainder of this document as ECE].

2. See Vatican Council II, Dogmatic Constitution on the Church *(Lumen Gentium),* 4, 7, 9–29 (Chapter II: the People of God) and *passim;* Congregation for the Doctrine of the Faith, "Letter to the Bishops of the Catholic Church on Some Aspects of the Church Understood as Communion," *Origins* 22 (1992), 108–112; Catechism of the Catholic Church, 787–801 and *passim;* 1985 Extraordinary Synod of Bishops, "A Message to the People of God," *Origins* 15 (1985), 441–444, and "The Final Report," *Origins* 15 (1985), 444–450.

3. ECE, II, Art 5, § 1.

4. ECE, I, 43. See also ECE, I, 49. For purposes of stylistic simplicity this document, in both the "Theological and Pastoral Principles" and "Particular Norms," uses the word *university* as a generic term to include universities, colleges and other institutions of higher learning.

5. ECE, I, 13, quoting from "The Catholic University in the Modern World," the final document of the Second International Congress of Delegates of Catholic Universities, Rome, Nov. 20–29, 1972, Sec. 1.

6. ECE, Introduction, 7.

7. "The Church's Presence in the University and in University Culture," II, §2, *Origins,* June 16, 1994, 74–80.

8. ECE, I, 27–29, 31.

9. Ibid., I, 32–37.

10. Ibid., I, 12, 37; II, Art. 7, §§1–2.

11. Ibid., I, 28. The citation at the end is from John Paul II, Address to Leaders of Catholic Higher Education, Xavier University of Louisiana, Sept. 12, 1987, 4: *AAS* 80 (1988) 764.

12. ECE, I, 28.

13. Pope John Paul II, address at the Catholic University of America to presidents of Catholic colleges and universities and other members of the academic community, Oct. 6, 1979, *AAS* 71:13 (1979) 1260.

14. ECE, I, 13 [quoting "The Catholic University in the Modern World," Sec. 1].

15. See ECE, I, 12 and Footnote 15; Vatican Council II, Pastoral Constitution on the Church in the Modern World *(Gaudium et Spes)* 59; Declaration on Catholic Education *(Gravissimum Educationis)* 10.

16. See ECE, II, Art. 2, §§4–5.

17. ECE, I, 4.

18. See ECE, II, Art. 1, §§1&2.

19. ECE, II, Art. 11: "Any particular laws or customs presently in effect that are contrary to this constitution are abolished. Also, any privileges granted up to this day by the Holy See whether to physical or moral persons that are contrary to this present constitution are abolished." These particular norms are not applicable to ecclesiastical universities and faculties insofar as they are governed by the apostolic constitution *Sapientia Christiana.*

20. See ECE, II, Art. 1, §3.

21. See ECE, II, Art. 3, §4.

22. See Canon 807 and ECE, Art. 3; Congregation for Catholic Education, "Directives to Assist in the Formulation of the Ordinances for the Apostolic Constitution *Ex Corde Ecclesiae,* not dated [Jan. 21, 1991; see Doc. 3], B1.

23. See above Footnote 15.

24. *Gaudium et Spes,* 62. A university's commitment to Catholic ideals, principles and attitudes is not only consistent with academic freedom and the integrity of secular subjects, it requires "[f]reedom in research and teaching" and respect for "the principles and methods of each individual discipline." ECE, II, Art. 2, §5.

25. Canon 218.

26. See ECE, II, Art. 2, §5.

27. Though thoroughly imbued with Christian inspiration, the university's Catholic identity should in no way be construed as an excuse for religious indoctrination or proselytization. See Vatican Council II, Declaration on Religious Liberty *(Dignitatis Humanae),* 2–4.

28. See Footnote 31 for a listing of canonical categories.

29. In this regard, the university may wish to establish a "mission effectiveness committee" or some other appropriate structure to develop methods by which Catholics may promote the university's Catholic identity and those who are not Catholic may acknowledge and respect this identity.

30. ECE, II, Art. 3, §§1–3, cf. Canon 808. Note that under Canon 322 private associations of the faithful can acquire juridic personality by the issuance of a formal decree of competent ecclesiastical authority (§1) and approval of their statutes, retaining, all the while, their private character (§2).

31. A Catholic university may be established by various ecclesiastical authorities or entities (e.g., the Holy See) or by individual Catholics. Moreover, the university may be erected as a self-standing public juridic person or it may be simply a complex "activity" or "apostolate" of a public juridic person. The following alternatives outline different categories that describe a Catholic university from the canonical perspective:

(*a*) *The university as an apostolate of the Holy See.* The Holy See may erect a university or approve an already-established university as an apostolate of the Holy See itself. Such universities, which are sometimes granted the title of *pontifical,* are erected or approved by a decree of the Holy See and their statutes must be approved by the Holy See. The "competent ecclesiastical authority" to which such universities are related is the Holy See through the Congregation for Catholic Education.

(*b*) *The university as an apostolate of the National Conference of Catholic Bishops.* An episcopal conference has the right to erect a university or approve an already-established university as an apostolate of the conference itself through the issuance of a decree and approval of its statutes. The "competent ecclesiastical authority" to which such a university is related is the NCCB.

(c) The university as an apostolate of a diocesan bishop or a group of diocesan bishops. Diocesan bishops, acting individually or jointly, have the right to erect a university or approve an already-established university as a diocesan or interdiocesan apostolate through the issuance of a decree and approval of its statutes. The "competent ecclesiastical authority" to which such a university is related is the individual diocesan bishop or the group of diocesan bishops establishing or approving it.

(d) The university as an apostolate of a public juridic person. A university may be established or approved as an apostolate of a public juridic person (such as a religious institute). In such cases the consent of the bishop of the diocese in which the seat of the university is situated (or of a group of bishops, the NCCB or the Holy See) and approval of its statutes are required. Such a university relates to the public juridic person that established or approved it and to the diocesan bishop (or group of bishops, the NCCB or the Holy See) as its "competent ecclesiastical authority."

(e) The university as a public juridic person. A university may itself be erected as a public association of the faithful or some other type of public juridic person *(universitas rerum* or *universitas personarum).* Such juridic personality requires the issuance of a decree of erection and approval of the statutes by the Holy See, the NCCB, or an individual or group of diocesan bishops.

(f) The university established by individuals. Individual Catholics may found a university or convert an existing university into a Catholic institution without its being established or approved by the Holy See, the NCCB, individual diocesan bishops or a public juridic person. Nonetheless, in accordance with Canon 808, such a university may refer to itself as Catholic only with the consent of the competent ecclesiastical authority.

32. ECE, II, Art. 3, §4.

33. Canon 808.

34. ECE, II, Art. 4, §1. In these norms the phrases *board of trustees, president* and *administration* are used to denote the highest bodies of governance within the university's corporate and operational structure. If, in an individual case, the university's governance uses a different structure or other titles, the norms should be applied accordingly.

35. In individual situations, it may be possible and appropriate to invite the diocesan bishop or his delegate to be a member of the board itself. In other cases arranging periodic meetings to address the university's Catholic identity and mission may prove more practical and effective.

36. Upon assuming the office of president for the first time, a Catholic should express his or her commitment to the university's Catholic identity and to the Catholic faith in accordance with Canon 833, §7 (see also *AAS* 81 [1989] 104–106, 1169). When a candidate who is not a Catholic is being considered for appointment as president of a Catholic university, the university should consult with the competent ecclesiastical authority about the matter. In all cases, the president should express his or her commitment to the university's Catholic mission and identity.

37. The identity of a Catholic university is essentially linked to the quality of its professors and to respect for Catholic doctrine. The church's expectation of "respect for Catholic doctrine" should not, however, be misconstrued to imply that a Catholic university's task is to indoctrinate or proselytize its students. Secular subjects are taught for their intrinsic value, and the teaching of secular subjects is to be measured by the norms and professional standards applicable and appropriate to the individual disciplines. See ECE, II, Art. 4, §1 and above Footnotes 24 and 27.

38. Canon 810, §1.

39. *Gravissimum Educationis,* 10.

40. Canon 812 and ECE, II, Art. 4, §3.

41. *Mandatum* is a technical term referring to the juridic expression of the ecclesial relationship of communion that exists between the church and the Catholic teacher of a theological discipline in the Catholic university. The prescription of Canon 812 is grounded in the right and responsibility of bishops to safeguard the faithful teaching of Catholic doctrine to the people of God and to assure the authentic presentation of the church's magisterium. Those with such a *mandatum* are not agents of the magisterium; they teach in their own name, not in the name of the bishop. Nonetheless, they are not separate from the church's teaching mission. Responding to their baptismal call, their ecclesial task is to teach, write and research for the benefit of the church and within its communion. The *mandatum* is essentially the recognition of an ecclesial relationship between the professor and the church (see Canon 229, §3).

Moreover, it is not the responsibility of a Catholic university to seek the *mandatum;* this is a personal obligation of each professor. If a particular professor lacks a *mandatum* and continues to teach a theological discipline, the university must determine what further action may be taken in accordance with its own mission and statutes (see Canon 810, §1).

42. The attestation or declaration of the professor that he or she will teach in communion with the church can be expressed by the profession of faith and oath of fidelity or in any other reasonable manner acceptable to the one issuing the *mandatum.*

43. Administrative acts in the external forum must be in writing (Canon 37). The writing not only demonstrates the fulfillment of Canon 812, but in cases of denial or removal it permits the person who considers his or her rights to have been injured to seek recourse. See Canons 1732–1739.

44. In *Gravissimum Educationis,* 10, the Vatican Council expressed the hope that students in Catholic institutions of higher learning will become "truly outstanding in learning, ready to shoulder society's heavier burdens and to witness the faith to the world."

45. See above Footnotes 27 and 37.

46. See ECE, I, 38 ff. and Footnote 44.

47. See ECE, I, 48–49.

48. See ECE, II, Art. 5, §2.

49. The following are some suggestions for collaboration:

—Arranging for the diocesan bishop or his delegate and members of the religious institute to be involved in the university's governance, perhaps through representation on the board of trustees or in some other appropriate manner.

—Sharing the university's annual report with the diocesan bishop and the religious institute, especially in regard to matters affecting Catholic identity and the religious institute's charism.

—Scheduling regular pastoral visits to the university on the part of the diocesan bishop and the religious institute's leadership, and involving the members of the diocese and the institute in campus ministry.

—Collaborating on evangelization and on the special works of the religious institute.

—Conducting dialogues on matters of doctrine and pastoral practice and on the development of spirituality in accordance with the religious institute's charism.

—Resolving issues affecting the university's Catholic identity in accordance with established procedures. (See ECE, II, Art. 5, §2 and ECE Footnote 51.)

—Participating together in ecumenical and interfaith endeavors.

—Contributing to the diocesan process of formulating the quinquennial report to the Holy See.

50. See NCCB, "Doctrinal Responsibilities: Approaches to Promoting Cooperation and Resolving Misunderstandings Between Bishops and Theologians," June 17, 1989, Washington, D.C.: USCC, III, C, pp. 16–22. When such disputes are not resolved within the limits of informal or formal dialogue, they should be addressed in a timely manner by the competent ecclesiastical authority through appropriate doctrinal and administrative actions, taking into account the requirements of the common good and the rights of the individuals and institutions involved.

51. See ECE, II, Art. 6, §2.

52. See NCCB, "Sons and Daughters of the Light: A Pastoral Plan for Ministry with Young Adults," *Origins*, Nov. 28, 1996, 384–402, especially 398–401; "Letter to College Students," *Origins*, Dec. 7, 1995, 429–430; "Empowered by the Spirit," Washington, D.C.: USCC, 1985.

53. See ECE, I, 35.

54. See ECE, I, 32–35.

55. Ibid., Introduction, 11.

41 | *Recognitio,* May 3, 2000 (Latin and English Texts)

CONGREGATIO PRO EPISCOPIS

FOEDERATARUM CIVITATUM AMERICAE SEPTENTRIONALIS
De Conferentiae Episcoporum decreti generalis recognitione

DECRETUM

Exc.mus P.D. Josephus A. Fiorenza, Conferentiae Episcoporum Foederatarum Civitatum Americae Septentrionalis Praeses, ipsius Conferentiae nomine, ab Apostolica Sede postulavit ut peculiares normae exsecutivae Apostolicae Constitutionis "Ex Corde Ecclesiae", a conventu plenario Conferentiae ad normam iuris approbatae, rite recognoscerentur.

Congregatio pro Episcopis, vi facultatum sibi articulo 82 Constitutionis Apostolicae "Pastor Bonus" tributarum et collatis consiliis cum Congregatione pro Educatione Catholica atque Pontificio Consilio de Legum Textibus Interpretandis, memoratas normas, prout in adnexo exemplari continentur, iuri canonico universali accommodatas repperit et ratas habet.

Quapropter eaedem normae, modis ac temporibus a memorata Conferentia determinatis, promulgari poterunt.

Datum Romae, ex Aedibus Congregationis pro Episcopis, die 3 maii anno 2000.

From the files of USCCB.

Unofficial Translation

CONGREGATION FOR BISHOPS

DECREE

**Recognition of the General Decree of
the Episcopal Conference of the United States of America**

His Excellency, the Most Reverend Joseph A. Fiorenza, President of the Conference of Bishops of the United States of America, in the name of that Conference, has petitioned the Apostolic See that the particular executive norms of the Apostolic Constitution "Ex Corde Ecclesiae," approved according to the norm of law by a plenary session of the Conference, be duly granted recognition.

The Congregation for Bishops, by virtue of the faculties granted it in Article 82 of the Apostolic Constitution "Pastor Bonus" and after consultation with the Congregation for Catholic Education and the Pontifical Council for the Interpretation of Legislative Texts, finds the above-mentioned norms, as contained in the attached copy, in conformity with universal Canon Law and declares them valid.

Therefore, these norms can be promulgated in the manner and at the time determined by the above-mentioned Conference.

Given in Rome, at the Congregation for Bishops, May 3, 2000.

✝ Lucas Cardinal Moreira Neves, O.P.
Prefect
✝ Archbishop Francesco Monterisi
Secretary

42 | Decree of Promulgation and a Statement on the *Recognitio* by Bishop Joseph A. Fiorenza

June 1, 2000

NATIONAL CONFERENCE OF CATHOLIC BISHOPS UNITED STATES OF AMERICA

DECREE OF PROMULGATION

On November 17, 1999, the Catholic Bishops of the United States, meeting in Plenary Session of the National Conference of Catholic Bishops, approved *Ex corde Ecclesiae: An Application for the United States* implementing the Apostolic Constitution *Ex corde Ecclesiae,* according to the norm of law.

The action was granted *recognitio* by the Congregation for Bishops in accord with article 82 of the Apostolic Constitution *Pastor Bonus* and issued by Decree of the Congregation for Bishops signed by His Eminence Lucas Cardinal Moreira Neves, Prefect, and His Excellency Most Reverend Francisco Monterisi, Secretary, and dated May 3, 2000.

As President of the National Conference of Catholic Bishops, I hereby decree that *Ex corde Ecclesiae: An Application for the United States* will be in force as particular law for the United States on May 3, 2001.

Given at the offices of the National Conference of Catholic Bishops in Washington, DC, on June 1, 2000.

Most Reverend Joseph A. Fiorenza   Reverend Monsignor Dennis M. Schnurr
Bishop of Galveston-Houston   General Secretary
President, NCCB

From the files of USCCB.

STATEMENT OF BISHOP FIORENZA ON
RECOGNITIO FOR *EX CORDE ECCLESIAE*

The United States Catholic Bishops' Conference has received the *recognitio* or formal approval by the Holy See of its *Application* of *Ex corde Ecclesiae* ("From the heart of the Church") to Catholic higher education in the United States.

The Conference is profoundly grateful to the Holy Father for the wisdom and insight with which he has addressed the question of Catholic higher education in both *Sapientia Christiana,* which deals with ecclesiastical universities and faculties that grant their degrees in the name of the Holy See, and *Ex corde Ecclesiae* which is the first papal document to discuss in detail and provide norms for the other Catholic institutions of higher learning.

Clearly the Holy Father addressed this issue from his own heart, since as a priest and bishop he dedicated a considerable part of his ministry to Catholic higher education. As universal pastor, he brings to his office of teaching and governing a wealth of personal experience and commitment to the importance of Catholic higher education.

Even before the draft of an application had been submitted to the Bishops, *Ex corde Ecclesiae* had made an enormous contribution to Catholic higher education in the United States by providing the focus for the first sustained discussions in the U.S. between bishops and college and university presidents. In this period of development of the *Application,* a renewed awareness grew of how important Catholic identity is for our colleges and universities. The dialogue between bishops and presidents throughout our country was important in itself and as a contribution to preparing the *Application.* The continuation of this dialogue should be a permanent result of applying *Ex corde Ecclesiae* to Catholic higher education in the United States.

I wish to acknowledge, in particular, the Ad Hoc Committee on the Implementation of *Ex corde Ecclesiae,* its resource persons, consultants, and project directors. I want to recognize especially the outstanding leadership of the Committee's chairman, Bishop John J. Leibrecht of Springfield–Cape Girardeau, throughout this nine year process. He has been extraordinarily perceptive and prudent in dealing with a complex matter whose ramifications extend from theology and canon law to issues of academic administration and civil law.

The essential contribution of the members of the Subcommittee on the Implementation should also be singled out for thanks and gratitude. Under the leadership of Cardinal Anthony Bevilacqua of Philadelphia, who brought to the task his vast understanding of the issues involved as well as his expertise in canon and civil law, this Subcommittee's contribution to the final draft was crucial.

Our thanks go as well to the prefects and officials of the Congregation for Catholic Education in Rome with whom the Implementation Committee and Subcommittee closely collaborated. Cardinal Pio Laghi, who brought to the matter extensive familiarity with Catholic higher education in the United States from his service here as Apostolic Nuncio, and Archbishop Zenon Grocholewski, who recently succeeded Cardinal Laghi, both played significant roles in the successful outcome.

As for the ways in which the *Application* will affect Catholic higher education in the United States, the purpose of *Ex corde Ecclesiae* and the U.S. Bishops' *Application* is, above all, to strengthen our Catholic colleges and universities, especially by helping them to maintain their Catholic identity. Few dimensions of service are as closely associated with the Church as education. The Church contributes to the work of higher education not only vast experience but also a focus on matters which are of the utmost importance to living a worthy life in this world and to our destiny in the next. At a time when many people—including young people at the dawn of their adult careers—are tempted to allow the quest for material success to dominate all other concerns, educational institutions which raise the fundamental questions of human existence are a vital necessity to our society.

Ex corde Ecclesiae and its *Application* envisage Catholic higher educational institutions—while maintaining their own proper autonomy—working in communion with the entire Church community through the ministry of the Bishop to provide our society with this kind of alternative.

As for some practical matters of implementation about which inquiries have been made, especially the granting of the mandatum to teach theological disciplines in Catholic colleges and universities, the date of granting the *recognitio,* May 3, 2000, began a year-long period of implementation during which the issues behind many of these inquiries will be addressed in dialogue with college and university presidents, theologians, and canonists.

The Bishops are keenly aware of the diversity and complexity of the world of Catholic higher education which in this country is comprised of over 230 individual institutions of various size and forms of governance. We hope that when the *Application* comes into full effect on May 3, 2001, that the practical effects will have been clarified and that implementation will proceed appropriately.

I ask all Catholics to pray during this implementation period for its success. Many Catholics are proud graduates of these institutions and continue to support them to this day. Others benefit from their existence, since many of their graduates assume leadership in their fields and in the church and secular communities.

The Bishops of the United States join in prayer that Catholic higher education, which has been one of the prides of the Church in our nation, will be united in even greater communion with and draw its sustenance and strength from the heart of the Church community.

> The Most Reverend Joseph A. Fiorenza
> Bishop of Galveston-Houston
> President
> U.S. Catholic Bishops' Conference

43 | Theologians, Catholic Higher Education, and the *Mandatum*

Report by the Ad Hoc Committee of
the Catholic Theological Society of America

September 11, 2000

INTRODUCTION

In November of 1999, the National Conference of Catholic Bishops approved its *Application* of *Ex corde ecclesiae* for the United States.[1] In it, the bishops included norms for a juridical instrument, the *mandatum*, that Catholic theologians at Catholic colleges and universities are required to have, in accord with Canon 812. In anticipation of approval of the *Application* by the Roman Curia (which occurred in May of 2000), the Catholic Theological Society of America appointed an ad hoc committee on the *mandatum* to assess the feasibility, theological appropriateness, and ecclesiastical status of such a requirement and to provide a response to the committee of bishops appointed to develop concrete procedures for its implementation. Any assessment of the *mandatum* must examine the role and work of theologians but it must begin with the character and tradition of the institutions where these theologians teach and conduct research.

Catholic colleges and universities in the United States have a long history of service to the church as places "where culture and faith intersect."[2] By original design and ongoing development, these institutions of higher education are communities of discourse dedicated to the search for truth rooted ultimately in the one Creator. Within them, the wisdom of Christian faith encounters the pressing issues and dominant intellectual perspectives of the day. As Pope John Paul II has expressed it, Catholic colleges and universities "unite existentially by intellectual effort two orders of reality that too frequently tend to be placed

From the author's files.

in opposition as though they were antithetical: the search for truth, and the certainty of already knowing the fount of truth. [3]

There is little doubt that the world today is in grave need of the dialogue between Christian faith and the breadth of human undertaking: science and technology, literature and the arts, political and economic life, to name a few. At the same time, in the eyes of many prominent leaders in all these fields, religion is often discredited as a cultural remnant of pre-modern superstition. Theological discourse, so central to the dialogue between the church and the world, is too often misunderstood as anti-intellectual fundamentalism, disreputably marketing out-dated beliefs under the guise of academic respectability.

Catholic colleges and universities have made impressive progress over the past century in countering many mistaken prejudices about religious faith and the Christian intellectual life. Many secular universities that once looked disparagingly at Catholic higher education are coming to view Catholic universities as their peers. Influential "think tanks" and the media now more often turn to scholars from Catholic colleges and universities as partners in intellectual conversation about the issues of the day. This notable improvement in dialogue with the world represents a great service by these Catholic institutions—and by theology as an academic discipline—to the church in its fundamental mission to the world.

Such developments were rightly celebrated in the apostolic constitution on Catholic higher education, *Ex corde ecclesiae,* of Pope John Paul II. Catholic colleges and universities have a challenging mission:

> "to explore courageously the riches of revelation and nature so that the united endeavor of intelligence and faith will enable people to come to the full measure of their humanity, created in the image and likeness of God, renewed even more marvelously after sin in Christ and called to shine forth in the light of the Spirit."[4]

In every nation, institutions of higher education must be formed in the scriptures, steeped in the Catholic tradition, and faithful to the church's magisterium—in order to present the wisdom of the church to the world. At the same time, they must be shaped by standards of intellectual rigor, imbued with the insights of secular discourse, and courageously committed to "its mission of freely searching for all truth"[5]—to present the wisdom of the world to the church. This essential balance of sometimes-conflicting commitments is even more difficult for Catholic colleges and universities in the United States, where higher education standards for the intellectual credibility of any discipline have historically included the freedom from outside interference or control.[6] To theology, as an academic discipline, falls responsibility for sustaining and, where necessary, initiating this conversation between church and world.

For these reasons, the current plan for implementing *Ex corde ecclesiae* presents both promise and danger to Catholic higher education. The promise is at the very core of the bishops' goal, like that of Pope John Paul II: the Catholic identity of these institutions. This commitment is shared by those colleges and universities and by the members of the Catholic Theological Society of America. The bishops' interest in deepening that commitment across each campus is welcome. The danger to Catholic higher education comes from the plan for the *mandatum*. The juridical judgment by the local bishop (who in most cases has no juridical role in the administration of the institution) about individual members of a theology or religious studies department raises several problems. Put in the broadest terms, the risk is that the *mandatum* will upset the creative balance that has made American Catholic higher education so vital and has served the church so well.

Differing contexts, perceptions, and judgments make a difference here. The relevant Catholic institutions range from small four-year colleges to large PhD-granting research universities. A few institutions were established by a local bishop, but the vast majority were independently founded by a religious order. A one-size-fits-all approach will not be pastorally adequate. There are also honest differences of perception and judgment—among theologians and among bishops—as to the likely beneficial and detrimental effects of the *mandatum*. Everyone involved in this process should recognize that at the source of disagreement here are faithful but conflicting views of what will best serve the church and its mission.

This document is written to contribute to the discussion of the implementation of the *Application* by offering the following reflections, in five sections. Part I addresses a brief history of the issue. Part II investigates the character of theological scholarship in the academy and the church. Part III addresses problems with the *mandatum*. Part IV provides principles proposed to the bishops as they implement the *mandatum*. Part V offers final recommendations. An Appendix includes procedures for the implementation of the *mandatum*. There are a multitude of other important issues arising from *Ex corde ecclesiae* and the NCCB's *Application,* and the theologians of the Catholic Theological Society of America are deeply involved in these, both in their home institutions and at a regional and national level. Our focus here is more narrowly on the *mandatum,* not because the others are unimportant but due to the urgency of the issue.

PART I: A BRIEF HISTORY OF THE ISSUE

The background to the current discussion about the identity of Catholic institutions of higher education and the role of theologians is reflected in documents by the presidents of Catholic colleges and universities and also by the Congregation for Catholic Education. A brief history of these texts provides a perspective from which to approach the topic of the *mandatum*.[7]

The Second Vatican Council voiced the Church's commitment to the appropriate autonomy of human affairs in general and in the pursuit of learning in particular. *Gaudium et spes* (December 8, 1965) acknowledges the validity of free inquiry in pursuit of the truth when it states: "Consequently, methodical research in all branches of science, provided it is carried out in a truly scientific manner and does not override moral laws, can never conflict with the faith, because the things of the world and the things of faith derive from the same God."[8] *Gravissimum educationis* (October 28, 1965) makes concrete this principle of the rightful autonomy of scholarly inquiry. Regarding Catholic institutions of higher education, the declaration states: "Indeed, in the institutions under its control the Church endeavors systematically to ensure that the treatment of the individual disciplines is consonant with their own principles, their own methods, and with a true liberty of scientific inquiry" (art. 10).

Since the Second Vatican Council, the International Federation of Catholic Universities (IFCU) has sought to clarify and implement the Council's vision for Catholic higher education around the world. At a regional meeting of the IFCU at Land O'Lakes, Wisconsin, in June 1967, presidents of Catholic colleges and universities in North America agreed on some of the basic elements of a Catholic university. They declared that "the Catholic university must have a true autonomy and academic freedom in the face of authority of whatever kind, lay or clerical, external to the academy." They also stated that a Catholic college or university must be a community "in which Catholicism is perceptibly present and effectively operative." Moreover, they explained that the Catholic university serves as "the critical reflective intelligence" of the Church as well as of society.[9]

The entire IFCU subsequently endorsed and amplified the views in the Land O'Lakes statement of 1967. Its congresses of 1969 and 1972 produced the document, "The Catholic University in the Modern World" (1973). After specifying a Catholic university's four "essential characteristics," it recognizes that since there are various kinds of Catholic universities and since each university must adapt to the culture of its region, colleges and universities will realize their Catholic identity in different ways. Moreover, distinguishing between institutions that are juridically independent of the bishops and those that are not, the document affirms that the former "must have true autonomy and academic freedom."[10] Applying this principle to theological studies, "The Catholic University in the Modern World" states: "The academic freedom which is essential if the science of theology is to be pursued and developed on a truly university level postulates that hierarchical authority intervene only when it judges the truth of the Christian message to be at stake." It adds:

> While no one will deny to bishops the right to judge and declare whether a teaching that is publicly endorsed as Catholic is in fact such, still the judgment concerning the product of a theologian's scholarly research will normally be left to his peers. The scholarly criticism of a theologian's views by his colleagues will in many cases constitute a kind of self-regulation of the Catholic academic community, which may well render unnecessary any direct intervention by ecclesiastical authority.[11]

In a letter that accompanied "The Catholic University in the Modern World," Cardinal Garrone, Prefect of the Sacred Congregation for Catholic Education, conveyed the Congregation's evaluation of this document. He explained that while "The Catholic University in the Modern World" has many praiseworthy elements, it contains "lacunae." In particular, it neglects to treat two points:

> (a) on the necessity for each Catholic university to set out formally and without equivocation, either in its statutes or in some other internal document, its character and commitment as "Catholic"; (b) on the necessity for every Catholic university to create within itself appropriate and efficacious instruments so as to be able to put into effect proper self-regulation in the sectors of faith, morality, and discipline.[12]

Cardinal Garrone expressed a view that has persisted in the Roman Curia, namely that the Church must have a juridical mechanism by which to ensure the Catholic character of institutions of higher education and the proper teaching by Catholic theologians. Although the *Code of Canon Law* of 1917 contains no canons concerning Catholic universities, the Curia's Commission for the Revision of Canon Law included in its drafts of the revised *Code,* which began to appear in 1976, regulations concerning non-pontifical universities and their theologians. As these drafts were made available to the presidents and officials of Catholic institutions of higher education, they were criticized by these leaders for threatening the academic freedom and institutional autonomy of Catholic colleges and universities. The presidents of the Catholic institutions of higher education in the United States expressed their views through the Association of Catholic Colleges and Universities (ACCU), which was formerly the College and University Department of the National Catholic Education Association. As a result of their dissatisfaction, representatives of the ACCU voiced their concerns directly to Pope John Paul II on March 18, 1982.

Nevertheless, the revised *Code* (1983) contains canons that trouble the members of the ACCU. Canon 810 requires academic authorities to assess theologians' "integrity of doctrine" and "probity of life." Canon 812 declares that "those who teach theological disciplines in any institute of higher studies must have a mandate from the competent ecclesiastical authority." The inclusion of Canon 812 was vigorously fought by the presidents and members of the ACCU. They have argued that it is incompatible with academic freedom as understood and practiced in the United States. Also, they have insisted that this canon could jeopardize the accreditation status of Catholic institutions and their eligibility for federal funding.

Subsequently, the Roman Curia's effort to find juridical means to oversee the independent colleges and universities and their theologians manifested itself in the Congregation for Catholic Education's proposed Schema (April 15, 1985) for a pontifical document on Catholic institutions of higher education, which called for juridical procedures by which bishops and the Roman Curia could formally relate to institutions and their teachers.[13] It reiterated Canon 812, which had not been implemented in the United States.

In response to the Congregation for Catholic Education's request, the ACCU explained its disagreements with the Schema of 1985. In particular, it reiterated the superiority of pastoral approaches to issues of Catholic identity and doctrinal orthodoxy, again expressing its concern that juridical methods would jeopardize the academic freedom and institutional autonomy of Catholic colleges and universities.[14] Concurring with this view, the IFCU at its congresses of 1985 and 1989 reiterated that Church authorities should not rely on juridical means to convey their views concerning issues of governance and teaching at the colleges and universities that are not chartered by the Holy See.

Catholic theologians have been intensely involved in efforts to develop cooperative, non-juridical relations between theologians and bishops. The Catholic Theological Society of America has commissioned or contributed to statements in this regard at various times. These efforts include its 1982 statement, with the Canon Law Society, on the relation of theologians and the magisterium,[15] the close cooperation with the NCCB in developing its 1986 statement

"Doctrinal Responsibilities: Approaches to Promoting Cooperation and Resolving Misunderstandings Between Bishops and Theologians,"[16] as well as the 1990 CTSA statement on the profession of faith and oath of fidelity.[17] Other theological societies have also been active.[18] In addition, many individual theologians have served their own institution and its president as consultants, both locally and in the work of the ACCU and the IFCU.

By 1990, it had become clear that the IFCU, the ACCU, and professional societies such as the CTSA, on the one hand, and the Roman Curia, on the other, represented two differing positions on the best way to ensure a Catholic institution's academic freedom in pursuit of the truth and its theologians' consonance with Church teachings.

Ex corde ecclesiae (1990) does not specify the concrete means by which institutions should implement the pope's vision of Catholic higher education. It points out that bishops will fulfill their role of assisting schools in preserving their Catholic character "if close personal and pastoral relationships exist between university and church authorities characterized by mutual trust, close and consistent cooperation and continuing dialogue" (# 28). At the same time, it acknowledges that "general norms are to be applied concretely at the local and regional levels by episcopal conferences and other assemblies of Catholic hierarchy in conformity with the *Code* and complementary church legislation, taking into account the statutes of each university or institute and, as far as possible and appropriate, civil law" (art 1.2). The document stops short, however, of specifying the approaches for implementing the pope's vision of a Catholic university.

Seeking to apply *Ex corde ecclesiae* to the United States, the U.S. bishops implicitly recognized the tension between the positions of the IFCU and the ACCU, on the one hand, and of the Roman Curia, on the other. They initially adopted, by a vote of 224-6, a "pastoral approach" to Catholic higher education in their *Application* of November 13, 1996. This document did not, however, receive the *recognitio* of the Congregation of Catholic Education, which regarded it as a "first draft." Accepting the Congregation's decision, the U.S. bishops set out to revise their *Application* of 1996 in light of the Congregation's recommendations. In response to the bishops' invitation, the ACCU reiterated the dangers of the Church's use of a "juridical instrument" in relating to Catholic institutions of higher education and their theologians; it even did so as recently as April 28, 1999.[19] However, by a vote of 223-31, the U.S. bishops adopted the revised *Application* on November 17, 1999, which includes juridical procedures. Hence, they took the position that the implementation of the juridical instrument would not threaten the institutional autonomy and academic freedom of Catholic colleges and universities and their theologians. The Congregation for Catholic Education approved this *Application* on May 3, 2000.

This history of the unfolding of the issue of Catholic identity and academic freedom shows the challenges that face all men and women who seek to strengthen the academic integrity and credibility of Catholic colleges and universities while simultaneously trying to nurture the Catholicism of these institutions. In light of this complex history, three specific observations are appropriate.

First, the IFCU and the ACCU have been right: whenever possible, Church authorities should adopt pastoral approaches to Catholic colleges and universities that have not been erected by the Holy See or a diocesan bishop. The principle of subsidiarity, as expressed in Pope Pius XI's encyclical *Quadragesimo anno* (1931), would make a non-juridical approach preferable.

Second, there are serious ambiguities in the *Application* of 2000. For example, the document states that Church authorities will respect the institutional autonomy of Catholic institutions of higher education and the academic freedom of their theologians. Yet by adopting a juridical mechanism for implementing the *mandatum,* the *Application* in fact opens the door for Church officials to interfere in the governance of colleges and universities that are not chartered by the Holy See.

Third, the decision by the Congregation of Catholic Education concerning the *Application* of 1996, and the U.S. bishops' subsequent revision of this *Application,* is theologically problematic, for it raises the issue about the authority of the national conference of bishops in relation to the Roman Curia—an issue that has been highlighted by retired Archbishop John R. Quinn.[20]

PART II: THEOLOGICAL SCHOLARSHIP IN ACADEMY AND CHURCH

"Grounded in the commitment of their ecclesial faith and trained in the skills of scholarship, theologians systematically explore the nature and foundations of God's revelation and the teaching of the church."[21] Theologians undertake this exploration with the firm conviction that God's truth is one and that what reason comes to clarify cannot ultimately conflict with divine revelation. "The constructive critical quality of theological scholarship does not compromise its fidelity to the church and its magisterium but indicates the disciplined reflection characteristic of genuine scholarly investigation."[22]

The teaching and research of theologians occurs in relation to but distinct from the work of bishops in the church. Bishops, "united with the pope, have the mission of authentically teaching the message of Christ."[23] Both bishops and theologians "participate in the community's experience of faith and both seek to promote greater understanding of the word of God."[24] At the same time, the difference in roles of bishops and theologians and in the character of their differing modes of teaching are critically important. "Thus, diverse gifts, ministries and authority exist for the full development of the church's unity in life and mission. They require an ecclesiological application of shared responsibility, legitimate diversity and subsidiarity."[25]

Any understanding of the meaning of the *mandatum* for theology in Catholic colleges and universities must begin with a consideration of the character of theology in these institutions.

A. The Character of Academic Theology

Theology is "an intellectual discipline, i.e., an ordered body of knowledge about God."[26] Theology is a complex reality; it appears in different forms and methods in different contexts: in a high school classroom, in a bishop's teaching, in a PhD dissertation, in a parish adult education class, or in a scholarly lecture. Among the various forms of theology is academic theology. ("Academic" here does not mean "abstruse" or "unrelated to the world," as the word has unfortunately come to be used popularly, but "rooted in the academy.")

In the academy, theologians teach and conduct research. It is essential to realize that the term "teach" here does not have the same meaning as in the context of the episcopal or pastoral roles. Pastoral teaching, by bishops and parish ministers, quite appropriately articulates a single perspective: that of the Roman Catholic church. Catholic academic theologians are committed "to teach authentic Catholic doctrine and to refrain putting forth as Catholic teaching anything contrary to the church's magisterium."[27] But there is an important difference between pastoral and academic teaching.

Academic theologians teach in the sense of inducting others into the practices of scholarly research, in a critical community of scholars. Students in college or graduate school, according to their level and competence, are exposed to diverse, even conflicting and unorthodox, points of view, not simply a single correct perspective. Catholic academic theologians deeply desire that their students come to a full appreciation of the truth and wisdom of the faith. They undertake a disciplined search for a deeper understanding of what we believe and this requires attending to students' (and others') experience of God, one another, and the world. Yet unlike the pastoral situation, the focus of theological scholarship (both in research and in the classroom) is on the systematic analysis and development of a tradition, a thinker, or a body of scholarship. Some who see danger in the intellectual openness of the academic setting forget that the classroom is not the sum total of a student's contact with the church. Like every other believer, the faithful student at a Catholic college or university has manifold contacts with the church, including sacramental celebrations, church-related activities, interaction with peers, communication with family—in sum, many sources of formation besides classroom instruction.

Academic theologians also conduct research. This is tested among other theologians through presentations at professional societies and in scholarly articles and books. Like Catholic higher education itself, Catholic theological research occurs in a balance, employing both ecclesial and academic principles, in spite of the tension between them. For example, church documents are typically published only when they are judged to be a correct statement of the position of the church. Within the guild of scholars, however, publication is not presumed to indicate the truth. Rather, it is through the process of review, reaction, and subsequent publication by others that academic theology as a whole moves to a more adequate understanding of God's truth. All new insights are tested in this manner. Catholic theologians endorse the right and authority of the bishops ultimately to reject theological positions contrary to Catholic faith. Yet foreclosure of the academic review process prematurely by authoritative intervention undercuts the credibility of both church authorities among theologians and of theologians among outside conversation partners in the dialogue between church and world.

When emphasizing the communion that should exist between academic theologians and the institutional church, people sometimes say that the theologian and the bishop share a mission of "proclaiming the gospel." In one sense, of course, this is true; Catholic academic theologians play an important role in this proclamation by illuminating over time the meaning of that message. They plumb the depths of our tradition, leading to understanding in faith and action in hope and love. However, speaking of a joint mission unfortunately tends to assimilate academic theologians to an evangelical, pastoral, or catechetical role that does not capture what academic theology is or does.

Academic theology takes the matter of faith as its point of departure, and reflects upon it. But evangelical proclamation is not primary to the academic theologian's role as theologian. These theologians provide careful reflection, understanding, probing, questioning, and systematization of tradition, doctrines, and practices, aiming for a cumulative and differentiated "ordered body of knowledge about God."[28] Academic Catholic theology exists in a reciprocal, communal, and mutually supportive relation with the proclamation of faith, but it is not reducible to it. Many of the goals of academic theology—and the credibility of Catholic higher education and the church more broadly—are threatened when this critical difference is overlooked.

A century ago, nearly all the theologians in a diocese were priests, whose education the bishop had arranged for and whose work occurred at the diocesan seminary, a place the bishop knew well. With the burgeoning of Catholic colleges and universities and a dramatic drop in the number of diocesan seminaries, things have changed significantly. A century ago, seminary professors easily outdistanced other Catholic theologians, both in their numbers and in the weight of their scholarly publications. Today there are far more theologians—including many lay men and women—in college and university contexts and many of these are leaders in Catholic theological scholarship.

Catholic theologians remain committed to accountability, both within the university and the church. In addition to work at the level of the individual college or university, another appropriate form of accountability among theologians involves the professional theological societies, such as the Catholic Biblical Association, the Canon Law Society of America, the College Theology Society, and the Catholic Theological Society of America. Accountability of this sort, which could be made more formal within these respective societies, would parallel the kind of accountability that exists in the United States among lawyers, physicians, and psychologists. For example, these professional societies could establish a procedure by which a bishop, or the NCCB's Committee on Doctrine, could ask that the society conduct a symposium to explore a controversial work.

B. THE ESSENTIAL BALANCE THAT CHARACTERIZES CATHOLIC HIGHER EDUCATION

The balance required of Catholic academic theology is founded on the institutional balance of the colleges and universities where it takes place. Although many outside of Catholic colleges and universities do not understand, these institutions exist only because they balance two commitments: one ecclesial, the other academic. Without the first, they would be secular institutions. Without the second, they would be centers of catechetical instruction. Catholic colleges and universities in the United States face the complex issue of maturing as respected institutions of higher education while simultaneously nurturing their commitment to Catholicism.

In *Ex corde ecclesiae,* Pope John Paul II acknowledged the challenge of maintaining the proper balance between, on the one hand, institutional autonomy and academic freedom, and, on the other, faithfulness to the Catholic tradition. He wrote: "The responsibility for maintaining and strengthening the Catholic identity of the university rests primarily with the university itself" (art. 4.1). And, he added: "Every Catholic university is to maintain communion with the universal church and the Holy See; it is to be in close communion with the local church and in particular with the diocesan bishops of the region or nation in which it is located" (art. 5.1). The U.S. bishops also recognized this challenge when in the *Application* they declared that Catholic colleges and universities must balance a "twofold relationship" to the church and to society. In their words: "Catholic universities are participants in the life of the universal church, the local church, the higher education community of the United States and the civic community" (Part 1, III).

At times in its history, the discipline of theology has had to fight within the academy against a secular skepticism so strong as to deny that theology deserves a place in any university. Catholic colleges and universities have similarly had to struggle against a skeptical attitude of secular institutions of higher education. At times over the years, a secular academic view has proposed an interpretation of the university, often focusing on the character of academic freedom, that would define church-related colleges and universities out of higher education. It would be a great loss to the church if the standards of academic inquiry ever came to be defined in a way that would not include Catholic colleges and universities. Catholic intellectuals are active in this conversation within academe and work to ensure that this will not occur.

A similar blow would be struck if the institutional church were to insist on ecclesiastical control of Catholic institutions of higher education or of the professors who teach there. For this reason, it is essential that university statutes not include the *mandatum* as a requirement for employment as a Catholic theologian. In general, the canons of the *Code* on higher education were designed and drafted so as to safeguard the academic integrity of the individual institutions. That is, the canons manifest a respect for the autonomy appropriate to universities and other institutes of higher studies. They are governed by their own statutes and administered by their own internal authorities. This autonomy is explicitly affirmed both in *Ex corde ecclesiae* and in the *Application.*[29] More specifically, in regard to the appointment and removal of teaching faculty, the canons explicitly state that it is "the authority competent according to the statutes" who are to take such actions, and that in doing so "the manner of proceeding defined in the statutes is to be observed."[30]

Some have argued that the *mandatum* is simply another form of external certification, similar to professional certification in law, medicine, public accounting. But there is a critical difference. These other certifications judge academic competence, which does not present a problem. Loyalty to church teaching is quite different in character. Professional theologians expect professional and ecclesial accountability, but they question the juridical and unilateral form of the *mandatum*.

Although not as great a threat as changing institutional statutes to require a *mandatum* as a condition of employment, the very granting of a *mandatum* by a bishop to a Catholic theologian outside the juridical structure of the theologian's college or university presents a grave risk in the American context. Intellectual respectability and credibility are tied to the strength of ideas. This is true not only among academics but among educated people more generally. Even strong ideas take on the blight of disrepute when they are enforced—or are perceived to be enforced—by institutional power instead of reasoned argument.

The Catholic character of our institutions is critically important, but it is and must remain the responsibility of each institution: its board of trustees, administrators, faculty and staff. The genius of Catholic higher education in the United States is founded on a balance between the institutions of church and academy. Upsetting that balance, by either side, would upend the enterprise. It would be an unthinkable loss to the church if Catholic colleges and universities found themselves forced off this historic path. It would be a tragedy if they were to go down the road taken by many formerly Christian but now secular institutions that self-consciously moved away from their sponsoring churches, often in response to ecclesiastical pressure. Similarly grievous would be a move to become sectarian educational centers, so focused on the correct training of youth that the dialogue with the world loses its credibility with thoughtful leaders in science and technology, the arts and culture, social, political and economic life.

c. The Importance of Credibility for Catholic Academic Theology

The dictionary defines "credibility" as "the quality, capacity, or power to elicit belief." Credibility is a relational idea; a person "has" credibility only if others respond with belief. Credibility differs from expertise. An expert, by definition, knows a lot—and knowledge is an important part of credibility—but some experts lack the capacity to elicit belief in their listeners. Good teachers know the importance of being credible: proclaiming the truth is not the same as proclaiming the truth with credibility.

In the academy, intellectual credibility is the coin of the realm. Academics regularly present their research to other scholars. Knowing a lot is not enough. One must also know the related research and engage the arguments of others who see things differently. In scholarly exchange, intellectual argument—presented for critique by others—is a prerequisite for credibility. Scholars make mistakes, of course, but the fundamental conviction underlying the academy is that reason moves us closer to truth through an ongoing cycle of analysis and critique. One reads and converses widely, develops an argument, presents it to others, receives a critique, and subsequently either abandons or refines the argument prior to another cycle.

The participation of Catholic scholars in this process has been an important part of the church's mission to the world. Engagement with contemporary intellectual argument began in the early church, with the highly educated leaders we now know as the Fathers. It reached a new stage with the appearance of the medieval university. It has become even more important with the rapid rise in the number of college-educated Catholics in the past fifty years. Especially in the United States, more and more lay Catholics are well educated; many are professionals. They expect an intellectually engaging dialogue.

The danger for the church presented by the *mandatum* is that its implementation threatens to undermine the credibility of the church and Catholic intellectuals—both with others in the academy and derivatively with the modern world more broadly. Central here is the credibility of academic theology. The task of making a credible case for Catholic theology rests, of course, with Catholic theologians. Nonetheless, there are two outcomes which, if they accompany the implementation of the *mandatum,* can seriously undermine this effort. The first is the use of juridical authority without reasoned argument to enforce doctrinal discipline. The second is the effect on credibility caused by the denial of due process in the investigation of theologians.

The concern here is credibility—of theologians, of bishops, and of the church as a whole.

1) Actions that Undermine Intellectual Credibility

Official Roman Catholic documents have long emphasized the importance of the dialogue between Christian intellectuals and their peers in the secular world. In this regard, the intellectual credibility—the ability to elicit belief—of Catholic theology is essential. A danger arises when some church leaders attempt to resolve difficulties with individual theologians in a manner which in itself is not intellectually accountable. Beyond the juridical requirements of due process, all participants in such a process need a commitment to intellectual engagement.

Perhaps the most critical issue here is the matter of the empirically obvious changes that have occurred in the teaching of the magisterium of the church over the centuries. "The theologian, who cannot pursue his discipline well without a certain competence in history, is aware of the filtering which occurs with the passage of time . . . Only time has permitted discernment and, after deeper study, the attainment of true doctrinal progress."[31]

The development of doctrine is a complex issue that has been the object of a multitude of essays and books over the years. Among the most vivid examples are the changes of church teaching on slavery, usury, religious freedom, and the authorship of the scriptures. A report of this nature is unable to examine this question thoroughly, but two conflicting values, both of which must be preserved, are readily identifiable. The first is faithfulness to the tradition; through the work of the Holy Spirit, God has brought humanity to a deeper understanding of the Divine Plan for all creation. It is the right and duty of the bishops to guard the integrity of faith in their dioceses. The second is that every attempt by humans to describe the truth is by necessity expressed in a particular language at a particular point in human history—and every language and epoch of history has its own distinctive characteristics and context.

The church's magisterium in our day has rightfully been quite articulate in defending the insight into truth represented by current church teaching, but it has been largely silent about the development of doctrine. This silence threatens the intellectual credibility of the magisterium in the minds of many scholars, Catholic, Protestant, and secular. Any intellectual perspective that cannot account for its own history undermines its credibility, its own capacity to elicit belief.

Any "success" that church leaders might have in altering the opinion of theologians through juridical procedures and a process of enforcement without authentic intellectual engagement will further undermine the intellectual respect that others—both inside Catholic theology and out—had previously rendered to them. As Karl Rahner argued,

> Especially since the (First) Vatican Council the magisterium knows its own authority to be expressly recognized, even as an object of faith, and it can more easily be tempted to suppress heretical systems of ideas simply by its formal authority without making sure that they are overcome on principles relevant to the particular case. In this way the temptation arises to combat heresy to a certain extent only by administrative means, by putting books

on the Index, dismissing suspect professors and so on, instead of by means of the teaching office, that is by such positive formulation of the true doctrine that the error is really supplanted.[32]

2) *The Role of Due Process in Intellectual Credibility*

The Appendix of this report will address the due process requirements that should be part of the implementation of the *mandatum*. The primary reason for this concern is the importance of a guarantee of justice for the individuals involved, as endorsed by the universal law of the church. There is, however, another important reason for a stress on due process: it is essential to the intellectual credibility of both Catholic theology and the institutional church itself.

In a democratic society the absence of due process is widely interpreted as prima facie evidence not only of an abuse of power but also of an absence of intellectual credibility. Thus, when a Roman congregation intervenes with a theologian but does not respect widely acknowledged standards for due process, this denial of due process undermines not only the congregation's position but also the position of all of Catholic theology in its aftermath. Similarly, any refusal to give reasons when disciplining a theologian weakens the intellectual credibility of church leadership as a whole. It becomes harder to elicit belief in other situations. The same is true when a Roman congregation overrules the considered judgment of an individual bishop or conference of bishops without engaging any reasoned argument on the matter.[33] The insistence that an individual not even speak publicly about the denial of due process procedures is one of the most serious violations of due process itself and leads many unbiased onlookers to question both the credibility of this process and the integrity of Catholicism's broader commitment to reasoned discourse. It is not only theologians—and not only Catholics—who notice.

The procedures for granting or withdrawing a *mandatum* are still to be worked out by the bishops of the United States, presumably with attention to the requirements of due process. Nonetheless, many theologians are inclined to skepticism in light of the general disuse into which has fallen the carefully crafted document, "Doctrinal Responsibilities," which the U.S. Catholic Bishops developed, with the assistance of the Catholic Theological Society of America and the Canon Law Society of America, and subsequently approved.[34] In addition, the disinclination of individual bishops to speak up when curial authorities ignore fundamental standards of due process in dealing with theologians within their dioceses leaves many people—and not only theologians—skeptical about the likely results of further conversation about the standards of due process in the implementation of the *mandatum*.

Due process is a fundamental requirement of justice within the church, but that is not the issue here. Any violation of due process weakens the intellectual credibility of church leadership at all levels. Derivatively, the credibility of Catholic theology in dialogue with other scholars is greatly weakened when church leaders violate so fundamental a principle of justice with impunity. A church that believes that "knowledge and reason are sure ministers to faith"[35] must remain committed to reasoned discourse at all times.

D. SUMMARY

The work of a Catholic academic theologian in investigating the insights of church teaching in the classroom and in scholarly work is related to but different from the work of bishops in teaching and defending that same church doctrine. Theologians and bishops, each in their own ways, are responsible for serving the truth that is founded in the one God we worship. Though bishop and theologian "teach" in different ways, both are called by Christ to teach with credibility.

Bishops have a critically important role as guardians of the apostolic faith, passed down from generation to generation. At the same time, the manner in which bishops guard and teach that core of truth will have a great impact on how effectively the word of Christ is embodied in the church and the world. Acting in ways that diminish intellectual credibility, by employing juridical power rather than intellectual argument, undermines not only the persuasiveness of the insight being enforced. Especially in a democratic society and especially among the well educated, it undercuts the broader message of the church to the world.

PART III: PROBLEMS WITH THE *MANDATUM*

Given the many difficulties that surround the *mandatum*, many theologians committed to ecclesial accountability may nonetheless decide against requesting one. Decisions by theologians not to request a *mandatum* might be open to misinterpretation by church leaders and it will be helpful to recount several of the various reasons that seem to be leading many theologians toward this decision.

a) Many theologians are deeply concerned by the lack of clarity in the description of the *mandatum* they are being asked to request. The *Application* incorporates several ambiguities. The *mandatum* is described as an acknowledgement that the theologian is "in full communion with the church,"[36] but this phrase has typically been employed to describe either the relation of whole churches with the church of Rome or the relation of Catholics who are not excommunicated. Presumably, however, a denial or withdrawal of a *mandatum* has nothing to do with excommunication. Is the local bishop left to decide when communion is "full"? Would the hierarchy of truths be respected?[37] The notion of "full communion" between theologian and church is itself a theological novelty and is not a sufficiently clear basis for a juridical procedure that could threaten the good reputation of a theologian.

Further, as the *Application* notes, theologians teach in their own name in virtue of their baptism and professional competence. In addition, the *Application* asserts that "the *mandatum* should not be construed as an appointment, authorization, delegation or approbation of one's teaching by church authorities."[38] But approbation seems to be precisely what the *Application* envisions.[39] Does this then mean that one's *teaching* is not to be considered by the bishop but only one's *writing*? But isn't this a form of teaching as well? At least one widely respected theologian has described the idea of the *mandatum* in the *Application* as "incoherent."

b) Many theologians are deeply concerned that the *mandatum* presses forward a juridical relationship between bishops and theologians and subverts a more beneficial relation of communion. The *mandatum* appears aimed at developing the type of hierarchical control over theologians that a bishop has over members of the clergy in his diocese. Lay theologians come to be treated as quasi-clerics, accountable to the bishop in the performance of their academic duties. The relationship is vertical and unilateral, with bishops acting as judges and theologians being evaluated. The *Application* employs the language of "communion" at times, but the actual relation implicit in the *mandatum* lacks the reciprocity that real communion always entails.

A more appropriate model for the relationship between bishops and theologians, as between bishops and Catholic universities, is a relation of dialogue, collaboration, and mutual listening, with each respectful of the distinctive mission of the other. This would be a relation of communion. Pope John Paul II has called for this.[40] The U.S. bishops have called for this.[41] The theological community has consistently encouraged this.[42] The *mandatum*, however, moves in a contrary direction, juridicizing the role of theologians while making no practical proposal for advancing a dialogical communion.

c) Many theologians are deeply concerned that the internal logic of the *mandatum* does not recognize sufficiently the character of academic theology. The *Application* asserts that theologians at Catholic colleges and universities do not teach "in the name of the bishop or of the church's magisterium,"[43] but the prevailing presumption seems to be that they should not truly be considered "Catholic" theologians without this seal of approval from the bishop.

As members of the academy, academic theologians serve the church and the broader society by inducting students into the study of theology as an academic and scholarly discipline in a way that is consistent with the highest professional and intellectual standards. In their teaching, their role is to induce inquiry, to open horizons, to encourage students to "think things through." In their scholarly research, academic theologians investigate both old and new insights and press for an expression of ancient truths accessible to the modern world. Open dialogue with other points of view is characteristic of university scholarship and interchange and requires freedom to explore and test new insights.

Some have described the *mandatum* as a sort of "truth in advertising" technique: Students and parents have the right to know which Catholic theologians are "true" Catholic theologians and which are not. But this greatly oversimplifies the nature of academic theology and misrepresents what the *mandatum* is, as the many concerns of theologians already cited in this section indicate. In addition, the *Application* itself asserts that the *mandatum* is *not* an approbation of a theologian's teaching, which presumably is the concern of students and parents.

d) Many theologians are deeply concerned by the importation of a European model of church/university relations into the North American context where an entirely different history prevails. In Europe, bishops often have a quite direct and legally sanctioned relation to Catholic theologians teaching in universities, often controlling the appointment of theologians even in universities financed by the national government. In the United States, most Catholic colleges and universities are governed by predominantly lay Boards of Trustees,[44] without the local bishop having any juridical role.

College and university presidents are well aware of the importance of protecting institutional autonomy and the academic freedom of faculty members. Infringement of these fundamental principles can affect the legal status of the institution, its accreditation, and its economic stability.[45] Presidents and members of Boards, mindful of their fiduciary responsibilities, have been careful to observe the laws of the nation and protect both institutional autonomy and academic freedom.[46] The presidents with whom the bishops consulted in recent years put it this way:

We cannot speak for Catholic institutions in other lands; their circumstances and culture differ from ours. We can only say that juridical, canonical, statutory relationships which would infringe upon proper institutional autonomy are not in keeping with our circumstances, and would make no positive contribution to our efforts to maintain and strengthen Catholic higher education and its service to the American church.[47]

e) Many theologians are deeply concerned that the establishment of procedures for the *mandatum* will be only a first step toward the far more objectionable expectation that colleges and universities alter their statutes to include a *mandatum* from the local bishop as a requirement for employment of Catholic theologians. Should the current, "personal" requirement of a *mandatum* further develop in such a way as to affect appointment, rank, or tenure, or the assignment of classes, or other matters internal to the university, it would be a violation of institutional autonomy and academic freedom.

This would constitute a violation of institutional autonomy because it introduces an external, non-academic agent into the internal academic processes of the university. Only the faculty and academic administration of a university are competent to make these decisions.[48] It would entail a violation of academic freedom because, in the U.S. context, academic freedom includes in its meaning that the institution and its faculty are immune from direct intervention by outside authorities of any kind, including political and religious authorities, in the fulfillment of their academic responsibilities.

Like the protection of religious freedom in the U.S. Constitution, academic freedom is a civic principle, not a religious one. As John Courtney Murray argued, such principles are ordered to the common good in a pluralistic society and serve religion indirectly but quite importantly nonetheless. Academic freedom and institutional autonomy are hallmarks of colleges and universities. To the extent that the implementation of the *mandatum* would be an opening wedge for a violation of these principles, it threatens the essence of Catholic higher education.

f) Many theologians are deeply concerned about a troubling overcentralization of ecclesiastical decision-making in Rome and the attempt by some forces within the church to impede, if not block, the vision of the Second Vatican Council.[49] The implementation of the *mandatum* in this context reinforces in university circles the image of a reactionary ecclesiastical leadership intolerant of the freedom of thought and expression that characterizes North American higher education.[50] The rising level of concern about overcentralization is reflected in the scholarly papers and discussions following the promulgation of Pope John Paul II's encyclical *Ut Unum Sint.*[51]

Instead of promoting dialogue between Catholicism and culture, such over-centralization contributes to the isolation of North American Catholic intellectual life from the society it is attempting to converse with and influence. Instead of integrating theology into the whole academic enterprise, it tends to remove theology from creative intellectual commerce with other academic departments.[52]

g) Many theologians are deeply concerned that should the *mandatum* become a condition for employment it would unfairly threaten the livelihood of lay theologians, who in some departments already constitute a majority. Historically bishops are accustomed to dealing with theologians who were diocesan clergy or members of religious orders. In that situation, "difficulties" of all kinds—whether of behavior, belief, or professional incompetence—were dealt with largely as personnel problems, where a job reassignment by one's immediate superior was the typical solution.

Lay theologians, however, do not have the economic and institutional resources of a diocese or religious order to support them. Usually they have family members dependent upon them. They experience a call to deepen their knowledge of theology, frequently in the course of pursuing other careers and intellectual interests. They pay for their own education, at considerable financial cost, and secure a teaching position at a Catholic college or university without the involvement of a bishop or religious superior. An economic threat would exert great and inappropriate influence on a parent responsible for his or her family's economic well being.

h) Many theologians are deeply concerned that any due process guarantees with which the U.S. bishops may agree are nonetheless too likely to be subverted if a curial office decides to intervene and unilaterally directs a bishop to withdraw a *mandatum*. In Germany, for example, where the process is governed by Concordat, members of the Roman Curia have repeatedly overridden a bishop's decision to grant the *nihil obstat* to an applicant for a position.[53] It seems unlikely that a U.S. bishop would be able to defend a theologian in the face of curial insistence, no matter how justified the cause. U.S. theologians are already concerned about the episcopal disuse of the procedures of "Doctrinal Responsibilities," which bishops and theologians developed and the NCCB approved in 1989.[54]

Catholic bishops have the right and responsibility to defend Catholic doctrine. The *mandatum,* however, sets up a deeply flawed system where many hundreds of fully faithful theologians must be "processed," all out of a concern for dealing with a small number with whom the bishops may have doctrinal concerns. As a result, the fact that a theologian decides not to seek a *mandatum* ought not to be interpreted as a sign of infidelity. There are a number of serious problems with the *mandatum,* the process leading up to it, and its potential impact on the church. These are very critical concerns, so serious that some have questioned whether the law should be "received."[55]

PART IV: A CANONICAL ANALYSIS OF THE *MANDATUM*

As a juridical instrument, the *mandatum* seems more likely to endanger than enhance the relationship between bishops and theologians. Still, the U.S. bishops are planning to develop procedures and norms for its implementation. Given this, the following four sections offer principles and reflections on this matter. The first concerns the character of a *mandatum*. The second asks who is required to have a *mandatum*. The third concerns the ecclesiastical authority competent to grant a *mandatum*. The fourth addresses basic principles needed to guide any choice of procedures for the granting, denying, or withdrawing a *mandatum*. A proposed set of procedures appears in the Appendix to this report.

A) What Is a Mandatum?

The 1983 Code of Canon Law introduced a requirement for those who teach theological disciplines: They are to possess a *mandatum* from competent ecclesiastical authority.[56] The *mandatum* is described in the *Application* in terms of "communion."[57]

Communion is a basic theological reality, rooted in the communion of trinitarian life, made visible in the communion of the divine and human natures of Christ, and present in us through the indwelling of the Holy Spirit through whom we are sharers in the communion of divine life. This communion, always a relation of reciprocity, is expressed most fundamentally in the celebration of the Eucharist, a Holy Communion in which we share in the sacred species and are sanctified. Eucharistic communion is sustained through the communion of those who preside at the Eucharist, especially the communion of the bishops with the other members of the College of Bishops and with their head, the Bishop of Rome.

Communion has various ecclesiological meanings. The church of Christ consists in the communion of the particular churches in which and from which the one church of Christ exists.[58] This church of Christ subsists in the Catholic church.[59] Other churches and ecclesial communities are in real but imperfect communion with the Catholic church.[60] Individual believers are incorporated into the church of Christ through baptism. Believers in the full communion of the Catholic church, having the Spirit of Christ, are joined to Christ through the visible bonds of profession of faith, sacraments, and ecclesiastical discipline.[61]

The determination of whether someone is in this full communion is not an isolated judgment; it takes place in a complex setting of communion, to which the bishop himself is bound (canon 209). Because such a judgment entails the determination of the visible bonds of profession of faith, sacraments, and ecclesiastical government, it must be subject to a strict (i.e., narrow) interpretation. There are two reasons for this. The first is expressed in the ancient principle that "no burden is to be imposed beyond the indispensable."[62] The second reason for restraint here is that breaking full communion restricts rights (canons 18 & 96).[63] Thus, for example, the hierarchy of truths must be respected as well as the different levels of teaching authority by the magisterium (canons 750–753), as well as the limits imposed by heresy or apostasy. Similarly, there must be respect for the distinction between difficulties with non-irreformable magisterial teaching and organized public dissent.[64]

According to the *Application,* these principles are applied to the meaning of the *mandatum* in two ways. First, the *mandatum* is given only to one who *is* in full communion; that is, it is restricted to Roman Catholics.[65] Second, it expresses the fact that a Catholic who teaches theological disciplines will act within the communion of the church,[66] will respect the obligations and rights which arise from this fact,[67] and will do so in the context of academic freedom assured them in the church's law.[68] Thus "the *mandatum* recognizes the professor's commitment and responsibility to teach authentic Catholic doctrine and to refrain from putting forth as Catholic teaching anything contrary to the church's magisterium."[69]

The understanding of the *mandatum* is further clarified in the *Application* by statements of what it is not:

> The *mandatum* should not be construed as an appointment, authorization, delegation or approbation of one's teaching by church authorities.[70]

> Those who have received a *mandatum* teach in their own name in virtue of their baptism and their academic and professional competence, not in the name of the Bishop or of the church's magisterium.[71]

Thus the *mandatum* is not what in English is called a "mandate," and careful usage will not employ this false cognate.

In addition, the *mandatum* is not an academic requirement, but an ecclesial one. Therefore, "it is not the responsibility of a Catholic university to seek the *mandatum;* this is a personal obligation of each professor."[72] The *mandatum* is also not based on private or devotional life, but whether the theologian "will teach in communion with the church"[73] in the areas of academic competence of the theologian, the disciplinary subjects in which the theologian teaches and writes.

It would have been helpful if the *Application* had been clearer about its use of the phrase "in full communion with the church"[74] as applied to theologians. The status of a theologian, as a theologian, must not be confused with the ecclesial status of a member of the church who is "in full communion." Similarly, the withdrawal of the *mandatum* is not the same as an imposition of the penalty of excommunication. Thus this novel use of the phrase "in full communion" to describe a theologian's relation to the church remains open to unfortunate ambiguity.

b) Who Is Required to Have a Mandatum?

Canonically, the requirement for a *mandatum* is in the nature of a restriction upon the rights of those engaged in sacred disciplines to freedom of inquiry and prudent expression (canon 218). As a result, it is subject to strict interpretation; that is "whenever the text of canon 812 is subject to differing interpretations, the stricter or narrower meaning should be given because of the context of the canon as a restriction upon the free exercise of rights."[75]

Thus the requirement for a *mandatum* applies only to Roman Catholic theologians in Catholic colleges and universities.[76] It does not apply to non-Catholic theologians who teach in Catholic institutions nor does it apply to Catholic theologians who teach in non-Catholic colleges or universities. It applies to the individual, and not to the institution where the individual teaches.[77]

The *Application* refers to "Catholic professors" as those who "have the duty to be faithful to the church's magisterium."[78] According to customary academic usage in the United States, the term "professor" includes assistant professors, associate professors, and full (or "ordinary") professors. However, only tenured faculty members form the long-term core of the faculty at each institution. Other instructors are part-time or short-term (e.g., lecturers, adjuncts replacing faculty on sabbatical, graduate students who are teaching assistants, etc.) or are still on probation prior to a decision about tenure (i.e., "on tenure track"). The academy has not yet accepted probationary faculty as full and equal partners on the faculty. Thus it would be appropriate that the *mandatum* apply only to tenured professors, whatever their rank.[79]

The history of the drafting of canon 812 makes it clear that the *mandatum* applies to those who teach "theological disciplines" but not to those who may teach related disciplines.[80] The 1983 *Code, Ex corde ecclesiae,* and the *Application* do not address which are the "theological disciplines." The "Norms of Application" from the Congregation for Catholic Education, which accompanied the apostolic constitution *Sapientia christiana,* do address this issue. The list includes sacred scripture, fundamental theology, dogmatic theology, moral and spiritual theology, pastoral theology, liturgy, church history, patrology, archeology, and canon law.[81] Only those who will teach properly theological disciplines are to obtain a *mandatum*.[82]

The *Application*'s requirement for a *mandatum*, like nearly all canonical provisions,[83] is not retroactive. It is a new obligation as of May 3, 2001, when the *Application* becomes effective. Hence it affects only those teachers of theological disciplines who, after the *Application* goes into effect, enter into a position covered by the scope of the *mandatum*.[84]

c) The Competent Ecclesiastical Authority

The *Application* specifies that "the competent ecclesiastical authority to grant the *mandatum* is the bishop of the diocese in which the Catholic university is located."[85] This provision is an exception to the usual norm that Catholics are subject to the diocesan bishop of their place of domicile or quasi-domicile (canon 107 §1), since the person may not have a domicile or quasi-domicile in the diocese in which the Catholic university is located. As an exception to the law, this provision is subject to a strict interpretation (canon 18), and applies to the place of the principal seat of the university rather than to any of its extensions or off-campus programs. Bishops of dioceses where off-campus programs are held are not competent to grant or withdraw the *mandatum*.

Because the granting of the *mandatum* has effects within canon law, granting the *mandatum* must include "those things which essentially constitute the act itself as well as the formalities and requirements imposed by law for the validity of the act" (canon 125). Thus, the one who is to grant or withdraw the *mandatum* is to seek out the necessary information and to hear those whose rights can be affected by this act.[86] The diocesan bishop "may grant the *mandatum* personally or through a delegate."[87] The granting of the *mandatum* is to be in writing.[88]

d) Canonical Principles to Guide Procedures for the *Mandatum*

Any inquiry or response related to the granting, denial, or withdrawal of a *mandatum* to teach theological disciplines takes place within the context of several critical principles.

i.) The theologian, like other Catholics in full communion with the church, participates in the prophetic role of Christ, under the guidance of the Holy Spirit. That is, in virtue of the sacraments of initiation the theologian possesses a "sense of the faith (*sensus fidei*) aroused and sustained by the Spirit of truth." Indeed, the theologian fully shares the task of God's holy people as "it penetrates more deeply into that same faith through right judgment and applies it more fully to life."[89]

ii.) In embracing their theological vocation, Catholic men and women respond to the gifts, special graces, and charisms given by the Spirit for the renewal and upbuilding of the church. In so doing, they gratefully accept and earnestly pursue these manifestations of the Spirit given to each for the common good.[90] The Second Vatican Council recognized that everyone of the faithful has the right and duty to exercise, in the church and in the world, the gifts and charisms of the Holy Spirit.[91]

iii.) Theologians enjoy the same human rights and religious freedom as all others. They cannot be compelled to act against their consciences in religious matters, whether in private or in public. They, like everyone else, are morally obliged to seek the truth, above all religious truth; in order to do so, they must have both psychological freedom and freedom from external coercion. Truth is sought by free inquiry, by means of teaching, communication, and dialogue through which people assist each other in their search.[92]

iv.) Teachers of theological disciplines have the same basic freedom of expression as other Catholics. That is, they should make known to their pastors "their needs and desires with that freedom and confidence which befits children of God and sisters and brothers in Christ." In matters pertaining to the good of the church, they have the right and duty to make their opinions known to their pastors and to the rest of the Christian faithful. In fact, because of their special knowledge and competence, they have greater prerogatives than others in this regard.[93]

v.) The church's canonical system provides a special protection for its theologians: "Those engaged in the sacred disciplines have a lawful freedom of inquiry and of expressing their opinion prudently on those matters in which they have expertise, while observing a due respect for the magisterium of the church."[94] This right to theological freedom of inquiry and expression is found among the basic "Obligations and Rights of All the Christian Faithful" which are stated in the *Code* at the beginning of the book entitled "The People of God."[95]

vi.) The role and function of the theologian in the church is not an "ecclesiastical office" like those of bishop, pastor, or ecclesiastical judge. The theologian is not a part of the church's hierarchical structure. Those who are "engaged in the sacred disciplines" or who function as "teachers of sacred sciences" or "teachers of disciplines pertaining to faith or morals," are acknowledged in canon law,[96] but their status is nowhere defined. They do not receive a "canonical mission" to teach in the name of the church. Rather they teach in their own name, with their own responsibility, in virtue of their own academic and professional competence.[97]

vii.) The role of theologian also brings responsibilities. Catholic academic theologians are responsible "to teach authentic Catholic doctrine and to refrain from putting forth as Catholic teaching anything contrary to the church's magisterium."[98] Their focus on the systematic analysis and development of the tradition should be done with deep respect for the authority of the magisterium. "The constructive critical quality of theological scholarship does not compromise its fidelity to the church and its magisterium but indicates the disciplined reflection characteristic of genuine scholarly investigation."[99]

viii.) The action of granting or revoking a *mandatum* falls within the canonical category of "juridic acts," hence it is subject to the norms governing juridic acts.[100] More specifically, the resulting document is an "individual decree," and it must conform to the canonical requirements for such decrees.[101] Since the consequences of giving, withholding, or removing a *mandatum* are so serious both personally and professionally, the procedures provided in contested cases must be correspondingly careful and completely fair.

ix.) The bishops are charged with safeguarding the revelation that has been given to the whole church. This is an essential element in the sacramental ministry of the episcopacy. Yet, as Ladislas Örsy, S.J., has put it, "the specific vocation of the popes and bishops is to be witnesses to the truth of evangelical doctrine . . . which does not necessarily include the capacity to have the deepest insight into the content of the mysteries."[102] Given the range of scholarly specialties in contemporary theology, an individual bishop may need to assess the work of a theologian in an area where the bishop is not an expert. As a result, the following steps are important:

a) The authority of bishops and the credibility of the church in the United States will be jeopardized if criteria and procedures by which a bishop grants a *mandatum* remain ambiguous, ideological, or idiosyncratic. Criteria and procedures must be agreed upon nationally.

b) Before a bishop withdraws a *mandatum* or refuses to issue one when it is requested, a panel of recognized theologians should be consulted. An appropriate body to arrange such a review could be the NCCB Committee on Doctrine, which, working with scholarly theological societies, would retain a slate of respected theologians for this purpose.

c) If bishops are to act with credibility, it will also be necessary that every bishop explain his theological reasons and sources if he decides against granting a *mandatum*, or if he subsequently decides to withdraw it.

x.) In all matters concerning the *mandatum*, professors and bishops need to keep in mind the provisions of *Ex corde ecclesiae* 29:

The Church, accepting "the legitimate autonomy of human culture and especially of the sciences," recognizes the academic freedom of scholars in each discipline in accordance with its own principles and proper methods,[103] and within the confines of the truth and the common good.

Theology has its legitimate place in the university alongside other disciplines. It has proper principles and methods which define it as a branch of knowledge. Theologians enjoy this same freedom so long as they are faithful to these principles and methods.

Bishops should encourage the creative work of theologians. They serve the Church through research done in a way that respects theological method. They seek to understand better, further develop and more effectively communicate the meaning of Christian revelation as transmitted in Scripture and tradition and in the Church's magisterium. They also investigate the ways in which theology can shed light on specific questions raised by contemporary culture. At the same time, since theology seeks an understanding of revealed truth whose authentic interpretation is entrusted to the bishops of the Church,[104] it is intrinsic to the principles and methods of their research and teaching in their academic discipline that theologians respect the authority of the bishops and assent to Catholic doctrine according to the degree of authority with which it is taught.[105] Because of their interrelated roles, dialogue between bishops and theologians is essential; this is especially true today, when the results of research are so quickly and so widely communicated through the media.[106]

PART V: FINAL RECOMMENDATIONS

This report has proposed a number of recommendations, both above and in the Appendix. Three general recommendations stand out as most important.

1. National Procedures and Criteria

Although each local bishop is charged with making the decision about the granting of a mandate, standards of justice would require that both the procedures and criteria for the granting, denying, and withdrawal of a mandate should be common throughout all the dioceses of the United States. The "portability" of a *mandatum* from one diocese to another[107] also argues for national, not local, criteria and procedures. In addition, an appeal procedure at the national level must exist to insure that due process and other requirements of justice are respected.

2. Consultation about Implementation

Given the seriousness of concerns of theologians and institutions, the bishops should develop implementation procedures and criteria for granting and withdrawing a *mandatum* in close conversation with theologians at Catholic colleges and universities and representatives of professional theological societies. The plan of the NCCB Committee on the *Mandatum* to include in their consultation representatives of professional theological societies is very helpful but not in itself sufficient. Prudence would dictate that the bishops move deliberately and without haste, with an intermediate draft that then becomes the topic of local consultations between every bishop who has one or more Catholic colleges or universities in his diocese with the theologians who teach there. Bishops and theologians involved in such consultations should invite the bishops of nearby dioceses which may not have within them a Catholic college or university. Every diocese in the nation has a stake in this conversation.

3. Ongoing Dialogue Between Bishops and Theologians

All magisterial documents related to *Ex corde ecclesiae* have helpfully insisted on the importance of an ongoing dialogue between each bishop and the theologians working in his diocese. Unfortunately, this dialogue has rarely occurred. At most Catholic colleges and universities, there has never been a meeting of the theology or religious studies department with the local bishop. Real dialogue on important theological issues, without the presence of a crisis, should occur regularly so that mutual understanding and trust can grow over time. Both bishops and Catholic theologians should make this dialogue a priority. There can be no doubt that common perspectives, interests, and goals of bishops and Catholic theologians far outweigh the few areas where there are differences.

CONCLUSION

Catholic theologians at Catholic colleges and universities in the United States share a deep sense of fidelity to the church. At the same time they are committed members of the scholarly guild. Behind this double commitment is the conviction that "it is in the context of the impartial search for truth that the relationship between faith and reason is brought to light and meaning."[108] The work of Catholic theologians here is critical for the church's mission to the world, particularly as more and more ordinary Catholics seek education in Catholic college or graduate school programs and take leadership roles throughout North American society.

Whatever practical tensions there may be between ecclesiastical and academic commitments, Catholic colleges and universities—and academic theology within these institutions—exhibit an underlying coherence that is based in the conviction that "knowledge and reason are sure ministers to faith."[109] The members of the CTSA are convinced that these very tensions can be deeply creative, conducive to the vitality of these institutions. Great effort in coming to mutual understanding will be needed to sustain this project, but the promise for the church and for the church's mission to the world calls us all to participate wholeheartedly.

Members of the Drafting Committee:
John P. Boyle, University of Iowa
Lisa Sowle Cahill, Boston College
James A. Coriden, Washington Theological Union
Daniel Rush Finn, Chair, St. John's University
Robert A. Krieg, University of Notre Dame
M. Theresa Moser, RSCJ, University of San Francisco
James H. Provost, Catholic University of America

APPENDIX:
SUGGESTED PROCEDURES FOR
IMPLEMENTING THE *MANDATUM*

The Catholic character of Catholic colleges and universities within the United States is critically important both to these institutions and to the church as a whole. Theologians across the nation enthusiastically support the call of Pope John Paul II and of the U.S. Catholic Bishops to broaden and deepen the attention to the Catholic character of Catholic higher education. At the same time, most Catholic theologians in the United States agree with the advice presented to the bishops by the presidents of Catholic colleges and universities who were consulted in the process of developing the *Application*. The juridicization of the relation between bishop and theologian may be intended to strengthen the Catholic character of higher education, but it represents an imposition of a European model of university structure. In the North American context, the *mandatum* threatens both the character of Catholic colleges and universities and the mission of the church in the modern world. Thus, this Appendix should not be misconstrued as an endorsement of the *mandatum*.

At the same time, we recognize that the National Conference of Catholic Bishops has decided to proceed with the implementation of the *mandatum*, and thus we propose a number of concrete recommendations in that regard.

USUAL PROCEDURES FOR GRANTING A *MANDATUM*

The ordinary procedure for requesting a *mandatum* should be a letter to the bishop from the Catholic professor. In it, the professor should inform the bishop of his or her status as a Catholic, and should make clear "that he or she will teach in communion with the church."[110] The usual presumption of full communion for any Catholic also applies to a Catholic professor seeking a *mandatum*. Only if there is weighty evidence against that person's willingness to teach in communion with the church would any further investigation or assurances be necessary. Given the theological uncertainties surrounding the profession of faith (as described in the next section), its use as an assurance of communion required for receiving a *mandatum* would be inappropriate.

SPECIAL PROCEDURES FOR GRANTING, DENYING, OR WITHDRAWING A *MANDATUM*

Although the usual procedure for the granting of a *mandatum* would not entail an investigation of a theologian's work, there may from time to time arise a situation where a bishop has good reason to believe a theologian may not qualify for a *mandatum*.[111] This could occur when a theologian requests a *mandatum* or at some time after the bishop has granted one. In either case, an inquiry into the theologian's work is required. Such a process is a complex one, particularly if the rights of both the theologian and the bishop are to be fully respected. A number of elements of this process require careful attention.

A.) THE SCOPE OF INQUIRY

The range of any theological questioning related to the *mandatum* must not exceed certain limits.

i.) The Hierarchy of Truths.

Vatican II reminded Catholic theologians that there is "an order or 'hierarchy' of truths, since they vary in their relationship to the foundation of the Christian faith."[112] The "hierarchy of truths" in *Unitatis redintegratio* does not refer to the distinction between definitive dogma and nondefinitive doctrine, but rather to a hierarchy that exists among the dogmas of the Church, some being central and foundational dogmas and others that might be termed confirmatory dogmas.[113] In addition to this hierarchy within dogmas of the Church, however, one can also speak more broadly of a hierarchy between doctrine taught infallibly and church teaching that is fallible.

On account of these different kinds and levels of truth,[114] various responses are asked of the faithful, depending on the authoritative weight of a particular teaching. Thus those truths requiring an assent of faith (credenda) are those truths that are divinely revealed. The hierarchy of truths is reflected in the *Code,* where "full communion" requires profession of faith, and faith means the truths which must be believed (credenda).[115] Vatican II also taught that a religious submission ("religiosum voluntatis et intellectus obsequium") is due to the teaching of the Roman Pontiff, even when a particular teaching is not proposed as infallible.[116]

Recently, the Congregation for the Doctrine of the Faith prescribed a Profession of Faith and Oath of Fidelity for certain members of the Church. The

Profession embraces three kinds of truths and three corresponding levels of assent: "firma fide. . . . credo," "firmiter . . . amplector ac retineo," and "religioso voluntatis et intellectus obsequi. . . . adhaereo."[117]

Until the pontificate of John Paul II, those truths "to be held definitively" were truths taught infallibly. Pope John Paul II, however, began to use this phrase in a way that suggested yet another level of authority lying somewhere between infallible teaching and non-infallible teaching.[118] In 1998, Pope John Paul II added a new paragraph to c. 750, stipulating that anyone who rejected a proposition "which [is] to be held definitively is opposed to the doctrine of the Catholic Church."[119]

What is not at all clear at this moment in church history is the process for discerning and declaring a doctrine "to be definitively held." The process is clear concerning the infallible pronouncement of a pope teaching *ex cathedra* or the definition of an ecumenical council.[120] The process is not clear for definitive teaching that has been developed and promulgated differently. The Pope issued such a teaching in an apostolic letter. Recently the Pontifical Council for the Family declared the condemnation of contraception "to be held as definitive and irreformable."[121]

These instances are novel and confusing since "definitive and irreformable" is language previously reserved for infallible teaching. Does a pontifical council have the authority to issue definitive teaching or to define earlier teaching as definitive? The pope only teaches infallibly under certain conditions. What are the conditions required for his definitive, non-infallible teaching? These questions demand greater clarity—and the careful study necessary to achieve it—since at issue is the very identification of church doctrine, the response required of the faithful, and the conditions for communion with the Church.

The Holy See's initiatives in the matter of "definitive" teaching have provoked disquiet and discussion among Catholic theologians throughout the world, since this category of truths has no clear conciliar or canonical antecedents. The CTSA commissioned an extensive analysis of the main issues raised by the Profession and the Oath,[122] but there have been additional developments since then. There is an important literature on *Ad tuendam fidem*, and at least one international conference has been held on the difficulties it raises.[123] In an institution whose identity is rooted in a theological tradition reaching back two millennia, it is not surprising that more than a few years are required to address ambiguities that arise from recent theological developments.

The key point here, however, is that both the nature and status of truths to be held definitively are still quite cloudy theologically and canonically. Therefore, in no case should the Profession of Faith and the Oath of Fidelity be made a condition for granting a *mandatum,* as footnote 42 of the *Application* suggests.

ii.) Relevance.

Teachers of theological disciplines ought not to be questioned about matters unrelated to their areas of training, teaching, and professional research. Issues of concern are those reasonably within the theologian's disciplinary specialization or teaching assignments.[124]

iii.) Inculturation and Plurality of Theological Expression.

Among the theologian's tasks is that of listening to and interpreting the voices of our day and searching for better expressions of revealed truth so that the message of Christ may be more effectively communicated to the people of our time. A legitimate freedom of expression, even in the elaboration of revealed truths, must be maintained.[125]

iv.) Legitimate Dissent.

Reasoned and respectful disagreement with teachings that have not been taught infallibly is a practice of long standing and legitimacy in the church. The Congregation for the Doctrine of the Faith explicitly acknowledges the legitimacy of dissent:

> It can happen, however, that a theologian may, according to the case, raise questions regarding the timeliness, the form or even the content of magisterial interventions. . . . When it comes to the question of interventions in the prudential order, it could happen that some magisterial documents might not be free from all deficiencies.[126]

The Congregation admits "that tensions may arise between the theologian and the magisterium." Such tensions "can become a dynamic factor, a stimulus to both the magisterium and the theologians to fulfill their respective roles while practicing dialogue."[127]

The Congregation envisions "the case of the theologian who might have serious difficulties, for reasons which appear to him or her to be well founded, in accepting a non-irreformable magisterial teaching." "It can also happen that at the conclusion of a serious study . . . the theologian's difficulty remains because the arguments to the contrary seem more persuasive to him or her."[128] Theologians may be faced with propositions to which they feel they cannot give intellectual assent. However, they should remain open to a deeper examination of the question. A theologian should take care not to "present his own opinions or divergent hypotheses as though they were nonarguable conclusions."[129]

Dissent becomes a "problem" for the Congregation when it is in public opposition to the magisterium, appeals to the mass media, and attempts to exert the pressure of public opinion.[130] Both bishops and theologians must keep in mind that

> All in the church must preserve unity in essentials. But let all, according to the gifts that they have received, maintain a proper freedom in their spiritual life and discipline . . . and even in their theological elaborations of revealed truth. In all things let charity prevail.[131]

b.) Limits on Self-Disclosure:

Any inquiry related to the *mandatum* should be confined within legitimate boundaries.

i.) The Dignity of the Human Person and the Right to Privacy

The church's canonical system recognizes this fundamental right of each one of the Christian faithful: "No one is permitted to harm unlawfully the good reputation which a person enjoys nor to violate the right of any person to protect his or her own privacy."[132] It is one of the basic rights articulated in the 1983 *Code*.

One's private opinions, convictions, doubts, suspended judgments, and confusions are precisely that, private matters. They need not be shared, and they may not be compelled. Their revelation may not be demanded, even of a teacher of theological disciplines. Theological writings and other formal communications are the public expressions of a person's professional views and judgments. Personal thoughts and musings are in the private domain. As the CDF statement indicates, the judgment of the magisterium "does not concern the person of the theologian, but the intellectual positions which he or she has publicly espoused."[133]

ii.) Manifestation of Conscience

The primacy and inviolability of conscience is essential to church teaching. The Council taught that "conscience is the most intimate center and sanctuary of a person, in which he or she is alone with God whose voice echoes within them."[134] The liberty and dignity of the children of God implies and demands absolute respect for conscience.[135] The *Code of Canon Law* recognizes the autonomy and privacy of personal conscience when it forbids religious superiors from inducing their subjects in any way to make a manifestation of conscience to them.[136] This strong assertion of the inviolability of personal conscience, even in the singularly close and trusting spiritual relationships within religious communities, signals the respect due to the internal forum of conscience in the church's canonical system.[137]

Theologians no less than other Christians enjoy the privacy of their consciences. *Ex corde ecclesiae* itself affirms a full respect for freedom of conscience.[138]

iii.) The Rights of Those under Scrutiny

The canons recognize, in penal proceedings, the rights of the accused to be provided with counsel, the right to speak or write last, and the right not to be required to take an oath or to confess.[139] The procedure to deny or withdraw a *mandatum* is technically not penal in nature; that is, its purpose is not to impose a canonical penalty. However, since its outcome could result in a serious sanction, similar safeguards must be insisted upon and provided.

iv.) Publications

Writings, that is, published books and articles, are the normal objects of doctrinal investigations.[140] Other forms of communication that are publicly distributed, e.g., audio or video recordings offered for sale, could also be included. However, classroom teaching, lectures, conferences, seminars, discussions, dialogues, and the like, are not subject to scrutiny. Consequently, class notes or outlines provided for the private use of students ("ad usum privatum"), as well as notes taken by students or by others, are also excluded.

c.) Definitions

i.) "The theologian" refers to an individual Catholic theologian teaching at a Catholic college or university who either is requesting a *mandatum* from the bishop or whose *mandatum* is under consideration for withdrawal by the bishop.

ii.) "The bishop" means the bishop of the diocese in which is located the main campus of the Catholic college or university at which the theologian teaches.[141]

iii.) The "objectionable text" refers to one or more particular passages from the theologian's written work or from a public presentation by the theologian offered for public distribution through audio or video recordings. The granting or withdrawing of a *mandatum* "does not concern the person of the theologian but the intellectual positions which he has publicly espoused."[142]

iv.) "The consonance of the theologian's position with the Catholic tradition" refers to a multi-faceted judgment based on a view of both the objectionable text and the Catholic tradition. The objectionable text must be assessed at three levels: its meaning and context in the theologian's broader work, its consonance with the Catholic tradition, and its implications for the life of the church. The Catholic tradition includes the whole range of church teachings, based in the Scriptures and received in the church over the centuries. The magisterium serves the word of God, with the help of the Holy Spirit, by proposing doctrines at various levels of teaching authority. Great care must be taken concerning

> the historical context and development of church teaching, an understanding of the hierarchy of truths, an evaluation of the various levels of teaching authority, an appreciation of the distinction between the substance of the faith and its expression, and the degree to which the church has committed itself in this matter.[143]

v.) "The Committee on Doctrine" refers to the National Conference on Catholic Bishops' Committee on Doctrine.

vi.) "The slate of available experts" refers to a listing of theologians of national repute available for consultation when a bishop considers withholding or withdrawing a *mandatum*. The Committee on Doctrine develops the slate of theological experts after soliciting nominations of appropriate persons from Catholic colleges and universities and Catholic professional theological societies. Any individual named to the slate should hold an appointment at a Catholic college or university and should be fully in accord with the faith of the church. Individual theologians should serve on the slate for a fixed term. The slate of names should be publicly available.

vii.) "The panel of experts" refers to a two person panel composed of theologians from the slate of available experts invited to serve in the investigation by the Committee on Doctrine when an individual bishop is considering withholding or withdrawing a *mandatum*.

viii.) "The appeal panel" is a panel of two bishops from the Committee on Doctrine and one theologian appointed from the slate of experts. This panel is called upon to evaluate the record and make a recommendation to the Committee on Doctrine concerning the theologian's appeal of the bishop's decision.

D.) PRESUMPTIONS

i.) The foundation of faith and theology, Jesus Christ, taught his disciples: "By this all men will know that you are my disciples, if you love one another" (John 13:35). As the Congregation for the Doctrine of the Faith has advised, "If it happens that they [theologians] encounter difficulties due to the character of their research, they should seek their solution in trustful dialogue with the Pastors, in the spirit of truth and charity which is that of the communion of the Church."[144] In all matters related to the *mandatum,* the bonds of charity are paramount and mutual respect must be maintained.

ii.) The presumption is that a baptized Catholic who holds an appointment in the theological disciplines at a Catholic college or university teaches in communion with the Church.[145] The ordinary procedure for requesting a *mandatum* (a simple letter from the theologian to the bishop) acknowledges this presumption. In further recognition of this presumption, any decision by a bishop to withhold a *mandatum* or to withdraw one already issued is a serious matter and should be preceded by a process of consultation and investigation.

iii.) If a problem does develop concerning the consonance of the theologian's position with the Catholic tradition, a bishop will ordinarily hear about this problem through complaints from third parties. Although such reports may be true, it is common experience that many such complaints are based on incomplete information or misinterpretation. In light of their obligations,[146] bishops should insist on accountability from complainants: complaints must be in writing, must specify particular texts, and must explain why these are objectionable. When controversy is involved, particularly if the complainant has a history in the controversy, great care is needed.

iv.) The bishop and theologian must take great care in communicating with each other during both informal and formal attempts to resolve their differences. Timelines indicated in the procedures proposed below are intended to foster deliberate but steady progress on the issue. Any theologian involved in this process should make clear to the bishop the most appropriate means of contact for the coming months, particularly if the theologian anticipates an absence from the diocese. Written communication during this process should be delivered by a service that provides a confirmation of receipt by the other party.

v.) Sides "harden" in the light of public attention, so standards of confidentiality should be developed by mutual agreement.

vi.) Any procedures specified as normative for the granting or withdrawing of a *mandatum* may be altered by the mutual consent of the bishop and the theologian.

e.) Step One: Informal Resolution

i.) If, in the context of granting or withdrawing of a *mandatum,* a bishop has weighty evidence calling into question the consonance of the theologian's position with the Catholic tradition, he should first attempt to resolve the apparent differences informally. Whenever possible, this should occur through a meeting between the bishop and the theologian.[147] If the matter remains unresolved, the bishop should send to the theologian a written statement of his concerns.

ii.) The statement of concerns from the bishop should articulate the meaning of the objectionable text as the bishop sees it, its departure from the Catholic tradition, and its implications for the pastoral life of the Church. All three of these elements are essential to the judgment. Included in this document should be explicit reference to particular objectionable texts. General dissatisfaction is insufficient.

iii.) Once the written statement of concerns is issued, a copy of the complete record must be provided to the theologian. This includes access to any complaints that came from third parties.

iv.) Once the theologian has received the statement of concerns from the bishop, a written response is made, clarifying the meaning of the text, its relation to the Catholic tradition, and its implications for the life of the Church. This response is to be sent to the bishop within three months.

v.) It is possible that this exchange of statements will clarify the issue and answer the bishop's concerns. If, however, the bishop still has serious concerns regarding the granting or withdrawing of the *mandatum*, a meeting between the bishop and theologian should occur. The bishop, at his discretion, may be assisted by others, and the theologian will have the option of bringing an advisor. In some situations, the use of a mutually agreed upon facilitator, theologically astute though perhaps not an expert, can assist in the process. More than one meeting is possible.

vi.) At this point the process for informal resolution ends. If the bishop's concerns are resolved, he proceeds to grant a *mandatum* or declines to withdraw a *mandatum.* If serious concerns remain for the bishop, he moves forward to the process of formal resolution below.

F.) STEP TWO: FORMAL RESOLUTION

i.) If the process of informal resolution of differences between the bishop and the theologian has not allayed the concerns of the bishop, he proceeds to a formal process of resolution through a written request to the NCCB Committee on Doctrine to form a panel of experts to investigate. In a written statement, the bishop identifies his concerns with the theologian's work. A copy of the full record, including all documentation and correspondence between the bishop and the theologian should accompany the statement. Simultaneously, the bishop sends a copy of his letter to the Committee on Doctrine to the theologian, along with anything else sent to the committee that the theologian has not had access to. The theologian may, within thirty days of receipt of the materials and access to the full record, send an additional written statement to the Committee.

ii.) Within two months of receiving the materials from the bishop, the Committee on Doctrine appoints a two-person panel of experts from the slate of experts the Committee keeps on hand. In making this appointment, the Committee will take into consideration the fields of expertise of the theologian under investigation and the fields of the available experts. If there are not appropriate theological experts available, the Committee will request names of suitable persons from the leadership of professional theological societies and will subsequently make an appointment of theological experts appropriate for the task at hand. To prevent an adversarial character for the inquiry, theological experts known to be in conflict with the theologian, either personally or academically, should not be appointed. Both the bishop and the theologian have the right to exclude one member of the panel, in which case the Committee will complete the panel from other available theologians on the slate of experts. The Committee will appoint one of the two experts as convener for the panel.

iii.) The panel of experts will receive from the Committee on Doctrine all the materials sent from the bishop. The panel reviews the record and the objectionable text and any other work of the theologian they think appropriate. The experts may communicate with the bishop and/or the theologian if they judge this appropriate. They are to clarify the meaning of the text, determine the relation to the Catholic tradition, and articulate the implications of the text for the life of the church. Within three months from the time of their appointment, the panel members will send a report on these matters to the bishop and the theologian. If the experts find inadequacies in the consonance of the theologian's position with the Catholic tradition, they should also include in their report recommendations as to what the theologian might do to address this issue. A copy of the report will be sent to the Committee on Doctrine.

iv.) Within thirty days of receipt of the report from the panel of experts, the bishop should write to the theologian. If his concerns are resolved, the bishop simply indicates this. If there is unambiguous evidence of a lack of consonance of the theologian's position with the Catholic tradition, the bishop articulates those concerns, identifies actions that the theologian might take to address them, and invites a final reaction by the theologian to the experts' report and the bishop's response to it. A meeting between the bishop and theologian (again with the option of an advisor present) to discuss the situation may be helpful. The theologian then has thirty days (either after receipt of the letter or the meeting, whichever is later) to respond in writing to the bishop.

v.) Within thirty days of receipt of the theologian's response, the bishop writes to the theologian indicating either that his concerns have been met or that he plans formally to decide to withhold or withdraw the *mandatum* at the end of the next thirty-day period. The bishop must include in this letter the reasons for his decision. The theologian then has this next thirty-day period to initiate an appeal process. If the bishop does not receive notice of appeal within that thirty-day period, he takes the action he planned and sends a final letter to the theologian announcing this.

g.) Step Three: Appeal Procedure

i.) In accord with the standards of due process, a theologian may appeal the announced plan of the bishop to withhold or withdraw a *mandatum* by means of a letter written to the Committee on Doctrine. The theologian makes clear the reasons for appeal and includes all relevant materials in the case. The theologian sends to the bishop a copy of this letter of appeal along with copies of all material submitted which the bishop does not already possess.

ii.) In the earlier stage of the procedure the Committee on Doctrine acted only as a facilitator in forming the panel of experts. At this point the Committee on Doctrine becomes actively involved in a decision on the merits of the case. To conduct its inquiry, the Committee on Doctrine appoints an appeal panel consisting of two bishops from the Committee on Doctrine and a theologian, chosen by the Committee from the slate of experts, who did not serve on the panel of experts and who was not excluded from the panel of experts by either the bishop or the theologian. It is the task of the appeal panel to review the complete record. If it has happened that one of the complaints of the theologian is that the bishop has held part of the record in secrecy, the committee should make a formal request through the Committee on Doctrine to the bishop for access to the complete record. At its discretion, the appeal panel may consult with the bishop, the theologian, or with the panel of experts earlier involved. The appeal panel sends a written report, including a recommendation, to the Committee on Doctrine, simultaneously sending a copy of their report to the bishop and the theologian.

The Committee on Doctrine receives the report of the appeal panel and makes a decision. If the Committee supports the bishop's decision, it will write to the bishop and the theologian announcing this, giving reasons for this judgment. It is at that point appropriate for the bishop to make his authoritative judgment concerning withholding or withdrawing a *mandatum,* announcing this to the theologian in writing. If the Committee on Doctrine concludes in the theologian's favor, it will issue a written formal recommendation to the bishop that he grant the *mandatum* or alter his plans for withdrawing it. This recommendation will include the reason for the Committee's judgment. A copy of this recommendation will be sent to the theologian. Within thirty days the bishop should respond in writing to the Committee on Doctrine indicating whether he has complied with the committee's recommendation.

NOTES

1. "*Ex corde ecclesiae*: An Application to the United States," *Origins,* vol. 29, no. 25, December 2, 1999. (Hereafter designated as *Application.*) The final version was approved on May 3, 2000 and announced on June 7, 2000. All references to the *Application* will be to the final version, *Origins,* vol. 30, no. 5, June 15, 2000.

2. *Application,* Introduction.

3. John Paul II, *Ex corde ecclesiae,* para. 1, *Origins,* vol. 20, no. 17, Oct. 4, 1990.

4. Ibid., para. 5.

5. *Application,* part 2, art. 2, para. 1.

6. For the classic 1940 "Statement of Principles on Academic Freedom and Tenure" endorsed by nearly every scholarly association in every discipline and by all organizations of colleges and universities, see *Policy, Documents, and Reports,* 1995 edition, American Association of University Professors, Washington DC, pp3 ff.

7. See James L. Heft, "Have Catholic Colleges Reached an Impasse?," *The Chronicle of Higher Education* (November 12, 1999): B6–B7; Alice Gallin, *Negotiating Identity: Catholic Higher Education since 1960* (Notre Dame: University of Notre Dame Press, 2000); idem, *Independence and a New Partnership in Catholic Higher Education* (Notre Dame: University of Notre Dame Press, 1996); idem (ed.), *American Catholic Higher Education: Essential Documents, 1967–1990* (Notre Dame, Indiana: University of Notre Dame Press, 1992).

8. *Gaudium et spes,* art. 36; cf. art. 41.

9. "Land O'Lakes Statement" (1967), in Gallin (ed.), *American Catholic Higher Education,* pp. 7 and 9.

10. "The Catholic University in the Modern World" (1973) in Gallin (ed.), *American Catholic Higher Education,* pp. 37–57, 43.

11. Ibid., p. 55.

12. "A Letter from Gabriel Marie Cardinal Garrone" (April 25, 1973), in Gallin (ed.), *American Catholic Higher Education,* pp. 59–61.

13. Congregation for Catholic Education, "Proposed Schema for a Pontifical Document on Catholic Universities" (April 15, 1985), in *Origins* 15 (April 10, 1986): 706–711.

14. "Catholic College and University Presidents Respond to Proposed Vatican Schema," in *Origins* 15 (April 10, 1986): 697, 699–704; Congregation for Catholic Education, "Summary of Responses to Draft Schema on Catholic Universities," *Origins* 17 (March 24, 1988): 695, 697–705.

15. *Cooperation Between Theologians and the Ecclesiastical Magisterium,* a Report of the Joint Committee of the Canon Law Society of America and the Catholic Theological Society of America, edited by Leo J. O'Donovan, S.J., 1982.

16. NCCB, "Doctrinal Responsibilities: Approaches to Promoting Cooperation and Resolving Misunderstandings Between Bishops and Theologians," *Origins,* vol. 19, no. 7, June 29, 1989.

17. Michael Buckley, et al., *Report of the Catholic Theological Society of America, Committee on the Profession of Faith and Oath of Fidelity,* April 15, 1990.

18. See, for example, M. Theresa Moser, RSCJ et al., "Preliminary Report of the CTS Committee on Profession of Faith/Oath of Fidelity," *Horizons: The Journal of the College Theology Society* (Spring 1990): 103–127.

19. See "ACCU Alternative Proposals: Ex corde ecclesiae," www.accunet.org; J. Donald Monan and Edward A. Malloy, "'Ex corde ecclesiae' Creates an Impasse," 181 *America* (January 30, 1999): 6–12.

20. John R. Quinn, *The Reform of the Papacy* (New York: Crossroad, 1999); See also Hermann J. Pottmeyer, "Primacy in Communion," *America* 182 (June 3–10, 2000): 15–18.

21. NCCB, "Doctrinal Responsibilities," p. 101.

22. Ibid.

23. Ibid., p. 100.

24. Ibid.

25. Ibid.

26. William Hill, OP, in *The New Dictionary of Theology* (ed. Komonchak, Collins, Lane), p. 1011.

27. *Application,* art. 4, 4, e, 2.

28. Hill, p. 1011.

29. *Ex corde ecclesiae,* I, 12; *"Application,"* VII and Norms, art. 4, 1.

30. *CIC,* c. 810.1.

31. CDF, "Instruction on the Ecclesial Vocation of the Theologian," para. 24, May 24, 1990, *Origins* 20:8 (July 5, 1990). On the hierarchy of truths, see J. Komonchak, M. Collins and D. Lane, eds., *The New Dictionary of Theology* (Wilmington: Michael Glazier, 1987) s.v. "Hierarchy of Truths" (William Henn, OFM.cap) 464–466.

32. From "On Heresy," in *Inquiries* (New York: Herder & Herder, 1964), p. 458. This position of Rahner's is cited in John P. Boyle, "The Rights and Responsibilities of Bishops:

A Theological Perspective," in Leo J. O'Donovan, S.J., *Cooperation Between Theologians and the Ecclesiastical Magisterium,* p. 26.

33. Wolfgang Seibel, S.J., "Besetzung theologischer Lehrstuehle," ["The Filling of Teaching Positions in Theology"] *Stimmen der Zeit* 218 (May 2000): 289–90. Translated by Robert A. Krieg, University of Notre Dame. Forthcoming in *America.*

34. NCCB, "Doctrinal Responsibilities."

35. *Ex corde ecclesiae,* para. 4.

36. *Application,* art. 4, 4, e, 1.

37. For a treatment of the hierarchy of truths, see section a, i. in the Appendix to this report.

38. *Application,* art. 4, 4, e, 2.

39. The *Application* asserts that "the *mandatum* is fundamentally an acknowledgment by Church authority that a Catholic professor of a theological discipline is a teacher within the full communion of the Catholic Church," art. 4, 4, e, 1.

40. *Ex corde ecclesiae,* 39.

41. NCCB, "Doctrinal Responsibilities," I, A.

42. See, for example, O'Donovan, *passim.*

43. Ibid., art. 4, 4, e, 2.

44. Alice Gallin, O.S.U., *Independence and a New Partnership in Catholic Higher Education* (Notre Dame, Indiana: University of Notre Dame Press, 1996) describes the evolution to government by lay Boards of Trustees.

45. In two major court challenges involving the constitutionality of federal and state grants to church-affiliated colleges and universities, the Supreme Court distinguished between the primarily secular mission of the colleges and universities and the proselytizing mission of elementary and secondary schools. To qualify for federal aid, the colleges and universities have to meet the following criteria: "persons other than Catholics are admitted to the student body and faculty; attendance at religious services is not required; the institutions do not proselytize; the college adheres to the principle of academic freedom." Charles Curran, *Catholic Higher Education, Authority and Academic Freedom* (Notre Dame: University of Notre Dame Press, 1990), p. 113. And Philip Burling and Gregory T. Moffat, "Notes from the Other Side of the Wall," in *Catholic Universities in Church and Society: A Dialogue on Ex corde ecclesiae,* Ed. John Langan, Foreword by Leo O'Donovan, S.J. (Washington, D.C.: Georgetown University Press, 1993): 172–73. n. 33.

46. Cf. Paul Saunders, "A Cautionary Tale: Academic Freedom, 'Ex Corde,' & the Curran Case," *Commonweal* (April 21, 2000): 12–16.

47. Alice Gallin, Ed., "Relations of American Colleges and Universities with the Church: Position Paper of the College and University Department, National Catholic Educational Association," in *American Catholic Higher Education: Essential Documents 1967–1990* (Notre Dame: University of Notre Dame Press, 1992): 71–86 and at 83.

48. Alice Gallin, O.S.U., *Negotiating Identity: Catholic Higher Education since 1960* (Notre Dame: University of Notre Dame Press, 2000) explains the developments within Catholic higher education regarding institutional autonomy, academic freedom, and Catholic identity. See also Richard P. McBrien, "Why I Shall Not Seek a Mandate," *America* (February 12, 2000):14.

49. Quinn, especially pp. 169–170.

50. Beth McMurtrie, "Vatican Backs Rules for Catholic Colleges That Spur Concerns About Academic Freedom," *The Chronicle of Higher Education* (June 16, 2000): A18; and

American Association of University Professors, "AAUP Annual Meeting Urges American Catholic Bishops to Preserve Academic Freedom when Implementing Ex corde ecclesiae," Press Release, June 13, 2000, at http://www.aaup.org. The text of the Resolution is as follows: "The American Association of University Professors' 1999 Annual Meeting commended the Association of Catholic Colleges and Universities, the Association of Jesuit Colleges and Universities, the Catholic Theological Society of America, the College Theology Society and the Catholic Biblical Association for their efforts to produce alternative proposals for the implementation of the Apostolic Constitution, *Ex corde ecclesiae,* in the United States. The Association's Committee A on Academic Freedom and Tenure, at its November 7, 1999 meeting, expressed 'its deep concern and substantial reservations' about the draft implementation document for *Ex corde ecclesiae* then shortly to be considered by the National Conference of Catholic Bishops. The committee urged the bishops to defer a final decision. The Conference of Bishops approved the proposed implementation document on November 17, 1999 and submitted it to the Congregation for Catholic Education for approval. The approval, which was given in May, was made public on June 7, 2000. The implementation norms take effect in one year. In light of the above, the Eighty-sixth Annual Meeting of the American Association of University Professors urges the American Catholic bishops and other appropriate church authorities to engage in substantive discussions directly with the faculty and administrations of the Catholic colleges and universities in their dioceses concerning the implementation of *Ex corde ecclesiae* and its implications for academic freedom and institutional autonomy. This Annual Meeting further calls upon the academic community to scrutinize the actions taken to implement *Ex corde ecclesiae* to make certain that they are consistent with the basic principles upon which higher education in this country rests."

51. Examples include: Archbishop John R. Quinn, *The Exercise of the Primacy: Continuing the Dialogue,* Ut Unum Sint: Studies on the Papal Primacy, Edited by Phyllis Zagano and Terrence W. Tilley (New York: Crossroad, 1998); Michael J. Buckley, S.J., *Papal Primacy and the Episcopate: Towards a Relational Understanding,* Ut Unum Sint: Studies on the Papal Primacy (New York: Crossroad, 1998); Hermann J. Pottmeyer, *Towards a Papacy in Communion: Perspectives From Vatican Council I & II,* Translated by Michael J. O'Connell (New York: Crossroad, 1998); and William Henn, OFM Cap, *The Honor of My Brothers: A Brief History of the Relationship Between the Pope and the Bishops,* Ut Unum Sint: Studies on Papal Primacy (New York: Crossroad, 2000).

52. "The CTSA and the Proposed Schema on Catholic Universities," in *Proceedings of the Forty-First Annual Convention* 41, 1986, p. 206

53. Seibel, "Besetzung theologischer Lehrstuehle."

54. NCCB, "Doctrinal Responsibilities."

55. For treatments of reception, see Yves Congar, "Reception as an Ecclesiological Reality," *Concilium,* 77 (1972) 43–68; Geoffrey King, "The Acceptance of Law by the Community: A Study in the Writings of Canonists and Theologians," *Jurist* 37 (1977) 233–265; James Coriden, "The Canonical Doctrine of Reception," *Jurist* 50 (1990) 58–82; John Huels, "Nonreception of Canon Law by the Community," *New Theology Review,* 4 (1991) 47–61; Ladislas Örsy, "The Reception of Laws by the People of God: A Theological and Canonical Inquiry in the Light of Vatican Council II," *Jurist* 55 (1995) 504–526.

56. 1983 *Code,* canon 812. For a detailed commentary see Sharon A. Euart in *New Commentary on the Code of Canon Law,* ed. John P. Beal et al. (New York/Mahwah, NJ: Paulist Press, 2000), pp. 966–971.

57. *Application,* art. 4, 4, e, 1. The concept of "communio" has received considerable attention in recent years. See John Paul II, apostolic exhortation *Christifideles laici,* December 30, 1988, n. 19: *AAS* 81 (1989) 422–425; Congregation for the Doctrine of the Faith, "Letter to the Bishops of the Catholic Church on Some Aspects of the Church Understood as Communion," May 28, 1992: *Origins* 22 (June 15, 1992) 108–112; Pontifical Council for Promoting Christian Unity, *Directory for the Application of Principles and Norms on Ecumenism,* March 25, 1993, nn. 13–17. See also Jean M.-R. Tillard, *Church of Churches: The Ecclesiology of Communion* (Collegeville, MN: Liturgical Press, 1992); Joseph A. Komonchak, "Concepts of Communion. Past and Present," *Cristianesimo nella storia* 16 (1995) 321–340; Robert J. Kaslyn, *"Communion with the Church" and the Code of Canon Law* (Lewiston: Edwin Mellen Press, 1994); Severino Dianich, *La Chiesa mistero di comunione,* 7th ed. (Genoa: Marietti, 1990); James H. Provost, ed., *The Church as Communion* (Washington: CLSA, 1984).

58. *LG,* 23.

59. *LG,* 8.

60. *UR,* 3.

61. *LG,* 14.

62. Acts 15:28; see *UR,* 18.

63. See Robert J. Kaslyn in *New Commentary on the Code of Canon Law,* ed. John P. Beal et al. (New York/Mahwah, NJ: Paulist Press, 2000) p. 248.

64. See CDF, Instruction on the Ecclesial Vocation of the Theologian, May 24, 1990, para. 28–38. On the hierarchy of truths, see J. Komonchak, M. Collins and D. Lane, eds., *The New Dictionary of Theology* (Wilmington: Michael Glazier, 1987) s.v. "Hierarchy of Truths" (William Henn, OFM.cap) 464–466.

65. See *Application:* "The *mandatum* is fundamentally an acknowledgment by church authority that a Catholic professor of a theological discipline is a teacher within the full communion of the Catholic church" (art. 4, 4, e, 1); "'*Mandatum*' is a technical term referring to the juridical expression of the ecclesial relationship of communion that exists between the church and the Catholic teacher of a theological discipline in the Catholic university" (note 41); "The *mandatum* is essentially the recognition of an ecclesial relationship between the professor and the church (*See* canon 229, §3)" (note 41).

66. Observing canon 209: "§1. The Christian faithful, even in their own manner of acting, are always obliged to maintain communion with the church. §2. With great diligence they are to fulfill the duties which they owe to the universal church and the particular church to which they belong according to the prescripts of the law."

67. See especially canon 212: "§1. Conscious of their own responsibility, the Christian faithful are bound to follow with Christian obedience those things which the sacred pastors, inasmuch as they represent Christ, declare as teachers of the faith or establish as rulers of the church. §2. The Christian faithful are free to make known to the pastors of the church their needs, especially spiritual ones, and their desires. §3. According to the knowledge, competence, and prestige which they possess, they have the right and even at times the duty to manifest to the sacred pastors their opinion on matters which pertain to the good of the church and to make their opinion known to the rest of the Christian faithful, without prejudice to the integrity of faith and morals, with reverence toward their pastors, and attentive to common advantage and the dignity of persons."

68. See canon 218: "Those engaged in the sacred disciplines have a just freedom of inquiry and of expressing their opinion prudently on those matters in which they pos-

sess expertise, while observing the *obsequium* due to the magisterium of the church." See also the bishop's obligation to respect this freedom in canon 386 §2: "Through more suitable means, he is firmly to protect the integrity and unity of the faith to be believed, while nonetheless acknowledging a just freedom in further investigating its truths."

69. *Application,* art. 4, 4, e, 3.

70. Ibid., art. 4, 4, e, 2.

71. Ibid., art. 4, 4, e, 2. This is further emphasized in note 41: "Those with such a *mandatum* are not agents of the magisterium; they teach in their own name, not in the name of the bishop."

72. Ibid., note 41.

73. Ibid., note 42.

74. Ibid., art. 4, 4, e, 1.

75. Euart, 969.

76. Ibid.; also see *Ex corde ecclesiae,* General Norms. art. 4, §3.

77. The *Application,* note 41, makes this clear: "It is not the responsibility of a Catholic university to seek the *mandatum;* this is a personal obligation of each professor" note 41.

78. *Application,* art. 4, 4, d.

79. This distinction is parallel to one made in the *Ordinationes* for *Sapientia Christiana:* Between those who are "ordinary" members of the faculty, namely those who are "stabiliter adscripti, pleno ac firmo jure cooptati sunt," and "extraordinary" faculty, and others who can be usefully employed (art. 16, i). Congregation for Catholic Education, "Ordinationes ad Constitutionem Apostolicam 'Sapientia christiana'" (Normae speciales), art. 51, April 29, 1979: *AAS* 71 (1979) 513; English translation in John Paul II, *On Ecclesiastical Universities and Faculties,* April 15, 1979 (Washington: USCC, 1979).

80. See "Relatio Complectens Synthesim Animadversionum ab Em.mis atque Exc.mis Patribus Commissionis ad Novissimum Schema Codicis Iuris Canonici Exhibitarum, cum Responsionibus a Secretaria et Consultoribus Datis," *Communicationes* 15 (1983) 104–105.

81. *Ordinationes* for *Sapientia Christiana,* 69–70.

82. Euart, 970, comments: "Program of study focusing on pastoral ministry, methodology of religious education, comparative religion, and history and sociology of religion, for example, would seem not to be considered 'theological disciplines' in the strict sense and, therefore, would be beyond the scope of canon 812."

83. *CIC,* c. 9.

84. Some might contend that the obligation actually began with canon 812 of the 1983 *Code* and hence obliges those hired after November 27, 1983. However, that is not the case. The *mandatum* requirement of canon 812 never went into effect in the United States. It was never observed, never urged, and never even made available, for a period of over seventeen years. This respectful non-observance, on the part of American bishops as well as theologians, is a classic example of the operation of the canonical principle of reception. (Consult the sources in note 55 above.) The canon's legitimate non-reception by the community caused it to lose obligatory force. The requirement of the *mandatum* is now being urged as a new obligation, it will be a new burden under a new formality, namely that of *Application* (part II, art. 4, 4, e).

85. *Application,* art. 4, 4, e, 4, a.

86. See canon 50.

87. *Application,* art. 4, 4, e, 4.

88. Ibid., note 44.

89. *LG,* 12; confer *CIC,* cc. 204.1 and 747.

90. *LG,* 12; 1 Cor 12, 7.

91. *AA,* 3.

92. *DH,* 1–3; *CIC,* c. 748.

93. *LG,* 37; *CIC,* 212.2 & 3. The canon explicitly recognizes "the knowledge, competence, and prestige which they (the Christian faithful) possess."

94. *CIC,* c. 218; *CCEO,* 21; see *GE,* 10 and *GS,* 59.

95. The apostolic constitution *Ex corde ecclesiae* explicitly acknowledges freedom in research and teaching in Catholic universities. It bases its assertion on *GS,* 57 & 59 and on *GE,* 10. (General Norms, art. 2.5; *Origins* 274.)

96. *CIC,* cc. 218, 229, 253, 812, and 883 are instances.

97. This understanding of the theologian's role is affirmed in the *Application,* art. 4, 4, d, 2.

98. *Application,* art. 4, 4, e, 2.

99. Ibid.

100. *CIC,* cc. 124–128, e.g., acts placed by persons with authority, observing requisite formalities, not acting out of force or fear, not acting out of ignorance or error, consulting those who must be consulted, liable for damage inflicted.

101. *CIC,* cc. 48–58, e.g., a decision made after information and evidence has been gathered, and after having heard interested parties, the decision given in writing, with supporting reasons, that obliges only the one for whom it is given, etc.

102. Ladislas Örsy, SJ, *The Church: Learning and Teaching* (Wilmington, Delaware: Michael Glazier, 1987), p. 65.

103. *GS,* 59.

104. *Dei verbum,* 8–10.

105. *LG,* 25.

106. CDF, "Ecclesial Vocation."

107. *Application,* art. 4, 4, e, b.

108. *Ex corde ecclesiae,* no. 5.

109. Ibid., no. 4.

110. *Application,* note 42.

111. The process of granting, denying, or withdrawing a *mandatum* is not the place to deal with issues of "probity of life" (*CIC,* 810), "witness . . . of authentic Christian life" (*ECE,* 22) or "good character" (*Application,* 4, 4, b), as important as these personal and moral concerns are. The statutes of the institution on impermissible activities (e.g., sexual harassment), as well as federal, state, and local criminal statutes must be applied where serious moral failure or criminal activity is alleged. The *mandatum* is an acknowledgement that a Catholic professor is a teacher within the full communion of the Catholic Church. It is not a certification of moral virtue or good conduct. The judgment about the *mandatum* relates to being and teaching within the Catholic communion, not to moral worthiness.

112. *UR,* 11.

113. Richard R. Gaillardetz, *Teaching with Authority: A Theology of the Magisterium in the Church* (Collegeville: The Liturgical Press, 1997) 115–116. The Marian dogmas would be an example of confirmatory dogmas: the doctrine of the immaculate conception of Mary, confirming the nature of Christ's saving work, and the doc-

trine of the bodily assumption of Mary confirming the promise of the integral bodily resurrection of all. The infallibility of the Pope is confirmatory of the indefectibility of the Church.

114. As Margaret O'Gara puts it, there is a distinction in Roman Catholic teaching in what is central to the faith and what is less central. Not everything is of the same importance: "Statues of Mary, the divinity of Christ, the discipline of obligatory celibacy for clergy in the West, the existence of God, the teaching against abortion, the small vigil candles in some churches, the teaching against artificial contraception, the injunction against idolatry, the refusal to ordain women, the doctrine of the Trinity: all of these have their place in present Roman Catholic life, but they do not all have the same weight of authority.... Creeping infallibility tends to collapse all of these together and surround them with the aura of equal authority." "Shifts below the Surface of the Debate: Ecumenism, Dissent and the Roman Catholic Church," *Jurist* 56 (1996): 386–87.

115. *CIC*, cc. 205; 750.1.

116. *LG*, 25.

117. *Report of the Catholic Theological Society of America, Committee on the Profession of Faith and Oath of Fidelity,* April 15, 1990, pp. 74–92.

118. See the apostolic letter, "On Reserving Priestly Ordination to Men Alone" (1994) that declared that the judgment that the Church has no authority to ordain women to the priesthood "must be definitively held by all the Church's faithful." The letter did not claim infallible authority for this teaching. The Congregation for the Doctrine of the Faith only later claimed such authority for this teaching according to the universal ordinary magisterium in its reply to the *dubium* in 1995.

119. *Ad tuendam fidem* (May 18, 1998), 4, A. See *Origins* 28.8 (July 16, 1998), 115.

120. However, Francis Sullivan has shown the intricacies of interpreting conciliar statements in *Creative Fidelity: Weighing and Interpreting Documents of the Magisterium* (New York: Paulist Press, 1996).

121. The Pontifical Council for the Family, "Vademecum for Confessors Concerning Some Aspects of the Morality of Conjugal Life" (February 17, 1997). There it declared that "the intrinsic evil of contraception, that is, of every marital act intentionally rendered unfruitful," is a teaching "to be held as definitive and irreformable" (2.4).

122. Michael Buckley et al., Report of the Catholic Theological Society of America on the Profession of Faith and the Oath of Fidelity, April 15, 1990.

123. "Die zentrale und entscheidende Frage dieser Debatte, wie sie von vielen Theologen wahrgenommen wird, ist diese: Bedeutet die Einfuehrung der Kategorie 'endgueltige Lehre' eine Ausdehnung der Lehre der papstlichen Unfehlbarkeit?" Ladislas Orsy, "Antwort an Kardinal Ratzinger," *Stimmen der Zeit* 217.5 (May 1999), 306. See also his essay "Von der Autoritaet kirchlicher Dokumente," *Stimmen der Zeit* 216.11 (November 1998), 735–740, as well as Joseph Cardinal Ratzinger, "Stellungnahme," *Stimmen der Zeit* 217.3 (March 1999), 169–171.

124. For instance, church historians should not be asked about the morality of in vitro fertilization.

125. *GS*, 44, 62; *UR*, 4. The conciliar theme of legitimate theological inculturation has been developed by Paul VI in the apostolic constitution *Evangelii nuntiandi* (December 8, 1975, n. 63; *AAS* 68 [1976]: 53–54) and John Paul II in the encyclical *Redemptoris missio* (December 7, 1990; *AAS* 83 [1991]: 299–301).

Unique formulations of non-defined doctrines must not be insisted upon or imposed as "personal professions of faith," e.g., "homosexual acts are intrinsically disordered." Clear and unambiguous expressions of equivalent meaning are acceptable.

126. Private dissent is anticipated and countenanced in the CDF's "Instruction of the Ecclesial Vocation of the Theologian," May 24, 1990, no. 24; (*Origins* 20:8 [July 5, 1990]: 123).

127. Ibid., no. 25.

128. Ibid., nos. 28 & 31.

129. Ibid., no. 27.

130. Ibid., nos. 30 & 32.

131. *UR*, 4; *DH*, 14.

132. *CIC*, c. 220; *GS*, 26.

133. CDF, "Ecclesial Vocation," no. 37; (*Origins*, 125).

134. *GS*, 16; *DH*, 2. Confer Joseph Ratzinger's use of Newman on obedience to conscience before all else "if necessary even against the requirement of ecclesiastical authority" in commenting on the *GS* text, H. Vorgrimler (ed.), *Commentary on the Documents of Vatican II* (New York: Herder and Herder, 1969) v. 5, 134.

Bernard Häring's teaching on "The Magisterium and the Inviolability of Conscience" has been described in these terms: ". . . personal conscience and its exercise are inviolable. Although never guaranteed to be correct, conscience itself, as the inner heart of a person where God reveals the truth of all things, is never to be hindered or coerced." Robert J. Smith, *Conscience and Catholicism: The Nature and Function of Conscience in Contemporary Roman Catholic Moral Theology* (Lanham, MD: University Press of America, 1998), p. 93.

135. Bernard Häring, *Faith and Morality in the Secular Age* (Garden City, NY: Doubleday, 1973), p. 129.

136. *CIC*, c. 630.5.

137. É. Jombart, "Manifestation de Conscience," *Dictionnaire de Droit Canonique*, VI (Paris: Letouzey et Ané, 1957) 719–723.

138. General Norms, 2.4 (*Origins*, 274).

139. *CIC*, cc. 1723, 1728.2, 1725.

140. *CIC*, c. 824.2 includes "any writings whatsoever which are destined for public distribution" when it treats of books requiring prior approval. Congregation for the Doctrine of the Faith, "Regulations for Doctrinal Examination" (June 29, 1997; *Origins* 27:13 [Sept. 11, 1997] 221–222) speak of "writing and opinions" (art. 1) and "writings or teachings, in whatever way they are disseminated" (art. 3). In practice the CDF does not judge private communications, but only those publicly disseminated. The Congregation's "Ecclesial Vocation" limits the magisterium's judgment to "intellectual positions . . . publicly espoused" (no. 37; *Origins*, 125).

141. *Application*, art. 4, 4, e, 4, a.

142. CDF, "Ecclesial Vocation," para. 37.

143. NCCB, "Doctrinal Responsibilities," pp. 107–108.

144. CDF, "Ecclesial Vocation," para. 40.

145. NCCB, "Doctrinal Responsibilities," p. 105.

146. *Application*, art. 2, 3.

147. NCCB, "Doctrinal Responsibilities," p. 105.

44 | Guidelines Concerning the Academic *Mandatum* in Catholic Universities (Canon 812)

NCCB, 2001

PREFACE

On Nov. 17, 1999, the Catholic bishops of the United States approved "The Application of *Ex Corde Ecclesiae* for the United States," implementing the apostolic constitution *Ex Corde Ecclesiae*. This action received the *recognitio* from the Congregation for Bishops on May 3, 2000. Bishop Joseph A. Fiorenza, president of the National Conference of Catholic Bishops, decreed that the application would have the force of particular law for the United States on May 3, 2001.

GUIDELINES

Pope John Paul II's constitution *Ex Corde Ecclesiae* of 1990 fostered a productive dialogue between the bishops of the United States and the leaders of Catholic colleges and universities. It is anticipated that this recently approved "Application of *Ex Corde Ecclesiae* for the United States" will further that conversation and build a community of trust and dialogue between bishops and theologians. Without ongoing and respectful communication, the implementation of the *mandatum* might appear to be only a juridical constriction of the work of theologians. Both bishops and theologians are engaged in a necessary though complementary service to the church that requires ongoing and mutually respectful dialogue.

From *Origins* 31, no. 7 (June 28, 2001): 128–130.

Article 4, 4, e, iv, of the application states that "a detailed procedure will be developed outlining the process of requesting and granting (or withdrawing) the *mandatum*." These guidelines are intended to explain and serve as a resource for the conferral of the *mandatum*. Only those guidelines herein that repeat a norm of the application have the force of particular law. They were accepted for distribution to the members of the NCCB on June 15, 2001, by the conference's general membership.

1. Nature of the *mandatum*.

a. The *mandatum* is fundamentally an acknowledgment by church authority that a Catholic professor of a theological discipline is teaching within the full communion of the Catholic Church (Application: Article 4, 4, e, iii).

b. The object of the *mandatum* is the content of the professor's teaching, and thus the *mandatum* recognizes both the professor's "lawful freedom of inquiry" (Application: Article 2.2) and the professor's commitment and responsibility to teach authentic Catholic doctrine and to refrain from putting forth as Catholic teaching anything contrary to the church's magisterium (cf. Application: Article 4, 4, e, iii).

c. The *mandatum* should not be construed as an appointment, authorization, delegation or approbation of one's teaching by church authorities. Theologians who have received a *mandatum* are not catechists; they teach in their own name in virtue of their baptism and their academic and professional competence, not in the name of the bishop or of the church's magisterium (Application: Article 4, 4, e, ii).

2. Who is required to have the *mandatum*?

a. All Catholics who teach Catholic theological disciplines in a Catholic university are required to have a *mandatum* (Canon 812 and Application: Article 4, 4, e).

b. In accord with Canon 812, the *mandatum* is an obligation of the professor, not of the university.

c. *Teaching* in this context signifies regular presentation (by full-time or part-time professors) of academic material in an academic institution. Occasional lectures as well as preaching and counseling are not within the meaning of the application and these guidelines.

d. *Catholic theological disciplines* in this context signifies sacred Scripture, dogmatic theology, moral theology, pastoral theology, canon law, liturgy and church history (cf. Canon 252).

e. *University* in this context signifies not only institutions that bear the title *university* but also Catholic colleges and other institutions of higher learning.

3. Who is to grant the *mandatum*?

a. The *mandatum* is to be granted by the diocesan bishop of the diocese in which the Catholic university is located, generally understood to be where the president and central administration offices are located (cf. Application: Article 4, 4, e, iv, [1]).

b. The competent ecclesiastical authority may grant the *mandatum* personally or through a delegate (Application: Article 4, 4, e, iv, [1]).

4. How is the *mandatum* to be granted?

a. A request for a *mandatum* by a professor of a Catholic theological discipline should be in writing and should include a declaration that the teacher will teach in full communion with the church.

b. The ecclesiastical authority should respond in writing (Application: Article 4, 4, e, iv, [3]) (see Appendix for samples).

c. An ecclesiastical authority has the right to offer the *mandatum* on his own initiative (which requires an acceptance), provided that the commitment to teach in full communion with the church is clear.

d. A professor already hired by the effective date (May 3, 2001) of the application is required to obtain the *mandatum* by June 1, 2002.

A professor hired after the effective date of the application is required to obtain the *mandatum* within the academic year or within six months of the date of being hired, whichever is longer.

If the professor does not obtain the *mandatum* within the time period given above, the competent ecclesiastical authority should notify the appropriate authority in the college or university.

e. Without prejudice to the rights of the diocesan bishop, a *mandatum*, once granted, remains in effect wherever and as long as the professor teaches unless and until it is withdrawn by the competent ecclesiastical authority (Application: Article 4, 4, e, iv, [2]). Although there is no need for the *mandatum*, once granted, to be granted again by another diocesan bishop, every diocesan bishop has the right to require otherwise in his own diocese (Application: Footnote 43).

f. If the bishop is contemplating the denial or withdrawal of the *mandatum*, he should discuss this informally with the theologian, listing the reasons and identifying the sources, and allowing the theologian to make all appropriate responses.

5. Grounds and process for withholding or withdrawing the *mandatum.*

a. If all the conditions for granting the *mandatum* are fulfilled, the professor has the right to receive it, and ecclesiastical authority has an obligation in justice to grant it.

b. Right intentions and right conduct are to be presumed until the contrary is proven. Hence the ecclesiastical authority should presume, until the contrary is proven, that those who attest that they teach in full communion with the church actually do so.

c. Ecclesiastical authorities who, after discussion with the professor in question, withhold or withdraw the *mandatum* must state their reasons in writing and otherwise enable the person who believes that his or her rights have been violated to seek recourse (Application: Article 4, 4, e, [3]; Footnote 44). Such withholding or withdrawal should be based on specific and detailed evidence that the teacher does not fulfill the conditions of the *mandatum* (these guidelines: 1, b, and c, *supra;* Application: Article 4, 4, e, iii; NCCB, "Doctrinal Responsibilities: Approaches to Promoting Cooperation and Resolving Misunderstandings Between Bishops and Theologians" [Washington, D.C.: USCC, 1989], III, C, 4).

d. Any negative judgment concerning an objectionable portion of a professor's work should be assessed at three levels: (1) the significance of that portion of the professor's work within the context of his or her overall theological contribution; (2) its relationship to the larger Catholic tradition; (3) its implications for the life of the church (cf. "Doctrinal Responsibilities," III, C, 4).

6. Appeals and resolution of disputes.

a. Because the decision to withhold or withdraw the *mandatum* touches on the rights of theologians, the general principles of canon law should be adhered to in seeking recourse and in the process of appeal.

b. In the resolution of disputes about the withholding or withdrawal of the *mandatum,* it is important for both parties to have competent canonical and theological counsel.

c. For the resolution of disputes about the withholding or withdrawal of the *mandatum,* there should be that contact between the bishop and the professor as urged in Canon 1733 §1. The process set forth in "Doctrinal Responsibilities" should be followed. The right of all parties to good reputation must always be honored (cf. Canon 220).

d. Other means for conflict resolution on the diocesan, regional or provincial levels (not excluding local mediation procedures) can also be invoked (cf. Canon 1733).

e. While the use of informal procedures is preferable, the aggrieved party always has the right to formal recourse against the denial or withdrawal of a *mandatum* in accordance with the canonical norms for "Recourse Against Administrative Decrees" (Canons 1732–1739).

7. Diocesan bishops who have Catholic colleges or universities in their dioceses are encouraged to be available to meet with professors of Catholic theological disciplines to review concrete procedures for the granting, withholding or withdrawal of the *mandatum* and to discuss other matters of common interest.

8. The members of the NCCB Committee of Bishops and Catholic Colleges and Universities Presidents and its staff will serve as resource personnel for information and guidance on matters connected with the *mandatum*.

9. These guidelines are to be reviewed after five years by a committee appointed by the conference president.

Epilogue

In describing the reception and implementation of *Ex Corde Ecclesiae,* I have focused on the work of the bishops, especially the Implementation Committee, and the documents they examined and developed during a ten-year period from 1990 to 2000. They had the task of applying the apostolic letter, including its norms, to the Catholic colleges and universities in the United States. Their work culminated in the Application of November 1999 and the subsequent *recognitio* granted in 2000. Finally, the bishops approved the "Guidelines Concerning the Academic Mandatum" in 2001.

During the same decade, the Catholic higher education community as a whole also demonstrated a renewed interest in the Catholic intellectual tradition and in ways of making their Catholic character more visible. Although its leaders were spurred on by the message of John Paul II, there were additional reasons for this increased attention to the specifically "Catholic" mission of their institutions. They shared some of these reasons with other church-related colleges and universities in the United States, which were also struggling to maintain their religious identity and emphasize their unique contributions to American higher education. A conference held at the Kennedy School of Government of Harvard University in October 2000 on the theme "The Future of Religious Colleges," for example, included speakers from both Protestant and Roman Catholic institutions. The importance of such a conference was described in the preparatory materials: "Shaped by changing currents in public policy, demographics, economic realities, intellectual fashion and church priorities, religiously affiliated colleges and universities experienced significant change during the second half of the twentieth century." In the new-found circumstances, "most of these colleges became more religiously diverse in the composition of their faculty, staff and student body and more secular in character and content."

In addition to these commonly experienced changes, a reason more specific to Catholic colleges and universities was the presence of new ecclesiological questions within the Roman Catholic church, especially those concerning lay governance and control of Catholic colleges and universities. The fundamental question Rome asked was, "What makes these colleges Catholic?" Since the 1960s, Catholic colleges had made great strides in adapting to the standards of American higher education. In the 1980s the questions for Catholics were, "Are our colleges and universities also engaged in a work of transformative influence on the cultural environment in which they exist?" "How do they manifest their esteem for their Catholic heritage?" and "How do they envision their responsibility to hand it on to the next generation?"

Under pressure to conform to the standards of academia, the approximately 235 Catholic colleges and universities in the United States had sometimes tended to minimize their Catholic roots. Court cases in the 1960s and 1970s made them wary of being "pervasively sectarian," and their increasing dependence on funding from government and major foundation sources made it advisable for them to place less emphasis on their religious mission. This created a tension that was difficult to resolve. On the one hand, voices from Rome, urged on by some American Catholics, challenged Catholic theologians as to their orthodoxy. On the other hand, the American Association of University Professors and the American Civil Liberties Union were ever ready to censor policies regarding faculty and students that were based on religious traditions and beliefs.

How did Catholic colleges and universities react to this ambiguity concerning their place in American higher education? The answer is, in many different ways. The very diversity of these institutions in size, kinds of programs and curricula, student body, number and quality of faculty, religious sponsorship, and financial situation mandated a variety of responses to the call to be visibly "Catholic." The tension created by efforts to preserve a Catholic identity in American culture while, at the same time, achieving academic integrity and public recognition as legitimate institutions of higher education colored the reaction of American Catholic colleges and universities to Roman efforts to define a juridical relationship between them and the Catholic Church. The long struggle to find an acceptable description of this relationship culminated in *Ex Corde Ecclesiae,* and it had preoccupied both university and church officials for almost twenty years. The further search for common ground in applying that document to the United States consumed them for yet another ten years. Nevertheless, there have been many other ways in recent decades in which colleges and universities have revisited their Catholic intellectual tradition and sought to articulate their unique character in the wider world of American higher education. Areas in which they took new steps toward clarifying their identity include:

1. Publications (written by faculty and administrators) as well as university brochures treating of their mission;
2. Grants and other funding for writing histories of individual colleges as well as of Catholic education as a whole; funding for seminars and workshops on the issue of Catholic identity;

3. New centers and institutes;
4. Orientation programs for trustees, faculty, administrators, and students that stress the Catholic identity and mission of the colleges and universities; one topic frequently cited in this context is the exploration of the meaning of inculturation and the role of the Catholic university in mediating faith to cultures;
5. Peace and justice studies based on the social teaching of the church;
6. Recognition of the new importance of the laity according to the teaching of Vatican Council II, by addressing the question of formation of lay leadership; related to this were changes in academic government and discipline in ways that encouraged participatory decision-making within the framework of Christian values.

Other ways of clarifying Catholic identity could be explored, but these suffice to show the degree to which colleges and universities have paid attention to the issues raised in *Ex Corde Ecclesiae.*

PUBLICATIONS

The best and most recent bibliography on this period is one prepared by Dr. Philip Gleason for the *Handbook of Research on Catholic Higher Education,* edited by Thomas C. Hunt, Ronald James Nuzzi, Ellis A. Joseph, and John D. Geiger (2003), 101–117. As Gleason points out, most of the writing on the period since the 1960s consists of commentaries and contemporary analyses, with few attempts at historical perspective. Overall there was an increase in the quality of books and journals published by Catholic university presses, and several institutions, such as Sacred Heart University in Bridgeport and Stonehill College, have set up their own presses. Several new periodicals appeared from Catholic colleges and universities. The well-known publications *Commonweal* and *America* paid greater attention to higher education. A new periodical, *First Things,* became an important resource for criticism of the direction in which Catholic higher education was moving. The Jesuit universities began a journal called *Conversations on Jesuit Higher Education,* under the direction of their National Seminar on Jesuit Higher Education. The Center for Catholic Studies at the University of St. Thomas in St. Paul, Minnesota, began publication of the journal *Perspectives.* The Institute for Catholic Studies at John Carroll University initiated *Prism,* a self-described effort to "illuminate the diversity of Catholic intellectual life" using as a prism the two thousand years of

Catholic history. Another new periodical, *Catholic Education,* was founded at the University of Dayton and is currently supported by sixteen Catholic universities; it is now housed in the Alliance for Catholic Education Program at the University of Notre Dame. This journal addresses issues across the entire spectrum of Catholic schools.

Philip Gleason's work *Contending with Modernity* (1995) set a model for historical writing on Catholic higher education in the twentieth century and encouraged many other scholars to pursue related topics. Alice Gallin's collection of documents, *American Catholic Higher Education: Essential Documents, 1967–1990* (1992), provided the raw material for a study of the development of *Ex Corde Ecclesiae,* and her *Independence and a New Partnership in Catholic Higher Education* (1996) and *Negotiating Identity* (2000) provide the historical context for the ongoing dialogue about the purposes and mission of Catholic higher education in the United States. David O'Brien's *From the Heart of the American Church* (1994) portrays the tension between being American and being Catholic and underscores the importance of recognizing the unique aspects of American Catholic institutions. A collection of personal essays by faculty on their experiences in a Catholic university can be found in *The Challenge and Promise of a Catholic University,* edited by Theodore M. Hesburgh, C.S.C. (2001). Publications of various institutes and centers for Catholic Studies that were founded in the 1990s, as well as papers delivered at various symposia, such as that at Fordham University in 1992 and Georgetown University in 1993 (discussed in the introduction to this volume), have added considerably to the relevant resources. The Association of Catholic Colleges and Universities (ACCU) has presented many thoughtful essays dealing with the question of Catholic mission and identity in its journal, *Current Issues in Catholic Higher Education*; it also provides regular brief accounts of activities on campuses and in the national and international world of higher education in its newsletter, *Update* (www.accunet.org/publications).

GRANTS

Many of the publications and other innovative projects on Catholic campuses have relied on outside financial support. A major source of grants supporting Catholic higher education has been the Lilly Endowment. In 1989 the Religion Division of the Lilly Endowment launched an initiative in the area of religion and higher education, which between 1989 and 2001 has been responsible for seventy awards totaling $15.6 million for approximately forty-five projects, many of them on Catholic campuses. Of eight published works listed in the Winter 2002 newsletter of the Lilly Endowment as having received Lilly support, seven dealt with Catholic higher education: Alice Gallin, *Independence and a New Partnership* (1996) and *Negotiating Identity* (2000); Donald J. Kirby et al., *Ambitious Dreams: The Values Program at Le Moyne College* (1990); Thomas M. Landy, ed., *As Leaven in the World: Catholic Perspectives on Faith, Vocation, and the Intellectual Life* (2001); Tracy Schier and Cynthia Russett, eds., *Catholic Women's Colleges in America* (2002); William M. Shea, ed., with Daniel Van Slyke, *Trying Times: Essays in Catholic Higher Education in the 20th Century* (2002); and John R. Wilcox and Irene King, eds., *Enhancing Religious Identity: Best Practices from Catholic Campuses* (2000).

An evaluation of the general impact of the Lilly initiative by Kathleen A. Mahoney, John Schmalzbauer, and James Youniss in 2000 and a follow-up evaluation by Alice Gallin in 2002 can be viewed on the Lilly Endowment web page under www.resourcingchristianity.org (under "search/view all essays," see "Revitalizing Religion in the Academy" and "The Impact of the Lilly-funded Research on Catholic Colleges and Universities," respectively).

Grants from the Lilly Endowment assisted not only individual scholars but also institutions wishing to highlight their heritage through various creative efforts. An example of the latter was a $12 million grant to Saint Mary's College in Indiana, underwriting a program to train leaders "for a world of different cultures." Another Lilly project gave a total of $171.3 million to eighty-eight American colleges and universities to support programs addressing the question of vocations and helping students discern their vocations in life. (The final round of three rounds of grants was made in 2003.) St. Bonaventure University, for instance, received almost $2 million in January 2003 for their "Journey Project," which focuses on creating a campus culture linking faith, service, and vocation. In addition, the assistance of the Lilly Endowment in setting up institutes and seminars on related topics will be noted below. Lilly also funded a five-college consortium consisting of Rivier College (New Hampshire), St. Mary of the Woods (Indiana), Incarnate Word (Texas), St. Paul's College (Episcopal, Virginia), and Dordt College (Christian Reformed, Iowa), which was set up in 1996 as a collaborative effort to bring in speakers and to host symposia addressing the topic "the role of service within curriculum and religious mission at church-related institutions."

Many other foundations also supported efforts to redefine the Catholic identity of institutions of higher learning. Several were members of FADICA (Foundations and Donors Interested in Catholic Activities). They also include the Kroc Foundation (especially for efforts in peace education and international understanding), the Pew Charitable Foundation, and the Olin Foundation. A project on trusteeship was undertaken by the Association of Governing Boards, the Association of Catholic Colleges and Universities, and the Association of Jesuit Colleges and Universities, which received funding from the Teagle Foundation, several members of FADICA, George E. Doty, Sr., and an anonymous foundation. This project resulted in workshops and a publication, *Mission and Identity: A Handbook for Trustees of Catholic Colleges and Universities* (2003). Funding support is currently being sought for an Institute of Advanced Catholic Studies, mentioned below.

The history of Catholic philanthropy directed toward higher education is one of slow evolution. As more alumni/ae have gained wealth, the support they have given to their alma maters has been increasingly generous. Now, a particular need is funding for joint projects that will serve not merely one institution but Catholic higher education as a whole and, through the colleges and universities, meet the wider needs of society and church.

During the 1990s the founding/sponsoring religious communities of colleges also provided funds, especially in support of campus ministry, peace education, Catholic studies, faculty and trustee seminar programs on the particular heritage of the group, and meetings for faculty off campus on relevant topics. Religious communities often gave or lent money to the colleges or universities in times of financial need. They have continued to make contributions to annual fund drives and also, where feasible, continued to support members of the community in pursuing Ph.D. degrees and encourage them to serve as faculty and administrators. The significant decrease in the number of members of religious communities serving within colleges and universities sponsored by those communities has had a financial impact that is difficult to calculate, but it explains, in part, the colleges' need for greater outside funding.

NEW CENTERS AND INSTITUTES

As indicated above, a number of new publications were linked to institutes or other kinds of organizations that focused on particular audiences. Since 1993, Collegium has sponsored week-long summer programs whose purpose is to interest junior faculty and graduate students in the mission of Catholic colleges and universities. Collegium was begun under the leadership of Dr. Thomas Landy at Fairfield University and was supported by ACCU and several universities and colleges. As of 2004 it had sixty-three member institutions and was planning programs through at least 2007. Its activities have led to a lengthy list of alumni/ae and a newsletter that shares their achievements. It is described in Landy's work, *As Leaven in the World* (2004), noted in the section above. Another summer program was begun in 1996 by Dr. Sandra Estanek, in collaboration with John Carroll University, Ursuline College, and the ACCU, for the student affairs officers on Catholic campuses. Known as the Institute for Student Affairs Offices on Catholic College Campuses (ISACC), its goal was to meet the expressed needs of those involved in such offices, particularly in updating their knowledge of Catholic moral teaching, which often impacts decisions in an institution with a Catholic heritage and mission. In 1999 it evolved into an Association of Student Affairs Officers at Catholic Colleges and Universities (ASACCU) and was located at the Catholic University of America. Estanek describes this program in her volume, *Understanding Student Affairs in Catholic Colleges and Universities: A Comprehensive Resource* (2002).

Other resources went to new or ongoing programs, such as the Jesuit Institute at Boston College, the Alliance for Catholic Education, the Cushwa Center for the Study of Catholicism, various Catholic Studies programs on campuses, faculty orientation programs in individual colleges, and the Catholic Scholars Council in Florida. Other well-established institutes have existed at the University of Notre Dame for many years: The Joan B. Kroc Institute for International Peace Studies, which engages in research and teaching that focus on the Catholic tradition of social thought and its impact on justice and the advocacy of human rights; the Erasmus Institute, which supports research grounded in the Catholic intellectual tradition and its relation to contemporary humanities, arts, and social sciences; the Institute for Church Life, which attempts to link programs on campus with the interests of the church community; and the Helen Kellogg Institute for International Studies, which engages in comparative international research with special reference to Latin America. The John S. Ryan Institute for Catholic Social Thought at the University of St. Thomas in St. Paul, Minnesota, is a significant resource for the Catholic Studies Program on both graduate and undergraduate levels on that campus and for the active role the university has played in encouraging other colleges' Catholic Studies programs.

A major project undertaken in 1997 was the convening of a Commission on Catholic Scholarship to consider the possibility of a residential center for collaborative research. By 1998 an Institute for Advanced Catholic Studies (IACS) had been set up, and by 2000 it had a board of trustees with the tasks of raising an endowment, finding an appropriate location, and presenting programs that would bring scholars together around themes of common interest. The institute was committed to interdisciplinary projects looking at contemporary culture from the perspective of the Catholic intellectual tradition. The work would occur in a residential setting of invited scholars, both recognized and beginning researchers. By 2004 the institute had found a location near the University of Southern California, a very gracious and welcoming neighbor, and had successfully sponsored three major conferences with subsequent publications. The chair of IACS (see www.ifacs.com) is Rev. James Heft, S.M., on leave from the University of Dayton.

Several colleges have "centers" for promotion of programs which deal with the broad mission of Catholic institutions. An example is the Center for Religion, Ethics, and Culture at the College of the Holy Cross in Worcester, Massachusetts. The center's activities during the recent years have included sponsoring guest lecturers on a wide variety of topics, a faculty study group, an interdisciplinary faculty dialogue, the Lilly-funded Vocation project, and presentations on Jesuit scholars such as the late Walter Ong and John Courtney Murray. It arranges interfaith conversations and joint projects with other local religious groups for both faculty and students. Several other colleges are attempting similar institutes or centers, according to their interests and resources.

ORIENTATION PROGRAMS

There is widespread recognition that unless faculty, administrators, and trustees are firmly committed to the mission of a college or university as both Catholic and academic, the hope of maintaining its Catholic identity is small. The work of the Implementation Committee for *Ex Corde Ecclesiae* involved numerous consultations with bishops, presidents, learned societies, theologians, and leaders of religious communities, and these consultations were the impetus for extensive dialogues on campuses among the various parties. In itself, this process was a significant factor in the acceptance of the apostolic letter. It also opened the way for continued dialogue on the topic of Catholic identity and mission. Some institutions appointed a vice president to monitor ongoing efforts related to the institution's mission. Others developed special materials, such as video presentations at Saint Louis University, on the history of the founding religious community and its special character, and these presentations were used to stimulate group discussions among faculty and administrators. Another creative approach was that at the University of Dayton, where an eight-month interdisciplinary faculty seminar dealing with ethics and religion across the spectrum of disciplines was set up by Rev. James Heft, S.M. (described in *Current Issues in Catholic Higher Education*, Spring 1998). A project at St. Bonaventure

University in the mid-1990s, the development of a core curriculum for all students in Clare College (a division of the university), also had the benefit of orienting all faculty toward the Franciscan heritage of the college as they collaborated on the curriculum.

The role of the Catholic university, according to John Paul II, is to mediate the faith to cultures. Such a vision opens up vistas to be explored—how do we "mediate faith" to the cultures of twenty-first-century America? What cultures are we talking about? What does authentic "inculturation" involve? This is an area of dialogue that might well bring faculty and students together for debate both in the classroom and in co-curricular activities. Finding out whether prospective faculty and administrators are interested in such conversation has become part of the hiring process in some universities. Orientation programs offered to new presidents by ACCU and other groups often lay the foundation for retreats in connection with strategic planning for the institution.

PEACE AND JUSTICE STUDIES AND
THE SOCIAL TEACHING OF THE CHURCH

Beginning in the late 1960s and early 1970s, some Catholic colleges focused on peace studies. Partly as a result of Vietnam and the Civil Rights Movement, questions about just war theory and human rights were of particular contemporary importance. Manhattan College founded an Institute for Peace Studies in 1971, the same year that the World Synod of Bishops proclaimed in the introduction to its document "Justice in the World" that "action on behalf of justice and participation in the transformation of the world fully appear to us as a constitutive dimension of the preaching of the Gospel." The ACCU established an advisory board for peace and justice studies in the late 1970s and helped set up seven pilot projects on campuses to integrate the social teaching of the church with the many service-oriented projects in which students and some faculty participated. On many campuses today, work at local shelters for the homeless or after-school programs for children often involve faculty and students. Spring break "plunges" in large cities or elsewhere away from campus afford opportunities for students, and also for the alumni/ae who offer them hospitality. Education for Service is included in many college mission statements.

By 1998, when a national symposium on peace and justice education at Catholic colleges and universities was held at Iona College, some 117 institutions answered a preliminary survey reporting that they offered some course or program on Catholic social teaching. Unfortunately, only about ten or fifteen of these programs had significant "institutional" standing—there was often little budget support and no academic credit. This is an area in need of attention.

Each year ACCU sponsors a "wraparound" session at the USCCB Social Ministry Meeting, thus engaging participants in reflection on the work of the church in providing services for the needy and on the faith basis for social action. Social action is one of the most visible signs of the Catholic identity of an institution. The task is described by John Paul II: "Just as every individual Christian, so also every Catholic institution of higher education has a duty to help promote development in emerging nations; of equal importance is that each Catholic institution of higher education, through means within its own competence as a center of learning, contribute to the progress of the specific society in which it is located. It will be incarnated in the local culture, assuming it, healing it, elevating and transforming it according to the values and principles of the Gospel. The task of development is to remedy the causes of poverty, whether material, cultural, or spiritual" (*Ex Corde Ecclesiae*, para. 67)

Many Catholic colleges have joined with other American colleges in promoting community services, under the auspices of an organization called "Campus Compact." A further dimension sought at some Catholic institutions is the grounding of such action in the social teaching of the church. Here, there is still much work to be done. In October 2003, for example, a conference at the University of St. Thomas in St. Paul, Minnesota, addressed the theme of "Catholic Social Teaching across the Curriculum." ACCU has also promoted collaboration with the USCCB Task Force on Social Justice Teaching. The annual meeting of ACCU in 2003 was focused on the relation of Catholic higher education to the common good.

EMPHASIS ON THE ROLE OF THE LAITY

Catholic colleges and universities in the United States owe their existence and development to various religious orders and dioceses that founded them, but from the beginning they depended on lay men and women who were willing to share in their mission. The enormous expansion in college student population after World War II required more lay faculty and staff, and the documents of Vatican Council II, especially *Lumen Gentium* and *Gaudium et Spes,* highlighted the vocation of the laity as scholars and teachers. A partnership evolved in which the laity and members of religious orders worked side by side. Over the past thirty years this relationship has led to a remarkable increase in lay presidents and other administrators of Catholic colleges, as well as increased lay membership on boards of trustees. Apparently, the field of higher education is one in which Catholic laity have achieved more responsibilities and authority than in any other area in the church. The work on *Ex Corde Ecclesiae*, with its widespread consultations, is a clear example of that. However, one fact that became clear in the process of implementation of the apostolic letter was the importance of orientation programs like those mentioned above.

As numbers of religious men and women continue to decline, laypersons are needed more than ever in positions of leadership. They recognize their need to understand the relationship of the college or university to the church as a whole and the ways that values central to the institution's mission have been handed on to new generations. Many have also discovered their need for help in developing their own spiritual gifts, if they are to lead an institution committed to the Catholic intellectual tradition. An effort to meet these needs was evident in the presentations and discussions at two summer workshops held at Sacred Heart University (see the two-volume *Examining the Catholic Intellectual Tradition,* edited by Anthony J. Cernera and Oliver J. Morgan, 2000 and 2002).

To promote a continuing dialogue between bishops and leaders of Catholic higher education (now mostly laypersons), the ACCU has invited several bishops to celebrate the liturgy or give keynote addresses at its annual meetings. The reorganization of NCCB in 2001 led to a renewed but different Bishops and Presidents' Committee. Founded in 1974, the original committee had been defined as a "joint" committee of NCCB and ACCU, and the membership was chosen by the two organizations. ACCU members over the years have included many sisters, brothers, and lay men and women. Hence, the meetings of this committee, and particularly its work in developing the 1980 pastoral letter on Catholic higher education, provided a forum where women religious and lay men and women found their voices. Since 2001, however, the Bishops and Presidents' Committee has been defined as a committee of USCCB, and the bylaws work against equality among members. If it can regain its former identity, it would be a vehicle for the dialogue that both bishops and presidents have asked for.

This may seem a small point, but the experience on the Implementation Committee was a positive one partly because the attitude of the bishop members toward those who were technically "consultants" (the presidents and resource persons) was one of respect for their intelligence and faith and a genuine willingness to negotiate points of difference when they surfaced, without stressing the fact that strictly, only the bishops were members of the committee. It is important for both bishops and presidents to recognize the significant role played by each others' constituents, those to whom they are accountable, and to acknowledge the culture of American life and the post–Vatican Council II church, which place high priority on freedom and accountability. Internal structures of colleges and universities have become more collaborative, and the "identity" of the institution no longer depends on a religious community with strong ties to the original mission of the founding community. Instead, it depends on the trustees and administrators who assume their responsibilities, respectful of that mission but perhaps envisioning it in slightly different form.

Since 1990 there has been a remarkable expansion in the awareness of the complexities of "mediating faith to cultures," but Catholic colleges and universities in the United States provide many illustrations of how the task can be approached. The challenge of handing on the Catholic intellectual tradition has led to serious study of what that tradition includes and to countless conversations about how the "handing on" can be accomplished. We can only be grateful to all those who have made efforts during the past decade to implement *Ex Corde Ecclesiae* in the real world of everyday campus life and who now need encouragement to continue their efforts.